Y0-CBF-083

**Of
Children**

Of
Children

An Introduction to
Child Development

SEVENTH EDITION

Guy R. Lefrançois
University of Alberta

Wadsworth Publishing Company
Belmont, California ▣ A Division of Wadsworth, Inc.

Editor: Suzanna Brabrant
Development Editor: John Bergez
Editorial Assistant: Dana Lipsky
Production Editor: Karen Garrison
Designer: Andrew H. Ogus
Print Buyer: Karen Hunt
Art Editor: Nancy Spellman
Permissions Editor: Robert Kauser
Copy Editor: Joan Pendleton
Photo Researchers: Judy Mason and Stephen Forsling
Technical Illustrator: DBA Design and Illustration
Cover: Andrew H. Ogus
Compositor: Thompson Type, Inc.
Printer: Arcata Graphics/Fairfield
Cover Painting: *Under the Horse Chestnut*, ca. 1898, Mary Stevenson
Cassatt. Color print with drypoint and aquatint, 15⅞ × 11¼ inches.
Bequest of W. G. Russell Allen. Courtesy, Museum of Fine Arts, Boston.

1 2 3 4 5 6 7 8 9 10−96 95 94 93 92

Library of Congress Cataloging in Publication Data

Lefrançois, Guy R.
    Of children : an introduction to child development / Guy R.
  Lefrançois. — 7th ed.
      p. cm.
    Includes bibliographical references and index.
    ISBN 0-534-16824-8
    1. Child development. I. Title.
  RJ131.L38 1991
  305.23'1 − dc20   91-27667

This book is affectionately dedicated to Laurier, Claire, and Rémi,
beautiful children, and to all things beautiful.

1972

1976

1979

1982

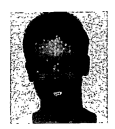

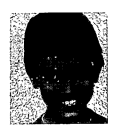

1985

1988

1991

Brief Contents

Detailed Contents

V   MIDDLE CHILDHOOD   435

Thematic Contents

Tis strange — but true;
for truth is always strange
Stranger than fiction.
Lord Byron, *Don Juan*

Preface

Dear Reader,

This is the story about this book. My grandmother knew about people, but I was studying psychology and I figured I knew stuff she didn't know. So to put me in my place, she asked me a question: "Let's suppose," she said, "that you had a kid like Gerry Bisson.* Could you have known beforehand how he was going to turn out?"

I used to love that kind of question. It's the kind of question against which you can throw the entire weight of organized psychology. So I gave my grandmother what I thought was psychology's best answer, which was about the kinds of tests and evaluations we have to do with youngsters to find out exactly why some are at greater risk of developmental problems than others.

"Then we can predict what's going to happen," I said, "and maybe we can do something about it."

My grandmother was a gardener. She summarized her response to my answer with a garden analogy.

"Take an aspen seedling," she said. "You can look at it, test it all you want, figure out exactly what its genes are, see if there's anything wrong with it. But can you tell me for sure how it's going to grow? How fast? How tall? How straight? Will it have broken branches?"

What my grandmother was saying was that it would be absurd to try to predict from a seedling exactly what a tree will be like when it's grown. As she explained, it depends on the kind of soil in which it's planted, the amount of rain that falls, whether bears deposit fertilizers at its roots, and whether wild cows scar it or break its branches as they lean drunkenly against it. It depends on windstorms and lightning, on frost and hail, on insect infestations and winter storms. It has to do with woodpeckers pounding on its trunk, beavers chewing its bark, songbirds nesting among its leaves.

"Most important," she concluded, "you have to realize that seedlings respond to these things differently. Some need more rain than others, or different fertilizers; some are stronger in windstorms and tougher in the winter."

The lesson is simple: The important point is that what happens to the seedling is not entirely within the plant itself or in the conditions that surround it; its growth is mostly a function of the *relationship* between the two. In other words, its growth is a function of its ecology.

---

*Gerry experienced some developmental problems, the outcome of which put him in jail.

So, too, with children. The growth and development *of children* is not explained by things entirely within children. It is influenced by their ecologies — by their relationships and interactions within the systems that nurture and shape them: family, school, friends, relatives, society, culture. We need to ask how the individual characteristics of children interact with the characteristics of these systems.

WHAT IS OF CHILDREN, SEVENTH EDITION?

This book is an answer to my grandmother's question. It's an introductory textbook in child development. It deals with physical, social, emotional, and intellectual development from infancy to adolescence. My goal is to present the most important and useful information about children simply and clearly, to communicate how fascinating the subject can be and also how provocative, challenging, and sometimes controversial.

Although the organization of *Of Children, Seventh Edition* is primarily chronological, chapters can be read independently rather than in sequence. Accordingly, it is simple to rearrange chapters to conform to a topical approach using the detailed thematic table of contents included on pages 16–17.

WHAT'S NEW IN THIS EDITION?

Of Children, Seventh Edition recognizes more clearly the importance of our contexts and especially of our relationships and interactions within these contexts. That is, it's more ecologically oriented — as is evident in the addition of sections on Bronfenbrenner and Vygotsky in Chapter 2 and in a greater emphasis on interactions within the family, school, and peer systems throughout the text.

In addition, the many new or significantly expanded topics include children's rights, self-efficacy, molecular genetics, infant memory, AIDS and other sexually transmitted diseases, biological contributions to development, mother/father and infant interaction, infant perceptual development, English as a second language, family violence and child maltreatment, the development of self and of notions of self-worth, gender roles, social cognition, adolescent sexuality, violent gangs, adolescent drug use, and much more (nearly 400 new references, most published within the last three years).

All primarily textual boxed inserts have been eliminated in this edition in an effort to eliminate the confusion that often arises over whether boxes contain material that is so important that it needs to be set aside or so unimportant that it need not be part of the main text. These have been replaced with brief, primarily visual features (labeled *At A Glance*) that summarize important facts and trends. Many new concept-organizing tables have also been included.

SPECIAL FEATURES

A number of features are designed to make *Of Children* a better teaching/learning tool. These include chapter outlines that depict clearly where the chapter is going; comprehensive, point-form chapter summaries that can be used as textbook notes; annotated readings at the end of each chapter as suggestions for clarification and further information; and a glossary of important terms at the end of the book. They include, as well, emphasis on clear, simple writing, the liberal use of illustration (both conceptual and graphic), and the use of motivational, vignette-type chapter introductions. In addition, a full complement of teaching-learning aids accompanies *Of Children*, including test items and a student study guide.

GRANDMA

Of course, you can't tell exactly what a seedling will be like, Grandma. Like you said, it depends on a lot of things. But if I let you choose the soil, the location, the fertilizers, and if I let you fence out bad things like wild cows — if I let you match all these things to *this* specific seedling because we know that some seedlings grow better with different soils, different fertilizers — you can certainly increase the chances that your seedlings will turn out to be fine specimens.

So, too, with children.

Except, as you said so often, seedlings are even simpler than children. There is less mystery in their growth. And perhaps less magic as well.

Acknowledgments

There are more people than I can name whose help, guidance, and inspiration have nurtured the growth of *Of Children*. These are some of them:

- Richard Greenberg, who helped shape the first edition, and who was among the first to glimpse the wolf and to give it a resounding boot.
- Ken King, editor, who skillfully oversaw the next four editions.
- Suzanna Brabant, who provided new enthusiasm for the sixth and now the seventh edition.

- Karen Garrison, production editor, who patiently and expertly guided the transition from manuscript to book.
- Joan Pendleton, copy editor, who challenged and corrected many imperfections.
- John Bergez, development editor, whose talent, taste, and understanding contributed much to these pages.
- Andrew Ogus, who designed a clean, uncluttered, and attractive book.
- A legion of Wadsworth reps, past and current, without whose efforts the wolf would be much happier.
- My maternal grandmother with whom I lived in early adolescence, whose wisdom and wit affect me still.
- The many reviewers of the previous half-dozen editions, whose influence is still apparent in these pages.
- The reviewers of this seventh edition, whose more recent influence is considerable: Vernon P. Estes, Jr., San Antonio College; Peggy Glider, University of Arizona; Derl Keen, Fresno City College; Susan Mantyla, Santa Barbara City College; Richard Passman, University of Wisconsin-Milwaukee; and Lisa M. Reboy, University of Kansas.

To each of you, my sincere thanks.

Grown-ups love figures.

Antoine de Saint-Exupéry, *The Little Prince*

i

Introduction

"When you tell them that you have made a new friend," Antoine de Saint-Exupéry continues, "they never ask you any questions about essential matters." They never say, "What does his voice sound like? What games does he love best? Does he collect butterflies?" Instead, they demand: "How old is he? How many brothers has he? How much does he weigh? How much money does his father make?" Only from these figures do they think they have learned anything about him.

"What does his voice sound like? . . . Does he collect butterflies?" Grown-up that it is, science, too, seldom asks these questions.

Why? Is the science that studies children not interested in such matters? Is it so preoccupied with its research designs and its measurements, its theories and its hypotheses, that it has no time to wonder what it's like, really like, to be a child?

The simple answer is yes. Yes, science cannot allow itself to wonder about such things. Science needs to be impersonal and objective. It doesn't have time to stop and notice that Filbert carries small marbles in his pocket because he likes their smooth, cold touch; that rainbows and dewdrops and frosty blades of grass make Marilyn want to sing and write poetry; that Jerry's voice booms from his little chest as though it were a hollow drum; that Ashley cries at night for reasons she is too ashamed to put into words.

As is made clear in the two introductory chapters that make up Part I, the science of children deals with "average" children. It describes typical behavior at different ages. It invents theories that explain the most common ways of thinking and behaving, the most usual reactions, the most widespread beliefs and attitudes. It deals with what is common, normal, predictable, average.

But there is no average child. The concept is a convenient invention, a necessary creation if we are to speak coherently and meaningfully of all children. We must always keep in mind that each child is a unique individual, that each is different from the "average," in countless ways, and that no one theory will ever account for all behavior. Children are incredibly more complex than even the most extensive theoretical description of them. A theory — and a book — can deal only with the objective details of the lives of children, not with their essence.

Still, in this text we will stop ourselves occasionally to notice that Scott collects butterflies and that roses make Marilyn happy. And we will ask too what it is that makes Ashley cry.

Child! Do not throw this book about;
Refrain from the unholy pleasure
Of cutting all the pictures out!
Preserve it as your chiefest treasure.

Hilaire Belloc
Bad Child's Book of Beasts

Studying the Child

Jason is 5; he's in Marie's kindergarten class. He's a solemn little guy, wide-eyed and earnest, and dead serious about most things.

During circle time in Marie's kindergarten, children share things. It was Jason's turn one day last week, and he brought to class something nobody there had ever seen before: a *live* black widow spider. He had gotten it from an uncle who lives down by Medicine Hat. "Where my uncle lives," he proudly told the class, "there's things that can kill you like rattlesnakes and black widow spiders." He didn't mention wild cows.

It was a very large, female black widow spider; the entire class crowded in to have a close look. "They're the only ones that can kill you," Jason explained. "See the red thing on its belly. My uncle got bit by one, and he almost died."

"Is there anything else you want to say about the spider before we put it away?" Marie asked. "Oh yes," Jason announced solemnly. "My uncle keeps my aunt under his bed."

There were gasps of amazement; nobody laughed.

"Why?" they asked Jason. He shrugged. "He does, you know," he answered.

"No," someone said, less in disbelief than in wonder.

"Really. I heard her," said Jason.

"But not really," Marie said. "It's just a joke, Jason. Nobody keeps anybody under any bed."

"My uncle really does," said Jason. "He does."

He's such a solemn little child, so honest, so serious. What if . . . what if his uncle really . . . ? Shouldn't someone do something?

"Yeah," I said to Marie, "let's go to Medicine Hat and look under the bed; it's only a 6-hour drive."

We didn't go. But earlier this week there were parent-teacher interviews at Marie's school and Jason's mother came. Marie mentioned the spider, said how excited the class was to see it, how well-informed Jason was. This was all by way of sneaking in the question, Jason's uncle doesn't really keep an aunt under his bed, does he, heh, heh?

He doesn't. But for some reason — he may have somebody else under there — he didn't want Jason and his sister to go under the bed. So he told them that's where their aunt was and when they went to look, he projected his voice and croaked in a high-pitched tone, "If you come any closer little children, I'll bloody eat you!"

So they didn't go any closer and nothing bloody ate them.

GROWING UP

You and I are grown up; we're not scared of things under the bed, are we? Unlike little children, we know very well that there's nothing under the bed; we can look if we want to and nothing will eat us. You can't fool us just by projecting your voice. We recognize lies, and we know that magic isn't real, and we know there are some things people don't do. Don't we?

Little children don't know these things. Part of growing up is learning them — learning what to expect; becoming familiar with what's out there; sorting fact from fancy, reality from wishes, tears from laughter.

Describing and explaining differences among infants, children, adolescents, and adults is mostly what this text is all about.

THIS TEXT

Of Children is divided into seven major sections. The first is an introduction: It explains what developmental psychology is and how psychologists study children, and it introduces some of the most important theories that are used to explain developmental change. The first chapter in Part II deals with our genetic origins; the second looks at systematic changes that occur from conception through birth and at important influences on the unborn child. Parts III through VI look at physical, intellectual (cognitive), and emotional changes and processes during each of the major pre-adult periods: infancy (birth to 2); early childhood (2 to 6 or 7); middle childhood (6 or 7 to 11 or 12); and adolescence (11 or 12 to 19 or 20). And Part VII is simply an ending (see Table 1.1).

Some Definitions

Psychology is a general term for the science that studies human behavior and thought.* **Developmental psychology** is the division of psychology that is concerned specifically with changes that occur over time and with the processes and influences that account for these changes. In other words, *development* refers to changes in behavior with the passage of time. The task of the developmental psychologist is twofold: to describe changes and to discover their

---

*Boldfaced terms are defined in the Glossary in the back of the book.

Table 1.1
Organization of *Of Children*

Period/part	Ages	Chapters
I Introduction		1 Studying the child
		2 Theories of development
II Biological beginnings		3 Genetics and context
		4 Prenatal development and birth
III Infancy	Birth to 2 years	5 Physical and cognitive development
		6 Social development
IV Early childhood	2 to 6 or 7	7 Physical and cognitive development
		8 Social development
V Middle childhood	6 or 7 to 11 or 12	9 Physical and cognitive development
		10 Social development
VI Adolescence	11 or 12 to 19 or 20	11 Physical and cognitive development
		12 Social development
VII Epilogue		13 The end

underlying causes. A third, closely related task is to advance theories that organize and interpret observations and that can be used to make predictions.

There are several important concepts in the study of children. These include *growth, maturation,* and *learning.* Put another way, to develop is to grow, to mature, and to learn. **Growth** ordinarily refers to physical changes, which are primarily quantitative because they involve addition rather than transformation. Such changes as increasing height or enlargement of the nose are clear examples of growth.

Maturation is a less precise term used to describe changes that are relatively independent of the child's environment. These changes are often attributed to heredity. In almost all aspects of human development, however, maturation and learning interact. Learning to walk, for example, requires not only that the child's physical strength and muscular coordination be sufficiently developed but also that there be an opportunity to practice the different skills involved.

Learning is defined as the result of experience rather than as a maturational process. All changes in behavior resulting from experience are examples of learning, provided these changes are not simply the temporary effects of drugs or fatigue.

In summary, **development** is the total process whereby an individual adapts to his or her environment; and because we adapt by growing, maturing, and learning, these are all aspects of development. (See Table 1.2.) The main

Table 1.2
Important Definitions

Psychology	The science that studies human thought and behavior
Developmental psychology	Division of psychology concerned with changes that occur over time and with the processes and influences that account for these changes
Development involves	
Growth	Physical changes; primarily quantitative
Maturation	Naturally unfolding changes, relatively independent of the environment (for example, pubescence — the changes of adolescence that lead to sexual maturity)
Learning	Relatively permanent changes in behavior that result from experience (rather than from maturation, fatigue, or drugs)

difference between learning and development is simply that learning is concerned with immediate, short-term adaptation, whereas development refers to gradual adaptation over a period of years. *Developmental psychology,* then, has as its subject the human from conception to death (although in this text we do not deal with the entire life span but stop instead somewhere in adolescence). It undertakes two essential tasks: observing humans and their progress in adapting to the world and formulating an explanation of that adaptation.

A BRIEF HISTORY

The attitudes toward children reflected in this text are warm, positive, interested, sympathetic, concerned — all the good things we think of as characteristic of our enlightened, twentieth-century attitudes toward children. It has not always been so. In fact, even yet, it isn't always and everywhere entirely so.

Before the Eighteenth Century

Nature has been stingy with her ancient records. There are vast gaps in our knowledge about the origins of plants and animals, long series of missing links about which we can only guess.

We do not fare all that much better with human history even when the questions we ask deal with relatively modern rather than very ancient events. There are few reliable records of what life might have been like prior to the "print cultures" — those societies that regularly produce written artifacts.

When Aries (1962) attempted to uncover what the lives of medieval children were like, he was forced to put together fragments gathered from many sources — historical paintings, school and university regulations, Doctor Heroard's description of the upbringing of the French king Louis XIII. The result is a dramatic account of conditions and attitudes vastly different from those we assume to be contemporary.

In the Middle Ages, Aries informs us, childhood did not exist as we know it. Early paintings depict children as miniature adults — as little things to be used when useful and discarded or ignored when not. True, there was a period of dependency early in the child's life, a period during which the infant needed a parent or some other caregiver to survive. Sadly, however, a vast number did not survive. Aries describes one scene where a mother has just given birth to her fifth child. She is depressed; there is now one more mouth to feed, one more body to clothe and look after. There had not been enough to go around before. What will it be like now? The neighbor consoles her: "Before they are old enough to bother you," she says, "you will have lost half of them, or perhaps all of them" (Aries, 1962, p. 38).

The implication is clearly that the children's dying is somehow preferable to the burdens of caring for them. And the logical inference is that the mother's emotional attachment to her children does not compare with the emotional links that bind today's mother and child.

If you are not strongly attached to the child, there is little need to worry that it might suffer or die. And those children who do manage to survive would be expected to be working long before what we now consider adulthood — or even adolescence. You see, the medieval child, Aries tells us, did not have a childhood — at least, not a prolonged childhood. Children had just those short few years of dependence and then direct entry into the world of adults. In the Middle Ages, teen marriages were the rule rather than the exception.

This is admittedly an incomplete sketch of medieval childhood. It reflects a cold, callous, unfeeling attitude toward children. We do not know for certain how accurate the portrayal is, but we do know that like many historical accounts, it omits exceptions and, as a result, it exaggerates. We do know that there were many exceptions, that many children were much loved and tenderly reared.

Did the number of exceptions increase with the passage of time?

The Eighteenth and Nineteenth Centuries

Through the early 1700s, written and printed records became increasingly common as literacy was achieved slowly around the world. Accordingly, available accounts of attitudes toward children are far more reliable than are those for earlier periods. But in some ways, they are no less shocking. Laws and courts had not yet begun to grant children rights or protection; by today's standards, childrearing practices were often cruel and unforgiving; and child labor flourished throughout Europe and North America.

In 1761, the British courts sentenced one Anne Martin to two years in Newgate prison. Her crime? She habitually poked out the eyes of the children she took begging with her; it increased their success — and hers. Aha, you say, the courts did offer some protection to children! True, but it was skimpy protection indeed. As Pinchbeck and Hewitt (1973) point out, Anne Martin's case was unusual in that the children whose eyes she removed were not her own. Had they been her own children, it is likely that no one would have paid any attention. Parents could generally treat their own children any way they wanted.

Nor were the courts above severely punishing children for infractions of laws. Siegel and White (1982) report the case of a 7-year-old girl who stole a petticoat — surely not that great a crime. Still, she was brought to trial, convicted, sentenced — and hanged!

Eighteenth-century attitudes toward children are evident not only in the ways children were treated by the courts, but also in the ways children were treated by parents. In the crowded and diseased slums of eighteenth-century European cities, thousands of parents, ignorant of all but the most primitive birth control methods, bore children whom they promptly abandoned in the streets or on the doorsteps of churches and orphanages. Foundling homes sprang up all over Europe in an attempt to care for these children, but the majority died in **infancy** (before the age of 2 years). Kessen (1965) reports that of 10,272 infants admitted to one foundling home in Dublin in the last quarter of the eighteenth century, only 45 survived. Indeed, until the turn of that century, even if a child were not abandoned, chances of surviving till the age of 5 were less than one in two.

The high mortality rate of abandoned children was not restricted to eighteenth-century Europe but was characteristic of nineteenth-century America as well. Bakwin (1949) cites evidence indicating that with few exceptions children in infant homes (asylums) in the United States before 1915 died before the age of 2.

In the face of this tragic mortality rate, it is perhaps true that many parents did not become emotionally attached to their children. It was not unusual for children to be left on other people's doorsteps. And perhaps nowhere was parental indifference to the fate of their children as obvious as in the practice of burying them in the yard like a dog or a cat (Aries, 1962).

The nineteenth century brought some improvement in the status of children in Europe; abandonments decreased drastically. Unfortunately, this may have been less an index of increasing love and concern for children than of their economic value. In nineteenth-century Europe children had become highly prized as workers. In thousands of factories and mines, children as young as 5 or 6 years, male and female, worked 10 hours a day or more at grueling labor in conditions so hazardous that many became ill and died (Kessen, 1965). At that time, children were employed extensively in the coal mines of the British countryside. Most of these mines were underground, and the tunnels that led to the workings were often no more than 22 to 28 inches in height; the tunnels were poorly ventilated and were sometimes filled with 3 or 4 inches of water. Children were particularly valuable in the coal mines because they were small enough to crawl through these tiny tunnels, dragging baskets loaded with coal behind them by means of a "girdle and chain." The seventh earl of Shaftesbury (Anthony Ashley Cooper) described this contraption (in Kessen, 1965, p. 49):

> a girdle bound round its [the child's] waist, to which is attached a chain, which passes under the legs, and is attached to the [coal] cart. The child is obliged to pass on all fours, and the chain passes under what, therefore, in that posture, might be called the hind legs; and thus they have to pass through avenues not so good as a common sewer, quite as wet, and oftentimes more contracted.

The earl also described the blisters and the wounds that resulted from this device, the illnesses and diseases that children suffered in the mines, the physical and mental abuse, the beatings, the injuries. He begged the British House of Commons to pass a bill that would establish the age of 13 as a minimum age for male employment in the coal mines and that would completely prohibit the employment of females underground. Following considerable debate, and in spite of strong opposition, the bill prohibiting females from working underground was passed. But the House was convinced by the argument that children whose fathers are miners were more likely to profit from an education in the mines than from a "reading" education; as long as they had reached the age of 10, boys could continue to be employed in the mines.

Conditions in North America were, in some instances, not vastly different from those that prevailed in parts of Europe. Children were employed in great numbers in factories and cotton mills, in fields and in shops. But profound social and economic changes would soon alter all that.

The Twentieth Century

Infanticide, the murder of children, was, we are told, not uncommon in ancient times (DeMause, 1975). And, as we saw, abandonment and various forms of child use and abuse have been common until very recently. But our contemporary attitudes toward children are vastly different from those that permitted these things. We think.

The industrialized world. In the industrialized Western world, it is no longer common to abandon children for fear they will prove too much of an economic burden. We no longer send them into mines and factories when they are scarcely out of diapers. Children have now assumed an importance that is apparent not only in the home, but also in the courts, in the schools, and even at the highest levels of government. Among the many manifestations of this new importance are the thousands of programs that have sprung up since the United Nations' designation of 1979 as the International Year of the Child

(IYC), showing increasing concern with the social, emotional, and intellectual welfare of children and with their legal rights. A 1990 United Nations World Summit conference on the plights and the rights of the world's children reemphasized this importance.

The absolute control that parents and various agencies have long had over the lives and affairs of children has been weakened, although it is far from removed — nor, of course, should it be, because in a majority of cases the control that parents and others exercise over children is to their advantage. Unfortunately, however, such control is still abused. Farleger (1977) reports numerous instances in which children have been "voluntarily" committed to mental institutions by their parents or legal guardians ("voluntarily" because their parents "volunteered" them). Until recently, these children had virtually no legal recourse, no matter how badly they felt they had been treated, and they simply remained in the institution until psychiatrists and guardians judged it appropriate to release them.

Increasingly, major court decisions have begun to change this situation. In almost all cases in which institutionalized children have obtained legal aid in an attempt to establish their right to adequate care or to release, they have been successful. The overriding theme of these court decisions is that laws and their application must protect children rather than the rights of their parents; that societies have a responsibility for the welfare of children that transcends the wishes of parents when these are not in the best interests of the child; that, in short, the rights and privileges that have been guaranteed to adults by law also extend to children.

Evidence of increasing concern with the rights of children is also apparent in the adoption of ethical principles guiding research with children (published by the Society for Research in Child Development; Ethical standards for research with children, 1973). Establishment of these principles was motivated in part by the observation that research procedures with children can, in fact, be unethical if they involve coercion, if they subject the child to stress or other potentially damaging conditions, if they involve an invasion of privacy, and so on. The principles specify not only that the consent of parents must be obtained before conducting research with children but also that the children themselves must consent. Furthermore, their consent must be "informed" in the sense that they are made aware beforehand of any aspect of the research that might affect their willingness to participate.

In spite of the progress that has been made in the rights of children in the Western industrialized world, there are some who believe that much more must be done. According to Bronfenbrenner (1977a) the family is rapidly falling apart. Increasing numbers of people are marrying much later. The number of never-married 20- to 24-year-old women increased from 30 to 50 percent between 1960 and 1980 (Stein, P. J., 1983). By 1986, the percentage of never-married 20- to 24-year-old females had increased to over 65 (U.S. Bureau of the Census, 1988). In addition, divorce rates increased dramatically until 1980. In 1948, perhaps one child in 14 was raised in a single-parent family; at present, somewhere close to half of all children spend an average of six years in a one-parent family. In 90 percent of these families, the mother is the single parent (U.S. Bureau of the Census, 1988).

The eighties have seen other changes in the structure of Western societies that impact directly on the lives of children. Among these are important demographic (population) changes that have resulted in smaller families, reduced birthrates, larger numbers of childless couples, and a greater proportion of young adults (following the post–World War II baby boom) and of elderly people (resulting from medical advances). Another important change, the effects of which are discussed in detail in Chapter 10, is associated with the role of television in people's lives — and especially in children's lives.

Some argue that the net effect of these, and other, changes is that current decades are less child-centered than had been anticipated. Packard (1983), for example, advances the somewhat chilling thesis that being a child in the 1980s, and presumably in the 1990s as well, may be a very lonely experience. Among other things, childhood in these times brings with it a high probability of being looked after by a stranger, or more often by a series of strangers. And this is most likely to occur outside the comfort of the child's home. Childhood now also includes the probability of losing a father for much of the growing-up period, or perhaps of losing a mother, or of losing them in alternating fashion — or of losing much of their interest and attention and maybe their affection as well — as they struggle to cope with stressful personal and cultural changes. Childhood now entails the possibility of major readjustments when (and if) one or the other of the parents remarries, particularly if stepsiblings are brought into the family.

There was a time, not very long ago, when the things that most children feared were highly predictable: pain, death, spinach, darkness, and things that go bump in the night. The eighties have added some new fears: concerns over whether or not the parents will divorce; fears related to being left alone; fears associated with the likelihood of having to make new adjustments. In addition, there are some less private, new fears associated with our brutal and unceasing assaults on our world and the mounting environmental damage that results; there are fears, too, of possible nuclear annihilation.

But lest this paint too bleak a picture, let me hasten to point out that the changes of these times do not overwhelm all children and are not always a source of loneliness or despair. For many, they may be a challenge that results in strength rather than in weakness. Keep in mind too that these changes have little to do with the lives of many children.

The developing world. Clearly, not all children were abused and murdered in those very dark ages we call antiquity. Nor were all children abandoned through the Middle Ages. The children of Europe's eighteenth and nineteenth centuries weren't all beaten into the coal mines, and North America's children weren't all driven into the cotton fields and the textile factories. Of course, there have always been warm, loving parents. Historical accounts are typically painted with very broad strokes, the vividness of the colors exaggerated. We tend to concentrate on single themes and ignore what doesn't fit.

Sometimes we do the same thing when history isn't to blame. The twentieth century, we say piously, is characterized by a loving and helping attitude toward children. We are tempted to assume that in our contemporary wisdom we have corrected most of the evils of a more ignorant age. The assumption is naive, misleading, and dangerous.

The twentieth century too has its share of ignorance, of cruelty, of needless pain and suffering. About 15 million of the world's infants and children die each year from preventable causes. An astounding 4 million of these die from diarrheal dehydration (World Health Organization, 1989), and some 3 million die from easily preventable diseases — more than half of these from measles (see Figure 1.1). The majority of the remainder die from inadequate nutrition.

Sadly, in the early 1990s, these numbers have hardly changed. *Le Monde* reports United Nations data which indicate that some 8,000 infants die each day from measles, tetanus, and whooping cough — and another 7,000 from diarrheal dehydration: Pneumonia adds significantly to this total, and starvation more than doubles it. As a result, even in 1990 more than 30,000 children died each day from preventable causes (*Le monde au chevet de l'enfance menacée*, 1990).

At a theoretical level, the solutions for these social crimes seem simple and technically feasible. Vaccine-preventable diseases require proper and timely immunization. Nutrition-related suffering and dying can be relieved through a redistribution of our food surpluses. Diarrheal infection can be lessened through sanitation, and its effects can be countered or ameliorated through oral rehydration therapy (ORT). (ORT involves attempting to increase the infected child's fluid intake and to replace essential salts. ORT solutions can be made from specially prepared packets that are dissolved in water, or can be made from a proportionate solution of salts, sugar, or rice powder.) And the effects of each of these causes of infant and child death — vaccine-preventable diseases, diarrheal infection, and poor nutrition — can be lessened enormously through something as simple as breast-feeding. Incidence of diarrhea among breast-fed infants is far lower than among bottle-fed infants (Breast milk prevents disease, 1984). In addition, breast milk provides infants with a degree of immunity to various other diseases and supplies nutritious food in hygienic conditions (David & David, 1984). (Clearly, these arguments for breast-feeding are not entirely relevant in developed societies where malnutrition, poor sanitation, and gastrointestinal infections are less common.)

The majority of the 15 million children who die of preventable causes each year are born in the world's poorer countries. In many of these countries immunization is difficult, nutritious food is scarce, and drinking water is often contaminated. Compounding these problems, in many underdeveloped areas women work approximately twice as many hours a day as men, especially if they are responsible for agricultural as well as domestic tasks (Grant, 1986). As

Infant Survival

| Measles 2,000,000 | Tetanus 803,000 | Pertussis (whooping cough) 606,000 | |

Estimated deaths from
all vaccine-preventable diseases—
3,450,000

Other
41,000

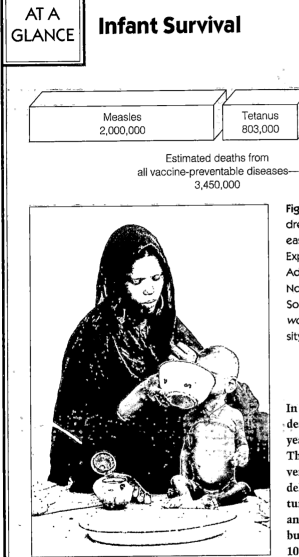

Figure 1.1   Estimated number of deaths in children under age 5 from vaccine-preventable diseases. Information is based on the report of the Expanded Programme on Immunizations, Global Advisory Group Meeting, UNICEF, Copenhagen, November 1985.
Source: Grant (1986), p. 3. *The state of the world's children: 1986.* New York: Oxford University Press.

In many parts of the world, infant mortality — defined in terms of death prior to the age of 1 year — exceeds 100 for every 1,000 live births. The vast majority of these infants die of preventable causes such as measles or diarrheal dehydration. At the turn of the twentieth century, infant mortality rates in the United States and in Canada were also about 100 per 1,000, but they have now been reduced to fewer than 10 per 1,000.

a result, they have little time or energy to devote to improving the lot of their children. And to save having to come home from the fields, they are likely to bottle-feed rather than breast-feed their infants. In fact, with the increasing availability of infant formulas, breast-feeding has declined dramatically in some areas (see Figure 1.2).

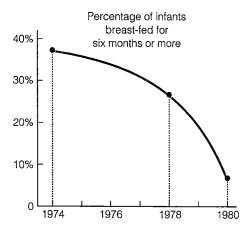

Figure 1.2

Decline in breast-feeding, São Paulo, Brazil, 1974–1980. Information is from a report by the International Union of Nutrition Scientists, Ad Hoc Task Force on Rethinking Infant Nutrition Policies, March 1982.

Source: Published for UNICEF in James P. Grant, Executive Director of the United Nations Children's Fund (1986). *The state of the world's children: 1986.* New York: Oxford University Press, p. 25.

Not surprisingly, one of the important factors in infant mortality is the mother's education. There is a growing consensus that female schooling can be a direct *cause* of reductions both in birthrate and in infant death (Levine, 1987). An analysis of information collected by the World Bank from some 99 different third world countries shows a very high relationship between the proportion of a country's females enrolled in primary schools and infant mortality rates some 22 years later (Caldwell, 1986). These data reveal that even incomplete primary schooling often leads to smaller families and to the loss of fewer children, even where sanitation, nutrition, and medical attention have not improved noticeably. Levine (1987) also reports that verbal interaction between mother and infant and maternal responsiveness to infant vocalizations are significantly higher for mothers with more schooling.

Unfortunately, in most developing countries, and especially in Africa, fewer than 50 percent of all children enroll in primary schools. And even at this level, dropout rates are extremely high, quality of education is very low, and the relative cost of education is high (Tsang, 1988). And, as Grant (1986) points out:

> it is the poor, those whose need is greatest, who have the least surplus of resources — of money, time, energy, health, knowledge, and confidence — to invest in improvements. That is the catch-22 of poverty . . . and so the cycle goes on. (p. 41)

But the cycle needn't go on forever. Nutrition, education, immunization, and medical care can break it. The cost? *Le Monde* (*Le monde au chevet de . . .*)

reports a UNICEF estimate that an expenditure of 2.5 billion dollars per year through this decade would save the lives of some 50 million children — and that is roughly what the major cigarette manufacturers spend each year on advertising!

CHILDREN'S RIGHTS

DeMause (1975) traces six historical trends in the way society has treated children — six trends that reflect changing attitudes toward children:

1. In antiquity, infanticide was a common way of dealing with millions of children.
2. In the Middle Ages, children were more likely to be abandoned than murdered.
3. The Renaissance appears to have been marked by an ambivalent attitude toward children.
4. With the growth of industrialization, children became like chattel — things to be used, to be benefited from economically.
5. The nineteenth century saw a continuation of many of the abuses and cruelty of the preceding century, but also heralded increasing concern with the plights of children.
6. And now, according to DeMause, we are at the threshold of a deep-seated helping attitude toward children (Table 1.3).

Contemporary industrialized societies' attitudes toward children are reflected in the efforts of various advocacy groups to establish the rights of children and to make society responsible for ensuring that these rights are safeguarded. Parents no longer have absolute jurisdiction and control over the lives of their children; where the rights of children are violated, various social and judicial agencies may intervene.

What are the rights of children? A list proclaimed by the United Nations in 1979 includes the child's right to:

- adequate medical care
- adequate nutrition
- affection, love, and understanding
- education
- the opportunity for play and recreation
- special care if required
- a peaceful environment
- the opportunity to develop individual abilities

As Caldwell (1989) notes, the rights of children are geared toward providing the optimal, growth-fostering conditions for them. In general, they are rights of *protection* rather than rights of *choice*. That is, children need to be protected from the dangers to which their immaturity exposes them, and their access to a growth-fostering environment needs to be safeguarded. But in many instances, they lack the maturity and the knowledge required for making the best choices in their own lives. My fourteen-year-old has the right to adequate nutrition, medical care, and education; but, understandably, he does not have the right to make all his own nutritional, educational, and medical choices. Many of those choices are my responsibility — or his mother's. We might not be able to convince him that he should eat his spinach, that it is good for him, but we can at least point him toward school each morning carrying a well-balanced meal in his lunch-bag (and a pocketful of coin that he can exchange for his own nutritional choices).

This does not mean, of course, that children have no responsibilities. As Caldwell (1989) points out, society expects its children to assimilate dominant cultural values and eventually foster the continuation of the culture. In addition, of course, society expects that its children will take advantage of the rights and opportunities provided for them — that they will mature and learn. (See Figure 1.3 for a summary of the relationships among the rights and responsibilities of parents, society, and children; and Figure 1.4 for a look at child poverty.)

PIONEERS IN CHILD DEVELOPMENT

The study of children is a relatively recent enterprise. The widespread social changes that manifested themselves in seventeenth- and eighteenth-century attitudes toward children — together with intellectual movements reflected in the writings of philosophers and early scientists, advances in biology and medicine, and the increasing availability of elementary education — all contributed significantly to the development of child psychology.

Early Pioneers

Closely associated with these intellectual movements were people such as John Locke and Jean-Jacques Rousseau. Locke, writing in the late seventeenth century, argued that the child is essentially a rational creature, born with a mind comparable to a blank slate *(tabula rasa)* upon which experience writes messages. The child described by Locke is a passive recipient of knowledge, information, and habits and is highly responsive to rewards and punishments. In Locke's (1699) words, "If you take away the Rod on one hand, and these little Encouragements which they are taken with, on the other, How then (will you say) shall Children be govern'd? Remove Hope and Fear, and there is an end of all Discipline."

Rousseau's child, described in the book *Emile* (1762), is a direct contrast to the child described by Locke. The Rousseau child is active and inquiring. Furthermore, this child is not a "blank slate," neither good nor bad until the rewards and punishments of experience exert their influence, but is innately

Table 1.3
Six Historical Trends in Treatment of Children

Antiquity	Little evidence of strong parental attachment; occasional infanticide socially acceptable
Middle Ages	Poverty and emotional indifference lead to widespread abandonment of infants; very high infant mortality rates
Renaissance	Ambivalent attitude toward children
Eighteenth century	Industrialization contributes to widespread use of children as manual laborers in factories, mines, fields, shops, etc.
Nineteenth century	Child labor continues to flourish; beginnings of important medical and educational changes
Twentieth century	Child-centered, especially in the industrialized world; concern with the rights and plights of children. But still many instances of abuse, starvation, exploitation, and unnecessary mortality

Source: Based in part on de Mause (1975).

Note: Although these trends and attitudes are descriptive of some cultures and of some families during the periods in question, they are sometimes not very general. Clearly, although infanticide might once have been acceptable under some circumstances, no society permitted all its infants to be killed. Similarly, even at the height of the period of child labor in the eighteenth century, there were many well-cared-for children who played and went to school and had carefree childhoods in loving homes.

good – a "noble savage." Rousseau insists that if children were allowed to develop in their own fashion, untainted by the corruption and evil in the world, they would certainly be good when grown: "God makes all things good; man meddles with them and they become evil."

Although both Locke and Rousseau are closely associated with the beginning of the study of children, their ideas have led to fundamentally different conceptions of childhood. Locke's description of the child as a passive creature, molded by the rewards and punishments of experience, has a close parallel in learning theory descriptions of development, particularly as exemplified in the works of Skinner and Bandura (described in Chapter 2). Rousseau's view of an active, exploring child developing through deliberate interaction with the environment finds an important place in the work of Jean Piaget (also described in Chapter 2).

Later Pioneers

Although the science of child psychology owes a great deal to early "child philosophers" such as Rousseau and Locke, its beginnings are usually attributed to the first systematic observations and written accounts of children, such as Preyer's (1882) detailed observations of his own children and Darwin's (1877) biography of his son (Cairns & Valsiner, 1984). Preyer and Darwin were among

Our conceptions of children and childhood have evolved over the centuries. By the time of Willem Van Mieris's *The Happy Mother (Allegory of the Senses)* in 1707 (left), children were no longer seem simply as miniature adults. But close study of children dates back to the late 19th century, when Western society was becoming more child-centered, as reflected in Mary Cassatt's *Women Admiring a Child,* painted in 1891 (right).

the first to undertake detailed, systematic, and relatively objective investigations of children developing.

Hard on the heels of these two pioneers followed G. Stanley Hall (1891), who became the first president of the American Psychological Association. Hall was profoundly influenced by Darwin's theories of evolution. "Ontogeny recapitulates phylogeny," he informed his colleagues, summarizing in one short phrase his conviction that the development of a single individual in a species parallels the evolution of the entire species (an idea now largely discredited). As evidence for this theory, Hall described the evolution of children's interests in games, noting how these seem to correspond to the evolution of human occupations and life-styles. Notice, insisted Hall, how the child is, in sequence, interested in games corresponding to each of the following: an arboreal existence (for example, climbing on chairs and tables); a cave-dwelling existence (crawling into small spaces, making tiny shelters with old blankets); a pastoral existence (playing with animals); an agricultural existence (tending flowers and plants); and finally an industrial existence (playing with vehicles).

Hall pioneered the use of the questionnaire as a tool for studying children, questioning them at great length in an attempt to discover something of their behavior and their thoughts. Often, too, he presented his questionnaires to adults to try to get them to remember what they had felt and thought as

Figure 1.3

Caldwell's triadic
model of the rights
and responsibilities
of parents, children,
and society in rela-
tion to each other.
Source: Caldwell, B. M.
(1980). Balancing chil-
dren's rights and
parents' rights.[1]

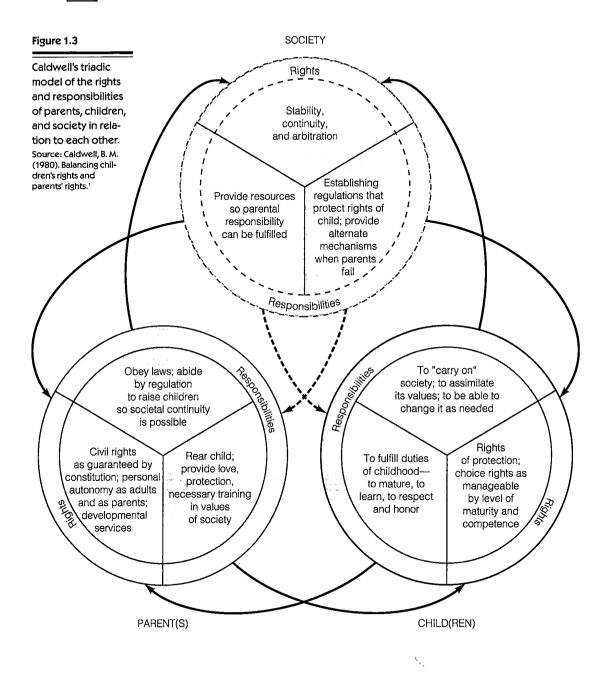

SOCIETY

Rights

Stability,
continuity,
and arbitration

Provide resources
so parental
responsibility
can be fulfilled

Establishing
regulations that
protect rights of
child; provide
alternate
mechanisms
when parents
fail

Responsibilities

Obey laws; abide
by regulation
to raise children
so societal continuity
is possible

Responsibilities

Responsibilities

To "carry on"
society; to assimilate
its values; to be able to
change it as needed

Civil rights
as guaranteed by
constitution; personal
autonomy as adults
and as parents;
developmental
services

Rights

Rear child;
provide love,
protection,
necessary training
in values
of society

To fulfill duties
of childhood—
to mature, to
learn, to respect
and honor

Rights
of protection;
choice rights as
manageable
by level of
maturity and
competence

Rights

PARENT(S)

CHILD(REN)

---

[1]In R. Haskins & J. J. Gallagher (Eds.), *Care and education of young children in
America: Policy, politics and social science* (p. 37). Norwood, NJ: Ablex. Reprinted
by permission of the publisher.

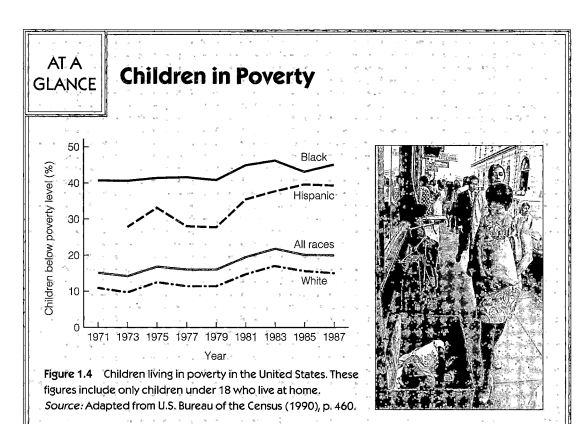

AT A GLANCE

Children in Poverty

Figure 1.4 Children living in poverty in the United States. These figures include only children under 18 who live at home. *Source:* Adapted from U.S. Bureau of the Census (1990), p. 460.

Not only do children have a right to be protected from harm, proclaims the United Nations, but their right to access a growth-fostering environment also needs to be safeguarded. Children's rights include the right to adequate medical care, nutrition, education, and special care if required – and the right to a peaceful environment and to affection, love, and understanding. But even in the wealthiest and most child-centered of the world's nations, millions of children are poor. Strangely, although the percentage of Americans over age 65 living in poverty declined from 24.6 to 12.2 between 1970 and 1987, during that same period the percentage of American children below poverty level increased from 14.9 to 20. That means about 12.5 million children in the United States live in poverty.

children. Always, he summed, tabulated, averaged, and compared the results of his questionnaires, a true pioneer of the application of scientific procedures and principles to the study of human development.

Another pioneer of child psychology was John B. Watson (1914), who introduced an experimental, learning theory–based approach to the study of development. Following his influence, as well as that of Skinner, this model came to dominate child study through the early part of the twentieth century. It was a model that looked for the causes of developmental change among the rewards and punishments of the environment and viewed the child as the passive recipient of these influences.

Child Study Today

Economic and social changes have done a great deal to change our attitudes toward children. Advances in medicine and hygiene have saved children from early deaths and made it less traumatic for us to love them. Legislation has gone a considerable distance toward assuring them their legal rights and protecting them from various forms of abuse. Children, for most people in our society, are no longer an economic burden or necessity. We, and they, have the advantage of a wealthier and perhaps kinder age. As a result, our industrialized societies can aptly be described as child-centered (DeMause, 1975).

In this child-centered age, we study children for a variety of reasons, not least because we want to understand how we become what we are. Our hope is that with greater understanding, we will be better able to ensure the development of happy, productive, healthy individuals. It should not be surprising, then, to find that child psychology is highly applied, in the sense that it is directed toward practical as well as theoretical concerns. The questions that have traditionally seemed most important are those dealing with the welfare of children. Accordingly, child psychologists have addressed themselves directly to questions relating to instruction, discipline and behavior problems, emotional disorders, perceptual problems, language acquisition, social development, morality, and a variety of other topics that are important to teachers, nurses, counselors, physicians, child welfare professionals, religious personnel, and parents.

To simplify, our study of developmental processes is intended to provide us with information about: (1) the sorts of behaviors we might expect from children at different ages; (2) the optimal experiences for children at different developmental levels; and (3) the nature of developmental problems and the best treatments for them.

3   RECURRING QUESTIONS

A number of important questions have served as recurring themes in developmental psychology and have guided much of its research and theorizing. The Locke-Rousseau question is one of them:

1. Is it best to view the child as an active, exploring organism, discovering or inventing meaning for the world, as Rousseau argued? Or is it more useful to emphasize, as did Locke, the effects of rewards and punishments on a

more passive recipient? Rousseau and Locke clearly felt very strongly about this question — and disagreed very strongly. Most contemporary developmental psychologists do not adhere to one or the other point of view so passionately. Clearly, however, the predominant view is one of an active, exploring child, deliberately attempting to create meaning out of the world — and also trying to become meaningful in the sense of *meaning* something to important others (Kegan, 1982). At the same time, most developmental psychologists recognize the important influence of reward and punishment.

2. What are the relative effects of genetics and of environments on the developmental process? This question raises an issue that has been the source of great controversy throughout the history of psychology — an issue often referred to as the **nature-nurture controversy** or the **heredity** versus **environment** question. Extreme points of view on this issue would maintain either that the environment is solely responsible for whatever children become (nurture) or that genetic background (nature) determines the outcome of the developmental process. Although neither of these extreme positions is completely valid, the issue continues to be debated and is discussed in detail in Chapter 3.

3. Is development a continuous, relatively uninterrupted process, or does it consist of separate stages? This question, like most of the recurring questions in human development, does not have a simple answer — especially not one that can be presented clearly in a handful of short paragraphs. Here, as elsewhere, the answer depends to a large extent on how the terms in question are defined. **Stages** in developmental psychology, are typically defined as separate, sequential steps in the evolution of abilities, understandings, or competencies — these steps being closely related to age. As we will see in the next chapter, many important developmental theories are stage theories (for example, Piaget or Freud). But as we will also see, it has been difficult to identify abilities or competencies that *invariably* develop in a fixed, predictable sequence, appearing at a predetermined age. Nor, in most areas of human activity, is it simple to discover developmental phenomena that are sufficiently discrete or separate to allow researchers to identify universally accepted stages. We do not develop like caterpillars, cocoon to butterfly to egg to caterpillar to cocoon to butterfly, each stage undeniably different from the one that precedes or follows it. Nevertheless, stage theories are useful in organizing the *facts* of human development and in helping us understand and talk about them.

None of these issues has been completely resolved. Perhaps they cannot be; and perhaps history will show that they were not particularly important in any case. What is important, however, is to keep in mind that what we think and say about children — indeed, the questions we ask and sometimes the answers we are prepared to accept — are strongly influenced by our assumptions and beliefs.

BASIC BELIEFS

Developmental psychology is much more than a handful of questions; there are also a number of widely held beliefs about some of the important characteristics and causes of human development. These are fundamental to understanding contemporary developmental psychology.

1. As we noted earlier, most psychologists view the child as active, exploring, and engaged in trying to create meaning — not simply as the passive recipient of external forces, responding blindly to the rewards and punishments that life provides and ingesting information as it is provided.

2. The causes of development are to be found in the *interaction* of environmental and genetic factors (rather than in their *separate* effects).

3. Development occurs in a specific historical and cultural context (that is, in a specific environment) and is profoundly influenced by the interaction between the person's characteristics and properties of the environment.

4. Some common threads appear to run through the developmental paths that different individuals take. These commonalities allow developmental psychologists to describe developmental stages or phases and to make generalizations for *groups* with identifiable characteristics.

5. At the same time, there are pronounced differences among individuals even from very similar contexts and genetic histories. The differences become even greater where context and genetic history are more dissimilar.

6. Change is what human development is all about. The quest to describe and understand changes that occur with age and experience is based on the belief that some of the personal and environmental factors that influence change, and some of the processes involved, are identifiable and their effects predictable.

METHODS OF STUDYING CHILDREN

The scientific study of children is relatively recent. Indeed, for many years animals such as dogs, horses, and sheep were more likely to be the subject of detailed observation than were children. And when children did become the focus of psychological investigation, new methodological problems arose. It is unfortunate that in attempting to make sense of the mind and emotions of infants, we can no longer remember what it was like to be an infant — nor can infants tell us in words. Much of what we know of the private life of preverbal children is based on inferences that we make. However, these inferences are based not on speculation, inspiration, or the prejudices of grandparents but on careful, controlled, and replicable observation.

Observers of human development may focus on natural events, such as children playing in a playground; they may collect information on less natu-

Table 1.4
Naturalistic Methods of Observing Children

Method	Description	Main Uses
Diary description	Fairly regular (often daily or weekly) descriptions of important events and changes	Detecting and understanding major changes and developmental sequences
Specimen description	Detailed description of sequences of behavior, detailing all aspects of behavior	Studying individual children in depth; not restricted to only one or two predetermined characteristics
Time sampling	Behaviors are recorded intermittently during short but regular periods of time	Detecting and assessing changes in specific behaviors over time
Event sampling	Specific behaviors (events) are recorded during the observational period and other behaviors are ignored	Understanding the nature and frequency of specific behaviors (events)

Source: Based in part on Wright (1960).

rally occurring events, such as controlled experiments or children being interviewed. In addition, developmental research is usually either longitudinal (following the same subjects over a long period of time) or cross-sectional (using a sample of subjects that differ in age at one point in time). Each of these approaches is described in the following sections. Note that these are not mutually exclusive categories. For example, a study of development might be experimental and longitudinal or cross-sectional simultaneously.

Observations

Observation is the basis of all science. The study of children always begins with observation.

Observations are termed *naturalistic* when children are observed *without interference* in natural rather than contrived situations — for example, in the playground or in school. Psychologists who observe children and write **diary descriptions** of their behavior (sequential descriptions of behavior at predetermined intervals) are making use of naturalistic observation. Similarly, those who describe continuous sequences of behavior (**specimen descriptions**), behaviors during specified time intervals (**time sampling**), or specific behaviors only (**event sampling**) are using naturalistic observation (Wright, 1960; see Table 1.4). Note that in each of these methods, the child's behavior is unaffected by the observation.

Time and event sampling are often used together. Time sampling specifies *when* observations will be made; event sampling specifies *what* behavior will be observed. If, for example, an investigator wanted to determine whether a new approach to teaching encourages student participation, a combination of time and event sampling would be appropriate. During specified intervals of time over a number of days (time sampling), the investigator would record instances of student participation (event sampling). Subsequently, observed participation before and after introduction of the new teaching method would be compared.

In nonnaturalistic observations, the investigation affects the child's behavior. Nonnaturalistic observations are sometimes called *clinical* if they involve the use of interviews or questionnaires. If they attempt to manipulate or change the child's environment, they are called *experimental*. Experiments are described in some detail in the next section.

In practice, the methods used by those who investigate child development are determined by the questions they want to answer. Some questions can best be answered with one approach; others, with another. And some questions, of course, lend themselves to more than one approach. If you are interested in knowing whether children have more affection for cats than dogs, you might simply compare the number of children who have dogs with the number who have cats (naturalistic observation). Alternately, you might *ask* a sample of children which they like best (interview technique). Or you might arrange for different children, alone and in groups, to meet different cats and dogs — also alone and in groups (experimental approach) — and assess their reactions (through simple visual observation or perhaps by measuring their heartrates and other physiological functions).

Note that each of these approaches might lead to somewhat different answers for the same questions. Perhaps there are more cats than dogs in the homes of your subjects — many parents think cats are less demanding — but children really like dogs better. And maybe, even if they do like dogs better, more would be afraid of dogs than of cats because strange dogs are somewhat more frightening than strange cats.

In short, answers are sometimes partly a function of the research methods, and the answers might have been different had the investigation been different. That is an important point to keep in mind as you go through some of the studies described in this text.

In many cases, the study of children involves a combination of methods rather than a single method. Experiments typically require observations. Hence interviews and questionnaires are often part of an experiment.

Experiments

Science's most powerful tool for gathering useful observations is the **experiment**. What distinguishes an experiment from other observations is the requirement that the observer systematically manipulate some aspect of a situation to detect and measure the effects of doing so. More precisely, in an experiment the observer controls certain **variables** (characteristics that can vary) — termed **independent** — to investigate their effect, or lack of effect, on other variables — termed **dependent.** For example, in an experiment designed to investigate the relationship between two teaching methods and the development of language skills, the experimenter can manipulate (control) the variable *teaching method* by arranging for the use of teaching method A with one group of students and teaching method B with a second group. In addition, if we are to have faith in the results of the experiment, subjects must be assigned to methods A or B randomly to guard against the possibility that students in one group might have some systematic advantage over students in the other.

   In this illustration, teaching method is the independent variable; it is under the experimenter's control. Measures of the subjects' language skills are a dependent variable; the experimenter's hypothesis (scientific prediction) is that the independent variable (teaching method) will affect the dependent variable (language skills).

   Experimental procedures often use **experimental groups** and **control groups.** Experimental groups are ordinarily made up of subjects who are treated in some special way. The object is usually to discover whether the special treatment (independent variable) has a predictable effect on some outcome (dependent variable). To ensure that any changes in the dependent variable are due to the treatment, it is often necessary to use a second group — the *control* or *no-treatment group.* This second group must be as similar as possible to the experimental group in all relevant ways except that it does not experience the treatment. The effect of the special treatment is then assessed by comparing the two groups with respect to some outcome (dependent variable) after the experimental group has been given the treatment.*

   Bear in mind that a careful, well-controlled experiment that can be replicated — that is, whose outcomes are the same on different occasions — is science's only reliable method for determining causes and effects. Experiments that cannot be replicated tell us nothing about causes and effects. Science pays little attention to things that happen only once.

An example. According to a theory of emotions developed by Carroll Izard (1977), expressions of emotion by one member of a **dyad** (two people interacting) can elicit similar emotions in the other member. The theory also argues that feelings are powerful human motivators that can lead to predictable kinds of behaviors. For example, emotions associated with interest might lead to exploration, play, learning, or other sorts of approach behaviors; in contrast, sadness typically leads to a slowing or cessation of exploration or play or to other kinds of avoidance behaviors.

   Considerable evidence has been gathered to support and clarify this theory with respect to adults and children. However, relatively little has been done

---

*This is only one of a large variety of experimental designs that are employed in psychological research. For others, see Ray and Ravizza (1985).

with infants, partly because of difficulties involved in identifying and measuring infant emotions.

In an experiment conducted by Termine and Izard (1988), 36 9-month-old infants were brought into a laboratory setting on two separate occasions (nonnaturalistic observation). On each occasion, they were placed in a high chair directly in front of their mothers, and their behaviors and facial expressions, as well as those of their mothers, were videotaped for later analysis. In one experimental manipulation, mothers were instructed to show *sadness* both verbally and facially. They were asked to recall a sad incident and to talk about it, and they were instructed in the basic components of a sad face (for example, turning down the corners of the mouth). After two minutes of sad expression and vocalization, an experimenter entered and presented the infant with a series of toys, all of which were removed some three minutes later. During this period, mothers were reminded at 30-second intervals, via earphones, to continue to look sad and to occasionally say something sad like, "I feel so sad today."

In the second experimental manipulation, the same infants were brought into an identical situation except that the mothers were now instructed to sound and look joyful. Half the infants were exposed to the *sad* situation first; the other half, to the *joy* situation.

This experiment permits a comparison of the effects of two sets of independent variables (*sad* facial expressions and vocalizations on the one hand and expressions of *joy* on the other) on a set of dependent variables having to do with infant responses to their mothers. Specifically, three separate **hypotheses** (scientific predictions) were examined: (1) infants would show more joy in the *joy* situation and more sadness in the *sad* condition, (2) infants would look at their mothers less in the *sad* condition (an avoidance behavior) and more in the *joy* situation (an approach behavior), and (3) infants would play more in the *joy* than in the *sad* condition.

Measures of infant emotions, of the extent to which they looked at their mothers, and of their play behavior, were obtained by having two trained observers analyze videotapes of each experimental session. It is especially important to note that a **blind procedure** was used; that is, the observers, working independently, were unaware of the experimental condition to which each infant had been exposed. As explained in a later section of this chapter, this is an important safeguard against the possibility that the observer's expectations might affect experimental outcomes.

Analysis of the results support the investigators' principal expectations. First, infants in the *joy* condition expressed significantly more joy; those in the *sad* condition, more sadness. Perhaps not surprisingly, infants in the *sad* condition also displayed more anger, perhaps because, as Termine and Izard (1988) suggest, anger and sadness are related emotions.

Second, as is shown in Figure 1.5, infants in the *sad* condition looked at their mothers significantly less during the initial two minutes, during which time the mother was actively attempting to induce an emotional state. After

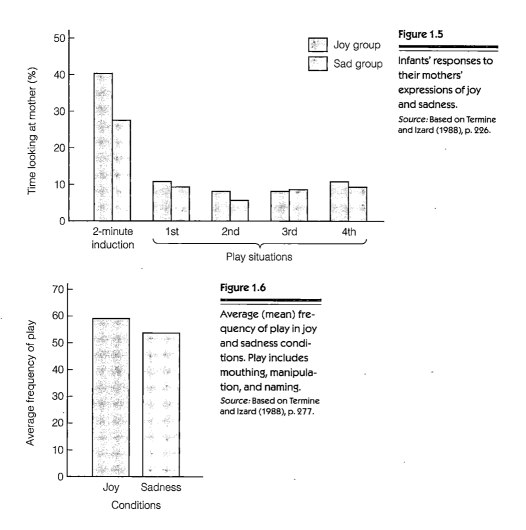

Figure 1.5

Infants' responses to their mothers' expressions of joy and sadness.

Source: Based on Termine and Izard (1988), p. 226.

Figure 1.6

Average (mean) frequency of play in joy and sadness conditions. Play includes mouthing, manipulation, and naming.

Source: Based on Termine and Izard (1988), p. 277.

the presentation of the toys, infants in both groups look at their mothers only very briefly.

Finally, infants in· the *joy* condition played more with the toys than did infants in the *sad* condition (Figure 1.6).

A single experiment does not *prove* anything. In fact, a whole battery of related experiments might not *prove* very much either; absolute fact is a rare luxury in science. Still, experiments such as this, carefully controlled and replicated, are, as we have noted, science's only reliable way of investigating cause-and-effect relationships. They are science's best source of information, the foundation for its most logical and useful conclusions. But in many situations experiments are not possible or would be quite unethical. In some of these situations, **correlational studies** might be used.

Correlational Studies

A great deal of child development research may be described as follows: Researchers decide to investigate the sources (causes) of specific characteristics in a group of children; children with these characteristics are identified; a comparison group of children without these characteristics is also identified. An attempt is now made to obtain historical information about these children (for example, home environment, presence or absence of a father, intelligence, presence of similar characteristics in biological ancestors, and so on). Researchers now compare the two groups on these historical variables. In the end, a relationship (**correlation**†) will be found to exist between specific historical variables and present characteristics or no relationship will be found.

Largely through studies such as these, research has established relationships between socioeconomic variables such as poverty and delinquency or between the personality characteristics of parents and those of children. Many such studies, sometimes termed *retrospective,* are described in this text. They are called retrospective because they try to establish relationships by looking backward at the child's history (*retro* means backward) to see how factors in the child's past are related to present behavior.

One caution is extremely important here. One of the most common errors in the interpretation of research results stems from the apparently logical but false assumption that if two events are related (correlated), one causes the other. It might be possible to demonstrate, for example, that in many areas there is a high positive correlation between the number of police personnel in a city and the number of criminal arrests among students. The more police officers, the more arrests. Should we conclude that there is something about police officers that causes criminal behavior among students?

By the same token, if we find that measures of home background (socioeconomic indicators such as family income, parental education, and so on) are correlated with school achievement, can we conclude that these *cause* high or low achievement? No. At best, correlational studies show relationships or their absence; they do not establish causation.

Although correlational studies cannot establish that one thing leads to and therefore causes another, it is nevertheless true that presence of a correlation is a *necessary* condition for inferring causality; but it is not a *sufficient* condition. If, as my grandmother believed, it is true that having freckles causes people to have violent tempers, then there *must* be a correlation between presence of freckles and bad tempers. If there is no such correlation, then my grandmother is dead wrong: Freckles do not cause bad tempers. Unfortunately, however, even if this correlation exists and is very high, she might still be wrong. Freckles

---

†A *correlation* is a mathematical measure of relationship. It is usually expressed as a number ranging from $+1.00$ (a perfect *positive* relationship; as one variable increases, so does the other), through 0 (no relationship) to -1.00 (a perfect *inverse* relationship; as one variable increases, the other decreases).

might simply be the work of the same fairies who mischievously hand out uncontrollable tempers. Or they might be nothing more than genetic accidents in my grandmother's sample.

So, knowing whether or not there is a correlation between two things is necessary if we are to determine whether one causes the other. But a correlational relationship is still not proof of a causal relationship, although a carefully controlled experiment might be.

These comments do not mean that correlational studies should be avoided and that only experiments should be conducted. Not only are correlational studies often highly informative (when interpreted cautiously), but experiments also are often impossible for practical and ethical reasons. Consider, for example, an experiment designed to investigate the effects of poverty. Such an experiment would require that investigators assign randomly selected (or highly similar) children to precisely defined conditions of wealth or poverty at some critical and presumably early stage in their lives and that these children be examined and compared later. For this and many other investigations, an experiment is clearly not in order.

Longitudinal and Cross-Sectional Research

There are two general approaches to the study of human development: the longitudinal and the cross-sectional. A longitudinal study is based on observation of the same subjects over a period of time; a cross-sectional study is based on the comparison of different subjects of different developmental levels at the same time. There are two ways, for example, of arriving at some notion about the different rules employed in games played by 2-year-old children and 6-year-old children. One method is to observe a group of 2-year-old children at play and four years later repeat the same procedure with the same children. This is the longitudinal approach. The same results could be obtained by observing several groups of 2- and 6-year-old children at the same time and comparing them directly. There are occasions, however, when a longitudinal approach is necessary despite the fact that it is time consuming. If investigators want to discover whether intelligence test scores change with age or remain stable, they can do this by observing the same children at different times. This question cannot be answered by employing a cross-sectional approach.

Cross-sectional and longitudinal approaches are both essential for studying human development. Each, however, has some weaknesses and limitations. As we noted, a cross-sectional approach cannot give us information about changes that occur over time within a single individual, because it looks at each individual only once.

Among the problems associated with longitudinal research are its higher cost, the fact that instruments and methods may become outdated before completion, the possibility that some of the research questions will be answered in some other way before the project is finished, and the tremendous amount of time that is sometimes required. Often an experiment must be designed to go

beyond the lifetime of a single investigator (or team of investigators). This is
the case with the Terman study of giftedness, which began in the early 1920s
and which continues today (Terman et al., 1925). This kind of study encounters
an additional problem related to subject mortality. The death of subjects not
only reduces the size of samples but may also serve to bias the results. If, for
example, individuals of a certain personality type die younger than do others,
a longitudinal assessment of personality change might reveal some significant
changes with old age when such is, in fact, not the case. As a purely hypothetical illustration, if aggressive people die before those who are nonaggressive, we
might be led to believe that people become less aggressive as they age.

Perhaps the most serious limitation of longitudinal studies is that they
must frequently assume that currently valid measures will be equally valid in
the future. This problem is particularly evident in longitudinal studies of vocabulary growth, intelligence, and related variables where rapidly changing
cultural conditions may significantly affect the appropriateness of measures
employed. Cross-sectional studies sometimes suffer from a similar problem,
stemming from their assumption that children at one age level now are comparable to children at that age level at another time. With respect to intelligence, for example, drastic improvements in educational experiences and
perhaps in television fare can affect children sufficiently over a period of time
that measures of intelligence obtained at one time cannot easily be compared
with measures obtained some years earlier.

It should be noted that many of the problems associated with longitudinal
research (for example, subject mortality, higher cost, greater time requirement,
changing contexts in the lives of subjects) apply only to *longer*-term research.
But not all longitudinal research is long term. For example, longitudinal studies
of infant development might span only weeks, or perhaps only days or hours.
However, because human development spans a huge spread of years, much of
our longitudinal research necessarily is long term (see Table 1.5).

Age, time, and cohort. Cross-sectional and longitudinal studies look at three
separate sources of variation. First are changes related to age. Bear in mind,
however, that age is neither a cause nor an explanation for human development,
although we often treat it that way. Second are influences related to time of
testing. Third is the influence of the **cohort.**

A cohort is a group of individuals who have in common the fact that they
were born within the same range of time. The 1970 cohort includes all individuals who were born during the year 1970; the December 1970 cohort includes
all individuals born during December 1970; and the cohort of the eighth decade
in the twentieth century includes all individuals born in the 10-year period
between January 1970 and December 1979. A cohort is therefore of a specific
size and composition initially. It does not normally increase in size, but rather
decreases as members die until it has completely disappeared. Its composition
also changes gradually in other ways. Because men die sooner than women, the

Table 1.5
Methods of Studying Children

Observation	The basis of all science. Observation is naturalistic when children are observed without interference in natural rather than contrived situations. Naturalistic observation may involve time or event sampling, diary descriptions, or specimen descriptions (see Table 1.4). Nonnaturalistic observation may be clinical when it involves structured interviews or questionnaires.
Experiment	Science's most powerful means of gathering observations. Experiments involve systematic attempts to manipulate the environment to observe what the effects of specific independent variables are on given dependent variables.
Correlational study	A look at relationships among two or more variables. A correlation exists when changes in one variable are accompanied by systematic changes in another (for example, during childhood increasing age is correlated *positively* with increasing strength). The existence of a correlation is necessary but *insufficient* for inferring causality.

Developmental research can be:

Longitudinal	where the same subjects are followed over a period of time
Cross-sectional	where subjects of different ages are studied at one point in time

male-female ratio of a cohort usually changes over time. Similarly, racial composition might also change as a result of different mortality rates.

What is most important for the developmental psychologist is not that individuals of a single cohort are of the same age so much as that they may be subject to a variety of experiences very different from those to which members of other cohorts are exposed. For example, cohort groups such as that of my grandmother date to the turn of this century and include people who were born into a world without electricity, without television, without computers, and without automobiles. These rather obvious cohort-related influences might be important in attempting to understand why an 8-year-old in 1990 might be quite different from an 8-year-old in 2028 or in 1928. Less obvious cohort-related influences would also include changes in medical practices (including the general use of a variety of inoculations), in nutrition, in leisure-time activities, in work roles, in morality, and so on. Because of these influences, cohorts that are scarcely separated in time might turn out to be very different in some important ways.

One of the most serious problems that developmental researchers have faced is the difficulty of separating the effects of age, time, and cohort. Often these sources of variation cannot be distinguished. In a cross-sectional design it may be impossible to determine whether differences between two age groups are age-related or whether they are due to generational factors because two different cohorts are being examined. In a simple longitudinal study it may be impossible to separate the effects of time of testing from those of age. In addition, generalizations derived from a longitudinal study might be applicable only to the specific cohort under investigation.

One way of overcoming these important research problems is to use what are termed *sequential* designs (Schaie, 1965). Essentially, these involve taking sequences of samples at different times of measurement. One well-known sequential design is the **time-lag study** in which different cohorts are compared at different times. For example, a time-lag study might compare 10-year-olds in 1991 with 10-year-olds in 1993, 1995, and 1997. Because subjects are of the same age when tested, but were born in different years, they belong to different cohorts. Consequently, observed differences among the groups might reveal important cohort-related influences (see Figure 1.7).

EVALUATING DEVELOPMENTAL RESEARCH

Truth in psychology, as in most disciplines, is relative. It is occasionally approximated but seldom attained. Hence the validity of conclusions derived from research can seldom by judged in terms of some absolute degree of rightness or wrongness, but must instead be interpreted in terms of usefulness, clarity, logical consistency, and **generalizability** (generality). Of all these, perhaps generalizability is most important. Too often, results of a specific research project apply only to the situation in which they were obtained; they cannot be generalized to other, similar situations. The value of such conclusions is limited.

Sampling

Research in psychology attempts to reach conclusions that are generalizable to entire **populations** — that is, to entire collections of individuals (or objects or situations) with similar characteristics. For example, the entire collection of North American fifth-grade children defines a population; all left-handed, brown-eyed infants make up another population. In most cases, the populations that are of interest to the researcher are too large to be investigated in their entirety. Consider, for example, the problem of determining possible relationships between measurements of creative potential and intelligence for the population of elementary-school boys and girls in North America. It would be extremely expensive, not to mention virtually impossible, to measure creativity and intelligence for the entire population. What the investigator does, instead, is select a *sample* from this larger population. A sample is simply a subset

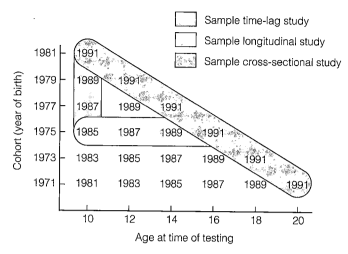

Figure 1.7

Schematic representation of three research designs. Years inside the figure indicate time of testing. Vertical columns represent possible time-lag studies (different cohorts; different times of measurement; same ages). Horizontal rows represent possible longitudinal studies (same cohort measured at different times). Diagonals represent possible cross-sectional studies (different cohorts examined at one point in time).

of a larger population, carefully chosen to be representative of the entire population.

Clearly, it would be very difficult to obtain valid information concerning the moral beliefs and behaviors of American children by interviewing and observing a sample comprising subjects from San Francisco or Boston alone. If the results are to be generalized to the entire population, subjects should represent all major geographical areas in the nation. In addition, care must be taken to ensure that all nationalities, major religious groups, socioeconomic levels, occupations, and ages are represented in proportions similar to the entire population. One of the simplest and most effective ways of ensuring this is to select subjects at random from a group that does represent the entire population — in many cases, from the entire population itself.

Ecological and Cross-Cultural Validity

Children, like other humans, are not "islands unto themselves." We sometimes lose sight of the fact that children exist and function in specific, multidimensional, and sometimes highly influential environments. These environments (ecosystems) might be quite different for different children, as well as for the same child at different times. It seems obvious that my behavior will be predictably (and perhaps justifiably) different in church than it might be at a

Bacchanalian festival. It is perhaps not so obvious, but no less true, that children might behave quite differently in schools, clinics, or their homes. The important point is that observations made in one environment might not be generalizable to another. Hence the phrase **ecological validity.** A generalization may be said to be ecologically valid to the extent that it is applicable and accurate in the circumstances to which it is applied. For example, numerous studies of language differences, particularly between black and white groups, have indicated language deficits for blacks (relative to whites). The tendency was to generalize this finding by concluding that certain groups of blacks were *generally* inferior to certain groups of whites in language development or usage. Other studies have shown, however, that black children are usually as proficient in the use of *their* language as whites are in the use of theirs, and that if white children were tested on their understanding and usage of black idiom, it is the whites who would appear to be disadvantaged (see Carroll, 1986). In short, the initial generalizations lacked ecological validity: They were not limited to the environments in which they were valid.

The notion of ecological validity has also raised an important issue concerning the universality of some of our more cherished findings in child development. Most of the research on which our more general findings are based has been conducted with white, predominantly middle-class American or European children. Cross-cultural research is finding, at a sometimes alarming rate, that many of these "general" findings are perhaps not so general after all.

Memory

Studies of the ages at which girls experience their first menstrual period (**menarche**) have frequently had to rely on the memories of women for whom the event may not be entirely recent; investigations of the ages at which children first walk or talk often base their conclusions on the memories of mothers. Unfortunately, the human memory is far from perfect. Not only does it forget, but it also distorts — sometimes in predictable ways, sometimes not.

Honesty

Having to rely on the honesty of subjects is a particularly severe problem with questionnaires and interviews, especially when highly personal areas are being researched. Comparisons of contemporary adolescent sexual behavior with behavior characteristic of adolescents several generations ago are typically unreliable primarily for this reason. Given prevailing attitudes toward sexual behavior, it is not unreasonable to suppose that today's adolescent is more likely to be honest about sexual behavior than the adolescent of the 1920s might have been. Hence the finding that there is considerably more premarital sexual activity among contemporary adolescents than there was when their parents were adolescents may be partly due to differences in subject honesty.

Experimenter Bias

Some research indicates that investigators sometimes unconsciously bias their observations to conform to their expectations. One effective means of guarding against experimenter bias is the **double-blind procedure.** This requires simply that the experimenters and examiners, as well as the subjects, not be aware of the expected outcomes of the research or of which subjects are experimental subjects and which are members of the control group.

Subject Bias

Subject bias may also have an effect on the outcomes of an experiment. In a highly publicized experiment, two psychologists (Roethlisberger & Dickson, 1939) compared a number of ways to increase productivity among workers in the Hawthorne plant of the Western Electric Company in Chicago. In successive experiments, the workers were subjected to shorter working periods, longer working periods, better lighting conditions, poorer lighting conditions, long periods of rest, short periods of rest, work incentives such as bonuses, and a variety of other conditions. Under most of these conditions, productivity apparently increased. This observation led to the conclusion that if subjects are aware that they are members of an experimental group, performance may improve simply because of that fact.

  Although the **Hawthorne effect,** as it is now called, is usually accepted as fact in social science research, its existence has not been well established — in spite of the experiments just described. Following a careful reexamination of the original experiments and interviews with some of the people who were involved at that time, Rice (1982) found little evidence of a Hawthorne effect. He reports that productivity did not increase in many of the experiments, but that later reports of the study usually concentrated on only one experiment where there was some easily explained improvement over the 5-year course of the study. Adair, Sharpe, and Huynh (1989) analyzed 86 studies for the presence of a Hawthorne effect. They conclude that in most research, this effect is rare or trivial (see Table 1.6).

What Does It All Mean?

When you consider all these aspects of research, you realize that you have to be careful when you interpret the results of psychological research. Ideally, you should ask a number of questions:

1. Is the sample representative of the population to which the research is generalized?
2. Can the results be applied to other groups within the culture or to other cultures, or are they specific to this environment — this ecological reality?

Table 1.6
Checklist for Evaluating Developmental Research

The *usefulness, clarity, logical consistency,* and *generalizability* of research results are influenced by:

Sampling	Is the sample a good representation of the population to which the observations and conclusions are meant to apply?
Ecosystem	Is there something special or unique about the social, cultural, or historical context in which observations are made? Do the characteristics of the context *in interaction with* the characteristics of the individuals reduce the generalizability of the findings?
Memory	Does the investigation have to rely on human memories? Has the possibility of systematic or random distortion been taken into account?
Honesty	Does the validity of the observations depend on the honesty of subjects? Do they have a reason to consciously or unconsciously distort facts?
Experimenter or Subject Bias	Is there a possibility that experimenter or subject expectations might have influenced observations?

3. Do the observations rely on the memory and honesty of the subjects? Are they objective and replicable?

4. Has the possibility of experimenter or subject bias been taken into consideration?

And then, of course, you need to ask: Are the questions important or are they merely trivial? Do the answers really matter?

If you do not ask this most fundamental question, there is a danger that, like those grown-ups who love figures so much, you may eventually forget to ask about essential matters. You may cease to remember the wonder of butterfly wings in the sunshine of a barefooted morning. Or the electric touch of the cool skin of a prized cat's eye, with heart pounding, standing on the edge of the great spring marble circle.

It is worth reminding ourselves, now and again, that this book is *of children.*

MAIN POINTS

1. This text deals with the development of individuals from birth to maturity.

2. Development is the total process whereby children adapt to their environment. It includes maturation (genetically programmed unfolding), growth (quantitative changes), and learning (changes due to experience).

3. There is evidence that in medieval times, the concept of childhood did not exist as we know it; instead, children were considered miniature adults whose presence in the family did not give rise to strong feelings of parental attachment — perhaps because infant mortality was very high.

4. Through the eighteenth and nineteenth centuries, child labor flourished, child-rearing practices were often harsh and cruel by current North American standards, and the courts provided children with little protection against parental and societal abuses.

5. The twentieth century brought about increasing concern with the social, physical, and intellectual welfare of children, especially in the industrialized world.

6. There are indications that recent demographic and social changes such as lower birthrates, greater numbers of childless young couples and of older couples, delayed marriages, increasing numbers of one-parent families, and the impact of television have altered the experience of childhood. As a result, recent decades may not be as child-oriented as might have been expected. For many, childhood may be a lonely and difficult time.

7. In many nonindustrialized, underdeveloped areas of the world, millions of children die each year — primarily from three causes: malnutrition; vaccine-preventable causes such as measles and tetanus; and diarrheal dehydration. In many of these areas, formal education is substandard or nonexistent, and physical and mental abuse of children is common.

8. The legal rights of children in contemporary developed societies are primarily rights of protection (rights to adequate medical and educational care, to affection and love, to a peaceful environment, to the opportunity to develop) rather than adult rights of choice that entail adult responsibilities.

9. Among early pioneers of the scientific study of children were John Locke (*tabula rasa*) and Jean-Jacques Rousseau ("noble savage"). Later pioneers included Charles Darwin (baby biography; evolution), G. Stanley Hall ("ontogeny recapitulates phylogeny"), and John B. Watson (we become what we are as a function of our experiences).

10. Among recurring themes in studies of development are questions dealing with the relative influence of heredity and environment, with whether development is continuous or progresses in discrete stages, and with whether we should view children as primarily active or passive.

11. Some basic current beliefs that drive developmental research and theorizing include the beliefs that: the child is active and creates meaning; the causes of development involve a complex *interaction* between the environment (context or ecosystem) and specific characteristics of an individual; in spite of marked individual differences, especially where context and genetic backgrounds are very dissimilar, there are some commonalities in the developmental patterns of different individuals that allow researchers to identify predictable patterns of growth or stages.

12. Naturalistic observation of children occurs when children are observed without interference — for example, *diary descriptions* (regular descriptions of

interesting observations), *specimen descriptions* (continuous sequences of behavior), *event sampling* (recordings of predetermined behaviors), and *time sampling* (recordings during predetermined time intervals).

13. Nonnaturalistic observations may be clinical (questionnaires or interviews) or experimental (deliberately manipulating the child's environment). In many cases, investigations involve a combination of approaches rather than only one.

14. In an experiment, the investigator randomly assigns subjects to groups and controls relevant variables in an effort to determine whether independent variables (those that are controlled) affect dependent variables (outcomes). Experiments are useful for investigating cause-and-effect relationships.

15. Correlational studies look at relationships among variables and provide useful information about causes and effects, although a correlation is not by itself proof of causation.

16. There are two general approaches to child development studies: longitudinal studies compare the same children at different periods in their lives; cross-sectional studies compare different children at the same time.

17. A cohort is a group of individuals born during a single time span. Not only are these individuals of similar ages but they might also have been exposed to a variety of influences that are unique to their cohort and that might account for important differences between them and members of other cohorts. In research, it is sometimes difficult to separate influences of the cohort from the effects of age.

18. One way of separating cohort and age effects is to use a *sequential* design where sequences of samples are taken, thus permitting different combinations of longitudinal, cross-sectional, and time-lag studies. In a *time-lag* study, different cohorts are compared at different times (for instance 7-year-olds in 1991 are compared with 7-year-olds in 1995, 1999, and 2003).

19. The value and generalizability of research results are subject to the influences of sample size and representativeness, subject memory and honesty, experimenter bias, ecological validity, and other factors. Truth, here as elsewhere, is relative.

Further Readings

Fascinating descriptions of changes in the status of children throughout history are provided by:

Aries, P. (1962). *Centuries of childhood: A social history of family life* (R. Baldick, Trans.). New York: Alfred A. Knopf. (Originally published 1960.)

Kessen, W. (1965). *The child.* New York: John Wiley.

Eckardt, G., Bringman, W. G., & Sprung, L. (Eds.). (1985). *Contributions to a history of developmental psychology.* Berlin: Morton.

Science, both as a method and as an attitude, need not be nearly so esoteric and difficult as we sometimes imagine. For an entertaining, highly readable, and pertinent discussion of the role of research in the behavioral sciences, see:

Ray, W. J., & Ravizza, R. (1988). *Methods toward a science of behavior and experience* (3rd ed.). Belmont, Calif.: Wadsworth.

Not everyone believes that science is the only, or even the best, way of knowing. For a provocative and sometimes challenging view of science and our conception of reality, see:

Pearce, J. C. (1971). *The crack in the cosmic egg.* New York: Fawcett.

Kegan's book is an intriguing, well-written book whose central theme is that we are *meaning-making* organisms. Not only do we try to discover and invent what things mean, but we also struggle to mean something to others.

Kegan, R. (1982). *The evolving self: Problem and process in human development.* Cambridge, Mass.: Harvard University Press.

A highly practical guide to observing children, particularly useful for teachers and parents, is the following:

Cohen, D. H., Stern, V., & Balaban, N. (1983). *Observing and recording the behavior of young children* (3rd ed.). New York: Teachers College, Columbia University.

The following presents a somewhat chilling account of infant and child mortality in the underdeveloped world. It also includes important abstracts of research on strategies intended to protect the world's children:

Grant, J. P. [Executive Director of the United Nation's Children's Fund (UNICEF)]. (1986). *The state of the world's children: 1986.* New York: Oxford University Press.

A belief is not true because it is useful.
Henri-Frederic Amiel, *Journal*

Theories of Development

ven now, I still have some difficulty reacting appropriately to the term *theory*. It is an awesome term; sometimes it frightens me. This is a reaction conditioned by long hours in my grandmother's kitchen, where she would repeatedly stop my ramblings with, "Yes, but that's just theory. Have you looked at the facts?" And then she would tell me what the facts were; they always contradicted my "theory."

I might, to this day, have remained convinced that facts and theory are completely different, and that theory is what one resorts to only when the facts are unknown, had it not been for the old lady's theory of wastes. (My cousins and I were less polite then; we called it Grandma's ——— theory.)

We had been sitting on the porch one June night, she knitting and I dreaming, both looking at the garden — a fine garden with potatoes only two hills to a pail and carrots big as my arm. Interrupting my dreams of incredible future glories, I commented on the excellence of my grandmother's garden, being careful to observe that Tremblay's potatoes were never so large or plentiful and that his carrots were like shoestrings next to hers.

"It's the horse manure," she said matter-of-factly. The word is somewhat less offensive in French than in English. *Merde.*

"He uses manure too," I said, always ready to contradict the old lady.

"Cow manure."

"Cow manure? It's manure too. Why shouldn't his garden be as good? He uses a lot of it."

"I have a theory about that," said my grandmother. It was my chance, and I jumped right in.

"A theory?" Politely, of course. "But facts, Grandma. We should speak of facts, not theory."

"The facts," she informed me calmly, "are that I have a far better garden than Tremblay, that I use horse manure, and that he uses cow manure."

And the theory, as she explained in detail, simply accounted for the facts: It explained why horse manure favors potatoes and carrots; why small chicken droppings invigorate cabbages; why flattened and dried circles of cow dung excite flowers. It is not a simple theory; nor would it be of much interest to you, sophisticated as you are. But for my grandmother, a proud woman — proud of her favored potatoes and carrots, her invigorated cabbages, her excited flowers — it was of considerable interest.

THEORY AND SCIENCE

And for me, it was a lesson in theory — a lesson that I now pass on. Theory need not be an exotic collection of obscure pronouncements; nor does it substitute for facts in the absence of the latter. In its simplest sense, a theory is no more than an explanation of facts. As Thomas (1985) put it, specifically with respect to theories of child development, to theorize is to suggest "(1) which facts are most important for understanding children and (2) what sorts of relationships among facts are most significant for producing this understanding" (p. 4).

Put another way, a theory is a collection of related statements that are intended to organize and explain a set of observations. But the goal of theorizing goes somewhat beyond explanation: In addition, it involves prediction and control. If my grandmother *understands* why specific manures affect certain crops in given ways, she can not only predict these effects but also exercise a high degree of control over her garden (barring such acts of God as severe storms, locust infestations, or small boys chasing cats among the turnips).

Theories in child development are also intended to explain (hence, to lead to understanding); similarly, if they explain adequately, prediction and control should result. For example, if a theory explains why it is that some children are happy and others are not, then it should be possible, given relevant facts, to predict which children will be happy. Also, if the circumstances affecting happiness are under our control, it should also be possible to bring happiness to saddened lives. Thus theories may have a very practical aspect. At the same time, they are one of science's primary guides for doing research. In large part, it is a theory — sometimes crude, but sometimes elegant and refined — that tells the researcher where to look for a cure for cancer, what the cure will look like when it is found, and how it might be used. In the same way, psychology's theories tell the researcher where and how to look for personality or intellectual change in the course of development. They suggest as well what some of the causes of change might be and how change may be brought about.

Developing a Theory

Theories are seldom handed to philosophers and scientists carved in pieces of rock — or even written on pieces of paper. They arise, instead, from observations that are assumed to be factual and that are important enough to require explanation. Because they arise from observations, and because what different individuals choose to observe (that is, what they consider to be important and in need of explanation) may vary a great deal, there are many different theories in most areas of research.

The types of observations on which scientific theories are based are seldom of the kind that were of such intimate interest to my grandmother. Science, if nothing else, insists upon a kind of objectivity, precision, and **replicability** (repeatability) that would have been difficult, to say the least, in my grand-mother's garden. We can accurately say, in fact, that science is less a collection of methods than an attitude. The "scientific method" that you might have been asked to learn in school (statement of problem, prediction, material, method, observation, conclusion) is simply a means of ensuring that observations are made under sufficiently controlled circumstances that they could be made by anyone else — that, in short, they can be replicated and confirmed. The attitude that characterizes science's search for explanation is precisely one that empha-sizes the replicability of observations and that demands precision in measuring and observing; hence the importance of the research methods described in the first chapter. Clearly, if the facts on which theories are based are themselves suspect, the theory is not likely to be very useful.

Evaluating Theories

Why, you might ask, must there be a variety of theories if a theory is simply an explanation of fact? Some of the reasons for this state of affairs have already been mentioned. Different theories may be used to explain quite different facts. And even very general theories of development — those that attempt to explain all of development — are not all based on the same observations; that is, theo-rists select observations that need to be explained. Furthermore, given the same set of observations, not all theorists will arrive at the same sets of explanations. Finally, fact (or truth) is no more obvious in developmental psychology than it is elsewhere. Our observations are often more or less accurate depending on the precision of our observation (or measurement); they are often relevant only in specific circumstances and sometimes for specific individuals; and they are colored by our expectations — in other words, by our theories and our assump-tions. As Scarr (1985, p. 499) put it, "we do not discover scientific facts; we invent them." Nor do we always generalize appropriately — and it is on gener-alizations that our theories are based.

　　We cannot easily determine whether a theory is right or wrong, whether it is accurate and truthful. But we can evaluate it in other ways, most of which have to do with its usefulness. In other words, theories do not have to be accurate explanations of selected observations; they can be nothing more than useful attempts to explain important things. And two theories that present different explanations for the same observations might both be useful — or useless. Sometimes the differences result from the fact that the theories present different levels of analyses, are based on different assumptions, or emphasize different aspects of human functioning.

　　Thomas (1985) suggests a number of criteria that might be used to judge the "goodness" of a theory of child development. A theory is good, says Thomas, if it (1) accurately reflects the facts, (2) is expressed in a clearly understandable way, (3) is useful for predicting future events as well as explaining past ones,

(4) can be applied in a practical sense (that is, has real value for counselors, teachers, pediatricians, and so on), (5) is consistent within itself rather than self-contradictory, and (6) is not based on a great number of assumptions (unproven beliefs).

We might also add that a good theory should be thought provoking and should have *heuristic* value — that is, it should be useful in our quest for knowledge. It should lead to new ideas, new discoveries, new applications.

MODELS IN CHILD DEVELOPMENT

Imagine that you have just been presented with this problem: Your instructor has brought into class a smallish thing inside a larger glass thing. You do not know what this smallish thing is. Your task is to decide what would be the best way to discover all you can about this thing. Think about the problem for a moment before reading on.

Is there enough information presented in the preceding paragraph for you to make some reasonably intelligent suggestions? Consider now what the nature of your suggestions might be had I written: "Your instructor has brought into class a smallish animal inside a glass cage" or "Your instructor has brought into class a small piece of machinery inside a glass box" or again, "Your instructor has brought into class a strange new fruit in a glass container." Why is the task of investigating the object so much easier in the last three cases? Simply because you have been given information that allows you to classify the object in terms of a something about whose properties and functioning you already know a great deal. You have, in your view of the world, a mental **model,** or pattern, of what animals, fruits, and machines are like.

Psychologists investigating human development are, in some ways, in the same position as a student presented with a "thing." Initially, it is very difficult to know what questions would be the best ones to ask. But if we could look at development in terms of something more familiar, many questions might suggest themselves, not to mention a few answers. This is, in effect, the starting point of all systematic investigation. We begin with a metaphor — a comparison. We say this is *like* that, and it might therefore work in the same way as that. The *that* serves as our model.

Models exist at various levels of generality (Reese & Overton, 1970). For example, at a simple level, there are models that describe how a mechanical system might work. At a more complex level, there are models that serve as specific analogies or comparisons (a computer program might be used as a model of human problem-solving processes). At the most general level, there are models that represent our world views — our presuppositions about how things are.

Machine-Organism Models

Many of the theories in developmental psychology reflect one of two basic underlying models: the organismic or the mechanistic (Fischer & Silvern, 1985). The organismic model assumes that it is useful to view people as though they are like active organisms; the mechanistic model reflects the belief that it is useful to view people as though they are like machines. In the first instance, the model is primarily *active*; in the second, the model is *reactive*.

These underlying models are extremely important in the development of theory. In effect, they suggest what the theorist will investigate and what the resulting theory will look like. An organismic view (Piaget's, for example) will describe development as a process resulting from self-initiated activities and will look for regularities in behavior to understand the wholeness and unity of the organism. In contrast, a mechanistic view (early behaviorism, for example) will describe development as a process resulting from reactions to external events and will search for the machinelike predictability that might result given sufficient knowledge about how the machine reacts to external forces.

Theorists do not usually decide before the fact that theirs will be a mechanistic or an organismic theory. That a theory can be described as being more one or the other simply reflects the theorist's basic underlying views about human nature and human development. And it is important to stress that these two models are metaphors, not literal beliefs. No theorist actually believes that people are machines; but there are some who think it useful to emphasize some apparently machinelike qualities of human functioning.

A Contextual or Ecological Model

An increasing number of contemporary developmental psychologists are profoundly influenced by a third view: the **contextual model** (Kleinginna & Kleinginna, 1988), also termed the *ecological* model (Bronfenbrenner, 1989). This view emphasizes the role of society, culture, and family and recognizes the importance of the historical period in which the individual develops, as well as the importance of events that are unique to the individual. That is, the model takes into consideration the environmental *context* in which development occurs.

The contextual model shares characteristics of both the organismic and the mechanistic models. It is organismic because it sees development as the product of organism-environment interaction and because it looks for universal principles that might be useful for describing development (Lerner, 1985). It is mechanistic because it is concerned with the influence of the environment on the developing organism.

One of the important characteristics of a contextual model is that it is based on an **open systems** view of human development (Bertalanffy, 1950). An open system is one that depends on interaction (in contrast to a *closed* system, which is completely predictable and totally unaffected by its environment). Thus an open system is constantly subject to change. It is fundamentally dependent on its context and adapts continually as a function of interacting with its context. Accordingly, it is impossible to predict precisely what the final adaptation will be in an open system.

All biological, psychological, and social systems are open systems, says Valsiner (1987). Hence all developmental research should ideally be based on models that take into consideration interaction between the person's characteristics and characteristics of the environment.

The contextual or ecological model is exemplified in Bronfenbrenner's *ecological systems theory* described later in this chapter. It is also the model most apparent throughout this text, which — with Bronfenbrenner — views development as the progressive adaptation of active, growing human beings to changing environments. Our emphasis is on understanding development as an interactive process involving individuals with different characteristics in a range of different ecological systems or contexts. Thus the emphasis on the importance of the family, the school, peers, siblings, and other significant aspects of context. Thus, too, the emphasis on the importance of the social and interactive nature of the processes of development.

We might ask, as this point, whether one of these three models — the mechanistic, the organismic, or the contextual/ecological — is correct and, by implication, the others incorrect. But the question is irrelevant. The models are simply metaphors — implied comparisons. They direct our research and shape our beliefs and our theories — and perhaps our textbooks too. But we should not judge them correct or incorrect. We might as well ask whether "The moon was a ghostly galleon, tossed upon cloudy seas" is more accurate than "That orbed maiden with white fire laden, Whom mortals call the moon." Metaphors are apt and useful or they are clumsy and useless. We might judge our poetic metaphors in terms of the images and feelings they give rise to; we can judge our scientific metaphors only in terms of their usefulness (see Table 2.1).

THEORIES OF CHILD DEVELOPMENT

This chapter presents some of the most important and distinct theoretical approaches to the study of child development. These theories are just a few of the many that have been proposed in this area; nor is coverage of each approach exhaustive. The theories presented are grouped according to six major orientations: psychoanalytic, behavioristic, cognitive, biological, ecological, and humanistic. Although these labels are useful in making distinctions among different concerns and orientations, they can also be misleading if interpreted too narrowly. As will become apparent, most of the theoretical approaches described share at least some of the characteristics of other approaches.

Table 2.1
Three Basic Models in Developmental Psychology

	Organismic	Mechanistic	Ecological
Metaphor	A biological organism	A machine	Strong, resilient, adaptive, open system
Perception	Sees individual as active, self-directed	Sees individual as reactive, responsive to environment	Sees individual as interactive
Developmental process	Tends toward final adult stage, describable in terms of adult thought structures (logical characteristics of adult thought)	Described in terms of learning and problem solving; no clearly described end goal	Involves person-context-process. Adaptation influenced by the individual's specific social, historical, personal context.
Theories	Age-related stage theories emphasizing similarities of thought at each level	Theories emphasizing the continuity of development	Theories emphasizing the interaction of age, historical variables, important life events, culture, and other aspects of context with individual characteristics
Emphasis	Attention to similarities	Attention to individual differences	Attention to context- and person-related differences
Theorists	Jean Piaget	Early behaviorists	Bronfenbrenner; Vygotsky

PSYCHOANALYTIC APPROACHES: FREUD

Psychoanalytic theory, developed initially by Sigmund Freud, arises from a single basic assumption: Among the most important causes of human behavior and personality are deep-seated, usually unconscious forces within individuals. Freud believed that these forces, some of which represent conflict between desires and conscience, are at the root of mental disorders. He also believed that therapists (psychoanalysts) could help restore mental health by helping patients understand these unconscious forces and the conflicts that result from them. Among the techniques that he found most useful for this — techniques that soon became part of standard psychoanalytic procedure — were free association; the analysis of dreams and of the unintended use of words and expressions (popularly referred to as *Freudian slips*), both of which were assumed to reflect unconscious desires or fears; hypnosis; and painstaking analysis of childhood experiences — especially those of a sexual or traumatic (intensely frightening) nature.

Not surprisingly, then, Freudian psychoanalytic theory has traditionally been most useful in treating mental disorder. However, there is much in the theory that is developmental in nature. And although the most important beliefs of psychoanalytic theory are no longer an important part of current developmental theories, their historical importance and their influence on the thinking of later theorists justifies their inclusion here. Accordingly, the following sections present a very abbreviated account of what is, in fact, an incredibly complex, sometimes bewildering, but always fascinating view of the development and machinations of human personality.

While going through these brief sections, it is worth keeping in mind that Freudian theory is very much a product of the Victorian era in which it was developed — an era that by contemporary standards can only be described as one of extreme sexual repression and masculine domination. These cultural factors greatly influenced Freud's theory and are reflected in the importance he gave sexual motives and behaviors, as well as in the masculine orientation of the theory. Much of what Freud initially thought about development applied primarily to male children — and to females only as a sometimes very hasty and incomplete afterthought (Gilligan, 1982).

Basic Ideas

Among the most fundamental Freudian ideas is the notion that human behavior, and consequently the direction that personality development takes, derives from two powerful tendencies: the urge to survive and the urge to procreate (Roazen, 1975). The survival instinct is of secondary importance because it is not usually endangered by our environments (the Freudian term for environment is *reality*). The urge to procreate, however, is constantly being discouraged and even prevented by reality; this is what accounts for the tremendous importance of sexuality in Freud's description of human development.

Sexuality is a very broad term in Freud's writings. It means not only those activities that are clearly associated with sex but all other activities that may be linked with body pleasure, however remotely (for example, behaviors such as thumb sucking or smoking). Sexual urges are sufficiently important in Freud's system that they are given a special term — **libido.** The libido is the source of energy for sexual urges; accordingly, the urges themselves are referred to as libidinal urges. However, satisfaction of sexual impulses need not involve the sexual regions of the body.

Three Levels of Personality

The newborn infant has a simple, undeveloped personality, consisting solely of primitive, unlearned urges that will be a lifetime source of what Freud called *psychic energy,* the urges and desires that account for behavior. Freud's label for the child's earliest personality is **id.** The urges that define id are primarily sexual.

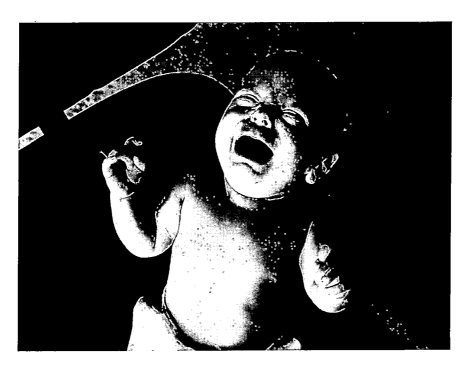

For Freud, an infant is all id—"a bundle of instincts and reflexes."

The Freudian infant is all instincts (unlearned tendencies) and reflexes, a bundle of unbridled psychic energy seeking almost desperately to satisfy urges that are based on a need to survive and to procreate. An infant has no idea of what is possible or impossible, no sense of reality, no conscience, no internal moral rules that govern conduct. The most powerful urge at this stage is to seek immediate satisfaction of impulses. A child who is hungry does not wait. *Now* is the time for the nipple and the sucking!

Almost from birth, the child's instinctual urges collide with reality. The hunger urge (linked with survival) cannot always be satisfied immediately. The reality of the situation is that the mother is often occupied elsewhere, and the infant's satisfaction has to be delayed or denied. Similarly, the child eventually learns that defecation cannot occur anywhere and at any time; parental demands conflict with the child's impulses. This constant conflict between id impulses and reality develops the second level of personality, the **ego.**

The ego grows out of a realization of what is possible and what is not; it is the rational level of human personality. It develops as a result of the child's experiences, and it comes to include the realization that delaying gratification is often a desirable thing, that long-term goals sometimes require the denial of short-term goals. Although the id wants immediate gratification, the ego channels these desires in the most profitable direction for the individual. Note that the levels of personality represented by the id and the ego are not in opposition.

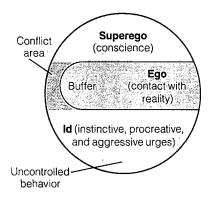

Figure 2.1

The Freudian conception of the three levels of personality: id, ego, and superego. The id, consisting of instinctive urges, develops first. The ego and superego (conscience) develop later. In normal personality development, the ego acts as a buffer between the id and superego, which are in conflict with each other. Personality disorders may arise from unrestricted conflict when the ego fails to mediate successfully.

They work together toward the samel goal — satisfying the needs and urges of the individual.

The third level of personality — labeled the **superego** — sets itself up in opposition to the first two. The term *superego* refers to the moral aspects of personality. Like the ego, the superego develops from contact with reality, but it is more concerned with social than physical reality. The development of the superego (or conscience) does not occur until early childhood. Freud assumed that it resulted principally from a process of identifying with parents, most especially with the like-sexed parent. To identify in a Freudian sense is to attempt to become like others — to adopt their values and beliefs as well as their behaviors. By identifying with their parents, children learn the religious and cultural rules that govern their parents' behaviors. These rules then become part of the child's superego. It is significant that many religious rules, as well as many social and cultural rules, oppose the urges of the id. Hence the superego and the id are generally in conflict. Freud assumed that this conflict accounts for much deviant behavior.

In summary, Freud's theory describes three levels of personality: the id, the ego, and the superego (Figure 2.1). The first is the source of psychic energy deriving from instincts of survival and procreation. The ego is reality-oriented and intervenes between the id and the superego to maintain a balance between the id's urges and the superego's rules. It is as though the id were continually saying, "I want that almond torte right now; I want to be caressed immediately; I want that Ferrari today; I want to punch that guy's lights out," while the superego chides, "Don't you dare; deny your desires; thou shalt not steal; fighting is a sin." And the ego, seated between these warring forces, attempts calmly to make peace. "Have you considered eating only at mealtime and with some moderation? Take a bus if you can't have a Ferrari. As for that idiot, let the courts handle it. You can watch. How would that be?"

Psychosexual Stages

Freud's account of the development of the three levels of personality is a description of **psychosexual development.** Stages in psychosexual development are distinguishable by the objects or activities necessary for the satisfaction of urges during that stage. The labels for each stage reflect changes in the areas of sexual satisfaction as the child matures (see Table 2.2).

The **oral stage** lasts through infancy (approximately to the age of 18 months). It is characterized by the infant's preoccupation with the mouth and with sucking. During this first stage, the child's personality consists mainly of id. Children seek constantly to satisfy their urges and are incapable of deliberately delaying gratification.

Toward the end of the first year, the area of sexual gratification shifts gradually from the oral to the anal region. According to Freud, in the early part of the **anal stage** the child derives pleasure from bowel movements. Later in this stage the child acquires control of sphincter muscles and may then derive considerable pleasure from withholding bowel movements to increase anal sensation. Both of these behaviors oppose the mother's wishes. As a result of these conflicts, the child begins to develop an ego — a sense of reality, an awareness that some things are possible whereas others are not, coupled with the ability to delay gratification to some extent.

The third stage, which lasts roughly from ages 2 to 6, is labeled **phallic,** because the zone of sexuality has now shifted from the anal to the genital region and because the phallus (the male genital) is of primary importance in the sexuality of girls as well as boys. Whereas gratification had been obtained earlier by sucking or by expelling or withholding feces, children now often masturbate (manipulate their genitalia).

According to Freud, normal development now takes the male child through the **Oedipus complex,** when his increasing awareness of the sexual meanings of his genital area leads him to desire his mother (and to unconsciously wish to replace his father). For girls at 4 to 6 years, there is the **Electra complex,** in which a girl's sexual feelings for her father lead her to become jealous of her mother.

The resolution of the Oedipus complex marks the transition from the phallic stage to the period of sexual **latency** that follows (from age 6 to 11). This period is marked by a loss of sexual interest and a continued **identification** with the like-sexed parent. The process of identification is very important in Freud's

Table 2.2

Freud's Stages of Psychosexual Development

Stage	Approximate Ages	Characteristics
Oral	0–18 months	Sources of pleasure include sucking, biting, swallowing, playing with lips. Preoccupation with immediate gratification of impulses. Id is dominant.
Anal	18 months–2 or 3 years	Sources of sexual gratification include expelling feces and urination, as well as retaining feces. Id and ego.
Phallic	2 or 3–6 years	Child becomes concerned with genitals. Source of sexual pleasure involves manipulating genitals. Period of Oedipus or Electra complex. Id, ego, and superego.
Latency	6–11 years	Loss of interest in sexual gratification. Identification with like-sexed parent. Id, ego, and superego.
Genital	11 and older	Concern with adult modes of sexual pleasure, barring fixations or regressions.

system. It not only involves attempts to behave like the parent with whom the child is identifying but also implies attempting to be like the object of identification in terms of beliefs and values. In this way, the child begins to develop a superego.

Following this lengthy period of sexual neutrality, the child enters the stage of adult sexuality, the **genital stage** (at around age 11), and begins to establish heterosexual attachments. Also during this last developmental stage, the superego (conscience), which has previously been very rigid, becomes progressively more flexible.

Defense Mechanisms

Mention of Freud's theories is incomplete without a consideration of **defense mechanisms** — the irrational and sometimes unhealthy methods some employ to compensate for their inability to satisfy the demands of the id and to overcome the anxiety that accompanies the continual struggle between the id and the superego (A. Freud, 1946). Defense mechanisms are invented by the ego in its role as a mediator between the id and the superego; they are the ego's attempt to establish peace between the two so that the personality can continue to operate in an apparently healthy manner. Defense mechanisms are particularly

Freud's emphasis on the importance and pervasiveness of sexual motives is not shared by all his followers.

important for understanding disturbed personalities, although they are not at all uncommon in the lives of those who have no clearly recognizable disturbances. It is only when people rely on them excessively that defense mechanisms become unhealthy (see Table 2.3).

Freud in Review

Freud paints a dark and often cynical picture of human nature: Primitive forces over which we have no control drive us relentlessly toward the satisfaction of instinctual urges and bring us into repeated conflict with reality. From the very moment of birth, our most basic selves — our ids — react with anxiety and fear. We fear that our overpowering urges to survive (and eventually to procreate) will not be satisfied, and we suffer from the anxiety accompanying that fear. According to Freud, this *trauma of birth* leads to all our adult anxieties.

Hofer (1981) describes Freud's theory as one of the most comprehensive and influential of all human psychological theories. It has had tremendous impact on our attitudes toward children and childrearing. More than anyone else, Freud was responsible for making parents realize how important the experiences of the early years can be. The importance of Freudian theory is not limited to its direct impact on parents, educators, physicians, and others but

Freud viewed toilet training as critically important to the child's development. He said nothing of toy dogs.

Table 2.3
Defense Mechanisms

Mechanism	Example
Displacement A suppressed behavior appears in a more acceptable form.	A potential murderer hunts predatory animals or becomes a mercenary soldier.
Reaction formation Behavior is the opposite of what the individual would like it to be.	A woman loves an unobtainable man and behaves as though she dislikes him.
Intellectualization Behavior is stripped of its emotional concomitants.	A man who loves his aunt too dearly treats her with extreme consideration, kindness, and devotion but convinces himself that he is motivated by duty and not by love.
Projection People come to believe that their own undesirable feelings or inclinations are more descriptive of others than of themselves.	A person who is extremely jealous of his brother and unconsciously wishes him harm believes that it is others who have those feelings.
Denial Reality is distorted to make it conform to the individual's wishes.	A heavy smoker is unable to give up the habit and decides that there is no substantial evidence linking nicotine with human diseases.
Repression Unpleasant experiences are stored deep in the subconscious mind and become inaccessible to waking memory.	A soldier comes very close to death but remembers no details of the event.

includes its tremendous influence on the development of other theories (such as those of Erikson and Bowlby). However, many of Freud's students and followers have not accepted the theory entirely.

Freud's theory is clearly weak from a scientific point of view, based as it is on a limited number of observations collected by a single individual (Freud himself) and not subjected to any rigorous analysis; it uses difficult and important terms and concepts, such as *unconscious*, in confusing and ambiguous ways; it leads to contradictory predictions; and it places excessive emphasis on sexual and aggressive impulses (Rothstein, 1980).

In spite of these criticisms, Freud's theorizing still stands as an immensely rich basis for thinking about and understanding human personality. In summarizing the contributions of psychoanalysis, Kegan (1982) notes that it remains the single most important guide for mental health practitioners in clinics and in hospitals. Ironically, however, its status in academic psychology is considerably more tarnished. In contrast, theories such as Piaget's cognitivism are an ongoing source of debate and research in academic circles; but these theories have remarkably little influence on the application of psychology in the real world.

PSYCHOANALYTIC APPROACHES: ERIKSON

Freud's influence can be found among the many theories developed by some of his followers. Perhaps the most important of these for understanding human development is the theory advanced by Erik Erikson (1956, 1959, 1961, 1968). It draws heavily from Freud's work, but also departs from it in several important ways.

Recall that Freud's primary emphasis was on the role of sexuality (libido) and on the importance of conflicts involving different levels of personality (id, ego, superego). In contrast, Erikson downplays the role of sexuality and of psychodynamic conflicts and instead emphasizes the importance of the child's social environment. His theory is a theory of **psychosocial development** rather than a theory of *psychosexual development.*

A second departure from Freudian theory is Erikson's focus on the role of the ego rather than the superego. Third, Erikson was more concerned than Freud with the development of a healthy ego (or identity, in Erikson's words) rather than with the resolution of powerful internal conflicts.

Psychosocial Stages

Erikson describes human development in terms of eight psychosocial stages, the first five of which span infancy, childhood, and adolescence. The last three describe maturity. Unlike other theorists, Erikson does not assume that the developmental process ends with adolescence, but maintains instead that there remain a number of crucial stages through which the individual must progress.

Each of Erikson's stages is described in terms of a basic conflict, brought about primarily by the child's need to adapt to the social environment. Resolution of this conflict results in the development of a sense of competence. Although Erikson's first five stages closely parallel Freud's psychosexual stages in terms of ages, his descriptions and his emphases are quite different. The first five stages are described here and are summarized in Table 2.4.

Trust versus mistrust. One of the most basic components of a healthy personality is a sense of trust. This sense of trust toward oneself and toward others develops in the first year of life (Erikson, 1959). The infant is initially faced with a fundamental conflict between mistrust of a world about which very little is known and an inclination to develop a trusting attitude toward that world.

The most important person in the infant's life at this stage is the primary caregiver – usually the mother. Successful resolution of the conflict between trust and mistrust depends largely on the infant's relationship with this caregiver, and on the gradual realization that the world is predictable, safe, and loving. According to Erikson, if the world is unpredictable and the caregiver rejecting, the infant may grow up to be mistrustful and anxious.

Autonomy versus shame and doubt. During this stage, corresponding to Freud's anal stage, children begin to realize they are authors of their own actions. With the recognition that they can carry out some of the behaviors they intend, children develop a sense of autonomy. However, this autonomy is threatened by children's inclination not to accept responsibility for their own actions, but to go back to the comfort and security that characterized the first stage – an inclination that gives rise to feelings of shame and doubt (Erikson, 1961).

If the child is to successfully resolve this conflict and develop a sense of autonomy, it is important that parents encourage attempts to explore and that they provide opportunities for independence. Overprotectiveness can lead to doubt and uncertainty in dealing with the world later.

Initiative versus guilt. By the age of 4 or 5, children have resolved the crisis of autonomy. In short, they have discovered that they are somebody; during the next stage, they must discover who it is that they are (Erikson, 1959). True to his Freudian orientation, Erikson assumes that children try to discover who they are by attempting to be like their parents. During this stage they establish a wider physical environment, made possible by their greater freedom of movement. Their language development is sufficiently advanced for them to ask questions, understand answers, and also imagine all sorts of possibilities. With their increasing exploration of the environment, children develop a sense of initiative. Not only are they autonomous, but they are also responsible for their behavior.

Table 2.4
The First Five of Erikson's Eight Psychosocial Stages

Erikson's Psychosocial Stages	Corresponding Freudian Psychosexual Stage	Principal Developmental Task	Important Influences for Positive Developmental Outcome
Trust vs. mistrust	Oral (0 — 18 months)	Developing sufficient trust in the world to explore it	Mother; warm, loving interaction
Autonomy vs. shame and doubt	Anal (18 months—2 or 3 years)	Developing feeling of control over behavior; realizing that intentions can be acted out	Supportive parents; imitation
Initiative vs. guilt	Phallic (2 or 3—6 years)	Developing a sense of self through identification with parents and a sense of responsibility for own actions	Supportive parents; identification
Industry vs. inferiority	Latency (6–11 years)	Developing a sense of self-worth through interaction with peers	Schools, teachers; learning and education; encouragement
Identity vs. identity diffusion	Genital (11 years and older)	Developing a strong sense of identity — of ego (self); selecting among various potential selves	Peers and role models; social pressure

Source: Based in part on Erikson (1959).

Because the central process involved in resolving the initiative versus guilt conflict is one of identification, parents and family continue to be the most important influences in the child's development. It is important for them to encourage the young child's sense of initiative and to nurture a sense of responsibility.

Industry versus inferiority. The fourth developmental phase, corresponding to Freud's latency period, is marked by the child's increasing need to interact with and be accepted by peers. It now becomes crucial for children to discover that their selves, their identities, are significant; that they can do things; in short, that they are competent. Children now avail themselves of all opportunities to learn those things they think are of importance to their culture, hoping that by so doing they will become *someone*. This is the source of their rising need for accomplishment through industrious behavior. Although this stage corresponds to Freud's period of latency, Erikson points out clearly that the only sense in which the child may be considered "latent" is in terms of the formation of heterosexual attachments. In all other ways, children are much more active than latent.

Successful resolution of this stage's conflict depends to a large extent on the responses of significant social agencies — especially schools and teachers — to the child's efforts. If the child's work is continually demeaned and seldom praised, the outcome may be a lasting sense of inferiority.

Identity versus identity diffusion. Erikson's fifth developmental stage, corresponding to Freud's genital period and spanning adolescence, involves the development of a strong sense of identity. Here, Erikson's emphasis on the ego becomes most evident. The development of a strong sense of identity implies the development of a strong ego: hence, Erikson's expression *ego identity*. The crisis implicit in this stage concerns a conflict between a strong sense of **self** and the diffusion of self-concepts.

At a simple level, the formation of an identity appears to involve arriving at a notion, not so much of who one is but rather of who one can be — in other words, of developing one of several potential selves. The source of conflict lies in the various possibilities open to the child — possibilities that are magnified by the variety of cultural models in the environment. Conflict and doubt over choice of identity lead to what Erikson terms *identity diffusion*. It is as though adolescents are torn between early acceptance of a clearly defined self and the dissipation of their energies as they experiment with a variety of roles. One of the primary functions of adolescence is to serve as a period during which the child need not make a final decision concerning self (as a *moratorium*, in Erikson's words). The development of identity during adolescence is discussed in detail in Chapter 12.

Adult stages. Erikson's description of development does not end with adolescence but continues through the entire life span. He describes three additional psychosocial conflicts that occur during adulthood and old age, requiring new competencies and adjustments. The first of these, *intimacy and solidarity versus isolation*, relates to the need to develop intimate relationships with others (as opposed to being isolated) and is particularly important for marriage and parenthood. The second, *generativity versus self-absorption*, describes a need to assume social, work, and community responsibilities that will be beneficial to others (that will be generative), rather than remaining absorbed in self. The third, *integrity versus despair*, has to do with facing the inevitability of our own ends and the need to realize that life has meaning — that we should not despair because its end is imminent.

Erikson in Review

Erikson's theory is referred to as a theory of the life cycle, of ego psychology, of psychosocial development, or as a psychoanalytically oriented theory concerned mainly with the development of healthy personality. He describes development in terms of a series of crises through which the individual progresses. Each of these involves a conflict between new abilities or attitudes and inclinations that oppose them. Resolution of conflict results in the development of a sense of competence with respect to a specific capability that is primarily social; hense *psychosocial* development. The resolution of conflicts is never perfected during one developmental phase but continues through succeeding stages; hence the concept of *life cycle*. Perhaps the most crucial crisis involves the development of a strong sense of identity; hence the concept *ego psychology.*

We should note that although Erikson assigns ages to each of these psychosocial stages, the ages do little more than indicate a very general sequence. This is particularly true during adulthood when important social, physical, and emotional events such as retirement, children leaving home, illness, and death occur at widely varying ages and sometimes in totally unpredictable sequence. Some of the important social and physical changes of childhood are more predictable; hence, ages tied to the psychosocial crises of childhood are more accurate.

Erikson's theory, like Freud's, does not lend itself well to experimental validation. What Erikson's theory provides is a very general framework for describing and interpreting some of the major changes that occur in the life span. Its usefulness rests largely in the insights that may result from examining the lives of individuals within the context of the theory.

A COGNITIVE APPROACH: PIAGET

Whereas psychoanalytic theorists are concerned primarily with personality development, other theorists focus on the intellectual (cognitive) development of children. **Cognition,** my dictionary informs me, is the art or faculty of knowing. Cognitive theorists are concerned with how we know — that is, with how we obtain, process, and use information. Flavell (1985) suggests that there are two principal orientations in the study of cognitive processes: the information-processing approach and Piaget's approach. The information-processing approach is concerned mainly with processes involved in memory — processes such as deriving information, abstracting, sorting, organizing, analyzing, and retrieving, for example. Piaget's approach deals with the same basic questions (specifically, how do we learn, remember, and consequently *know?*), but is more interested in the developmental aspects of cognition. That is, it looks at how the child's interaction with the environment leads to the progressive development of cognitive abilities.

Important basic aspects of Piaget's theory are introduced briefly in the following sections. More specific details of Piaget's theory and the contributions of information-processing approaches are discussed in subsequent chapters that deal chronologically with the child's cognitive development (chapters 5, 7, 9, and 11).

Basic Ideas

Piaget was trained as a biologist, not a psychologist. Consistent with his early training, he began his study of children by posing two of the fundamental questions of biology: (1) What is it that enables organisms to adapt to their environments and to survive? (2) What is the most useful way of classifying living organisms?

The questions of biology can be rephrased and applied to the development of children: (1) What are the characteristics and capabilities of children that allow them to adapt to their environments? (2) What is the most useful way of classifying or ordering child development? Piaget's answers for these two questions form the basis for his theory. He developed these answers over an extraordinarily prolific career spanning more than six decades (he died in 1980 at the age of 84). As a result, they are very complex in scope and detail. But they can be simplified.

Assimilation and accommodation permit adaptation. The newborn infant that Piaget describes is in some ways a helpless little organism, unaware that the world out there is real, with no storehouse of thoughts with which to reason, no capacity for intentional behaviors, only a few simple reflexes. But infants are much more than this. They are also remarkable little sensing machines that seem to be naturally predisposed to acquiring and processing a tremendous amount of information. They continually seek out and respond to stimulation. As a result, the sucking, reaching, grasping, and other reflexes that were present at birth become more complex, more coordinated, and eventually more purposeful. The process by which this occurs is *adaptation*. And to answer the first of the questions of biology as simply as possible, **assimilation** and **accommodation** are the processes that make adaptation possible.

Assimilation involves responding to situations in terms of activities or knowledge that have already been learned or that are present at birth. For example, an infant is born with the capability to suck — with a sucking **scheme** in Piaget's terms (sometimes used interchangeably with **schema**, which is pluralized as **schemata**). The sucking schema allows the infant to assimilate a nipple to the behavior of sucking. Similarly, a child who has learned the rules of addition can assimilate a problem such as 2 + 2 (can respond appropriately in terms of previous learning). Often, however, our understanding of the world is insufficient to deal with the present situation. The newborn's sucking schema is adequate for ordinary nipples but does not work for fingers and toes; the preschooler's understanding of number is sufficient for keeping track of

The sucking scheme.

toys but is inadequate for impressing kindergarten teachers. Changes are required in information and behavior. These changes define *accommodation*. In short, assimilation involves reacting on the basis of previous learning and understanding; accommodation involves a change in understanding. And the interplay of assimilation and accommodation leads to adaptation (see Chapter 5 for further illustration of these concepts).

Development can be ordered in stages. The second of biology's questions asks what is the most useful way of organizing and classifying child development. Piaget's answer is found in his description of the stages through which each child passes. There are four major stages in this description, each marked by strikingly different perceptions of the world and by different adaptations to it. Each is the product of learning that occurred in earlier stages, and each is a preparation for the next stage.

Note that although Piaget's theory is most easily explained and understood in terms of stages, he nevertheless viewed development as a *continuous* process of successive changes. Development does not consist of abrupt, clearly recognizable changes like steps on a stairway; it is more like a gradual incline. Although cognitive development moves along relatively smoothly, it is useful and simpler to divide it into stages. Doing so allows us to compare behaviors and capabilities that are characteristic of different levels and sometimes leads

Table 2.5
Piaget's Stages of Cognitive Development

Stage	Appropriate Age	Some Major Characteristics
Sensorimotor	0–2 years	Intelligence in action World of the here and now No language, no thought, no notion of objective reality at beginning of stage
Preoperational	2–7 years	Egocentric thought Reason dominated by perception Intuitive rather than logical solutions Inability to conserve
Concrete operations	7–11 or 12 years	Ability to conserve Logic of classes and relations Understanding of numbers Thinking bound to concrete Development of reversibility in thought
Formal operations	11 or 12–14 or 15 years	Complete generality of thought Propositional thinking Ability to deal with the hypothetical Development of strong idealism

Note: Each of these characteristics is detailed in appropriate sections of Chapters 5, 7, 9, and 11.

to discoveries about the processes underlying change. Note, too, that the ages Piaget assigned to each stage are simply averages reflecting the behaviors of upper-middle-class Swiss children through the middle of the twentieth century. Children from different cultural contexts and with different characteristics sometimes pass through these stages much earlier or much later than Piaget's norms would suggest.

The Stages

Piaget's major stages are shown in Table 2.5 and summarized very briefly here. (There is more detail in chapters 5, 7, 9, and 11.)

Sensorimotor period. The first two years of life are labeled the **sensorimotor period,** so called because during this time the child understands the world largely through immediate action and sensation. For the infant, the world exists here and now. It is real only when it is being acted on and sensed. When the ball is no longer being chewed, it doesn't exist. Only toward the end of the second year do children finally realize that objects have a permanence and an identity of their own — that they continue to exist when they are not in view. Toward the end of the first two years, the child begins to acquire language and progresses slowly from a sensorimotor to a more cognitive intelligence.

Preoperational thinking. Following the acquisition of language, the child enters the period of **preoperational thought** (ages 2 to 7). Among the various characteristics of the child's thinking during the preoperational period, one of the more interesting is an excessive reliance on perception rather than on logic. Piaget illustrates this in his famous **conservation** experiments. In one of these experiments, for example, children are presented with two glasses, each of which contains an equal amount of water. The experimenter then pours the contents of one glass into a tall, thin tube — or, alternately, into a lower, flatter dish. The child is now asked whether each of the containers still has the same amount of water or whether one has more than the other. Preoperational children, relying on the appearance of the two containers, almost invariably say that the tall tube has more because it is higher (or less because it is thinner) — or that the flat dish has more because it is "fatter" (or less because it is shorter). Even when they realize that the water could be poured back into the original container so that both would then be equal, preoperational children continue to rely on perception (on actual appearance) rather than on reasoning (see Chapter 7 for more details).

Concrete operations. The major acquisition of the next period of development is the ability to think operationally (**concrete operations,** ages 7 or 8 to 11 or 12). An *operation* is a thought — what Piaget called an internalized action. In this sense, it is a mental action or, more precisely, an operation performed on ideas according to certain rules of logic. These rules of logic permit the concrete operational child to scoff at the ridiculous simplicity of a conservation problem. Of course, there is the same amount of water in both containers because none has been added or taken away, because one misleading dimension is compensated for by the other (it is taller but thinner), and because the act of pouring the water from one container to the other can be reversed to prove that quantity has not changed. Concrete operational children are capable of this kind of logic. But it is a logic that is tied to real, concrete objects and events. They are still unable to reason logically about hypothetical situations or events and cannot go from the real to the merely possible or from the possible to the actual. Thought is bound to the real world, the concrete — hence *concrete operations* (see Chapter 9).

Formal operations. When children finally liberate themselves from the restrictions that have bound them to the concrete world, they enter the last stage of cognitive development — **formal operations,** characterized by the ability to manipulate abstract ideas — beginning around age 11 or 12. During this stage the child's thought becomes as logical as it will ever be; it is the culmination of a decade spent in preparation for it (Chapter 11).

Piaget in Review

Child development, in Piaget's view, is best described as the emergence of progressively more logical forms of thought — that is, as the development of ways of thinking that become increasingly more effective in freeing children from the present and allowing them to use powerful symbol systems to understand and manipulate the environment. According to the theory, the major characteristics of thinking in each of the four developmental stages influence all aspects of children's understanding of the world, including their notion of space, time, numbers, reality, causality, and so on.

A theory such as Piaget's is considerably easier to evaluate objectively than are the psychoanalytic approaches. It makes very specific predictions about how average children function intellectually at different age levels; and an enormous number of these predictions have been tested by researchers. In general, this research confirms many of Piaget's initial findings, particularly about the order of stages, although it is clear that the ages at which different children reach specific stages can vary considerably.

Evidence suggests that Piaget underestimated the information-processing capabilities of infants and young children (Flavell, 1985). However, this is due less to weaknesses in the theory than to Piaget's lack of tools and instruments with sufficient sensitivity to detect the infant's cognitive capacities. Recent studies of the infant's responsiveness to stimulation often make use of sophisticated instruments that measure changes in heart and respiration rate, movements of the eyeballs, changes in pupil size, brainwave activity, and so on — all devices not available to Piaget in the 1920s and 30s.

Another weakness in Piaget's theorizing is that he overestimated the importance of motor activity in the infant's cognitive development and underplayed the importance of perception, most especially of visual perception (Bullinger, 1985). Others criticize Piaget because his theory says relatively little about individual differences among children, about the factors that might account for these differences, or about what can be done to promote intellectual development. In addition, the language and concepts of the theory are sometimes difficult, and it is not always clear that terms such as *assimilation* and *accommodation* add significantly to our understanding of human behavior. In spite of these criticisms, Piagetian theory has clearly been the most dominant cognitive developmental theory of this century and continues to have a profound influence on current research and practice.

BEHAVIORISTIC APPROACHES

The three child development theories presented so far (Freud, Erikson, and Piaget) describe development in terms of progression through a relatively fixed sequence of stages. Freud's emphasis is on the development of personality; Erikson looks at the development of social competence; and Piaget is concerned with intellectual development. Each of these theories views the child's actions as important to the outcome of the developmental process. In addition, each makes some important assumptions about the biological (inherited) aspects of behavior and personality.

In contrast, most **behavioristic theories** of development make few assumptions about inherited tendencies; nor are they very concerned with the historical causes of behavior. Instead, they focus on the child's immediate behavior and on the environmental forces that affect it. In other words, they look at relationships between experience and behavior and consequently make extensive use of concepts such as reinforcement and punishment, which describe how behavior may be encouraged or discouraged.

Several fundamental assumptions underlie behavioristic approaches to development (also referred to as learning theory approaches). Most important among these is the belief that behavior is reducible to responses or actions that can be observed, measured, and analyzed. The label *behaviorism* derives from the behaviorist's concern with responses (behaviors).

Another important behavioristic assumption is the belief that responses are a function of such things as reinforcement (usually rewards) and punishment. Accordingly, one of the main goals of behavioristic theorists has been to discover the rules that govern relationships between stimuli (conditions that lead to behavior) and responses and to learn how responses can be controlled through the administration of rewards and punishments.

Note that many of these assumptions are assumptions of the mechanistic model, which views the child as more passive than active. According to this model, experiences and circumstances — especially those that are reinforced or punished — are among the most important factors in shaping the course of our development. In some ways, our behavior is like the functioning of a machine, the model insists. As long as we understand how the machine works, we are in a position to predict its actions, given sufficient knowledge of immediate circumstances. The goal of the behavioristic theorist is to understand the human machine so well that with sufficient knowledge of past functioning and of immediate circumstances, it would be possible to predict behavior accurately and, in some instances, to control it as well.

The behavioristic approach is not only somewhat mechanistic, but is also fundamentally contextualist in its emphasis on the importance of environmental influences (see Bijou, 1989). The rewards and punishments that are the causes and consequences of behavior are, in fact, *context.*

The behavioristic approach was introduced into American psychology through the work of John B. Watson and B. F. Skinner and led to a dramatic upheaval in psychology, the effects of which are still being felt (Cairns, 1983). Both theorists believed strongly in the importance of the environment as the principal force in shaping development. Both believed that development could be understood through an analysis of specific behaviors, the circumstances leading to them, and their consequences. Watson is associated with a learning theory based on a model of **classical conditioning;** Skinner developed a model of **operant conditioning. Conditioning** refers to a simple kind of learning whereby certain behaviors are affected by the environment, becoming more or less probable and predictable. Classical and operant conditioning are described and illustrated in the following sections.

Classical Conditioning

Among early contributors to modern knowledge about human learning was the Russian psychologist Ivan Pavlov. In the course of research that he was doing with dogs, Pavlov (1927) noticed that the older and more experienced animals in his laboratory began to salivate when they saw their keeper approaching. Because none of the dogs had ever tasted the keeper, Pavlov reasoned that they were salivating, not because they expected to eat him now, but probably because they had formed some sort of **association,** or link, between the sight of the keeper and the presentation of food. This observation led Pavlov to a series of investigations of a simple form of learning called *classical conditioning.*

The model. The psychology of learning has its own language for the stimuli and responses of classical conditioning. The stimulus that is part of the original stimulus-response link (the reflex) is termed the **unconditioned stimulus** (UCS). Food in the mouth of Pavlov's dog is an unconditioned stimulus. It leads to a response without any new learning having taken place. The stimulus that is originally neutral but comes to be effective through repeated pairing with the unconditioned stimulus is called the conditioning or **conditioned stimulus** (CS). The bell or buzzer is a conditioned stimulus. Eventually, it gives rise to responses similar to those originally made only for unconditioned stimuli. Corresponding responses are termed the **unconditioned response** (UCR) or the **conditioned response** (CR), depending on whether they occur in response to the unconditioned or the conditioned stimulus. Salivating in response to a buzzer is a conditioned response. The process involved in classical conditioning is illustrated in Figure 2.2.

An example. A well-known study demonstrating classical conditioning of emotional responses in children is reported by Watson and Rayner (1920). Watson knew that infants react with fear to loud noises, and he reasoned that it should be possible to make a child fear any other distinctive stimulus simply by pairing it often enough with a loud noise. In this case, the noise is an unconditioned stimulus because it elicits a fear response without any learning having taken place; the responses associated with fear are therefore unconditioned responses. The neutral stimulus that Watson and Rayner chose was a white rat, a stimulus that does not ordinarily frighten most young children. The unwitting subject was an unfortunate 11-month-old infant named Albert.

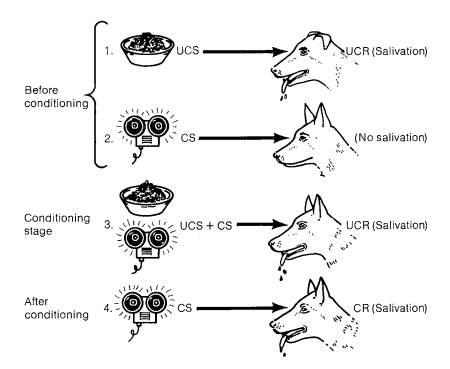

Before conditioning

1. UCS ──────→ UCR (Salivation)

2. CS ──────→ (No salivation)

Conditioning stage

3. UCS + CS ──────→ UCR (Salivation)

After conditioning

4. CS ──────→ CR (Salivation)

Figure 2.2

Classical conditioning. In *(1)* an unconditioned stimulus leads to an unconditioned response; whereas in *(2)* a conditioning stimulus does not lead to the same response. In *(3)* the unconditioned stimulus is paired with the conditioning stimulus a number of times so that eventually the conditioning stimulus alone elicits the original response, as in *(4)*.

To demonstrate the effectiveness of classical conditioning in producing emotional reactions, each time Watson and Rayner presented Little Albert with the rat, they made a loud noise behind Albert. The poor infant reacted with a great deal of fear, as was expected. After repeating the procedure seven times, Watson and Rayner ceased making the noise, but simply presented the rat to Albert. Now, as soon as the child saw the rat, he was terrified and began to whimper, attempting to crawl away. Unfortunately Little Albert was removed from the hospital before Watson could cure him, although a conditioning procedure could have been used for that as well (Jones, Albert, & Watson, 1974).

Although Watson and Rayner's experiment with Little Albert is more systematic than most situations in which we acquire emotional responses, the results can nevertheless be generalized. There is considerable evidence that emotional reactions do transfer from one situation to another. People who react with fear to the sound of a dentist's drill are not fearful because the *sound* of the drill has caused them pain in the past. But the sound of the drill (a conditioned stimulus) may have been associated with pain and now elicits related reactions. Similarly, children who dislike their teacher and who react negatively to the teacher's presence may eventually react negatively to the classroom, to school-related activities, to voices that sound like the teacher's, to adults who resemble her, to students who look like other students in the class, to pencils, and so on.

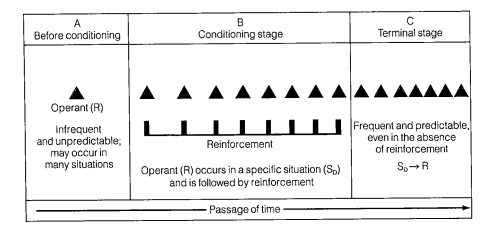

A Before conditioning	B Conditioning stage	C Terminal stage
▲ Operant (R) Infrequent and unpredictable; may occur in many situations	▲ ▲ ▲ ▲ ▲ ▲ ▲ ⌐_⌐_⌐_⌐_⌐_⌐_⌐_ Reinforcement Operant (R) occurs in a specific situation (S_D) and is followed by reinforcement	▲▲ ▲▲▲▲▲ Frequent and predictable, even in the absence of reinforcement $S_D \rightarrow R$

─────────── Passage of time ───────────►

Figure 2.3

Schematic model of operant conditioning. In *(A)* the operant behavior alone is not rewarded. In *(B)* conditioning begins. The operant behavior takes place by chance; it is immediately reinforced. It occurs again, by chance or deliberately, and the reinforcement is repeated. As the timeline chart shows, repetition becomes more and more frequent as the learner catches on. Eventually, the operant behavior continues even without reinforcement at the terminal stage *(C)*.

Operant Conditioning

A classical conditioning model is sometimes useful for explaining the learning of simple behaviors that occur in response to specific stimuli. As Skinner (1953, 1957, 1961) has pointed out, however, many human behaviors or responses are not **elicited,** or brought about, by any obvious stimuli, but appear instead to be **emitted,** or issued, by the organism, for whatever reason. Skinner labeled such behavior **operant;** a response elicited by stimuli, he labeled a **respondent.** His major work is an attempt to explain how operants are learned.

The simplest explanation of operant conditioning is that the consequences of a response determine whether it is likely to be learned. Put simply, behaviors that are reinforced will tend to be repeated; those that are not reinforced (or that are punished) are less likely to be repeated (see Figure 2.3). This is fundamentally different from saying that learning will occur as a function of the pairing of stimuli, regardless of its consequences. Clearly, when Little Albert reacted with fear to the rat, it was not because his fear responses led to pleasant consequences but because the rat was paired with some other fear-producing situation.

Reinforcement. One of Skinner's first tasks was to define the nature of **reinforcement.** Because he was determined to be objective, he advanced a simple and objective definition for the term: Whatever increases the probability of a response occurring is reinforcing. A **reinforcer** is the stimulus that reinforces; reinforcement is the effect of a reinforcer. **Negative reinforcement** is one kind of reinforcement; **positive reinforcement** is the other. *Both* positive and negative reinforcement *increase* the probability of a response occurring. The difference between the two is that positive reinforcement is effective as a result of a

reward being added to a situation after the behavior has occurred, whereas negative reinforcement is effective through the removal of an unpleasant stimulus. A simple way of remembering the difference between the two is to remember that positive reinforcement involves a *reward* for behavior; negative reinforcement involves *relief* from something unpleasant.

Unfortunately, real-life situations are more complicated than this black-and-white terminology suggests. Subjective judgments such as "pleasant" and "unpleasant," although they make our understanding simpler, are misleading. Reinforcement and punishment have to do with *effects* rather than with perceived pleasantness. Thus a parent or teacher who keeps "punishing" a child but who observes that the punished behavior becomes more rather than less frequent may well be reinforcing that behavior — or something (someone) else is. Similarly, there are occasions where a teacher's praise of a student's behavior will lead to a drastic reduction of that behavior. Reinforcement? No. By definition, punishment. The important point is that pleasantness and unpleasantness are subjective — they exist *in the eye of the beholder;* reinforcement and punishment are objective phenomena defined in terms of increases or decreases in the frequency of behavior.

Punishment. Both reinforcement and punishment are defined by their effects. Whereas reinforcement, whether positive or negative, serves to make a response more likely, punishment does not.

There are several kinds of punishment. The kind that we usually think of first involves a clearly unpleasant consequence. Being beaten with a hickory stick is an example of this kind of punishment. Another kind of punishment involves taking away something that is pleasant. Being prevented from watching television (called a *time-out procedure*) or having to give up something desirable like money or privileges (called *response-cost punishment*) are both examples of this kind of punishment (see Chapter 10). Distinctions among the various kinds of reinforcement and punishment are illustrated in Figure 2.4. As the illustration makes clear, both may involve stimuli with pleasant or unpleasant effects, but whether these stimuli are added to or removed from the situation determines whether they are reinforcing or punishing. It is worth emphasizing again that both reinforcement and punishment are defined by their effects.

Types of reinforcers. Skinner distinguishes between two types of reinforcers, each of which can be either positive or negative. Some stimuli such as food and drink are naturally reinforcing. We don't have to learn that these are pleasant. (Sex is in the same category.) These stimuli are referred to as **primary reinforcers** because they are related to primary (unlearned) **needs** (such as for food and drink). Other stimuli are not naturally reinforcing, but if they are paired with primary reinforcers they often become reinforcing in a number of situations

Figure 2.4
The four alternatives that define punishment and reinforcement.

Nature of stimulus effect

	Pleasant	Unpleasant
Added to the situation	*Positive reinforcement:* Wendy is given a jelly bean for being "good"	*Punishment:* Wendy has her nose tweaked for being "bad"
Removed from the situation	*Punishment:* Wendy has her jelly bean taken away for being "bad"	*Negative reinforcement:* Wendy has her nose released because she says "I'm sorry"

☐ Response increases

☐ Response decreases

and for a variety of different behaviors. These are acquired or **generalized reinforcers.** Examples are plentiful: Praise, social prestige, money, power, and many other consequences are reinforcing in almost any situation and for nearly any behavior.

There are other ways of classifying reinforcement. Bijou and Sturges (1959) list five classes of reinforcement that may affect the child's behavior. First there are *consumables* — meat and potatoes, milk, water, and chocolate. Their effectiveness in influencing behavior is not so obvious for well-fed children as it might be for poorer children who actually lack consumables. Most of our children are sufficiently nourished that they do not need to engage in many behaviors that are designed to get them food, particularly after they have passed through their infancy. However, it is no secret that babies who cry when they are hungry, awakening their mothers and bringing them running, will soon learn to cry whenever they want their mothers. Nor is it a secret that the behavior of children can frequently be controlled by rewarding them with candies and other consumables.

A second class of reinforcers that has been used in experimental situations (but that also occurs frequently in a child's daily activities) is called *manipulatables.* These include all the objects a child finds pleasant to play with, chief among them toys.

The third class of reinforcers, *visual and auditory* stimuli, includes sights and sounds that are employed deliberately and systematically to reinforce behavior. Bells that are rung by happy teachers or displays of lights and sirens that signal success with a one-armed bandit are examples of this class of reinforcers.

The fourth category of reinforcers is *social* stimuli: smiles, verbal praise, physical contact such as a pat on the back or a handshake. These are probably among the most powerful reinforcers for people, but are not as important for bears, who often prefer blueberries.

Skinner, a pigeon,
and many pigeons
watching.

Fifth are *token* reinforcers: chips, disks, counters, or anything that can be exchanged for some more meaningful reinforcer. Token reinforcers have been used successfully in many experiments, especially with mentally retarded children.

Another category of reinforcement is implicit in Premack's (1965) definition of the Premack Principle: Behaviors that occur frequently and spontaneously can be employed to reinforce other behavior. An application of this principle is illustrated by teachers who allow their students to read their favorite books when they complete their assignments. In this case, reading occurs frequently and spontaneously; therefore, it can be used to reinforce a lower probability behavior (see Table 2.6).

Table 2.6
Five Classes of Reinforcers with Examples

Reinforcers	Examples
Consumables	Candy, drinks, chocolates, fruit
Manipulatables	Toys, games, puzzles
Visual and auditory stimuli	Bells, buzzers, smiling puppets, green lights
Social stimuli	Praise, a pat on the back, a smile, applause
Token reinforcers	Coins, counters, points, or other tokens that can be exchanged for other reinforcers
Premack principle	Activities that occur frequently — and that are presumably pleasant (reading; watching television) can be used to reinforce other, less frequently occurring activities (studying)

Sources: Bijou and Sturges (1959), Premack (1965).

Behavioristic Approaches in Review

Learning theory explanations for human development emphasize the role of the environment in shaping our personalities and our behaviors. Unlike psychoanalytic approaches, they are not concerned with psychodynamic conflicts and other hidden causes of behavior; and unlike the more cognitive approaches, they do not often pay much attention to concepts such as *understanding* and *knowing*. Instead, they focus on the role of reinforcement and punishment and on the extent to which behavior can be shaped by its consequences.

One of the principal criticisms of these approaches is that they are poorly suited to explain what are referred to as higher mental processes — thinking, feeling, analyzing, problem solving, evaluating, and so on. Their emphasis, and their principal usefulness, relates to actual behavior rather than to conceptual processes.

A second criticism of behavioristic approaches is that by emphasizing the machinelike qualities of human functioning, they rob us of what we consider most human — namely, our ability to think and imagine and our ability (real or imagined) to exercise significant control over our own behaviors. In brief, critics have claimed that in its attempts to reduce behavior to a handful of observable stimuli and responses, behaviorism dehumanizes us.

Although these criticisms may be reasonable and fair with respect to older and more extreme interpretations of behaviorism, they are less pertinent for more current positions. Bijou (1989), for example, notes that whereas Watson's theory describes an essentially passive organism, contemporary behaviorism sees the individual "as *always* being in an interactive relationship with the environment" (p. 68). In his words, the individual is *adjustive* rather than simply reactive. However Bijou's contemporary behaviorist does not view our ability to think, to imagine, or to feel as a *cause* of behavior. Bijou labels these cognitive activities *implicit interactions*. The primary concern of the behaviorist is not so much these implicit — hence, unobservable — interactions as it is the more observable interactions between stimuli and responses. Bijou cautions, however, that insofar as the contemporary behaviorist views people as adjustive rather than simply reactive, the environment is given a less important role in determining behavior. The causes of behavior, he claims, will be found not in the environment alone, but rather in all the factors that are involved in a person's interactions, including history of past interactions.

On a more positive note, behavioristic approaches to development are sometimes very useful not only for understanding developmental change, but also for controlling it. The deliberate application of conditioning principles to change behavior (termed **behavior modification**) has proven extremely useful in a variety of settings, including the classroom and psychotherapy.

Theories, we should remember, are inventions whose purpose is to simplify, to explain, sometimes to predict. Unlike traditional religions, they don't have to be accepted or rejected in their entirety. Elements from different theories can sometimes be combined to produce new theories, new insights, that go far beyond the original theories. A case in point is Albert Bandura's theorizing, which in some ways serves as a transition between behaviorism and cognitivism.

SOCIAL COGNITIVE THEORY

At one level, Bandura's (1977, 1986) theory is a behavioristic theory of imitation based on the assumption that much important learning involves models of various kinds that act as social influences on the child. At another level, it is a cognitive theory that gives an important role to the child's ability to symbolize — that is, to reason, to imagine, to ferret out cause-and-effect relationships, to anticipate the outcomes of behavior. There is no doubt, Bandura (1977) assures us, that reinforcement controls much of our behavior. But it does not control us blindly. Its effects depend largely on our *awareness* of the relationship between our behavior and its outcomes. As Bruner (1985) points out, reinforcement often occurs a long time after the behavior it follows — as happens, for example, when you study for an examination. In such cases, it is not reinforcement (or the possibility of punishment) that affects behavior directly so much as it is the individual's ability to anticipate the consequences of behavior.

Bandura's social learning theory is a theory of **observational learning** (or **imitation**). It can be summarized simply as follows:

1. Much human learning and behavior is a function of observing the behavior of others or of symbolic models such as fictional characters and television or folk heroes.

2. Imitation is often reinforced.

3. Observational learning can therefore be explained largely through operant conditioning principles.

The Processes of Observational Learning

Bandura (1986) emphasizes that the effects of models are due largely to their *informative function*. From observing models, we learn not only *how* to do certain things, but also what the *consequences* of our behaviors are likely to be. Accordingly, there are four distinct processes involved in observational learning.

First there are *attentional processes*. It seems clear that children are not likely to learn very much from a model if they pay no attention to important aspects of that model's behavior. Whether or not they will attend, Bandura informs us, depends a great deal on the **value** (judgment about the desirability of certain behavior) of the model's behavior. (Is it important for the observer to be able to swear like that? Throw a ball in that way? Cock his head in just that fashion?) It also depends on other factors such as the distinctiveness of the behavior, its prevalence, and its complexity, as well as on such things as the motor, perceptual, and cognitive capacities of the observer and learned preferences.

Not only are there attention processes involved, but also *retention processes*. The child must attend and must then be able to remember. This, says Bandura, implies being able to represent mentally, either in terms of images or words and therefore depends on the child's cognitive skills.

Observational learning also requires appropriate *production processes*. That is, in order to imitate, the observer must be able to translate what has been retained (represented mentally) into an actual sequence of behavior. This might require certain motor and physical capabilities, as well as the ability to monitor and correct one's own behavior.

Finally, in observational learning, as in all learning, there must be relevant *motivational processes*. That is, in the absence of appropriate motivation (reasons for behavior), many behaviors that are observed and potentially learned will not be performed. In this connection, learning theorists make an important distinction between *acquisition* and *performance*. Much is acquired (learned, in other words), but does not become part of behavior (see Figure 2.5).

Manifestations of Observational Learning

The term *model* may refer to an actual (perhaps very ordinary) person whose behavior serves as a guide, a blueprint, an inspiration for somebody else. A model might also be **symbolic.** Symbolic models include such things as books, verbal or written instructions, pictures, mental images, cartoon or film characters, television programs, and so on.

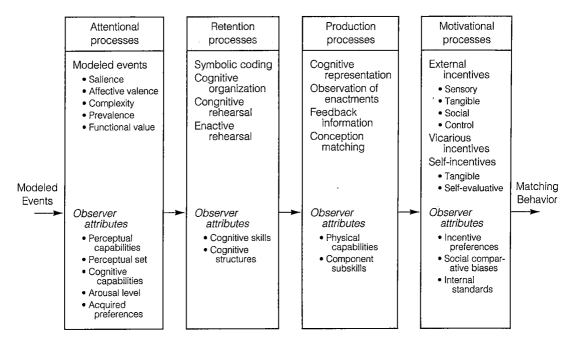

Attentional processes	Retention processes	Production processes	Motivational processes
Modeled events • Salience • Affective valence • Complexity • Prevalence • Functional value	Symbolic coding Cognitive organization Congnitive rehearsal Enactive rehearsal	Cognitive representation Observation of enactments Feedback information Conception matching	External incentives • Sensory • Tangible • Social • Control Vicarious incentives Self-incentives • Tangible • Self-evaluative

Modeled Events → Observer attributes • Perceptual capabilities • Perceptual set • Cognitive capabilities • Arousal level • Acquired preferences → Observer attributes • Cognitive skills • Cognitive structures → Observer attributes • Physical capabilities • Component subskills → Observer attributes • Incentive preferences • Social comparative biases • Internal standards → Matching Behavior

Figure 2.5

Subprocesses governing observational learning in Bandura's social cognitive theory.

From Albert Bandura (1989). Social cognitive theory. In Ross Vasta (Ed), *Annals of Child Development*, Vol. 6, p. 16. JAI Press. Reprinted by permission of the publisher.

Bandura and Walters (1963) describe three different effects of imitation on learning in children. The first is the learning of *novel* behavior; it is labeled the **modeling effect.** One important manifestation of the modeling effect is the acquisition of some aspects of language. That Eskimo children learn Eskimo rather than Greek is evidence that they model the language that surrounds them. (There is much more than imitation involved in language learning.) (See Chapter 5.)

The effects of imitation are also found in the phenomena labeled the **inhibitory effect** (the suppression of deviant behavior) and the **disinhibitory effect** (the appearance of previously suppressed deviant behavior). These effects are usually the result of punishment or reward to the model for engaging in deviant behavior. Consider the hypothetical case of a teenager from an upstanding, conservative, middle-class family, whose friends have recently discovered marijuana. The behavior is deviant by the child's own standards, but the amount of reinforcement (in terms of social prestige, acceptance by the group, and so on) that others appear to derive from smoking marijuana may well disinhibit this behavior in the child. There is really no new learning involved, as in modeling, but merely the disinhibition of previously suppressed behavior. If this teenager later observes members of her peer group punished by law, parents, or school authorities, or experiencing ill effects of the drug, she might suddenly cease engaging in this behavior. Again, there is no new learning involved, although there is a change in behavior resulting from the influence of models; thus this change illustrates the inhibitory effect.

A third effect of imitation is known as the **eliciting effect:** The behavior engaged in by learners as a result of observing a model is not identical to the

Table 2.7
Three Effects of Imitation

Modeling	Acquiring *new* behavior as a result of observing a model
Inhibitory-Disinhibitory	Ceasing or starting some *deviant* behavior as a result of seeing a model punished or rewarded for similar behavior
Eliciting	Engaging in behavior *related* to that of a model

model's behavior, nor deviant, nor novel, but is simply related to it. It is as though the model's behavior suggests some response to the observer and therefore *elicits* that response. A child "acting up" in school may elicit misbehavior in her classmates; they may not imitate her behavior precisely, but simply engage in the same general type of behavior — or misbehavior (see Table 2.7).

Self-Efficacy

Theories in psychology, as elsewhere, are not often static, unchanging things — unless the theorist has lost interest, moved to other things, or died. And even then, if the theory is at all compelling or important, there will be others who will chew at it, who will try to change its shape to fit new facts and to answer new questions.

Albert Bandura's theorizing is a case in point. His early ideas stemmed very directly from a behavioristic orientation. Thus his imitation-based theory of social learning attempts to explain the complex effects of modeling in terms of rewards and punishments, either actual or anticipated. But when a behavioristic theorist speaks of *anticipating*, of *imagining* the consequences of a behavior, either for a model or for the self, that theorist has stepped far beyond the carefully prescribed limits of traditional behaviorism. There is little room for imagining among the objective, observable, and measurable stimuli, responses, and reinforcement schedules of the early behaviorist.

So, as we saw, Bandura's social-learning theory has become progressively more *cognitive* (more concerned with *knowing, understanding, thinking,* and other mental processes). It gives an increasingly important role to the *informative* function of models. It is what the observer imagines and anticipates that is fundamentally important in learning through imitation.

Recently, Bandura's research and theorizing has taken yet another turn — one that is even more clearly cognitive (Bandura, 1981, 1986; Evans, 1989). It has to do with what is termed **self-referent** thought — thought that has to do with our *selves*, with our own mental processes. Among other things, self-referent thought deals with our estimates of our abilities, with our notions about how capable and how *effective* we are in our dealings with the world and

Parents are often the most accessible real-life models for young children; television characters, books, cartoons, film, and pictures are powerful symbolic models.

with others. And a very specific term has been coined to describe our estimates of our effectiveness: **self-efficacy.**

Definition. In a nutshell, efficacy signifies competence in dealing with the environment. The most *efficacious* people are those who can most effectively deal with a variety of situations even when these situations are ambiguous or highly stressful. Thus self-efficacy has two separate but related components: One includes the skills that are required for the successful performance of a behavior; the other consists of the individual's beliefs about personal effectiveness. From a psychological point of view, it is not so much the skills component that is important, but rather the person's own evaluations of personal efficacy. *Self*-efficacy is the term that refers more precisely to the judgments we make about how *efficacious* we are likely to be in given situations. Among the most important of all the different aspects of self-knowledge, Bandura insists, is our conception of personal efficacy.

Implications of self-efficacy judgments. Why? Because our judgments about our personal effectiveness are extremely important in determining what we do and don't do. In fact, in some situations, self-efficacy may be a better predictor of behavior than relevant skills are (Schunk, 1984). Under most circumstances, children, and adults, do not seek out and undertake activities in which they expect to perform badly.

Judgments of personal efficacy affect not only our choices of activities and settings, but also the amount of effort individuals are willing to expend when faced with difficulties. The stronger an individual's perceptions of efficacy, the more likely that individual is to persist and the greater will be the effort expended. But if notions of self-efficacy are not highly favorable, difficult activities may be abandoned after very little effort and time.

Finally, perceived self-efficacy influences our thoughts and emotions. Those whose assessment of their effectiveness is low are more likely to evaluate their behaviors negatively and to see themselves as being inadequate.

Sources of efficacy judgments. Judgements of personal efficacy, Bandura (1986) suggests, stem from four main sources. First, there are the direct effects of the individual's behavior. Whether we succeed or not must surely have some effect on our estimates of how efficacious we are. However, the inferential processes involved in judgments of self-efficacy are not always simple and linear. That is, the individual who is mostly successful does not invariably arrive at highly positive judgments of self-efficacy; nor does lack of success always correspond to negative judgments. As Weiner (1980b) points out, there are a number of factors to which success — or lack of success — can be attributed. Some of these, such as ability and effort, are under personal control and reflect directly on the efficacy of the individual. Others, such as luck or the difficulty of the task, are not under personal control and do not, therefore, have very direct implications for judgments of self-efficacy. Some individuals are prone to attribute the outcomes of their behaviors to factors over which they have control. Dweck (1975) refers to these people as *mastery-oriented*. Others are more likely to attribute their failures and successes to luck or to the task's being too difficult or too easy. Dweck describes these individuals as being characterized by *helplessness* rather than by a mastery orientation.

One source of influence for judgments of personal efficacy, then, are personal accomplishments and especially individual attributions concerning the reasons for these accomplishments. A second influence is vicarious (secondhand); it derives from observing the performance of others. Even as children, we arrive at notions of how effective we are partly on the basis of comparisons we make between ourselves and others. And, as Bandura (1981) suggests, the most informative comparisons we can make are those that involve others whose performance is similar to ours. A 12-year-old who demolishes his 6-year-old brother in a game of skill and intelligence learns very little about his personal effectiveness. Similarly, if he, in turn, is blown away by his father, he may not have learned much more — except, perhaps, for a touch of humility.

A third source of influence on self-judgments, Bandura (1986) argues, is persuasion. "You can do it, Guy. I know you can. Sing for us. We love the way you sing." (This is a totally fictitious illustration; even very dumb animals do not love the way I sing.) Persuasion, depending on the characteristics of the persuader and on the relationship between persuader and the person being persuaded, can sometimes change an individual's judgments of self-efficacy and lead that individual to attempt things that would not otherwise be attempted — or to decide not to attempt them:"Guy, they're just flattering you. Please don't sing."

The fourth source of influence on judgments of self-efficacy is the person's **arousal** level. The term *arousal* has many meanings. In this context, its most important meaning has to do with alertness or with intensity of immediate emotional reaction. Situations that produce very high arousal are those that are shocking, sudden, frightening, intensely exciting, deeply moving — in short, those that lead to profound positive or negative emotions. High arousal can significantly affect self-judgments — in either direction. For example, extreme fear might conceivably lead to specific judgments of high or low efficacy. A mountain climber might, because of fear that threatens to turn her legs to jelly, decide that she is not capable of completing her climb. In contrast, a father who finds his child trapped beneath an overturned automobile might, in a sudden surge of emotion, decide that he is capable of lifting the vehicle off his son.

At a less extreme level, whether arousal will have positive or negative effects on the individual's self-judgments may depend largely on experiences the individual has had in situations of high or low arousal. There are those who find that moderately high arousal helps their performance; others react in the opposite way. For example, the trepidation that precedes speaking in public may be seen as helpful by some speakers and as highly negative by others.

In summary, four separate sources of influence can have an effect on the individual's judgments of self-efficacy. Bandura describes these as *enactive* (based on the outcome of the individual's own actions); *vicarious* (based on comparisons between the person's performance and the performance of others); *persuasory* (the result of persuasion); and *emotive* (the result of arousal or emotion).

Development of self-efficacy. Not long ago, my oldest son, who is now 23, said something that surprised and alarmed me. We were talking about the various foolish things we had each done when we were very young. I had little to say. My memories about those early years are perhaps a little fuzzier than his; they reach back through a longer and probably dimmer space.

"Do you remember the house we had in Carmel?" he asked. I did. "Well," he said, "I used to think I'd be able to fly from the upstairs window if I held a nice clean sheet over my head like Superman's cape. One day I decided I'd try it. I looked all over the house, but I didn't know where the sheets were, and I thought mom would be mad if I took one off the bed, and I wasn't sure it would work with a dirty sheet. So I didn't jump."

If he had, there is little doubt he would have injured himself seriously (unless, of course, he was right, and he could have flown . . .).

Young children don't have a very good notion of their personal capabilities. Their self-judgment, and their corresponding self-guidance, is less than perfect. As a result, without external controls, they, like my son, would often be in danger of severely hurting themselves. Instead of imposing on themselves the internal *self-judgment*, "I can't do that," they require the external judgment, "*You* can't do that."

The sense of personal control over behavior that is essential for judgments of personal efficacy begins to develop very early in infancy. Some of its roots lie in the infant's discovery that looking at the mother makes her look back in return, that smiling or crying draws her attention, that waving a hand makes her smile. Later, as infants begin to move around freely, they begin to learn more about the *effects* of their behaviors — and also more about their *effectiveness* as behavers. Language provides them a means to analyze and think about themselves and a means to symbolize and anticipate the consequences of their behaviors.

In the early stages, Bandura (1986) informs us, the most important sources of information for the development of self-referential thought is the family. Soon, however, peers begin to increase in importance. Now the behavior of others, as well as their response to our behavior, is factored into our personal estimates of our efficacy. Eventually schools, too, exert their powerful influences. Teachers tell us a great deal about how well we can do things — or how badly. So, too, does the response of our classmates and the response of our parents to the evidence we bring home of our merit in school, of our intelligence, of our ability to do the things that teachers require in ways that please them.

And so it continues throughout life. In adolescence we are faced with new tasks, new challenges — as we are through adulthood and into old age. At every step these new challenges require new competencies and new behaviors — and new judgments of personal effectiveness.

Among the judgments of efficacy that are perhaps most important to the individual at all stages of life are those that have to do with our ability to capture the attention, the interest, the affection of others. As Kegan (1982) argues, we strive to *mean* something. We want people to pay attention to us, to like us, to want to be with us, listen to us, do things with us. Put another way, we need to feel that we are capable of eliciting these feelings on the part of others — that we are *socially effective*. Hence the central role of self-efficacy judgments in our lives and in our happiness.

BIOLOGICAL AND ECOLOGICAL APPROACHES

Biological approaches to understanding human development stress the importance of innate, predetermined behavior patterns or tendencies. These approaches often stem from research conducted with nonhuman animals, where genetic influences are sometimes more readily apparent than they are among humans.

Ecological approaches emphasize the importance of the individual's context — hence the importance of the environment. But for contemporary ecological theorists, it is not so much the context as the interaction between the person's characteristics and specific characteristics of the environment that are important. As Bronfenbrenner (1989) insists, the most useful ecologically oriented model is one that takes the person into account jointly with the context and that looks for processes to explain changes in development — therefore, the label, *process-person-context* model.

The following sections look at Bowlby's biologically based theory of attachment; at sociobiology, which attempts to uncover the biological basis of social behaviors; and at Bronfenbrenner's ecological systems theory, which emphasizes the importance of the accommodation between changing human beings and changing aspects of their environments.

Ethology and Bowlby's Attachment Theory

The role of biology (of heredity) in determining animal behavior has long been accepted. I accept without question that my English setter is reasonably adept at sniffing out certain potent-smelling birds precisely because she *is* an English setter. I would not expect the same behavior of Boris, our rather useless cat. Even if their early experiences, Boris's and the setter's, had been identical, I still would not expect Boris to enjoy walking at my heels or to drool at the prospect of a cold swim in a reedy pond. We know that many of the behaviors and habits characteristic of an individual of some nonhuman animal species are not acquired solely as a function of experience. A moth does not fly into a flame because it has learned to do so; dead moths don't fly. We can therefore assume that the attraction light has for a moth, like the overpowering urge of a goose to fly south or a salmon to swim up river, is the result of inherited tendencies.

Are we, in at least some ways, like moths and salmon? If so, what are our flames? Our rivers?

Ethologists (scientists whose principal concern is with studying behavior in natural situations) think yes, we are just a little like moths. And although the flames that entice us might be less obvious than those that draw the moth, they are perhaps no less powerful.

Lorenz's (1952) study of **imprinting** in ducks and geese was among the first to draw parallels between animal and human behavior. Imprinting is the tendency of newly hatched geese (or chickens, ducks, and related birds) to follow the first moving object they see during a **critical period,** which occurs shortly after hatching. The period is *critical* because exposure to the same moving object (a *releaser*) before or after this period does not ordinarily result in the appearance of the same imprinted behavior (Figure 2.6).

Imprinting among newly hatched birds clearly has survival value. The gosling's chances of survival are far better if it, along with all its fellow goslings, follows its mother. Of course, the gosling does not follow the mother because it is aware of a genetic relationship between this big bird and itself. It follows

Figure 2.6

A model of imprinting. Under appropriate environmental conditions, exposure to a releaser during the critical period leads to imprinting, which is manifested in predictable behaviors in response to specific environmental conditions. Imprinting does not occur in the absence of a releaser or if the releaser is presented too early or too late.

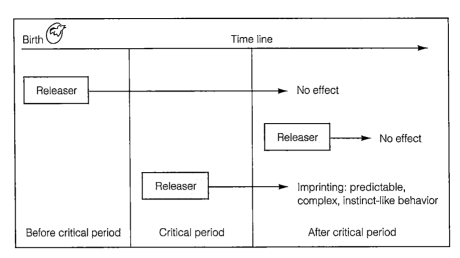

its mother simply because she happened to be the first moving object it saw during the critical few hours following hatching. Ethologists have repeatedly demonstrated that if some other object such as a balloon were to replace the mother goose, the young gosling would quite happily follow it instead. When Lorenz substituted himself for the mother goose, the young goslings followed him much as they would have their mother.

The critical period is all important. Newly hatched geese or chickens that are not exposed to a moving object during this critical period fail to become imprinted and will subsequently not follow their mothers. Similarly, lambs that are removed from their mothers after birth and not brought back for a week or more do not ordinarily show any evidence of attachment to them. Perhaps even more striking, the mothers themselves do not appear to be attached to their kids under these circumstances and will sometimes butt them out of the way if they insist on coming too close (Thorpe, 1963).

Although the search for imprinted behaviors among humans has not led to the discovery of behaviors as obvious as "following" among geese some theorists argue that the ethologists' emphasis on observation and on genetic contributions to behavior are important, especially when the individual's social *relationships* are also taken into account (Hinde, 1989). Other theorists, such as John Bowlby (1979, 1980, 1982), suggest that there are important parallels between the findings of ethologists and the development of attachment between mother and infant. Bowlby's research with young infants indicates that we have a natural (inherited) tendency to form emotional bonds with our mothers or with some other permanent caregiver. Such bonds, Bowlby argues, would clearly have been important for the infant's survival in a less civilized age. The need for them is evident in the infant's attempts to maintain physical contact, to cling, and to stay in visual contact with the mother (Bowlby, 1979). It is

"Mother" Lorenz.

evident as well in the effects of separating mother and infant — effects that, in Bowlby's (1979) words, are marked by "emotional distress and personality disturbance, including anxiety, anger, depression, and emotional detachment" (p. 127).

Although researchers have not identified specific critical periods during which a mother or other caregiver must be present for the infant to form strong attachment bonds, many speak of a *sensitive period*. According to Bowlby, this sensitive period spans the first six months of life. Although attachment behaviors (clinging, looking) tend to be directed indiscriminately toward anyone in the early months, by the age of 6 months, infants who have been given the opportunity to do so will have formed strong bonds with their mother. Abrupt disruptions of these bonds after the age of 6 months can be extremely distressing (see Chapter 6). However, in the normal course of development, the bonds become less intense as the child matures. Although the mother usually remains the dominant figure until well into the third year of life, by then the child will experience progressively less anxiety during her temporary absences and will have begun to form important attachments to others.

Bowlby's Attachment Theory in Review

Although Bowlby's ethological theory provides an intriguing biological explanation for mother-infant attachment, it has not been without its critics. One criticism is that he has overemphasized the role of the mother and neglected that of the father. But as Ainsworth (1979) points out, Bowlby has focused on the role of the mother primarily because she is typically the principal caregiver. In fact, his theory is quite compatible with the belief that in the absence of the mother, the father or some other caregiver may substitute for her.

A more serious criticism of Bowlby's theory centers on his belief that failure to form strong attachments during infancy causes later adjustment problems and difficulties in establishing loving relationships as an adult. If this were inevitably true, children who are raised without contact with their mothers for prolonged periods (in institutions or even in daycare centers or foster homes) would be expected to experience problems. Research suggests, however, that this is not always the case. For example, in a longitudinal study designed to compare home-raised infants with those raised in daycare centers, Kagan, Kearsley, and Zelazo (1978) found no systematic differences between these two groups, even on measures of attachment to their mothers.

What these and related criticisms point out most clearly is that the concepts and language of animal imprinting are not always entirely appropriate for understanding human behavior. Human attachment is not as predictable a behavior as "following" in geese; nor is there as definite a critical period during which the appropriate stimulus must be presented if the relevant behavior is to appear. In addition, the implications of not forming an attachment bond with a primary caregiver early in life are not as clear for an infant as for a gosling. The gosling that fails to imprint on its mother is likely to become lost and perish; our infants often fare better. (See Chapter 6 for a more detailed discussion of attachment among humans.)

Sociobiology

Bowlby is only one of a large number of theorists who have become progressively interested in applying knowledge of biology (more specifically, of genetics and evolution) to an understanding of human development and behavior.

A group of ethologically oriented scientists is attempting to explain the development of all social behavior in terms of genes: these researchers call themselves sociobiologists.

Led by such people as E. O. Wilson (1975) they argue that science has neglected the role of heredity in determining many of the behaviors that we attribute to our environments and upbringing. **Sociobiology** is defined as "the systematic study of the biological basis of all social behavior" (Wilson, 1975, p. 4). Its single most striking and most controversial belief is that human social behavior is the product of a lengthy evolutionary history — that it is therefore genetically based. Among other things, sociobiologists explain altruistic behavior (helping, self-sacrificing) in terms of the evolutionary concept of survival. Nature, as Dawkins (1976) points out, does not care for the individual except insofar as the survival of the individual contributes to the survival of a group of individuals with related genes. The fundamental unit in the Darwinian law of survival of the fittest is the gene (or, more precisely, the DNA material that defines the gene's hereditary characteristics). Thus altruism makes evolutionary sense whenever an altruistic act increases the probability that some related genetic material will survive. In Wilson's (1975) terms, "the ruling

Sociobiologists argue that patterns of organization among humans and animals are determined by evolutionary forces. It is thought we are genetically programmed to behave in certain ways.

principle [is] the maximum *average* survival and fertility of the group as a whole" (p. 107). In the same way as it makes adaptive sense for a honeybee to sting an invader, thereby protecting a hive, even though the stinging bee must now die, so it makes sense for a human being to be altruistic even if doing so lessens the individual's probability of surviving, provided it increases the probability that others with related genes will themselves survive. As Haldane (a British biologist) reportedly put it, "I would gladly lay down my life for two brothers or eight cousins" (Hofer, 1981, p. 20). It is in this sense that the "maximum average survival" of the group is improved.

In much the same way as altruism might be explained by reference to the "selfishness" of genes (it is, after all, genetic material that survives), sociobiological theory can be used to explain maternal love, sexual mores, aggression, spitefulness — indeed, the entire range of human social behaviors.

Sociobiology in Review

Not surprisingly, sociobiological theory has provoked considerable controversy and a great deal of negative reaction. Critics have been quick to point out that the theory is highly speculative and is based on a handful of assumptions that have not been tested and that are probably untestable in any case (Eckland, 1977). As Masur (1977) notes, the theory assumes that behaviors occur because they increase the genetic survival of a group (or the probability that genetic material will survive). How do we know this is so? Because the behavior occurred. Why did the behavior occur? Because it increases average genetic survival. This type of circular reasoning offers no hope of proof. To validate the theory, it would, in fact, be necessary to establish the presence of "altruistic" genes, for example, by some means unrelated to the behaviors these genes are intended to explain. That has yet to be done.

This does not mean that genetics are therefore irrelevant to understanding human behavior. In fact, as is made clear in Chapter 3, our genes are fundamentally involved in everything we do. What it does mean is that science has not yet succeeded in showing that there are specific genes, or combinations of genes, that directly cause specific individual behaviors. The fundamental error in sociobiological theory has to do with level of explanation. Evolutionary theory, the basis of sociobiology, is designed to explain variation at broad zoological levels such as classes, orders, families, or species (Plomin, 1987). It can rarely predict individual behaviors.

Culture and Ecology

Ethologists (and sociobiologists) emphasize the importance of biological or genetic contributions to development; ecologically-oriented theorists stress the importance of culture or context. However, the differences between ethological and ecological positions frequently have to do more with different emphases than with different beliefs. Most theorists readily accept that both ecological (cultural or environmental) influences and biological tendencies are intimately involved in determining human development. In Hinde's (1989) words, "the futility of a dichotomy between the biological and social aspects of human nature is now generally recognized." It is still true, however, that many theories continue to emphasize one at the expense of the other. Vygotsky and Bronfenbrenner present approaches that are, in some ways, a synthesis of the two orientations.

Vygotsky's Cultural-Historical Approach

The Russian psychologist Vygotsky was a major force in Soviet psychology by the time he was 28; that was in 1924. Sadly, 10 years later, he died of tuberculosis. But many of his ideas, old as they are now, still seem fresh and important.

Among the most central of Vygotsky's ideas is the belief that human development is fundamentally different from the development of animals. Why? Because humans can use tools and symbols; as a result, they create cultures. And cultures have a vitality, a life of their own. They grow and change, and they exert a very powerful influence on their members. They determine the end result of competent development — the sorts of things that its members have to learn, the ways they should think, the things they are most likely to believe. As Bronfenbrenner (1989) puts it, we are not only culture-producing, but also culture-produced.

There are several underlying themes that run through Vygotsky's theorizing. One, just mentioned, has to do with the centrality of culture in human development; a second deals with the functions of language; and a third relates to the developing child's relationship with the environment — a relationship Vygotsky described as the **zone of proximal growth.** We look at each of these briefly.

Culture. Culture, Vygotsky insists, is what most clearly separates us from animals. It is the manifestation of our ability to think and to invent symbol systems (Vygotsky, 1986). It permits humans to have a history and perhaps a future as well.

There is an important distinction, says Vygotsky, between *elementary* mental functions and *higher* mental functions. Elementary functions are our natural, unlearned capacities. They are evident in the newborn's ability to attend to human sounds and to discriminate among them. They are apparent in the ability to remember the smell of the mother or in the capacity to goo and gurgle, to scream and cry. In time, however, these elementary capacities are gradually transformed into *higher* mental functions — that is, they change from natural, unlearned functions, to more sophisticated, learned behaviors and capacities. This transformation, which is absolutely fundamental to human development, is made possible through language.

The role of language. Language, after all, is what makes thinking possible, Vygotsky insists (see Wertsch, 1985). During the preverbal stage of development, the child's intelligence is much like that of, say, an ape. It is purely natural, purely practical — elementary, in other words. But language changes all that.

Vygotsky describes three forms of language that develop sequentially; each has different functions. The first, social (or external) speech, is common until around the age of 3. It is the most primitive form of speech, whose function is largely to control the behavior of others (as in "I want candy!") or to express simple concepts.

Egocentric speech dominates the child's life between ages 3 and approximately 7. This type of speech is a sort of bridge between the social speech of the preceding period and the more internal (inner) speech of the next period. Egocentric speech often serves to control the child's own behavior, but is frequently spoken out loud. For example, young children often talk to themselves as they are trying to do something: "Push. Okay, now turn. Turn. Tu . . . push. . . ."

Inner speech is our private self talk — what James (1890) called our stream of consciousness. According to Vygotsky, inner speech is what makes thought possible. It is the basis of all higher mental functioning (see Table 2.8).

Zone of proximal growth. Language is a cultural invention. It is one of the most important ways in which the environment, the child's context, influences and shapes the course of development. For Vygotsky, development is a function

Table 2.8
Vygotsky's Theory of the Role of Language

Stage	Function
Social (external) *(to age 3)*	Controls the behavior of others; expresses simple thoughts and emotions
Egocentric *(3 to 7)*	Bridge between external and inner speech; serves to control own behavior, but spoken out loud
Inner *(7 onwards)*	Self-talk; makes possible the direction of our thinking and our behavior; involved in all higher mental functioning

of the interaction between culture and the child's basic biological capacities and maturational timetables. But, insisted Vygotsky, it is the environmental context (the culture) that is most important — not biological maturation (Valsiner, 1987). Development (or growth) takes place when environmental opportunities and demands are appropriate for the child. In a sense, the environment *instructs* the child in the ways of development. But the instruction is effective only if the child's biological maturation and present developmental level are sufficiently advanced. For every child, says Vygotsky, there is a *zone of proximal growth* — a sort of potential for development (Belmont, 1989). Demands that are in advance of this zone — in other words, that are beyond the child's capacities — are ineffective in promoting growth. Similarly, demands that are too simple are wasteful.

In summary, Vygotsky's developmental theory underscores the role of culture and especially of its most important invention, language. The zone of proximal development — a sort of label for developmental potential — expresses Vygotsky's belief in the interdependence between the processes of child development and the resources that cultures provide (Valsiner, 1987). A second approach that also emphasizes the importance of context/person interaction is Bronfenbrenner's.

Bronfenbrenner's Ecological Systems Theory

Psychological, biological, and social systems are *open* systems, we insisted near the beginning of this chapter. This means that their existence depends on interaction and that they are constantly subject to change as a function of interaction. The Piagetian infant, born with a small number of primitive reflexes, adapts and changes as a function of interacting with the environment — in Piaget's terms, as a result of assimilating and accommodating. It is infant/

environment interaction that results in the notion that objects are permanent, that symbols represent, that quantities can be added and subtracted, that there is a fine and elegant logic that governs physics and chemistry.

Bronfenbrenner refers to the interaction of the individual with the environment as the *ecology of human development* (also the title of his 1979 book). Here is the cornerstone of his theory, expressed in his own words in what he labels *definition I* (Bronfenbrenner, 1989):

> The ecology of human development is the scientific study of the progressive, mutual accommodation, through the life course, between an active, growing human being, and the changing properties of the immediate settings in which the developing person lives, as this process is affected by the relations between these settings, and by the larger contexts in which the settings are embedded. (p. 188)

The emphasis in this theory is clearly on understanding development as an interactive function of the person and the environment. That is, Bronfenbrenner's ecological system is not out *there* in the environment, but is to be found in interactions. Hence the Bronfenbrenner model has three components: the person, the context in which behavior occurs, and the processes that account for developmental change. It is, in Bronfenbrenner's words, a *process-person-context* model. And development is simply the processes through which "properties of the person and the environment interact to produce constancy and change in the characteristics of the person. . . ." (p. 191).

One of the basic principles of Bronfenbrenner's ecological systems theory is that differences in intellectual performance between different groups are a function of interacting with different cultures or subcultures that may be characterized by different types of cognitive processes. It follows that a person's cognitive competence is always culturally relative. A very intelligent, well-adapted bushman of the Cameroon jungles would not necessarily function very intelligently in downtown Chicago. But then a Chicago lawyer might quickly lose his bearings — and perhaps his marbles — in the Cameroon jungle.

Not only are we influenced by our contexts, but we also influence them in turn. If infant Ronald cries more than is polite or expected, he may change some significant aspects of the environment with which he interacts. His mother may come running sooner than she otherwise would; his nurse might become more irritable, more impatient; his father might pay less attention to him — or more; his siblings might openly resent his intrusion in the family; even the dog might be annoyed. And each of these changing aspects of context might, in turn, alter Ronald's behavior. That his mother runs to soothe his cries might encourage his crying even more. But now, perhaps the mother senses what is happening and comes more slowly, more reluctantly, and again the interaction changes. Thus the mother's personality and her beliefs about child-rearing interact with Ronald's personality and his behavior in a constantly changing, *open* system — in Bronfenbrenner's terms, an ecological system. There is always an interplay between the person's characteristics and those of the environment, says Bronfenbrenner. "The one cannot be defined without reference to the other" (p. 225). He also makes the point that some characteristics (termed *developmentally instigative*) are more important than others in influencing contexts. Temperament, low birth weight, physical characteristics such as size or appearance, age, sex, race, developmental handicaps, and many other factors tend to provoke important reactions — hence, changes — in context. These, in turn, affect the individual.

One of Bronfenbrenner's important contributions to the study of child development lies in his description of the parameters of the context in which development occurs. The ecological system of which he speaks consists of interactions with four different levels of context. From nearest (most proximal) to most remote, these are the **microsystem,** the **mesosystem,** the **exosystem,** and the **macrosystem.**

The microsystem. Interactions that occur at an immediate, face-to-face level define the microsystem. The complex patterns of behaviors, roles, and relationships within the home, the school, the peer group, the workplace, the playground, and so on, are the microsystem component of the individual's ecological system. Most important within the microsystem are the personality characteristics, the attitudes, the customary behaviors, and so on, of *other people* in these contexts. The interaction of Ronald's crying with the behaviors of mother, father, siblings, and dog illustrates what is meant by a microsystem. Everybody in a microsystem influences everybody else.

The mesosystem. In turn, microsystems may influence each other in important ways. For example, the home does not exist in isolation from other elements of the microsystem. How parents treat children is influenced by schools, by teachers, perhaps by the church. Similarly, homes and churches influence schools, and how schools treat children reflects some of these influences. Interactions between elements of the microsystem that include the developing person define what is meant by the mesosystem.

The exosystem. Interactions between an element of the microsystem that ordinarily includes the developing child and an element of the wider context that does not include the child define the exosystem. For example, interactions between the school and such formal trappings of contemporary contexts as legal or welfare systems, or between the home and federal taxation departments, are exosystem interactions that might have important influences on the child. Also, interactions between less formal contexts such as fishing buddies or colleagues and mother or father are potentially significant exosystem interactions.

Table 2.9

Levels of Context in Bronfenbrenner's Ecological (Open) System Theory

Microsystem	Child in immediate, face-to-face interaction
Mesosystem	Relationships between two or more microsystems
Exosystem	Linkages and relationships between two or more settings, one of which does not include the child
Macrosystem	The totality of all other systems, evident in the beliefs, the options, the life-styles, the values, the mores of a culture or subculture

The macrosystem. All the interactive systems — micro, meso, and exo — that characterize cultures (or subcultures) define the macrosystem. Macrosystems are describable in terms of beliefs, values, customary ways of doing things, expected behaviors, social roles, status assignment, life-styles, religions, and so on, as these are reflected in interactions among systems. In Bronfenbrenner's (1989) words, the macrosystem "may be thought of as a societal blueprint for a particular culture, subculture, or other broader social context" (p. 228). Macrosystems may be identified in terms of such things as common beliefs, values, resources, goals, life-styles, and ambitions.

Macrosystems can change over time, and sometimes these changes are very significant for the developing individual. For example, within the last few decades of this century, there have been profound changes in family employment patterns (from one to two wage earners), in family structure (from two- to one-parent families), in childrearing styles (from home-rearing to other childcare options), in age of marriage (from younger to older), in age of childbearing (also from younger to older), in range of expected school attendance (from kindergarten being optional to postsecondary education being expected of most). Clearly, many of these macrosystem changes directly affect the microsystems the child participates in — the family, the home, the school (see Table 2.9).

Bronfenbrenner's Ecological
Systems Theory in Review

Although most contemporary developmental theorists pay lip service to the importance of taking context, person, and interaction into account, many researchers continue to operate within more traditional models. Two such models have dominated much of our thinking and research. One says that the causes of developmental change are to be found primarily within the individual; the other insists that the individual's environment is a more important cause of change. It is, of course, the old nature-nurture debate (about which we say more in the next chapter).

The model that underlies our thinking is tremendously important to our research and our conclusions. One model says that if Johnny turns out to be an unmanageable scoundrel, we should look for the cause and the explanation in his temperament and his personality characteristics; the other says we should look to his environment. But neither of these models says that we should look at how Johnny's characteristics influence his environment and at how, in turn, his environment influences him. Neither insists that the cause is to be found in the progressive changes in the *interactions* that take place between Johnny and his alcoholic mother, his overworked and indifferent teachers, his peers (the microsystem). Neither suggests that the aborted love affair between Johnny's mother and his kindergarten teacher is of consequence (the mesosystem). Neither is concerned with interactions that might have occurred between Johnny's mother and her employer, leading to a reduction in her pay and chronic, irrepressible disgruntlement (the exosystem). Neither asks the researcher to look at how society's encouragement of the changing structure of the family affects Johnny's well-being (the macrosystem). Not asking these questions is a weakness in some of our traditional approaches to understanding child development; asking these questions is among the strengths of Bronfenbrenner's ecological systems theory.

But posing these questions is also among its weaknesses. Explanations based on ecological systems theory require the analysis of an almost infinite number of highly complex interactions. Identifying these interactions, observing and quantifying them, sorting out relationships among them, teasing out the reciprocal influences between individuals and their micro-, meso-, and exosystems, and determining how changing cultural values and options impinge on the individual — these are difficult tasks. But perhaps if we chew at them long enough, we may find that they are not impossible. Bronfenbrenner's ecological systems theory at least suggests where we should begin.

HUMANISTIC APPROACHES

Had I spoken of Piaget or Freud, of Skinner or sociobiology, of ethology or ecology, in my grandmother's kitchen, the old lady would have listened politely. She was always polite. But in the end she would probably have said, "That's theory. It's all very nice, but what about Frank?" Why Frank? Simply because he was a unique child. And although there is little doubt that Freud, Skinner, and Piaget might each have had something very intelligent, and perhaps even useful, to say about Frank's habits of stealing chicken eggs, writing poetry, and dancing little jigs in mudholes, they would have been hard pressed to convince my grandmother that they knew more about Frank than she did. My grandmother was a **humanist.**

Humanistic psychologists concern themselves with the uniqueness of the individual child. A prevalent humanistic notion is that it is impossible to describe the environment, much less a child, in a truly meaningful way because the important features of the environment are particular to each individual. To understand the behavior of children, we must attempt to perceive the world as they see it — from the perspective of their knowledge, their experiences, their goals and aspirations (Rogers, 1951). Such an orientation does not imply that it is impossible to understand human nature or human behavior generally, although it renders the task more difficult. It does imply, however, that understanding human behavior in a general sense may be of relatively little value for understanding the behavior of one child. As we noted earlier, the individual child is not an average. There is no average child.

Humanistic concerns with the uniqueness of the individual do not lend themselves easily to the formulation of theories that are both highly specific and widely applicable. But they do suggest an attitude toward children and toward the process of developing that is of tremendous potential value to those concerned with the welfare of children. Humanistic orientations tend to personalize (to humanize?) our attitudes toward children; they restore some of the dynamism of the developmental process that our more static and more complex theories might otherwise remove.

Maslow (1970), one of the individuals closely associated with the humanistic movement in psychology, was primarily concerned with the development of the healthy personality. Fundamental to his position is a belief that we are moved by two systems of needs. The **basic needs** are physiological (food, drink) and psychological (security, love, esteem). The **metaneeds** are described as higher-level needs. They show themselves in our desire to know, in our appreciation of truth and beauty, and in our tendencies toward growth and fulfillment — termed *self-actualization* (Figure 2.7). The basic needs are also termed *deficiency needs* because, when they are not satisfied, individuals engage in behaviors designed to remedy a lack (for example, hunger represents a deficiency that can be satisfied by eating). The metaneeds are also termed *growth needs* because activities that relate to them do not fulfill a lack but lead toward growth.

These needs are assumed to be hierarchically arranged in the sense that the metaneeds will not be attended to unless the basic needs are reasonably well satisfied. In other words, we pay attention to beauty, truth, and the development of our potential when we are no longer hungry and unloved (at least not terribly so).

Chief among Maslow's metaneeds, and central to Rogers's humanistic theory as well, is **self-actualization.** Maslow suggests that self-actualization is characterized by absence of "neurosis, psychopathic personality, psychosis, or strong tendencies in these directions" (1970, p. 150). On the more positive side, he claims that self-actualized people "may be loosely described as [making] full use and exploitation of talents, capacities, potentialities, etc." (p. 150). Using this loose definition, Maslow searched among a group of 3,000 college students and found only one person he considered to be actualized (although there were several dozen "potentials").

For our purposes, we can view self-actualization as a process that guides the direction of development rather than as a state that we can attain. The view that children are directed by a need to *become* (to actualize) and that the process of actualization is essentially positive and self-directed presents a subtle but important contrast to the more mechanistic, more passive, and less inner-directed theories that we have considered so far. Although humanistic theory does not address itself to the specifics of the developmental process, it might in the end serve to explain facts that are not easily accounted for by other theories (see Chapter 13 for more about humanism).

A FINAL WORD ABOUT THEORIES

We began this chapter by insisting that facts and theories are not worlds apart in terms of "truthfulness" — that theories are intended as explanations of facts. From these explanations, scientists strive for understanding, for prediction, and sometimes for control. But theories do more than explain facts. As Thomas

(1985) notes, they suggest which facts are most important for understanding and what relationships among these facts are most likely to lead to understanding. More than that, they guide our invention of "facts" and give them meaning (Scarr, 1985). Theories lead us to accept certain things as true — specifically, those things that fit our beliefs and expectations. By the same token, theories also lead us to ignore contradictory or apparently irrelevant observations.

Table 2.10 summarizes the approaches to developmental theory discussed in this chapter. History, as is so often its custom, will inform us later about the fruitfulness of these approaches.

MAIN POINTS

1. A theory is a collection of related statements that are intended to organize and explain observations. Theories are best evaluated in terms of usefulness rather than truthfulness. They should reflect "facts," be understandable, and be useful for predicting events as well as for explaining the past.

2. Theories are based on fundamental underlying assumptions about human nature and behavior: the mechanistic (it is useful to view children as machine-like and highly reactive to external stimulation); the organismic (it is useful to view children as active and exploring); or contextual (it is useful to emphasize the role of the environmental context in which development occurs *in interaction with* the child's characteristics).

3. Sexual urges, or libido, are fundamentally important in Freud's system. The three levels of personality he describes are the id (primitive sexual and survival urges), the ego (reality-oriented, growing out of collisions between unbridled id-related urges and a growing understanding of what is possible and what isn't), and the superego (conscience — the moral aspect of personality growing out of identification with parents and the incorporation of societal norms).

4. Freud describes development as a progression through five stages, each differentiated from the other primarily by the areas of the child's body that are the principal sources of sexual gratification at that time. In sequence, these are the oral, the anal, the phallic, latency, and the genital stage.

5. Freud's theory reflects the sexual repression and masculine domination of the Victorian era in which he lived. For these reasons, and also because of its scientific and methodological weaknesses, it has sometimes been severely criticized.

6. Erikson has advanced a psychosocial, ego-oriented theory of child development premised partly on Freud's theories but more culturally based. According to Erikson, the child progresses through a series of stages characterized by basic conflicts, the resolution of which results in the appearance of new capabilities and attitudes.

7. Erikson's stages are, in order, trust versus mistrust, autonomy versus shame and doubt, initiative versus guilt, industry versus inferiority, identity versus

Table 2.10
Approaches to Developmental Theory

Approach	Representative Theorist	Major Assumptions (theoretical beliefs)	Key Terms
Psychoanalytic	Freud	Individual is motivated by instinctual urges that are primarily sexual and aggressive.	Id, ego, superego, psychosexual, fixation, regression
	Erikson	Child progresses through developmental stages by resolving conflicts that arise from a need to adapt to the sociocultural environment.	Competence, social environment, developmental tasks, psychosocial
Cognitive	Piaget	Child develops cognitive skills through active interaction with the environment.	Stages, assimilation, accommodation, adaptation, schema
Behavioristic	Watson Skinner	Changes in behavior are a function of reinforcement and punishment.	Reinforcement, punishment, stimuli, responses
Social cognitive	Bandura	Observational learning leads to developmental change; our ability to symbolize and to anticipate the consequences of our behavior is fundamental as are our estimates of our self-efficacy.	Imitation, modeling, eliciting, self-efficacy
Biological	Bowlby Wilson	Social behaviors have a biological basis understandable in evolutionary terms. The formation of attachment bonds is one example.	Attachment bonds, biological fitness, survival value, altruistic genes, sensitive period
Ecological systems	Bronfenbrenner	The ecology of development is the study of accommodations between a person and the environment, taking the changing characteristics of each into account.	Open systems, ecology, microsystem, mesosystem, exosystem, macrosystem
Humanistic	Maslow Rogers	All individuals are unique but strive toward the fullest development of their potential.	Self, positive growth, metaneeds, self-actualization

    identity diffusion, intimacy versus isolation, generativity versus stagnation, and integrity versus despair.

8. Piaget's theory describes the child's cognitive development, how the child knows or understands. Biologically based, it inquires about the process of adaptation and about how intellectual development can be classified.

9. Piaget believes that adaptation results from the interaction of the child with the environment through using activities that are already in the child's repertoire (assimilation) and changing activities to conform to environmental demands (accommodation).

10. Piaget describes the child's cognitive development in terms of sequential progression through four major stages: sensorimotor (world of here and now; intelligence in action); preoperational (egocentric thought; perception-dominated; intuitive rather than logical); concrete operations (logical thought operations applied to real objects and events); and formal operations (propositional thinking; potentially logical thought; hypothetical, idealistic reasoning).

11. Behavioristic theories focus on the child's immediate behavior and on the environmental forces that affect it. The most important concepts in learning-based developmental theories are conditioning and imitation.

12. In classical conditioning, a neutral stimulus (conditioned stimulus or CS) is paired repeatedly with a second stimulus (unconditioned stimulus or UCS) that reliably brings about a response (unconditional response or UCR) until presentation of the CS by itself is sufficient to bring about the response (now termed a conditioned response or CR). It is well illustrated by Pavlov's dog learning to salivate in response to a tone.

13. In its simplest sense, operant conditioning changes the probability of a response occurring, as a function of its consequences. Before conditioning, the operant is erratic and unpredictable. Following its emission and reinforcement, however, its frequency may increase dramatically in specific situations.

14. A reinforcer is whatever increases the probability of a response occurring; reinforcement is the effect of a reinforcer. Positive reinforcers increase the probability of a response as a function of being added to a situation; negative reinforcers have the same effect when they are taken away from a situation.

15. Punishment, unlike negative reinforcement, does not ordinarily increase the probability of a response but has the opposite effect. It might add something unpleasant or remove something pleasant.

16. The most important reinforcers for humans are generalized social reinforcers. Other reinforcers include consumables, manipulatables, visual and auditory stimuli, and tokens. In addition, a pleasant activity may be employed to reinforce another activity (the Premack Principle).

17. Bandura's observational (social) learning theory is an application of operant conditioning based on the effects of imitation. He describes four processes involved in observational learning: attentional processes (where important aspects of the model's behaviors are attended to); retention processes (where

the observer mentally represents, in images or words, and stores in memory what has been observed); production processes (which make possible the performance of the observed behavior); and motivational processes (which lead to actual *performance* rather than simply *acquisition* without performance).

18. The three manifestations of observational learning are the acquisition of novel responses (the *modeling effect*), the inhibition or disinhibition of deviant responses (the *inhibitory* or *disinhibitory effect*), and the encouragement of behaviors that are neither novel nor deviant but that are directly related to those of a model (the *eliciting effect*).

19. Self-referent thought has to do with our estimates of our selves, our capabilities, our effectiveness. *Self-efficacy* refers specifically to judgments about personal effectiveness. Notions of self-efficacy are important in determining the behaviors we undertake, the amount of effort we are willing to expend on a given task, and our feelings about ourselves.

20. Judgments of self-efficacy derive from four sources: enactive (based on the outcome of our own behaviors); vicarious (based on comparisons between the self and similar others); persuasory (the result of others persuading, cajoling, pleading, bribing); and emotive (the function of arousal or high emotion).

21. The ability to judge personal effectiveness (self-efficacy) does not exist in infancy, but develops slowly as a function of the eventual discovery that we can control our behaviors, that they have an effect, and that we can, to some extent, control that effect — hence, our effectiveness or efficacy.

22. Biological approaches to development look at the role of biology (heredity) in determining development and behavior; ecological approaches emphasize the importance of interaction in changing contexts; ethologists are biologically oriented scientists who study behavior in natural situations.

23. Bowlby has adapted some of the concepts and principles of ethology (specifically of imprinting) to explain the development and importance of the attachment bond that forms between mothers (or other principal caregivers) and their infants.

24. Sociobiology argues for the biological basis of social behavior and attempts to explain such behaviors — for example, altruism — in terms of their group survival value.

25. Vygotsky's cultural/historical approach emphasizes the importance of culture and especially language. The zone of proximal growth, an expression of Vygotsky's belief in the interdependence of development and environment, is the child's potential for development in a given context.

26. Bronfenbrenner's ecological systems theory looks at the interaction and progressive mutual accommodation between the growing child and changing environmental contexts. It is a process-person-context model where context is described in terms of four levels: the microsystem (the child in face-to-face interaction with, for example, family members or teachers); the mesosystem (interactions among contexts in the child's microsystem; for example, between parents and teachers); the exosystem (interactions between one of the

child's microsystem contexts and another context with which the child does not ordinarily interact; for example, interactions between a parent and a government agency); and the macrosystem (the totality of all contexts relevant to the child's life and identifiable in terms of the major beliefs, values, options, and life-styles that make up a culture or a cultural subgroup).

27. Humanistic theory is concerned with the uniqueness of the individual child and with the development of human potential (self-actualization). Maslow and Rogers are important representatives of humanistic concerns.

Further Readings

Freud, Erikson, and Piaget were voluminous writers. It is often easier and sometimes more valuable to use secondary sources for information about their theories. The following are particularly useful starting points:

Baldwin, A. L. (1980). *Theories of child development* (2nd ed.). New York: John Wiley.

Brill, A. A. (Ed.). (1938). *The basic writings of Sigmund Freud.* New York: Random House.

Wadsworth, B. J. (1989). *Piaget's theory of cognitive and affective development* (4th ed.). New York: Longman.

An imitation-based theory of social learning is presented simply and clearly in:

Bandura, A., & Walters, R. (1963). *Social learning and personality development.* New York: Holt, Rinehart & Winston.

The first of the next two references is an excellent summary of Bandura's social-cognitive theory. The second is a fascinating and insightful view of the theorist and a remarkably clear exposition of his beliefs:

Bandura, A. (1986). *Social foundations of thought and action: A social cognitive theory.* Englewood Cliffs, N.J.: Prentice-Hall.

Evans, R. I. (1989). *Albert Bandura: The man and his ideas — a dialogue.* New York: Praeger.

An excellent introduction to the role of biology in development is presented by:

Hofer, M. A. (1981). *The roots of human behavior: An introduction to the psychobiology of early development.* San Francisco: W. H. Freeman.

The predominant textbook in sociobiology is Wilson's massive and detailed attempt to compile and interpret most of the information that might be relevant to the biological basis of social behavior. Dawkins's book is simpler and much shorter, but it is less complete:

Dawkins, R. (1976). *The selfish gene.* New York: Oxford University Press.

Wilson, E. O. (1975). *Sociobiology: The new synthesis.* Cambridge, Mass.: Belknap Press.

For more detailed information about Bronfenbrenner's ecological systems theory, see either the following book or, for a more recent account, see the relevant chapter in the Vasta book listed later:

Bronfenbrenner, U. (1979). *The ecology of human development.* Cambridge, Mass.: Harvard University Press.

Maslow's humanistic psychology is well explained in:

Maslow, A. H. (1970). *Motivation and personality* (2nd ed.). New York: Harper & Row.

Loevinger's book is an excellent general summary and comparison of most of the major theoretical approaches discussed here. The collection edited by Vasta is an authoritative exposition of important current theoretical positions in child development.

Loevinger, J. (1987). *Paradigms of personality.* New York: W. H. Freeman.

Vasta, R. (Ed.). *Annals of child development* (Vol 6). Greenwich, Conn.: JAI Press.

❖

Biological Beginnings

I'm afraid you've got a bad egg, Mr. Jones.

Oh no, my Lord, I assure you! Parts of it are excellent!

Punch, 1895

That's what you and I were in the beginning. An egg. Not a big, oval chicken egg like the one Mr. Jones had on his plate; instead, this microscopic, itty-bitty thing of an egg. And, of course, a sperm. Of the millions that had begun

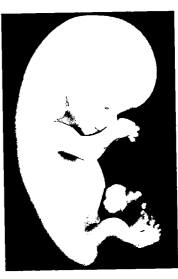

the journey, this was the only sperm to finish, the only one to butt its tiny head hard enough, long enough, to succeed in penetrating the egg's tough shell.

Those were our biological beginnings, yours and mine.

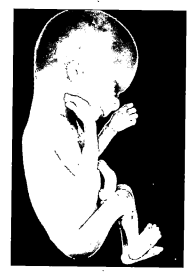

But what if we had got a bad egg, my lord? Or a bad sperm, for that matter? Is that possible?

As we shall see in the next two chapters, science says that yes, it is sometimes possible for an egg or a sperm to be defective. And it is possible, too, for what started out as a good egg to be spoiled. You see, our physical and psychological development start long before we are born. It is important that our mothers not smoke or drink too much, that they eat well, and that they avoid nuclear (and other) accidents. It is also important that they take care of themselves emotionally as well as physically, and that they see to it that their nests — their ecological systems — are prepared for the delivery of our ripened eggs.

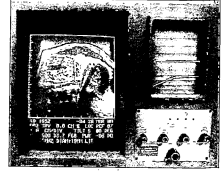

Fortunately, most of the time we can, like Mr. Jones, claim that our eggs — or at least some parts of them — are most excellent!

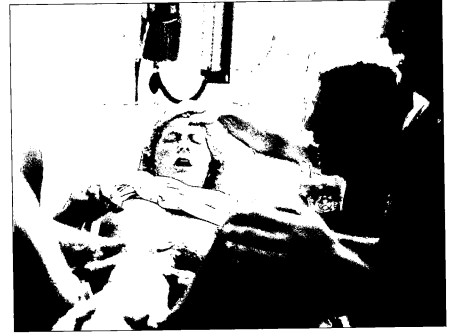

Men's natures are alike; it is their habits that carry them far apart.
Confucius, *Analects*

Genetics and Context

onight I write to you from a cabin far up in the Northern woods. It's a pot-bellied stove kind of January night; outside the winds shriek through the frozen aspen. I am reminded of other places, other times, when I listened to the voices of the wind. My grandmother used to tell me that the wolf lives where the winds are born, and that if you listen, you can hear his howling mixed in with the crying of the winds. Even now, I sometimes listen for him.

Snow sifts in beneath the door, building little ridges on the mat. The patterns of the ridges catch my attention. Strangely, the snow doesn't drift in evenly under the door. Instead, the ridges pile up at either end.

I know it can't be true, but . . . perhaps . . . might there be a *wolf* on my step? A wolf whose gaunt body, huddled shivering against my door, blocks the drifting of the snow?

A strange creature, the wolf. Wild and secretive, fearfully alone — yet almost literate, so well does he read the signs of his wild, secluded places. How desperate his hunger would have to be to drive him from his lair on a night such as this. Or is the wolf lonely?

I know it's only my imagination that sees him whimpering against my door. I know that he's not here, that he's far away, huddled in his solitude. Still, sometimes I wonder whether . . . dare I say it? . . . I sometimes wonder whether he might not have a child in his secret place. Yes, a human child.

It is perhaps not so farfetched. There is, for example, the story of Amala and Kamala, two children who were reportedly dug out of a wolf's den (Singh & Zingg, 1942). According to the story, these children had been abandoned by their parents at some tender age, and a mother wolf who had sensed their helplessness had taken them in as her own. When they were dragged from the wolf's den, Amala and Kamala were as wild as any wolf. They scurried about on all fours, growling at people, refusing cooked foods, preferring to gnaw on bones and chew raw meat. In captivity, they soon languished and died. Neither ever learned to speak.

Amala and Kamala aren't alone, Singh and Zingg tell us. Of the more than 30 cases of wild children they discovered in the literature, not a single child learned to speak, very few learned to socialize with adults or other children, and only a small number learned to walk and laugh and eat vegetables like carrots and spinach. (Sometimes I think my youngest one is partly wolf-child.)

COMMON WOLF.

FERAL CHILDREN

But perhaps we should not take these stories too seriously. The evidence surrounding reports of what are called *feral* children is highly circumstantial. In fact, as Dennis (1941, 1951) points out, there is not a single documented case of a child actually having been raised by a wild animal. The evidence is drawn from reports of children apparently being found with animals or in animal lairs. The identity of these children usually has been unknown, so that the length of time they spent in isolation can only be guessed; and in no case has anyone actually observed them with their supposed adoptive parents. Dennis suggests it is likely that the so-called wild children were initially brain-damaged or otherwise retarded, and this might explain why they were abandoned by their parents in the first place. Hence no reliable conclusions can be drawn from stories of wild children.

But there are other accounts of abandoned children that are more reliable. One is the story of Genie, a less dramatic story, perhaps, but no less sad. Genie, unlike Amala and Kamala, was not deserted in the wilds. Instead, at the age of 20 months, she was abandoned in a small upstairs bedroom in her own home. The reasons for her abandonment are complex and unclear. They include a subservient and frightened mother who became increasingly blind and helpless with the passing years, and a cruel and dominating father who was afraid that Genie would be mentally retarded (although pediatric reports indicate that her development had been normal during the first few months of her life). Except for brief periods when she was still a toddler, Genie would not leave her room for 12 years.

Genie's room was barren and completely unfurnished save for a small crib entirely covered with wire mesh, and an infant potty. The little girl was left in this room, day after day, week after week, year after year — alone and naked except for a sturdy leather harness strapped to her body and fastened to the potty so that she was forced to sit on it hour after hour after hour. At night, when she was not forgotten on the potty, she would be stuffed into a sleeping bag, specially made to restrain her like a straightjacket, and placed inside the crib, completely imprisoned within the wire mesh. On occasion, someone, usually her father, would come in and feed her — almost always either baby food, soupy cereal, or a soft-boiled egg. Her father insisted that contact with her be minimal and that no one speak to her, so feeding times were extremely rushed; whoever fed her simply stuffed as much food as possible into her mouth. If she spit some of it out, her face would be rubbed in it. And if she cried or whimpered, or made some other noise, perhaps with her potty or her crib, her father would come in and beat her with a stick. Nor did he ever speak to her. Instead, he pretended he was a dog, barking and growling at her, and sometimes scratching her with his fingernails. If he wanted just to threaten her, he would stand outside her door and make his most vicious dog noises.

When Genie was 13½ years old, following an especially violent fight with the father, the mother finally took her and left. Shortly after that, Genie was discovered, charges were laid against the parents, and Genie was admitted to a hospital. Genie's father committed suicide on the day he was to be brought to trial. And although Genie made some progress, her language and social development remained far below normal (see Curtiss, 1977, for more complete details).

GENETICS AND CONTEXT
IN INTERACTION

From a psychological point of view, Genie's story is important because it provides evidence relevant to the ancient nature-nurture (or heredity-environment) issue. The issue, simply stated, concerns the relative contributions of our genes (heredity or nature) on the one hand, and of our experiences (interaction in context) on the other. If the problem were simply one of determining which of these two forces is responsible for this specific characteristic or that — or for a certain percentage of this characteristic and a different percentage of that — cases such as that of Genie would provide us with some pretty useful information. Whatever characteristics these children share with others who are brought up in more "normal" environments we would assume to result from genetic influences; and whatever human characteristics they failed to develop, we would attribute to environmental forces. Thus, we might separate the relative contributions of each to our development.

But the issue is not quite so simple. It concerns, as Anastasi (1958) put it, not "what" or "how much" but "how."

Nor is the answer very simple. In fact, there are at least two sorts of answers reflecting two different points of view (Overton, 1973): the additive and the interactive. The additive point of view assumes that the effects of heredity and environment are, in a sense, additive. That is, heredity accounts for a certain percentage of the *variation* in a characteristic; environment is responsible for the remainder. Add them together and you get the entire characteristic. This model has governed the research and speculation of people such as Jensen (1968), who argues, for example, that approximately 80 percent of the variation in measured intelligence is accounted for by genetic factors and the remaining 20 percent is influenced by the environment.

The interactive model, currently the more favored of the two models, argues that heredity and environment do not influence development in a linear, additive way, but *interact* instead. And the interaction is not simple and highly predictable, but is a complex, nonadditive phenomenon. Take something as simple as water and temperature. We know that water and temperature interact to form ice; but can we understand the hardness of ice, its taste, its effect on our skin, solely by understanding temperature and water? Is it not true that steam also results from the interaction of water and temperature? The interaction becomes more complex, but it still appears linear and predictable: More heat equals steam; less heat equals ice. Even here, however, interaction is not quite so simple. With changes in air pressure, the interaction of water and temperature change. Now more or less heat is required for the same effect.

So, too, with genetics, context, and human behavior. Interaction is not a simple additive affair. Relative contributions of heredity and environment may change with age, may be different in different environments, and may vary from one individual to another. As we saw in Chapter 2, Bronfenbrenner's ecological systems theory is based squarely on this notion. In this system, it is the interaction that is all important — in fact, human ecology *is* interaction. But Bronfenbrenner (1989) recognizes very emphatically that both the characteristics of the person *and* those of the context need to be taken into account.

An Illustration

A dramatic illustration of context-person interaction is found in Elder, Nguyen, and Caspi's (1985) analysis of the effects of the Great Depression (during the 1930s) on children's lives. The analysis is based on a longitudinal study of 167 children born in 1920 and 1921 and who were therefore in the second decade of their lives during the depression. Earlier investigations of these children had suggested that the severe economic hardships accompanying the depression had profound effects on the lives of parents and children (Elder, 1974). Fathers, in particular, seemed to be most affected, probably because they were usually the ones who lost their jobs and consequently their ability to care for their families as they had before. As a result, many women and older children were forced to work. These changes, says Elder (1979), increased the tendency for some fathers to become punitive and perhaps exploitive; others became more rejecting and indifferent. In contrast, mothers, for whom loss of the husband's job would be an economic but not a personal blow, seemed relatively unaffected. Their relationships with their children did not change in very noticeable ways.

In a later analysis of some of the earlier data, Elder et al. (1985) looked at the effects of the depression on the experiences and lives of adolescents, paying particular attention to specific and important adolescent characteristics such as sex and physical attractiveness. This analysis indicates that, like younger children, many adolescents suffered during the depression and that their relationships with parents changed in systematic ways. For example, boys' perceptions of the power and attractiveness of their fathers tended to decline, whereas their peers became more appealing. This change was especially true in the more deprived homes, where boys were even more likely to stress the importance of being with peers and to minimize the importance and the influence of the father. Interestingly, however, adolescent boys did not appear to suffer in terms of confidence, aspirations, and positive self-concept. In contrast, girls tended to lower their aspirations and their self-esteem and to experience increased moodiness and unhappiness.

Elder et al. (1985) found that these negative effects, which were more serious for girls than for boys, were linked less to the economic hardships of their lives than to the rejecting behavior of the fathers. And what is perhaps most striking and pertinent here is that the least attractive girls suffered most. In Elder, Nguyen, and Caspi's words, "If girls were unattractive, family hardship accentuated fathers' overly demanding, exploitive behavior . . . [but] only when girls were rated as unattractive" (p. 371). In fact, Elder et al. report that, in some cases, economic hardship actually *increased* the extent to which fathers were warm and supportive of their attractive daughters, sacrificing and going out of their way to provide for them.

The lesson to be learned from studies such as this is clear: If we are to understand the development and the lives of children, it is essential that we take into account the contexts in which they are born and live. In Bronfenbrenner's terms, the interactions that define the child's changing ecology are fundamentally important. They need to be considered at a variety of levels: the microsystem (for example, in this study, the adolescent in interaction with father, mother, peers); the mesosystem (family interactions with school or with adolescent's workplaces); the exosystem (for example, the father's changed relationship with his work setting); and the macrosystem (for instance, the dramatic changes in social and economic conditions that defined the Great Depression). And at each level — and perhaps especially that of the microsystem — the researcher has to take into consideration the characteristics of the individuals involved. In this study, for example, sex is clearly an important factor; furthermore, girls' physical attractiveness is especially important in influencing the father's behavior.

An ecological approach to understanding development not only emphasizes the importance of the interactions that define the child's ecological system, but also underscores the importance of the characteristics of individuals and settings in interaction. And it provides a framework for beginning to understand how characteristics that have a strong genetic basis (physical appearance, for example), can influence interactions in systems that are also influenced by other environmental factors (such as economic conditions).

We return to the ecology of human genetics and human contexts later in this chapter; first, a look at heredity.

THE MECHANICS OF HEREDITY

The mechanics of heredity are complex and impressive. We know that human life begins with the joining of the mother's **egg cell (ovum)** and the father's **sperm cell.** For life to occur, this union is necessary; and because two people of opposite sexes are involved, it ordinarily requires a physical union between a male and a female as well — ordinarily, but not always. Conception is also possible with **artificial insemination,** a clinical procedure wherein the father's sperm is introduced directly into the mother. If viable, the husband's sperm is typically used; at other times, donor sperm may be used, either alone or combined with the husband's sperm so that who the biological father is may never be clear. At other times, too, an ovum from a female donor may be inserted in a woman whose Fallopian tubes are blocked. Still another possibility is conception that occurs completely outside the mother's body, either in another woman's body or *in vitro* (literally, meaning "in glass"). The fertilized egg can then be implanted in the mother to develop as it normally would.

None of these procedures is a certain solution for all childless couples. To begin with, none is a *cure* for the causes of childlessness. But when successful, they do remove the *symptom:* childlessness. At present, however, the average success rate of most North American fertility clinics is about 10 percent.

Another medical solution for childlessness involves the use of fertility drugs — drugs whose effects are typically to stimulate the production of mature ova. In these cases, pregnancy typically comes about as a result of the male/female union to which we referred earlier in this section.

A single ovum is released by a mature and healthy woman usually once every 28 days (ordinarily between the tenth and the eighteenth day of her menstrual cycle). Sometimes two or more eggs are produced at once or a single fertilized egg divides, thus making possible multiple births.

Interestingly, all of the woman's ova are present in her ovaries at birth — perhaps as many as a million of them. These are primitive and immature, and more than half of them atrophy before **puberty** (the beginning of sexual maturity). Of those that remain, approximately 400 will mature and be released between puberty and menopause (cessation of menstruation).

In contrast with a woman, a man produces sperm at the rate of several billion a month (200 to 300 million every four days or so) and usually continues to produce them from puberty until death.

The ovum is the largest cell in the human body. It is approximately 0.15 millimeters in diameter — about half the size of each period (.) on this page. The sperm cell, by contrast, is one of the smallest cells in the body, 0.005 millimeters in diameter. What the sperm cell lacks in size is made up by the length of its tail — fully 12 times longer than the main part of the cell to which it is attached. It is this long tail that enables the sperm to swim toward the ovum.

Protein, DNA, Chromosomes, and Genes

The egg cell and the sperm cell, called **gametes,** are the immediate origins of new life. Not only do they give rise to the development of a new human, but they also carry the instructions or the blueprints that determine what that individual will inherit. **Genetics** is the science that studies heredity.

The complex field of genetics is among the fastest growing of all modern disciplines. To try to simplify it accurately in a few paragraphs, or a few pages, is somewhat presumptuous. But we have no choice; so we will strive for clarity and simplicity, if not completeness.

The basis of all human life — the living, functioning cells of which we are composed — can be reduced to complicated molecules called **proteins.** These, in turn, are made up of different amino acids, of which there are perhaps 20 or so. These 20-odd amino acids are arranged in any number of combinations and sequences. A specific combination determines the nature and function of the protein it makes up. And the number of possible combinations is astronomical. Consider that the 26 letters that make up the alphabet by means of which you and I are now communicating allows us to generate new combinations of sentences, paragraphs, chapters, even books, virtually indefinitely.

The basis of life is proteins; the nature and function of proteins is determined by amino acid combinations and sequences. In turn, these combinations and sequences are determined by a special code contained in a substance called **deoxyribonucleic acid** or **DNA.** This substance consists mainly of four components, which are arranged in different sequences of pairs in a structure resembling what is termed a **double helix** (see Figure 3.1). In effect, this arrangement of DNA components is the blueprint or *genetic code* that determines our heredity.

All normal cells in our body contain identical genetic information. That is, all have the same assortment of DNA molecules — the same genetic code. These DNA molecules are located on rodlike structures called **chromosomes.** Every human body cell has 23 pairs of these chromosomes.

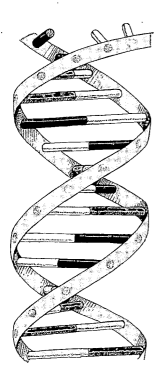

Figure 3.1

DNA molecules are arranged in sequences of pairs in a spiraling, double-helix structure. Genes, labels for carriers of specific hereditary information, can be thought of as locations or addresses on a segment of DNA molecule.

The smallest units of heredity, which are defined by particular types and combinations of DNA molecules, are called **genes.** It is useful to think of genes as specific locations on segments of DNA molecules.

Sperm and Ovum

There are two types of cells in our bodies: body cells and sex cells. Body cells each contain identical genetic information. That is, each of our body cells contains an identical complement of 23 pairs of chromosomes (each contains identical sequences of DNA molecules). We have inherited one member of each pair of chromosomes from our mothers and the other member of each pair from our fathers — in other words, 23 chromosomes from each of our parents (46 chromosomes total). The division of body cells involves what is called **mitosis** — a process that results in genetically identical pairs of cells.

Unlike body cells, mature sex cells (sperm and ovum) each contain 23 chromosomes rather than 23 pairs (46 chromosomes). This is because the gametes (sex cells) result from a special kind of cell division termed **meiosis,** which results in daughter cells that have only half the number of chromosomes of the parent cell.

It is especially important to note that when chromosome pairs in the parent cell divide to form mature sperm (in males) or ova (in females), they do so randomly. That is, individual members of chromosome pairs wind up in any of a mind-boggling number of different possible combinations — in fact, some 2^{23} different possibilities. And because there are two parents involved, the total number of different individuals that can theoretically result from a single human mating is some almost meaningless number larger than 60 trillion. *

So should we be amazed that we are so much like our parents and siblings? Not really. You see, in these over 60 trillion theoretically possible combinations, there will be a vast amount of redundant information. And much of that redundant information is absolutely fundamental to our humanity. Among other things, it is expressed in the fact that most of us have a single head, two eyes, a brain with a marvelously developed cortex, limbs, digits, and on and on.

But genetics, which is the science of heredity, deals less with our sameness than with our variability. It is concerned with the chemistry and the biology that account for differences among individuals of the same species.

One very noticeable and very important difference among individuals is sex. Genetics, too, is interested.

Sex Chromosomes

Of the 23 chromosomes contained in each sperm and each ovum, one, labeled the **sex chromosome,** determines whether the offspring will be male or female (the other 22 are called **autosomes**). As shown in Figure 3.2, the father produces two types of sperm, one type with a larger sex chromosome labeled X and one type with a smaller chromosome labeled Y. If the sperm that fertilizes the ovum contains an X chromosome, the offspring will be a girl; if the sperm cell contains a Y chromosome, the result will be a boy. Because the mother produces only X chromosomes, it is accurate to say that only the father's sperm can determine the sex of the offspring (a fact of which Henry VIII was probably ignorant as he disposed of his wives for failing to give him sons). The X chromosome that is contributed by the mother to her son is sometimes the carrier of sex-linked, predominantly male defects and illnesses such as color blindness, hereditary baldness, and hemophilia.

The ratio of males to females at birth is about 105 to 100 (U.S. Bureau of the Census, 1990). But males are more susceptible to various illnesses and diseases so that, by the age of 5, there are almost as many girls as boys. By age 75, women outnumber men about 2 to 1.

---

* And that does not even take into account that during meiosis segments of chromosomes sometimes *cross over* and exchange places, thereby increasing the number of possible combinations astronomically.

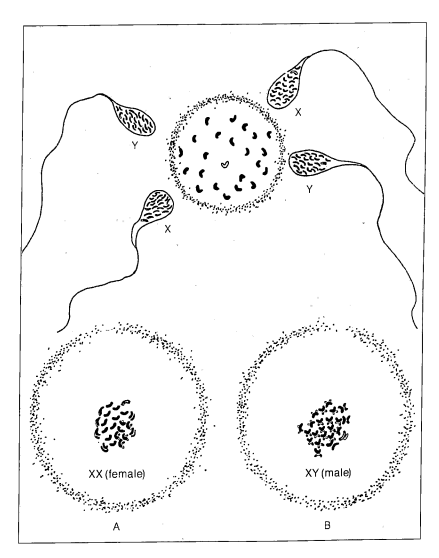

Figure 3.2

Sex determination at fertilization. At the top of the figure are an ovum and four sperm, two with the large X sex chromosome and two with the smaller Y sex chromosome. The ovum always contains only the X sex chromosome. (The sex chromosomes are outlined.) In *(A)* the zygote (fertilized egg) contains an X sperm and will result in a girl. In *(B)* the zygote contains a Y sperm and will therefore be a boy.

Genes

The units of heredity carried by the chromosomes are called genes. Some of our 23 chromosomes contain between 50,000 and 100,000 genes; others, especially the sex chromosomes, contain far fewer (Snyder, Freifelder, & Hartl, 1985). These genes, either in pairs or in complex combinations of pairs, determine our potential for inherited characteristics. There are, for example, pairs of genes that correspond to eye color, hair characteristics, and virtually every other physical characteristic of an individual. In addition, other combinations of genes appear to be related to personality characteristics such as intelligence — although the ways in which genes affect personality are not as obvious or as easily measured as the ways in which they affect physical characteristics.

A simple explanation of gene functioning involves dominance and recessiveness. From studies of animals and plants (particularly fruit flies and peas), as well as from observations of humans and other animals, scientists have discovered that certain members of pairs of genes may be **dominant** over their corresponding member. When a dominant gene is paired with a corresponding **recessive** gene, the characteristics corresponding to the dominant gene will appear in the individual. We know, for example, that the gene for normally pigmented skin is dominant over the gene for albinism (unpigmented skin). Hence an individual who inherits a gene for normal skin from one parent and one for albinism from the other will nevertheless have pigmented skin. A true albino (completely unpigmented skin) will have inherited a recessive gene for unpigmented skin from each parent. It follows as well that two albino parents will inevitably produce albino children. (See Figure 3.3 for an illustration of a characteristic related to the presence of a dominant gene.)

If human genetics were limited to the effects of single pairs of genes and their dominance or recessiveness, genetics would be far simpler. In fact, however, many characteristics are a function of an undetermined number of pairs of genes acting in combination. In addition, genes are seldom completely dominant or recessive under all circumstances. Some genes appear to be dominant over a specific gene but recessive with respect to another. Furthermore, the material of which genes consist (deoxyribonucleic acid, or DNA) occasionally undergoes *mutations* — changes that may be brought about through X-rays, drugs such as thalidomide, or other known and unknown causes.

Molecular Genetics

Molecular cell biology, a new kind of biology that combines the fields of biochemistry, cell biology, and genetics, represents the forward edge of a field that is moving back the frontiers of science at a dizzying rate. It is the science that studies the chemistry and the functioning of genetic material — the science that has made it possible to examine chromosomes, to look at sequences of DNA molecules, to identify their specific chemical components, to locate chemical segments that correspond to genes.

How is this done? Among important new techniques that have come out of molecular genetics, and specifically out of recombinant DNA research, is the use of certain enzymes that serve to cut through sequences of DNA, producing, in effect, microscopic DNA fragments. Where two individuals have identical DNA sequences, the length of the resulting fragments will be exactly the same; but if the sequences are different, the resulting fragments will be of different lengths (called *restriction fragment length polymorphisms* or RFLPs).

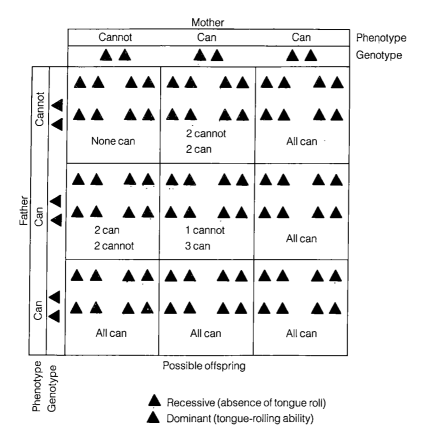

Figure 3.3

Can you roll your tongue as shown? An illustration of dominance and recessiveness. If you can roll your tongue, would you be prepared to wager that either your mother or your father can also? See the discussion of phenotypes and genotypes in the chapter.

Thus RFLPs (pronounced "riff-lips") allow geneticists to identify genes on specific chromosomes that are associated with the presence or absence of some observable characteristic. These genes are termed **marker genes.** Plomin (1987) reports that marker genes have now been discovered for all chromosomes and that they continue to be discovered at the rate of two or more a month. Some examples are the location of marker genes for Huntington's disease on chromosome 4 and for some forms of schizophrenia on chromosome 6 (Loehlin, Willerman, & Horn, 1988). Similarly, some manifestations of manic depression are clearly linked to a portion of chromosome 11 (Egeland et al., 1987); others appear to be linked to a deficiency on the X chromosome (Baron et al., 1978).

For traits that result from the effects of a large number of genes, it is possible to use a series of RFLPs to begin to sort out genetic contributions. The approach is complex, but incredibly promising. It brings with it the possibility not only of discovering the location and composition of DNA sequences that underlie human defects as well as human strengths, but perhaps also of correcting defective genes or, at the very least, of identifying their presence early — perhaps even before conception.

As of March 1989, some 4,550 genes had been identified. A massive federally funded genetics project is now underway in the United States. Its goal is eventually to provide a complete genetic map of the human being — a map of what is termed the **genome,** the complete set of genetic instructions contained in our cells ("The Gene Hunt," 1989).

The implications of success in this endeavor are staggering. Correcting genetic defects might be possible, and so could accurately predicting the outcome of different gene pairings. What happens next? Does medicine play God? Do governments engineer genes to produce the kinds of people they want? Do chromosomal tests become mandatory? Do they become part of who we are, like our Social Security numbers?

GENOTYPE AND PHENOTYPE

Your genetic makeup is your **genotype;** it consists of all the genes you have inherited from your parents. Your manifested characteristics define your **phenotype.** That is, phenotype is what you see — what is on the outside; genotype is hidden and has to be inferred from phenotype — or can sometimes be determined through an examination of a person's DNA. Sometimes it's possible to make accurate inferences about genotype directly from phenotype. Some characteristics such as certain eye colors appear to be determined by the absence or presence of specific dominant or recessive genes. Normally, for example, (but not always) the gene for brown eyes is dominant over that for blue eyes. Therefore, we can infer that individuals whose phenotype (manifested characteristics) includes blue eyes must have two recessive genes for blue eyes (genotype). On the other hand, the corresponding genotype for brown-eyed individuals cannot be inferred with certainty from their phenotype since they might have two dominant genes for brown eyes or a dominant gene for brown eyes and a corresponding gene for blue eyes (see Figure 3.4). Even here, however, the effects of genotype on phenotype are not quite so simple. In fact, most human characteristics, including eye color, are often the result of combinations of genes (polygenic). The effects of polygenetic determination, as Plomin (1987) points out, are not either-or (for example, either blue or brown), but include a whole range of possibilities. And so individuals are not simply blue- or brown-eyed, but can also have eyes that are green, hazel, blue-green, or a variety of other related shades.

According to Plomin, three important conclusions summarize the relationship between genotype (inherited genetic structure) and phenotype (manifested characteristics):

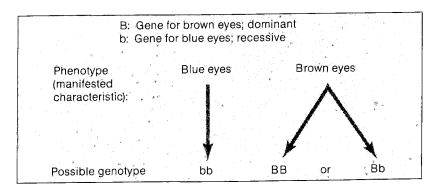

B: Gene for brown eyes; dominant
b: Gene for blue eyes; recessive

Phenotype (manifested characteristic):

Blue eyes   Brown eyes

Possible genotype   bb   BB   or   Bb

Figure 3.4

Phenotype (manifested characteristics) is influenced by genotype (genetic makeup). But genotype cannot always be inferred from phenotype. A brown-eyed person might have two genes for brown eyes or just one, with a recessive gene for blue eyes.

1. First, genetic differences (genotype) lead to phenotypic differences.

2. Second, characteristics that are influenced by more than one gene tend not to be dichotomous (black or white) but are distributed in a manner that approximates what is referred to as the **normal curve** (a bell-shaped curve where the majority of cases cluster near the average, with fewer and fewer cases deviating further and further from the average).

3. The environment also makes an important difference to manifested characteristics.

Canalization and Reaction Range

With respect to Plomin's last point, it is worth emphasizing again that for some characteristics, the environment makes a great deal of difference (language learning, for example); for others, it makes little apparent difference (eye color, for example). That is, some manifested characteristics seem to correspond much more closely than others to underlying genetic material. The appearance of these characteristics is, in one sense, predetermined by genotype. This phenomenon is described as **canalization** (Waddington, 1975). Characteristics that are strongly canalized are less affected by environmental forces. Thus for a highly canalized characteristic, phenotype corresponds closely to genotype. For characteristics that are not highly canalized, phenotype may be very different from what might have been predicted on the basis of genetic makeup. Eye color is a highly canalized characteristic; it typically corresponds to genotype and is unaffected by experience. In contrast, many complex intellectual abilities (the ability to learn to speak several languages, for example) do not appear to be highly canalized but result from specific experiences.

Described in evolutionary terms, canalization may be seen as a genetic tendency toward predictable regularity. This predictable regularity ensures that individuals of one species will be much more similar than dissimilar.

.e 3.5

Waddington's epigenetic landscape, a graphic analogy depicting the interaction between environmental and genetic forces. Genetic forces are represented by the valleys and contours of the landscape; they make certain outcomes more probable than others. Environmental forces are represented by changes in the tilt of the landscape.
Source: Based on Waddington (1975).

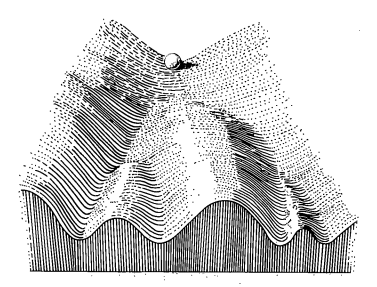

Figure 3.5 presents Waddington's (1975) *epigentic landscape,* a well-known analogy he uses to illustrate the relationship of genetic and environmental forces in development. His "landscape" makes the term *canalization* meaningful. In this illustration, genetic forces are represented by the canals that run down the landscape; the tilt of the figure represents environmental forces; and the ball represents some characteristic of the developing organism. Where the ball ends up represents the final state of that characteristic.

The analogy makes several important points. First, shifts (different tilts) in the environment can change the ball's path and dramatically affect the final outcome; second, for highly canalized traits (deeper channels) far greater environmental forces (changes in tilt) will be needed to influence the final outcome; and third, subtle environmental forces are more likely to significantly affect the course of development early (top of the figure) rather than late in development (bottom of the figure, where all channels are deeper).

Even for highly canalized characteristics, phenotype (manifested characteristics) seldom results only from predetermined genetic influences, but is usually influenced by environmental factors as well. That is, **epigenesis,** the unfolding of genetically influenced characteristics, is brought about by the interaction of genes and environment. In a sense, it is as though genetic influences (genotypes) make possible a *range* of different outcomes, with some being more probable than others; as these genetic influences interact with environmental forces, the outcomes become manifest (phenotypic). Gottesman (1974) introduces the concept of **reaction range** to illustrate this. Simply stated, the reaction range for a particular characteristic includes all the possible outcomes for that characteristic given variations in the nature and timing of environmental influences. The existence of a reaction range for any given characteristic makes it possible for the same genotype to give rise to very different outcomes (different phenotypes). By the same token, highly similar phenotypes need not reflect identical genotypes. One of the important tasks of the psychologist is to determine the nature and timing of experiences that are most likely to have a beneficial influence on phenotype.

GENETIC DEFECTS

In addition to their role in determining the course of normal development and in assuring that we are more alike than different, genes are also sometimes responsible for certain diseases and defects. In most cases, these disorders are linked with recessive rather than dominant genes. The reason for this is simple: Any abnormality that is linked with a dominant gene will always be manifested in all carriers and will have relatively little chance of being passed on to offspring (particularly if it leads to early death). In contrast, abnormalities that are linked to recessive genes will be manifested only when the carrier has inherited the two related recessive genes. Many individuals may be carriers of a single recessive gene for some abnormality without manifesting the abnormality. Their offspring will, likewise, not manifest the abnormality unless *both* parents carry the relevant recessive gene *and* each passes it on to the offspring.

The risk of genetic disorders among the children of biologically related parents is considerably higher than for children whose parents are not related: If genetic disorders linked to a recessive gene are present in a family, matings among family members will have a higher probability of producing offspring with a pair of the recessive genes (or gene groupings) in question. In contrast, if a member of this family, who is a carrier of the recessive gene, mates with someone outside the family who does not carry the gene, there is only one chance in four that the offspring will inherit the gene and no chance that this offspring will manifest the disorder (since the gene is recessive). Thus continued matings among individuals who are not biologically related may, over a period of generations, eventually succeed in eradicating or greatly reducing the incidence of the recessive gene in question. By the same token, continued matings among family members might lead to a proliferation of the gene and a corresponding increase in the manifestation of the disorder it underlies.

Hemophilia-A is a sex-linked recessive genetic disorder. Males who carry the recessive gene on their X-chromosome are always affected: Their blood-clotting mechanisms do not work properly, and they run the risk of dying from untreated bruises, cuts, or internal bleeding. Females who carry the recessive gene can pass it on to their children. Many of the royal families of nineteenth-century Europe carried the gene. Queen Victoria of England was a carrier, and so were two of her daughters (see Figure 3.6).

Figure 3.6

Descendants of Queen Victoria, showing female carriers and affected males.

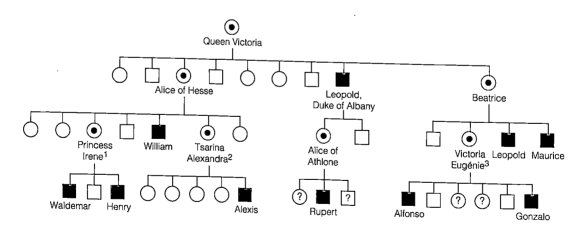

[1] Married to Prince Henry (Prussia)

[2] Married to Tsar Nikolas II (Russia)

[3] Married to Alfonso XIII (Spain)

⊙ Female carrier

■ Hemophiliac male

? Status uncertain

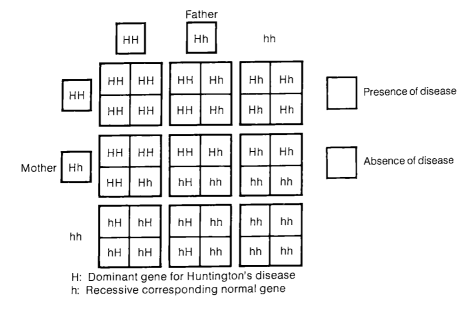

Father

H: Dominant gene for Huntington's disease
h: Recessive corresponding normal gene

Mother

Presence of disease

Absence of disease

Figure 3.7

Huntington's disease (H), a disorder involving neurological deterioration and eventual death whose onset is usually after the age of 20, is caused by a dominant gene. Hence only where at least one of the parents suffers from the disorder can the offspring be affected. The matrix illustrates the possible results of matings between parents who are homozygous for Huntington's disease (HH), heterozygous for the disorder (Hh—these individuals will also suffer from the disease because the gene is dominant), and those who are homozygous for normality (hh).

Huntington's Disease

Most very serious or fatal genetic disorders, as we just noted, are linked with recessive genes; if they were associated with dominant genes, all carriers would be affected and would either die before having children or would be aware of the risks involved and refrain from parenthood. One exception to this general rule, however, is **Huntington's disease** (also called Huntington's chorea), a disease that is both fatal and associated with a dominant gene. The disorder is still present because it does not ordinarily manifest itself until the age of 30 or 40 (see Figure 3.7). When it does appear, it leads to rapid neurological deterioration and eventual death.

Until recently, there was no way of determining whether an individual carried the dominant gene for Huntington's disease. Thus a person whose parents, uncles and aunts, siblings or grandparents had cases of Huntington's could only wait to see whether the disease would eventually strike. Now, however, using the RLFP technology described earlier, geneticists have succeeded in locating the gene for the disorder, making it possible to detect its presence (or absence) in an individual before it becomes manifest. Ultimately it might also be possible to replace this defective DNA sequence with a normal gene spliced to a harmless virus (Loehlin et al., 1988).

On the left, normal
oxygenated red
blood cells; on the
right, sickle cells.

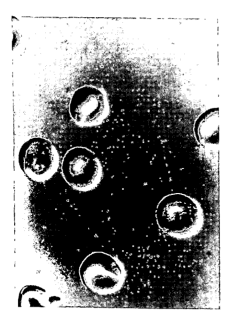

Sickle-Cell Anemia

Sickle-cell anemia is a genetic disorder linked to a recessive gene. Approximately 10 percent of all blacks in the United States, and a much lower proportion of whites, carry the recessive gene for sickle-cell anemia (Snyder, Freifelder, & Hartl, 1985). Figure 3.8 illustrates the recessive gene action associated with sickle-cell anemia. These 10 percent are *heterozygous* for this gene (having one normal and one abnormal gene); another 0.25 percent of the black population is *homozygous* (carrying two defective genes). Effects of the defective gene are clearly apparent in abnormally shaped red blood cells (sickle shaped rather than circular), which multiply with lack of oxygen. Sickle-shaped cells tend to clot together, carrying even less oxygen, thereby increasing in number and reducing oxygen still more. Individuals who are homozygous for this gene often die in childhood or are severely ill throughout life. Those who are heterozygous for the gene are ordinarily healthy except in conditions of low oxygen such as at high altitudes; here they may become quite ill, indicating that the normal gene is not completely dominant.

The fact that sickle-cell anemia is so common among blacks, particularly in tribes living in Central African coastal areas (40 percent heterozygous and 4 percent homozygous) would, on the surface, appear to be a contradiction of evolutionary theory; we would expect most of these individuals to have disappeared over generations. However, following the discovery that individuals who are heterozygous for sickle-cell anemia are also resistant to malaria, it becomes

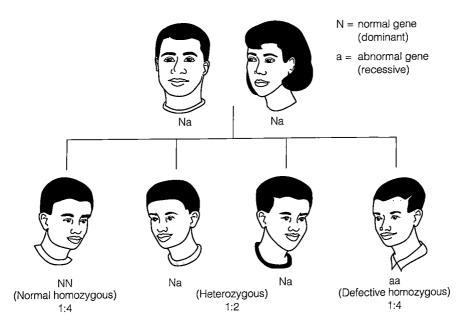

N = normal gene
(dominant)

a = abnormal gene
(recessive)

Na   Na

NN
(Normal homozygous)
1:4

Na
(Heterozygous)
1:2

Na

aa
(Defective homozygous)
1:4

Figure 3.8

An illustration of re-
cessive gene action
in the determination
of sickle-cell anemia.
Parents are heterozy-
gous; that is, they
possess one normal
(N) and one defec-
tive (a) gene and will
therefore not suffer
from the disease. A
child born to these
parents will have 1
chance in 4 of not
carrying the defec-
tive gene, 1 chance
in 2 of being het-
erozygous, and 1
chance in 4 of pos-
sessing two defective
genes and therefore
suffering from sickle-
cell anemia.

clear that the high incidence of this defective gene in malaria-prone areas is, in
fact, a dramatic example of current evolution. Not surprisingly, incidence of
the disease is now decreasing among blacks in the United States.

PKU

Phenylketonuria or **PKU** is a genetic defect associated with the presence of two
recessive genes. Specifically, in individuals suffering from this disease, the liver
enzyme responsible for breaking down phenylalanine into usable substances
(tyrosine, skin pigments, and neurotransmitters) is absent or inactive. Infants
who inherit the two recessive genes for PKU appear normal at birth, but with
the continued ingestion of phenylalanine (which makes up about 5 percent of
the weight of protein), their nervous system deteriorates irreversibly, and they
become increasingly mentally retarded. Fortunately, however, PKU is easily
detected at birth, and its onset can be prevented by providing infants with diets
low in phenylalanine (Springer, 1982). Here, then, is a disorder that is clearly
genetic, but that does not become manifest (phenotypic) until the occurrence
of specific environmental events (ingestion of phenylalanine). Furthermore, in
the absence of these environmental influences (that is, given a special diet low
in phenylalanine), the individual's *genotype* (presence of relevant recessive
genes) will not be reflected in the *phenotype* (manifested characteristics).

Other Genetic Defects

There are a large number of other genetic defects; in fact, nearly 2,000 have now been identified and catalogued (McKusick, 1986). Some of these, like Huntington's disease, are associated with a dominant gene; others, like sickle-cell anemia, result from the presence of two recessive genes; and some are multifactorial. They result from genetic factors in combination with specific environmental factors, either pre- or postnatal, such as the ingestion of phenylalanine by individuals who carry the genes for PKU.

Another disorder caused by a recessive gene is **Tay-Sachs disease.** This enzyme disorder results in the brain's inability to break down certain fats. Eventually these build up, preventing neural transmission and leading to the degeneration of brain cells. Affected individuals commonly die before the age of 3. Tay-Sachs disease can be detected before birth but cannot yet be prevented or cured.

Muscular dystrophy, a degenerative muscular disorder of which there are a variety of forms, is, in many of its forms, linked to a recessive gene or is multifactorial. It usually involves an inability to walk and may lead to death. Similarly, some forms of **diabetes,** an insulin deficiency disease, are associated with recessive genes, as are **neural tube defects.** Neural tube defects may take the form of *spina bifida*, where the spine remains open at the bottom, or of *anencephaly*, where portions of the skull and brain are absent. Neural tube defects often lead to severe retardation or death. Although genetically linked, the causes of these defects are multifactorial. They generally develop very early in pregnancy (as early as the first week) and can be detected by means of what is termed the **AFP** test — a test that looks at the level of *alphafetoprotein* in the mother's blood. If this substance is present in concentrations higher than usual, further tests such as ultrasound or fetoscopy (described later) are performed to determine whether there is a neural tube defect. In some jurisdictions, AFP screening is routine or even mandatory (as are tests for PKU).

In addition to a large number of medical conditions that are clearly genetically linked, there is increasing evidence of a genetic basis for at least some manifestations of emotional and behavior problems such as alcoholism, depression, anorexia nervosa, infantile autism, and schizophrenia (Loehlin et al., 1988). For some of these conditions, specific marker genes have been located. However, their causes are multifactorial; and, accordingly, they are highly susceptible to environmental influence.

CHROMOSOMAL DISORDERS

Genetic defects are linked to specific recessive or dominant genes or to a combination of genes; they may also be importantly related to certain environmental conditions. **Chromosomal disorders,** on the other hand, are associated not with specific genes but with errors in chromosomes. Many of these errors result from improper divisions and recombinations during meiosis. Several of the most common chromosomal disorders are described in the following sections.

Down Syndrome

Down syndrome (sometimes referred to as *Down's syndrome* and *mongolism*) is the most common chromosomal birth defect. It affects approximately 10 percent of all children institutionalized for mental retardation (1 in 750 live births — Snyder, Freifelder, & Hartl, 1985). Down syndrome children tend to be short and stocky, have small squarish heads, defective hearts, protruding tongues, and characteristic loose folds of skin over the corners of the eyes, producing an Oriental appearance: hence the term *mongolism*. Mental retardation is common among these children. Because not all children affected by Down syndrome manifest all (or most) of these symptoms, they cannot always be easily identified at birth. However, a chromosomal examination provides a certain diagnosis: Children suffering from this defect have an extra chromosome; they have three copies of chromosome 21 (as they are numbered by geneticists) rather than a pair. Thus the alternative medical label *Trisomy 21*.

Most cases of Down syndrome are due to what is termed *nondisjunction* of the twenty-first chromosome pair during meiosis — that is, to the failure of this pair of chromosomes to separate. Therefore, the resulting gamete (sex cell) has an extra copy of chromosome 21. The result is that when this gamete is combined with the other gamete during fertilization, the resulting zygote has an extra twenty-first chromosome. A smaller number of cases are due to *translocation* of chromosome 21 material to another chromosome (Emery, 1984).

For unknown reasons, nondisjunction of the twenty-first chromosome most often occurs during meiosis of the ovum rather than of the sperm. Accordingly, Down syndrome is usually associated with the mother rather than the father. Not surprisingly, the probability of producing a child with Down syndrome has been directly linked with the age of the mother. The incidence ranges from 1 in 1,500 for mothers aged 15 to 24 to 1 in 38 for mothers over 45 (Brock, 1982). The age of the father too appears to be linked to the incidence of the defect, with fathers older than 55 having a 20 to 30 percent greater chance of fathering children with Down syndrome (Erickson & Bjerkedal, 1981; Matsunaga et al., 1978). In these instances, disjunction failure occurs during meiosis of the sperm rather than the egg.

The extra twenty-first chromosome that is present in Down syndrome has led to an important discovery with respect to **Alzheimer's disease,** some forms of which appear to be inherited. Alzheimer's disease is a serious illness that typically occurs between the ages of 40 and 80 or more. Its principal symptoms include progressive loss of memory and eventual deterioration of brain func-

Down syndrome, whose effects vary considerably in severity, is the most common of chromosomal defects. Although this child may never be what we consider normal, he can still experience the exhilaration of running a good race.

tion leading to death. Physiologically, it involves a tangling and plaquing of nerve fibers. These plaques are composed primarily of *amyloid* filaments. Investigators noticed that middle-aged individuals with Down syndrome typically display the same development of amyloid filaments as Alzheimer's patients. Further research revealed that the gene underlying the production of amyloid is located on the twenty-first chromosome (Goldgaber et al., 1987). It appears that, at least in some cases, Alzheimer's may result from a defective gene on the twenty-first chromosome.

Turner's Syndrome

A number of chromosomal defects are linked to the sex chromosome. Of these, Turner's syndrome affects 1 out of 5,000 female children (Thompson, 1975). These children are born with a missing sex chromosome (45, X or XO rather than 46, XX. The 45 indicates the total number of chromosomes). Most such children are aborted spontaneously; those that do survive typically have underdeveloped secondary sexual characteristics, although this is not evident until puberty (Money, 1975). Possible symptoms of the disorder include swelling in the extremities that disappears with age — leaving loose folds of skin (webbing) particularly in the neck region, fingers, and toes — and dwarfism. Mental ability is usually normal. Injections of the female sex hormone *estrogen* before puberty are sometimes helpful in bringing about greater sexual maturation (Timiras, 1972).

Klinefelter's Syndrome

A second chromosomal aberration linked to the sex chromosome involves the presence of an extra X chromosome in a male child (47, XXY) and is called Klinefelter's syndrome. It is considerably more common than Turner's syndrome (1 out of 400 males; Thompson, 1975) and is marked by the presence of both male and female secondary sexual characteristics. Children suffering from this disorder typically have small, undeveloped testicles, more highly developed breasts than is còmmon among boys, high-pitched voices, and little or no facial hair after puberty. Therapy with the male sex hormone *testosterone* is often effective in enhancing the development of masculine characteristics and in increasing sex drive (Johnson et al., 1970). Without therapy, many children suffering from Klinefelter's syndrome remain infertile throughout life.

XYY Syndrome

Males with an extra Y chromosome (47, XYY), sometimes referred to as "super males" because they possess one extra male chromosome, are characteristically tall; frequently, they are also of lower than average intelligence. Some research evidence (for example, Telfer et al., 1968) has linked this syndrome with criminality following the observation that considerably more of the tall men in prisons are of the XYY type than is true of tall men in the general society. The theory is that the extra chromosome is linked with greater aggressiveness and hence greater tendencies toward violent crimes. In fact, the syndrome was first discovered among prisoners with violent histories, where its incidence is between 2 and 12 percent; only 0.1 percent of the normal population has the syndrome (Jarvik, Klodin, & Matsuyama, 1973). The conclusion that the XYY syndrome is linked with criminality remains tentative, however

(Falek, 1975). Certainly, not all XYY individuals manifest undue aggression. In fact, Witkin et al. (1976) found that imprisoned XYY individuals were most often guilty of nonviolent crimes. Kalat (1981) suggests that one reason why more of these individuals are in jail may be their lower intelligence rather than their greater aggressiveness.

FETAL DIAGNOSIS

More than 3,000 chromosomal aberrations and other disorders can now be detected in the fetus as a result of advances in medical knowledge and technology (Emery, 1984). There are four principal techniques for fetal diagnosis: **amniocentesis, chorion biopsy, ultrasound,** and **fetoscopy.**

In amniocentesis a hollow needle is inserted into the amniotic fluid surrounding the fetus, allowing the physician to obtain fluid containing fetal cells. An examination of chromosomes in these cells reveals the absence of chromosomes or the presence of extra chromosomes. In addition, the blood type of the fetus and the chemical composition of the amniotic fluid may be detected in this manner; these may provide evidence of other diseases that might affect the unborn child. Because the procedure involves a slight risk of infection, it is commonly employed only in those cases where the pregnant woman is older and where there is a probability of fetal abnormality or other complications. Amniocentesis is not usually performed until the fifteenth or sixteenth week of pregnancy (Raeburn, 1984).

Chorion biopsy (*chorionic villus biopsy* or *CVS*) is a relatively new medical procedure for obtaining and examining fetal cells. In CVS, a plastic tube is inserted through the vagina to obtain a sample of the chorion, which is a precursor of the placenta and which contains the same genetic information as does amniotic fluid. The great advantage of a chorion biopsy over amniocentesis is that it can be performed as early as seven weeks after conception. In addition, it yields results faster than does amniocentesis. If these results lead to a decision to terminate the pregnancy, this can be accomplished more simply and more safely in the first trimester of pregnancy. Amniocentesis, as we saw, cannot be performed and does not provide results until well into the second trimester of pregnancy.

Chorion biopsy procedures are somewhat more experimental than amniocentesis and carry a slightly higher risk of complications. Neither is used routinely.

The use of ultrasound (sometimes called *sonogram*) is another important technique for diagnosis of fetal defects. Not only is it among the least harmful and least traumatic of techniques currently available, but it is also the method of choice to prove the presence of a living fetus. In addition, it is the most exact means for estimating fetal age, detecting the position of the fetus, discerning changes in fetal position, detecting multiple pregnancies, and identifying a variety of growth disorders and malformations. Ultrasound images of the fetus in "real time" make it possible to see the beginnings of fetal activity including such behaviors as thumb sucking. They also allow the physician to examine bone structure, to assess length of bones, to determine relationships among the size and growth of various bodily structures, and even to count fingers and toes (Galjaard, 1982). Ultrasound is always used with amniocentesis or CVS to guide the physician.

Fetoscopy is a surgical procedure that allows the physician to see the fetus. It is employed primarily to obtain samples of tissues from the fetus itself, the most important being blood. Fetoscopy can furnish the physician with a tremendous amount of information about the status of the fetus (Golbus, 1982; Rodeck, 1982). Because it is a more exacting surgical procedure than amniocentesis and carries higher risks, it is most likely to be used when the probability of defects and disease is known to be high.

Although amniocentesis, chorion biopsy, ultrasound, and fetoscopy are powerful tools for detecting possible abnormalities in offspring, not all risks can be eliminated by these means. When family background or abnormalities in one or both of the parents or siblings indicate a higher-than-chance probability of some defect, parents and physicians may be faced with decisions involving serious ethical questions. In these situations genetic counseling offers a needed service.

GENETIC COUNSELING

Genetic counseling is a branch of medicine and of psychology that attempts to provide counsel to physicians and parents. Such counseling typically strives to assess the probability of a defect's occurring, its likely seriousness, the extent to which it can be treated and even reversed, and the best courses of action to follow once a decision has been made about whether or not to have a child. In many instances, genetic counseling will take place before conception and might take into account the age and health of the mother as well as the presence of genetic abnormalities in ancestors or in siblings. In other cases, genetic counseling will occur after conception (see Table 3.1).

In spite of the availability of genetic counseling in a number of medical, research, university, and community centers, there is still a relatively widespread lack of knowledge about such counseling, on the part of both physicians and potential clients. In addition, psychological barriers such as fear, social stigma, and values that stress God's will, as well as financial considerations, act to limit the use of genetic counseling and to reduce its effectiveness even when it is available

Prenatal fetal diagnosis also presents some potential for abuse. In the Ganxiao district of the province of Hubei in northern China, as elsewhere in China, parents take tremendous pride in male children. Accordingly, government regulations limiting parents to a single child led to the widespread killing of baby girls. In addition, many parents are having the sex of the fetus

Table 3.1
Probability of Some Common Genetic Defects

Genetic Defect	Incidence (per 1,000 Population)	Sex Ratio M:F	Normal Parents Having a Second Affected Child (%)	Affected Parent Having an Affected Child (%)	Affected Parent Having a Second Affected Child (%)
Asthma	30–40	1:1	10	26	—
Cerebral palsy	2.0	3:2	1	—	—
Cleft palate only	0.4	2:3	2	7	15
Cleft lip and/or cleft palate	1.0	3:2	4	4	10
Club foot	1.0	2:1	3	3	10
Congenital heart disease (all types)	5.0	1:1	1–4	1–4	10
Diabetes mellitus (juvenile, insulin-dependent)	2.0	1:1	6	1–2	—
Dislocation of hip	0.7	1:6	6	12	36
Epilepsy ("idiopathic")	5.0	1:1	5	5	10
Hydrocephalus	0.05	1:1	3	—	—
Manic-depressive psychosis	4.0	2:3	10–15	10–15	—
Mental retardation (of unknown cause)	3.0–5.0	1:1	3–5	10	20
Profound childhood deafness	1.0	1:1	10	8	—
Schizophrenia	10–20	1:1	10	16	—
Spina bifida (neural tube defect)	3.0	2:3	5	4	—
Tracheo-esophageal fistula	0.3	1:1	1	1	—

Source: Adapted from *Elements of Medical Genetics* (6th ed.) by A. E. H. Emery. Edinburgh and London: Churchill-Livingstone, 1983. Used by permission.
— means no data

determined before birth so that female fetuses can be aborted (see Figure 3.9). As a result, by 1983, there were as many as five boys for every girl under the age of 5 in the Ganxiao district (China fears sexual imbalance, 1983).

INVESTIGATING GENE-CONTEXT INTERACTION

Genesis refers to the beginning; it refers, as well, to the development or unfolding of something. In one sense, our genes, aptly named, are our beginnings. Not only do they account for a great many of our obvious physical characteristics but they are also related to the fact that most of us go through similar developmental sequences. This phenomenon is sometimes referred to as epigenesis and is clearly evident in the maturational processes that occur at adolescence. In other words, epigenesis is the unfolding of those aspects of human development that appear to be genetically determined.

Earlier in this chapter we looked at Waddington's *epigenetic landscape,* an analogy that attempts to clarify the interaction of genetic and environmental forces in human development (Figure 3.5). What the analogy says is that the genetic potential for certain characteristics is highly probable; these are more highly canalized characteristics. But other characteristics are not so canalized; the ridges and channels of the epigenetic landscape are shallow, and there are many alternative paths leading to different outcomes.

The analogy of the epigenetic landscape makes another important point: All genetically influenced characteristics, whether or not they are highly canalized (highly probable), can be influenced by environmental forces. Thus, as the landscape tilts one way or the other (as the environment exerts forces of varying strength), the outcomes of the developmental process may change.

There are a number of ways to sort out the relative contributions of heredity and environment in human development. Most of these do not provide simple answers — perhaps because interactions are complex and variable, and correct answers are therefore not simple.

Many of the answers, and much of the speculation, that have resulted from science's attempts to understand gene-environment interactions have been highly controversial — even inflammatory. This is especially true of theories and research dealing with the development of intelligence.

In the following brief sections, we look at the various approaches that science has employed to investigate the role of genes and contexts in interaction.

Historical Family Studies

One way to investigate the role of genes is to look at differences and similarities among members of families. Why? Simply because family members share a number of common genes. As Plomin (1987) points out, there is 100 percent genetic similarity between pairs of identical twins, approximately 50 percent similarity among siblings who share both parents, and somewhere around 25 percent similarity among siblings who share only one parent. In actuality, however, what is called *assortative* mating — the tendency of mates to select each other on the basis of similarity — increases genetic relatedness even more.

This high degree of genetic relatedness among members of families led Francis Galton, Charles Darwin's cousin, to conclude that intelligence is largely hereditary. He had noticed that most of England's outstanding scientists came from a small number of families. Not very good research, surely. Even if Galton's observations were entirely accurate (and accuracy of observations is

Abortion Rates in the United States

Figure 3.9
Legal abortions in
the United States
(per 1,000 women
ages 15–44) be-
tween 1972 and
1985. *Source:* U.S.
Bureau of the Census
(1988), p. 68.

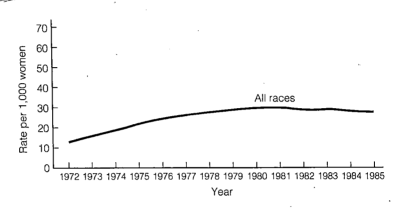

The rate of legal abortions in the United States increased dramatically between 1972 and 1980 but has since leveled off. It is probable that the number of *illegal* abortions declined as legal abortions became more widely available. However, the legal availability of abortion remains an extremely controversial issue. In the United States, the highest abortion rate is for teenagers, ages 15 to 19; they account for more than one-quarter of all abortions. The abortion rate for black women is about twice as high as for white women (U.S. Bureau of the Census, 1988, p. 70).

Psychology has not found it easy to understand the combined effects of heredity and environment on the intellectual, physical, emotional, even musical aspects of human development.

fundamental to good research), they don't prove his point. An environmentalist might argue, for example, that the reason these families produced outstanding scientists was simply that they provided childen with environments conducive to the development of genius. Still, Galton was convinced of the heritability of intelligence and argued that parents should be selected for favorable genetic characteristics — a practice termed **eugenics.**

Animal Studies

There are a number of reasons why gene/environment interactions can sometimes be studied more easily with animals than with humans. First, certain physiological measurements are sometimes possible with animals but not with humans (brain dissections, for example). Second, animal environments can be controlled far more completely than can human environments — in terms of environmental stimulation, food, social contacts, and so on. Third, animal matings can be controlled precisely, and many generations can be produced and studied within a relatively short period of time. Not so with humans.

There are, of course, some serious limitations to animal studies in this area, not the least of which is the difficulty of generalizing findings from animals to humans. This text is about humans; we mention rats and other animals only in passing.

Figure 3.10

A representation of Tryon's attempt to breed rats for maze-learning ability. After 18 generations, the two groups no longer overlapped.
Source: Tryon (1940), p. 113.

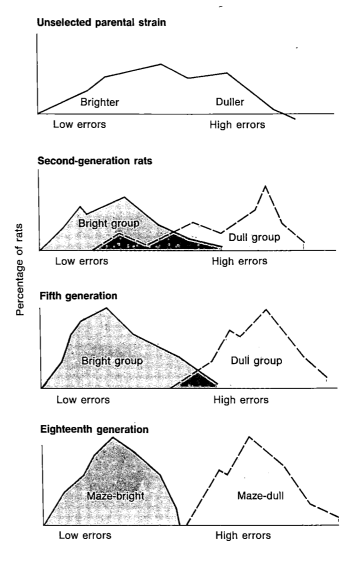

A classical study of genetic influence in rats is that of Tryon (1940), who began by testing his rats' intelligence by having them learn a maze. Fast learners were then mated with other fast learners, and slow learners were paired with other slow learners. After only 18 generations, there was no longer any overlap between the groups. The dullest rats among the bright group were now brighter than the smartest of the dull group — and vice versa (see Figure 3.10).

Many other animal studies have demonstrated that it is possible to breed different strains of the same species that are predictably different in some identifiable characteristic. For example, in only a few generations mice can be bred for aggression, emotionality, preference for alcohol, and other character- istics (see Cairns, Gariépy, & Hood, 1990). In much the same way, various "personality" characteristics have been developed in different breeds of dogs: fierceness and fighting ability in pit bull terriers; vigilance in German shep- herds; obstinacy and contrariness in the Lefrançois hound.

But even in rats and dogs and other nonhuman animals, genetics by itself tells only part of the story. Consider, for example, the case of the song thrush, which dearly loves to eat snails. This bird grabs the snail by the foot and smashes its shell against a rock by means of a rapid, sideways motion of its head, back and forth, back and forth (Weisfeld, 1982). This appears to be a genetically influenced behavior because the European blackbird, a close rela- tive of the song thrush that also loves to eat snails, doesn't seem to be able to learn the same smash-the-snail's-shell behavior. But it is also an environmen- tally influenced behavior because the young song thrush doesn't instinctively know how to smash a snail shell, and learns to do so largely by trial and error during a critical period early in its life. If it's not given an opportunity to learn during this critical period, it goes through life never knowing how to eat a snail properly, the way other song thrushes do it.

What investigations such as these illustrate most clearly is the complexity of gene/environment interaction, even with respect to behaviors that we might otherwise naively assume to be entirely genetically based. In addition, the study of genetic and contextual forces in animals and in humans leads to the very important observation that these forces are *not* in opposition, but collab- orate in an effort to bring about physical and social adaptation (Cairns et al., 1990). Finally, animal studies suggest that behaviors that have important adap- tive functions become more probable through succeeding generations. Because these behaviors have to do with biological adaptation and the survival and propagation of species, they are typically related to feeding, rest, defense, repro- duction, or elimination (Weisfeld, 1982). Are there similar, genetically ordained behaviors among humans?

Some researchers think so. These behaviors, they argue, are common to all members of the species — hence common to all human cultures. In addition, they occur in the absence of experiences that might otherwise explain their acquisition.

Specifically, what behaviors might these be? Weisfeld (1982) suggests they might include such things as the infant's distress at being separated from the mother or other caregiver (more about this in Chapter 6); the tendency of mothers in all cultures to hold their infants on the left side, whether or not they are right-handed; a variety of facial expressions that have identical emotional connotations everywhere, such as the human smile, which occurs in blind as well as in sighted infants; and human vocalizations, which are initially iden- tical in deaf and in hearing infants.

Figure 3.11

Comparisons between Mountain children and contrast groups on some measures of intelligence.

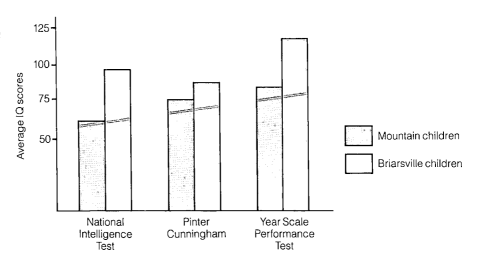

Intervention Studies

Another way of studying gene/environment interactions is through various kinds of interventions. It is possible, for example, to deprive individuals of important experiences and to measure the effects of this deprivation. Another possibility is to enrich the individual's environment, to provide special experiences.

An early study by Sherman and Key (1932) provides tentative evidence of the effects of intervention. The study compared the intelligence test scores of groups of isolated children (the Mountain children) with those of a control group in a more normal environment (the Briarsville children). Most of the Mountain children had been exposed to very little schooling and came from homes devoid of newspapers, magazines, most forms of reading material, or any consistent source of contact with the outside world. Briarsville children had been exposed to normal schooling and had access to the offerings of the wider culture through newspapers and other sources. Results of the comparison are shown in Figure 3.11. Note that the Briarsville children performed significantly better than the Mountain children on all three measures of intellectual performance.

Sherman and Key argue that these differences reflect the effects of environmental pressures. Is that the only, or even the best, explanation? Probably not. We don't know, for example, whether the parents of these children were comparable in terms of intelligence; none was tested. It is possible that the parents who chose to isolate themselves in the mountains were less intelligent than those who lived closer to the cultural mainstream. It's also possible that they were more intelligent.

More recent and better controlled interventions are abundant in the child development literature. Many of them involve preschool children, perhaps largely because of research and theorizing that led to the belief that the pre-school period is a critical period during which environmental influences will be most potent (for example, Bloom, 1964). One example is Project Head Start, a massive, federally funded American program designed to alleviate, through intervention, some of the possible disadvantages of being born and raised in homes less advantaged economically, socially, and intellectually.

There have been more than 2,000 different Head Start programs (Zigler & Freedman, 1987). Many of these lasted only a few hours a day, and many did not expose children to systematic, well-thought-out experiences. Not surprisingly, some evaluations of Head Start have concluded that intelligence is perhaps not as plastic and malleable as had been hoped (see Lazar et al., 1982). In general, however, indications are that higher quality programs are effective in increasing measured intelligence and that children exposed to such programs often do better in subjects such as mathematics. In addition, there are usually improvements in areas that are more difficult to measure, such as social functioning (Zigler & Freedman, 1987).

Studies of Twins

"If I had any desire to lead a life of indolent ease," Gould (1981) tells us, "I would wish to be an identical twin, separated at birth from my brother and raised in a different social class. We could hire ourselves out to a host of social scientists and practically name our fee. For we would be exceedingly rare representatives of the only really adequate natural experiment for separating genetic from environmental effects in humans" (p. 234).

Why is this so? Because identical twins are the only genetically identical individuals that it is possible for two humans to produce. They are genetically identical because they result from the splitting of a single zygote, a fertilized ovum, that has already obtained its full complement of chromosomes from the sperm and from the ovum. This segmentation results in two fertilized eggs, each with an identical genetic makeup, producing **identical (monozygotic) twins.** The other type of twins, **fraternal** or **dizygotic,** results from the fertilization of two different egg cells by two different spermatozoa. This is possible only when the mother produces more than one egg and results in twins who are no more alike genetically than ordinary **siblings** (sisters and brothers). In studying the interaction of heredity and environment, however, we often assume that fraternal twins have environments that are probably more similar than those of most siblings, if only because they share the same womb at the same time and because they are of the same age as they develop. Identical twins too usually have highly similar environments.

If the environments of fraternal twins are as similar as those of identical twins, it follows that any greater similarity between identical twins than between same-sex fraternal twins will be due to the influence of heredity. By the same token, if fraternal twins are more alike than ordinary siblings it would

The incidence of twins is low — approximately one in every 86 births. Identical twins are even rarer — perhaps one in every 300 or so births among Caucasians, but far fewer among Chinese and Japanese. The study of twins is an important source of information about the interactions of genes and environment. Triplets, such as the Koralja trio, who are Jersey City policemen, are even rarer than twins.

not be due to their greater genetic similarity but to their more nearly identical environments, both prenatally and postnatally. Unfortunately for research, the incidence of twins is relatively low — approximately one case in every 86 births. Furthermore, identical twins are much rarer than fraternal twins. The precise causes of twin birth are not known, although it appears that there is a hereditary factor because twins are found relatively frequently in some families and not at all in others. Also, older parents are more likely to have twins than are younger parents (Ernst & Angst, 1983).

Intelligence. Many of the large number of twin studies conducted have looked at correlations for intelligence test scores. A correlation coefficient is a measure of relationship. It can be expressed in numbers ranging from 0 to + or −1. A *high* positive correlation — say, +.75 to +1.00 — means that if one twin has a low intelligence test score, the corresponding twin is likely also to have a low score (or both are likely to have high or mediocre scores). A high *negative* correlation — say, −.75 to −1.00 — means that a low score for one would be associated with a high score for the other.

Bouchard and McGue (1981), Scarr and Kidd (1983), Loehlin, Willerman, and Horn (1988), and others have summarized some of the twin study correlations. In general, the median correlation for intelligence test scores for identical twins is above +0.80 whereas that for fraternal twins is below +0.60 (see Figure 3.12). If members of identical and fraternal twin pairs have had similar environments, these correlations may be interpreted as evidence that measured

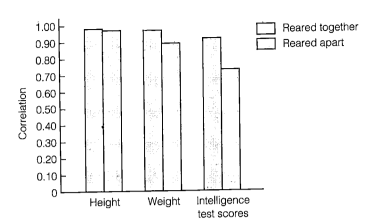

Figure 3.12

Correlations for intelligence, weight, and height for identical twins reared together and apart.

Source: Data from Newman, Freeman, and Holzinger, *Twins: A study of heredity and environment,* p. 347. Copyright 1937 by the University of Chicago Press. Used by permission.

intelligence is influenced by heredity. Related to these studies is the observation that with decreasing genetic similarity, there is a corresponding decrease in similarity between intelligence scores. Figure 3.13 is a summary of a number of correlations for intelligence test scores.

These data also support the belief that contexts influence measured intelligence. Since most sets of identical twins have more similar environments than do cousins or siblings, the higher correlation between various intelligence measures for identical twins may be due at least in part to their more nearly identical environments.

And the difference between identical twins reared together and those reared apart is additional evidence that environment influences development. Figure 3.13, for example, reports median correlations of 0.85 and 0.67 for intelligence test scores of identical twins raised together and apart respectively. Because these twins are genetically identical, environmental forces are clearly important. It is also revealing that as identical twins grow up, their phenotypes (manifested characteristics) become less similar; but, of course, their genotypes remain identical. It seems that the interaction of these identical genotypes with somewhat different contexts leads to progressively more dissimilar developmental outcomes (McCartney, Bernieri, & Harris, 1990).

Personality. Twin studies have also compared attributes other than intelligence. And increasingly, these studies provide evidence that a host of personality characteristics are strongly influenced by genetic factors in interaction with context (Plomin, 1989). In an Australian survey of 3,810 pairs of adult identical and fraternal twins, for example, Martin and Jardine (1986) found that personality characteristics such as anxiety, depression, conservatism, and introversion/extroversion are strongly influenced by genetic factors. Similar

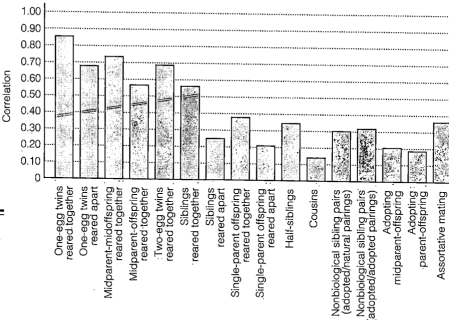

Figure 3.13

Median correlation coefficients for intelligence test scores from a large number of studies. The high correlation for identical twins shows the strong genetic basis of measured intelligence. The greater correlation for siblings or twins reared together compared with those reared apart supports the view that environmental forces are also important in determining similarity of intelligence test scores. *Midparent* refers to the average measured IQ of two parents. *Midoffspring* refers to the average measured IQ of children.

Source: From T. J. Bouchard and M. McGue (1981). Familial studies of intelligence: A review, *Science,* 212, 1055–1059. © 1981 by The AAAS. Used by permission.

results have also been reported in a survey of American adult twins (Pogue-Geile & Rose, 1985).

Perhaps more striking is evidence that various types of mental disorders appear to have a genetic basis. Gottesman and Shields (1982) found a significantly higher concordance for schizophrenia between members of identical twin pairs than for members of fraternal twin pairs. They found that of 28 pairs of identical twins there was 42 percent concordance for schizophrenia. The procedure was to identify members of twin pairs from among a population of schizophrenic patients and then to determine how many of these individuals had a twin who was also schizophrenic (of all members of twin pairs who were schizophrenic, 42 percent had a schizophrenic twin). The concordance between members of fraternal twin pairs was only 9 percent, from a sample of 34 pairs.

Studies of adopted children and studies of mental disorders among related family members also confirm the finding that some forms of schizophrenia, as well as manic depression, have a genetic component (see Loehlin, Willerman, & Horn, 1988). Similarly, there appears to be little doubt that heredity is often involved in the onset of alcoholism, and there is evidence, as well, that it may be implicated in such disorders as Alzheimer's disease, infantile autism (a schizophrenialike disorder first apparent in early infancy), and anorexia nervosa (see Chapter 11).

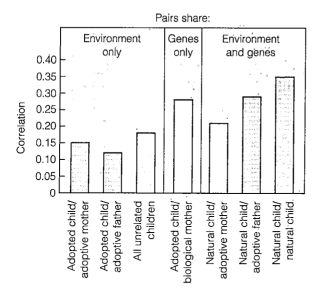

Figure 3.14

IQ correlations from the Texas Adoption project.

Source: Data from J. M. Horn, The Texas Adoption Project, *Child Development,* 1983, *54,* 268–275. Reprinted by permission of The Society for Research in Child Development, Inc.

Adopted Children Studies

Adopted children studies are another rich source of information about the interaction of contexts and biology. When it is possible to obtain information about biological as well as adoptive parents, and about natural and adopted children, these studies permit a wide range of comparisons that make it easier to untangle the interaction of genes and context.

In the Texas Adoption Project, which began in 1973, investigators have had access to data that include physical as well as cognitive measures of the adopted children's biological mothers (and sometimes fathers as well), in addition to similar measures for the children themselves, their adoptive parents, and other natural children in the adoptive home (Horn, 1983; Willerman, 1979; Loehlin, 1985). This makes it possible to compare relationships between adopted children and their biological mothers with those between the adopted children and their adoptive mothers. Furthermore, these relationships can also be compared with those that exist between the adoptive parents and their natural children. In other words, the design of this study makes it possible to look at correlations where the members of a pair have common genes but different environments (adopted children and their biological mothers), where members of a pair share an environment but are genetically unrelated (adopted children and their adoptive parents), and where there is some commonality of both genes and the environment (adoptive parents and their natural children).

Some of the results of the Texas Adoption Project are summarized in Figure 3.14. What is most striking about these findings is that the correlations between adopted children and their biological mothers is higher than those between the adopted children and their adoptive parents. Also, the relationship between adopted children and their biological mothers is about the same as that between adoptive parents and their own children in spite of the fact that the adopted children, unlike the natural children, are not raised by their own mothers. Eysenck (Eysenck & Kamin, 1981) claims this is strong evidence that genetics is the principal determiner of variation in intelligence. We should note, however, that these correlations are very low — they do not by themselves account for very much variation in intelligence. But as geneticists would be quick to point out, the degree of genetic relatedness between a child and a natural parent is not nearly as high as that between siblings and even less than that between identical twins.

There are several other studies of adopted children, many of them employing longitudinal designs, that have begun to contribute significantly to our knowledge of the ways in which heredity and environment interact to determine changes during the course of development. One of the Minnesota Adoption Studies, for example, found that black children adopted into white homes performed as well on IQ tests as the natural white children in the adoptive homes (Scarr & Weinberg, 1983). That is, these black children adopted into white homes had higher average intelligence test scores than their biological parents. Significantly, however, their measured intelligence was more closely related to that of their biological than their adoptive parents. What this means is that if the biological parents were ranked according to measured IQ, and then their children were ranked in the same way, the correspondence between the two rankings would be high (the correlation would be high). Put simply, variations in measured intelligence are more easily explained in terms of genetics than environment (Plomin, 1989).

THE CONTINUING CONTROVERSY

When Snyderman and Rothman (1987) questioned 1,020 American experts, they found that most believed that intelligence is inherited to a significant degree. This, of course, does not contradict the fundamental position, elaborated earlier in this chapter, that all human characteristics are influenced by the *interaction* of genes and changing contexts.

So what is the controversy? Essentially, it is still the same old nurture-nature question: the question of whether certain traits are influenced primarily by heredity or by the environment, and the question of how important each is. It is a controversy that stems from an extreme and often emotional belief that we are — or at the very least *should be* — equal. And if we are equal, then it cannot be that Gerry has an assortment of genes highly likely to lead to charm and intelligence and grace while Philip starts out life with an assortment of genes that propel him blindly toward stupidity or schizophrenia.

Or can it? Science suggests that yes, our genes are different, and yes, we have different probabilities of reaching certain outcomes. But science also tells us that genes, by themselves, determine little. They simply underlie potential, making some outcomes more probable than others. But even in the face of highly probable (highly canalized) outcomes, environmental forces can lead to surprising and wonderful things.

PLASTICITY

Those surprising and wonderful outcomes are the essence of Gottesman's (1974) concept of reaction range, which we described earlier in this chapter. Reaction range is the range of possibilities implicit in our genes. It includes all the outcomes possible for any characteristic, given variations in the timing and nature of environmental influences.

What the concept of reaction range recognizes, in effect, is our plasticity. Plasticity, or adaptability, is one of our most fundamental characteristics. But, as Lerner (1987) notes, our malleability does have limits. It is as though our genetic makeup, our biology, sets a range of possible outcomes. Ultimately, it is the complex interplay between our contexts and our characteristics that gradually shapes our developmental paths. If, for example, we are attractive adolescent females, perhaps things like great economic depressions will affect us far less than if our genetic makeup had made us less attractive (Elder et al., 1985). The ecologies defined by our face-to-face interactions — in what Bronfenbrenner (1989) calls microsystems — always reflect our personal characteristics as well as the characteristics of the contexts with which we are interacting. The processes are complex, the systems "open," and our developmental outcomes are never completely predictable.

The concept of human plasticity is simplified by Stern (1956) in what he calls the "rubber band hypothesis" (Figure 3.15):

> The genetic endowment in respect to any one trait has been compared to a rubber band and the trait itself to the length which the rubber band assumes when it is stretched by outside forces. Different people initially may have been given different lengths of unstretched endowment, but the natural forces of the environment may have stretched their expression to equal length, or led to differences in attained length sometimes corresponding to their innate differences and at other times in reverse of the relation. (p. 53)

In brief, the Stern hypothesis suggests that our manifested intelligence can be compared to the length of a rubber band. Genetics determines the original

Figure 3.15

The Stern hypothesis, an example of gene-environment interaction. Individuals with different inherited potentials for intellectual development can manifest a wide range of measured intelligence as a function of environment-gene interaction.

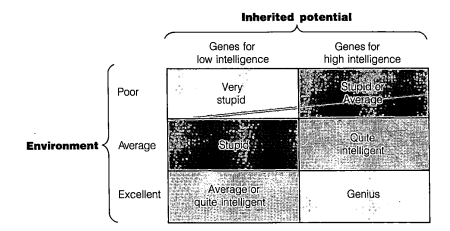

length of the band, but the environment can make it much longer. Thus those who are born with good bands and into good environments will be the most intelligent; those born with inferior bands into inadequate environments will be least intelligent.

Do highly demanding environments break bands? Do old bands become frayed and brittle? Do bands stretch more easily when new? Unfortunately, analogies are simply comparisons; they provide no logical answers for questions such as these.

THE FUTURE

Molecular genetics, as we saw earlier, is a rapidly developing and tremendously exciting field. Almost daily, there are new discoveries. Science is at the threshold of being able to detect genetic weaknesses, as well as strengths, from the very earliest moments of life. It is at the threshold, too, of altering genetic messages, of rewriting the code to enhance the possibilities implicit in our genetic ranges. Our mushrooming knowledge of cell biology at the molecular level is opening new doors into the vast and almost uncharted world of genetic engineering. Recombinant DNA techniques now make it possible for scientists to use bacteria to reproduce specific sequences of genetic material. The results include new medications, new refining and manufacturing processes, new products . . .

Science is breaking the code. It's learning to read the messages that direct the arrangements of the amino acids that, in turn, define the structure and function of the protein molecules that are the fundamental units of our biological lives.

Ethical issues are involved here — important ethical issues. Some have to do with the potential dangers of experiments that can, theoretically, produce new forms of life, the consequences of which cannot really be imagined because the nature of that life may be unknown before its creation.

Other issues have to do with the morality of altering genetic codes, with the ethics of decisions relating to creating or ending life, with the legality and morality of surrogate mothering and artificial insemination, maybe even with the very definition of life. Perhaps in another decade these issues will have become more important than the science that gave them birth, and another new discipline will have arisen to deal with them.

MAIN POINTS

1. Accounts of the lives of feral children are sometimes used as support for the argument that human experiences are critical to the development of human characteristics.

2. *Nature* refers to biology or genetics; *nurture* to the environment or context. The nature-nurture question concerns the ways in which heredity and environment interact to determine human development.

3. There are two points of view with respect to gene-environment contributions to human development. The additive view assumes that genes contribute a certain percentage and environment contributes the remainder. The interactive model assumes a more complex relationship between genes and environment, such that neither alone accounts for anything.

4. The basis of biological life is *protein* molecules whose function is determined by the arrangement of the 20 or so amino acids of which they are composed. In turn, arrangements of the amino acids are determined by a special genetic code contained in sequences of *deoxyribonucleic acid* (DNA) molecules located on rodlike structures called *chromosomes*. The hereditary basis of life resides in the egg (ovum) and the sperm cell, each of which contains half the number of chromosomes found in ordinary human body cells. In the chromosomes are the carriers of heredity, the genes.

5. Two chromosomes of special importance are the sex chromosomes, X and Y. Only the male can produce a Y chromosome, whereas both females and males produce X chromosomes. The presence of a Y chromosome in the fertilized egg determines that the offspring will be male; two X chromosomes determine a female.

6. Genes, in pairs or in combinations of pairs, interact with the environment to determine the potential for certain characteristics. At the simplest level, characteristics corresponding to dominant genes will be manifested in the individual except where two recessive genes are paired together.

7. Molecular genetics, which looks at the structure and function of sex cells (gametes), has succeeded in locating a large number of "marker genes" — specific

segments of DNA that are associated with some identifiable characteristic. One technique by which this is accomplished involves the use of enzymes to produce short segments of DNA material. If the sequences are not identical — that is, if they contain different genetic material — resulting segments are unequal (called restriction fragment length polymorphism or RFLPs).

8. Genetic makeup defines *genotype; phenotype* refers to manifested characteristics. Manifested characteristics (phenotype) that typically correspond closely to underlying genetic makeup (genotype) are said to be highly *canalized.* Canalization is an evolutionary biological phenomenon that tends to ensure a high degree of similarity among members of a species. *Reaction range* refers to the range of possibilities implicit in genotype. The nature of the characteristics manifested (phenotype) are a function of gene-environment interaction, within the limits of the trait's reaction range.

9. Waddington's *epigenetic landscape* presents an analogy for understanding gene-environment interaction. In this analogy, developmental possibilities implicit in genotype are represented by a tilted landscape with grooves and channels of varying depth and pitch; development of specific characteristics is represented by a ball rolling through these channels; and environmental forces tilt the entire landscape in various ways and at different times.

10. Genetic defects are associated with defective genes or with genes or combinations of genes that underlie defects. Many genetic defects (approximately 2,000 have been identified) are associated with recessive genes and will therefore not be manifest unless the individual inherits the genes (or gene combinations) from both parents. Chromosomal disorders result from errors in chromosomes rather than from defective genes.

11. Genetic defects include Huntington's chorea (a dominant-gene, usually fatal neurological disorder not manifested until later in life); sickle-cell anemia (a blood disorder); PKU (a metabolic disorder leading to mental retardation but preventable through diet); and other diseases such as Tay-Sachs disease, muscular dystrophy, some forms of diabetes, and neural tube defects.

12. Among the better-understood and more common chromosomal abnormalities are Down syndrome resulting from an extra twenty-first chromosome; Turner's syndrome affecting girls only and linked to an absent sex chromosome (XO rather than XX); the XYY syndrome affecting men only; the Klinefelter's syndrome affecting men with an extra X chromosome (XXY).

13. Many genetic abnormalities and fetal diseases can be detected before birth by means of amniocentesis (analysis of amniotic fluid withdrawn through a needle), chorionic villus biopsy (CVS; analysis of a sample of the chorion), fetoscopy (a surgical procedure employed to obtain fetal blood or skin samples), or ultrasound (use of sonar techniques to detect physical characteristics as well as fetal movement). These techniques are sometimes used as an adjunct to genetic counseling.

14. Based on the observation that members of family resemble each other in important ways, Galton concluded that intelligence is largely inherited. Studies with rats and mice have demonstrated that it is possible to selectively breed

for intelligence, aggressiveness, emotionality, and other characteristics. But even in animals, gene-context interaction is complex, and highly canalized outcomes often depend on appropriate experiences.

15. Studies of isolated children, as well as intervention studies (often conducted in preschool settings) indicate that early experiences can have long-lasting influences on children. However, intelligence is perhaps not as completely plastic and malleable as many researchers had believed.

16. On various physical and psychological measures, scores for fraternal twins are often more closely related than those for siblings. Because fraternal twins are no more alike genetically than siblings, and because their environments are in most cases similar, this greater similarity may be evidence of the environment's influence in determining the measured traits.

17. Studies of twins also offer evidence that intelligence as well as physical characteristics, some personality traits, and even mental disorders have a genetic basis. The most striking supportive evidence is that the correlation between intelligence test scores of identical twins is above $+0.80$, whereas for fraternal twins it is around $+0.60$.

18. Studies of adopted children typically report higher (although modest) correlations for measured intelligence between biological mothers and the children they have given up for adoption than between the adopted children and their adoptive mothers (and/or fathers).

19. The Stern hypothesis presents a summary of the evidence relating to the nature-nurture controversy by stating that genetic endowment is like a rubber band that assumes its final length (the actual performance of an individual) as it interacts with the environment. Implicit in this summary is the notion that it is easier to stretch a long band than one that was short to begin with.

20. The possibilities implicit in recombinant DNA technology and in various other facets of genetic engineering give rise to important ethical issues.

Further Readings

For a fascinating, tragic, and contemporary account of an abandoned child, see:

Curtiss, S. (1977). *Genie: A psycholinguistic study of a modern-day wild child.* New York: Academic Press.

A comprehensive summary of current research on the heritability of intelligence, personality characteristics, and psychopathologies such as schizophrenia, alcoholism, and Alzheimer's disease is the following:

Loehlin, J. C., Willerman, L., & Horn, J. M. (1988). Human behavior genetics. *Annual Review of Psychology, 39,* 101–133.

For those interested in the biological details of heredity, there are a wide assortment of comprehensive textbooks available in this rapidly changing field.

For example:

Snyder, L. A., Freifelder, D., & Hartl, D. L. (1985). *General genetics*. Boston: Jones and Bartlett.

Darnell, J., Lodish, H., & Baltimore, D. (1986). *Molecular cell biology: Revised printing with expanded index*. New York: Scientific American Books.

Eysenck and Kamin present two of the more extreme points of view in the classical nature-nurture debate in:

Eysenck, H. J., & Kamin, L. (1981). *Intelligence: The battle for the mind*. London: Macmillan.

Stephen Jay Gould gives a fascinating account of the history of mental measurement and a strong indictment of historical and sometimes current beliefs about the IQ and its heritability in his aptly titled book:

Gould, S. J. (1981). *The mismeasure of man*. New York: W. W. Norton.

Our genes are not simply limits; they are potential. They make possible our uniqueness and our flexibility. The following collection explores the potential implicit in our adaptability:

Gallagher, J. J., & Ramey, C. T. (Eds.). (1987). *The malleability of children*. Baltimore: Brookes.

Take her up tenderly,
Lift her with care;
Fashioned so slenderly,
Young, and so fair!

Thomas Hood, *The Bridge of Sighs*

Prenatal Development and Birth

As a child, I remained ignorant of reproductive matters for an embarrassingly long time. That, of course, had something to do with my parents. Being products of their times, they would not have dreamed of speaking with their children about what they would surely have referred to as the "birds and the bees" — had they dared say even that much. "Some matters are much better left alone. There will be plenty of time for *that* kind of thing when he's grown up."

So I was kept far away from horses foaling and cows calving: from dogs whelping and pigs littering — and most especially, from all these animals when, as my grandmother so poetically put it, "the heat is on them!" But, nobody ever bothered to keep me from the chickens; they felt that there was nothing very suggestive about the laying of an egg — nor even about its hatching. In retrospect, I think they might have been wrong.

What finally brought matters to a head was a new game that some aspiring delinquents had taught my older brother, Maurice. He then taught it to me. A simple game: All you do is put two index fingers in the mouth, one in each corner, and stretch the lips thin and wide. Then you try to say "puck."

I played the game at the dinner table. "Puck! Puck! Puck!" I said to my grandmother as clearly as I could — which was not easy with my fingers in my mouth.

My father was embarrassed and angry. "What!" he roared at me. Luckily, I knew he didn't mean for me to repeat what I had said.

"It's time you had a talk with your son about 'you know what,'" he said then to my mother.

"He's far too young, isn't he?" she said to her mother. My grandmother shrugged. She seemed mildly amused.

"I know he's too young," my mother repeated again. My dad nodded; I had nothing more to say.

Not long after this my grandmother pointed out to me a pair of mating dragonflies — surely as titillating a sight as I have ever seen.

"The heat's on them," she said by way of preface. "That means they're gonna have little ones." This, by way of explanation.

The secret was out! In spite of my parents' reluctance to discuss these important matters openly, I had finally learned about birds and dragonflies.

But it was not, as I found out shortly after my fifth birthday, the whole secret. There is more to these matters than is revealed by the sight of a pair of dragonflies clutching each other on a May morning in what cannot be anything but ecstasy. There were secrets yet to be uncovered and savored.

CONCEPTION

That's what this chapter is about: savory secrets. Secrets like that of conception.

Recall from Chapter 3 that at conception, the newly fertilized egg cell (termed a zygote) contains the individual's entire genetic endowment in the arrangement of the DNA molecules that make up its 23 pairs of chromosomes. Normally, all changes that take place in this cell's development will result from the interaction of genetic predispositions with the environment, both before and after birth. As we saw in Chapter 3, it is difficult to separate these two effects; they are not, in fact, separate and additive, but combined and interactive. Nevertheless, it is possible to isolate and describe the effects of specific experiences at certain times and under certain circumstances. For example, during prenatal development, some drugs and chemicals and other environmental conditions can have markedly harmful effects on the fetus.

This chapter traces the normal course of prenatal development from conception through birth and looks at some of the important factors that can affect the fetus.

DETECTING PREGNANCY

Women find it valuable to be able to detect **pregnancy** (the condition of a woman with a fertilized ovum) before the actual birth of the baby. Although there are few indications of pregnancy that an expectant mother can interpret with certainty before the later stages of **prenatal development** (development beginning at conception and ending at birth), some less certain signs appear relatively soon after conception. They can include cessation of **menses** (menstruation), morning sickness, changes in the breasts, and **quickening** (fetal motion). Most of these symptoms do not occur very early in pregnancy. Cessation of menses is not usually noticed until at least two weeks of pregnancy have passed because conception ordinarily occurs approximately two weeks after the last menstrual period. Nor is this a certain sign of pregnancy — many other factors may cause it. Morning sickness, although it affects approximately two-thirds of all pregnant women, does not ordinarily begin until about two weeks after the missed period and can easily be mistaken for some other ailment. Frequently during the early stages the breasts enlarge and become slightly painful, and the aureoles darken. Because these symptoms are highly subjective, they are quite unreliable. Quickening, the movement of the **fetus** in the womb, is not usually noticed by the mother until the fourth or fifth month, and by then most women have realized for some time that they are pregnant.

In addition to these probable signs of pregnancy, there are some more **positive symptoms.** One of these is the fetal heartbeat, which can be heard with the aid of a stethoscope. Similarly, fetal movements can be detected by feeling the abdomen or sometimes simply by observing it. Other methods of ascertaining the presence of a fetus are to X-ray the mother to detect its outline, to feel it manually through the abdominal wall, or to use *ultrasound,* a high-frequency sonic device that shows the body structures of the fetus without any of the dangers of X-rays.

Several decades ago, the surest early medical test of pregnancy required the aid of a rabbit, a frog, a mouse, or some other poor creature. A small amount of urine from the suspecting mother was injected into an unsuspecting, immature mouse or a virgin rabbit (if such an animal could be found). If the woman was four or more weeks into her pregnancy, she would have begun to produce *human chorionic gonadotropin* (HCG), traces of which would be present in her urine. Injections of urine containing HCG would cause a rupturing of the follicles on the animal's ovaries. This test (called the **rabbit test**) required killing the animal, a procedure that many physicians did not feel was warranted, given that they could detect pregnancy fairly accurately by other means after eight weeks of gestation.

Fortunately for virgin rabbits and mice, chemical pregnancy tests are now widely available, even in kit form for in-home use. These kits detect HCG in the woman's urine through a chemical reaction. Some of the tests boast that they can detect pregnancy as early as one day following the day when the woman's menstrual period would have begun. Positive indications in early pregnancy tests are highly reliable. Negative readings are less accurate, however, and should be followed by a second test a week or so later if the menstrual period has still not begun.

STAGES OF PRENATAL DEVELOPMENT

It is nothing short of phenomenal that as physically insignificant an object as a fertilized egg can become as complex and sophisticated an organism as a child within a period of nine calendar months. The **gestation period** (the time between conception and birth) for different species varies considerably: For bovines it is similar to humans; elephants require no fewer than 600 days; dogs come to term in approximately 63 days, rabbits in 31, and chickens in 21.

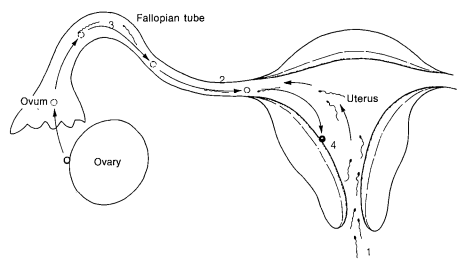

Fallopian tube

Ovum

Ovary

Uterus

Figure 4.1

Fertilization and implantation. At (*1*) many millions of sperm cells have entered the vagina and are finding their way into the uterus. At (*2*) some of these sperm are moving up the Fallopian tube (there is a similar tube on the other side) toward the ovum. At (*3*) fertilization occurs. The fertilized ovum drifts down the tube, dividing and forming new cells as it goes, until it implants itself in the wall of the uterus (*4*) by the seventh or eighth day after fertilization.

Fertilization in the woman usually occurs in the **Fallopian tubes** that link the **ovaries** to the **uterus** (Figure 4.1). It results from the invasion of the tubes by sperm cells, one of which successfully penetrates the outer covering of the ovum and unites with it. It is estimated that the male must ejaculate 20 million or more sperm cells if one is to succeed in reaching and fertilizing the egg. Once a single sperm has penetrated the ovum's outer shell, the egg then becomes impenetrable to other sperm. From that moment a human child begins to form, but it will be approximately 266 days before this individual is finally born.

The gestation period is usually calculated in lunar months, each month consisting of 28 days — hence 10 lunar months or 280 days for pregnancy when these days are counted from the onset of the last menstrual period, as they usually are. The true gestation period is nevertheless approximately 266 days because fertilization usually cannot occur until 12 to 14 days later when ovulation takes place.

The American College of Obstetrics and Gynecology has standardized the terminology used to describe prenatal development by identifying three developmental stages with clear time boundaries (Table 4.1). The stage of the **fertilized ovum** or **zygote** (also called the **germinal** stage) begins at fertilization and ends with implantation in the uterus at approximately the end of the first week. The **embryo** stage follows and terminates at the end of the eighth week (calculated from the onset of the last menses rather than from fertilization). The final stage, the **fetus,** lasts from the end of the second lunar month until the birth of the baby.

Table 4.1
Stages of Gestation (Prenatal Development)

Stage	Description
The fertilized ovum	Also termed the *germinal stage* or the period of the *zygote;* begins at fertilization and ends with implantation of the zygote (fertilized egg) in the uterine wall about one week later. Still microscopic.
Embryonic stage	From implantation to the end of the eighth week following last menses. The embryonic stage therefore lasts about 5 weeks. During this stage most of the important morphological (pertaining to form) changes occur. Accordingly, teratogens (influences that cause malformations and defects) are most influential during this period. At the end of this period, the embryo is close to 2 inches (4.5 cm) long and weighs about ⅔ ounce (19 grams).
Period of the fetus	From the end of the second lunar month until birth — usually 8 lunar months (224) days later. Accelerating growth curves toward the end of this period.

The Fertilized Ovum

After fertilization, the ovum is carried toward the uterus by currents in the Fallopian tubes, a process requiring between five and nine days. Cell divisions occur during this time, so that the fertilized ovum, which initially consisted of a single egg cell and a single sperm cell, now contains many more cells. It is hardly larger at the end of the first week than it was at the time of fertilization, mainly because the cells of which it consists are considerably smaller in size than they originally were. This is not surprising, because the ovum has received no nourishment from any source other than itself. At the end of the first week, the ovum is ready to implant itself in the uterine wall.

The Embryo

The embryo stage begins with the implantation of the fertilized ovum in the wall of the uterus. The ovum facilitates this process by secreting certain enzymes and producing tiny, tentaclelike growths, called *villi*, that implant themselves in the lining of the uterus to obtain nutrients from blood vessels. This is the beginning of the **placenta** — the organ that, while keeping the blood of the mother and of the fetus separate, allows nutrients to pass to the fetus and allows waste materials to be removed. In time, the placenta and the fetus are connected by the **umbilical cord,** a long, thick cord that is attached at one end to the placenta and at the other to what will be the child's navel. The umbilical cord consists of two arteries and one large vein and is approximately 20 inches

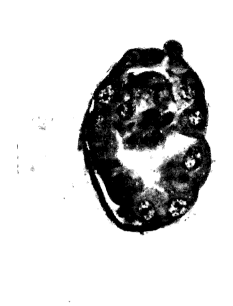

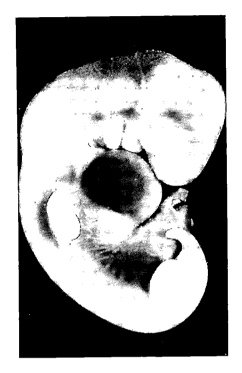

3 days after
conception

32 days

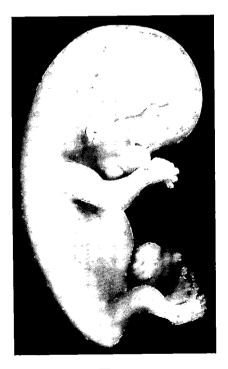

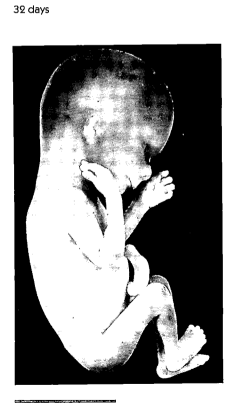

8½ weeks

15 weeks

long. It contains no nerve cells, so that there is no connection between the mother's nervous system and that of the child **in utero** (a common medical term meaning "in the uterus"). Note that the placenta serves as a link between mother and fetus, whereas the umbilical cord links the fetus to the placenta.

The normal course of physiological development in utero is highly predictable and regular. By the end of the first lunar month (very early in the embryonic stage), the embryo is still only a fraction of an inch long and weighs much less than an ounce. Despite the size, not only has there been cell differentiation into future skin cells, nerves, bone, and other body tissue but also the rudiments of eyes, ears, and nose have begun to appear. In addition, some of the internal organs are beginning to develop. In fact, by the end of the first month, a primitive heart is already beating! By the end of the second lunar month (the end of the period of embryonic development), the embryo is between 1½ and 2 inches long and weighs close to ⅔ of an ounce. All the organs are now present, the whole mass has assumed the curled shape characteristic of the fetus, and the embryo is clearly recognizable as human. Arm and limb buds have appeared and begun to grow, resembling short, awkward paddles. External **genitalia** (sex organs) have also appeared.

The Fetus

It is now the end of the second lunar month; the woman is six weeks pregnant. She has missed two menstrual periods or is currently missing her second. She is definitely pregnant, although the absolute mass of the organism that she carries inside her is still quite unimpressive. By the end of the third month, it may reach a length of 3 inches but will still weigh less than an ounce. The head of the fetus is one-third of its entire length; this will have changed to one-fourth by the end of the sixth lunar month and slightly less than that at birth.

During the third month of pregnancy, the fetus is sufficiently developed that if it is aborted it will make breathing movements and will give evidence of a primitive **sucking reflex** and of the **Babinski reflex** (the infant's tendency to fan its toes when ticked on the soles of its feet) if stimulated appropriately. However, the fetus will have no chance of survival if born at this stage of development.

During the fourth lunar month of pregnancy, the fetus grows to a length of 6 inches and weighs approximately 4 ounces. The bones have begun to form, all organs are clearly differentiated, and there may even be evidence of some **intrauterine** (within the uterus) movement. During the fifth month a downy covering, called **lanugo,** begins to grow over most of the fetus's body. This covering is usually shed during the seventh month but is occasionally still present at birth. The fetus weighs approximately 11 ounces and may have reached a length of 10 inches by the end of the fifth lunar month.

Toward the end of the sixth month, it is possible to palpate (feel by touch) the baby through the mother's abdomen. The heartbeat, faintly discernible in the fifth month, can now be heard clearly with the aid of a stethoscope. The eyelids have now separated so that the fetus can open and close its eyes. It is approximately a foot long and weighs close to 20 ounces. If born now, it would have some chance of surviving in a modern hospital with sophisticated care to compensate for the immaturity of its digestive and respiratory systems.

The fetus's growth in size and weight becomes more dramatic in the last few months of the final stage. Brain development is also particularly crucial during the last three months of pregnancy, as it will continue to be after birth, especially for the first two years of life. The unborn child's sensitivity to malnutrition is assumed to be related to neurological growth during the late stages of fetal development. This sensitivity is sometimes evident in lower developmental scores during infancy and impaired mental functioning among children born to malnourished mothers (Lewin, 1975).

Most of the physical changes that occur after the seventh month are quantitative (Table 4.2). It is now a matter of sheer physical growth: from 15 inches and 2.6 pounds in the seventh month (37.5 cm; 1.2 kg) to 16 inches and 4 pounds in the eighth (40 cm; 1.8 kg); from 17.5 inches and 4.7 pounds in the ninth (44 cm; 2.1 kg) to 20 inches and 7.5 pounds at end of the tenth (50 cm; 3.4 kg).

Two terms that are sometimes used to describe the general pattern of fetal development are **proximodistal** and **cephalocaudal.** Literally, these terms mean "from near to far" (proximodistal) and "from the head to the tail" (cephalocaudal). They refer to the fact that among the first aspects of the fetus to develop are the head and internal organs; the last are the limbs and digits.

After 266 days of intrauterine development, the fetus is ready to be born — although some appear to be ready earlier and some later. But before we look at birth, we turn to a discussion of the factors that may be important to the normal or abnormal development of the fetus.

FACTORS AFFECTING
PRENATAL DEVELOPMENT

External influences that cause malformations and physical defects in the fetus are referred to as **teratogens** (from *teras*, the Greek word for "monster," so called because such substances were thought to be capable of producing monsters). Accordingly, the study of birth defects is called **teratology.**

Among the most commonly recognized teratogens are various maternal illnesses, drugs, chemicals and minerals, and radiation. However, it is difficult to give a complete listing of the factors that influence prenatal development because of the highly circumstantial nature of much of the evidence. There is a lot of confusion about such factors, not only because they are extremely complex but also because many potentially helpful experiments cannot be performed for ethical or moral reasons. Consider, for example, the apparently simple problem of determining whether a particular drug affects the fetus. It

Table 4.2

Prenatal Development According to Lunar Months (Weight and Length Approximate)

Lunar Month	Weight	Length	Characteristics
1	Negligible	Negligible	Cell differentiation into those that will be bones, nerves, or other cells
2	⅔ oz. (19 g)	1½–2 in. (3.75–5 cm)	All organs present; leg buds and external genitalia just appearing
3	⅞ oz. (24.5 g)	3 in. (7.5 cm)	If aborted, will make primitive breathing movements and suck; bones forming, organs differentiated
4	4 oz. (112 g)	6 in. (15 cm)	
5	11 oz. (308 g)	10 in. (25 cm)	Fetal movement (quickening); lanugo appears
6	20 oz. (560 g)	12 in. (30 cm)	Heartbeat clearly discernible; eyelids present
7	2.6 lb. (1.2 kg)	15 in. (37.5 cm)	
8	4 lb. (1.8 kg)	16 in. (40 cm)	All major changes have now occurred; development is largely a matter of increasing weight and length
9	4.7 lb. (2.1 kg)	17.5 in. (44 cm)	
10	7.5 lb. (3.4 kg)	20 in. (50 cm)	

would appear that all that is required is to obtain a group of women to whom the drug has been administered and observe their offspring for any signs of possible effects of the drug. However, the women have usually been given the drug for a particular reason. As a result the investigator is often unable to

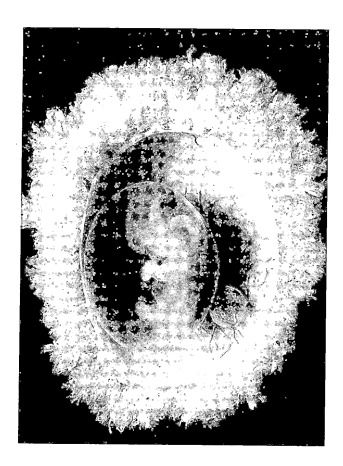

The world in utero, at 48 days.

determine whether differences between the children born to women who have taken the drug and a control group are due to the ailment for which the drug was administered or are due to the drug itself. For obvious ethical reasons, it is not usually possible to administer the drug simply to observe its effect. Furthermore, the effects of prenatal environments are sometimes so subtle that they are not easily detected. Despite difficulties like these, however, a good deal of valid information about the various effects of prenatal conditions on the development of the fetus is now available.

It is important to note at the outset that the effects of many teratogens often depend on a variety of factors, both environmental and genetic. That is, the occurrence and the severity of a defect associated with a particular teratogen are often determined by the fetus's genetic background as well as by the stresses that might result from the combined presence of other teratogens — not to mention the effects of other external *positive* influences. Accordingly, the effects of the same teratogen can vary widely from one fetus to another.

Not all external factors that affect the fetus are teratogens (produce defects). There are many possible influences on the developing fetus. Reassuringly, approximately 97 out of every 100 infants born in North America are normal and healthy. In the following sections, however, we focus more on teratogens than on positive influences.

Maternal Emotions and Stress

A once-common folk belief was that the mother's emotional states could be communicated directly to the child. If the pregnant woman worried too much, her child would be born with a frown; if she had a particularly traumatic experience, it would mark the infant, perhaps for life; if she was frightened by a rabbit, the result might be a child with a harelip. She must try to be happy and have pleasant experiences so that the child could be born free of negative influences. In point of fact, most of these tales about pregnancy are simply tales. Because there is no direct link between the mother's nervous system and the child's, there is little possibility that the mother's emotional states or disorders would be communicated directly to the unborn child. However, because of the close relationship between the mother and the fetus, a number of investigators have pursued the idea that stimuli affecting her will also have some effect on the child, however indirect.

There is some evidence that maternal emotions affect the child. Increases in fetal activity have been observed following emotional tension in the mother. In addition, mothers who are anxious during much of their pregnancy frequently have infants who are more irritable and more hyperactive and have more feeding problems. This is especially true if the mother experiences long-term stress rather than isolated episodes (Spezzano, 1981). One prevalent theory is that an anxious mother's chemical balance affects the child physiologically and therefore, indirectly, psychologically.

These findings must be viewed as highly tentative. Not only is it extremely difficult to arrive at valid and useful measures of emotional states in mother and infant but it is also often impossible to control a variety of other factors that might be related. For example, some of the factors sometimes associated with high maternal stress (poverty, inadequate diet, medical problems) might also be associated with fetal problems. Hence conclusive statements about the influence of maternal emotional states on the unborn are not warranted.

Prescription Drugs

Investigating the effects of **drugs** on the fetus presents a number of scientific, ethical, and moral problems. It is clearly impossible to use human subjects in controlled investigations with chemical substances whose effects may be injurious to the fetus. Our information is therefore based on studies of animals or observations of human infants in poorly controlled situations. Generalizing from studies of animals to humans in the case of drugs presents an additional problem, because certain drugs have dramatically different effects on members of different animal species, as well as on children relative to adults (Bowes et al., 1970). Also, normal adult doses of a drug might well represent huge doses for a fetus weighing only ounces, particularly if the drug crosses the placental barrier easily.

The frequency of drug use by pregnant women and the variety of drugs they consume is relatively high. Heinonen, Slone, and Shapiro (1983) gathered data on more than 50,000 pregnant women in the United States and found that the average number of different prescription drugs taken during pregnancy was 3.8. A study of pregnant women in Scotland revealed that 82 percent took at least one prescription drug during pregnancy (Lewis, 1983). In addition, an estimated 75 percent of pregnant women take a variety of nonprescription drugs such as analgesics (painkillers such as headache tablets) and cough or cold preparations (Rayburn et al., 1982). There are indications that extent of drug use by pregnant women — and the problem of overprescribing by the medical profession — may be declining following increasing awareness of the possibly harmful effects of some drugs on the fetus (Schardein, 1985).

Among the better-known teratogens (drugs that cause malformations and physical defects in the fetus) are thalidomide, which causes severe physical changes in the embryo; quinine, which is associated with congenital deafness; barbiturates and other painkillers that reduce the body's oxygen supply, resulting in varying degrees of brain damage; and various anesthetics that appear to cross the placental barrier easily and rapidly and cause depression of fetal respiration and decreased responsiveness in the infant (Schardein, 1985). Note that the most serious structural changes (physical deformities and abnormalities) that are sometimes associated with drug intake, as well as with other factors such as maternal malnutrition, can occur only during the embryonic stage of development. After this stage, the fetus's basic structure has already been formed and is not as vulnerable to external influences (see Figure 4.2)

Among nonprescription drugs that may also have negative effects on the fetus are aspirin, which may increase the tendency to bleed in both mother and fetus (Stockman, 1990) and which is clearly linked with physical deformities among experimental animals (Vorhees & Mollnow, 1987). Also, megadoses of vitamins C, D, A, K, and B_6 have been linked with birth defects (Scher & Dix, 1983).

The prescription drugs mentioned in this section are only a few of the drugs that are known to be harmful to the fetus. There are many others that do not seem to have any immediate negative effects, but whose long-term effects are still unclear. **Diethylstilbestrol (DES)**, for example, is a drug that was heavily prescribed through the 1940s and 1950s for women who were at risk for spontaneous abortions. Not until several decades later did medical researchers discover a link between DES use by pregnant women and vaginal cancer among girls subsequently born to these women. Because the effect occurs so long after taking the drug and because it is manifested in only a small percentage of the

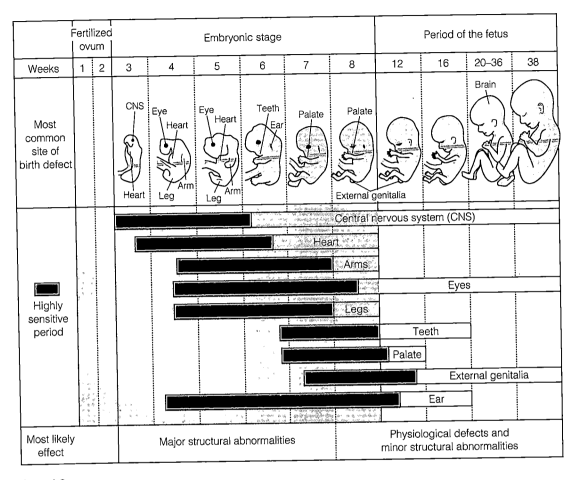

Figure 4.2

The most serious structural defects in prenatal development are most likely to occur in the first 8 weeks, although teratogens can have serious consequences throughout gestation.

offspring, it is extremely difficult to detect. For this reason, many medical practitioners discourage the use of any prescription drugs by pregnant women unless absolutely necessary.

Chemicals

The effects of chemicals on mother and fetus are also very difficult to ascertain. This is partly because the effects of many chemicals are sometimes too subtle and not sufficiently widespread to be easily noticed. It is also because there are so many chemicals in our environments that it is almost impossible to separate their individual effects from one another (Elkington, 1986). Would you believe that there are some 60,000 chemicals currently in use in North America, and that several thousand *new* chemicals are introduced each year (Sloan, Shapiro, & Mitchell, 1980)? Although the majority of these are "contained" in one way or another — that is, they do not find their way into our air, our water, or our food — and are essentially harmless, we are exposed to others on a daily basis in the form of water, air, or food pollutants, or as toxic wastes of various kinds. Unfortunately, their ultimate effects on our lives or on the lives of those not yet born are not fully understood.

We do know, however, that the ingestion of mercury by expectant mothers may result in severe retardation and physical deformities in their children. Although mercury occurs naturally in some areas, it is most often a problem where it is an industrial waste. It is also sometimes used to treat seed grains. Its effects received worldwide attention following the births of a large number of severely deformed and retarded infants in Minimata Bay, Japan. The deformities were traced to the presence of high levels of mercury in the fish that inhabitants of this community consumed in great quantities; the mercury was, in this case, an industrial waste. The effects of mercury are now known as Minimata disease.

Other chemicals that are known to be harmful include a range of hydrocarbons that are used as herbicides or insecticides. These include dioxin and PCB, both of which appear to be associated with a higher incidence of miscarriage and with physical deformities. Agent orange, a chemical widely used to defoliate trees during the Vietnam War, is a dioxinlike chemical. It too has been linked with fetal abnormalities and death.

In addition to the chemicals known to be harmful to the fetus, there are many toxic chemicals whose effects on fetal development are unknown, although we know how they affect children and adults. Lead is one example. It is present in some fuel emissions, in some paints, in certain metal products, and elsewhere. It accumulates slowly in the body; and when it reaches sufficiently high concentrations, it can lead to serious physical and mental problems in children and adults (Weisskopf, 1987).

We might want to think that these terrible things happen only to other people, strangers, who live in faraway places. That is not true. They happen where I am and where you are. When, in the spring of 1986, the nuclear reactor in Chernobyl spewed radioactive particles into the air, their presence could be felt and measured in Norway, in Poland, in France, and yes, even in North America. And we do know that radiation is an extremely powerful teratogen and that relatively low levels can lead to abortion, stillbirths, and physical abnormalities.

Even here, in the pristine Northern wilderness, it seems I have not escaped the contamination. A lake on the shores of which I have a small shelter is cited in the current fishing regulations. My government informs me that certain species of fish in that lake have unusually high levels of mercury. In its wisdom, it cautions me that I should not eat of these fish more than once a week, and that those who are pregnant should avoid them altogether. It makes me sad. And angry.

Nicotine

The harmful effects of smoking on the smoker, and the effects of "sidestream" smoke on the nonsmoker, have been well documented. Some of its effects on the fetus also seem clear.

The Surgeon General, following an extensive review of the literature on cigarette smoking during pregnancy, summarizes some of its most important and consistent effects (U.S. Department of Health & Human Services, 1981). Cigarette smoking, the Surgeon General concludes, is linked with a higher probability of placental problems where the placenta becomes detached from the uterine wall, often leading to fetal death or stillbirth; it is associated with significantly lower birthweight, which, in turn, is associated with a higher probability of subsequent complications; it is linked with a higher risk of miscarriage and fetal death; and it is related to a higher incidence of early childhood respiratory infections and diseases. In brief, cigarette smoking is clearly harmful not only to the mother, but also to the fetus, the placenta, the infant, and the child.

Caffeine

The effects of caffeine on the fetus remain somewhat unclear — perhaps because these effects are different for different individuals and because they do not appear to be very dramatic. Nevertheless, large doses of caffeine given to pregnant rats have been associated with birth defects in their offspring. And some research indicates that the probability of premature delivery is somewhat higher among mothers who consume higher levels of caffeine (Jacobson et al., 1985). However, current evidence suggests that caffeine is not a human teratogen, although extremely high consumption might be toxic for the fetus (Brendt & Beckman, 1990).

Alcohol

Alcohol consumption by pregnant women may be associated with various defects in their offspring, collectively labeled **fetal alcohol syndrome** (Streissguth, Barr, & Martin, 1983). The major features of this syndrome are central nervous system problems sometimes manifested in mental retardation, as well as retarded physical growth, and cranial and facial malformations. These malformations typically include a low forehead, widely spaced eyes, a short nose and long upper lip, and absence of a marked infranasal depression (the typical depression in the center of the upper lip, going upward toward the nose) (Abel, 1984).

With humans it is difficult to conduct the types of experiments that would allow researchers to determine precisely what amounts of alcohol, at what stage of development, will have these effects. Nor is it possible to separate

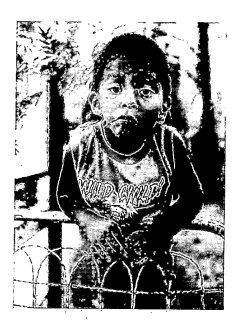

Fetal alcohol syndrome, most often apparent in central nervous system problems including mental retardation, may also be evident in facial and cranial malformations including widely spaced eyes, low forehead, long upper lip, and absence of distinct infranasal depression.

completely the effects of alcohol from those of other drugs that might accompany alcohol use or from the effects of malnutrition, also a possible corollary of alcohol use. However, a number of studies have looked at FAS among animals and have found, to no one's great surprise, that injections of ethanol (the type of alcohol that is drunk as opposed to the type that might be rubbed on a horse's sore muscles or burned in an engine) in pregnant mice quite readily produce what appears to be FAS in their offspring. Not only are these offspring less likely to be born alive but also many of them will display facial and skull deformations highly similar to those characteristic of FAS children (Rosett & Sander, 1979).

How much can a pregnant woman drink, and when? The current consensus is that even in small amounts, alcohol may be harmful to the fetus although it may not necessarily lead to fetal alcohol syndrome. Accordingly, some researchers speak of *fetal alcohol effects* rather than of FAS. For example, one study compared the effects of heavy drinking (four or more drinks a day) with the effects of more moderate drinking (two to four drinks a day) and with those of lighter drinking (fewer than two drinks a day) (Streissguth et al., 1980). Some of the symptoms associated with FAS were found in 19 percent of the children born to mothers in the first group, 11 percent of those in the second, and only 2 percent of those in the third.

How much can a pregnant woman drink, and when? The evidence is not all in, and the conclusions are still tentative. However, in summarizing the effects of alcohol on the developing fetus, Brendt and Beckman (1990) cite evidence that consuming six drinks or more of alcohol per day constitutes a high risk, but that fewer than two drinks per day is not likely to lead to fetal alcohol syndrome. And Graham (1985) suggests that binge drinking may be especially harmful to the fetus in the early stages of pregnancy and that it might be associated with neural tube defects.

A longitudinal study of 449 children found a significant relationship between *moderate* use of alcohol by their mothers when pregnant and children's motor performance on a battery of tests administered at the age of 4. Specifically, children made more errors on fine and gross motor tasks, responded more slowly, and had poorer balance (Barr et al., 1990).

Given these findings, corroborated by a large number of other investigations, it should come as no surprise that an increasing number of medical practitioners recommend that pregnant women refrain completely from alcohol use.

Substance Abuse

Narcotics. Babies born to narcotics addicts are themselves addicted. These infants suffer a clearly recognizable withdrawal syndrome labeled the **neonatal abstinence syndrome.** Its symptoms may include tremors, restlessness, hyperactive reflexes, high-pitched cries, vomiting, fevers, sweating, rapid respiration, seizures, and sometimes death (Chasnoff, 1986). Frequently, these symptoms don't reach a peak until the infant is 3 or 4 days of age. Some physicians recommend methadone maintenance in low doses for the mother during the later stages of pregnancy and gradual weaning of the infant from methadone after birth (Iennarella, Chisum, & Bianchi, 1986).

In addition to their addictive effects evident in the neonatal abstinence syndrome, the use of narcotics has also been linked with prematurity and low birthweight and with behavior problems such as hyperactivity (Kolata, 1978).

LSD and marijuana. The effects of substances such as LSD and marijuana remain somewhat uncertain. Although research with pregnant monkeys who were given LSD has found chromosomal damage in the mothers and a high rate of stillbirths and early deaths among infants (Kato, 1970), these results cannot easily be corroborated among humans. As Bolton (1983) points out, mothers who use one or both of these drugs typically consume alcohol as well — and may also use a number of other drugs. In addition, many of them receive little prenatal medical care, some suffer from drug-related diseases and deficiencies, and many have severely deficient diets. The causes of higher incidence of prematurity, fetal and infant death, and physical or mental abnormality among this group cannot easily be sorted out.

One attempt to look at the effects of marijuana use on the human fetus and infant involved a longitudinal investigation of 700 pregnant women (Fried, 1986). These were women who had been informed of the study by their physicians and who had volunteered to participate. Subsequently, each woman was interviewed three times during her pregnancy, once in each trimester. Detailed questioning touched on past and present alcohol, caffeine, and nicotine use, with particular emphasis on marijuana use. For the study, women were classified as nonusers, irregular users (one or fewer joints per week), moderate users (two to five joints per week), and heavy users (five or more joints per week). In this sample, 80 percent of the women were nonusers, 12 percent were irregular users, 1 percent were moderate users, and 3 percent were heavy users.

Fried (1986) reports that for this sample, there were no differences between marijuana users and nonusers with respect to rate of miscarriages, birth complications, or physical anomalies at birth. The study did find, however, that the gestational period was an average of 1.1 weeks shorter for heavy users. In addition, newborns whose mothers were regular heavy marijuana smokers exhibited more tremors and more intense startle reactions; and they were less responsive to a light directed at their eyes. Fried (1986) speculates that this may reflect minor neurological dysfunction and perhaps an immature nervous system. However, tests of motor and cognitive functioning do not ordinarily reveal any differences between infants of marijuana users and nonusers. Fried suggests the tests might not be sufficiently sensitive to detect differences that could exist. Additional evidence that the nervous systems of infants of heavy marijuana users may mature more slowly is apparent in the somewhat higher rate of visual problems among these children when they are tested between three and six years later.

Cocaine. A more recent and perhaps increasingly common kind of pregnant drug abuser is the cocaine user. Chasnoff, Burns, Schnoll, and Burns (1985) identified 23 pregnant cocaine users who were part of an ongoing study on the effects of drugs. Twelve of these women used only cocaine; the others also used alcohol or other drugs.

Infants born to cocaine users manifested more startle reactions and more tremors, much like children of heavy marijuana users. In addition, many of their reflexes and motor behaviors were significantly different from those of a control group whose mothers were not cocaine users. These differences included common reflexes such as the Moro reaction (startle reflex), age of standing, age of pulling up to a sitting position, and visual and auditory orientation.

Maternal Health

The mother's health inevitably affects the occupant of her womb; she is responsible for the fetus's comfort and nourishment. A wide range of diseases and infections are also known to affect the fetus. The best known is probably rubella (German measles); others are syphilis, gonorrhea, and poliomyelitis, each of which can cause mental deficiency, blindness, deafness, or miscarriages. Cretinism (subnormal mental development, undeveloped bones, a protruding abdomen, and rough, coarse skin) may be related to a thyroid malfunction in the mother or to an iodine deficiency in her diet. If the deficiency is not too extreme, it can sometimes be alleviated in the child through continuous medication after birth.

Diabetes is another maternal condition that can have serious consequences for the fetus (see Hare, 1989). Prior to the discovery of insulin, fetal and maternal death were very high. Now, however, mortality rates among diabetic mothers are about the same as those among nonpregnant diabetic women. And with timely diagnosis and proper medical management, fetal deaths are generally below 5 percent (Coustan, 1990). Management involves careful monitoring of mother and fetus to assess and control sugar levels (glycemic control). Simple, self-monitoring procedures are available for in-home use.

Although fetal death as a complication of maternal diabetes has been greatly reduced, the rate of birth defects among these infants is still two to four times higher than that of the general population. The most common defects include congenital heart disease, cleft palates, neural tube defects, and other neurological problems (Barss, 1989). Most of these birth defects result from influences that occur early in pregnancy. Hence the importance of careful monitoring from the outset (Coustan, 1990).

Herpes can also have serious effects on the fetus, particularly if the mother's infection is active at the time of delivery. The probability of the infant's contracting the virus during birth is extremely high — 40 to 60 percent (Eden et al., 1990). In addition, evidence suggests that as many as 50 percent of mothers suffering from active herpes infections give birth prematurely (Babson et al., 1980). Because the newborn does not possess many of the immunities that are common among older children and adults, the herpes virus may attack the infant's internal organs, leading to visual or nervous system problems or death in about 50 percent of cases (Eden et al., 1990). As a result, infants born to mothers infected with the herpes virus are often delivered through cesarean section to prevent infection from occurring.

Acquired Immune Deficiency Syndrome (or **AIDS**), another sexually transmitted disease, is of considerable current concern. First reported in the United States in 1981, as of now, it remains incurable and fatal. By October 20, 1986, 24,424 males in the United States had been diagnosed as having AIDS (31 percent living in New York State); at that date, 1,775 women in the United States had developed AIDS (47 percent were residents of New York State). Estimates are that some 60,000 American men and women have now developed the disease (Trofatter, 1990). And the prognosis is that virtually all will eventually die from resulting complications.

AIDS is transmitted through the exchange of body fluids, primarily through blood/blood exchange or through semen/blood exchange. Accordingly, transmission occurs mainly through anal intercourse (because of the thinness of rectal tissues, which frequently tear during intercourse), through blood transfusions involving infected blood, and through the communal use of hypodermic syringes. Not surprisingly, AIDS is most common among homosexual males and among intravenous drug users.

By 1987, more than 400 children in the United States had developed AIDS (Long, 1987). Most of these children had mothers who were intravenous drug users. And the great majority of them acquired AIDS directly from their mothers through blood exchange in the uterus or during birth. The risk of transmission from infected mother to fetus ranges from 35 percent to 60 percent (Trofatter, 1990). Prognosis for an infected newborn is poor, with survival typically being considerably shorter than the 11 to 15 months that is the average survival period for adults (ACOG Technical Bulletin, 1988).

Clearly, high-risk women (current or past intravenous drug users; those whose sexual partners include bisexual males and/or men who have been or are intravenous drug users) should be tested for the AIDS antibody before considering pregnancy (see Figure 4.3).

Older Mothers

The mother's age also appears to be related to the well-being of the fetus. We know (as was pointed out in Chapter 3) that the incidence of Trisomy 21 (Down syndrome) is approximately 1 in 1,500 live births for mothers between the ages of 15 and 24 but increases to 1 in 38 for mothers over 45 (Brock, 1982). We know, as well, that the probability of fathering a child with Down syndrome is 20 to 30 percent higher for fathers over the age of 55. Nor is Trisomy 21 the only chromosomal disorder related to age. For example, Klinefelter's syndrome as well as Trisomies 13 and 18 increase dramatically with the mother's age (Hsu, 1986). Both Trisomies 13 and 18 may be associated with neural tube defects, congenital heart disease, growth retardation, and other problems.

Another chromosomal abnormality that increases with the mother's age is a defect on one arm of the X chromosome. This abnormality, labeled the **fragile X syndrome,** is second only to Trisomy 21 as a cause of mental retardation, occurring in approximately 1 out of every 1,000 live births (Herbst & Miller, 1980). It is a sex-linked, primarily male disorder that often underlies a history of retardation among male children in some families (Silverstein & Johnston, 1990).

However, given the availability of prenatal procedures such as chorion biopsy or amniocentesis that now make it possible to determine the presence of a number of chromosomal abnormalities and other defects or diseases, increasing numbers of women, and men, are making the decision to have a family later. Kopp and Kaler (1989) point out that the greatest increase in fertility rates in recent years has been among women in their early thirties. However, fewer than 7 percent of all births occur to women over the age of 35 (Drugan, Johnson, & Evans, 1990).

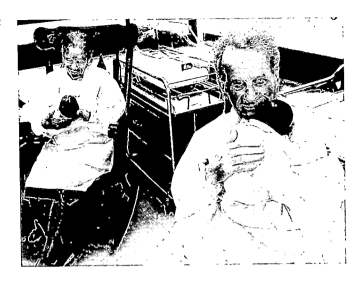

Volunteers with AIDS babies.

In spite of the association between the mother's age and some chromosomal abnormalities, modern health care makes it possible for many women to deliver healthy, full-term babies at ages that would have entailed much higher risk a few decades ago. In fact, when Spellacy, Miller, and Winegar (1986) compared outcomes for 511 pregnancies of women over 40 with more than 26,000 pregnancies of women between 20 and 30, they found that age posed little risk when factors such as cigarette smoking and maternal weight were taken into account.

Teenage Mothers

It appears too that more women are having children at younger ages — that the numbers of teenage pregnancies have increased dramatically in recent decades. In fact, however, the appearance may be somewhat misleading. Brooks-Gunn and Furstenberg (1986) report that the fertility rate for teenagers has actually declined since 1960 — from 80 births per 1,000 white American girls aged 15 to 19 in 1960 to fewer than 50 births per 1,000 in 1982. Corresponding numbers for nonwhite teenage American girls declined from 160 per 1,000 to approximately 100 per 1,000.

In spite of these declines in fertility rate, the number of births to unwed teenage girls remains very high relative to the number of births in the rest of the population. In fact, some 14 percent of all births are to girls aged 15 to 19 (U.S. Bureau of the Census, 1988). And more than half of these are to unmarried teenage parents (National Center for Health Statistics, 1981). The teenage birthrate in the United States is among the highest in the world — approximately 17

AT A
GLANCE

Pediatric AIDS Mortality

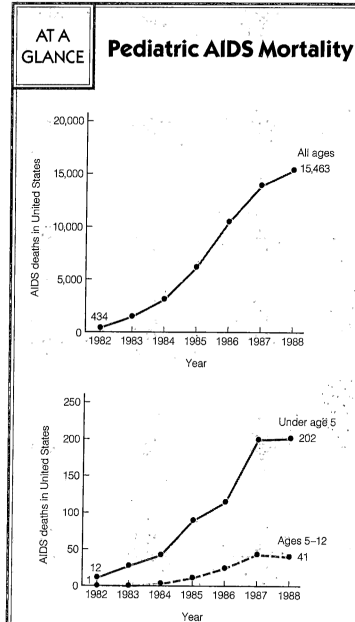

Acquired Immune Deficiency
Syndrome (AIDS) is a fatal
disease transmitted through
the exchange of body fluids. Most
cases of pediatric (childhood)
AIDS are transmitted directly
from mother to fetus. In later
childhood, AIDS is acquired
primarily through blood transfusions and is consequently
rarer. With increasing sexual
activity after adolescence,
incidence of AIDS rises
dramatically. Male AIDS
cases outnumbered female
cases by a factor of almost 10
to 1 in 1988.

Figure 4.3   Rising number of deaths from AIDS in the
United States, 1982 to 1988. Reported cases of AIDS
are much higher. *Source:* Adapted from U.S.
Bureau of the Census (1990), p. 83.

times higher than in Japan and 3 times higher than in the Soviet Union (Davis & Harris, 1982).

Research indicates that children born to younger teenage mothers are often at a physical, emotional, and intellectual disadvantage relative to children born to older mothers. There are more miscarriages, premature births, and stillbirths among teenage mothers, and surviving infants are more often the targets of abuse and neglect. Their developmental scores on various measures are often retarded (Smith, Weinman, & Malinak, 1984).

As Lamb and Elster (1985) point out, however, much of this research fails to take into account the social circumstances of teenage parenthood — the poverty and the lack of social, educational, and medical assistance. In retrospect, it seems that it is not the age of the teenage parent that is the important factor, but the health care available to the expectant mother both before and after the birth of her child. All other things being equal, unless she is very young (below age 15), if a teenage mother and her infant receive the same medical attention as an older mother, the health and developmental status of her infant will be normal (McCormick, Shapiro, & Starfield, 1984).

But all other things are not often equal for teenage mothers. And they will not be equal, argues Grow (1979), unless various agencies provide comprehensive services for teenage parents who keep their children. In the absence of such services, the economic and social conditions under which the majority of teenage mothers are forced to live and the emotional stresses that accompany these conditions — as well as the demands of pregnancy and of childrearing — present many with serious disadvantages. (See Chapter 12 for a more detailed discussion of teenage pregnancy.)

Maternal Nutrition

During the German siege of Leningrad in World War II, many Russians lived near starvation in bitterly cold, unheated homes. And many died. But perhaps most striking, in one clinic that had seen an average of 3,867 births a year for the preceding three years, only 493 infants were born in 1942 (Shanklin & Hoden, 1979). Most of these were born in the first half of the year, and would have been conceived before the famine was at its height; only 79 were born in the second half of the year. In addition to this dramatic decline in birthrates, there were also great increases in *amenorrhea* (cessation of menstruation, which, incidentally, is not uncommon among anorexic women), low levels of fertility, and an increase in miscarriages.

Similarly, during the great Dutch famine (1944–45), birthrates declined dramatically, more than 50 percent of childbearing women became amenorrheic, neonates (newborns) were smaller, and rates of infant mortality and malformations increased (Smith, 1947).

There is little doubt that starvation, and extreme malnutrition, can have serious negative consequences for the fetus. Malnutrition and starvation, if they do not lead to fetal death, may result in prematurity, physical abnormalities, epilepsy, cerebral palsy, or deficits in motor and cognitive development (Parmelee & Sigman, 1983).

Unfortunately, research on malnutrition among humans is seldom experimental; that is, investigators have no control over assigning subjects to groups or over the manipulation of treatments. We know that most naturally occurring instances of malnutrition involve many other factors, often including lower socioeconomic levels, lower educational levels, lower intellectual stimulation, and so on. The effects sometimes attributed solely to malnutrition might also, at least in part, be related to these other factors. In addition, malnutrition is seldom limited to the period of prenatal development but usually continues into infancy and even childhood. As Stein et al. (1975) note, perhaps the most plausible conclusion is that the effects of malnutrition are a complex interaction of the severity and nature of deprivation, its timing, and its duration. It is not improbable, as Lewin (1975) suggests, that long-term intellectual deficits may result from malnutrition that begins before birth and continues for some time afterward; and it is possible that some of the short-term effects associated with prenatal malnutrition are reversible given adequate nourishment after birth.

During pregnancy, the mother's energy requirements and her metabolism change. The presence of a growing fetus means that the mother requires somewhere between 10 and 15 percent more calories. In addition, there are important metabolic changes, including an increased synthesis of protein, which is important for the formation of the placenta and enlargement of the uterus; a reduction in carbohydrate use, the effect of which is to provide sufficient glucose for the fetus; and increased storage of fat to satisfy the mother's energy requirements (Chez & Chervenak, 1990).

Not only must the pregnant woman increase her protein intake, but there is also an increased need for important minerals (for example, calcium, magnesium, iron, iodine, phosphorus) and vitamins (such as A, D, E, C, and some of the B's). Recommended dietary allowances for pregnant women range from 25 to 50 percent above those for nonpregnant women (*Recommended Dietary Allowances*, 1980).

Current medical advice emphasizes that *what* the woman eats is more important than *how much*. With respect to brain growth, protein appears to be among the most important ingredients of a good diet. In studies of both humans and rats where expectant mothers had protein-deficient diets, the offspring developed fewer brain cells or performed more poorly on subsequent tests of intellectual performance (McKay et al., 1978).

A second aspect of current medical advice contradicts the long-held belief that the woman should be careful to minimize her weight gain during pregnancy. Infant mortality is often lower in countries where pregnant women gain significantly more weight than do pregnant women in the United States or Canada. Maternal weight gain leads to higher fetal weight and reduces the risk of illness and infection. Accordingly, doctors who once cautioned women to limit their weight gain to about 10 pounds now suggest that the optimal weight gain for a woman who begins pregnancy at an average weight is somewhere between 22 and 28 pounds (Chez & Chervenak, 1990); it is even higher for women who are initially underweight. For women who are initially over-weight, recommended gains are correspondingly lower.

Unfortunately, this medical advice is most likely relevant to those least likely to be exposed to it and to those least able to take advantage of it. Malnu-trition and starvation are seldom a deliberate choice. There are important issues and responsibilities here for our social consciences. (See Table 4.3 for a description of some influences on the fetus and Figure 4.2 for a timetable of influences.)

Social Class

The greatest single cause of infant death is premature birth. Prematurity is among the most direct causes of cerebral palsy and various mental defects. The factor most closely related to premature births is social rather than medical. These facts are relatively well documented and highly significant (Kopp & Parmelee, 1979). Although social class does not by itself explain anything, the high correlation between low social class and higher incidence of premature birth suggests that the living conditions and associated emotional and health consequences of membership in the lower class are not conducive to the pro-duction of healthy full-term babies (Baker & Mednick, 1984). Research re-viewed in this chapter on the effects of maternal malnutrition on the fetus, and subsequently on the infant, is directly relevant here. There is little doubt that prenatal care of mothers who live in poverty is not often comparable to that afforded middle-class mothers — nor is postnatal health care. General diet, pro-tein intake, and mineral and vitamin intake are frequently significantly infe-rior; and the effects of these factors are too often the harsh consequences of an infant's being born poor. Social and moral implications should be clear.

Rh(D) Immunization

There is a particular quality of blood in Rhesus monkeys that is often, but not always, present in human blood. Because this factor was first discovered in the Rhesus monkey, it is called the Rh factor. Individuals who are missing this factor are termed Rh-negative; those whose blood contains the factor are termed Rh-positive. More precisely, however, it is a specific component of the Rh blood group, labeled D, that is important for the pregnant mother and her fetus. Introduction of Rh(D)-positive blood into an individual who is Rh-negative leads to the formation of antibodies to counteract the D factor — a process termed *immunization* (Bowman, 1990). If these antibodies are then introduced into an individual with Rh(D)-positive blood, they attack that per-

Table 4.3
Influences on the Fetus

Agent	Some Reported Effects or Associations
Alcohol	Fetal alcohol syndrome; intrauterine growth retardation; microcephaly; mental retardation
Diethylstilbestrol (DES)	Anomalies of cervix and uterus; higher risk of cervical cancer
Lithium carbonate	Heart and blood vessel defects; neural tube defects
Methylmercury	Minamata disease; cerebral palsy; microcephaly; mental retardation; blindness; death
Polychlorinated biphenyls	Cola-colored children; gum, nail, and groin pigmentation; can affect offspring for up to 4 years after maternal exposure
Radiation	Microcephaly; mental retardation; eye anomalies; visceral malformations
Street drugs	Fetal and pregnancy complications sometimes leading to death; no reported association with malformations
Tetracycline	Tooth and bone staining if exposed during last two-thirds of pregnancy
Thalidomide	Limb reduction defects; anomalies of external ears, kidneys, and heart
Iodine deficiency	Hypothyroidism or goiter; neurological damage
Mechanical (constraint in womb)	Defects involving limb development and position; neural tube, lip, palate, or abdominal defects
Maternal starvation	Intrauterine growth retardation; central nervous system anomalies; fetal death
Diabetes	Malformations involving internal organs; caudal dysplasia
Rubella	Mental retardation; deafness; cardiovascular malformations; cataracts
Herpes simplex	Microcephaly; eye defects
Aspirin	Heavy use associated with lowered birthrate; no increase in malformation
Caffeine	Not likely to be a teratogen, although excess consumption may be toxic
Nicotine	Placental lesions; intrauterine growth retardation; increased mortality
Vitamin A	Urogenital anomalies associated with massive doses; ear malformations; neural tube defects; cleft palate; facial abnormalities
Vitamin D	Heart defects; facial malformation; mental retardation

Source: Based on R. L. Brendt & D. A. Beckman. (1990). Teratology. In R. D. Eden, F. H. Boehm, & M. Haire (Eds.), *Assessment and care of the fetus: Physiological, clinical, and medicolegal principles* (Table 17-4, pp. 227–28). Norwalk, Conn.: Appleton & Lange. Reprinted by permission of the publisher.

son's blood cells, causing a depletion of oxygen and, in the absence of medical intervention, death.

Unfortunately, this situation can occur in the fetus (termed fetal erythroblastosis) when the fetus has Rh(D)-positive blood and the mother is Rh-negative. Because the Rh factor is a dominant genetic trait, this situation will occur only when the father is Rh(D)-positive (and the mother Rh-negative). If blood from the fetus gets into the mother's bloodstream — termed transplacental hemorrhage — the mother's blood will begin to produce antibodies. These are usually not produced early enough or in sufficient quantities to affect the first child. Subsequent fetuses may be affected, however.

Transplacental hemorrhage occurs in approximately 50 percent of all pregnant women, either during pregnancy or immediately after birth (Knuppel & Angel, 1990). Hence the chances of Rh(D) immunization are very high — if, of course, the mother is Rh-negative and the father Rh(D)-positive. At one time, this condition was always fatal. Now, however, it is possible for the physician to monitor antibody levels in the mother's blood, determining when levels are high enough to endanger the fetus. At this point, there are several alternatives. If the fetus is sufficiently advanced (32 or 33 weeks, for example), labor might be induced or a cesarean delivery performed and the infant given a complete blood transfusion immediately (Bowman, 1990). If the fetus is not sufficiently advanced, a blood transfusion may be performed in utero.

Fortunately, this type of medical intervention is not often necessary, following the development of the drug *Rhogam (Rh Immune Globulin* or *RhIG)* in 1968. Rhogam is blood that already contains *passive* antibodies that prevent the formation of additional antibodies.

It has become routine, even mandatory, for all physicians to ascertain whether a pregnant woman is Rh-negative and whether she is at risk of immunization. This should be done at the time of the first prenatal visit. Bowman (1990) suggests that husbands or partners of Rh-negative women should then be screened. If they too are Rh-negative, there is little chance of fetal erythroblastosis. However, because of the possibility of an extramarital conception, mothers who are Rh-negative and their fetuses should be monitored closely throughout pregnancy.

When an expecting mother is at risk of immunization — that is, she is Rh-negative and the father is Rh(D)-positive — Rhogam is sometimes administered during the seventh month of gestation — even though the incidence of immunization before delivery is low (approximately 2 percent). Current medical guidelines say that all such women should be administered Rhogam within no more than 72 hours of delivery, as soon as it has been determined that the fetus is Rh-positive and that the mother is therefore at risk of Rh(D) immunization. Similarly, Rhogam should be administered in the event of the abortion or miscarriage of an Rh(D)-positive fetus if the mother is Rh-negative. The drug needs to be administered after the termination of every Rh-positive pregnancy (see Figure 4.4).

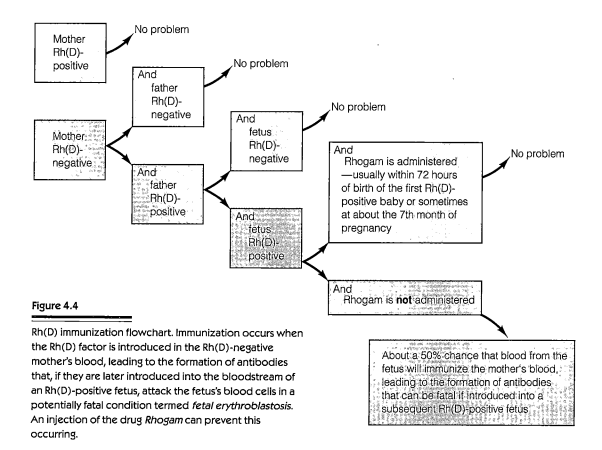

Figure 4.4

Rh(D) immunization flowchart. Immunization occurs when the Rh(D) factor is introduced in the Rh(D)-negative mother's blood, leading to the formation of antibodies that, if they are later introduced into the bloodstream of an Rh(D)-positive fetus, attack the fetus's blood cells in a potentially fatal condition termed *fetal erythroblastosis*. An injection of the drug *Rhogam* can prevent this occurring.

CHILDBIRTH

Childbirth is something that happens almost 4 million times a year in the United States — although fertility rates (proportion of women having children) have declined (U.S. Bureau of the Census, 1988).

Birth in today's industrialized nations is largely a medical procedure. Doctors and other medical personnel work to ensure the safety of the newborn as well as the safety and comfort of the mother. They have at their command techniques and procedures to induce labor, to accelerate it, even to stop it if necessary. They can administer drugs to lessen the mother's pain, perform blood transfusions on the infant, or deliver through cesarean section.

Elsewhere, and in earlier times, birth was a less sophisticated process. It occurred in birthing huts, in fields, and in forests. Sometimes it was a solitary experience; sometimes there were midwives, healers, or other attendants. We know too that it was often a tragic experience — infant mortality was high and

Figure 4.5

Declining maternal
mortality rates from
delivery and compli-
cations of pregnancy
and childbirth, 1960
to 1987.

Source: U.S. Bureau of the
Census (1990), p. 77.

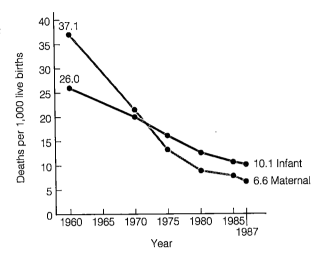

the death of the mother too was not uncommon. A century ago, more than 100 of every 1,000 infants died; that number has now been reduced by almost 90 percent (U.S. Dept. of Health and Human Services, 1989). The decline in infant mortality rates is due not only to medical advances, but also to improved sanitation and a consequent reduction in maternal and infant infections. Through the Middle Ages, high risk of death during childbirth (or of subsequent infections) made childbearing a relatively dangerous undertaking. Even as recently as 1960, of every 100,000 women giving birth in the United States, an average of 37 died (75 percent of these were nonwhites). By 1987, maternal mortality rates had been cut by more than 80 percent (still twice as high for black as for white mothers). During the same period, infant and fetal death rates were more than halved (see Figure 4.5).

The history of **obstetrics** (the medical art and science of assisting pregnant women) is a long struggle between the traditions and beliefs of generations of midwives and the inevitable progress of science. It begins with Hippocrates' attempt to separate labor from religious rites, progressing through the arduous efforts of men like Semmelweis to promote cleanliness in hospitals to combat the dreaded killer of women after childbirth, puerperal fever (dramatized in the novel *The Cry and the Covenant* by Morton Thompson), finally leading to modern hospital techniques and procedures. Through the early 1970s, however, North America saw a return to more "natural" forms of childbirth and a corresponding increase in midwifery and "birthing stations." There are indications that this trend has now reversed again — due in part to a tremendous increase

Table 4.4
A Résumé of the Development of Obstetrics

400 B.C.	Hippocrates attempts to separate labor from religious rites.
A.D. 200	Soranus teaches obstetrics to Roman midwives.
1513	The printing press is invented; the first book on obstetrics is published (Roesslin).
1560	Paré rediscovers and describes version and breech extraction.
1647	Chamberlen invents obstetric forceps.
1739	Smellie improves the teaching of obstetrics.
1807	Ergot is introduced in obstetrics.
1847	Holmes and Semmelweis fight puerperal fever.
1860	Pasteur discovers streptococci in puerperal fever.
1867	Lister describes asepsis (sterile procedures).
1900	The development of prenatal care and of obstetrics in nursing institutions and in schools of medicine advances rapidly.
1950	The use of drugs in "assisted" childbirth becomes widespread.
1970	"Natural" childbirth is newly popular. Midwifery flourishes and birthing stations spring up.
1980s–1990s	The pendulum swings again toward hospital births.

Source: Adapted in part from Bookmiller and Bowen (1967), pp. 17–18.

in malpractice suits (and corresponding increases in insurance premiums). (See Table 4.4 for a brief sketch of the history of obstetrics.)

Surprisingly, what causes the childbirth process to begin remains almost as much of a mystery today as it has always been. Hippocrates, writing more than 400 years B.C., thought he knew. The child starts the whole process, he informed his readers. When the fetus has grown too big, there simply isn't enough nourishment available, so it becomes agitated, it kicks around and moves its arms, and it ruptures the membranes that hold it in. And then it forces its way out, head first because, measured from the umbilicus, the head part is heavier than the bottom part (see Liggins, 1988).

Hippocrates was wrong, although there were many who believed his speculation right into the eighteenth century. We now know that fetuses that are dead may go through the process of labor — which would not be possible if they were responsible for initiating it.

There have been many other theories over the years; but, as Liggins (1988) concludes, we still don't have "the final chapter of the 2000-year-old search for the cause of labor" (p. 387). But although we don't know its cause, we do understand a lot about the process.

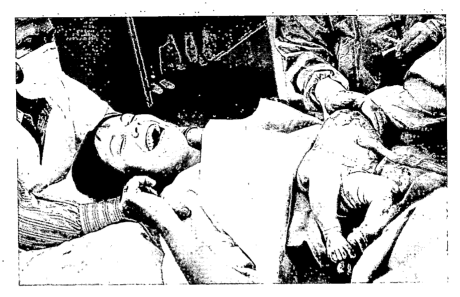

Some mothers find childbirth quite painful; however, many also find that the experience offers an intense and immediate emotional reward.

A Clinical View

Labor is the process whereby the fetus, the placenta, and other membranes are separated from the woman's body and expelled; it ordinarily occurs approximately 280 days after the beginning of the pregnant woman's last menstrual period, although it can also occur earlier than this or occasionally somewhat later. The physical status of the child has traditionally been classified according to the length of time spent in gestation and by weight. A fetus born before the twentieth week and weighing less than about 1 pound (500 grams) is termed an **abortion** (sometimes called a *miscarriage*). A fetus delivered between the twentieth and twenty-eighth week and weighing between 1 and 2 pounds (between 500 and 999 grams) is an **immature birth.** At one time, immature births invariably died; the majority still do, most of them from respiratory failure. But with modern medical procedures, an increasing number survive, some born as much as four months prematurely and weighing as little as 1½ pounds (750 grams) or less.

The birth of a baby between the twenty-ninth and the thirty-sixth weeks is called a **premature birth,** provided the child weighs between 2 and 5½ pounds (between 1,000 and 2,499 grams). Complications are more common if the child weighs less than 1,500 grams. A few decades ago, only 20 percent of premature infants (preemies) in the 2- to 5½-pound range survived. Now between 90 and 95 percent survive (Preemies' diet seen key to progress, 1988).

A **mature birth** occurs between the thirty-seventh and the forty-second week and results in an infant weighing over 5½ pounds (2,500 grams). A late delivery is called a **postmature birth.** All newborns, regardless of whether they

Table 4.5
Physical Status of Child at Birth

Classification by Gestation	Time	Average Weight
Abortion	Before 20th week	Less than 1 lb. (500 g)
Immature birth	20th–28th week	1–2 lb. (500–999 g)
Premature birth	29th–36th week	2–5½ lb. (1,000–2,499 g)
Mature birth	37th–42nd week	At least 5½ lb. (2,500 g)
Postmature birth	After 42 weeks	
Classification by Weight and Gestation		
SFD (small-for-date)	10 percent less than average for infants of same gestational age	
AFD (average-for-date)	Within 10 percent of average weight for gestational age	
LFD (large-for-date)	10 percent more than average infants of same gestational age	

are premature, are also classified as *small-for-date* (SFD) when they weigh 10 percent less than average newborns of the same gestational age; as *large-for-date* (LFD) when they weigh 10 percent more; or as *average-for-date* (AFD) (Table 4.5).

The onset of labor is usually gradual and may be described in three stages. That there are exceptions to the normal process has been substantiated by numerous fathers who were caught unawares, taxi drivers who drove too slowly, pilots who did not quite make it, and many others for whom nature would not wait. Although physicians can induce labor, as we saw, the precise natural cause of the beginning of labor remains unknown. Yet labor begins, more often than not, at the prescribed time.

The first stage of labor is the longest, lasting an average of 12 hours but varying greatly in length, depending as much on unknown individual factors as on whether the woman has had previous births. Generally, labor is longest and most difficult for the first delivery. The first stage consists of contractions that are at first of relatively low intensity and usually spaced quite far apart, becoming stronger and more frequent as labor continues. The initial contractions are described as feelings similar to having "butterflies" in one's stomach; they last only a few seconds and are relatively painless. Apparently, the "butterflies" become more painful and last considerably longer toward the end of the first stage of birth. In this first stage, the **cervix** (the opening to the uterus) dilates to allow passage of the baby from the uterus, down through the birth

Figure 4.6

This cross section shows the normal presentation and delivery of a baby.

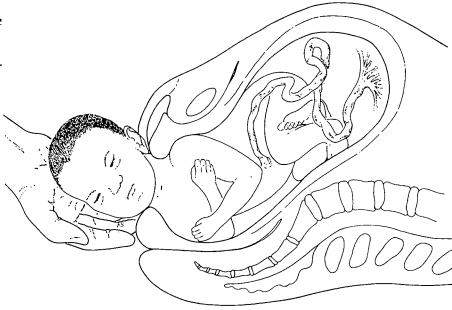

canal, and eventually into the world. Contractions are involuntary and exert a downward pressue on the fetus as well as a distending force on the cervix. If the **amniotic sac** (the sac filled with amniotic fluid in which the fetus develops) is still intact, it absorbs much of the pressure in the early stages and transmits some of the force of the contractions to the neck of the cervix. However, if the sac has ruptured or bursts in the early stages of labor, the baby's head will rest directly on the pelvic structure and cervix, serving as a sort of wedge.

The second stage of birth, **delivery,** begins when the cervix is sufficiently dilated. It starts with the baby's head emerging (in a normal delivery) at the cervical opening and terminates with the birth of the child (Figure 4.6). The second stage usually lasts no more than an hour and frequently ends in a few minutes. The fetus ordinarily presents itself head first and can usually be born without the intervention of a physician. On occasion, however, complications arise that require some sort of intervention. For example, the head of the fetus may be too large for the opening provided by the mother. In such a case the physician may make a small incision in the vaginal outlet (an **episiotomy**), which is sutured after the baby is born. Complications can also arise from abnormal presentations of the fetus: **breech** (buttocks first), **transverse** (crosswise), or a variety of other possible positions. Some of these can be corrected before birth by turning the fetus manually in the uterus (**version**). Sometimes the fetus is delivered just as it presents itself.

Toward the end of the delivery stage, the attending physician or nurse severs the neonate's umbilical cord; places silver nitrate or penicillin drops in its eyes to guard against gonococcal infection; and assures that its breathing, muscle tone, coloration, and reflexive activity are normal. Following this, the physician assists in the third and final stage of birth and evaluates the condition of the **neonate,** or newborn, perhaps by means of the Apgar scale (discussed next).

In this third stage, the **afterbirth** — the placenta and other membranes — is expelled. This process usually takes less than 5 minutes and seldom more than 15. The physician examines the afterbirth carefully to ensure that all of it has been expelled. If it is incomplete, surgical procedures (frequently **dilation and curetage,** or **D&C** — a scraping of the uterus) may be employed to remove remaining portions. At the end of the third stage of labor, the uterus should contract and remain contracted. It is sometimes necessary to massage the abdominal area or administer various drugs to stimulate contraction and to guard against the danger of postpartum (after-birth) hemorrhage.

In an increasing number of instances, medical intervention bypasses these three stages of birth through a cesarean delivery — almost one quarter of all births in the United States (Placek, 1986). In such cases, birth is accomplished by making an incision in the mother's abdomen and uterus and removing the baby. Cesarean deliveries may be undertaken when the baby's head is too large for the mother's pelvic opening (or the pelvic opening is abnormally small), when there is some immediate danger to the fetus or mother that requires delivery of the child, or when the normal process of birth cannot be accomplished for some other reason. Lieberman (1987) suggests that cesareans are most often indicated when the mother's labor fails to progress, if previous cesareans have been performed, when the fetus is in a breech presentation, or if the physician detects signs of fetal distress. Cesarean deliveries are ordinarily undertaken before the onset of labor, but can also be performed after labor has begun.

Cesarean deliveries have clearly saved the lives of many mothers and infants, and alleviated much pain and suffering, but the rapid increase in the proportion of cesarean births relative to nonsurgical births has been a source of some concern (deRegt et al., 1986). Although much of this increase clearly results from dramatic improvements in the physician's ability to monitor the fetus prior to birth and during labor, critics fear that not all cesarean deliveries are necessary. When they are unnecessary, they present potential disadvantages and dangers not part of a routine delivery: greater medical risk to the mother, a longer recovery period, and higher risk of infection. In addition, the use of anesthetics during surgery may depress neonatal responsiveness and may be related to the occasional respiratory problems of the infant delivered by cesarean. This problem may be compounded by the fact that infants delivered surgically do not normally experience the same surge of adrenaline-related hormones that is common among infants during normal labor. Among other

Figure 4.7

Cesarean deliveries in the United States, 1970 to 1987. (Numbers in parentheses are the rate of cesarean deliveries per 1,000 total deliveries.)

Source: Adapted from U.S. Bureau of the Census (1990), p. 66.

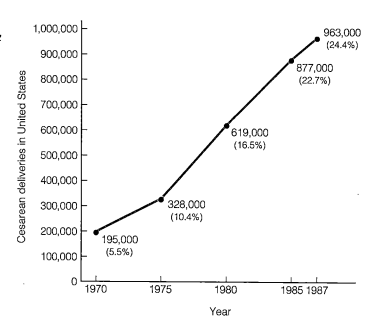

things, these hormones stimulate respiratory and cardiac activity (Lagercrantz & Slotkin; 1986) (Figure 4.7).

Lieberman (1987) reports that a number of hospitals have succeeded in dramatically reducing rates of cesarean deliveries without any increase in fetal or maternal problems. This is accomplished largely by reviewing the need for a cesarean delivery in cases where one might simply have been done routinely, as sometimes happens for breech births, twin births, or patients who have had previous cesareans.

Neonatal Scales

In almost all North American hospitals it has become routine to evaluate the condition of a newborn by means of the Apgar scale. The scale, shown in Table 4.6, is almost self-explanatory. Infants receive scores according to whether each of the appropriate signs is present. Maximum score is 10; average score is usually 7 or better; a score of 4 or less indicates that the neonate must be given special care immediately. The Apgar evaluation is administered at least twice – at 1 minute after birth and at 5 minutes after birth (and sometimes at 10 minutes after birth). Five- and 10-minute scores are often higher than 1-minute scores.

A second important scale for assessing the condition of a newborn infant is the Brazelton Neonatal Behavioral Assessment Scale (Brazelton, 1973). Like the Apgar scale, it may be used to detect problems immediately after birth. In addition, it provides useful indicators of central nervous system maturity as

Table 4.6
The Apgar Scale

Score	Heartrate	Respiratory Effort	Muscle Tone	Color	Reflex Irritability
0	Absent	Absent	Flaccid, limp	Blue, pale	No response
1	Slow (less than 100)	Irregular, slow	Weak, inactive	Body pink, extremities blue	Grimace
2	Rapid (over 100)	Good, crying	Strong, active	Entirely pink	Coughing, sneezing, crying

well as of social behavior. The Brazelton scale looks at a total of 26 specific behaviors including reaction to light, to cuddling, to voices, and to a pinprick; it also looks at the strength of various reflexes. The scale is particularly useful in identifying infants who might be prone to later psychological problems (Als et al., 1979). For example, parents of infants who are less responsive to cuddling and to other social stimulation might be alerted to this from the very beginning and might be able to compensate by providing the infant with more loving contact than might otherwise have been the case.

The Mother's Experience:
Prepared Childbirth

The preceding discussion of the delivery of a human child is admittedly clinical and perhaps somewhat like the cold, antiseptic hospitals in which most North American babies are born; it fails to uncover and transmit the magic of the process. We can recapture some of the mystery, however, by looking more closely at the mother's experience of childbirth. In preparation for this discussion, I spoke with several women whose experience qualified them to make subjective comments more valid than those my imagination might supply.

"What's it like, having a baby?" I asked politely.

"It's a piece of cake," my first expert assured me in her characteristic, cliché-ridden way. "It's as easy as rolling off a log."

"It hurts like #@*!!" my second expert insisted, in her typically profane manner. "It's a hell of a big log!"

Combining these impressions, an absolutely clear picture of the situation emerges.

The inexperienced mother sometimes approaches birth with some degree of apprehension; there is often some pain associated with childbirth. However, advocates of **natural childbirth** (also called *prepared childbirth*) claim that through a regimen of prenatal exercises and adequate psychological preparation, many women experience relatively painless childbirths.

Natural childbirth, a phrase coined by a British physician, Grantly Dick-Read (1972), refers to the process of having a child without anesthetics. The Dick-Read process recommends physical exercises, relaxation exercises, and psychological preparation for the arrival of the child, all directed toward delivery in which painkillers are unnecessary. Natural childbirth is based on the assumption that alleviating the fear of pain, together with training in relaxation, will result in less pain. Dick-Read's hypothesis has proved sound.

Two popular methods of prepared childbirth are the Lamaze and the Leboyer techniques. The Lamaze (1972) method teaches expectant mothers a variety of breathing and relaxation exercises. These are practiced repeatedly, often with the assistance of the father, until they become so habitual that they will be employed almost "naturally" during the actual process of birth.

The Leboyer method is concerned more with the delivery of the infant than with advance preparation of the mother. Leboyer (1975) advocates delivering the baby in a softly lit room, immersing the infant almost immediately in a lukewarm bath, often for a relatively long time, and then placing the baby directly on the mother's abdomen. These procedures are designed to ease the infant's transition from the womb to the world; thus the need for soft lights that do not contrast as harshly with the darkness of the womb as does conventional delivery-room lighting, and for a lukewarm bath to approximate the feeling of amniotic fluid. Leboyer claims that his procedures eliminate much of the shock of birth and result in better-adjusted individuals. Critics suggest that birth in dimly lit surroundings might contribute to the physician's failing to notice important signs of distress or injury and that the dangers of infection are greater under these circumstances than they are when more conventional hospital practices are employed.

Not only are many mothers choosing to have their babies by natural means but many are also deciding where birth will occur. For some, home is that choice; for others, hospital *birthing rooms* — a homier and more comfortable alternative than a conventional operating or delivery room — or hospital family suites where father and other siblings can actually stay. There is also some use of midwives in North America (Sagov et al., 1984), a practice that is more common in some European countries. Traditionally, in countries such as Britain, the majority of births were attended to by midwives rather than by physicians. However, with the medicalization of birth, the use of midwives has declined and their role has changed. An increasing number of births are attended to by physicians; and where midwives are used, they are often part of a medical team. Their role on that team has also declined dramatically in importance (Robinson, 1989). In many cases, midwives are used primarily as receptionists or to do routine tasks like weighing pregnant women and taking urine samples.

Although most North American births still occur in hospitals, length of hospitalization is considerably shorter than it once was (often only a matter of hours). Pearse (1982) reports that relative rates of in-hospital versus out-of-hospital births remained constant through the late 1970s.

For one mother, childbirth may be quite painful. For another mother, child-birth may be a slightly painful, but intensely rewarding and satisfying experience. Although the amount of pain can be controlled to some extent with anesthetics, the intensity of the immediate emotional reward will also be dulled by the drugs. In addition, sedatives employed may affect the infant. Children delivered without sedatives are frequently more alert, more responsive to the environment, and better able to cope with immediate environmental demands (Brackbill, 1979). In short, they may have a slight initial advantage, the long-range implications of which are unclear.

The Child's Experience

How do children, the heroes of this text, react to the process of birth? Consider the incredibly dramatic difference that birth makes. Before this moment the child has been living in a completely friendly and supportive environment. The provision of nourishment and oxygen and the elimination of waste products have been accomplished without effort. The uterus has been kept at exactly the right temperature, and the danger of bacterial infection has been relatively insignificant. In addition to the complete biological support furnished by the intrauterine environment, there have been no psychological threats. Now, at birth, the child is suddenly exposed to new physiological and perhaps psychological dangers. Once mucus is cleared from the mouth and throat, the newborn must breathe for the first time. As soon as the umbilical cord ceases to pulsate, it is unceremoniously clipped an inch or two above the abdomen and tied off with a clamp. The child is now completely alone — singularly dependent and helpless, to be sure, but no longer a parasite (biologically) on the mother.

Birth itself is not without danger for the newborn. Brain damage sometimes occurs during the birth of a child. Tremendous pressure is exerted upon the head during birth, particularly if labor is long and if the amniotic sac has been broken early, in which case the head, in a normal presentation, has been repeatedly pressed against the slowly dilating cervix. In addition, the infant has to pass through an opening so small that deformation of the head often results. (For most infants the head usually assumes a more normal appearance within a few days.)

An additional source of pressure on the child's head may be **forceps,** clamp-like instruments sometimes employed during delivery. Although the fetus can withstand considerable pressure on the head, the danger of such pressure is that it may rupture blood vessels and cause hemorrhaging. In severe cases, death may result; otherwise, there is a possibility of brain damage because cranial hemorrhage can restrict the supply of oxygen available for the brain.

The oxygen supply to the brain can be restricted in another way. The fetus is still dependent on the mother for oxygen during the birth process, obtaining this oxygen through the umbilical cord. There is a constant danger that the cord will become lodged between the child's body and the birth canal. If this happens, the flow of oxygen through the cord may be stopped (referred to as **prolapsed cord**). A shortage of oxygen to the brain is called **anoxia** and has been extensively researched in medicine. Correlation studies have long suggested that anoxia may be related to impaired neurological, psychological, and motor functioning. These findings have most often been explained in terms of brain damage that may have resulted from a temporary shortage of oxygen. Most of these studies have suffered from the difficulty of determining the actual contribution of anoxia to behaviors later observed in infants and children. Because other complications of birth may have caused the anoxia in the first place, it is hard to tell whether the complication itself or the resulting anoxia is the crucial variable.

In addition to the physiological **trauma,** or shock, that accompanies birth, there is a remote possibility of psychological trauma. Rank's (1929) theory of the trauma of birth maintains that the sudden change from a comfortable, parasitic existence to the cold and demanding world creates great anxiety for the newborn child, who is plagued forever after by a desire to return to the womb. Alleged evidence of this unconscious desire is found in the position assumed by many children and adults while sleeping or in times of stress — the characteristic curl of the fetus. However, there is no substantial evidence to support the theory of psychological birth trauma.

From the child's point of view, then, birth is an indifferent process: The infant cannot reason about it, cannot compare it with other more or less pleasant states, can do nothing deliberately to alter it, and will not even remember it.

PREMATURITY

Prematurity is defined by a short gestation period (36 weeks or less) and low birthweight (*small-for-date,* or SFD — less than 90 percent of average weight for term, usually less than 5½ pounds or 2,500 grams). It is one of the more serious possible complications of birth, affecting approximately 10 percent of all infants born in the United States. Incidence of prematurity is considerably higher in some other countries (Crowley, 1983).

Causes

We do not know the precise causes of premature delivery (Creasy, 1990). However, a number of factors are related to its occurrence. Malnutrition, which is implicated in other infant disadvantages, is one factor; drugs may also be involved. And, not surprisingly, social class, poverty, and race are also related to incidence of prematurity (Creasy, 1988). Note, however, that such factors as social class and race have no inherent explanatory value. Certainly, neither causes prematurity any more than they cause the environmental conditions of poverty, ill health, and lower social and economic opportunity with which they are often associated. But it is likely that such associated factors as poorer diet and poorer medical attention are directly related to prematurity. Hence the relationship between prematurity and social class (Figure 4.8).

Numerous studies have also implicated cigarette smoking with prematurity. In some studies, rate of prematurity among smoking mothers is almost twice as high as would normally be expected, with frequency of premature births increasing with amount smoked (see Bolton, 1983). Other related factors include toxemia and various other illnesses in the mother while she is pregnant. In addition, infants from multiple births are much more frequently premature than are infants from single births. Finally, a number of infants are preterm in the absence of any of these negative influences and in spite of excellent maternal care, nutrition, and health.

Effects

One of the most obvious possible effects of prematurity is death. Indeed, only a few decades ago the chances of death for a premature infant weighing between 4½ and 5½ pounds were approximately six times greater than for an infant weighing 6 pounds, 10 ounces or more. Now, however, the majority of premature infants weighing 4½ pounds or more (approximately 2,000 grams) survive. In fact, more than 90 percent of infants who weigh as little as 1,000 to 1,500 grams survive (Goldsmith, 1990). Most of these preterm infants spend the first two to three months of their lives in intensive care nurseries, often in incubators (also called isolettes) (Harrison, 1985). Chances of survival decrease 10 to 15 percent for each hundred grams below 1,000 (Goldsmith, 1990). However, half or more of those who weigh less than 1,250 grams suffer adverse consequences; one-third or more suffer from severe physical or mental handicaps (Allen & Jones, 1986).

Other possible effects of prematurity and/or of prolonged hospitalization following birth include lower intelligence, a higher incidence of cerebral palsy, and general developmental retardation. These effects, of course, are not found among all preterm babies, and are progressively less likely for those infants who are least premature and who weigh the most at birth. For example, in studies of premature identical twins, the heaviest of the twins tends to have higher measures of intelligence (Churchill, 1965). Among preterm infants who weigh 2,000 or more grams, subsequent complications are relatively rare.

In view of these rather alarming findings, and given the highly likely relationship between nutrition and prematurity, probably a great deal can be done for unborn children and their mothers through programs of education, nutrition, and housing. But it should also be pointed out that not all premature infants suffer noticeable disadvantages relative to their mature peers. Rawlings et al. (1971) examined 68 infants who had weighed less than 4 pounds at birth

Birthweight and Prenatal Influences

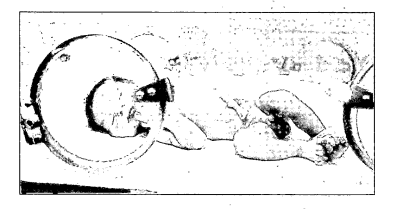

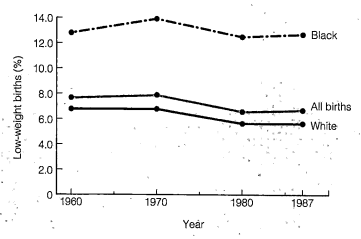

Figure 4.8   The relationship of race to low birthweight (less than or equal to 5 lb., 8 oz. for 1960 and 1970; less than 5 lb., 8 oz. for 1980 and 1987). *Source:* U.S. Bureau of the Census (1990), p. 66.

Prematurity and low birthweight are among the most serious complications of birth. Low birthweight may contribute to infant death or general developmental retardation, including lower intelligence. Factors implicated in low birthweight include smoking and use of other drugs, malnutrition, maternal age, socioeconomic status, and race. The relationship of age, social class, and race to low birthweight and prematurity is probably due primarily to other associated factors such as poorer nutrition and medical attention.

Stimulation of preterm infants, including the decoration of incubators with mobiles and stuffed animals, has proven beneficial to their emotional and physical development.

and found that 87 percent of them were apparently normal. A more pessimistic review of these findings would point out that 13 percent of them were not fully normal (in the sense that averages are considered normal) and that this number far exceeds the incidence of abnormality in the general population.

Prevention

Attempts to prevent the occurrence of preterm labor require being able to identify women who are at greater risk. This cannot be done with certainty since the precise causes of premature delivery are not usually known. However, it is possible to estimate degree of risk given knowledge of the woman's status with respect to the factors most often associated with prematurity—for example, previous preterm delivery, exposure to DES, the presence of more than one fetus, smoking, and uterine anomalies (see Table 4.7). It is also possible to monitor uterine activity in the home and sometimes to detect an increase in activity prior to the onset of preterm labor.

There are a number of different approaches to preventing preterm labor, including bed rest, avoiding sexual intercourse, the use of antibiotics and other drugs, and suturing the cervix. None of these has been clearly proven to be effective, although there is some evidence that each might sometimes be helpful (Goldsmith, 1990).

Table 4.7

Factors Associated with Higher Risk of Preterm Labor

Major Factors	Minor Factors
Multiple gestation	Febrile (fever) illness
DES exposure	Bleeding after 12 weeks
Uterine anomaly	More than 10 cigarettes per day
Cervix dilated more than 1 cm at 32 weeks	One previous second-trimester abortion
Two previous second-trimester abortions	More than two previous first-trimester abortions
Previous preterm delivery	
Previous labor during preterm, with term delivery	
Abdominal surgery during pregnancy	
Uterine irritability	

Source: Based on R. H. Holbrook, Jr., R. K. Laros, Jr., & R. K. Creasy (1988). Evaluation of a risk-scoring system for prediction of preterm labor. *American Journal of Perinatology,* pp. 6, 62. Reprinted by permission of Thieme Medical Publishers, Inc.

Care of Preterm Infants

Prematurity is not necessarily and inevitably linked with physical, psychological, or neurological inferiority. With adequate care, many premature infants fare as well as full-term infants. What are the dimensions of that care? First they include advances in medical knowledge and technology. Ventilators, for example, make possible the survival of infants whose hearts and lungs are not sufficiently developed to work on their own; so does intravenous feeding with what is termed *total parenteral nutrition* (TPN). The contents of this nutrition are especially important because they substitute for nutrients that the infant would ordinarily have received as a fetus. Certain fatty acids appear to be importantly involved in brain growth and neuron development during the last trimester of pregnancy — roughly the period of intrauterine growth that a 27-week preterm infant would miss (Preemies' diet seen key to progress, 1988). Accordingly, the premature infant's nutrition has to include these nutrients at the appropriate time and in the appropriate form.

In addition to important medical advances in the care of premature infants, a tremendous amount of research in the last 20 years has looked at the possibility that at least some of the adverse psychological consequences of prematurity might be due to the lack of stimulation the preterm infant receives in an intensive care nursery — or, perhaps more accurately, the inappropriateness of the stimulation. Scarr-Salapatek and Williams (1973) compared two groups of premature infants. The first of these was treated in the conventional manner; that is, the infants were kept in incubators with a minimum of human contact. This practice is premised on the belief that premature infants are particularly susceptible to infection and highly vulnerable once infected. The second group was also kept in incubators, but these infants were taken from the incubators for feeding and were talked to and fondled by their nurses. In addition, their incubators were decorated with mobiles, and in follow-up visits after they had left the hospital, they were provided with numerous toys at home. It is highly significant that by the age of 1 these infants were heavier than infants in the control group and scored higher on developmental scales.

Harrison (1985) summarizes 24 studies that have looked at various forms of "supplemental" stimulation for preterm infants. Some investigated the effects of tactile stimulation (stroking; holding); others looked at auditory stimulation (taped recordings of a mother's voice, for example), vestibulary stimulation (oscillating hammock or waterbed), gustatory stimulation (pacifier), or, as in the Scarr-Salapatek and Williams study described earlier, multimodal stimulation. The studies support the conclusion that additional stimulation of preterm infants is beneficial to their development. Positive effects include greater weight gains, shorter hospital stays, greater responsiveness, and higher developmental scores on various measures. The evidence is clear that the traditional hands-off treatment once given most premature infants is not the best of all possible worlds for them.

A REASSURING NOTE

It is often very disturbing for nonmedical people to consult medical journals and textbooks in search of explanations for their various complaints. Inevitably, they discover that they have all the symptoms for some vicious infection or exotic disease. So if you happen to be pregnant at this moment or are contemplating pregnancy, or are otherwise involved in the business, you might find yourself a little apprehensive. I draw this to your attention only to emphasize that it really isn't that bad (pregnancy, that is). The intrauterine world of the unborn infant is less threatening and less dangerous than our world. Also, it is perhaps reassuring that nature often provides for spontaneous abortions when the embryo or the fetus would have been grossly abnormal. In most cases the fetus comes to term; when it reaches this stage the probability that the child will be normal and healthy far outweighs the likelihood that it will suffer any of the defects or abnormalities described in this chapter.

MAIN POINTS

1. Early *probable* symptoms of pregnancy are uncertain, although in combination they provide relatively reliable information. Simple chemical urine tests can be performed very early in pregnancy — at home or by the physician — to detect human chorionic gonadotropin (HCG), a positive sign of pregnancy.

2. The gestation period for humans is 9 calendar months, which is more commonly computed as 10 lunar months (40 weeks or 280 days), beginning from the onset of the last menses. Prenatal physiological development occurs in three stages: the period of the fertilized ovum (1 week), the embryo (2 to 8 weeks), and the fetus (8 to 40 weeks).

3. The fertilized ovum moves from the Fallopian tubes to the uterus and embeds itself in the wall of the uterus approximately seven days after fertilization. From week 1 to week 8, the embryo develops from an almost microscopic speck to a little organism approximately 1½ to 2 inches long and weighing close to ⅔ of an ounce. By the end of the eighth week all the organs of the infant are present. No further structural changes will take place.

4. Fetal growth involves primarily physical changes in size and weight and neurological development. The fetus's chances of survival are low if born before the seventh lunar month. At full term, the average size of a newborn infant is approximately 20 inches (50 cm) and 7.5 pounds (3.4 kg).

5. A wide range of factors can affect the development of the fetus. External influences that cause malformations and physical defects are labeled *teratogens*. Effects of a single teratogen can vary widely from one fetus to another depending on genetic factors, the presence of other negative or positive influences, and their timing.

6. There is very tentative evidence that maternal emotions increase fetal activity and that maternal anxiety is sometimes reflected in more irritable infants.

7. A wide range of prescription drugs can act as teratogens. A number of these are no longer used — for example, thalidomide, which is associated with underdeveloped or absent limbs, and DES, which appears to be linked with higher incidence of cervical cancer among female offspring.

8. Among chemicals that can have detrimental effects on the fetus are mercury, which is associated with Minimata disease, symptoms of which include physical deformities and mental retardation of varying severity; a range of hydrocarbon compounds, including dioxin and PCB, which are linked with higher incidence of spontaneous abortions and physical deformities; and lead, whose effects on fetal development are still unclear, but which can lead to serious physical and mental problems in children and adults.

9. Nicotine is known to increase fetal heartrate and activity. Perhaps more important, it is associated with significant retardation of fetal growth, a significantly higher incidence of premature births, smaller birthweights, higher probability of placental problems, a higher risk of miscarriage and fetal death, and a higher incidence of childhood respiratory diseases. The effects of caffeine are unclear.

10. Alcohol consumption may lead to *fetal alcohol syndrome* (FAS), symptoms of which include mental retardation, retarded physical growth, and characteristic cranial and facial malformations (low forehead, widely spaced eyes, short nose, long upper lip, absence of a marked infranasal depression). Depending on the amount and timing of consumption, FAS may be full blown or only a few of the symptoms may be evident.

11. Infants born to narcotic addicts are themselves usually addicted at birth (neo-natal abstinence syndrome); in severe cases, they may die. Stimulants such as marijuana may be associated with slower maturation of the nervous system. Infants born to cocaine users manifest more startle reactions and tremors and are more likely to suffer from attentional and behavioral problems later in childhood.

12. Various maternal diseases and infections can have serious effects on the fetus. Diseases such as rubella, syphilis, gonorrhea, and diabetes can lead to mental deficiency, blindness, deafness, or fetal death. Herpes can be transmitted to the fetus during birth and can lead to serious complications including death (it can be prevented through a cesarean delivery). AIDS can also be transmitted from mother to fetus.

13. There is a higher probability of some chromosomal defects for older mothers (Trisomy 21; Trisomy 13 and 18; Klinefelter's syndrome; fragile X syndrome). Many of these defects can be detected early in pregnancy through chorion biopsy, amniocentesis, fetoscopy, or ultrasound.

14. Numbers of births to teenage mothers are relatively high in North America (some 16 percent of all births). Infants born to teenage mothers are at higher risk of physical, emotional, and intellectual disadvantage (more miscarriages, premature births, and stillbirths, and more emotional and physical abuse among those who survive). However, these outcomes are associated more with the social and medical circumstances of teenage parenthood than with the mother's age.

15. Maternal nutrition is closely implicated in the health and well-being of the fetus. Adequate nutrition may be especially critical to brain development during the spurt in brain growth in the later stages of fetal development (and in the first months and years of life). Social class, *because of related medical, nutritional, and drug use factors*, is associated with a higher incidence of prematurity and other complications.

16. In the absence of medical intervention, mothers who are negative for the Rh blood factor, where the father is Rh(D)-positive, would be at risk of giving birth to infants suffering from *fetal erythroblastosis*. This condition is routinely avoided in modern hospitals through injections of the drug Rhogam.

17. Birth ordinarily occurs 266 days after conception; the mature newborn weighs approximately 2,500 grams. Early deliveries are classified as *premature* (before the thirty-seventh week). Newborns are also classified as *small-for-date* (SFD) if they weigh 10 percent less than average newborns of the same gestational age.

18. Birth can be considered in three stages: *labor*, which involves dilation of the cervix in preparation for delivery (lasting an average of 9 to 12 hours); the actual *delivery* (usually accomplished within an hour); and the *afterbirth* — expulsion of the placenta and other membranes (soon after birth and lasting several minutes).

19. Newborns are routinely evaluated within 60 seconds of birth, as well as at 5 and occasionally 10 minutes, by means of the Apgar scale — a scale that looks

at their appearance (color), pulse (heartrate), grimace (reflex irritability), activity (muscle tone), and respiration (respiratory effort). *Note the mnemonic or memory device.*

20. Natural, or prepared, childbirth, pioneered by Dick-Read, refers to the preparation for and process of having a child without anesthetics. Two popular methods are the Lamaze and Leboyer techniques.

21. Birth poses some dangers for the neonate: cerebral hemorrhage resulting from extreme pressures in the uterus, in the birth canal, or from the forceps; and prolapse of the umbilical cord and anoxia (shortage of oxygen).

22. Prematurity appears to be linked to social class variables such as diet and poorer medical attention, the age of the mother, smoking, drugs, multiple gestations, and previous history of preterm deliveries. Its most apparent effects are the greater possibility of death, physical defects, hyperkinesis, and impaired mental functioning. Medical advances have made it possible for over 90 percent of premature infants weighing as little as 1,000 to 1,500 grams (2.2 to 3.3 pounds) to survive.

23. The severity of possible medical consequences of prematurity has been significantly ameliorated by medical advances — use of ventilators; carefully designed intravenous nutrition with TPN (*total parenteral nutrition*). In addition, the psychological consequences of prematurity can be offset through increased tactile (stroking, fondling), auditory, vestibulatory (rocking), gustatory (pacifier), or multimodal stimulation.

Further Readings

A good source for more detailed information on prenatal development and birth is:

Pritchard, J., & MacDonald, P. (1984). *Williams' obstetrics* (17th ed.). New York: Appleton-Century-Crofts.

The effects of maternal addiction on the fetus are explored in the following collection of articles:

Chasnoff, I. J. (Ed.). (1986). *Drug use in pregnancy: Mother and child.* Boston: MTP Press.

The clinical effects of alcohol on the fetus are examined in detail in:

Abel, E. L. (1984). *Fetal alcohol syndrome and fetal alcohol effects.* New York: Plenum.

The following is a massive collection of detailed medical information on the factors that influence prenatal development (including drugs, diseases, and genes) and on the various medical interventions that are possible:

Eden, R. D., Boehm, F. H., & Haire, M. (Eds.). (1990). *Assessment and care of the fetus: Physiological, clinical, and medicolegal principles.* Norwalk, Conn.: Appleton & Lange.

AIDS is a topic of considerable current interest — and misinformation. Long's book provides clear answers for 100 of the most common questions asked about AIDS. Anderson's little booklet deals most specifically with AIDS among children:

Long, R. E. (1987). *AIDS* (The Reference Shelf, Vol. 59, No. 3). New York: H. W. Wilson.

Anderson, G. R. (1986). *Children and AIDS: The challenge for child welfare.* Washington, D.C.: Child Welfare League of America, Inc.

Bellow's novel is an interesting change of pace from the usual fare of academic references. True, it's fiction. But it's also a chilling account of the potential dangers of lead in our environment. Schwarz and Yaffe's collection looks at the effects of other chemicals and drugs on fetal development and on infants.

Bellow, S. (1982). *The dean's December.* New York: Harper & Row.

Schwarz, R. H., & Yaffe, S. J. (Eds.). (1980). *Drug and chemical risks to the fetus and newborn.* New York: Alan R. Liss.

Those interested in alternative approaches to childbirth are referred to the originators of some of the more popular approaches:

Dick-Read, G. (1972). *Childbirth without fear: The original approach to natural childbirth* (4th ed.). (H. Wessel & H. F. Ellis, Eds.). New York: Harper & Row.

Lamaze, F. (1972). *Painless childbirth: The Lamaze method.* New York: Pocket Books.

Leboyer, F. (1975). *Birth without violence.* New York: Random House.

The following is a highly practical and very informative book for prospective parents that not only describes what to expect in normal and higher-risk pregnancies, but also explores the various choices available to parents:

Lieberman, A. B. (1987). *Giving birth.* New York: St. Martin's Press.

His lordship says he will turn it over in what he is

pleased to call his mind.

Richard Bethell (Baron Westbury), *Life of Westbury*

Infancy

What do you suppose *does* go on in his lordship's mind? Do you think that in the very beginning, our small lord pauses to ponder problems of quantum physics or Boolean algebra?

Not likely. You see, the world is an amazing and bewildering place for his lordship because he is totally unfamiliar with it. Much of the business of growing up is a matter

of becoming familiar with things. That is what occupies most of the first two years of life: becoming familiar with breasts and bottles, with cups and cats, with doors and dragons; learning when to cry, when to be afraid, when to laugh and smile; learning about mothers and fathers—and about strangers too; and learning to speak. This is what the next two chapters are about.

While reading these chapters, keep in mind that his little lordship is a real person; he is far more than just a compilation of science's hard-earned facts and speculations. Try to remember — or at least imagine — some of the feelings of being an infant. Is the world bewildering and frightening? Exciting and marvelous? Astonishing and delightful?

"There's no use trying," she said: "One can't believe impossible things."
"I dare say you haven't had much practice," said the Queen.
"When I was your age, I always did it for half an hour a day.
Why sometimes I've believed as many as six impossible things before breakfast."
Lewis Carroll, *Alice Through the Looking-Glass*

Physical and Cognitive Development

I have been advised that because you are bright and sophisticated, these chapter opening vignettes should be more cosmopolitan and worldly. They should speak not only of my rural childhood, but also of children in urban places with television sets and computers and sophisticated grandparents who drive expensive imports and struggle with post-Yuppie tendencies.

Good advice. Before we're done, I will have told you all about these wonderful things. Let me start right now, with my pre-Yuppie grandmother who, I swear it, owned an imported milking stool. (It had been imported all the way from Berlin, New Hampshire.)

One early spring day, shortly after my initiation into the mysteries of coupling dragonflies, my grandmother handed me that stool and asked me please would I go into the barn and start milking the cows; she would join me later, but first she had a pie to get into the oven.

"Yessir," I said, meaning no disrespect, neither my grandmother nor I yet being aware of the sexism of my simple remark. "Yessir, grammaw!"

I didn't know milking a cow from programming a computer. Except that I had seen it done — seen how my grandmother slid her stool next to the cow, squatting and squeezing the teats, two at a time, rhythmically, the milk spurting thin and hot into the pail between her knees, squeesh, squeesh, squeeesh-squeeesh, squeeeesh.

I slipped into the musty warmth of the barn, squinting till my eyes adjusted to the light. There were cracks between the wall boards; sunbeams streaked the semi-darkness. Little dust motes danced in the golden shafts; I imagined they might be fairies. A cow mooed, turned, looked at me with her cow eyes. Can cows see fairies?

"I'm gonna milk you, girl," I said. It's okay to speak to cows and horses and dogs and cats, though, for some strange reason, it's not okay to talk to oneself.

I slipped my imported milking stool next to Rosie, slid the milk pail between my knees, grabbed a pair of warm teats, one in each hand, and squeezed.

Nothing much happened. I squeezed again, pulled, tugged. A few drops of milk oozed slowly from one of the teats.

Milking a cow is not as simple as one might think. As I contemplated the problem, resting my head against the cow's flank, I was distracted by the sound of the cow in the next stall moving around. I leaned to my left (one *always* milks a cow on her right side) and peered into the neighboring stall. And several more pieces of the dragonfly puzzle fell — Bang! — into place.

The cow next door was in the process of delivering a calf. It hung there, half in, half out, wrapped in damp membranes, dripping amniotic matter.

I had been misled. I had no idea newborns were so gross.

WHAT IS A NEONATE?

The neonate (newborn infant) is not always very attractive. Its features are often wrinkled and distorted from passage through the birth canal. Its skull may be flattened, lengthened, or otherwise deformed. It is usually smeared with remnants of amniotic fluid, and mucus oozes from its mouth and nose. Its eyes are screwed shut and its breathing rasps and wheezes, as it utters its thin cries.

From the very moment of birth — perhaps even well before then — the newborn *means* something (Kegan, 1982). Helpless though neonates might be, they are the center of their little worlds, surrounded by people for whom they have very special meaning. As they grow and develop, their worlds expand and, for most, there will seldom again be periods when so many are concerned with their welfare — so many to whom they mean so much. Not surprisingly, much of social development throughout life is directed toward being meaningful — toward meaning something to others.

Do others also *mean* something to the neonate? Does the world have meaning? Does the newborn have primitive ideas, budding little concepts, some sort of pattern or blueprint that will govern its intellectual growth? What does it feel? Is there joy in the beating of its little heart? Is it capable of ecstasy? Does sadness drive its cries? Does purpose inform its movements?

What kind of creature is this little organism? These are not easy questions to answer. In fact, it will take us the remainder of this chapter and most of the next to describe the answers that science — and sometimes good sense — have begun to provide.

A Skeleton of an Answer

Let us start first with the bare bones of an answer. Imagine for a moment that you have been asked to design an organism that begins life in as primitive a condition as a neonate — that is, with as little physical and motor control as the infant has and with as unsophisticated an understanding of self and world. But you must design this organism in such a way that within two years it will be able to walk, talk, recognize its grandmother, ride a tricycle, laugh and sing. . . .

So what do you do? You program it for *change*. Because you're clever, you pay particular attention to change in three areas: biological, intellectual, and social. Biologically, you design a creature that is capable of converting raw proteins and carbohydrates, minerals and vitamins, and other foodstuffs into nutrients. And you program the effects of these nutrients into a sequence of biological growth and maturation that will, among other things, eventually lead to the organism's control of its movements. And because you are something of a poet, you put some grace, some exuberance, into those young movements.

Intellectually, you program your little organism to process an absolutely extraordinary amount of information (see Flavell, 1985). You program it in such a way that it will process this information regardless of whether it receives any immediate and tangible reward (such as food or a caress) for doing so. You provide it with an information-processing system that is automatically geared toward focusing on the most informative aspects of the environment. Accordingly, your little organism reacts strongly to surprise and novelty; it searches out the unexpected; it develops ways of organizing the information it gathers; it is programmed to invent concepts and ideas.

Socially, you program into the organism a wide range of emotions. These serve as motives for many of the things it does. And you arrange for complex ties between these emotions and the organism's relationships with other organisms of the same species (and sometimes with members of other species such as canines and felines and equines and bovines and porcines and crows). Socially, the organism is programmed to be gregarious, programmed to love, programmed eventually to try to spread its seed and contribute to the survival of its species — perhaps programmed, as well, to defend things that might be related to its survival and to that of others of its kind.

And a crowning achievement in your design of this creature is that you pretune it to attend to speech; you wire it so that it is capable of inventing language.

The bare bones of our answer to the question What is a neonate? may be summarized in this way:

> A newborn is a primitive, self-driven little sensing machine designed to mature and grow physically in a predetermined sequence and at a relatively predictable pace, programmed as an extraordinarily capable information-processing system, endowed with powerful gregarious tendencies and strong emotions to drive many of its actions, and pretuned to speech and to the development of language.

In this chapter we look at the newborn's growth and behavior, at motor development, and at perceptual and cognitive development. In the next chapter, we look at social relationships and attachments during infancy and at infant personality. These two chapters cover *infancy*, a period that lasts from the first few weeks of life to the age of 2.

CARE AND FEEDING OF THE NEONATE

Sadly, *Of Children* is not a childcare handbook. Still it begins this chapter with a look at three topics directly pertinent to the care of infants — and directly pertinent to their physical and psychological well-being: feeding; health and growth; and Sudden Infant Death Syndrome (SIDS).

Breast Versus Bottle

Kessen (1965) introduces a fascinating book on the history of child study with the statement that "the most persistent single note in the history of the child is the reluctance of mothers to suckle their babies" (p. 1). For many years battles were waged on this issue. On the one side were the many physicians and philosophers who insisted that mothers should breast-feed their own infants. Their arguments were varied. Some invoked nature. Breast-feeding is natural, they reasoned. All animals do it; therefore, human mothers should too. Others argued that breast milk was best for the child simply because "it became accustomed to it in the mother's womb" (S. de St. Marthe, 1797, quoted in Kessen, 1965, p. 2). There were some, too, who reasoned that maternal qualities might somehow be transmitted through breast milk. Especially to be guarded against was the milk of foster mothers of dubious virtue and morality, for "Who then, unless he be blind, does not see that babies imbibe, along with the alien milk of the foster mother, morals different from those of their parents?" (Comenius, 1633; quoted in Kessen, 1965, p. 3). Others invoked religion and duty: "The mother's breast is an infant's birthright and suckling a sacred duty, to neglect which is prejudicial to the mother and fatal to the child" (Davis, 1817, quoted in Kessen, 1965, p. 3).

On the other side of this apparent battle were the mothers who, for one reason or another, were reluctant to breast-feed their infants. Their arguments were generally more personal and more private, and their numbers varied through history, growing through certain decades and lessening again through others.

Is there still a conflict — a breast versus bottle controversy? There probably is, although most mothers see the issue as largely a matter of personal choice. The choice is sometimes made on the basis of convenience. It is simply not convenient for many working mothers to breast-feed their infants. Or it is not convenient for women who carry their infants on their backs, or take them to the fields, to also carry bottles with them — or to lead cows or goats around behind them.

At other times, the choice is made on the basis of current fashion. For example, through much of the early part of this century, breast-feeding declined in popularity in North America so that by the early 1970s, fewer than one in four mothers breast-fed their infants. But in the past several decades, breast-feeding has again increased in popularity (Eiger & Olds, 1987).

Among science's arguments for breast-feeding are the nutritional value of breast milk and the immunities it provides the infant. Breast-feeding has increased in popularity in recent decades.

What do physicians (and philosophers?) now recommend? Pretty well what they have recommended all along: when possible, mothers should breast-feed their infants (Lieberman, 1987). But their reasons have changed over the years. They no longer appeal to notions of maternal duty or sacred infant rights; nor do they argue that morals are transmitted along with the mother's milk. Science provides these crusty battlers with new ammunition. Mother's milk, science tells us, *is* the best of foods for most newborns. As Lieberman (1987) puts it, it is "species specific" and even infant specific. It contains just about the right combination of nutrients, the right proportion of fats and calories, the almost-perfect assortment of minerals and vitamins. Furthermore, it is easier to digest than cow's milk and less likely to lead to allergic reactions. And one additional benefit is that it provides infants with a measure of immunity against infections and diseases, and especially against diarrhea — which, as we saw in Chapter 1, is one of the principal causes of infant death in the developing world (Grant, 1986). Accordingly, the World Health Organization strongly recommends advising women in developing countries to return to breast-feeding where this practice has been abandoned. In addition, they advocate discouraging the distribution of infant formula. Not only is formula sometimes mixed with unsanitary water, often leading directly to infant diarrhea, but where money is scarce, there is also often insufficient formula available. As a result, it is sometimes diluted, thereby compounding malnutrition problems.

In spite of these compelling arguments for advocating breast-feeding, it would be misleading not to emphasize that in much of the industrialized world, where sanitation and nutrition are excellent, bottle-fed infants thrive every bit as well as those who are breast-fed. In addition, it is worth noting that breast milk is affected by what the mother eats as well as by any drugs or chemicals to which she is exposed. Alcohol, nicotine, barbiturates, stimulants such as caffeine, sedatives, and prescription drugs can each have an effect on the infant. Clearly, there are circumstances under which an infant might fare much better with a cow or a goat.

Unfortunately, a cow, a goat, or even a bottle, do not provide the same kind of *contact* for the infant as might a mother or a father. And, as we will note in some detail in Chapter 6, close contact between infants and their caregivers is important for their physical and psychological well-being. Breast-feeding requires physical contact; that is another of its benefits. But bottle-feeding can also provide for much the same kind of contact. Furthermore, it makes possible contact between fathers and infants rather than simply between mothers and infants. And that, too, might have its advantages.

Infant Health and Growth

As we saw in Chapter 4, in developed nations with high levels of medical service, the status of the newborn is routinely assessed at birth by means of some scale such as the Apgar score or the Brazelton Behavior Assessment Scale. In addition, fetal growth is typically monitored throughout pregnancy. As a result, some potential problems and disorders, such as PKU or Rh(D) incompatibility, can be corrected or even prevented. Not surprisingly, most infants are born in full health. And given adequate nourishment and care, most will remain healthy.

The neonate's central nervous system is functionally immature at birth. That is, although the brain is relatively large (approximately one fourth the size of the rest of the body compared with an adult ratio of around one eighth), much of it is not functioning. Brain activity at birth is relegated largely to the brain stem — which relates to physiological functions such as breathing, sleeping, waking, and temperature control — and to sensorimotor areas. Activity in the association areas of the brain (the cortex, where most of our adult brainwave activity occurs) increases during the first months of life, becoming common by the age of 7 months (Chugani & Phelps, 1986).

Optimal brain development appears to be influenced by two important factors. One is nutrition. Protein is especially important to normal brain development, both during the prenatal period and in the first year or so of life (Lewin, 1975). The other is sensory stimulation. There is considerable evidence from animal experimentation that exposure to sights and sounds is critical for normal development of the visual and auditory areas of the brain (Hubel and Wiesel, 1970). We look at sensory development in the infant later in this chapter.

Figure 5.1

Height and weight at 50th percentile for U.S. infants, birth to 24 months.

Source: Adapted from Health Department, Milwaukee, Wisconsin; based on data by H. C. Stuart and H. V. Meredith, prepared for use in the Children's Medical Center, Boston. Used by permission of the Milwaukee Health Department.

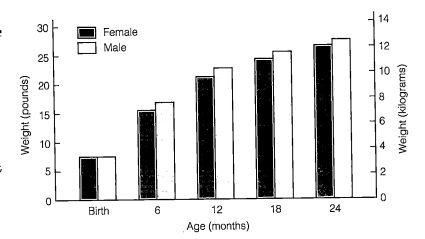

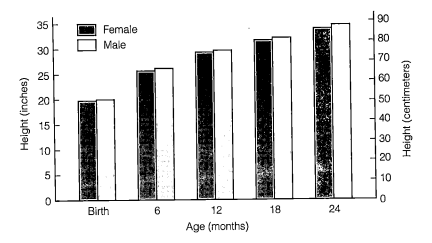

Physical growth in infancy is relatively predictable given adequate nourishment. However, because of our different genetic programs, identical nourishment will not make all infants exactly the same at all ages. Average physical development during infancy is shown in Figure 5.1. Note that these are median, or midpoint, values. In other words, 50 percent of all infants of a given age are expected to be taller than the indicated measurement, and 50 percent will be shorter. Nor is there anything intrinsically valuable or "normal" about being at or near these "norms" — or, conversely, anything negative about being some distance above or below the norms. Only when the infant is significantly above or below the average might there be cause for concern.

Unfortunately, as we saw in Chapter 1, many of the world's children *are* below the norm. Lozoff (1989) reports that 86 percent of all children are born in third world countries, and the World Health Organization estimates that well over half of these suffer from mild to severe malnutrition. Most serious is protein undernutrition, which may have long-term detrimental effects not only on physical growth and functioning, but also on cognitive functioning. Several long-term studies indicate that resulting deficiencies often cannot be entirely reversed with adequate nutrition later in life (Galler, 1984). One possible explanation for this is that undernourished infants tend to become apathetic and listless and to withdraw from environmental and social stimulation. The effects of this withdrawal are often compounded by the fact that many undernourished infants are born into families with little or no formal education and with a serious lack of stimulation in the first place. The effects of these circumstances, together with the possible contribution of protein deficiency to less than optimal development of brain cells, may be significant developmental disadvantage.

Lozoff (1989) suggests that although adequate nutrition in later life is clearly necessary if the effects of early under-nutrition are to be countered, nutrition alone is not sufficient. There is some hope that programs designed to assist mothers in providing emotional and cognitive stimulation for their children may be helpful. However, preventing this serious problem by providing adequate nutrition in the first place is clearly the most effective approach. In the long term, it may also be the most economical.

Sudden Infant Death

One of our local newspapers recently reported the death of a 3-month-old infant who had been found lifeless in his crib in the morning. The infant, a male child, had apparently been vigorous and healthy before his sudden death. Police described the death as "suspicious" and were investigating.

Several days later, the newspaper again reported on this death. Medical authorities had now determined that the infant had died of **sudden infant death syndrome** (or SIDS, sometimes popularly referred to as "crib death"), and all "suspicions" had been abandoned. In fact, however, a diagnosis of sudden infant death syndrome is really not a diagnosis at all; it is an admission that cause of death is unknown.

This mysterious cause of infant death accounts for approximately 2 deaths for every 1,000 live births. This makes SIDS the leading cause of death between the ages of 1 month and 1 year (Naeye, 1980); it accounts for somewhere between 10,000 and 20,000 deaths per year in the United States alone.

Although the cause of SIDS is still unknown, some SIDS victims share a number of characteristics. Among these, perhaps the most common is the presence of a mild upper-respiratory infection in perhaps slightly more than half of all victims (Kahn & Blum, 1982). In addition, victims are almost never in their first week of life; SIDS occurs most frequently between the ages of 1 and 4 months and very seldom after the age of 6 months. SIDS is more common among male than female infants and is somewhat more likely to occur among infants whose siblings have also been victims of the syndrome.

Medically, SIDS has often been associated with *apnea,* a sleep disorder characterized by cessation of breathing (Guilleminault et al., 1979). Apnea, which also occurs among a number of adults, seems to involve a temporary paralysis or a collapse of throat muscles and generally causes the person to awaken at once.

On occasion, parents of potential SIDS victims become aware that something is wrong and are able to revive the infant before death occurs. Some of these infants, termed "near misses for SIDS," have been used in studies that have attempted to discover the causes of SIDS or the combination of factors that might be most useful for identifying infants who are at risk for the syndrome. One such study conducted by Duffty and Bryan (1982) included 72 "near-miss" infants who had been revived by parents and referred to the investigation by their pediatricians. Another 52 infants were siblings of infants who had previously been victims of SIDS.

The procedure in this experiment was to teach parents resuscitation techniques and teach them as well the use of a monitor designed to detect cessation of breathing for a period longer than 20 seconds (in effect, an apnea detector) or a heartrate monitor that would be activated when the infant's heartrate dropped below 80 beats per minute. Parents were asked to keep track of the number of times the monitors sounded the alarms.

Among the 72 "near-miss" infants, 31 experienced prolonged apnea while being monitored at home. Fourteen of these required "vigorous stimulation" for revival on at least one occasion. Among the 52 siblings (those who had a sibling who had previously succumbed to SIDS), 16 had at least one episode, 7 of these requiring "vigorous" intervention. One died in spite of the fact that the mother, a trained nurse, had initially been able to revive the infant.

In the Duffty and Bryan study, a great many of the potential SIDS victims suffered more than one alarm episode. Indeed, some 45 percent experienced more than 10 such episodes. Also, in many of these infants, episodes occurred in clusters, perhaps three or four occurring in a period of as many days. Some 63 percent of these infants were also experiencing mild upper-respiratory infections at the time of these episodes, and a number had recently been exposed to stress through inoculations, traveling, teething, or overtiredness.

A relatively high incidence of respiratory infections among victims was also found by Kahn and Blum (1982). In addition, they report that many of these victims had been given phenothiazines (in the form of a cough syrup).

It is worth repeating that none of the factors most often associated with SIDS has been shown to cause it. Although the presence of these factors might be associated with increased risk, a large number of SIDS victims do not have colds, have never taken phenothiazines, have experienced no recent stress, and have no siblings who have been victims of SIDS. Small wonder that physicians and parents are baffled — and that law-enforcement personnel are occasionally suspicious (see Figure 5.2).

BEHAVIOR IN THE NEWBORN

One serious problem that researchers of early infancy face is the scarcity of behaviors for making observations and conclusions. Clearly, very young infants cannot be asked to interpret their own responses; nor can they be given instructions about how to behave in experimental situations. How, then, can the investigator determine whether the infant is curious, interested, bored, or confused? How do we know when and if learning has occurred?

The Orienting Response

Part of the answer lies in a group of subtle, sometimes almost imperceptible, behaviors that have played a significant role in the development of experimental child psychology. These behaviors are collectively labeled the **orienting response.** Defined simply, the orienting response is our tendency (and that of other animals and birds) to respond to new stimulation by becoming more alert — that is, by attending or *orienting* to it. It is, as Berg and Berg (1987) put it, a "mechanism that enhances the processing of information in all sensory systems" (p. 268).

In animals such as dogs and cats, the orienting response is clear. On hearing a new sound, for example, a dog will pause and its ears may perk up and turn slightly toward the sound; its attitude says, in effect, "What the heck was that?" The human infant may not respond so obviously, but distinct and measurable changes will take place; these in combination define the human orienting response. This reaction includes changes in pupil size, *cardiac* acceleration or deceleration (heartbeat), changes in the conductivity of the skin to electricity (*galvanic skin response*, or *GSR*; also termed *electrodermal response*), and other physiological changes that are observable by using sensitive instruments.

The value of the orienting response to the child psychologist is that it can be used as an indication of attention, because it occurs only in response to novel stimulation to which the individual is then attending. It can also be used as an indication of learning, because it stops when the stimulation is no longer novel. In other words, when an infant has learned a stimulus (when it has become familiar), the orienting reaction will no longer take place. In the same way, a dog might orient visibly when it first hears a cow in the distance, but will stop doing so when the sound has been identified. Such a decrease in the orienting reaction is termed *habituation*. lack of [illegible] reaction due to familiarization

An illustration of the use of the orienting reaction in infant research is provided by Moffett (1971). In this study, heartrates of infants aged 5 to 6 months

Infant Mortality in the United States

Approximately 10 of every 1,000 infants born in Canada and the United States die before the age of 1. Infant mortality in Canada is somewhat lower than in the United States: 7.9 compared with 10.06 in 1985. The difference is due largely to higher infant mortality among blacks and other races in the United States. The majority of infant mortalities occur before the end of the first month and are due to abnormalities that are congenital (present at birth; often associated with immaturity). For those who die later, the mysterious and unexplained condition labeled *sudden infant death syndrome* is the leading cause of death and is far more common among males than females.

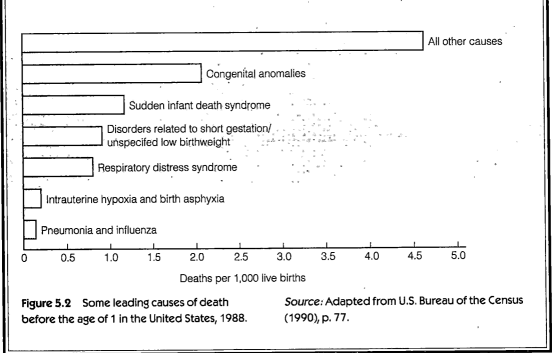

Deaths per 1,000 live births

Figure 5.2   Some leading causes of death before the age of 1 in the United States, 1988.

Source: Adapted from U.S. Bureau of the Census (1990), p. 77.

Table 5.1
Some Reflexive Behaviors of the Newborn

Reflex	Stimulus
Sucking	Object in the mouth
Head turning	Stroking the cheek or the corner of the mouth
Swallowing	Food in the mouth
Sneezing	Irritation in the nasal passages
Moro reflex	Sudden loud noise
Babinski reflex	Tickling the middle of the soles
Toe grasp	Tickling the soles just below the toes
Palmar grasp	Placing object in the infant's hand
Swimming reflex	Infant horizontal, supported by abdomen
Stepping reflex	Infant vertical, feet lightly touching flat surface

were monitored while the infants heard a repetitive taped recording of the sound *gah*. When infants first heard the sound, their heartrates slowed dramatically — clear indication of an orienting response (Clarkson & Berg, 1983). But with continued repetition of the same word (same voice, same tone, same volume), infants quickly habituated to the stimulus and heartrates rapidly returned to normal. Suddenly, with no break in inflection, tone, or volume, the taped recording changed: It said *bah* instead of *gah* Heartrates decelerated dramatically and immediately. The conclusion? Five- to 6-month-old infants are able to tell the difference between sounds as similar as *bah* and *gah*. Thus even though infants can't *tell* us whether *mother* sounds the same as *father*, whether the color blue looks like red, or whether salt tastes like sugar, we can turn to the orienting response and to other subtle behaviors for our answers.

Reflexes

Most of the behaviors in which the newborn engages are reflexive — that is, they do not require learning and can easily be elicited in the normal child by presenting the appropriate stimulus. Although neonates may engage in some activity that is not reflexive, it is probably true that they do not engage in any deliberate activity. In other words, some of the child's generalized behaviors such as squirming, waving the arms, and kicking are sometimes too complex and too spontaneous to be classified as reflexes, but they do not appear to be intentional (White, 1985).

Table 5.1 lists some of the newborn's common reflexes. Probably the best known of these is the sucking reflex, which is easily produced by placing an object in the child's mouth (a nipple is considered an appropriate stimulus). Reflexive behavior related to sucking is the **head-turning reflex** (also called the *rooting reflex*), which can be elicited by stroking the baby's cheek or the corner of the mouth. The infant will turn toward the side that is being stimulated. This reflex can be seen in breast-fed babies, who need to turn in the direction of stimulation if they are to reach the nipple. It is less important to the child who is presented with a bottle. Swallowing, hiccuping, sneezing, and vomiting can all be elicited by the appropriate nourishment-related stimulation. They are therefore referred to as the **vegetative reflexes.**

A number of common motor reflexes in the newborn have no particular survival value today, but might have been useful in humanity's early history. These include the startle reaction — throwing out the arms and feet symmetrically and then pulling them back toward the center of the body. Some have speculated that this reflex might be important for primate infants whose mothers live in trees. If they suddenly fall, but throw out their arms and legs while so doing, they might be lucky enough to catch a branch and save themselves. This response is labeled the **Moro reflex** and is sometimes useful in diagnosing brain damage because it ordinarily disappears during infancy in the normal child but is frequently present later in life among people with impaired motor function. In normal infants, these reflexes disappear with the development of the brain. As the infant develops control over motor actions, reflexes are inhibited (Hall & Oppenheim, 1987).

Other reflexes that disappear with time are the *Babinski reflex* — the typical fanning of the toes when the infant is tickled in the middle of the soles of the feet; the **palmar** (grasping) **reflex** (also called the *Darwinian reflex*), which is sometimes sufficiently pronounced that the neonate can be raised completely off a bed when grasping an adult's finger in each hand; and the *swimming* and *stepping* reflexes, which occur when one holds the baby balanced on the stomach or upright with the feet just touching a surface.

It is important to note that the infant's reflexive behaviors are not always entirely rigid, unmodifiable reactions to external conditions. True, a reflex is, by definition, a simple, unlearned, and largely uncontrollable response to a specific set of circumstances. When the nipple is in the mouth, the infant sucks. But two things are noteworthy here: First, very early, the infant begins to exercise a limited degree of control over some of the circumstances that lead to reflexive behaviors. When the stomach is full, the infant may avert its head or purse its lips tightly, thus avoiding the stimulation that might lead to the sucking response.

Second, beginning very early in life, the infant is capable of modifying some reflexive responses, including sucking. Sucking, Sameroff (1968) informs us, consists of at least two components: the squeezing pressure applied along the sides of the nipple and the negative pressure (vacuum suction) applied to the tip of the nipple.

In an intriguing study, Sameroff (1968) designed a nipple that could not only record the different pressures applied to the nipple (squeezing pressure and negative pressure at the tip), but that could also be controlled so that

Many fathers are now increasingly involved in the births and early lives of their infants, a fact that psychological research has begun to take into account.

it would deliver nutrients under specific conditions. For example, nutrients might be delivered to the infant only as a function of negative pressure at the tip (suction); or it might be delivered as a function of squeezing pressure. When Sameroff used his apparatus with 30 infants aged as young as 2 days, he discovered that even at this young age, infants were already able to adapt their sucking behavior in response to consequences. When nutrients resulted from squeezing the nipple hard between the tongue and the palate, that is exactly what the infant did; and when it resulted from suction created by negative pressure in the mouth, infants sucked rather than squeezed.

The human organism — programmed to process information, to learn, to change — begins to change very early.

MOTOR DEVELOPMENT

The helplessness of neonates results mainly from their limited ability to exercise control over motor movements. Their behavior is a far cry from that of the young of many nonhuman species, including some birds (like ducks) and most members of the deer family, who are able to follow their mothers and to make considerable efforts to obtain food almost immediately after birth. But the child does not remain physically helpless throughout infancy. One of the major acquisitions during this period is the ability to walk. Long before that the infant will have learned to move by creeping and before that will have developed the ability to sit with a little help.

Although the order in which children acquire motor skills is relatively invariable, the ages at which different abilities appear vary considerably from one child to another. It is useful nevertheless to have developmental **norms** (averages), not only as indications of sequence, but also as a standard by which to judge the child's rate of development.

A well-known description of motor development is provided by the Denver Developmental Screening Test (Figure 5.3). This test reflects the observation that children go through similar sequences in acquiring early motor skills. The sequence reflects two developmental principles mentioned in Chapter 4. The first is that development is *cephalocaudal* — it proceeds from the head toward the feet. Infants first acquire control over the head — for example, they can control eye movements and raise the head before acquiring control over the extremities. Fetal development proceeds in the same manner: The head, eyes, and internal organs develop in the embryo before the appearance of the limbs.

The second principle is that development proceeds in an inward-outward direction referred to as *proximodistal.* Development is said to be proximodistal because internal organs mature and function before external limbs develop and children acquire control over parts of the body closest to the center before they can control the extremities. Thus children are capable of gross motor movements before they can control hand or finger movement.

The sequence of early motor development probably reflects some sort of genetically influenced timetable. However, the infant's context can dramatically influence both the ages at which different motor skills are acquired and their quality. Gerber (1958) reports an investigation of 300 Ugandan infants who, a mere two days after birth (all home deliveries without anesthetics), could sit upright, heads held high, with only slight support of the elbows — a feat that most American children cannot accomplish until close to the age of 2 months (Bayley, 1969) — and all 300 Ugandan children were expert crawlers before they were 2 months old!

SENSATION AND PERCEPTUAL DEVELOPMENT

Our existence as human beings depends largely on our ability to make sense of the world and of our selves. In Kegan's (1982) terms, we struggle to discover meaning.

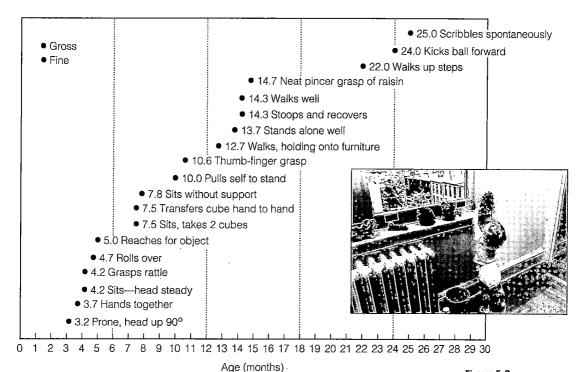

● Gross
● Fine

● 25.0 Scribbles spontaneously
● 24.0 Kicks ball forward
● 22.0 Walks up steps
● 14.7 Neat pincer grasp of raisin
● 14.3 Walks well
● 14.3 Stoops and recovers
● 13.7 Stands alone well
● 12.7 Walks, holding onto furniture
● 10.6 Thumb-finger grasp
● 10.0 Pulls self to stand
● 7.8 Sits without support
● 7.5 Transfers cube hand to hand
● 7.5 Sits, takes 2 cubes
● 5.0 Reaches for object
● 4.7 Rolls over
● 4.2 Grasps rattle
● 4.2 Sits—head steady
● 3.7 Hands together
● 3.2 Prone, head up 90°

0 1 2 3 4 5 6 7 8 9 10 11 12 13 14 15 16 17 18 19 20 21 22 23 24 25 26 27 28 29 30

Age (months)

Figure 5.3

Age (months) at which 90 percent of norming sample of infants accomplishes described task.

Source: Based on norms from Denver Developmental Screening Test. *Denver Developmental Screening Test Reference Manual: Revised 1975 Edition* by W. K. Frankenburg, J. B. Dodds, A. W. Fandal, E. Kazuk, and M. Cohrs, 1975, Denver, CO: University of Colorado Medical Center. Reprinted by permission of the publisher.

The infant's struggles to understand what things are and what they mean depend on three closely related processes: sensation, perception, and conceptualization. These are the topics discussed in the remainder of this chapter.

Sensation is what happens when physical stimuli are translated into neural impulses that can then be transmitted to the brain and interpreted. Thus sensation depends on the activity of one or more of our specialized sense organs — eyes, ears, and taste cells, for example.

In its simplest sense, **perception** is the brain's interpretation of physical sensation. Thus wavelengths corresponding to the color fuchsia affect our retinas in specific ways, causing electrical activity in our optic nerve. When this activity reaches the part of our brain that deals with vision, we *perceive* the color in question. That we can now conclude that we are seeing the color fuchsia and not avocado is a function of the third process, **conceptualization.**

To summarize, sensation is primarily a physiological process dependent on the senses and on neural transmission; conceptualization is a more cognitive (intellectual) process; and perception may be viewed as a bridge between the two. Investigating the sensory capacities and perceptual development of the young infant presents some difficult problems for researchers, most of which relate to the infant's inability to communicate directly the effects of sensory experience. Hence investigators have had to rely extensively on non-verbal infant behaviors, including movements of the eyes, amount of time spent looking at stimuli, gross bodily reactions to strong smells or tastes, subtle physiological changes with changing stimulation, and evidence of orienting to sounds (see Figure 5.4).

Vision

For years newborns were assumed to have poorly developed vision with little ability to discern patterns, form, or movement. More recent evidence has dispelled many of these early beliefs.

Visual acuity in the newborn. One way of describing **visual acuity** (sharpness of vision) is in terms of *Snellen ratings* – for example, 20/20, which indicates something close to normal human vision. A person with 20/20 vision sees at 20 feet what other individuals without visual defects see at 20 feet. A person with 20/100 vision sees approximately as well at 20 feet as people with normal vision see at 100 feet. There are individuals with better than 20/20 vision (20/15, for example, where the individual sees as clearly at 20 feet as others do at 15).

Among a number of complex and intriguing studies of infant visual perception are those that have attempted to determine the extent of the infant's visual acuity. Put more simply, how well can an infant see? Is the world fuzzy and blurred or is it crisp and clear? Is it 20/20 or better or worse? How can we find out?

Researchers sometimes report very different estimates of infant visual acuity depending on the methods used to assess the infant's vision. As a result, a small controversy clouds the field (see Norcia & Tyler, 1985). However, a number of important things are clear. First, infants are far from blind at birth, although some of their visual world may be somewhat fuzzy and blurred.

Second, there is a three to fourfold improvement in the infant's visual acuity between birth and the age of 1 year (Aslin & Smith, 1988). In fact, by the age of 6 months, the infant's visual acuity may be close to that of a normal adult.

And third, the newborn's visual accommodation is more limited than that of adults. It appears that newborns focus most accurately at a distance of approximately 12 inches (30 cm) (Banks, 1980). It is worth noting that 12 inches is approximately the distance of the mother's face when she is feeding the infant. This is one of the ways in which the neonate appears to be programmed to perceive important aspects of the environment; there are others.

Color vision, depth, and movement. Although it has not yet been possible to determine exactly when color vision is first present in the infant, we do know

Infants as Subjects

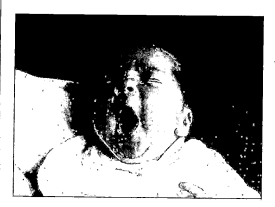

Young infants, and especially newborns, are not always very good experimental subjects. When Fantz (1963) wanted to see how newborns react to visual stimulation, one of the most important conditions for selecting subjects was whether they kept their eyes open long enough to be shown the stimuli. And when Meltzoff and Moore (1989) investigated the newborn's ability to imitate, even though they chose 93 well-fed infants who showed no signs of hunger and who remained wide-eyed and alert for at least 5 minutes before the testing, only 40 completed the brief test session.

The remainder fell asleep, cried, had spitting or choking fits, or, of all things, had a bowel movement!

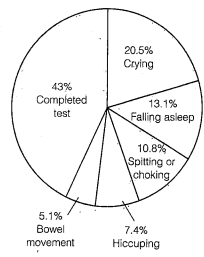

Figure 5.4   Difficulties in testing infants. Only 40 of 93 infants, aged 13.37 to 67.33 hours, completed an 8-minute test session. Testing had to be abandoned for the remaining 53 for the reasons shown. *Source:* Textual data from Meltzoff and Moore (1989), pp. 954–962.

that it is well developed by 2 to 4 months (Bornstein, 1979; Fagan, 1974). By the age of 4 months, infants even show a preference for certain colors; they spend more time looking at pure reds and blues than at other hues (Bornstein & Marks, 1982). **Pupillary reflexes,** changes in the size of the pupil caused by changes in the brightness of visual stimulation, demonstrate that the neonate is sensitive to light intensity, is capable of visually following a slowly moving object within a few days of birth, and is sensitive to patterns and contours as early as two days after birth (Fantz, 1965). There is evidence as well that infants

Figure 5.5

Use of the glass-floored visual cliff indicates that depth perception is developed at a very young age in human and other animal babies. In (a), an infant refuses to cross over even after receiving tactile assurance that the "cliff" is in fact a solid surface. In (b), the goat exhibits a similar reaction— although, unlike the human, it can jump to the other side. Goats show this response at the tender age of 1 day.

less than 2 months of age can perceive contours (or edges) providing they present sufficient contrast, but that they cannot yet perceive relationships among different contours or forms (Cohen, 1979).

In addition to perceiving color, movement, and form, and demonstrating preferences for these, young infants can also perceive depth. Gibson and Walk (1960) illustrate this in the "visual cliff" studies. The apparatus used in this experiment consists of a heavy sheet of glass over a patterned surface; half of this surface is flush with the glass and half is some three feet lower. An adult standing or sitting on the glass can plainly see a drop or cliff where the patterned material falls away from the glass. So can goats who, at the age of a mere day, avoid the deep side, either going around it or jumping over it when they can. So can infants, who, when they are old enough to crawl, typically refuse to cross the deep part, even when their mothers call them from the other side. Thus perception of depth is present at least from the time that the infant can crawl (Figure 5.5).

For a number of years, a test for depth perception before the infant was able to crawl seemed impossible. The refinement of physiological measures, however, has made it possible to look at changes in heartrate when infants who cannot crawl are simply moved from the shallow to the deep side of the visual

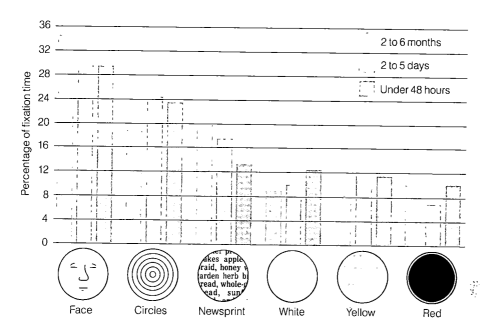

Figure 5.6

Relative percentage of time infants looked at six circular visual stimuli. The graph depicts infants' preference for the human face and the more complex stimuli.

Source: Based on data in Robert L. Fantz, Pattern vision in newborn infants, *Science,* 1963, *140,* 296–297. Copyright 1963 by the American Association for the Advancement of Science. Used by permission of the American Association for the Advancement of Science and the author.

cliff apparatus. Doing this, Campos, Langer, and Krowitz (1970) found heart deceleration in infants who were only a month and a half old. This might not mean they actually perceive depth, but it does indicate they are perceiving something new or unusual.

Visual Preferences

As we saw, if looking at these colors longer is an indication of preference, very young infants prefer reds and blues. It is possible, although perhaps not likely, that they really don't prefer these colors at all, but are simply puzzled or intrigued by them.

In another study of infant visual preference, 18 infants, ranging in age from 10 hours to 5 days, were shown six circular stimulus patterns of varying complexity, the most complex being a human face (Fantz, 1963). In diminishing order of complexity, the other stimuli included concentric circles, newspaper print, and three unpatterned circles of different colors. Figure 5.6 shows the relative percentage of total time spent by subjects looking at each of the stimulus figures. That the stimulus bearing the face was looked at for significantly longer periods of time indicates not only that infants can discriminate among the various figures but also that they prefer the more complex. From their first hours of life, infants' vision seems to be sufficiently developed to allow them to perceive many of the physical characteristics of their surroundings when they are awake (see Banks & Salapatek, 1983). Also, within a matter of weeks, they begin to respond differently to facelike patterns according to the number of elements contained in the patterns, typically spending more time looking at the more complex patterns (Haaf, Smith, & Smitley, 1983).

It might not seem very important that infants look at a face longer than at newsprint or at newsprint longer than at a blank circle. This, we suggested, might reflect their response to increasing complexity rather than to the human or humanlike stimulus. However, other research indicates that they prefer certain kinds of faces over others — and that may be very important.

In an intriguing study, 60 1-year-old infants were exposed to an experimenter wearing either of two professionally constructed, highly realistic masks — one attractive and one unattractive. Their responses to each were markedly different. They withdrew from the attractively masked person far less, played more, and generally showed more signs of positive emotions (Langlois, Roggman, & Rieser-Danner, 1990). Even at the age of 1, infants clearly seem to prefer attractive people and to react more positively to them.

In a second related study, Langlois et al. (1990) presented 1-year-old infants with attractive or unattractive dolls. Again, infants clearly preferred the attractive dolls, playing with them significantly longer than with the unattractive dolls.

The significance of these findings is twofold. First, it had long been thought that attractiveness is a learned and culturally determined quality, and that young infants would not likely have been exposed to enough models or to enough value judgments to have developed preferences. But this does not appear to be the case. Second, if infants *prefer* attractive faces, where does that leave ugly parents or grandparents — or brothers and sisters? Or even strangers? Recall the Elder et al. (1985) study of the effects of the 1930s depression on adolescents and their finding that attractive daughters were treated very differently by their fathers (see Chapter 3). Are attractive fathers and mothers treated differently by their infants? And later by their children? If so, what might the implications be for the ecological systems defined by the family?

Rules of Visual Perception

Earlier in this chapter you were asked to consider the problem of taking an organism as helpless and as primitive as a newborn and designing it in such a way that it would become as sophisticated as a 2-year-old — and eventually a 12-year-old, a 42-year-old, a 92-year-old. It is a useful exercise because it forces us to think of the perceptual, the physical, and the intellectual capacities the neonate must have.

In designing this little organism, we considered that, among other things, we would have to program it to become an extraordinarily capable information-processing system — a system tuned to notice and respond to the most important features of the environment, and predisposed, as well, to make sense of these features.

Does what we know about the infant's visual system conform to our design requirements? Haith (1980) says yes. The infant, he informs us, does not respond to the visual world in a simple, reflexive manner, response following stimulus in predictable mechanical fashion. Instead, infants behave as though preprogrammed to follow specific rules that seem to be geared to maximizing information. Haith's evidence is based on a series of five studies involving 16 full-term infants between the ages of 24 and 96 hours. In the studies, infants were shown various stimuli, including vertical and horizontal edges as well as blank fields. Infant eye fixations and eye movements were recorded using a video camera that responded to infrared light sources bounced off the infant's cornea.

So how do infants look? These, according to Haith's research, are some of the important facts and what they mean:

First, contrary to what we might have expected, infants move their eyes in the absence of light. They scan the darkness in a highly controlled manner, using small movements appropriate for finding shadows, edges, spots. When viewing a uniformly lit but unpatterned field, their eye movements are broader, sweeping movements, suitable for discovering bolder contours. Haith labels these searching patterns *ambient search routines* (ASR). It seems clear that from birth, visual scanning patterns are not simply under the control of external stimuli (after all, scanning occurs in darkness as well as in light), but are internally controlled. It is as though the infant, true to our speculative design, is preprogrammed to obtain information.

Second, newborns actually *look* at stimuli. That is, they position their eyeballs so that a maximum amount of visual information falls on the *fovea* — that part of the retina that has the greatest concentration of visual cells and therefore the greatest number of connections with the part of the brain concerned with vision (the visual cortex). It is as though the infant's scanning rules are designed to maximize stimulation — and, consequently, to maximize information.

Third, when the newborn looks at a simple stimulus (such as a vertical or a horizontal line), the eyes cross back and forth repeatedly over the edges of the stimulus. Haith labels this type of eye movement *inspection scan routine* (ISR). The effect of these eye movements is to maintain a high level of firing in the affected retinal cells and in the corresponding areas of the visual cortex. In the absence of eye movements, habituation to an unchanging stimulus occurs very rapidly and the retinal cells stop firing. But if the eye moves back and forth, different cells are affected and a high rate of firing is maintained.

Haith concludes that there appears to be a single important principle that governs the newborn's visual activity: *maximize neural firing*. It is a built-in (endogenous) principle that assures that the newborn's visual activity will lead to the greatest possible amount of information — a vital feature for an organism that has to be an outstanding information-processing system.

This principle — maximize neural firing — is manifested in the rules that babies look by (Haith, 1980, p. 96).

Rule 1. If awake and alert and light not too bright, open eyes.

Rule 2. If in darkness, maintain a controlled, detailed search.

Rule 3. If in light with no form, search for edges by relatively broad, jerky sweeps of the field.

Rule 4. If an edge is found, terminate the broad scan and stay in the general vicinity of that edge. Attempt to implement eye movements that cross the edge. If such eye movements are not possible in the region of the edge (as is the case for edges too distant from the center of the field), scan for other edges.

This view of the infant's visual perception as rule-governed and information-oriented rather than as stimulus-bound presents a dramatic departure from psychology's traditional approach to these matters. It is a departure that is evident in many other areas of child study as well. This decade's infant — and child — is no longer merely a passive recipient of external influences, but has become active, exploring, information-seeking. Happily, vision is not the infant's only source of information.

Hearing

Unlike the young of many nonhuman species (dogs, bears, and cats, for example), the neonate is not deaf at birth. In fact, physically the ear is fully grown and potentially functional a few months before birth. But just how sensitive the newborn is to auditory stimulation is still a matter of some debate, much of which arises because the results of investigations are often confounded by marked individual variations in responsiveness to sounds. In addition, a variety of indicators of sensitivity — changes in heartrate, respiration rate, EEG activity, electrical conductivity of the skin, as well as the more obvious indicators of attention such as blinking, turning, or startling — have been used in different studies and have sometimes led to contradictory conclusions.

In general, most investigations indicate that neonates are only slightly less sensitive than adults to sound intensity (loudness, measured in decibels; see Figure 5.7). Their hearing threshold averages somewhere between 20 and 30 decibels, or perhaps a little higher, depending on the types of measures used (Acredolo & Hake, 1982); that of a normal adult is at 0 decibels. The difference is not significant, particularly because the intensity level for a quiet conversation is usually above these thresholds (60 or more decibels).

Investigations of infant responsiveness to frequency (high or low pitch) have yielded somewhat inconsistent results, with some studies indicating that

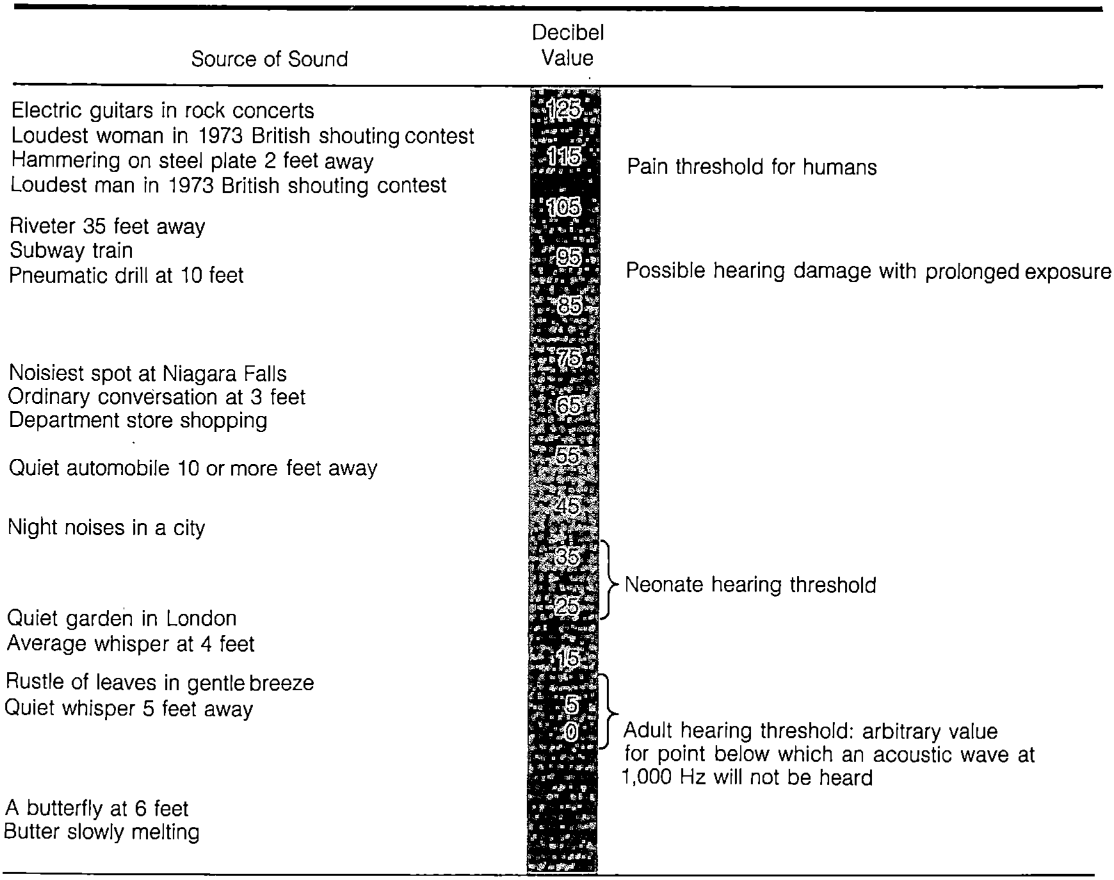

Source of Sound	Decibel Value	
Electric guitars in rock concerts Loudest woman in 1973 British shouting contest Hammering on steel plate 2 feet away Loudest man in 1973 British shouting contest	125 115 105	Pain threshold for humans
Riveter 35 feet away Subway train Pneumatic drill at 10 feet	95 85	Possible hearing damage with prolonged exposure
Noisiest spot at Niagara Falls Ordinary conversation at 3 feet Department store shopping	75 65	
Quiet automobile 10 or more feet away	55	
Night noises in a city	45 35	Neonate hearing threshold
Quiet garden in London Average whisper at 4 feet	25	
Rustle of leaves in gentle breeze Quiet whisper 5 feet away	15 5 0	Adult hearing threshold: arbitrary value for point below which an acoustic wave at 1,000 Hz will not be heard
A butterfly at 6 feet Butter slowly melting		

Figure 5.7

Decibel values of some ordinary sounds.
Source: Lefrançois (1983).

the newborn is most sensitive to lower frequencies (Berg & Berg, 1979) and others showing more sensitivity to higher frequencies (Kessen, Haith, & Sala-patek, 1970). Again, the contradictions seem to be due to the criteria employed, as well as to the ages of the subjects. Studies of older infants have typically shown that sensitivity to higher-frequency sounds increases with age (Schnei-der, Trehub, & Bull, 1980), and the general conclusion that infants (as opposed to newborns) are more sensitive to higher than to lower frequencies is widely accepted. Some researchers suggest that the common tendency of adults to raise the pitch of their voices when speaking to infants or young children is the result of an unconscious recognition of their greater sensitivity to higher frequencies (Fogel, 1984).

In addition to studies of newborns' sensitivity to loudness and frequency, there have been several investigations of their ability to recognize voices.

Amazingly, it appears that an infant as young as 3 days is able to discriminate among different voices and seems to prefer the sound of its mother's voice. In a study where systematic changes in an infant's sucking were reinforced with the sound of a woman reading a book, the infant responded to the sound of its mother but not to that of other women (DeCasper & Fifer, 1980). Have newborns, in the mere space of three days, learned to tell the difference between their mothers' voices and the voices of others? And have they developed a reliable preference for their mothers' voices so soon? DeCasper and Fifer think this unlikely. They suggest that these findings are evidence that the fetus can hear sounds while in the uterus and can distinguish among them. Moreover, if these findings and this interpretation are correct, they provide evidence of learning in utero (Aslin, Pisoni, & Jusczyk, 1983).

In summary, newborns are sensitive to a wide range of sounds and seem particularly sensitive to sounds that fall within the range of the human voice, almost as though their systems were pretuned to normal speech frequencies (Eisenberg, 1976).

Smell, Taste, and Touch

There is clear evidence that neonates are sensitive to odors, tastes, and touch. Within hours of birth, they will attempt to turn their faces when exposed to a powerful and unpleasant smell such as ammonia (Lipsitt, Engen, & Kaye, 1963). And their facial expressions are distinctly different when they are exposed to the smell of vanilla or of raw fish (Steiner, 1979). Like many adults, they like the smell of raw fish less than that of vanilla. Similarly, they react predictably when sweet, sour, or bitter substances are placed on their tongues, smacking their lips and sometimes protruding their tongues in reponse to sweet things, puckering their mouths in response to sour tastes, and opening them for bitter tastes (Steiner, 1979). These observations support Steiner's conclusion that taste and olfactory (smell) sensitivity is present at birth and that it does not depend on experience. The conclusion is further corroborated by studies that have shown that at the age of a single day, infants can differentiate among solutions varying in type and concentration of sweetener. Almost invariably, they prefer any of these sweeteners to plain water. And, contrary to what we might have been led to believe about the natural wisdom of the body, they prefer sweetened water to milk (Desor, Maller, & Green, 1978).

Early investigations of the infant's sensitivity to pain had concluded that the neonate is remarkably insensitive to much of the stimulation that children and adults would find quite painful (McGraw, 1943). Some of these studies had also reported that girls are somewhat more sensitive to pain than are boys (Lipsitt & Levy, 1959). These studies typically used electrodes or tiny pinpricks to assess the infant's sensitivity, and their results were somewhat confounded by differences in subcutaneous (below the skin) fat and in conductivity of the skin, as well as by the somewhat unpredictable concentration and location of nerve endings in the skin. In addition, for obvious ethical reasons the stimuli employed to elicit pain reactions have usually been very mild — nothing at all like the circumcision that so many male babies have almost routinely faced within a few days of birth. Boy babies do holler when circumcised!

More recent research has not established that the neonate is initially insensitive to pain, although there is some indication that pain sensitivity increases over the first few days of life (Haith, 1986). Nor is there any substantial evidence of sex differences. Studies that have used items from the Brazelton Newborn Behavioral Assessment Scale have found strong evidence of touch sensitivity in neonates with no discernible difference between the sexes. The relevant item in the Brazelton scale involves placing a cloth over the infant's face. Even at the age of 2 hours, the newborn usually responds with strong and abrupt movements that would ordinarily remove the cloth.

Neonates are remarkably alert and well suited to their environments. They can hear, see, and smell; they can turn in the direction of food, suck, swallow, digest, and eliminate; they can respond physically to a small range of stimuli; and they can cry and vomit. Still, they are singularly helpless creatures who would surely die if the environment did not include an adult intimately concerned with their survival.

A truly impressive distance lies between a human adult's responses to the world and the uncoordinated and apparently purposeless movements of a newborn child. The story of the child's progress toward adulthood continues.

COGNITIVE DEVELOPMENT

Throughout this text we occasionally pause to repeat that the child is really not composed of all the separate layers we have defined to simplify our study. We divide our subject to make it manageable, but we need to remember constantly that the child is much more than the sum of these layers.

So far in this chapter, we have looked at the simple, unlearned behaviors of the newborn and at motor and perceptual capabilities, as well as at the early development of these capabilities. One layer of paramount importance remains. It is closely linked with all other aspects of development, but we shall consider it in isolation: the intellectual development of the infant.

Maya Pines (1966) observed that for a long time psychology neglected the infant's mind, as though there was a tacit admission that babies did not really have minds or that whatever minds they possessed were unimportant at this stage of development. And Pearce (1977) suggests that we have hardly progressed, that we still think of infants as passive and impotent during the first few months after birth and that, as a result, we continue to neglect their minds. We, in Pearce's words, have yet to recognize the "magical child."

The first major theorists of child development were more concerned with physical and physiological development, acquisition of language, and

It is difficult to have a self-concept until the self is recognized. The little creature smiling back from the mirror will help this baby discover herself.

emotional and personality development than they were with intellectual development — with the exception of Jean Piaget. As far back as 1920, Piaget had begun to map the course of the child's intellectual development. Piaget's story of the growth of children's minds tells of their growing awareness of the world in which they live and their discovery or invention of ways of interacting with this world. It is a complex and fascinating story, but it is not the whole story; there are other theories of cognitive development, other explanations of how we come to *know*. Some of these are labeled *information-processing* approaches. They look at what is involved in memory: deriving information, abstracting, sorting, organizing, analyzing, and retrieving, for example. We look at memory processes in infancy before we turn to Piaget's theory of cognitive development.

Infant Memory

If neonates, ignorant and helpless as they are at birth, are ever to reach the level of competence of the 2-year-old, there is a great deal that they must learn and remember: what is edible and what isn't; how to put things in one's mouth; how to get from here to there, or there to here, or somewhere else; how to ask for things; how to get people's interest and attention; and much, much more.

The neonate's memory is not nearly as efficient and as powerful as yours or mine. In fact, a number of researchers have concluded that infant memory is very weak and that it is more often measured in terms of minutes or hours than days or months (Lipsitt, 1982). Clearly, however, from the very beginning, there must be some ability to learn and remember. This primitive ability must then eventually develop into the type of memory that is characteristic of the 2-year-old, the 40-year-old, the 90-year-old.

There are several ways of investigating infant memory. Some of these use components of the orienting response described earlier. For example, researchers might look at the infant's response to the same photograph, or other stimulus, presented on two different occasions. If the infant remembers something about the photograph, heartrate would not be expected to change in the same way as it might when the infant is presented with a completely new photograph.

A second approach is simply to look at how long it takes for the infant to *habituate* (become accustomed) to a stimulus. Habituation might be revealed in patterns of eye movements (the infant stops looking at the stimulus) or, again, in changes in components of the orienting response such as respiration or heartrate.

A third measure of infant memory involves the infant's behavior. For example, Rovee-Collier and her associates (1980) taught 3-month-old infants how to make a mobile turn by moving their feet (the infant's foot was fastened to a lever that, when moved, caused the mobile to move). Infants remembered the procedure several weeks later.

Using measures such as these, investigators have found that even newborns have memories. True, they are not very elaborate memories, but they are a beginning. Within days of birth, for example, newborns are able to recognize their mothers' smell (Macfarlane, 1975) and to discriminate among different speech sounds (Rovee-Collier, 1987) — clearly evidence of memory. But the infant's memory for most things appears to be of relatively short duration. For example, young infants who are conditioned to associate a puff of air with a tone or a feeding schedule with a bell may remember from one day to the next — or perhaps for 6 or 10 days. But without any reminders in the interim, all evidence of memory is likely to be gone within a few days (Rovee-Collier, 1987).

Perlmutter (1980) describes three sequential phases in the development of infant memory. In the first, the infant's memory appears to be largely a matter of neurons firing when a new stimulus is presented and the firing stopping with habituation. As the infant becomes more familiar with the stimulus (that is, learns and remembers), the period before habituation becomes shorter.

The second phase, which begins at around 3 months, is related to the infant's growing ability to accomplish *intended* actions. Infants now actively look and search; they begin to reach, even to grasp; they explore. And they show clear signs of *recognizing;* recognition is a sure sign of memory.

By the age of 8 or so months, infant memories have become much more like our own in being more abstract and more symbolic. They remember *classes* of things like fuzzy objects and big people and pets and building blocks and beets.

Memory in adults and in older children is greatly facilitated by certain strategies, the most important of which are *organization, grouping,* and *elaboration.* Infants do not systematically use any of these strategies. But if they are asked to remember something, they do use primitive strategies: They *try* to remember, and they *pay attention.* And these, says Wellman (1988), are strategies in their own right. Wellman notes, as well, that the 2-year-old infant already has some notions about what memory is and understands such mental-event terms as *remember, think, know,* and *pretend.*

There is a great distance between the immature memory of the week-old child who can, with appropriate instrumentation, demonstrate a vague recollection of a familiar smell or sound and that of the 1-year-old who *mistakenly* yells "Dada" when he sees a stranger's familiar-looking back in the supermarket. There is also a vast distance between this 1-year-old's memory and the memory of the 12-year-old whose cognitive (intellectual) strategies permit mental feats of which the 1-year-old cannot yet even dream. There is more about memory in Chapter 7. But first we look in more detail at Piaget's view of the development of the infant's mind.

Basic Piagetian Ideas

Jean Piaget describes the infant's world as a world of the *here and now.* That is, it is a world that makes sense and has meaning only in terms of the actions that infants can perform with it — primarily the simple sensory actions of looking, touching, tasting, smelling, and hearing. According to the Piagetian model of cognitive functioning, the infant does not have concepts — nor even a very large store of memories or hopes or dreams — no fund of information with which to think. .

But what the neonate possesses are the sensory systems and the cognitive inclinations that make it into a self-reinforcing, information-processing organism. That is basically the sort of system that Piaget describes when he speaks of the infant — a system that continually seeks out and responds to stimulation and that, by so doing, gradually builds up a repertoire of behaviors and capabilities.

Assimilation and accommodation. Initially, as we have seen, the infant's behaviors are largely limited to the simple reflexes with which the infant is born; but in time, these behaviors become more elaborate and more coordinated with one another. The process by which this occurs is one of adaptation. And the complementary processes that make adaptation possible are those of *assimilation* and *accommodation* (see Chapter 2).

To review briefly, assimilation and accommodation are highly active processes whereby the individual searches out, selects, and responds to information, the end result of which is the actual *construction* of knowledge. Imagine, for example, a young child walking on a windblown beach, stooping now and again to pick up pebbles and toss them onto the water. In Piaget's view, there is a *schema* involved here — a sort of mental or cognitive representation — that corresponds to the child's knowledge of the suitability of pebbles as objects to be thrown upon the waves, as well as other schemata that have to do with the activities involved in bending, retrieving, and throwing. The pebbles are, in a sense, being assimilated to appropriate schemata; they are understood and used in terms of the child's previous knowledge.

According to Piaget, activity includes both assimilation and accommodation. These processes involve seeking out, selecting, and responding to information, the end result of which (in this instance, a highly vocal response from an enraged feline?) is the construction of knowledge.

Imagine, now, that the child bends to retrieve another pebble but finds, instead, that she has picked up a wallet. The wallet is clearly not a pebble, and perhaps should not be responded to in the same way. But still, why not? The "throwing things on the big waves" schema is readily available, momentarily preferred. And so the wallet too is assimilated to the throwing schema, and the child tries to hurl it toward the water. But the new object's heaviness is sudden and surprising, the child's throwing motion inadequate, and the wallet falls again upon the sand. Now, when she picks it up again, she doesn't hurl it in quite the same way. She holds it in two hands, grasps it tightly with her pudgy little fingers, and pushes hard with her little legs as she throws. In Piaget's terms, she has accommodated to the characteristics of this object that make it different from the pebbles she has been throwing.

To simplify these sometimes difficult concepts, to assimilate is to respond in terms of preexisting information. It often involves ignoring some aspects of the situation in order to make it conform to aspects of the mental system. In contrast, to accommodate is to respond to external characteristics and to make changes in the mental system as a result.

Equilibration. It is important to note that these processes, assimilation and accommodation, are not separate and independent, but are, as Flavell (1985) put it, two sides of the same cognitive coin. According to Piaget, all activity involves both assimilation and accommodation. It is impossible to react to or understand something entirely new; everything is always understood, to some extent, in terms of existing information (assimilation). At the same time, everything to which the infant (or the adult) reacts presents something that is new and different and involves some change in information or structure (accommodation). The balance between accommodation and assimilation is labeled equilibrium. **Equilibration** is the process by which equilibrium is maintained. At one extreme, if an infant always assimilated, never accommodated, there would be no change in schemata (mental structure), no change in behavior. Everything would be assimilated to the sucking schema, the grasping schema, the looking schema (that is, everything would be sucked, or grasped, or simply looked at). Such a state of disequilibrium would result in little adaptation and little cognitive growth.

At the other extreme, if everything were accommodated to and not assimilated, schemata — and behavior — would be in a constant state of flux. Now the nipple would be sucked, now it would be chewed, now pinched, now swatted. . . . Again, an extreme state of disequilibrium would result in little adaptation.

For Piaget, equilibration is an internal tendency that governs the balance between assimilation and accommodation and that accounts for the *construction* of knowledge; that is, it accounts for adaptation and cognitive growth — throughout development.

Other factors. Several other factors are important in Piaget's (1961) description of the forces that shape development. *Maturation*, for example, refers to a sort of biologically determined unfolding of potential. Maturation — or biology — does not determine cognitive growth but is related to the unfolding of potential in a very general sense.

Active experience is essential to the child's progressive adaptation. In Piaget's view, development is dependent on the child's interaction with the world. Also important is *social interaction* — interaction with others — which helps the child develop ideas about things and about people as well as about the self.

These four factors — active experience, maturation, equilibration, and social interaction — are, in a sense, the cornerstones of Piaget's basic theory. In one sentence, cognitive growth results from assimilation and accommodation, governed by a need to achieve and maintain equilibrium, and occurring through active experience and social interaction broadly related to unfolding maturation.

It is a large mouthful conceptually.

The Object Concept

Perhaps we can chew its gristle a little more in this section.

So the infant's world begins as a world that, although not necessarily William James's "blooming, buzzing mass of confusion," exists only when it is being reacted to and is understood only in terms of those actions. A nipple exists for infants when they look at it, touch it, suck it, or otherwise respond to it; when it is removed from their immediate perception, it ceases to exist. In Piaget's terms, the infant at this stage has not yet achieved the **object concept** — the realization that objects continue to exist even when they are not being sensed. It is a concept that is so simple, so clear, so *inevitable* for us as adults that we take it completely for granted. Yet it is absolutely fundamental to our reasoning about the world; our very conception of the world demands that objects be real, out there, substantive, and independent of us. There is no "out there" for infants; they must discover the permanence and objectivity of objects for themselves. This discovery is one of the truly great achievements of infancy.

How do children discover the reality and the properties of objects? The processes are not clearly understood, but it seems evident that experience with, and exploration of, the real world are intimately involved. In a series of investigations, Stambak et al. (1989) videotaped young infants' responses to different objects such as nesting cups or hollow cubes or rods. Analysis of these videotapes reveals that even very young infants organize their behaviors in systematic ways, that their exploration is not simply the random exercising of behaviors. Thus, some subjects typically bang different objects with the rod; some explore the insides of the hollow cubes with their fingers or with their hands if the cubes are large enough. In a sense, it is as though they have already begun to invent questions and problems and to devise little experiments to find answers. In a series of naturalistic observations reported by Sinclair et al. (1989), infants often spent the entire 20-minute observation session coming back to the same *idea*.

Not only does the exploration of objects by young infants become increasingly systematic with advancing age, but it also involves more varied activities. As Rochat (1989) puts it, exploration becomes increasingly multimodal between the ages of 2 and 5 months. Initially, for example, exploration is primarily only visual or oral. Later, it also becomes manual. By the age of 3 or 4 months, most infants use both their hands *and* their mouths to explore. Significantly, however, the type of manipulation in which the infant engages becomes increasingly dependent on the objects being explored. Some things are more easily understood, more meaningful, when held in both hands, licked and drooled on, and gummed emphatically.

To investigate the infant's understanding of objects, Piaget (1954) devised an experiment in which the investigator shows the child an attractive object and then hides it from view. Piaget argues that if the object existed only when infants were perceiving it, they would make no effort to look for it even when they had seen it being hidden from view. When children begin to look for an object they can no longer see, this is definite evidence that they can imagine it. The object continues to exist for them even when it is unseen.

Piaget found that in the earliest stages, children do not respond to the object once it is removed; next, they progress through a number of stages during which they search for the object, but only in the place where they last saw it; and finally, they achieve a complete realization of object permanence and can look for objects in a variety of places. The final stage occurs near the middle of the second year of life.

A number of later investigations of the development of the object concept demonstrate that the age of acquisition is perhaps younger than Piaget suggests (see Norris, 1983). For example, Bower (1971, 1977) used the orienting response of very young infants to determine whether an object ceases to exist when it is removed from sight. In one study, the infant is shown a ball and then a screen is moved between the infant and the ball; a few seconds later, the screen is removed. On some trials, the ball is still there; on others, the ball has been taken away. When infants do not have object permanence, they should not be surprised if the ball is gone. But they would be surprised to see it gone if they expected it to be there — in other words, if they had acquired notions of object permanence. Bower measured surprise by noting changes in heartrate. His primary finding is that infants as young as 3 weeks of age appear to have some notion of object permanence, providing the object is hidden from view for only a few seconds. When the object is hidden for longer (15 seconds as opposed to 1½ seconds), infants at this age all show surprise when the ball is still present after the screen is removed.

In a related study, Baillargeon (1987) found that infants as young as 3½ months seemed to have some primitive notions about the solidity of objects. When one object moved through a space that should have been occupied by another object, they seemed surprised (if the fact that they looked longer at that *impossible* situation than at another comparable but *possible* situation can be interpreted as surprise).

Do such findings mean that Piaget was wrong? Do infants have a notion of the permanence and independent identity of objects a long time before the age of 18 months? In fact, they don't. What the studies indicate is that under the proper circumstances, infants appear to have a rudimentary and short-lived recollection of absent objects. However, it will still be a long time before the 3-week-old infant deliberately searches for an object that has not been present just recently (Haith & Campos, 1977; Ramsay & Campos, 1975).

Spatial Orientation

Acredolo (1978) corroborated Piaget's findings in a longitudinal investigation of 24 infants tested at the ages of 6, 11, and 16 months. Infants were placed in a small enclosure (10 by 10 feet). In the center was a table with a center pole to which was attached a baby chair on wheels. The chair could be rotated around the table so that the infant would be facing different walls in the enclosure. Small windows faced each other on two opposing walls. Initially, infants, accompanied by their mothers, were placed in the chair so that one window was on their immediate left, the other on the right. In the training portion of the study, a buzzer sounded and approximately 3 seconds later the experimenter peeked through one of the windows. The procedure was repeated a number of times, with the experimenter always peeking through the same window (to either the infant's right or left side). When infants had learned to expect a face at that window (indicated by looking at the window after the buzzer sounded, but before the appearance of the face), the chair was turned so that the window that had previously been on the left would now be on the right. Thus it was possible to determine whether the infants had learned only to turn to the left or right or whether they possessed sufficient knowledge of spatial orientation to interpret the situation objectively (as opposed to egocentrically). If, for example, infants had learned only their own response of turning to the left (or right), they would be expected to continue to do so in the testing situation, turning toward the wrong window. If, however, they had learned that it was at a particular window that a face would appear, they might be expected to turn in the opposite direction when they themselves had been turned 180 degrees, thus continuing to turn toward the same window.

Acredolo's findings, highly supportive of Piaget's observations, were that the 6- and 11-month-old infants continued to respond egocentrically; they had learned only to turn to *their* left or right, rather than to turn toward a specific window. By 16 months, however, responding had become progressively more objective. As long as the infant's interpretation of the world is largely egocentric, spatial orientation and the development of notions of objective reality are hampered.

Sensorimotor Development

Piaget believes that children's understanding of the world throughout most of infancy is restricted to the activities they can perform on it and to their perceptions of it — hence *sensori-motor*. Piaget simplifies the infant's cognitive development during this period by dividing it into six substages, summarized in Table 5.2 and described in the following sections (see also Table 5.3).

Exercising reflexes. There is little new learning in the first month of life. Infants spend most of their waking hours exercising the abilities with which they are born — they suck, look, grasp, and cry. Some children engage in a great deal of the latter activity. In addition to obvious survival functions of some of these activities, they have an important cognitive function. Through repeatedly performing these activities, the child eventually gains control over small aspects of the environment (as well as over the activities themselves). By the end of the first month, infants have become relatively proficient at each of them, although they still cannot execute more than one action to obtain a single goal. Infants presented with a visually appealing object can look at it but cannot reach toward it. The ability to look at an object and to continue looking at it when it moves (or when the child moves) precedes the ability to direct the hand toward the object (Provine & Westerman, 1979). Deliberately reaching and grasping is therefore a complex activity depending on the purposeful

Table 5.2
Piaget's Stages of Cognitive Development

Stage	Approximate Age	Some Major Characteristics
Sensorimotor	0–2 years	Motoric intelligence World of the here and now No language, no thought in early stages No notion of objective reality

Preoperational*
  Preconceptual
  Intuitive
	2–7 years
	2–4 years
	4–7 years
		Egocentric thought
		Reason dominated by perception
		Intuitive rather than logical solutions
		Inability to conserve

Concrete operations†	7–11 or 12 years	Ability to conserve Logic of classes and relations Understanding of number Thinking bound to concrete Development of reversibility in thought
Formal operations‡	11 or 12–14 or 15 years	Complete generality of thought Propositional thinking Ability to deal with the hypothetical Development of strong idealism

*Discussed in Chapter 7

†Discussed in Chapter 9.

‡Discussed in Chapter 11.

coordination of looking schemes, reaching schemes, and grasping schemes. This coordination is not usually apparent until after 3 to 5 months (Von Hofsten & Lindhagen, 1979).

Primary circular reactions. Early in infancy, children engage in many repetitive behaviors (thumb sucking, for example) called **primary circular reactions** (1–4 months). These reactions involve reflexive responses that serve as stimuli for their own repetition. For example, the child accidentally gets a hand or a finger into the mouth; this triggers the sucking response, which results in the sensation of the hand in the mouth. That sensation leads to a repetition of the response, which leads to a repetition of the sensation, which leads to a repetition of the response. This circle of action is called *primary* because it involves the infant's own body.

Despite the child's ability at this substage to acquire new behaviors (new adaptations through accommodation to different stimulation), these new be-

Table 5.3
Sensorimotor Development: The Six Substages

Substage and Approximate Age in Months	Principal Characteristics
1. Exercising reflexes (0–1)	Simple, unlearned behaviors (schemes) such as sucking and looking are practiced and become more deliberate.
2. Primary circular reactions (1–4)	Activities that center on the infant's body and that give rise to pleasant sensations are repeated (thumb sucking, for example).
3. Secondary circular reactions (4–8)	Activities that do not center on the child's body but that lead to interesting sights or sounds are repeated (repeatedly moving a mobile, for example).
4. Purposeful coordinations (8–12)	Separate schemes become coordinated (such as the ability to look at an object and reach for it); familiar people and objects are recognized; primitive understanding of causality begins, implicit in the use of signs to ancitipate events.
5. Tertiary circular reactions (12–18)	Repetition with variation (repeating a sound with a number of deliberate changes, for example) is experimented with.
6. Mental representation (18–24)	Transition between sensorimotor intelligence and a more cognitive intelligence is made; activity is internalized so that its consequences can be anticipated before its actual performance; language becomes increasingly important in cognitive development.

haviors come about accidentally and always involve the child's body. Interaction with the world is still highly one-sided; it is still a world of the here and now – a world that exists and has meaning when it is doing something to the child or when the child is doing something to it.

Secondary circular reactions. Another circular reaction appears during the third substage: the **secondary circular reaction** (4 to 8 months). Like the primary circular reaction, it is circular because the response stimulates its own repetition; but because it deals with objects in the environment rather than only with the child's body, it is called *secondary.* Six-month-old infants engage in many secondary circular reactions. They accidentally do something that is interesting or amusing and repeat it again and again. By kicking, Piaget's young son caused a row of dolls dangling above his bassinet to dance. The boy stopped to observe the dolls. Eventually, he repeated the kicking, not intentionally to make the dolls move, but more likely because they had ceased moving and no longer attracted his attention. The act of kicking had the same effect again, and again the boy paused to look at the row of dancing dolls. In a very short time he was repeating the behavior over and over — a circular reaction. This is an easily repeated illustration that Piaget describes as *behavior designed to make interesting sights and sounds last.*

Purposeful coordinations. One major achievement of the fourth substage (8 to 12 months) is particularly noteworthy: the development of the ability to coordinate previously unrelated behaviors to achieve some desired goal. Infants can now look at an object, reach for it, grasp it, and bring it to the mouth specifically to suck it. Throughout this sequence, there is clear evidence of intention.

Also during the fourth substage infants begin to demonstrate their ability to *recognize* familiar objects and people. Because of this, they may now become upset when a parent leaves or when a stranger appears (see Chapter 6).

At this time too the infant begins to use signs to anticipate events: Daddy putting on his jacket is a sign that he is leaving; mother putting on her pajamas is a sign that she is not. Understanding that certain events are *signs* that some other event is likely to occur is closely related to the ability to understand causality. For the young infant, whose logic is not always as perfect as yours or mine, the sign itself is often interpreted as the cause. In other words, a child who realizes that daddy will be leaving when he puts on his jacket *knows* that the cause of leaving is putting on the jacket — just as the cause of going to bed is taking a bath, putting on pajamas, the goodnight kiss, saying prayers, or whatever ritual is common.

Tertiary circular reactions. In the fifth substage (12 to 18 months), children begin to modify their repetitive behaviors *deliberately* to see what the effects will be. Rayna, Sinclair, and Stambak (1989) observed a 15-month-old girl whose current preoccupation was with fragmenting or breaking objects. Breaking something often seemed to lead to a repetition of the behavior (hence a circular response), but with deliberate variation (hence **tertiary**; recall that primary and secondary reactions are repetitive with occasional nondeliberate variations). For example, in one session, she picked up a ball of clay, scratched at it until a piece had come off, examined the piece, and then repeated the procedure several times, each time examining the clay on her finger. Next, she noticed a ball of cotton, picked it up, and pulled it into two halves; then she pulled one of the halves into two more pieces, and again, and again. Similarly, in another session, a 15-month-old boy who had been tearing apart bits of clay happened across a piece of spaghetti, pressed it to the floor, broke it, picked up the largest piece, broke it again, and repeated the process a number of times. Once finished, he attempted to break a short plastic stick and then a pipe cleaner; finally, he tore a sheet of paper into tiny bits.

The most important feature of tertiary circular reactions is that they are repetitive behaviors deliberately undertaken to see what their effects will be — that is, to explore.

Mental representation. Toward the end of the sensorimotor period, children begin to make a transition between the *motoric* intelligence of the first period and the progressively *cognitive* intelligence of the second. During this sub-stage, children begin to learn to represent objects and events mentally and combine these representations to arrive at mental solutions for problems. They are now able to anticipate the consequences of some of their activities before actually executing them. Their behavior is consequently no longer restricted to trial and error as it was previously but makes use of *mental representation.* In Piaget's terms, it is as though the child can now begin to internalize (represent mentally) actions and their consequences without having to actually carry them out.

An illustration of this growing ability to internalize actions before their execution is Piaget's description of his daughter's response to a matchbox problem. She had been given a partly open matchbox containing a small thimble. Because the opening was too small for her to withdraw the thimble, she had to open the box first. A younger infant would simply grope at the box, attempting clumsily to remove the thimble. But Piaget's daughter, then 22 months, appeared instead to be considering the problem. She opened and closed her mouth repeatedly as if displaying internal thought processes. Finally, she placed her finger directly into the box's partial opening, opened it, and removed the thimble.

The ability to conceptualize the environment is also reflected in infants' mushrooming language development, which, according to Piaget, is greatly facilitated by their imitative behavior.

Imitation in Infancy

In the earliest stages of imitation, infants are able to imitate objects, activities, or people that are immediately present. Stick your tongue out in front of a 3-month-old, and a tongue is likely to be stuck right back out at you; wink and the infant might well wink right back — but with both eyes, never just one.

Exactly when the ability to imitate first appears is a matter of some controversy. Some of the first studies in this area reported that at a mere 2 weeks of age, infants are already able to imitate simple things like an adult sticking out the tongue or opening the mouth wide (Meltzoff & Moore, 1977, 1979, 1983, 1989). Other studies have sometimes found even earlier instances of imitation. For example, Reissland (1988) looked at imitation among 12 neonates in the first *hour* after birth. All of these infants had been delivered without complications and without drugs, and all were awake and alert. Models bent over the infants and either widened their lips or pursed them. The results? Infants moved their lips in accordance with lip movements of the models significantly more often than at variance with them. There is evidence, Reissland concludes, that the ability to imitate is already present at birth.

In a slightly more complex study involving infants aged between 10 and 51 hours, Kaitz et al. (1988) looked at infants' ability to imitate facial expressions (happy, sad, or surprised) as well as tongue protrusion. Again, infants demonstrated modeling of tongue protrusion. But when they were shown happy, sad, or surprised faces, although they often responded by opening or pursing their mouths, their behaviors did not seem to be directly imitative. They were equally likely to open the mouth or purse it whether the model was happy, sad, or surprised. The conclusion? Perhaps infants do not truly imitate these facial gestures, but instead simply manifest a generalized, almost reflexive response.

A number of other researchers such as Masters (1979) and Jacobson and Kagan (1979) do not agree that young infants, and especially neonates, are actually imitating when they stick out their tongue or purse their lips in apparent response to a model doing the same thing. They argue that these behaviors are largely reflexive, related to feeding, and simply *released* by the nearness of the model rather than being an actual imitation.

Meltzoff and Moore (1989) disagree. In a recent study, they exposed 40 infants, aged 16 to 67 hours, to models who either protruded their tongues or shook their heads. Gestures lasted for 1 minute, followed by a 1-minute interval during which the model adopted an expressionless, "passive" face. Each gesture and passive-face sequence was repeated once (total testing time: 8 minutes). Infants were equally able to imitate head shaking — a nonvegetative behavior — and tongue protrusion. Furthermore, during the passive-face interludes, some continued to imitate the behavior they had previously seen. Meltzoff and Moore (1989) argue that the evidence supports the conclusion that infants have a general ability to match certain adult behaviors. However, they note that imitative behavior in the newborn is not completely automatic and easily triggered and that it is more easily brought about for certain behaviors than for others. They suggest, too, that the inborn capacity to match the behaviors of others may be very important for social and cognitive development.

Deferred Imitation

Many of the imitative behaviors of the very young infant do not continue when the model is no longer present. That is, the infant is initially capable of imitating only when the model is there or within a very short period of time thereafter, as in the Meltzoff and Moore (1989) study just described. This may be related to the difficulty infants experience in separating the objects they perceive from their perception of them — and their consequent failure to realize that objects continue to exist independently of them. It is largely for this reason that Piaget (1951) suggested that imitation is not likely to occur before the age of 9 to 12 months of age.

There is, in fact, no important contradiction here. Piaget was referring not to the simple imitation of a gesture or movement in the presence of a model, but to what is labeled **deferred imitation** — the ability to imitate something or someone no longer present. When two-year-old Amanda dresses up in her mother's shoes and struts in front of a mirror in the absence of her mother, she is practicing deferred imitation. This behavior is significant because to imitate a person who is absent the child must be able to represent that person mentally; similarly, to associate a name with an object not immediately present requires representing the object mentally.

A study by Meltzoff (1988) provides evidence of the kind of deferred imitation of which Piaget spoke. In this study, a group of 14-month-old infants were allowed to observe a model performing six different actions with six different objects. Some of these actions were clearly novel for the infant and would not occur in the course of their daily activities. Following these training sessions, the objects were removed immediately, without the infants having been given an opportunity to interact with them. When subjects were presented with the same six objects a full week later, they showed considerable evidence of precise imitative behavior.

The significance of deferred imitation is considerable for the cognitive development of the infant, depending, as it does, on the infant's ability to represent mentally and to remember. And, according to Piaget, it is one of the important abilities that underlies the acquisition of language.

LANGUAGE AND COMMUNICATION

Despite its tremendous power, **language** is not essential for **communication** (the transmission of messages). Animals that do not have language can nevertheless communicate danger. Whitetail deer wave their tails; pronghorn antelope bristle their rump patches; ground squirrels whistle. Some of these signals communicate danger to other members of the same species. Others, like the flag-waving of the whitetail deer, may also be examples of cross-species communication (Alcock, 1984). There is evidence that this behavior might not only signal danger to other deer, but might also serve as a signal to predators. It says, in effect, "Ha, ha, I've seen you so forget it." And the wolf, who is the deer's main predator in many areas, reads the signal. He knows he cannot ordinarily catch a healthy deer in a prolonged chase; so he lies down and licks his chops, or he goes snooping on people's doorsteps. Thus his reading of signals — his literacy — allows him to save his energy.

Communication between humans and other animals also occurs. An animal trainer who instructs his dog to roll over is communicating with the animal (at least when the dog obeys — and perhaps even when the dog does not obey). And the dog who walks to his empty dish, looks at his master, and then begins to growl is not only dangerous but is also communicating very effectively. This communication, however, is a far cry from that made possible by

Language is not always necessary for communication.

language. The parrot who can say "Polly wants a cracker" is not only boringly conventional but is also probably incapable of saying "A cracker wants Polly, heh, heh" with the intention of conveying a different meaning.

A DEFINITION OF LANGUAGE

The parrot merely mimics; it does not communicate. It is incapable of deliberately rearranging sounds according to established rules with the intention of conveying meaning. It does not know language.

Language may be defined as *the use of arbitrary sounds, with accepted referents, that can be arranged in sequences to convey different meanings.* This definition includes what Brown (1973) describes as the three essential characteristics of language: displacement, meaning, and productiveness.

Language involves *displacement* because it makes possible the representation of objects and events that are not immediate — that are displaced — in both time and space. "The moon was a ghostly galleon," we can say, "tossed upon cloudy seas." Yet neither ghosts nor galleons, nor even moons nor seas need be where we can touch them or see them. Indeed, what you and I can speak of need not even be where anybody has ever seen or touched them. We can speak of green blurbs and hypodrives in Scurrilian space vessels and other fantastic things that live only in our imaginations. There is virtually no limit to how far language can be displaced from the things it represents.

And still have **meaning.** That, in fact, is one of the primary functions of language: the communication of meaning (semantics). Unfortunately, the meaning of the concept "meaning" is by no means clear. The meaning of a verbal expression might relate to the objects or events for which it stands, to the mental images that are evoked, to the defining characteristics of the things to which it refers, to the emotional reactions associated with its referents, or to any combination of these. Although **psycholinguists** — those who study the relationship between language and human functioning — do not always agree about the best definition for meaning, we in our ordinary conversations tend to agree much more than disagree. Indeed, it is because you and I have similar meanings for words and sentences that we can communicate as we are now doing.

The third characteristic of language, **productiveness,** means that, given a handful of words, a set of mutually accepted rules about how they can be combined, and agreement about the significance of the various pauses, intonations, and other characteristics of speech, we can produce meanings forever. Language presents so many possibilities for meaningful combinations that almost every day of your life you will say something that no one else has ever said in exactly the same way. Language makes you creative.

ELEMENTS OF LANGUAGE

There are four basic components of language: **phonology, semantics, syntax, and pragmatics.** Each is essential for effective communication with language.

Phonology refers to the **phonemes** or sounds of a language. A phoneme is the simplest unit of language and is nothing more complex than a single sound such as that represented by a consonant or word. There are 45 phonemes in the English language.

Phonemes can be combined to form **morphemes,** which are the units of meaning in language, and therefore the building blocks of semanticity (meaning). Morphemes may be made up of sounds such as *ing* or *ed* — word endings that affect the meanings of words — or of whole words. Children cannot produce morphemes until they can first pronounce the phonemes. Simply making the sound is not enough; they must be able to make it when they intend to do so, and they must also be able to combine morphemes in meaningful combinations.

Organizing words into meaningful sentence units requires an intuitive knowledge of *syntax* — the grammar of language, the set of implicit rules governing the combinations of words that will be meaningful and correct for the speakers of that language.

As children practice and master sounds (phonemes), meanings (semantics), and grammatical rules (syntax), they must also learn a large number of unspoken rules and conventions governing conversation (Bates, 1976). Put another way, they must learn the *pragmatics* of language. An implicit knowledge of pragmatics is what tells children when and how they should speak. It includes uncounted rules and practices governing manners of expression, intonation, accents, and all the other subtle variations that give different meanings to the same morphemes and that might vary appreciably from one context to another. For example, that parents use shorter sentences, speak in higher-pitched voices, and use more concrete names and fewer abstractions when speaking with young children than with other adults is a function of their knowledge of pragmatics.

Phonology, semantics, syntax, and pragmatics are the elements of language. Most of us acquire these elements in an amazingly painless, effective, and efficient way without really being conscious of what we are doing.

LANGUAGE DEVELOPMENT IN INFANTS

Early studies of how children acquire language often concentrated on counting the number of words children had in their vocabularies at a given age. Psychologists soon found that children's passive vocabularies (their comprehension) far exceeded their active vocabularies (their production of speech); that is, in the early stages of language learning children can invariably understand many more words than they can use in their own speech. And before using words in speech, many also develop a wide range of communicative gestures (Bates et al., 1989).

A second way of approaching early language development is by examining the quality of the language acquired, rather than by estimating vocabulary size at different ages. Contemporary linguists treat the developing child as a fellow linguist; they examine the progression of children's knowledge of each of the elements of language not only to learn how the child acquires the ability to use language but also to learn more about language itself.

For convenience, language learning is frequently divided into two major stages: the prespeech stage and the speech stage. In the prespeech stage meaningful speech sounds are gradually developed; the speech stage is best described as a progression from sounds to words to grammar and pragmatics. The prespeech stage lasts from birth to about the end of the first year or the early part of the second and terminates with the utterance of single words. During this first stage, children engage in three different speech-related behaviors: They cry (sometimes a great deal), coo, and gurgle; they develop a repertoire of gestures, many of which are intended to communicate desires; and they practice **babbling** — the production of single sounds (see Table 5.4).

Table 5.4

Age at Which Infants Demonstrate a Given Language Capability

Capability	50% of infants	90% of infants
Responds to bell		1.6 mos.
Laughs	2.0 mos.	3.3 mos.
Squeals	2.2 mos.	4.5 mos.
Says "dada" or "mama," nonspecific	6.9 mos.	10.0 mos.
Imitates speech sounds	7.0 mos.	11.2 mos.
Says 3 words other than "mama," "dada"	12.8 mos.	20.5 mos.
Points to 1 named body part	17.0 mos.	23.0 mos.
Combines 2 different words	19.6 mos.	2.3 yrs.

Source: Based on norms from Denver Developmental Screening Test. *Denver Developmental Screening Test Reference Manual: Revised 1975 edition* by W. K. Frankenburg, J. B. Dodds, A. W. Fandal, E. Kazuk, and M. Cohrs, 1975, Denver, CO: University of Colorado Medical Center. Reprinted by permission of the publisher.

Early Achievements

Bates (1976) summarizes the language-related developments of the infant pre-speech period in terms of two critical achievements that generally occur between the ages of 9 and 13 months. The first is marked by the appearance of the intention to communicate and is evident in the conventional signals and gestures that clearly have meaning for both infant and caregiver. Squirming and gazing intently at the milk bottle are pragmatic (effective) ways of saying to mama, "If I don't get that *!!$@ing bottle soon, I'm gonna holler!"

The second critical achievement is the discovery of symbols — the discovery that things have names (Bates, 1976). This should not be confused with the simple ability to represent. As Mandler (1984) makes clear, there are two kinds of representation. *Simple representation* involves nothing more complex than memory. All that is in memory is represented. In this sense, the newborn's ability to suck involves representation. But this type of representation is a long distance from *symbolic representation* — the type of representation that defines semanticity (meaning) and that is essential for language. Symbolic representation begins with the infant's discovery that things can be named — can be symbolized with sounds. Ultimately, children learn to speak so they can communicate, Rice (1989) tells us. Thus they can achieve important social goals.

Infants begin to learn the rules of conversational turn-taking long before they can actually speak. This baby already understands that certain changes in his mother's voice and special head and hand movements are signals that it is his turn to make noises.

Language Origins

Research dealing with the origins of language has been particularly interested in the pragmatics and semantics of the infant's first gestures and sounds (Bates et al., 1981; Terrace, 1985). Researchers believe that the ability to use and to understand words grows out of a complex series of interactions between infant and parents. These interactions, referred to collectively as the *language acquisition support system* (LASS) by Bruner (1983), involve such things as learning how to make eye contact, how to direct attention through eye movements and gestures, and how to take turns.

Knowing when and how to take turns is basic to adult conversation. When we have conversations, we wait for the signals that tell us it is our turn; and we give others their signals — well, most of us do; there are some who simply shout a little louder. Most of us have learned the rules that govern turn-taking without really knowing that we have learned them and without, in most cases, being able to verbalize them. Duncan and Fiske (1977) inform us there are a handful of signals that tell us when we may speak and by which we tell others that it is their turn. These include an upward or downward change of pitch at the end of an utterance, the completion of a grammatical clause, a *drawl* on the last syllable, or the termination of a gesture. These are among the signals that children have to learn if they are eventually to converse in socially acceptable ways. And amazingly, they seem to have a relatively sophisticated awareness of turn-taking signals at very young ages. In one investigation, Mayer and Tronick (1985) found that even at the age of 2 months, infants and their mothers are already taking turns in their verbal interactions. They videotaped 10 mothers and their infants in face-to-face interaction for three-minute periods when the infants were 2, 3, and 5 months of age. Subsequent analysis of videotapes revealed that not only did infants rarely vocalize (other than for occasional "fussy" vocalizations) when their mothers were speaking, but they seemed to understand the mother's turn-taking signals. They responded not only to head and hand movements, but also to changes in intonation at the ends of utterances, to terminal drawls, and to the completion of grammatical clauses. Accordingly, they cooed and smiled mostly during the mother's pauses. Mothers, for their part, modified the number of turn-taking signals given depending on the child's responsiveness. This is very much what adults do. As Duncan and Fiske (1977) note, although a single turn-taking cue is often sufficient for smooth transitions in adult conversations, quite often more than one cue is given. The more cues given, the more likely it is that the listener will take a turn.

So, even here in the young months of the prespeech stage, the infant shows a readiness for language — even for conversation — that is little short of astounding. As Mayer and Tronick (1985) observe, it is as though the infant were "preadapted for social engagement" and as though the mother has an implicit knowledge of this fact.

First Sounds

It all begins with sounds — the ability of the infant to discriminate among them and the ability to produce them (see Table 5.5).

Sound discrimination. There is some evidence that infants have a built-in capacity to discriminate sounds. Recall, for example, the Moffitt (1971) experiment described earlier in this chapter in which the heartrates of 5- and 6-month-old infants were monitored while they were exposed to taped recordings of the sounds *bah* and *gah.* Changes in heartrate whenever the sound changed indicated that these infants could tell the difference between them.

These and related studies have led some to conclude that infants are innately able to discriminate equally easily among all distinct sounds. However, it appears that some sounds are far more difficult to tell apart than others. For example, infants experience considerable difficulty in telling *sa* from *za,* but they can much more easily tell the difference between *sa* and *fa* or *va* and *sa* (Eilers & Minifie, 1975). With language experience, however, children are eventually able to discriminate reliably among these sounds. In some cases, however, if the sounds are not part of their language, they may experience difficulty discriminating among them even as adults — the sounds *la* and *ra* for a native Japanese speaker, for example (Miyawaki et al., 1975).

Table 5.5
Stages in Children's Development of Grammar

Stage of Development	Nature of Development	Sample Utterances
1. Prespeech (before age 1)	Crying, cooing, babbling.	"Waaah," "dadadada."
2. Sentencelike word (holophrase) (by 12 months)	The word is combined with nonverbal cues (gestures and inflections).	"Mommy." (meaning: "Would you please come here, mother.")
3. Two-word sentences (duos) (by 18 months)	Modifiers are joined to topic words to form declarative, question, negative, and imperative structures.	"Pretty baby." (declarative) "Where Daddy?" (question) "No play." (negative) "More milk!" (imperative)
4. Multiple-word sentences (by 2 to 2½ years)	Both a subject and predicate are included in the sentence types. Grammatical morphemes are used to change meanings ("ing" or "ed," for example).	"She's a pretty baby." (declarative) "Where Daddy is?" (question) "I no can play." (negative) "I want more milk!" (imperative) "I running." "I runned."
5. More complex grammatical changes and word categories (between 2½ and 4 years)	Elements are added, embedded, and permuted within sentences. Word classes (nouns, verbs, and prepositions) are subdivided. Clauses are put together.	"Read it, my book." (conjunction) "Where is Daddy?" (embedding) "I can't play." (permutation) "I would like some milk." (use of "some" with mass noun) "Take me to the store." (use of preposition of place)
6. Adultlike structures (after 4 years)	Complex structural distinctions made, as with "ask-tell" and "promise."	"Ask what time it is." "He promised to help her."

Source: Based in part on Barbara S. Wood, Children and communication: Verbal and nonverbal language development (2nd ed.), © 1981, p. 142. Reprinted by permission of Prentice-Hall, Inc., Englewood Cliffs, New Jersey.

Sound production. Discriminating among sounds is only one part of early language learning; producing intended sounds is the other. It starts with the crying, the cooing, and the eventual babbling of the infant. Eventually it progresses to the word — and beyond.

It was long believed that all the sounds of every language in the world are uttered in the babbling of an infant, even in the babbling of deaf infants. This belief leads directly to the conclusion that the ability to produce speech sounds is innate, a conclusion that does not appear to be entirely true. For example, although the first sounds uttered by deaf infants are very similar to those of hearing children, their later vocalizations are typically quite different. These first sounds, say Eilers and Oller (1988), are precursors to the form of babbling in which infants finally utter well-formed syllables with clearly articulated consonants and vowels — a stage that does not occur until sometime between 7 and 10 months. Before then, infants make unarticulated noises; they goo, squeal, growl, whisper, and yell. And although it might be possible to discern many sounds that resemble those found in the world's 5,000 or so languages in these early infant sounds, their utterances remain unsystematic and do not obey the laws of syllables (requiring clarity and a complete vowel of adequate duration).

But by the age of 10 months, hearing children babble clearly, systematically, and repetitively. Deaf children do not reach this stage until later. "It cannot be maintained," say Eilers and Oller (1988), "that babbling is independent of hearing" (p. 23).

While it is true that certain sounds do appear in the babbling of virtually all infants, many other sounds are almost never heard, even though they are an important part of some languages. The most common sounds that infants babble are the ones that are easiest, given the anatomical structure of their vocal apparatus. Most common among these are certain consonants such as b's, d's, w's, and m's (described by linguists as *stop, glide,* or *nasal* consonants). Thus words like "mama," "papa," and "dada" are among the simplest for virtually all infants. And it should come as no surprise that these words are common to a variety of languages. Nor should it come as a surprise that, no matter the language involved, much of the infant's early speech consists of words that evolve directly from easy-to-babble sounds.

The first word. It is not usually easy to determine when infants say their first word. Expressions such as "bah," when they come to mean something for the child, may be considered words. However, most infants repeat a sound such as "bah" many times before it becomes associated with an object. The point at which the sound "bah" ceases to be babble and becomes a word ("ball," for example) is unclear. Somewhere near the age of 1 year, children do utter their first meaningful words, frequently created by repeating two identical sounds such as in "mama," "dada," or "bye bye." The appearance of the first word is rapidly followed by new words that the child practices incessantly. Most of an English-speaking child's first words are nouns: simple names for simple things — the simple things usually being objects or people that are part of the "here and now" that Piaget describes: "dog," "mama," "banket" (blanket), "yefant" (elephant). Verbs, adjectives, adverbs, and prepositions are acquired primarily in the order listed, with the greatest difficulty usually being the use of pronouns, especially the pronoun "I" (Boyd, 1976).

But before learning words, infants have begun to show signs that they understand much more than they can say — words that will not be part of their active vocabulary for some time, as well as entire sentences. "Stick out your tongue," she is told by a proud parent, and she sticks out her tongue. "Show Daddy your hand," and she shows it. "Can you wink?" Sure can. Two eyes, though.

For convenience, the learning of language is described in terms of six sequential stages (Wood, 1981). The first of these, the prespeech stage, lasts until approximately age 1. It consists of the crying, the gooing, the babbling just described. The next two stages — that of *the sentencelike word* and the *two-word sentence* are described in the following sections. The remaining three stages are detailed in Chapter 7 (see Table 5.5).

The Sentencelike Word

Sometime after the sixth month (usually around age 1) children utter their first meaningful word. This word's meaning is not limited to one event, action, or person but is interpreted as meaning something that an adult would require an entire sentence to communicate — hence the term *holophrase*. McNeill (1970) suggests that children's knowledge of grammar is innate — that they have notions of grammar long before they arrive at an understanding of how to express different grammatical forms in adultlike ways. Thus although most holophrases are nouns, they are not used simply for naming. When a child says "milk," she might mean, "There is the milk." She might also mean, "Give me some milk," "I'm thirsty," "I want you to hold me," "Sing me a song," or "Daddy is nice." A simple preposition such as "on" employed as a holophrase by my youngest linguist meant "Turn the light on," "Pick me up," "Put me on the chair," "Dress me," "Daddy is nice," and many other things.

Two-Word Sentences

Not surprisingly, the progression of speech development is from one word to two (roughly by the age of 18 months) — and later to more than two. There does not appear to be a three-word stage following this two-word stage, but rather a *multiword* stage where sentences range in length from two to perhaps five or more words (Brown, 1973).

Children continue to acquire words during the second year, but the range of syllables available to them is limited. Many of their words are one- or two-syllable words, which often repeat the same syllable in different combinations. For example, the child says, "mommy," "daddy," "baby," "seepy" (sleepy), "horsy," and "doggy." Even when it is incorrect to do so, the child may frequently repeat the syllable in a one-syllable word, as in "car car" or "kiss kiss." In an attempt to communicate with children on their level, parents sometimes exaggerate the trivial errors committed by their infants in the course of learning to speak. The result is occasionally something like, "Wou my itsy bitsy witta baby come to momsy womsy?" But there is no evidence that parental (or grandparental) models of this type hamper the rapid and correct acquisition of language. In the early stages, the warmth of the interaction may be more important than the nature of the language employed.

The transition from holophrases to two-word sentences generally occurs around 18 months. Bloom (1973) suggests this process begins slowly, with the relatively hesitant combining of familiar words, but that their use increases very rapidly once the child begins to understand the number of meanings that can be conveyed with two-word sentences. Speech at this stage is sometimes described as being *telegraphic*, because it eliminates a great many parts of speech while still managing to convey meanings. "Dog allgone" is a two-word utterance "telegraphed" from the lengthier adult equivalent, "The dog is not in this location at this time."

Whether precise grammatical functions can be accurately assigned to these two-word utterances is a matter of some debate. The functions of the words "fish" and "eat" in the two-word utterance "fish eat" are, in fact, dependent on the intended meaning. But because the child does not use number agreement (for example, "fish eats" to mean "the fish eats" and "fish eat" to mean "I eat fish") or order ("eat fish" versus "fish eat") to signal meaning, the psycholinguist can never be certain that children at this stage are aware of grammatical functions (Clark & Clark, 1977).

By the age of 2, infants have reached the point where they can name all the familiar objects and people in their environment. More than this, they can now combine words into meaningful sentencelike units. They can also use adjectives and adverbs, questions, simple negatives and affirmatives; and they have begun to learn a variety of subtle and implicit rules governing intonation, inflection, and the conventions that guide conversations.

But there is much more yet to be learned; there remain three stages in our six-stage description of the sequence of language acquisition. The story of that sequence continues in Chapter 7.

A Transition

The word *infant* derives from the Latin *infans*, meaning "without speech." Indeed, throughout much of the period that we arbitrarily label *infancy* the child is without speech. As noted earlier, the world of infants is initially a world of the here and now, a world populated only by those objects and feelings that are immediately perceived, a world that cannot be represented symbolically, but can only be acted on and felt. But the infant's capacities to act and to feel are far more impressive than we have long believed — perhaps even more impressive than most of us still believe (see Pearce, 1977; Pines, 1982).

Although the term *sensorimotor* describes well the predominant relationship between infant and world, it does not describe the most important cognitive achievements of the first two years of life. Some of these achievements are apparent in Table 5.6. By the time the child is 2, the world no longer exists only in the immediate, sensible present. Objects have achieved a permanence and an identity that no longer depend solely on the child's activities; there is a

Table 5.6

Average Ages for Mental Development in Infants

Month	Activity
0.2	Regards person momentarily, responding either to speech or to movements
0.7	Eyes follow moving person
0.7	Makes definite response to speaking voice
1.5	Smiles or laughs in response to another person's speaking to and smiling at him or her
2.0	Visually recognizes mother; expression changes when infant sees mother bending over to talk to him or her
2.6	Manipulates red ring placed in child's hand or grasped by child
3.8	Carries red ring to mouth during free play
3.8	Inspects own hands
4.1	Reaches for cube, even if not actually touching it
5.1	Laughs or shows pleasure when held and played with
5.8	Lifts cup with handle
6.0	Looks for spoon that has fallen
9.1	Responds to verbal request *not* accompanied by gesture.
12.0	Turns pages of book, even if effort is clumsy
14.2	Says two words meaningfully (approximations all right if clear)
20.6	Puts two or more words denoting two concepts into one sentence or phrase

Source: Adapted from *Bayley Scales of Infant Development* by N. Bayley, 1969. Reproduced by permission. Copyright © 1969 by The Psychological Corporation, New York, N.Y. All rights reserved.

dawning understanding of cause-and-effect relationships; language is rapidly exercising a profound effect on cognitive development. These achievements, together with children's recognition of their own identities — their selves — represent a dramatic transition from a quasi-animalistic existence to the world of thought and emotions as we know it. But although it is a dramatic transition, at least in its import, it is neither sudden nor startling. Those who follow the lives of individual children closely (and daily) never see the transition from sensorimotor intelligence to preoperational thought. It happens suddenly and irrevocably on the second birthday only in textbooks. Real life is less well organized.

MAIN POINTS

1. A newborn is a primitive, self-driven little sensing machine designed to mature and grow physically in a predetermined sequence and at a relatively predictable pace, programmed as an extraordinarily capable information-

processing system, endowed with powerful gregarious tendencies and strong emotions to drive many of its actions, and pretuned to speech and to the development of language.

2. Through history there has been a conflict between mothers who chose not to breast-feed their babies and others who insisted they should (for reasons including maternal duty, infant rights, the transmission of virtue, and natural goodness). Breast milk is among the best, most easily digested foods for infants and is useful in guarding against the possibility of illness and disease — especially diarrhea in developing countries. In much of the industrialized world where sanitation and medical care are adequate, the reasons for breast-feeding may not be as compelling or important as convenience and personal preference.

3. Optimal brain development in early infancy is profoundly influenced by nutrition (especially protein) and stimulation.

4. Sudden infant death syndrome accounts for the unexpected and largely unexplainable death of approximately 2 out of every 1,000 apparently healthy infants. It is more common among males, rarely occurs after the age of 6 months, and is sometimes associated with a mild upper-respiratory infection or with apnea (a sleep disorder involving sudden cessation of breathing).

5. The *orienting response,* a useful measure of attention, interest, and learning in infants, is defined by our tendency to respond to new stimulation by becoming more alert. It involves changes in physiological functions such as heartrate, respiration rate, electrical activity of the brain, and conductivity of the skin to electricity.

6. The repertoire of the neonate consists of a number of reflexes, some of which are important for survival: the sucking reflex; the Moro (startling); the Babinski (fanning and curling the toes); the palmar (grasping); and the swimming, stepping, swallowing, and sneezing reflexes. Many of these disappear with the development of the brain and the achievement of voluntary control over movements.

7. Motor capacities develop in sequence. Although there is wide individual variation in the age at which each ability is attained, the sequence appears to be similar among different infants.

8. Sensation is primarily a physiological process involving the senses and neural transmission; conceptualization is an intellectual process involving thinking and understanding; and perception, our interpretation of sensation, is a sort of bridge between sensation and conceptualization.

9. The perceptual equipment of the neonate is quite well developed at birth and matures rapidly with age. Depth perception, response to patterns, and the ability to recognize colors are all present early in life. The infant's visual acuity improves greatly in the first year of life. The infant's visual accommodation seems best for distances of approximately 12 inches.

10. Haith suggests that the infant's looking is governed by a need to maximize information (by maximizing neural firing). Two sorts of visual scanning routines are used: ambient search routines or ASR (broad, sweeping eye motions)

to discover shadows, edges, contours; and inspection scan routines or ISR (back-and-forth eye movements over edges) to examine specific stimuli. The rules that govern looking behavior are (1) if awake and alert, open eyes; (2) even in darkness, search with controlled eye movements (ASR); (3) in unpatterned light, search for edges, patterns, etc. (ASR); (4) if an edge is found, terminate ASR and go to ISR (short eye movements back and forth across edge, maximizing stimulation in foveal area).

11. Neonates are slightly less sensitive than adults to sound intensity (loudness). Sensitivity to higher frequencies increases with age, a fact that might explain why many adults make their voices higher when speaking to children. Infants appear to recognize and prefer their mother's voice at ages as young as 3 days.

12. Newborns prefer pleasant odors (such as vanilla) to less pleasant ones (ammonia or raw fish) almost from birth. Similarly, they prefer the sweet to the bland and appear to distinguish easily between sour and bitter tastes. Furthermore, they appear to be sensitive to touch (and to pain) at least within a few hours of birth.

13. There are two broad approaches to current explanations of cognition: the information-processing and the Piagetian. The information-processing approach looks at the processes involved in memory: deriving information, abstracting, sorting, organizing, analyzing, and developing strategies for learning and remembering.

14. The neonate's memory is not as efficient, as powerful, or as long-term as that of older children or adults. Nevertheless, even within days of birth, infants appear to remember something about what they have seen or smelled. By the age of 3 months, they actively look and search and show signs of recognition. By the age of 8 months, their memories have become more abstract.

15. In Piaget's theory, adaptation (cognitive growth) results from the interplay of assimilation (responding in a habitual and preferred way based primarily on preexisting information and well-practiced capabilities) and accommodation (adapting behavior to some external characteristic or quality). Equilibration is the governing force that strives to balance assimilation and accommodation. Other important factors in cognitive development include maturation, social interaction, and active experience.

16. The infant's world is a world of the here and now. The infant does not realize that objects continue to exist even when they are not being sensed. Piaget believed it was not until around 18 months that the child developed a complete understanding of object permanence (the *object concept*).

17. In the first of the six substages of the sensorimotor period (exercising reflexes: 0–1 month), there is little new learning, but infants repeatedly practice the simple reflexes with which they were born. Substage 2 (primary circular reactions: 1–4 months) is characterized by repetitive behaviors centering on the infant's body. In substage 3 (secondary circular reactions: 4–8 months), infants acquire new repetitive behaviors centering on the environment. Substage 4 (purposeful coordinations: 8–12 months) is marked by the coordination of activities in goal-oriented behaviors. In substage 5 (tertiary circular reactions: 12–18 months), infants explore the environment by deliberately modifying repetitive behaviors. And in substage 6 (mental representation:

    18–24 months), there is a gradual transition to a more symbolic, more conceptual intelligence.

18. There is evidence that even in the first days of life, infants are capable of imitating simple facial gestures such as opening the mouth, pursing the lips, or sticking out the tongue. These imitative behaviors may sometimes be due simply to the nearness of the experimenter. They are not completely automatic and easily triggered and are probably limited to a handful of behaviors. Evidence of *deferred imitation* (the ability to imitate a model who is no longer present) is seen by the age of 9–12 months, depends on the ability to represent mentally and to remember, and is therefore of considerable importance in cognitive development.

19. Language involves the use of arbitrary speech sounds that have accepted meanings. It is characterized by *displacement, meaning*, and *productiveness*.

20. The four basic elements of language are *phonology* (sounds), *semantics* (meanings of words); *syntax* (grammar or rules that govern relationships among parts of speech); and *pragmatics* (rules and conventions concerning how and when to speak).

21. There is evidence infants as young as 2 months of age have a relatively sophisticated awareness of turn-taking signals ordinarily employed in conversation. Most infants goo and babble in the pauses mothers leave following appropriate turn-taking signals, such as head and hand movements, changes of intonation at the ends of utterances, terminal drawls, and the completion of grammatical clauses.

22. There is some evidence that infants have a built-in capacity to discriminate certain sounds (some are more difficult than others or even impossible); also, they are able to produce a large variety of sounds in their babbling — but some sounds are more common than others among all infants, and some rarely appear. Babbling, involving well-formed syllables — as opposed to goos, squeals, and cries — becomes systematic by ages 7 to 10 months. Linguistic experience eventually modifies the infant's ability to discriminate and to produce sounds.

23. Two important achievements of the prespeech stage are the development of the intention to communicate and the discovery of symbols — the realization that things have names. The first word usually appears by the end of the first year — sometimes earlier, sometimes later. It is often sentencelike in nature (a holophrase).

24. Two-word sentences appear around the age of 18 months. These are telegraphic, condensing considerable information into two words.

Further Readings

An extremely simple, nontechnical description of development during the first three years of life, which offers numerous practical suggestions particularly useful for parents interested in understanding and promoting the intellectual development of their infants, is:

White, B. L. (1985). *The first three years of life* (Rev. ed.). Englewood Cliffs, N.J.: Prentice-Hall.

Although Piaget's writings are often difficult reading, there are a large number of relatively simple accounts of his principal findings and theoretical beliefs. The following is clear and useful:

Wadsworth, B. J. (1989). *Piaget's theory of cognitive and affective development* (4th ed.). New York: Longman.

The major premise of this captivating and sometimes disturbing book is that we have grossly underestimated the infant's intellectual capacities and that, worse still, we damage and even destroy much of that capacity:

Pearce, J. C. (1977). *Magical child: Rediscovering nature's plan for our children.* New York: Bantam Books.

The following two sources might be useful to those who want more information about physical, cognitive, and perceptual development in infancy. The first is a comprehensive textbook dealing solely with the first two years of life and providing for more research detail than is possible in a chapter such as this. The second is a look at the infant as a thinker.

Rosenblith, J. F., & Sims-Knight, J. E. (1985). *In the beginning: Development in the first two years.* Monterey, Calif.: Brooks/Cole.

Bradley, B. S. (1989). *Visions of infancy: A critical introduction to child psychology.* Cambridge, Eng.: Polity Press.

An outstandingly clear and well-written account of cognitive development that examines Piaget's theories in considerable detail is:

Flavell, J. H. (1985). *Cognitive development* (2nd ed.). Englewood Cliffs, N.J.: Prentice-Hall.

This short book by Haith presents an intriguing account of how the newborn uses vision as an information-gathering system:

Haith, M. H. (1980). *Rules that babies look by: The organization of newborn visual activity.* Hillsdale, N.J.: Lawrence Erlbaum.

The early development of language in infants is described in more detail in:

Wood, B. S. (1981). *Children and communication: Verbal and nonverbal language development* (2nd ed.). Englewood Cliffs, N.J.: Prentice-Hall.

Carroll, D. W. (1986). *Psychology of language.* Monterey, Calif.: Brooks/Cole.

An excellent analysis of pragmatics in language is:

Bates, E. (1976). *Language and context: The acquisition of pragmatics.* New York: Academic Press.

When the first baby laughed for the first time, the laugh broke into a thousand pieces and they all went skipping about, and that was the beginning of fairies.

James Matthew Barrie, *Peter Pan*

Social Development

hile I was sitting here, waiting for the inspiration that would begin this sixth chapter, a dog trotted into my office. I swear it. In fact, she is still here. She is a lovely, chocolate brown, German short-haired pointer puppy. She walked right in, smelled me, then curled into a little ball on the carpet by my feet. She will be my inspiration.

This dog reminds me of the wealth of experiments that psychologists, physiologists, medical researchers, and others have performed with her relatives. (Dogs have now salivated their way into almost every psychology textbook in the world.) One experiment in particular is important here. It begins with studies in which infant monkeys were taken from their mothers at birth and raised with substitute mothers — such as wire models of monkey mothers covered with soft terry cloth (Harlow, 1959). What the studies showed, among other things, was that infant monkeys can develop strong attachments even to inanimate objects, and that they will later respond to these objects as they might to their own mothers.

Several decades later a related study was performed by Mason and Kenney (1974). In this study, some infant monkeys were taken from their mothers at birth and were raised with cloth-covered surrogates; others were raised with a peer monkey; and a third group were allowed to stay with their mamas. As expected, all developed strong attachments to surrogate, peer, or mother.

Then, at ages ranging from 3 to 10 months, each of these infant monkeys was separated from mother, surrogate, or peer, and gradually exposed to — you guessed it — a dog. One would expect that under these circumstances, the little infant monkeys would be lonely and depressed. What, after all, can take the place of a mother (or a genuine mother substitute)?

The answer, strangely enough, is a *second* substitute. What happened in the Mason and Kenney study is that at first the infant monkeys were frightened. They had had no experience with dogs, and they found these creatures quite terrifying. But before long they overcame their fear and began to approach the dog. After a while, they began to cling to the dog, very much as they had previously clung to their mother, their surrogate, or their peer. Soon, they displayed all the usual signs of strong infant-mother attachment: clinging, following, running to the dog when frightened.

The conclusion? Objects of primary attachment are not necessarily permanent among some nonhuman primates. Even a creature like the little pointer puppy, who has just now left my office, might serve as a substitute for a monkey mother and bring comfort and joy into the life of a little monkey infant.

THIS CHAPTER

Might this dog also serve as a mother substitute for a human infant? How crucial are early contacts between infants and mothers and fathers? How do attachment bonds form? What are the consequences of disrupting them? Do we, as some psychoanalysts believe, go through life forever looking for something that will replace the first of our attachments?

    These are some of the questions we address in this chapter. We begin with a look at parent-infant attachment, discuss the development and meaning of infant emotions and of infant temperament, and examine how infants respond to strangers and how they react to separation from their parents. And in the end, we protest again that the average, normal infant of whom we speak is an invention. So we conclude with a look at infants who are not average — infants who have been especially favored by their biologies and their contexts, as well as infants who have been placed at risk by one or both.

INTERACTIONS IN THE FAMILY CONTEXT

Throughout much of child psychology's brief history, the principal emphasis has been on how parents affect their offspring. Although it is apparent that infants and children also affect parents' lives, these effects have not been considered important for infants and children themselves. After all, child psychology is about children, not about parents.

    Not so, ecological and culturally based theories such as Bronfenbrenner's and Vygotsky's inform us: Influence in development is interactional; it does not flow only one way. Not only do infants and children affect their parents, but these effects are often instrumental in changing how parents, in turn, affect their children. As an illustration, consider Sara, an especially difficult infant who cries a lot, refuses her mother's breast unpredictably, and soils her diaper at awkward times and with a wolfish grin as if to say, "There, that'll teach ya!" Her mother, in turn, is easily annoyed, impatient, highly emotional, and given to temper tantrums. Louis, on the other hand, is an angel of a baby. He sleeps regularly, seldom cries, loves his mother's breast, and soils his diaper only at regular intervals and always very politely with an apologetic little grimace as if to say, "Phugh and Yuk! I sure hate to have to do that!" and Louis' mother is a calm, enthusiastic, patient mama who is absolutely delighted with her infant.

    In Bronfenbrenner's terms, the ecology — the interactions — will be very different in each of these two *microsystems*. After all, the characteristics of both Louis and Sara, and their mothers, are very different; the interactions are not likely to be very similar.

A wide range of infant characteristics — and of parental characteristics — are especially important in determining the infant's developmental context. The infant's temperament is clearly important; physical appearance is also important (recall how fathers treated their attractive daughters more favorably than those less attractive).

And the infant's sex is important — as is the parent's sex. To illustrate: It appears that in general (but with many important exceptions) fathers engage in more physically exciting, stimulating play with infants than do mothers. They hold them primarily to play with them (see Hodapp and Mueller, 1982). In contrast, mothers hold them for nurturant, caregiving reasons — as well as to play. Also, infant responses to parents differ according to the sex of the parent. Fathers appear to elicit more positive emotions from their infants during play than do mothers. And perhaps most important, there appears to be a subtle fostering of sex-role differentiation involved in these early parent-infant interactions, especially after the infant has reached the age of 1. There is evidence that after that age, fathers tend to interact more with sons than with daughters. At about that time, it appears that sons begin to prefer their fathers, this preference being evident in the frequency with which they approach, touch, or ask to be picked up by one or the other parent. Similarly, there is a tendency, though somewhat less strong, for girls to show greater preference for their mothers (Lamb, 1980).

Discovering the nature of these interactions and influences is not simple; interpreting them is even more difficult. Do fathers and mothers treat sons and daughters differently because of sex-related differences in infant behaviors and interests? Or do differences in the behaviors and interests of the infants result from how their parents interact with them? Or both?

A Model of Influences

Questions such as these have led to some important changes in how researchers view the influence of the family on the developing child. Traditionally, the analysis has been of two-person or *dyadic* relationships: for example, mother-infant, father-infant, infant-sibling.

This model, useful though it continues to be, has one major shortcoming. It fails to take into consideration the *triadic* nature of the majority of the families into which infants are born, as well as the great variety of indirect effects that parents and families can have on infants. Our prevailing models have been dyadic and psychological, whereas alternative models proposed by individuals such as Parke (1979) and Belsky (1981) are triadic and partly sociological.

This new family-based triadic model differs from the traditional dyadic model in a number of important ways. First, it suggests that there are far more influences at work on the infant than just a mother on the one hand and a father on the other. There is also a family — a social unit made up of husband and wife (as opposed to just father and mother) and characterized by a marital relationship. Second, the model suggests there may be a great number of complex influences at play other than the obvious parent-infant links. Belsky (1981) refers to these as "second-order" effects. Some possible second-order effects include the influence that a father might have on a mother, which might then cause her to interact differently with the infant; the relationship that the mother has with the infant, which might influence the way the father interacts with the infant; the influence that the infant's arrival (or temperament) has on the marital relationship and the consequent effects on parenting; the influence of economic changes. Note that these "second-order" effects are what Bronfenbrenner (1989) labeled the meso-, exo-, and macrosystems.

This view suggests new lines of research and new interpretations of older research. It emphasizes the dynamic nature of the parenting unit and the fact that this unit is more than just mother and father. It reaffirms that even as parents influence children, so too do infants influence parents; and it goes even further in pointing out that what is influenced is more than two individuals; it includes a complex of relationships.

What does research tell us about these relationships? Perhaps not as much as we would like to know, because many of the results are still unclear or contradictory. To summarize briefly, Belsky (1981) reviews research indicating that the birth of an infant often changes the marital relationship (sometimes increasing stress and discord, sometimes having the opposite effect); that discordant and conflict-ridden marital relationships are sometimes related to the development of antisocial behavior in children; that highly supportive marital relationships are related to caregiving skills with young infants; that the birth of an infant can frequently make a good marriage better, although it is less likely to make a bad one good; and that among the most important qualities of parenting as it is reflected in cognitive development and adjustment are sensitive mothering (attentiveness, warmth, responsiveness, and stimulation) and involved fathering (doing things with infants, including caregiving and playing).

But, as Belsky points out, we still know "very little about the direct influence of the child on marital relations and even less about the reverse process of influence" (p. 17). The adoption of a contextual/ecological model may increase our knowledge considerably.

INFANT STATES

When discussing the characteristics of infants, we sometimes assume that all "normal" infants possess the same qualities, that all react in similar, predictable ways, and that individual differences observed in older children are not very apparent in the very young infant. In fact, however, individual differences are detectable very shortly after birth, are consistent, and are related to differences evident later in life. The term *infant state* is used to describe the general condition of a neonate; and it is when we examine a specific infant's predominant states that individual differences become most apparent.

Wolff (1966) presents a simple classification of infant states: regular sleep, disturbed or irregular sleep, drowsiness, alert inactivity, or focused activity. Additional states may sometimes be detected using physiological measures or more refined observational criteria. Wolff (1959) distinguishes between deep sleep and irregular sleep largely by heart and respiration rate. Similarly, he distinguishes between alert inactivity and focused activity by spontaneous changes in the infant's alert responsiveness. Inflexibly focused activity is, in effect, crying (see Table 6.1).

The most important observation from research on infant states is that infants vary consistently in the amount of time spent in each state. Brown (1964) studied states in six babies. Although this group of babies, on the average, spent approximately one-third of their time in stages of sleep, one infant slept 56 percent of the time. One child was in an alert state only 4 percent of the time; another, 37 percent of the time. One infant cried 39 percent of the time; another, only 17 percent of the time. Additional evidence of striking individual differences among these babies is that one infant responded to 86 percent of all auditory stimuli presented to her or that occurred randomly, regardless of her state. A low-intensity noise would cause her to open her eyes when in a state of apparently deep sleep.

Given these tremendous individual differences, knowledge of the average newborn's daily states is perhaps not too revealing. Hutt, Lenard, and Prechtl (1969) have found that this hypothetical infant sleeps between 75 and 80 percent of the time and that three-quarters of this time is spent in irregular sleep. The average newborn is drowsy or alert perhaps two or three hours of the day and engages in more intense, focused activity another hour or two. Crying occupies the remainder of the time.

Although the average neonate sleeps as much as 75 ot 80 percent of the time, for most young infants periods of sleep are relatively short and are interspersed with many brief periods of wakefulness. With increasing age, the infant sleeps somewhat less, but for longer periods of time.

It is not clear whether or not infants dream while they sleep; they cannot tell us. However, an extremely high proportion of the infant's sleeping time (as much as 50 percent) is characterized by rapid eye movements (termed *REM* sleep). And we do know that in children and adults, most dreams occur during REM sleep (Dement, 1974). Amount of REM sleep declines gradually during infancy. By the age of 2 years, approximately 25 percent of the infant's sleep is of the REM variety — very similar to the adult's average of 20 to 23 percent (Roffwarg, Muzio, & Dement, 1966).

Note that the concept of *infant state* refers to the infant's condition of alertness. That is, infant state simply takes into account whether the infant is sleeping, drowsy, alert, or crying. As we saw, however, infants differ in terms of the amount of time they characteristically spend in each of these states. These differences may, in fact, reflect basic, genetically influenced differences in temperament (or personality). They may also reflect the influence of different environments. Both of these possibilities are examined in more detail in a later section on temperament.

INFANT EMOTIONS

Any statements about an infant's emotions must be tentative for two reasons: Emotion is a subjective response that cannot easily be interpreted by an observer, particularly when subjects are still incapable of communicating their feelings in language more sophisticated than gurgles, wails, grunts, sighs, sobs, and belches; and situations that adults ordinarily interpret as emotion-producing cannot always be assumed to be emotion-related for infants. Until children are sufficiently developed that the emotional content of social and physical situations have meaning for them, investigating their emotions is a difficult task.

Nevertheless, beginning with the pioneering work of J. B. Watson (1914), a number of psychologists have assumed that the infant is capable of emotional responses from birth; that is, emotional responses are part of the reflexive repertoire. Watson identified three distinct emotional responses of a neonate: fear, rage, and love. He assumed that each of these was a reflex and could therefore be elicited by a specific stimulus. Rage was thought to result from being confined or from having movements restricted; fear, from a loud noise or from being dropped suddenly; and love resulted from being stroked or fondled. Sherman and Sherman (1929) later suggested that whenever investigators thought a child was reacting emotionally in response to a particular stimulation, they were subjectively interpreting the infant's behavior in terms of adult and personal predispositions. In other words, adults might be inferring motives and emotions with no valid basis for doing so.

More recently, theorists such as Izard and Malatesta (1987) suggest that human facial expressions reveal a number of distinct emotions including interest (or general excitement), joy, surprise, distress, anger, disgust, contempt, fear, shame, and guilt. They suggest as well that the facial expressions of infants indicate they may be capable of most of these feelings (Termine & Izard, 1988). Furthermore, some infants may have a distinct tendency to respond predictably in some situations, at least with respect to anger or sadness (see Collins & Gunnar, 1990). This may have implications for their personality development.

It is extremely difficult to separate such closely related emotions as joy and surprise (or distress, anger, and disgust — or shame and guilt). Accordingly,

Table 6.1
States Reflecting Infant's Responsiveness to Environment

State	Description	Responsiveness
Regular (deep) sleep	Largely motionless, eyes closed, regular breathing	No response to mild stimuli
Irregular sleep	Twitching motions, eyes closed, irregular breathing	Sounds or bright light can elicit grimace or smile
Drowsiness	Moderately active state precedes or follows sleep, eyes may be closed or open	Responsive to stimuli
Alert inactivity	Relative inactivity, eyes open, breathing more rapid than regular sleep, examining environment	Highly responsive; maintains examination of world
Focused activity (*includes* crying)	High activity, eyes open, low alertness, rapid breathing	Low responsiveness to stimuli

Source: Based on information in Wolff (1969).

much of the research on infant emotions has looked at behaviors such as crying, smiling, and fear reactions. We look briefly at each of these before considering infant temperament and attachments.

Crying

Wolff (1969) analyzed tape recordings of infants crying and identified a number of distinct cries that he interprets as expressions of different emotions. The most frequent cry is called the *rhythmic* cry. It is the type of cry to which most infants eventually revert after initially engaging in another type of crying. Most experienced parents apparently recognize their infant's rhythmic cries and typically interpret them as meaning that there is nothing seriously wrong. The *angry* cry is characterized by its protracted loudness and results from more air being forced through the vocal cords. A third distinguishable cry is that of *pain*, characterized by a long wail followed by a period of breath holding. Finally, there is the *hunger* cry.

What this research reveals most clearly is that infants' cries may be distinguished from one another and appear to fall into identifiable categories. The inference that a long wail followed by breath holding is an expression of pain rather than of anger, for example, can only be based on knowledge of the conditions that led to the cry.

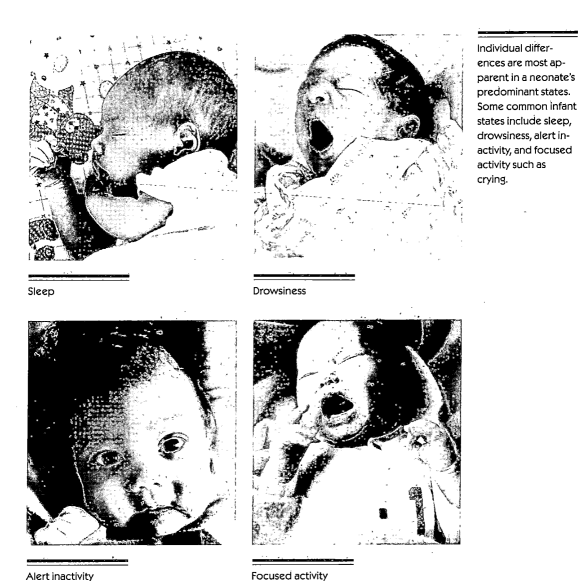

Sleep

Drowsiness

Alert inactivity

Focused activity

Mothers appear to be remarkably sensitive to the nature of infant cries, although here too there are individual differences (Ainsworth & Bell, 1969). Gustafson and Harris (1990) report that most mothers respond quickly to hunger cries or to cries of pain and that they readily discriminate between the two – although more mothers seem to be more sensitive to the general distress level of the infant than to the cause of the distress. Interestingly, first time parents tend to respond to infant crying sooner than parents who have more than one child. And mothers are more likely to be attentive than are fathers (Donate-Bartfield & Passman, 1985).

The meanings of an infant's cries are apparently not universal. Isabell and McKee (1980) observe that in many primitive cultures where the child is carried about constantly by the mother, mother-infant communication can occur through physical contact. In these cultures, there appears to be little need for the vocal signals of distress that we have come to expect from our infants. For instance, among South American Indian tribes in the northern Andes, infant crying is extremely rare and is invariably interpreted as a sign of illness. Why else would a warm, well-fed, and constantly embraced infant cry?

Smiling and Laughing

Smiling, a universal phenomenon among human cultures, is a fleeting response in the warm, well-fed infant and appears to occur as early as 2 to 12 hours after delivery (Wolff, 1963). In the weeks and months following birth, infants smile in response to an ever-widening range of sights and sounds. The social smile occurs first in response to a human voice (by the third week). By the age of 3½ months, infants smile more in response to familiar than unfamiliar faces (Gewirtz, 1965). Accordingly, Gewirtz identified three stages in the development of smiling behavior. The first phase, spontaneous or reflex smiling, occurs in the absence of readily identifiable stimuli and is often, though perhaps incorrectly, attributed to "gas pains." Social smiling, the second phase, takes place initially in response to auditory and visual stimuli that are social in nature — that is, related to other humans. Finally, the child displays the selective social smile, common among children and adults. It occurs in response to social stimuli that the child can identify as familiar. With the appearance of the selective social smile, children smile less often in response to an unfamiliar voice or face and display more withdrawal behavior and other signs of anxiety in the presence of strangers. (More about stranger anxiety in a later section of this chapter.)

Hodapp and Mueller (1982) note that the development of smiling in infants follows the same general pattern as the development of crying. Initially, infants smile and cry in response to internal states — primarily gastric disturbances. They use the term *endogenous* (related to internal states) to describe these smiles and cries. With the passage of time, however, the infant becomes more responsive to external stimulation, and both crying and smiling become more *exogenous* (responsive to external stimuli). By the age of 4 or 5 weeks, many infants will interrupt their feeding to smile when they hear their mother's voice. Similarly, crying now occurs in response to external sources of frustration such as having a pacifier presented and then taken away. In brief, the early development of these behaviors follows an internal to external progression. Whereas the first instances of smiling and crying might be considered to be

The true social smile occurs most frequently in response to a smiling face.

primarily physiological, within a short period of time, cognitive elements (such as are involved in recognizing a voice, a face, or an object) are clearly involved.

At about 4 months, infants begin to laugh in addition to smiling. At first, laughter is most likely to occur in response to physical stimulation such as tickling; later, infants laugh in response to more social and eventually more cognitive situations — seeing other children laughing, for example (Sroufe & Wunsch, 1972). Although the function of laughter in infants has never been very clear, perhaps because it has not been investigated very much, Sroufe and Waters (1976) suggest that it probably serves to release tension. Fear, by contrast, signifies a continued building up of tension.

Smiling and laughing are undoubtedly very important in parent-child interaction, particularly because we have come to recognize more clearly that parents and children have a mutual and interdependent effect on each other. In fact, both research evidence and common sense suggest that parents look for smiles and other nonverbal gestures in their infants as evidence that they are themselves worthwhile and loved. There is little reason to suppose that parents are not at least as sensitive as their children to feelings of rejection. A particularly significant though somewhat sad finding confirming these observations comes from the study of mothers interacting with their blind children

(Fraiberg, 1974, 1975, 1980). Blind children do not smile as often as do the sighted; it seems that the true social smile not only occurs in recognition of a familiar face or situation but appears also more readily in response to a smiling face than one that is not smiling. Perhaps it is not surprising that Fraiberg found that mothers of (less smiling) blind infants felt more distance — less attachment — with their babies.

Blind infants differ from normal infants not only in smiling but also in their lesser responsiveness to verbal controls (Greenberg, 1980; Henggeler & Cooper, 1983). Perhaps even more important, they cannot engage in mutual gazing. In the early stages of infancy, mutual gazing appears to be one of the most frequent and important types of interaction between infant and mother. It becomes less frequent with the infant's increasing ability to coordinate motor activities and to engage in behaviors to which the mother can respond in other ways (Hartup & Lempers, 1973).

The importance for children of visual contact with their mothers is further corroborated in a study where children aged 3 to 4½ years were observed in a playroom with their mothers present or with a silent, life-size, color film of their mothers or of some stranger (Passman & Erck, 1978). That children played as long in the presence of their "filmed" mother as they did in the actual presence of their mother indicates that visual contact alone has an important function in parent-child interactions. Significantly too, children whose mothers were present, either filmed or in actuality, played longer than did children whose mothers were not present or who were exposed to films of strange women.

The mutuality of mother-child influence can be seen in a variety of other situations. An infant's fretting and crying trigger soothing behavior in the mother: rocking, singing, talking quietly, and so on (Lewis & Lee-Painter, 1974). In turn, the mother's soothing behavior quiets the infant. Perhaps the infant's quiet behavior now leads to a mutual gaze. Has the infant learned to be quiet and loving in response to the mother's soothing behavior? Or has the mother learned to be soothing in response to the infant's crying? Probably both — again showing the bidirectionality of influence.

And what about fear? Does it, like crying and smiling, stem initially from internal conditions? Or is it always a response to the environment?

Wariness and Fear

Some years ago I went to a Halloween costume party. As part of my "costume," I attempted to grow a beard. After a number of months, I had succeeded in covering most of my face with hair. The remainder of my costume required little effort or imagination — just courage.

Shortly after the party, I shaved off all my whiskers. And when I walked out of the bathroom clean-shaven, my 1-year-old daughter took a wide-eyed look at me and turned crying to her mother.

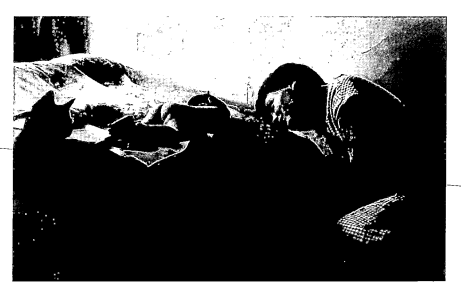

Mutual gazing is among the earliest forms of mother-infant interaction and appears to be very important in the formation of emotional bonds.

Although I was initially taken aback, my daughter's reaction should not have been unexpected; we know that young children often react to the unexpected with fear.

Fear reactions in infants and children have been investigated in some detail. Initially, as Watson and Rayner (1920) contended, it appears that infants react with fear to loud noises and sudden loss of support. Later, some infants come to fear a wide range of stimuli; others remain relatively unperturbed in the face of environmental changes. Fear of heights appears to be almost universal in infants by the age of 13 to 18 months and is present in more than 20 percent of all children by the age of 7 months (Scarr & Salapatek, 1970). Fear of strangers is not ordinarily seen before the age of 6 months and becomes most common by 2 years. Other situations that may evoke fear in an infant typically involve some unexpected change. For example, a Jack-in-the-box may be frightening; so might an experimenter or parent wearing a mask. In addition, separation from the mother is frightening for some infants, as are sounds presented in irregular fashion. As Hinde (1983) notes, it seems that as certain objects and people become familiar, infants begin to react with fear to strangers and to unfamiliar objects.

One of the classical studies of the roots of fear in infancy is Bronson's (1972) longitudinal study of wariness. In this context, the term *wariness* refers to an uneasiness that is somewhere between mild discomfort or distress and outright fear. The Bronson study used a relatively small sample of 16 male and 16 female infants. Infants were observed by one or more investigators at the ages of 3, 4, 6½, and 9 months. All observation sessions were videotaped so that they could be analyzed in detail later. In addition, parents were interviewed and questioned. Details of the observation sessions varied depending on the infants' ages. At 3 and 4 months, infants were observed while they lay on their backs in their cribs. During the observation session, they were presented with a number of novel objects such as a paper parasol being opened and closed and a mobile over their cribs. In addition, an adult male "stranger" leaned over the crib, smiled slightly at the infant, and asked the infant to smile, using the infant's name repeatedly. This episode lasted for approximately one minute unless the infant smiled broadly and repeatedly or began to cry.

At the age of 6½ months, infants were observed as they sat upright in an infant seat on the floor in a familiar room with the mother within view a short distance away. The experimenter hid behind a screen in back of the infant's seat and pushed a number of novel objects in front of the infant. Among these objects was a squarish box covered with red and white crepe paper and equipped with a sound device that transmitted random arrangements of short and long beeps. During the observation period, the experimenter, a male "stranger," walked out from behind the screen, squatted in front of the infant, and spoke quietly for one minute unless, again, the child cried or smiled continuously. At the end of the observation session, the stranger picked up the infants unless his presence had already elicited crying.

Observations at the age of 9 months took place with the baby on the floor and again involved the beeping object as well as the stranger. In the final episode of the observation, the stranger placed the infant on his knee for approximately one minute unless the infant had cried or smiled repeatedly earlier.

Examination of videotapes led to the development of a sequence of categories for classifying infant reactions ranging from smiling with delight (repeated smile) through smiling (less broad, noncontinuous smile), a neutral reaction (blank expression without vocalization), uneasiness (frowning, vocalizing, squirming, or trying to crawl away), and crying (Table 6.2).

A number of important findings resulted from this study. First, the most prevalent class of responses for 3- and 4-month-old infants is smiling rather than being uneasy or crying. By the age of 6½ months, however, there is increasing evidence of wariness; and by 9 months, evidence of *learned* fears. These findings are in agreement with many others indicating that infants are not likely to display marked *stranger anxiety* until after the age of 6 months.

A second intriguing finding relates to the effects of maternal care on the development of wariness in the infant. Observers identified two broad classes of maternal behavior in this study. At one extreme are those mothers who appear particularly adept at recognizing infant moods and needs, who respond sensitively, and who appear to enjoy interacting with their infants. At the other extreme are those who seem quite indifferent to infant needs and moods, whose interaction with infants appears more routine and less enjoyable, and who often limit interaction to essential caregiver tasks such as feeding, bathing, and diaper changing. For some reason, these two styles of mothering appear to be

Table 6.2
Categories for Describing Infant Reactions

Scale Point	Category Description	Criterion Behaviors for Each Age		
		3 and 4 Months	6½ Months	9 Months
1	Smiled with delight	Wiggled or vocalized as smiled	Repeated broad smiles or smiles with sounds of pleasure	
2	Smiled	————————————Smiled more than once, but not broadly————————		
3	Neutral	——————Predominantly blank expression and no vocalization————————		
4	Uneasy	Severe frown or puckering of chin	Frowned or sounded unhappy (or, on pickup, turned body away)	Frowned, sounded unhappy, or crawled to mother (or, on pickup, squirmed or turned body away)
5	Cried	——————————————Cried or whimpered————————		

Source: Adapted from G. W. Bronson, Infants' reactions to unfamiliar persons and novel objects. *Monographs of the Society for Research in Child Development,* 1972, 37, No. 3. © The Society for Research in Child Development, Inc. Used by permission.

far more critical for male than for female infants. Boys whose mothers were classified in the first group (sensitive and so on) were less likely to be wary of strangers and of novel objects. In this study as in an earlier Bronson (1971) study, style of mothering did not appear to be as important for female infants.

A third important finding is that at all ages, objects are far less potent than strangers in bringing about reactions of wariness or fear. By the age of 9 months, a number of infants had experienced fear reactions with strangers and seemed to have learned to associate specific features of a person with fear (beards or white smocks, for example). Similarly, wariness of novel objects was very rare before 9 months. By that age, mothers reported a number of instances in which many of the infants had responded with fear to something other than a strange person. Situations or objects that make loud noises or move suddenly are most likely to bring about fear reactions in infants (vacuum cleaners or a Jack-in-the-box, for example).

A fourth finding based on Bronson's investigation relates to the role of temperament (discussed next) and may help us understand how fear develops. Detailed interviews conducted during the first home visits included a number of questions about the infant's typical reactivity. Specifically, investigators looked at incidence and persistence of crying, distress reactions during bathing, frequency and intensity of startle reactions, and the incidence of blinking when presented with novel stimulation. Not surprisingly, infants with the most reactive temperaments, especially those who startled most easily, were more likely to be wary of strangers later.

Why are infants sometimes wary and sometimes not? The Bronson data suggest the reason lies in innate temperament interacting with various experiences. The relationship of age to the development of fear may at least partly reflect the fact that certain experiences are unlikely or less frequent at earlier ages — also that the meanings of some experiences depend on the infant's level of understanding. Clearly, a stranger is not a stranger until a familiar person can be recognized as familiar.

But why should some strangers and some novel objects elicit fear? One plausible explanation is Hebb's (1966) suggestion that infants develop certain expectations about their world and that violation of these expectations (*incongruence* is Hebb's term) may lead to fear.

Which might well be why my infant daughter ran crying to her mother. And then again . . .

Regulation of Emotions in Infancy

When you or I find ourselves in a frightening situation, when our hearts race and our knees turn to jelly, we do something to control or *regulate* our emotions. Perhaps we play cognitive games with ourselves: We tell ourselves that we really shouldn't be frightened, that we are such wonderful skydivers or musicians or public speakers that we will perform marvelously. Or we change the situation so that it isn't frightening anymore, perhaps by avoiding it or by redefining it.

There is a temptation to think that infants are not capable of this sort of control of emotions: that if they are frightened, all they can do is cry; and if they are delighted, then, like little automatons, they must smile. We sometimes think of them as responding almost blindly to the stimulation that the world provides, willy-nilly, for them.

We are wrong; they are not nearly so helpless. Beginning very early in life, infants are capable of what Gianino and Tronick (1988) label *self-directed* and *other-directed regulatory behaviors*. These behaviors are designed to regulate, or control, their emotions. As an example, Tronick (1989) describes a peek-a-boo game between a mother and her infant. In this little episode, the infant turns away from the mother just prior to the "peek" and begins to suck on his thumb, staring blankly into space. The mother sits back. Within a few seconds, the infant turns to the mother, pulls out the thumb, and contorts his body; his expression is clearly interested. The mother smiles, moves closer, says "Oh, now you're back!" The infant smiles and crows. Shortly, he goes back to sucking his thumb. But again, after a few seconds, he turns to the mother once more and smiles (p. 112).

The infant in this instance seems to be attempting to control the mother's behavior. This *other-directed* regulatory behavior is evident in how he turns back to the mother, how he crows and smiles, how he tries to make her do things that he finds exciting. In effect, what he is doing is controlling her behavior and, by the same token, exercising control over his own emotions. And when things become too exciting, too emotional, he can regulate his emotions by turning away from his mother. Now he distracts himself by sucking his thumb and by staring into space — evidence of *self-directed* regulatory behavior.

Tronick (1989) argues that the many emotion-regulating behaviors in which infants engage are evidence that the infant's behavior is goal-directed. When an emotional state is negative, infants turn their faces, suck their thumbs, stare at something neutral or pleasant; the goal is clearly to avoid the situation and to reduce the emotion. But when the emotional state is positive, the infant smiles, looks, reaches; the goal is now to maintain or heighten the emotion. Thus does the infant begin to learn not only how to regulate emotions, but also how to communicate them (see Chapter 8 for a more detailed discussion of the early socialization of emotions.)

TEMPERAMENT

When psychologists speak of differences in the customary ways of reacting and behaving that differentiate adults from each other, they generally speak of personality differences. The term *personality* includes all of the abilities, predispositions, habits, and other characteristics that make each of us different from one another.

When psychologists speak of differences among infants, they don't often use the term *personality.* The term is somewhat too global for the characteristics of young infants; it implies a degree of learning that has not yet had time to occur. Instead, psychologists speak of infant **temperament,** or characteristic emotional responses. The principal difference between *temperament* and *personality* is simply that temperament is assumed to have a primarily genetic basis (Chess & Thomas, 1989a), whereas personality has developed through interaction with the environment. Accordingly, Buss and Plomin (1985) define temperament as "inherited personality traits present in early childhood" (p. 84). Thus a child is born with a certain temperament rather than with a certain personality. We see this temperament in prevailing moods or the states we described earlier (crying, for example). The personality that later develops is an outgrowth of interaction between innate temperament and environmental influences (Carey, 1989).

Studying Infant Temperament

The classical studies of infant temperament are those of Thomas, Chess, and Birch (1968, 1970) and of Thomas and Chess (1977, 1981). These investigations, begun in 1956, are known as the New York Longitudinal Study (NYLS). Initial subjects for the NYLS consisted of 85 families, having a total of 141 children, from highly educated, professional backgrounds. Two important goals of the

Table 6.3
Nine Temperament Characteristics of Infants

1. Level and extent of motor activity
2. Rhythmicity (regularity of functions such as eating, sleeping, and eliminating)
3. Withdrawal or approach in new situations
4. Adaptability to change in the environment
5. Sensitivity to stimuli
6. Intensity (energy level) of responses
7. General mood or disposition (cheerful, cranky, friendly, and so on)
8. Distractibility (how easily infant may be distracted from ongoing activities)
9. Attention span and persistence in ongoing activities

study were to develop ways of identifying and classifying infant temperament and to examine the relationship of infant temperament to later adjustment and behavior. The principal data-gathering techniques used in early stages of the study were regular, structured interviews with parents and direct observations of the infants themselves. In later phases of the NYLS, a variety of testing, interview, and observational approaches was employed.

Types of Temperament

Analysis of the NYLS data suggests there are at least nine different infant characteristics that can be observed relatively easily and that can be used to differentiate among different infants (see Table 6.3). Parents or other observers can rate infants as being high, medium, or low on each of these characteristics, particularly after the infant is 2 or 3 months of age. Certain infants seem to have remarkably similar patterns of characteristics. There are three such patterns, each of which identifies a *type* of infant that parents seem to recognize readily. Infants who might be described as *difficult* are characterized by irregularity (lack of rhythmicity) in such things as eating, sleeping and toilet functions; withdrawal from unfamiliar situations; slow adaptation to change; and intense as well as negative moods. In contrast, an *easy* temperament is characterized by high rhythmicity (regularity in eating, sleeping, and so on); high approach tendencies in novel situations; high adaptability to change; and a preponderance of positive moods as well as low or moderate intensity of reaction. The third temperament type identified by Thomas, Chess, and Birch is labeled *slow to warm up* and is characterized by low activity level, high initial withdrawal from the unfamiliar, slow adaptation to change, somewhat negative in mood, but with a moderate or low intensity of reaction (Table 6.4).

Table 6.4
Infant Temperaments

Temperament	Description
Easy	Regularity in eating and sleeping (high rhythmicity); high approach tendencies in novel situations; high adaptability to change; preponderance of positive moods; low or moderate intensity of responses
Difficult	Irregularity in eating and sleeping (low rhythmicity); withdrawal in novel situations; slow adaptation to change; preponderance of negative moods; high intensity of reactions to stimulation
Slow to warm up	Low activity level; high initial withdrawal from unfamiliar; slow adaptation to change; somewhat negative mood; moderate or low intensity of reaction to stimulation
Varying mixtures; unclassified	

Easy 40%

Varying mixtures; unclassified 35%

Difficult 15%

Slow to warm up 10%

Approximate percentage of infants with each temperament

Source: Based on classifications used by Thomas, Chess, and Birch (1968, 1970) and Thomas and Chess (1981) in the New York Longitudinal Study (NYLS).

Note: Thomas and Chess (1981) caution that these three types do not exhaust all possibilities. In addition, although it is sometimes convenient to classify infants in these ways, there are wide ranges of behaviors within each category. *Easy* children don't all react the same way to the same situations; nor do all *difficult* children. Furthermore, some 35 percent of all infants appear not to fit into any of these categories.

Of the original 141 children in the NYLS, 65 percent could be classified as belonging to one of these three temperament types (40 percent *easy*; 15 percent *difficult*; 10 percent *slow to warm up*); the remaining 35 percent displayed varying mixtures of the nine temperament characteristics.

Temperament in Context

Temperament — that is, the neonate's tendency to be *easy* or *difficult* or *slow to warm up* — appears to have some genetic component (Chess & Thomas, 1989). One piece of evidence used in support of this is the observation that temperamental differences are present very shortly after birth. Nevertheless, it is also clear that experiences are important and that temperament is modified and shaped as a result of context.

Early experiences can play an important part in determining a child's temperament. The fact that Masai mothers are in close contact with their babies, often breast-feeding them until they are 2 or 3, may help explain why their infants are good-natured and have regular eating and sleeping habits.

One cross-cultural illustration is DeVries and Sameroff's (1984) study of infant temperament among three African tribes: the Kikuyu, the Digo, and the Masai. The Kikuyu are a relatively modern, wage-earning or farming society. They view infants as vulnerable, toilet train them later than other tribes, and expect them to develop motor skills at later ages. Among the Kikuyu, childcare involves a number of individuals and groups other than the mothers.

The Digo are a Bantu tribe who farm and fish and who have a much more leisurely life-style than the Kikuyu. They live in clusters of extended families in large dirt houses with grass roofs. Digo mothers monitor their infant closely and respond quickly to their cries. They expect a high level of motor and social development by the age of 3 to 5 months.

The Masai are a pastoral tribe; they live mostly on milk and meat from the herds they tend. Accordingly, their life centers on their cattle and, to some extent, on the corn crops they cultivate. They live in small mud huts in the center of their cattle corrals. Tuberculosis, trachoma, and other parasitic diseases are common among Masai children. Mothers spend most of their day with their children, breast-feeding them until the age of 2 or 3 years and carrying them on their backs until the children are old enough that others can care for them.

When deVries and Sameroff rated Masai, Kikuyu, and Digo infants with respect to temperament, using the dimensions used by Thomas, Chess, and Birch in the NYLS, they found a high relationship between temperament and cultural factors such as maternal orientation, childrearing customs, degree of modernization, and important events early in the child's life. Ratings for Masai and Digo infants were, on the whole, more positive, with significantly more infants being classed as *easy* rather than *difficult*. It should perhaps come as no surprise that Digo infants, reared in an easygoing, leisurely environment, should be marked by less "rhythmicity." The Digo, deVries and Sameroff inform us, are concerned with the "here and now" needs of their infants and are far less concerned with regularity in their patterns of feeding and sleeping. However, that the Kikuyu infants should be less adaptable, less approaching, more intensly reactive, and more negative than the Digo and the Masai is not as easily explained. What deVries and Sameroff (1984) conclude is that the data strongly support the hypothesis that "temperament is influenced by infant experiential factors" (p. 94). But they also caution that there are no simple interpretations for these findings.

Chess and Thomas (1989b) make the important point that although temperament has a biological basis, it is constantly evolving as a result of child-environment interaction. Consequently, developmental outcomes are not always easy to predict. The infant who is initially difficult may become an adolescent whose charm and grace and other good qualities make a mother blush with pride; and the one who is initially easy may, it's true, become a thoroughly reprehensible, no-good #@%^^&*. Or worse.

Implications of Infant Temperament

Still, Thomas and his associates (Chess & Thomas, 1989a, 1989b) suggest that being able to identify infants on the basis of predominant temperament may be useful for a number of reasons, including the fact that children of different temperaments may respond in quite different ways to parenting styles. *Easy* children, because of their high adaptability, may respond well to a variety of parenting styles (permissive or authoritarian, for example). In contrast, a more difficult infant may require more careful parenting. Because these children adapt more slowly and respond less well to novelty and change, they require consistent and patient parents. Also, given their more intense and more negative moods, they are not likely to react well to highly authoritarian or highly punitive parents. (Parenting style is discussed in Chapter 8.)

The contribution of temperament to the infant's own development, and its relationship to the behavior of parents, presents yet another example of the extent to which parent-infant influences are bidirectional. Consider, as an illustration, the case of the easy child. Such an infant adapts readily to changes, establishes predictable feeding and sleeping routines, is highly responsive to parents but not easily alarmed by change, and, perhaps most important, appears to be happy most of the time. As Thomas and Chess (1981) note, parents react with pleasure to such a child. They feel somehow responsible for what the child is; they think of themselves as wonderful parents. They smile and laugh as they tend their infant, and the infant smiles back. They gaze at each other, and everything they say and do tells the other how wonderful he or she is.

But the difficult child does not smile as much, cries more, is not so regular about eating and sleeping, fusses and whines and complains, and does not adapt as quickly to changes. Hence social progress seems slower, and the message the parent receives does not say, "You're wonderful, dear wonderful parent," quite so loudly; instead it might say, "As a parent, you're just so so"; or, worse yet, "As a parent, you ain't worth ———!" Not all parents will read the same message, of course. Nor will all react in the same way. But there are some who will feel anxious and guilty about their difficult or slow to warm up infant — some who will try too hard to change the infant, or who will silently give up and perhaps, without even knowing it, begin an insidious process of rejection.

Although the scenario is clearly exaggerated, it nevertheless makes an important point: The infant's temperament interacts in complex ways with the environment, resulting in a series of accommodations that change both the environment and the infant. Thus, from the very beginning, infants begin to serve as what Lerner and Busch-Rossnagel (1981) label "producers of their development."

Thomas and Chess (1981) also found there are some important long-term consequences of temperament. Specifically, infants of difficult temperament were far more likely to manifest problems requiring psychiatric attention. Indeed, of the 42 children (out of a sample of 141) who had such problems, 70 percent had been classified as *difficult* infants and only 18 percent as *easy* children. On a more positive note, Martin (1989) found that temperament characteristics such as adaptability, persistence, and low withdrawal were positively related to school achievement and to aptitude.

To the extent that infant characteristics are related to later behaviors, early identification of these characteristics might be of tremendous value for parents, educators, and others concerned with the welfare of children. The NYLS findings have led to attempts to identify "high-risk" infants and to suggestions about the best way of reacting to this risk. However, these attempts carry some potential dangers. As Rothbart (1982) notes, labeling infants as *difficult*, particularly when parents have not thought of them in that way, may lead parents to expect problems, might change their reactions to their infants, and might indirectly be related to the appearance of problems.

Goodness-of-Fit: Context and Temperament

Within an ecological model of child development, interactions and mutual accommodations are all important. Understanding the relationship between temperament and developmental outcomes requires taking into account accommodations that occur in the face-to-face interactions of infant and important others *(microsystem)*. In Lerner et al.'s (1986) terms, the most optimal situation is one where there is high *goodness-of-fit* between the infant and context. This situation exists when external demands and expectations are compatible with the infant's basic temperament — that is, with the infant's inclinations and customary ways of doing things. Conversely, there is a poor fit when the infant's temperament is not in accord with environmental demands.

As an example, Sara (who, you may recall, is a difficult infant) reacts loudly and impatiently to frustration. Her father is distressed and annoyed at this behavior because he expects and wants Sara to be more like Louis. There is a poor fit here, and the result is conflict and strain in the relationship between Sara and her father.

A cross-cultural illustration makes the point well. In the deVries and Sameroff (1984) study of temperament among three African tribes, the researchers assumed that difficult infants would be at higher risk of later problems than easy infants. This was the case in two of the tribes; but it was not true for the Masai. deVries (1989) reports that when the tribe was revisited between four and six months later, things were far better for the difficult infants. In fact, mortality was much higher among the easy infants. Why? There had been a serious drought in the region, and many infants had died or suffered malnutrition and disease. But the difficult infants had fared best. deVries speculates that these infants probably yelled and hollered more when they were frustrated and hungry — and succeeded more often in being fed. Thus a particular environmental characteristic "fit" better with the difficult temperament — a temperament that, under most circumstances in our culture, seldom "fits" as well as the easy temperament.

Difficult temperaments do not always lead to poor fit; nor does the easy temperament always result in high goodness-of-fit. Goodness-of-fit would be higher than expected, for example, if Sara's father took pride in his daughter's lustiness, her independence, her aggressiveness. And if Louis' parents were uncomfortable with how "easy" he is, afraid that he might not cope well in what they think is a dog-eat-dog world, goodness-of-fit between his temperament and his context might be unexpectedly poor.

Other Approaches to Temperament

The idea of an easy-difficult continuum in infant temperament initially appeared to make a great deal of sense both to parents and to researchers. After all, parents quickly recognize infants who are easy and those who are more difficult; they have no trouble agreeing about the most important characteristics of each. And it seems reasonable to expect that at least the more extreme of these temperaments should somehow be reflected in personality characteristics that might be found in later life. However, research has been far from unanimous in supporting these expectations. For this, and for other reasons, the concept of *difficult* temperament quickly became controversial.

As an alternative to the Thomas, Chess, and Birch description of the easy-difficult patterns of infant characteristics, Buss and Plomin (1985) describe three aspects of temperament: *emotionality, activity,* and *sociability* (also termed the *EAS approach*). Emotionality refers to the ease with which the infant becomes aroused, particularly in fear- or anger-inducing situations. As Buss and Plomin point out, these are two of the three emotions that can be described as *high-arousal* emotions; the other is sexual arousal. Not surprisingly, each is closely related to survival, and each would therefore be expected to have a strong genetic basis. By definition, temperament is largely inherited.

The second aspect of temperament, activity, refers to the characteristic "vigor and tempo" with which behavior is undertaken. And the third, sociability, refers to the infant's tendency to seek or to avoid the company of others. Low sociability should not be confused with shyness. Shyness denotes discomfort or fear in situations that require interacting with casual acquaintances or strangers; low sociability refers to a low need to interact. Accordingly, an individual can be very *un*shy and yet very low in sociability.

Another approach to investigating temperament is physiological. The approach is very common in Eastern Europe (for example, Strelau, 1989). It stems directly from Pavlov's observation that some individuals have more excited nervous sytems than others — that their physiological reactions to stimulation are different. Differences in physiological reactions such as brainwave activity, heartrate, or motor responses may underlie specific temperament characteristics. For example, Stifter and Fox (1990) have shown that measures of heartrate variability are closely related to infant reactivity in the first year of life. Infants with low but variable heartrates respond better to novelty than do infants with higher but less variable rates. However, there is very little relationship between physiological measures taken within 2 days of birth and those taken 5 months later. Stifter and Fox (1990) conclude that no single physiological measure reflects temperament very clearly and that, early in life, behavior is the clearest indicator of temperament.

Evaluating Infant Temperament Research

Kagan (1982) raises two important questions: Are there temperamental traits? How valid are parental reports? A third, absolutely critical question concerns the extent to which temperament is a consistent characteristic of human reaction and behavior and the extent to which it is related to later behaviors. In other words, are infants of certain temperament (if there is such a thing as temperament) at greater or lesser risk of psychological casualty later in life?

Answers to these three questions are still uncertain. Bates (1980), for example, insists that temperament does not exist within an individual but that it is a projection of the observer. Like a number of personality theorists (such as Mischel, 1979), he suggests that behavior is as much (or perhaps more) a function of the immediate environment as it is of characteristics within the individual. According to this view, infants are not intrinsically *easy* or *difficult*; parents, psychologists, and other observers simply see them that way.

Following an extensive evaluation of the NYLS and of the temperament measures used in that study, Buss and Plomin (1985) conclude that the scales measure only two, rather than nine, types of temperament and that classification of infants as difficult or easy on the scales is not highly predictive of future adjustment. However, easy-difficult ratings obtained when children are 4 and 5 years of age appear to be somewhat more reliable.

Kagen (1982), following an examination of these issues, concludes that sufficient evidence exists to accept that children differ in temperament for at least a few years, that reasonably educated parents can detect and accurately report on some of the more obvious of infant characteristics (such as fearfulness or fearlessness), and that knowledge of infant temperament might have important practical implications. In addition, evidence from studies of twins supports the view that some aspects of temperament, including Buss and Plomin's (1985) EAS approach (emotionality, activity, and sociability), have an important genetic basis. Buss and Plomin point out that these traits are therefore likely to be relatively stable throughout life, although they, like most other human characteristics, will also be modified by environmental influences.

ATTACHMENT

Attachment is a powerful emotional bond, not easily defined, impossible for an infant to describe for us, but tremendously important for the infant.

The infant has two principal tasks, say Greenspan and Lieberman (1989). The first is to achieve a balance between what the organism needs and what it assimilates — a balance that is termed *homeostasis.* At a biological level, homeostasis is maintained when the infant is not too hungry, thirsty, cold, or hot. Maintaining homeostasis is greatly facilitated by infants' increasing ability to regulate or control their behavior as they interact with the environment.

The second task, very closely related to maintaining homeostasis, is that of forming an attachment — generally with a principal caregiver to begin with, later with other individuals in the immediate environment (the microsystem). Within these attachments, developing infants learn to communicate, both through gestures and language, and begin their exposure to culture. Language and culture, Vygotsky insists, are what make all higher mental functions possible.

Studying Attachment

Measurements of infant attachment are necessarily indirect. They look at behaviors that are directed more often toward the object of attachment than elsewhere (crying, smiling, vocalization, following, clinging, holding, and so on); they focus on the infant's reaction to strange situations and on physical contact between parents and infant; or they look at the infant's reaction to being separated from a parent (Ainsworth et al., 1978).

One of the problems that affects research in this area is the practical impossibility of conducting the types of controlled experiments that would be most likely to lead to definite answers. Infants cannot be deliberately separated from their mothers at different times in their lives and for different periods of time to determine the effects of separation; nor can they be brought up in complete social isolation. Considerations such as these have led to a series of intriguing studies with infant monkeys and their mothers. In these studies, infant monkeys are taken from their mothers at birth and raised in isolation or with wire models vaguely resembling monkey mothers. Results indicate that depriving infant monkeys of their mothers can have serious negative consequences for their later adjustment, but that substitute mothers can prevent these consequences (see Figure 6.1). Unfortunately, however, such studies do not tell us very much about human infants — and perhaps not very much about infant monkeys either, according to Ainsworth (1984).

Mother-Infant Bonding

Until recently, most of the research on parent-infant interaction has focused on the effects of this interaction on infants rather than on parents. It has traditionally emphasized the attachment that children form to their parents and the effects of separation and deprivation on children. More recently, a number of researchers have examined attachment from the parents' point of view — especially from that of the mother. **Mother-infant-bonding,** the expression coined to label this interest, refers primarily to the very early, biologically based bond

Mother-Deprived Monkeys

Infant monkeys who are raised in isolation later experience serious developmental problems, often manifested in an inability to achieve sexual relations. Female monkeys raised under such conditions who then have infants of their own will often reject them. But when the mothers of infant monkeys are replaced with a substitute, infants typically form a strong attachment to the substitute. Research that has compared infant monkeys' attachment to cloth-covered and wire mother substitutes indicates that quality of physical contact is especially important for monkeys.

The infant monkey remains on the terry cloth mother even though he must stretch to the wire model in order to feed.

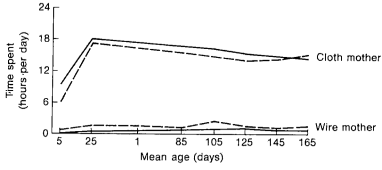

Figure 6.1 Amount of time spent by infant monkeys on cloth and wire surrogate mothers. The results show a strong preference for the cloth mother regardless of whether the infant was fed on the wire model (broken line) or on the cloth model (solid line). *Source:* From Harry F. Harlow, Love in infant monkeys, *Scientific American*, 1959, *200,* 68–74. Copyright 1959 by *Scientific American, Inc.* All rights reserved. Used by permission.

that the mother develops for her infant. Although the term *bond* is often used as though it were synonymous with *attachment*, *attachment* is a more general term that includes the host of *positive* emotions that link parents, children, and other people as well. Put another way, bonding is what happens to allow parents to love their infants; attachment is what happens to allow children to love their parents.

The term *bond* in this context is defined in much the same way as it is by ethologists (those who study animal behavior in natural settings) — that is, as a largely hereditary (hence biologically based) link that the mother forms for her offspring under appropriate circumstances. Among nonhuman species these "appropriate circumstances" generally involve nothing more complicated than the mother being exposed to her infant during some *critical period* that begins at birth and lasts for a short time thereafter. In the absence of appropriate experiences during this critical period, *bonding failure* occurs. When newborn lambs are taken from their mothers at birth and not returned to them for a week or more, the mothers refuse to accept them as their own (Thorpe, 1963). If the youngsters get in the way, they simply butt them aside! The mothers have failed to bond to their infants (see Chapter 2). Does it follow that mothers whose infants are taken away at birth, perhaps because they require intensive care or simply because of hospital routine, will not bond with these infants?

As we saw in Chapter 2, theorists such as Bowlby think that might be the case. And Klaus and Kennell (1983) agree with Bowlby that the mother-infant bond develops as a function of close contact and interaction with the infant from the earliest moments after birth. Although there is a biological predisposition toward the formation of this bond (and toward the interaction that leads to its development), it does not exist automatically as soon as the child is born. They suggest, as well, that the failure to establish a strong mother-infant bond is detrimental to the future adjustment and emotional health of the child and may be related to such things as child abuse or *growth failure* (a physical/psychological condition also known as "failure to thrive" and characterized by listlessness, apathy, loss of appetite, illness, and sometimes death).

Bonding Mechanisms

Some theorists (for example, Bowlby) argue that because of the importance of the mother-infant bond, there must be powerful genetic predispositions that ensure its formation. Clearly, no emotional bond links the infant to its mother immediately at birth. A neonate taken from its mother and given to another will surely never know the difference unless, of course, the facts are disclosed later.

But that a bond does form with the primary caregiver(s) is also clear. Schaffer (1984) points out that the infant has certain biological *preadaptations* that facilitate the development of this bond. There are two classes of such preadaptations: certain perceptual biases and certain response tendencies. We noted some of these important perceptual biases in Chapter 5. They include the infant's built-in visual accommodation for a distance of approximately 8 to 10 inches — about the distance of the caregiver's face during feeding. They include, as well, the young infant's apparent preference for the human face and a built-in sensitivity and responsiveness to the human voice.

Among the infant's preadaptive response tendencies that seem especially designed for social interaction are a number of reflexes. Like the young of most mammals, for example, the human infant clings and turns and roots and sucks. One of the functions of these vegetative reflexes is surely to ensure that the infant obtains nourishment and survives. But more than this, feeding is among the first important social interactions between caretaker and infant. Almost invariably, feeding leads to the mutual gaze, which is highly significant in the development of attachment and which appears to be universal between mothers and infants in different cultures (Fogel, Toda, & Kawai, 1988).

Schaffer (1984) also suggests that certain biological rhythms are geared to social interaction. Some, like those expressed in the infant states of waking and sleeping, are modifiable and eventually become attuned to the mother's cycles of waking and sleeping. Others, like the rhythms apparent in sucking behavior, seem to contain many of the elements of a dialogue and may underlie the learning of the turn-taking rules that are a fundamental part of conversations with language. It seems that infants suck in organized and relatively predictable patterns — short bursts of activity followed by pauses (Kaye, 1977). And the mother appears to be unconsciously attuned to these rhythms, adjusting her behaviors to those of the infant. During the sucking bursts, she is typically quiet; but during the pauses, she jiggles or strokes the infant, or she talks to it.

What other factors may be important in attachment? In Bowlby's (1958) ethological theory of attachment, smiling and crying play major roles. Bowlby suggests that attachment between mother and infant is the end product of an evolutionary process. Attachment had important survival value at a time when physical survival was threatened by the "hissing serpents and dragons of Eden" (Sagan, 1977). Given the importance of attachment for the infant's survival — and consequently for the survival of the race — it is reasonable to suppose there are powerful biological forces directing both mother and infant toward mutual attachment. Bowlby goes somewhat further and speculates that attachment is very much like imprinted behaviors such as "following" in some young birds. In the same way as imprinting occurs during a critical period, but only in the presence of a suitable stimulus, or releaser (see Chapter 2), attachment between a mother and infant occurs as a function of the crying and smiling behavior of the infant.

Other theoretical explanations for maternal attachment have also been advanced. Learning theory explanations maintain that attachment results from the mutual reinforcement that mother and infant give each other. From the infant's point of view, the most obvious source of reinforcement is the fact that the mother is the principal (sometimes the only) source of nourishment and comfort. From the mother's point of view, sources of reinforcement are more subtle but might include feelings of accomplishment, power, and worthwhileness that result from looking after someone who is virtually helpless. Gewirtz and Boyd (1976) suggest that learning theory explanations of attachment are not at all incompatible with ethological explanations. Although there might be some genetic tendencies in mother-infant attachment, they are nevertheless subject to environmental influence.

Importance of Bonding

A number of studies have looked at the formation and significance of mother-infant bonding. Klaus et al. (1972) randomly selected a group of 28 low-income mothers and gave half of them "extended" contact with their infants immediately after birth (one hour of the first two hours following birth) and five additional hours of contact with their infants on each of the first three days following birth. The remaining 14 mothers, serving as a control group, had contact with their infants according to hospital routine — that is, mainly at regular feeding times.

Follow-up interviews and filmed observations of mothers and infants one month later indicated that mothers in the extended-contact group were more attached to their infants, showed more concern for them, and expressed considerably more interest in them. These mothers tended to fondle their babies more, to engage in more verbal interaction with them, and to spend more time in mutual gazing. Further studies when the infants were aged 1 and 2 still revealed significant differences between extended-contact and control group mothers, not only in attachment but in verbal interaction as well (Ringler et al., 1975).

Looking only at these studies, it would be tempting to conclude that there is a critical period early in the lives of neonates during which contact with the mother (or perhaps some other important caregiver) is absolutely central. However, a raft of subsequent studies have failed to replicate the most important of the Klaus and Kennell findings (see, for example, Schaffer, 1984). Goldberg (1983), for one, concludes that the evidence of a critical period and of lasting harmful effects of "bonding failure" is totally unconvincing. It seems plausible, as Wasserman (1980) argues, that the formation of attachments is sufficiently important to human development that it is likely the infant and mother can take advantage of other opportunities for bonding without harmful consequences. Furthermore, the assumption that limited contact with infants immediately after birth — a common practice in many hospitals — may lead to "bonding failure" and subsequent health and adjustment problems has not been supported. In a careful investigation, Egeland and Vaughn (1981) found no greater incidence of abuse, child neglect, illness, or adjustment problems among children who had been separated from their mothers for a period of time immediately after birth. This does not mean that early contact between parents and infants is not highly desirable but simply that the importance of a "sensitive" few hours immediately after birth has not been established.

Through each of Bowlby's attachment phases, one simple principle rules: *Keep the attachment object close.*

Stages of Attachment

According to ethologists such as Bowlby, the "why" of infant attachment seems clear. After all, the infant's very survival demands a solicitous caregiver. What better way to assure that the caregiver will be there when needed than to program into the human gene-pool powerful parent-infant attachment tendencies? However, nature does not program the attachment itself. It seems clear that the infant is born without any strong attachment — indeed, without any way of readily identifying possible attachment objects. Nor do the infant's genes limit attachment to the biological mother and/or father.

Bowlby (1969) describes four phases in the infant's development of attachment. Through each of these phases, the infant's behavior seems to be guided by a single overriding principle: *Keep the attachment object close.* In most cases, that attachment object is the mother.

The first, a *pre-attachment* phase, spans the first few weeks of life. From the very beginning, the infant seems predisposed to identify and respond to stimulation from other people — and especially from mothers. From very shortly after birth, infants will often move their bodies in synchrony with adult human speech, but not in synchrony with disconnected vowel sounds or even rhythmic tapping sounds (Condon & Sander, 1974). Also, within the first month of life, not only are they able to discriminate their mother's voice from that of other women but they also show marked preference for their mother's voice (DeCasper & Fifer, 1980).

Not only can infants identify their mother's voice and respond to speech, but they are also capable of behaviors that promote contact with important adults. Very important among these behaviors are crying and smiling, both of which typically bring caregiver attention and response. Also important are a host of behaviors such as sucking, rooting, clinging, looking at, and following with the eyes.

Bowlby labels the second phase *attachment in the making*. It is marked by a gradual differentiation of the behaviors that promote contact and by the singling out of primary objects (persons) of attachment. The second phase culminates in clearly identifiable attachment sometime during the second half of the first year of life. At this time, the infant manifests the selective social smile — the smile that occurs in recognition of familiar faces. At the same time, smiling in response to unfamiliar faces becomes less common.

The third phase, *clearcut attachment*, becomes evident with the infant's development of locomotor abilities. Now infants are able to do far more than simply attract the mother's or father's attention through smiling, crying, reaching, and so on; they can crawl over and grab a leg; they can climb up and wrap themselves around a neck; they can cling to the strings that hang from the rear of old-fashioned, pre-Velcro aprons. (Some of us never want to let go. We hang on so desperately that our mothers have to resort to scissors to cut the strings.)

Some time in the second year, Bowlby informs us, the infant enters a phase of *goal-corrected attachment*. The infant has now developed notions of self and others as being separate and permanent and has begun to understand something of the point of view of others. Gradually, it becomes possible for infants to make inferences about the effects of their behaviors, as well as about their parents' behavior; and it becomes possible to affect the behavior of parents in ways more subtle than crying, smiling, yelling, or toddling over and grabbing hold.

In summary, Bowlby's account of the development of attachment during the first two years of life describes an initial *pre-attachment* phase where the infant attracts attention by crying, smiling, and looking; an *attachment in the making* phase where the infant's attachment behaviors become more selective, as is evidenced by the use of the selective social smile; a *clearcut attachment* phase where the infant demonstrates attachment repeatedly not only by attracting attention, but also by locomoting over to the attachment object; and a *goal-corrected* phase where the infant's behavior is controlled in complex ways by the dawning of the ability to understand means-end relationships and to make inferences about the behavior of others (see Table 6.5)

Ainsworth (1973) makes the important point that one of the major functions of the infant's early behavior is not only to foster and maintain a high degree of attachment, but also to permit exploration of the environment. For this reason, the infant has to strike a balance between proximity-seeking be-

Table 6.5
Sequential Phases in the Development of Infant Attachment

Phase	Approximate Age	Important Behaviors
Pre-attachment	First month	Crying, smiling, rooting, clinging, sucking, looking at; movements synchronized with adult speech; discrimination of mother's voice
Attachment in the making	Into second half of first year	Singling out objects of primary attachment; selective social smile — directed more toward attachment objects/persons than toward the unfamiliar
Clearcut attachment	Second half of first year	Continued use of behaviors designed to draw attention — smiling, crying, squirming; use of newly developed locomotor skills to approach attachment object/person
Goal-corrected attachment	Second year	Begins to adopt mother's point of view and to make inferences about mother's behavior; manipulation of mother's behavior in more subtle ways following gradual recognition of cause-and-effect relationships.

Source: Based on Bowlby (1969).

havior and exploratory behavior. At the same time, it is important to maintain a sense of security about the environment and about the attachment. Thus Ainsworth speaks of two related concepts that motivate much of what the infant does: the *attachment-exploration balance* and the *secure-base phenomenon*. It is noteworthy that in the absence of the mother's presence (or that of some other important attachment object/person), many infants will cease exploratory behavior. Others are less likely to do so; their attachments seem to be different.

Types of Attachment

Psychologists and child researchers, who are never stingy with classifications and stages, suggest a number of different ways in which infant attachments may be sorted. Perhaps the most useful of these classifications are those described by Ainsworth and her associates (1978). Before we describe them, let us look at the research that led to them.

How do you determine whether, to whom, and how strongly an infant is attached? One way is Ainsworth et al.'s (1978) *Strange Situation* procedure, a procedure sequenced as follows (each event lasts approximately three minutes):

1. Mother and baby enter a room.

2. Mother puts baby down; stranger enters, speaks with mother, shows baby a toy; mother leaves.

3. If baby cries, stranger attempts to comfort; if baby is passive, stranger attempts to interest in toy.

4. Mother returns, pauses in doorway; stranger leaves; mother leaves.

5. Baby is alone.

6. Stranger comes back.

7. Mother returns; stranger leaves.

What the Strange Situation provides is a way of assessing attachment under stress. It permits researchers to determine the infant's anxiety or security in these circumstances. When Ainsworth and her associates placed 1-year-old infants in the Strange Situation, they discovered attachment behaviors that sorted themselves into three categories.

Securely attached infants are those who use the mother as a base for exploration — who freely go out and play in the room, but who often reestablish contact, either by looking at the mother, interacting verbally, or actually returning to her physically. When the mother leaves, these infants are upset and often stop their exploration. During the reunion episodes of the Strange Situation, they greet the mother warmly and positively and try to reestablish physical contact or some sort of interaction with her. Securely attached infants manifest few, if any, negative reactions toward their mothers during these reunion episodes.

In contrast, anxious or insecurely attached infants are those who display significant negative behavior toward the mother during reunion events. Some of these infants, the *avoidant*, either ignore the mother's reentrance or actively avoid contact with her — sometimes by looking away, sometimes by pushing her away physically. Interestingly, they rarely cry when the mother leaves.

A second group of anxious infants, the *ambivalent*, are very upset when the mother leaves. Their behavior is apparent evidence of strong attachment. Strangely, however, they often display anger when the mother returns. For example, they might push the mother away even when they appear to want to be held (hence the ambivalence).

It is perhaps reassuring that the majority of the infants in Ainsworth's research — approximately two-thirds of them — can be classified as *securely attached*; it is less reassuring that approximately one-fifth are *avoidant* and the remainder, *ambivalent* (Table 6.6).

These patterns of attachment appear to reflect relatively stable qualities. Waters (1980) reports, for example, that there is little change in classification between the ages of 12 and 18 months. However, this is not the case when there are major changes in the infant's context, such as somebody leaving or dying (Waters, Hay, & Richters, 1986). Similarly, infants who are maltreated often display marked instability of attachment and are also more likely to be insecurely attached (Schneider-Rosen et al., 1985).

There is mounting evidence that securely attached infants — who, as we noted are in the majority in our cultures — fare better in the long term. These

Table 6.6
Types of Infant Attachment

Attachment Classification	Common Behavior When Mother Leaves or Returns
Secure	Use mother as base from which to explore; upset when she leaves; greets her return positively and reestablish physical contact
Insecure or Anxious Avoidant	Rarely cry when mother leaves; ignore mother when she returns or actively avoid her, sometimes pushing her away or pointedly not looking at her
Ambivalent	Very upset when mother leaves; often angry when she returns; may push her away while seeking proximity (hence ambivalence)

Source: Based on Bowlby (1969).

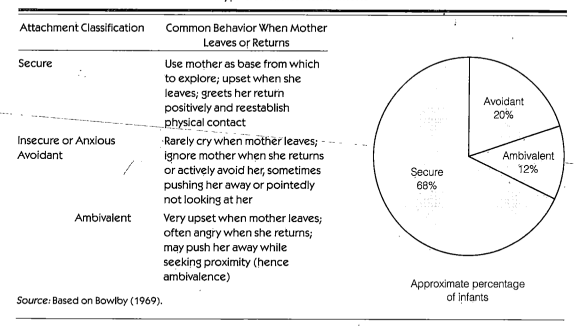

Approximate percentage of infants

infants are often more competent, better problem solvers, more independent, more curious, and perhaps more resilient. In contrast, insecurely attached infants are somewhat more likely to be overly dependent and to experience problems in school (see Collins & Gunnar, 1990).

It is clear that attachments are a function of interactions. It should also be clear that the nature of these interactions and their outcomes will be influenced by the characteristics of both infant and caregiver (or other significant people in the child's context). Hence the importance of the family—and of the culture in which the family is embedded, because it, too, influences childrearing practices and attitudes toward children. Our North American culture (macrosystem) is relatively child-centered; it emphasizes the rights of children, and it encourages parents to provide physically and psychologically safe environments. It should not be surprising that more than two-thirds of infants appear to be securely attached (perhaps it should be surprising that as many as one-third are not!).

Elsewhere in the world, cultures reflect different values; and sometimes child rearing practices and attitudes toward children are quite different. In some of these cultures, insecurely attached infants are far more common than in North America (for example, West Germany, Japan, and Israel; see Collins & Gunnar, 1990).

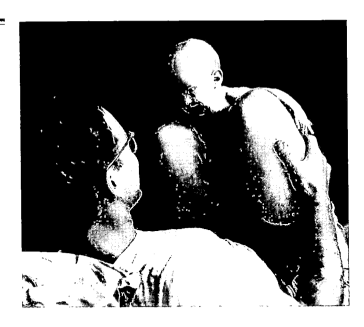

Fathers tend to engage in more physically exciting play with infants than do mothers; mothers are more involved in nurturant caregiving roles.

Whether parents should attempt to change their infants' predominant patterns of attachment — and whether they would be very effective in doing so — are important questions. Unfortunately, they are also very difficult to answer.

What is clear is that all infants should have the opportunity to develop attachments that will provide them with the security they need to engage in the exploration of a bewildering and exciting and sometimes frightening world. Those opportunities are found not only in the form of a mother; grandparents, siblings, uncles, and aunts can also be important. So can fathers.

Fathers and Infant Attachment

Our traditional views of the family and of mother/father roles have typically focused on the importance of the mother in the early social development of the infant — and on the father's relative unimportance. Most of our developmental theories (Freud's, for example) argue that the father becomes important after the age of 2 or 3. Further, because many of these theories have viewed the infant as largely incompetent — as passive and reflexive, moved by primitive physiological needs but seldom by a need to discover and to know — it is little wonder that the father, and often the mother as well, has not been seen as playing a very important role other than as a caregiver.

Some of these traditional values are still the norm in many of the world's cultures. For example, Ho (1987) reports that in China, looking after the young is still largely a female function; the father's role is more that of a disciplinarian. There, traditional values stress filial devotion and respect — that is, children, and especially sons, are taught to respect and obey fathers (and grandfathers).

Recently, however, there appears to have been a dramatic decline in some of these filial values. At the same time, fathers have begun to involve themselves more in childrearing.

In North America, too, important changes are rapidly altering our conception of the father's role. These changes include an increasing number of "father-assisted" childbirths, where the father often has an opportunity to interact with the infant as early as does the mother. In addition, changing work patterns and changing male-female responsibilities in the home have done a great deal to revise the role of the father vis-à-vis the infant. As Lamb and Elster (1985) note, mothers continue to be extremely important to the infant; but they are not unique. Fathers and other caregivers are also tremendously important. In fact, considerable research indicates that newborns and young infants may form attachments almost as strong with fathers as with mothers (Collins & Gunnar, 1990).

In summarizing the research on father-infant attachment, Collins and Gunnar (1990) conclude that fathers are as competent and as important as mothers in a caregiving role. But there are some systematic differences between mother-infant and father-infant interactions. Most obvious is the observation that fathers spend more time in play interactions with their infants; mothers spend more time in nurturant roles (feeding, bathing, changing). As a result, some infants — especially males — display more *affiliative* behaviors toward fathers than toward mothers (Lamb, 1980). Affiliative behaviors are defined as behaviors demonstrating a social relationship that stops short of being attachment. Evidence of affiliation includes smiling, looking at, laughing, and giving; evidence of attachment might include seeking to be close, clinging, wanting to be picked up, putting the head in the lap, snuggling, and so on.

In a study of 20 infants, Lamb (1980) found that fathers fared extremely well in the attachment and affiliation their infants displayed toward them. For younger infants (7 to 13 months), there was no difference in the amount of attachment behavior directed toward mother or father, although both were the object of far more attachment behavior than was a stranger. However, fathers were recipients of more affiliative behaviors (smiling, looking at, vocalizing, laughing, and giving) than were mothers. For older infants (15 to 24 months), fathers continued to have more affiliative behaviors directed toward them and were now also the objects of more attachment behaviors (seeking proximity, touching, approaching, wanting to be held). The differences between mothers and fathers in amount of affiliative and attachment behavior directed toward them by their infants was minimal, however. In fact, it was the boys who displayed most of these behaviors toward their fathers; girls were somewhat less predictable. Lamb suggests that here, at age 2, is evidence of the beginning of same-sex modeling.

Thus it appears that infants (especially males) begin to affiliate with their fathers at a very young age when given the opportunity to do so (Lamb et al., 1983). Fathers interact more (touching and verbalizing) with sons than daughters and with firstborns than with later children. Interestingly, in an unfamiliar

The unfamiliar and the unexpected may lead to anxiety and fear both in adults and in children. For young children newly learning about the world, there is more that is unfamiliar — hence more to fear. There is also more that is new and amazing and wonderful.

situation, the departure of both the father and the mother is followed by signs of distress, whereas the departure of a stranger leads to an increase in play behavior (Kotelchuck, 1976).

What these and a large number of related studies have established is that the father is far from irrelevant in the early development of the infant. It remains true, nevertheless, that the mother typically has considerably more contact with young infants than does the father.

STRANGERS AND SEPARATION

Investigations of parent-child attachment often look at the effects of parental deprivation and separation. Clearly, one indication of an infant's attachment to parents and of their importance may be derived from the infant's reactions when the parents are no longer there.

There are two broad groupings of studies of infant-parent separation. One deals with the effects of very short-term separations and attempts to measure what is termed *separation protest.* Ainsworth's Strange Situation, described earlier, is a good example of this type of study. The second type of study looks at the consequences of long-term separation from the principal caregiver. Studies of the effects of divorce on infants exemplify this approach.

In addition, there is a group of studies that has attempted to explore certain dimensions of parent-child attachment by studying the reactions of infants to strangers. If Orville's behavior is identical toward all adults, it is unlikely that he has formed a strong, specific attachment to his mother or father. If, however, he reacts with visible fear and anxiety in the presence of strangers, he has at least learned to equate the presence of his parents with comfort and security.

Stranger Anxiety

Fear of strangers occurs in many infants, but not usually before the age of 9 months (Eckerman & Whatley, 1975). As we saw earlier, lack of fear in the first few months of life is assumed to mean that children do not yet discriminate readily among adults who surround them and have not yet formed strong attachments to any particular person. That fear develops at all is perhaps a function of what has been labeled the *incongruity hypothesis* (Hebb, 1966). Essentially, this hypothesis maintains that once children have become familiar with their environment — can recognize it — they develop certain expectations of events that are most likely to occur. The appearance of the unexpected is incongruous with the infant's expectations and leads to anxiety.

An indirect test of the incongruity hypothesis is Schaffer's (1966) investigation of the onset of fear in children. Schaffer examined the relationship between a number of social interaction variables (maternal availability, number of siblings, exposure to strangers) and infant responses when confronted with strangers. He found only two variables to be related to incidence of stranger anxiety: number of siblings in the home and exposure to strangers. It appears that infants who are in contact with the largest number of people (strangers and siblings) are less likely to manifest fear, will react with the least amount of fear, and will cease to be afraid of strangers at an earlier age. This finding is consistent with the incongruity hypothesis because early exposure to a wide variety of strangers would necessarily eliminate or at least reduce incongruity associated with the presence of a stranger.

Additional corroboration of the incongruity hypothesis is provided by Kagan's (1976) investigations of the development of separation protest in four different cultural settings outside the United States: Ladino families in Guatemala; Indian families, also in Guatemala; Israeli kibbutzim infants; and Bushmen families in the Kalahari Desert. In all these groups, separation protest and fear of strangers was minimal prior to the age of 9 months, peaked between 12 and 15 months, and then declined. Kagan argues that the fact that separation anxiety becomes evident at about the same age in all infants is evidence that it is closely related to some maturational factors. He suggests that these factors are cognitive (related to mental processes, such as thinking and remembering) and that they relate specifically to the infant's ability to *represent* the parent's departure (or the stranger's appearance) — that is, to make inferences about its meaning and its consequences.

As we saw earlier in the Ainsworth et al. (1978) investigations of attachment, not all infants react the same way to the departure of a parent or the arrival of a stranger. In one study, Jacobson and Wille (1984) studied the reactions of 93 children, aged 15 to 18 months, to brief periods of separation from their mothers. They found that previous separation experience was closely related to the amount of distress the children manifested, but the relationship was *curvilinear* as opposed to linear. That is, distress did not increase in linear fashion with increasing separation experiences, but declined with moderate exposure to separation. Specifically, children who had experienced moderate amounts of maternal separation were best able to cope with the absence of their mothers; it was as though they had learned that the separation would only be temporary. Those who had experienced either very little or a great deal of separation were the most distressed — perhaps because they had had too little opportunity to learn about separation or because they had learned that separation would be frequent or prolonged.

As a practical aside, contrary to what we might expect, trying to prepare young preschoolers in advance for an upcoming separation from the mother does not always work as intended. Adams and Passman (1983) had one group of mothers of 2- to 2½-year-old children discuss their upcoming departure for three days preceding the event; a second group did not prepare their children in advance. And, at the time of departure, some of these mothers in both groups provided a brief explanation of their departure and then either left immediately or lingered for 1 minute; others left in their "natural" way. Interestingly, children who had not been prepared in advance showed less distress after the mother's departure than children whose mothers had discussed their departure during the previous three days. And those whose mothers did not linger after explaining they were leaving also showed less distress than those whose mothers lingered for 60 seconds. One possibility, argue Adams and Passman, is that the lengthy preparation actually teaches children to become alarmed. In the same way, lingering just prior to departure may teach the child that displaying anxiety might serve to delay the departure (Adams & Passman, 1981).

It follows from these studies that the child who is most likely to be free of strong anxiety and distress at the mother's absence (or at that of the father or other caregiver) and in the presence of strangers, is the one who has many siblings, who has frequently been exposed to strangers, whose mother leaves "naturally" without lingering and who has been separated from the mother for short periods of time moderately often. However, what is moderate for one infant is not necessarily moderate for another.

Security Blankets

A series of intriguing studies has examined the role of the blanket in the life of the American child. No less than half of all middle-class American children exhibit strong attachments to inanimate objects, the two most common of which are, not surprisingly, the blanket (60 percent of children) and the pacifier (66 percent; Passman & Halonen, 1979). Attachments to pacifiers lessen by age 2, but those to blankets remain high throughout most of the preschool period.

Reprinted by permission of UFS, Inc.

In one study, Passman and Weisberg (1975) compared the effectiveness of mothers and blankets in reducing a child's anxiety in a strange situation. They found that as long as they had their blankets close by, children who were attached to their blankets played and explored as much and displayed no more anxiety than children who were not attached to blankets but whose mothers were present. In fact, children who were attached to their blankets played and explored more than children who had no mother, favorite toy, or blanket present. Related studies (Passman, 1974, 1977) also found that a blanket was as effective as the mother in a learning situation for children who were attached to their blankets. Other research has shown, however, that in situations of higher stress (high arousal), the mother becomes more effective than a blanket or other inanimate attachment object in reducing anxiety (Passman, 1976; Passman & Adams, 1982). In play situations, pacifiers (Halonen & Passman, 1978), color films of mothers (Passman & Erck, 1978), black and white videotapes of mothers (Adams & Passman, 1979), and even Polaroid photographs of mothers (Passman & Longeway, 1982) are sometimes as effective as the actual presence of mothers.

Winnicott (1971) refers to objects such as teddy bears and blankets as **transitional objects** — so labeled because they become the focus of children's affection and attention while they are in transition between a state of high dependence on the parent and the development of a more independent *self*. According to this view, the development of self requires *separation* from the parent and **individuation** — the recognition of one's own individuality (Harter, 1983). The process of separating and becoming independent gives rise to anxiety; the blanket or the teddy bear serves to comfort the child.

To summarize, in North American cultures attachment to blankets, teddy bears, pacifiers, and other inanimate objects seems to be normal in the sense that a majority of children manifest these attachments. These objects are sometimes useful in reducing a child's anxiety in strange situations, and perhaps they bring comfort and joy to young hearts in less stressful situations too. But, some parents worry, is the child who is attached to these inanimate, nonsocial objects perhaps more insecure, less well adjusted, than the child whose attachments are more social?

Not likely, says Passman (1987). In a study of 108 preschoolers, he found little relationship between attachment to blankets and general fearfulness. "Blanket-attached children," he concludes, "are thus neither more insecure nor more secure than are others" (p. 829).

Long-Term Separation and Deprivation

Several naturally occurring situations have underscored the importance of the parents in the life of the child. Spitz (1945, 1954) and Bowlby (1940, 1953) are among many psychologists to describe the harmful effects of naturally occurring parent-child separation. Spitz (1945), reporting the fate of institutionalized children, claimed they had significantly higher mortality rates, they were retarded in physical development, and their emotional development was so severely thwarted by lack of mothering that they frequently withdrew, became depressed, and sometimes died as a result.

Related studies conclude that if children are separated from their mothers for a prolonged period of time, they will suffer severe emotional disturbances resulting from the lack of maternal love (see Bowlby, 1982). By implication, then, the studies support the hypothesis that maternal love or "mothering" is intimately involved not only in the child's emotional development but also in intellectual development and physical well-being. However, advocates of this hypothesis readily concede that love need not come only from the true mother but may also come from any person who devotes the time to the child that a mother customarily does. Note as well that the effects of separation are highly dependent on the age at which the infant is separated from parents. Maternal (or paternal) separation before the age of 6 months usually does not have the same consequences as later separation (Casler, 1961). Children separated from their parents after the age of 6 months are already likely to have formed a strong attachment to them. Any unhappy effects of institutionalization may be due to rupturing this affectional bond, rather than to the child's being deprived of a mother or father. If children are separated from their mothers before becoming strongly attached to them, we might expect that separation will not be as traumatic. In addition, regardless of the children's age when institutionalized, if the institution in which they are housed does not provide sufficient emotional and intellectual stimulation, any negative effect on the infants may be due to the nature of the care rather than to the lack of a mother.

Institutionalization is now much rarer than was once the case. Also, the care provided for infants in institutions is often characterized by a high degree of stimulation. Hence historical studies of the impact of institutionalization, particualarly when the institutions provided relatively deprived environments, may not be of great immediate relevance. Perhaps more relevant are studies of adopted children.

One study examined 70 adopted children between birth and 16 months of age (Yarrow & Goodwin, 1973). All these children were in foster homes before

Table 6.7
Immediate Impact of Long-Term Mother-Child Separation

Impact	Percentage
No disturbances	15
Mild disturbances	36
Moderate disturbances	23
Severe disturbances	20
Extreme disturbances	6

Source: Based on data provided by Yarrow and Goodwin (1973).

adoption, and all were assumed to have had normal environments both before and after adoption. The aim of this study was to discover the effects on the infant of separation from a parent figure. Because children were adopted at various ages, it was also possible to examine differences in their reactions as a function of age.

Not surprisingly, reactions were least apparent for children adopted under 3 months of age. This finding is consistent with the observation that before this age children have not formed any strong attachments. Only nine children were adopted before the age of 3 months, however; the remainder were placed at ages ranging from 3 to 16 months. Only 15 percent of all the children were completely free of all disturbances; the remainder showed disturbances of varying severity (Table 6.7). These disturbances were most obvious in the infant's sleeping schedule and were also evident in feeding behaviors, social reactions (withdrawal, for example), and emotional behavior (crying). Disruptions in social reactions were noted in three behaviors: decreased social responsiveness; increased stranger anxiety; and specific disturbances in interactions with the new mother figure expressed in feeding difficulties, colic, digestive upsets, and most strikingly, physical rejection of the new mother or excessive clinging to her. In addition, developmental scores, expressed in terms of IQ estimates, were lower in 56 percent of the cases following adoption. Apparently, separation from the mother or mother-figure has an adverse effect on most significant aspects of the infant's development.

Yarrow and Goodwin also examined the validity of the critical period hypothesis applied to maternal separation. This hypothesis maintains there is a period of time during which exposure to specific situations will lead to predictable behavior, but that exposure to the same situations before or after the critical period is less likely to lead to that behavior. It is fairly clear, for example, that maternal separation before the age of 3 months is not nearly so harmful as separation at 9 months. The relationship of age of separation to appearance of

Table 6.8
Severity of Reaction to Maternal Separation According to Age

Age	Slight or No Reaction	Moderately Severe to Very Severe Reaction
Less than 3 months	100%	0
3–4 months	60	40
4–5 months	28	72
6 months	9	91
9 months	0	100

Source: Based on data provided by Yarrow and Goodwin (1973).

disturbances in the Yarrow and Goodwin study is presented in Table 6.8. Although there does not appear to be a critical period before and after which maternal separation will have no effect, there is a definite relationship between age of separation and disturbances in the infant.

In conclusion, it is clear that permanent loss of a parent, as happens through death or sometimes through divorce, can have serious negative consequences for the infant — and for the older child as well (see Chapter 8). What about regular but temporary loss of parental contact, as happens in many forms of childcare?

INFANT DAYCARE

As many as one out of every two North American preschool children is now in daycare (Phillips, McCartney & Scarr, 1987). And, with increasing numbers of mothers going back to work within weeks of childbirth, the fastest growing type of daycare facility is *infant* daycare (see Table 6.9 and Figure 6.2). Given what we know about the importance of caretaker-infant interaction and attachment, questions relating to the effects of daycare on the social, emotional, and intellectual development of infants become critically important. (See Chapter 8 for a discussion of the effects of daycare on older children).

Gamble and Zigler (1986) summarize a large body of research that has looked at the effects of daycare on the infant's attachment to parents and on different aspects of social behavior. An important concern of this research has been to determine whether daycare can either prevent the formation of attachments between parent and infant or can serve to redirect that attachment toward a different caregiver. Reassuringly, all available evidence suggests not. It seems that the infant's primary attachment to parents can be established in a wide variety of circumstances and is highly resistant to disruption. Konner

Table 6.9
U.S. Establishments Assisting with Childcare (1987)

Type of Assistance	Private Sector (%)	Government (%)
Childcare benefits/services (such as daycare or assistance with expenses, referral services, counseling)	10.1	26.4
Varied work-schedule policies (such as flextime, voluntary part-time, job sharing, work at home, flexible leave)	61.4	57.2

Source: Adapted from U.S. Bureau of the Census (1990), p. 414.

(1982) reports that it occurs in societies as disparate as that of the Kung, where infants are in immediate contact with their mothers 24 hours a day, and in the Israeli kibbutzim, where infants have contact with their mothers for only a short period each afternoon and on weekends.

Still, even though daycare does not, *in general*, appear to disrupt parent-infant attachment bonds, there is evidence that the stress involved in repeated short-term separation from the mother might lead to the development of what Ainsworth labeled *anxious* or *insecure* rather than *secure* attachment (Belsky & Rovine, 1988). Vaughn, Gove, and Egeland (1980) found a high proportion of insecurely attached infants among those whose mothers had returned to work before they had reached the age of 1. They suggest that this effect might result in part from the mother's *emotional* unavailability as well as from her physical absence and that this unavailability might alter the quality of mother-infant interaction. We should hasten to point out, however, that some infants seem far less vulnerable than others to the stresses of separation from their mothers (Egeland & Sroufe, 1981). By the same token, some may be more vulnerable. Studies reviewed by Gamble and Zigler (1986) suggest that boys are more often in the vulnerable group than are girls.

In summarizing a number of studies on infant daycare, Clarke-Stewart (1989) draws two principal conclusions: First, the evidence suggests a somewhat higher probability that daycare infants will avoid their mothers after separation, that they will be insecurely attached; second, these children are sometimes less obedient later and may be more aggressive with their peers.

Clarke-Stewart cautions that the meanings of these findings are still unclear. We do not know whether slightly higher aggressiveness and independence are negative or whether they might even be marks of more rapid maturation —

Working Moms and Childcare

Since 1975, there has been a dramatic increase in the number of working mothers with children. Legislation in Canada makes it illegal to dismiss an employee because of pregnancy and grants mothers a 17-week maternity leave with full unemployment benefits and guarantee of employment at the end of that period. In addition, increasing numbers of employers are providing childcare benefits, sponsoring daycare facilities, promoting job-sharing arrangements, or allowing mothers to work at home.

Figure 6.2 Increase in percentage of mothers who live with husbands and work outside the home. Note by comparison that growth in employment is far more modest for wives without minor children at home. *Source:* Adapted from U.S. Bureau of the Census (1990), p. 385.

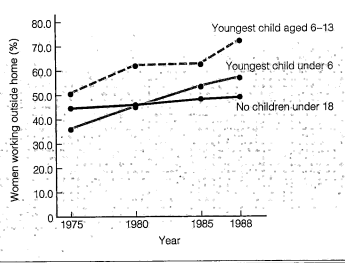

perhaps even an advantage. Here, as elsewhere, it is likely to depend on the individual child and the context in which the child interacts.

It is worth noting that where daycare does have apparently detrimental effects on infants, these effects are often associated with poorer quality daycare. In contrast, high-quality daycare is likely to have beneficial effects on most infants and older children (see Chapter 8 for a discussion of the characteristics of high-quality daycare).

PARENTING IN INFANCY

Belsky, Lerner, and Spanier (1984) summarize a vast body of research that has looked at the effects of parents on infants. They describe six dimensions of mothering (or parenting, or simply caregiving) that this research has shown to be most closely related to the infant's social, emotional, and intellectual well-being: *attentiveness, physical contact, verbal stimulation, material stimulation, responsive care,* and *restrictiveness.* The first five of these have positive effects; the last is more negative. Parents who are attentive to their children (for example, look at them more); who touch them, play with them, cradle and rock them; who speak to them and who provide them with objects to look at, to touch, to taste, to smell; and who are responsive to their cries and to their other signals of distress, amusement, interest, or amazement are more likely to have intellectually advanced and emotionally well-adjusted infants. Those who are restrictive in the sense that they verbally and physically limit the infant's freedom to explore may, to some extent, influence their intellectual development negatively.

In summary, Belsky et al. (1984) point out that those parents who are most likely to promote the most optimal cognitive development during infancy are those who serve as, or give the child access to, the greatest sources of stimulation (speaking, holding, touching, responding to, providing toys, and so on); those who are restrictive — that is, those who limit the amount of stimulation to which the infant is exposed — are likely to have an opposite effect. (See Chapter 8 for further discussion of parenting styles.)

Early Gender-Role Influences

Gender roles (or sex roles) are defined by the particular combination of attitudes, behaviors, and personality characteristics that a culture considers appropriate for the individual's anatomical sex — in other words, that is considered *masculine* or *feminine.* **Gender typing** is the psychological expression used to describe the process whereby boys and girls learn masculine and feminine roles.

Although it might be tempting to think that masculinity and femininity are primarily the products of genetically ordained physiological and hormonal differences between males and females, there is considerable evidence that this is only partly the case. In some cultures, behaviors that we might consider feminine are expected of men and are therefore masculine; at the same time, the aggressiveness and dominance that we think of as masculine characterize women (see Chapter 10 for more details). Clearly, cultures and families have a great deal to do with the eventual gender roles of their children.

When does gender typing begin? At the very beginning. When an infant is born, the attending physician or midwife doesn't say, "Holly jeepers, lady, it's a *baby!*"

No. The key word is not *baby*; it's *boy* or *girl.* The simple anatomical fact of being boy or girl tells mother and father and all the significant others what to think and how to react. The knowledge that it's a "boy" or "girl" even colors the parents' perceptions. When Rubin, Provenzano, and Luria (1974) asked 30 parents to describe their day-old infants as they would to a relative or a close friend, without any hesitation they spoke of their alert, strong, well-coordinated, firm and hardy sons. In contrast, they described their daughters as weaker, finer-featured, softer, less attentive, more delicate. Yet these parents, especially the fathers (who were most guilty of exaggerating the sex-appropriate characteristics of their sons), had scarcely had any opportunity to interact with and get to know their infants. And hospital records indicated clearly that these male and female infants were *indistinguishable* one from the other in terms of weight, muscle tone, activity, responsiveness, and so on.

Pogrebin (1980), in a provocative consideration of these issues, suggests that we are a little like the Mundugumor of New Guinea. The Mundugumor believed that a variety of signs could be used at birth to predict what the individual would become. For example, they were convinced that only those infants whose umbilical cords were wound around their necks at birth stood any chance of becoming great artists. Amazingly, they were right! All Mundugumor artists whose talents were accepted as outstanding had, in fact, been born with their umbilical cords twisted around their necks.

Our fortune-telling is not so primitive, is it? We know it is ridiculous to think that the position of the umbilical cord is of any consequence. Instead, we look for appendages between the legs of our infants. To a considerable extent, these tell us how to interact with our infants, what to expect of them, what sorts of toys they are most likely to enjoy, what their personalities should be. The anatomical features that determine sex also allow us to predict whether the infant will grow up to be strong and alert and aggressive — or weaker, more delicate, more sensitive, more emotional. And surprisingly often, our predictions are every bit as accurate as those of the Mundugumor. (More about the development of gender role differences in Chapters 8 and 12.)

EXCEPTIONALITY

This text deals primarily with the physical, intellectual, and social development of the average person from conception until death. It is worth repeating, however, that there is no average person, that the *average* is simply a mathematical invention, though a very useful one. If we had no average person about whom to speak, we would have to speak instead of individuals. And there are so many different ones — more than 5 billion now — that the task would be absolutely overwhelming.

Still, we need to keep in mind that our average is a fiction and that the individual — Robert, Shannon, Jennifer, David — is our reality and our main concern. We need to keep in mind, too, that some of these individuals depart so dramatically from our average that they are worthy of study in their own right. These individuals fall within the general category of **exceptionality.** Ex-

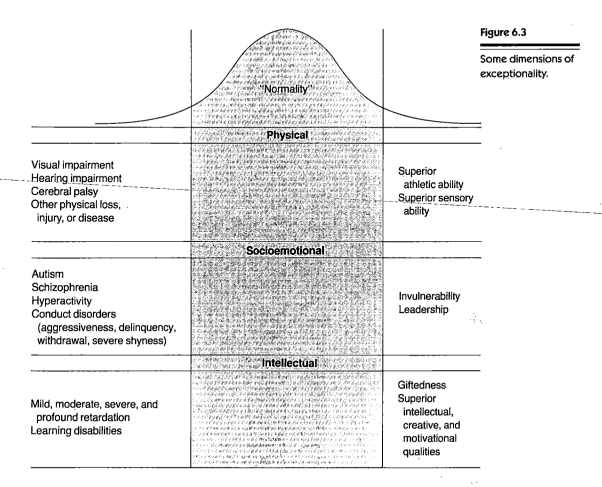

Figure 6.3

Some dimensions of exceptionality.

ceptionality is a two-sided concept: There are, on the one hand, those who are exceptionally gifted; on the other, there are those who lack normal abilities and competence. Furthermore, exceptionality is found in each of the three major areas of human development: social, physical, and intellectual (see Figure 6.3).

In this section, we deal briefly with some of the most common manifestations of social-emotional exceptionality in infancy. In Chapter 9, we look at physical and at intellectual exceptionality in childhood; and in Chapter 10, we discuss social-emotional exceptionality.

Cerebral Palsy

The condition labeled cerebral palsy (originally known as Little's disease after the surgeon who first described it) is not a disease but a collection of symptoms (a *syndrome*) that includes motor problems and may also include psychological problems, convulsions, or behavior disorders. An alternate label for this condition is *significant developmental motor disability* (Abroms & Panagakos, 1980). It is associated with brain damage and varies in severity from being so mild that it is virtually undetectable to being sufficiently serious that it is manifested in paralysis.

Cerebral palsy is most often a congenital disease; that is, it is present at birth in more than two-thirds of all cases (Verhaaren & Connor, 1981). It is often associated with anoxia (lack of oxygen during the birth process, or before or after birth). It can also result from maternal infection and disease, as well as from postnatal brain injury sometimes resulting from diseases such as meningitis or encephalitis.

Estimates of the prevalence of cerebral palsy are uncertain because many of the milder cases are not reported and because there is no "cure" for the condition. Estimates cited by Abroms and Panagakos (1980) vary from 1.63 to 7.5 cases for every 1,000 live births.

One of the most common symptoms of cerebral palsy is spasticity (inability to move voluntarily) in one or more limbs, or dyskinesia (abnormal movements) (see Table 6.10). These motor impairments are sometimes sufficiently severe that it is difficult to assess the child's intellectual ability. As a result, it was often assumed that intellectual deficits were common among those suffering from cerebral palsy. However, more recent evidence suggests that fewer than half of cerebral palsy victims are mentally retarded (Erickson, 1987).

Epilepsy

Also a neurological impairment, epilepsy is essentially a seizure disorder whose causes are unknown. Seizures involve abnormal electrical activity in the brain. The more serious forms of epilepsy (sometimes termed *grand mal* as opposed to *petit mal*) can often be controlled with drugs. Petit mal seizures, which last only between 1 and 30 seconds, are seen in a momentary "absentness" of the child and are often accompanied by rhythmic, fluttering movements of both eyelids (Abroms & Panagakos, 1980). These seizures may occur very often and are sometimes interpreted by parents or teachers as a sign that the student is deliberately not paying attention. Modern medication can successfully prevent the occurrence of petit mal seizures in more than 80 percent of cases (Love & Walthall, 1977). In more than 70 percent of all cases, petit mal seizures cease altogether by age 18 (Nealis, 1983).

Other Physical Problems

A large number of other physical problems sometimes require special education or services. These include diseases and conditions such as muscular dystrophy, cancer, asthma, diabetes, and the absence of one or more limbs, as well as paralysis, to name but a few. Some are congenital, some result from infections and diseases after birth, and others result from accidents of various kinds.

Table 6.10
Categories of Cerebral Palsy (Classified by Body Functioning)

Ataxia	Manifested in balance problems and an uncertain walk. Affects approximately one out of four of those with cerebral palsy.
Spastic	Characterized by loss of control over voluntary muscles. Movements tend to be jerky and uncontrolled. Some symptoms in two out of five cerebral palsy victims.
Athetosis	Marked by trembling, drooling, facial gestures, and other involuntary and purposeless muscle activity (fluttering of the hands, for instance — in contrast with the rigid, jerky movements of spasticity). Often affects speech as well. Frequently found in combination with spasticity. Affects one out of five cerebral palsy individuals.
Tremor	Involves shaky movements, most often of the hands, sometimes visible only when the individual is voluntarily attempting to do something. Involves less extensive movement than athetosis or spasticity.
Rigidity	Caused by strong opposing tension of flexor and extensor muscles, resulting in fixed and rigid bodily postures (sometimes referred to as *lead-pipe* cerebral palsy).
Mixed	Involves a combination of characteristics descriptive of one or more of the common classifications. Most cerebral palsy victims fall within this category, although the majority are described in terms of their most predominant combination of characteristics.

Note: It should be stressed that the effects of cerebral palsy are sometimes so mild as to be undetectable. At other times, they are serious enough to cause death in infancy.

Many cases are associated with serious emotional and social problems, which are often related to difficulties the child experiences in being accepted by others and in developing a positive self-concept. Hence a great deal of what special education programs, parents, and therapists can do for physically exceptional children relates to their emotional and social well-being.

Pervasive Developmental Disorders

Tim was an apparently normal, healthy child, the second child born to a couple in their early 20s. He was an "easy" infant who cried very little and who, in fact, appeared most content when left alone. The mother later recalled that he didn't smile as a young infant and that he didn't appear to recognize her. Still, he progressed apparently normally through his first year, learned to walk at the young age of 9 months, displaying advanced motor development, seldom tripping or falling, as most toddlers do.

But at the age of 2, he had still not learned to speak. An examination showed his hearing to be normal. His parents hoped he would be a "late bloomer." But even at the age of 3, Tim still did not respond to his parents' speech. In addition, he had developed few social skills, and he engaged in unusual and repetitive behaviors — behaviors like spinning the wheels of his toy car or sitting and rocking his body endlessly.

Tim's condition is rare; its occurrence is probably far less than 1 in 100,000 (Werry, 1972). It is among what are now labeled *childhood-onset pervasive developmental disorders* (formerly labeled childhood psychoses). Pervasive developmental disorders are defined by the American Psychiatric Association (1980) as: "disorders . . . characterized by distortions in the development of multiple basic psychological functions that are involved in the development of social skills and language, such as attention, perception, reality testing, and motor movement" (p. 86). The child's symptoms must meet the following criteria for diagnosis as childhood-onset pervasive developmental disorder:

1. Severe and consistent impairment in social relationships (for example, inappropriate emotional responses, lack of empathy, inappropriate clinging, asocial behavior)
2. At least three of:
   a. sudden episodes of "free-floating" anxiety, panic attacks, extreme reactions to ordinary occurrences
   b. inappropriate emotional reaction, lack of fear, excessive rage
   c. resistance to change
   d. bizarre motor movements such as posturing, walking on tiptoes, finger or hand movements
   e. speech abnormalities such as monotonous or "singing" voice
   f. extreme sensitivity or insensitivity to external stimuli
   g. self-mutilation such as pulling out hair, head banging, biting or hitting self
3. Onset between 30 months and 12 years
4. Absence of delusions, hallucinations, incoherence, or bizarre associations

Clinicians sometimes differentiate between two types of childhood-onset pervasive developmental disorder: childhood schizophrenia and autism. One of the main differences between the two is that autism manifests itself much earlier (before the age of 30 months). In addition, autism is characterized by extreme isolation or *aloneness*, manifested in lack of verbal and physical contact, as well as by an apparently strong need to have everything remain the same. Also the autistic child typically has grossly impaired or completely absent language development.

From a practical view, it is not very important to differentiate between autism and childhood schizophrenia because treatments are virtually identical, the more common being tranquilizers and antipsychotic drugs. Although we have little evidence that they are very effective in alleviating the condition, they are useful in making patients more manageable. Psychotherapy (psychoanalysis, for example) has not been demonstrated to be very effective. However, behavior therapies beginning early in the child's life and sustained over a long period of time are sometimes beneficial (see Erickson, 1987). But as Erickson notes, none of these therapies, including the behavior therapies, is very likely to make autistic children act normally.

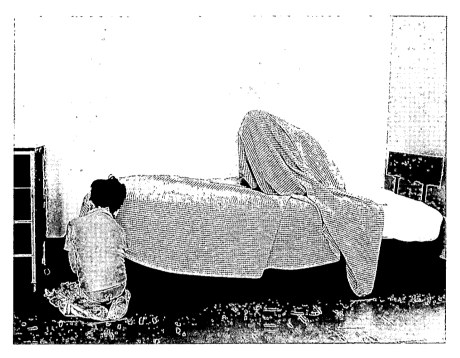

Children afflicted with autism and childhood schizophrenia, characterized primarily by withdrawal, social isolation, and bizarre behavior, generally require institutional care.

Follow-up studies of children diagnosed as having pervasive developmental disorders (autism or schizophrenia) have not given much reason for optimism. Combining several long-term studies that looked at these children between 5 and 10 years after initial diagnosis, DeMyer et al. (1973) found that only 1 to 2 percent of these had recovered sufficiently that they could be classed as normal. Another 5 to 15 percent were almost normal, 16 to 25 percent could be classed as "fair," and more than half were in poor condition. Not surprisingly, the prognosis is best for those who succeed in developing language skills.

THE WHOLE INFANT

There is something frustrating about fragmenting the developing child into such psychologically convenient categories as *description of capabilities, physical development, motor development, socioemotional development*, and *intellectual development*.

We lose the infant in the interminable and frequently confused array of beliefs, findings, tentative conclusions, convincing arguments, and suggestions. The theoretical infant is a hypothetical average. Although it is true that a great many infants are very close to the hypothetical average when they are 1 month old, fewer are still average at the age of 2 months, even fewer at 6 months, and by the age of 1 year, almost none. By the time the child becomes as old as you or I, the average individual will no longer exist but will appear only in the overly simplified theories of the social scientist or in the files of the market researcher who wants to know what the "average" person is wearing this spring.

Each person is a more or less integrated whole whose intellect, emotions, and physical being all interact; each part is inextricably linked with and dependent on every other part of the living organism. However, if we attempt to describe a child in that way, the sheer complexity of the task might overwhelm us. So we continue to speak of the isolated forces that affect human development as though they existed apart from the integrated, whole child. But it bears repeating that our divisions, although necessary, are artificial.

MAIN POINTS

1. Influence in infant-parent interactions is bidirectional and strongly influenced by the characteristics of both parent and infant (the microsystem) as well as by the larger context. Furthermore, relationships within the family are not simply *dyadic* (involving two people) but *triadic* (involving three units, one of which is often the family as a *system*) or even more complex.

2. Infant states reflect basic individual differences very early in life and may be related to personality differences observed later, as well as to inherited differences in *temperament*. Wolff describes some common infant states: regular sleep (no responsiveness to stimuli, motionless, regular breathing); irregular sleep (stimuli can elicit smile or grimace, eyes closed, twitching motions, irregular breathing); drowsiness (moderately active, eyes closed or open, responsive to stimuli); alert inactivity (eyes open, rapid breathing, examining environment, highly responsive to stimuli); and focused activity (includes crying, high anxiety, eyes open, low alertness, rapid breathing, low responsiveness to stimuli).

3. Statements about the young child's emotional responses are often subjective, although the research of Izard and others suggests that infants' facial expressions and other behaviors reveal they may be capable of feeling as many as 10 distinct emotions.

4. Infants' cries may be expressions of different underlying emotions. Mothers often appear to be able to differentiate among the emotions that different cries represent. Wolff identifies four infant cries: rhythmical (most frequent), hunger, anger, and pain.

5. The reflexive smile is often present only hours after birth, although the social smile, which usually occurs first in response to a human voice, is uncommon before the age of 3 weeks. By the age of 4 months, infants often laugh in addition to smiling.

6. Among newborn infants, fear responses may be brought about by loud noises or sudden loss of support. Among older infants, sudden presentation of the unexpected may give rise to fear — or at least to wariness. Fear of strangers is not common before the age of 6 months and appears to be related to the infant's ability to distinguish between familiar and unfamiliar people.

7. Infants exercise some control over their emotions through *other-directed reg-ulatory behaviors* (smiling, looking interested) and *self-directed regulatory behaviors* (turning away, thumb sucking, self-distraction).

8. Individual differences among adults are often referred to as *personality* differ-ences; those among infants, as differences in *temperament.* Temperament characteristics are assumed to have a strong genetic basis. The New York Longitudinal Study (NYLS, Thomas, Chess, & Birch) identified nine charac-teristics of infant temperament, particular combinations of which are associ-ated with three types of children: *difficult, easy,* and *slow to warm up.*

9. Some evidence suggests that *difficult* infants (characterized by lack of rhyth-micity, withdrawal from the unfamiliar, slow adaptation to change, and in-tense, negative moods) run a higher risk of behavior and emotional problems than do *easy* children. Although temperament appears to have a strong ge-netic basis, experiences are also important, as is evidenced in different cul-tures where infants manifest culture-related temperaments.

10. An ecological model of human development suggests that the "goodness-of-fit" between the infant's temperament and environmental demands may be a very important factor in determining the infant's ecology and consequently in affecting developmental outcome. Knowledge of goodness-of-fit might be im-portant in identifying infants who are vulnerable or whose contexts place them at risk. In our culture, "easy" infants usually fit better.

11. Buss and Plomin classify infant temperament in terms of three dimensions: emotionality (particularly as it is manifested in the survival-related, high-arousal emotions of fear, anger, and sexual arousal); activity (reflected in the "vigor and tempo" of behavior); and sociability (expressed in terms of a desire to be with others).

12. Forming an attachment (a strong, positive emotional relationship), usually with a primary caregiver (later with others), is one of the most important tasks of early infancy.

13. Mother-infant bonding appears to be important to the healthy development and adjustment of the infant. It has not been established, however, that there is a critical period during which this bonding must occur or that it can only occur with the mother. The infant has a number of apparent preadaptations that facilitate bonding.

14. Bowlby's ethological explanation of attachment between mothers and infants maintains that smiling and crying serve as releasers for attachment bonds, which are genetic in nature. Learning theory explanations of mother-infant attachment are based on the mutual reinforcement that mother and child give each other: nourishment and comfort for the child and possibly feelings of accomplishment and power for the mother.

15. Bowlby identifies four sequential phases in the development of infant attach-ment, each characterized by behaviors designed to bring about and maintain proximity between infant and caregiver: *pre-attachment* (first month: crying, smiling, clinging, sucking, responding to caregiver voice); *attachment in the making* (into second half of first year: selective social smile); *clearcut at-tachment* (after 6 months: use of newly developing motor skills to approach

attachment object); and *goal-corrected attachment* (second year: dawning of ability to adopt caregiver's point of view, more subtle manipulation of attachment person's behavior).

16. Ainsworth's Strange Situation studies reveal two major types of infant-parent attachment. *Securely attached* infants (use mother as a base from which to explore; upset when she leaves; react positively and attempt to reestablish contact when she returns); and *anxiously* or *insecurely attached* infants, who may be *avoidant* (rarely cry when mother leaves; ignore or avoid her when she returns), or *ambivalent* (very upset when mother leaves; often angry when she returns; seek proximity while attempting to avoid mother, sometimes by pushing her away).

17. Infants appear to become equally attached to their mothers and fathers when given the opportunity to do so but display more affiliative (let's be friends) behaviors toward their fathers. This is especially true of boys.

18. Fear of strangers occurs in many infants but is less pronounced in those who have been exposed to more people. It is not common before the age of 6 months.

19. Long-term infant separation from parents may have harmful effects on the child, particularly after 6 months of age but seldom before 3 months.

20. Infant daycare does not appear to disrupt parent-infant bonds or to prevent their formation. It has sometimes been associated with less securely attached infants and with infants who are less compliant and more aggressive with peers.

21. Among the most positive dimensions of parenting are attentiveness, physical contact, verbal stimulation, material stimulation, and responsive care; restrictiveness is more negative. From the very beginning, parents often exert a subtle influence on the gender-typing of their infants.

22. Exceptionality has both positive and negative dimensions. Exceptional children are those who require special education and related services to realize their full human potential.

23. Physical and motor problems sometimes requiring special services include cerebral palsy, epilepsy, a variety of diseases, congenital physical problems, and physical problems resulting from accidents.

24. Childhood-onset pervasive developmental disorders are rare but very serious early forms of emotional disorders (autism and schizophrenia are examples).

25. Although relatively fragmented aspects of the child have been discussed in this chapter, it is the whole person with whom we are concerned.

Further Readings

Valsiner's collection of articles is an excellent illustration of how contemporary developmental psychologists are taking into account the influence of cultural, historical, and family systems on developmental outcomes:

Valsiner, J. (Ed.). (1989). *Child development in cultural context.* Lewiston, N.Y.: Hogrefe and Huber.

A good summary of research and applications in temperament research is contained in:

Carey, W. B., & McDevitt, S. C. (Eds.). (1989). *Clinical and educational applications of temperament research.* Berwyn, Penn.: Swets North America.

In the following book, Bowlby examines mother-infant interaction with special emphasis on the development of attachment:

Bowlby, J. (1982). *Attachment and loss* (Vol. 1). New York: Basic Books.

An important view of mother-infant bonding is presented in:

Klaus, M. H., & Kennell, J. H. (1983). *Bonding: The beginnings of parent-infant attachment* (Rev. ed.). St. Louis: C. V. Mosby. (Originally published as *Maternal-infant bonding.*)

The first of the following books looks at the impact of father absence on children; the second presents a research-based collection of major studies of the role of the father in the young infant's social development:

Adams, P. L., Milner, J. R., & Schrepf, N. A. (Eds.). (1984). *Fatherless children.* New York: John Wiley.

Pedersen, F. A. (Ed.). (1980). *The father-infant relationship: Observational studies in the family setting.* New York: Praeger.

Excellent general coverage of many of the topics discussed in this chapter is provided by:

Campos, J. J., Barrett, K. C., Lamb, M. E., Goldsmith, H. H., & Stenberg, C. (1983). Socioemotional development. In P. H. Mussen (Ed.), *Handbook of child psychology* (4th ed.). Vol. 2, *Infancy and developmental psychobiology* (pp. 783–916). M. M. Haith & J. J. Campos (Eds.). (1983). New York: John Wiley.

Field, T. M., & Fox, N. A. (Eds.). (1985). *Social perception in infants.* Norwood, N.J.: Ablex.

Pogrebin's book is a provocative analysis of the role parents play in gender typing their infants:

Pogrebin, L. C. (1980). *Growing up free: Raising your child in the 80's.* New York: McGraw-Hill.

iv
Early Childhood

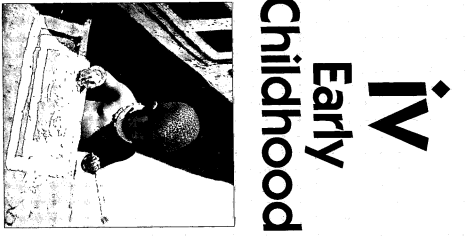

Bliss was it in that dawn to be alive,

But to be young was very heaven.

William Wordsworth, *A Poet's Epitaph*

If to be young is *very heaven,* does it follow that to be old is not? What is it that the young lose as they age? Now that you are old, do you remember what you might have lost? Do you think it was innocence?

Perhaps, but it was surely ignorance too, because there is a dramatic shedding of ignorance in the years from

2 to 6. In those years, there are astounding strides in the acquisition of language, in the ability to think clearly and logically, and in the ability to deal with complex things like numbers. There are major advances, as well, in the ability to interpret the emotions of others and to control the expression of feelings.

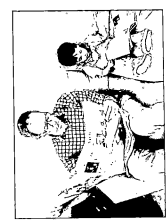

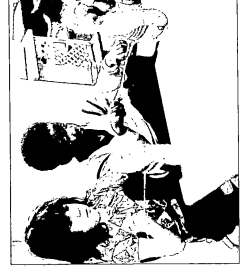

And there are some wonderful developments in the ability to stretch the imagination, to understand magical things, and to play.

Do you remember how you played?

Perhaps that is what the old forget that makes life less like heaven.

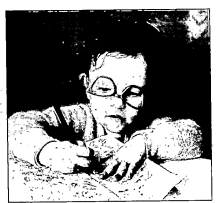

Childhood is measured out by sounds and smells
And sights, before the dark of reason grows.
John Betjeman, "Summonded by Bells"

Physical and Cognitive Development

A t Harry's place on Thanksgiving, we sat around a table heavy with what would surely have passed for a grand feast in medieval times. And as we filled our plates, Harry tried to impress upon his 4- and 6-year-old sons the many things for which they should be thankful. He spoke to them of pioneers and pilgrims in savage days when there were neither roads nor streets, neither theaters nor stores.

"If they needed a loaf of bread or some meat, they couldn't just go and buy it," Harry explained.

"There was no stores?" the younger one asked, not yet willing to believe in a world so primitive that it would have no stores. "Not even for candy?"

"No stores at all," Harry assured him. "They had to grow and make all their food."

"Gardens," the older one shouted. "They had gardens."

"Good!" Harry beamed. "They had gardens. Now, if you were a pilgrim and you had to grow all your own food, and you could never go to the store to get anything, what would you plant in your garden?"

"Corn!" the older one said.

"Good!"

"And peas!"

"Right! And what would you plant?" Harry asked the younger boy.

"Potatoes!" he answered, cleverly glancing at his plate.

"Good! Anything else? What else would you plant?"

The younger boy examined his plate carefully.

"I'd plant turkeys next," he announced solemnly.

MAGIC AND REALITY

"I'd plant turkeys next!"

The mind of the 4-year-old is sometimes wonderfully inventive. It is not limited by the rules that hem in our thoughts. The thinking of 4-year-olds, as Pearce (1977) put it, is *magical;* it does not always need to be checked against reality. In these early years, thinking is autistic, wishful, fantastic. It somehow assumes that reality can be changed by a thought. Thus it is that a magic spell can produce a witch or a princess, a silver thread or a pot of gold; a dream can be real, and perhaps reality too can be a dream; a wish can make a race car of a stone, a cave of a small corner, a giant sailing ship of a discarded matchbox.

But, Pearce tells us, we do not gladly accept, perhaps we do not even understand, the magical child. Our psychologies and our research ask instead: "How can the child be made to attend to reality? Or how can we make the child abandon magical thinking?" (p. xv).

Perhaps we should try to understand more, and control and change less.

In this chapter, we examine the early development of thinking and the growth of language. But first, we look at physical growth and motor development in the years from 2 to 6.

PHYSICAL GROWTH

A comparison of the 6-year-old with the 2-year-old offers some idea of developmental changes during the preschool years. The difference between the two is phenomenal, although the changes that occur from birth to the end of the child's second year are probably even more striking. Physical development during childhood is generally characterized by a marked slowing of development. For example, the rate of weight gain for the average child is greater during the first year than it is for any other year between the ages of 2 and 6.

Figure 7.1 traces the physical development of boys and girls from ages 2 to 6. These data reveal a dramatic deceleration in growth rates after the period of infancy, particularly in height. Although the growth rate between the second and fourth year declines, there is an increase in the rate of absolute weight gained between the fourth and the sixth year. However, the increase in weight gain is slight and does not significantly alter the general pattern of decelerated growth.

Different growth rates for different parts of the body help explain some of the changes that occur between the ages of 2 and 6. The thick layers of baby fat that give 1-year-old children their babyish appearance begin to disappear slowly during the second year of life and continue to recede gradually. These tissues grow much more slowly than other tissues, so that by the time children have reached age 6 their layers of fat are less than half as thick as they were at age 1. Partly because of this change, they begin to look more like adults.

Other changes, as well, account for the gradual transition from the appearance of infancy to the appearance of young boyhood or girlhood. Not only does the relative amount of fatty tissue change during the preschool years but its distribution also changes as a result of the more rapid growth of bone and muscle. The squat appearance of infants is explained by the fact that their waists are usually as large as their hips or chests. Six-year-old children, by contrast, have begun to develop waists that are smaller than their shoulders and hips. This becomes even more evident in early adolescence than at the end of the preschool period.

The larger infant waists are also due in part to the relative size of the internal organs, many of which grow at a much more rapid rate than other parts of the body. Given space limitations between the child's pelvis and diaphragm, their abdomens often protrude. This condition changes as they grow in height during the preschool years.

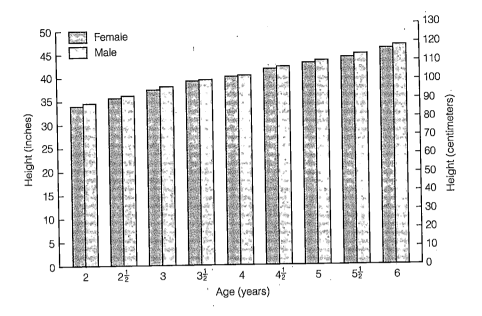

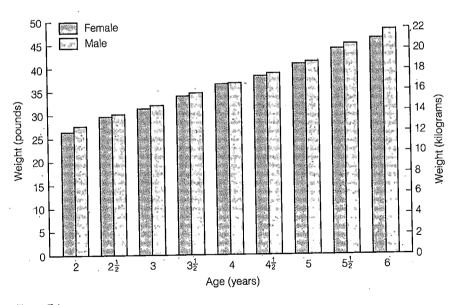

Figure 7.1

Height and weight at 50th percentile for U.S. children 2 to 6 years old.

Source: Adapted from the Health Department, Milwaukee, Wisconsin; based on data by H. C. Stuart and H. V. Meredith, prepared for use in Children's Medical Center, Boston. Used by permission of the Milwaukee Health Department.

Preschoolers' Health Problems

Most preschoolers occasionally suffer from illness or injury serious enough to require medical attention or to keep them home at least one
day (Figure 7.2). In fact, only 2 or 3 of every
100 preschoolers will *not* have an upper-
respiratory infection at least once (a cold, for
example), and almost one-third will suffer
some physical injury. Between ages 5 and 17,
the rates for all common health problems decline — except for injuries. At all ages except
after 65, rate of injuries is higher for males
than females.

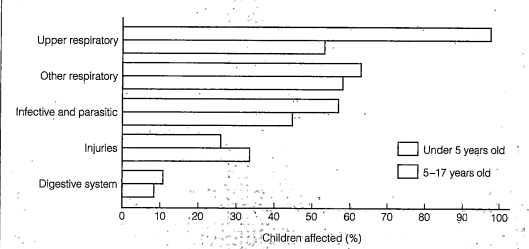

Figure 7.2   Preschoolers' and older children's
susceptibility to injury and illness. The graph
shows the percentage of children who will be affected at least once by the indicated condition.
Source: Adapted from U.S. Bureau of the Census
(1990), p. 118.

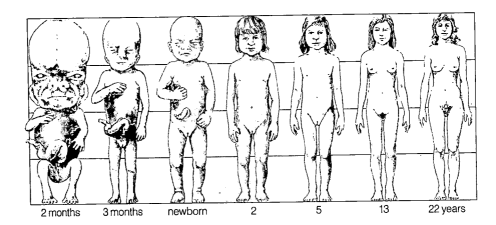

2 months   3 months   newborn   2   5   13   22 years

Figure 7.3

Changes in form and proportion of the human body during fetal and postnatal life.

(Reproduced with permission from Jensen et al., *Biology.* Belmont, Calif.: Wadsworth, 1979, p. 233.)

Other aspects of body proportions that account for the different appearance of the 6-year-old include changes in the ratio of head to body size. The head of a 2-month-old fetus is approximately half the length of the entire body — that is, it is equal in length to the remaining part of the organism. At birth the head is closer to one-fourth the size of the rest of the body. By the age of 6 it is close to one-eighth the size, which is a short step removed from the head-to-body relationship typical of the normal adult with a normal-sized head: one-tenth. From the age of 2 to 6 the head changes from approximately one-fifth to one-eighth of total body size — a significant enough change to be noticeable (Figure 7.3). Because of this change and changes in the distribution of fat and in the space that the child now has for internal organs, the 6-year-old looks remarkably like an adult; the 2-year-old looks more like a typical baby.

MOTOR DEVELOPMENT

Infants' most significant motor achievement is learning to walk. At the same time that they learn to walk, they also learn to coordinate other motor activities that they have been practicing, so that by age 2 they are remarkably adept at picking up objects, stacking blocks, unlacing shoes, and a host of other motor activities. The close relationship between motor and cognitive development during early childhood is evident in Jean Piaget's theory. It is through actual experience and activity with objects that children learn about the properties of objects — and about sorting, classifying, and counting. Hence the close alliance between activity and early intellectual development.

In infancy, the child acquires abilities such as those involved in locomotion and in grasping. In early childhood, children continue to progress in motor development, their locomotion becoming more certain as they lose the characteristic wide-footed stance of the **toddler** (from 18 months to 2½ years). As their equilibrium stabilizes and their feet move closer together, their arms and hands also move closer to their bodies. They lose both the wide stance and the

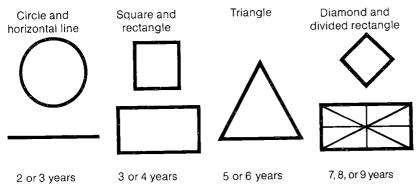

Circle and horizontal line	Square and rectangle	Triangle	Diamond and divided rectangle
2 or 3 years	3 or 4 years	5 or 6 years	7, 8, or 9 years

Figure 7.4

Usual order of difficulty for copying simple geometric designs reasonably well with very approximate ages. Because of the close relationships between motor and intellectual development in early childhood, some intelligence tests for young children include items such as these.

appearance of a tightrope walker; they no longer need to maintain a precarious balance with both arms and feet. As their walking improves, they acquire the ability to climb stairs standing upright and completely unassisted and eventually to hop with two feet and to skip.

Preschoolers also develop a variety of other motor skills that are closely related to increasing control and coordination of fine-muscle movements. Among these are the skills involved in tracing geometric figures or in copying them freehand. Gesell (1925), whose work maps out in detail the sequential progression of children's motor development, reports that before age 2 the child is usually incapable of copying a circle or a horizontal line although the 2- to 3-year-old can do so quite easily. By the age of 4, childen can also copy a cross but are unable to copy a diamond (see Figure 7.4).

As Broderick (1986) points out, successfully copying geometric figures is not simply a fine-motor task; it also requires important perceptual and cognitive abilities. For example, there are visual abilities involved in perceiving a shape to be copied and in comparing it with the child's own drawing; there are cognitive abilities at play when the child successfully interprets the requirements of the task, plans an approach, and evaluates its execution, sometimes modifying and correcting; and, of course, there are fine-motor abilities involved in carrying out the task.

Children as young as 1 or 2 can easily discriminate among different geometric forms, says Broderick (1986); but they cannot copy them. In an investigation of the drawing skills of 80 children, she found that although 5- and 6-year-olds can draw quite recognizable squares, they cannot draw diamonds. Strangely, even 12-year-olds and adults experience difficulty with diamonds. Although what they draw is usually clearly recognizable as a diamond, the figures are often oriented many degrees to one side or the other. In addition, even adults often make highly noticeable errors in angularity — that is, opposing angles of the diamonds are sometimes quite different from each other, although not nearly as much as is the case for younger children.

Given the close relationship between motor and cognitive development in early childhood and the highly predictable sequence for learning to copy geometric figures, it is not surprising that a large number of intelligence tests include such items (for example, the Stanford-Binet and the Wechsler).

Assessing Motor Development

All parents are concerned about the developmental progress of their infants and children. They feel proud of their offspring's accomplishments and are sometimes distressed and worried when their children do not develop as rapidly as they expect — or as rapidly as someone else's children.

Here, as in all areas of human development, there are no absolute norms, no definite, preestablished levels of performance that must be reached by certain ages. Our definitions of what is normal are vague and inexact. Still, psychology and medicine provide us with indications of what we might expect; and this information provides benchmarks against which to evaluate our children — if we must.

A variety of different scales of infant and child development might be used for these purposes. As we saw, there are neonatal scales with which to assess the physiological and neurological condition of the newborn (for example, the Brazelton Neonatal Behavioral Assessment Scale or the APGAR). There are also scales to assess motor and mental development in infancy (for example, the Bayley Scales of Infant Development). And there are developmental scales that span infancy and childhood (for example, the Denver Developmental Screening Test or the Gesell Developmental Schedules). Each of these instruments typically provides simple tasks that can be presented to the infant or child or describes observations that can be made. More important, each also provides specific tables of norms describing what sorts of infant or child behaviors can be expected at different ages.

The Denver Developmental Screening Test, for example, was initially designed primarily to permit identification of infants and children suffering from developmental delays (Frankenberg et al., 1981). Accordingly, age norms are provided corresponding to the levels at which 25, 50, 75, and 90 percent of children are expected to demonstrate a given capability. Four different areas are examined by the test: language; personal-social; fine-motor; and gross-motor. (See Table 7.1 for examples of fine-motor and gross-motor tasks pertinent to early childhood.) A child is considered to be developmentally delayed when incapable of a task of which 90 percent of children of the same age are capable. Isolated developmental delays are not considered serious. But when a child is delayed on two or more tasks *and* in more than one area, further assessment may be required.

Table 7.1
Age at Which Norming Sample of Children Accomplish Described Task.*

Task		Age (years)	
		50 percent of sample	90 percent of sample
Gross	Kicks ball forward	1.7	2.0
	Throws ball overhand	1.6	2.6
	Balance on 1 foot 1 second	2.5	3.2
	Pedals tricycle	2.0	3.0
	Broad jump	2.8	3.2
	Balance on 1 foot 5 seconds	3.2	4.3
	Catches bounced ball	3.9	5.5
	Walks backward heel to toe	4.7	6.3
Fine	Scribbles spontaneously	1.1	2.1
	Tower of 4 cubes	1.5	2.2
	Imitates vertical line within 30°	1.8	3.0
	Tower of 8 cubes	2.0	3.4
	Picks longer line 3 of 3	2.9	4.4
	Draws man, 3 parts	4.0	5.2
	Draws man, 6 parts	4.8	6.0

Source: From *Denver Developmental Screening Test Reference Manual: Revised 1975 Edition* by W. K. Frankenburg, J. B. Dodds, A. W. Fandal, E. Kazuk, and M. Cohrs, 1975, Denver, CO: University of Colorado Medical Center. Used with permission.
*Based on norms from Denver Developmental Screening Test.

Like most other instruments that attempt to measure psychological and motor functioning in the early years, the Denver Developmental Screening Test does not provide highly precise and completely reliable measurements. Research suggests that when used with infants and young children, it leads to a relatively high proportion of underreferrals — that is, it fails to identify a number of children with developmental problems (Francis, Self, & Horowitz, 1987).

Motor and Cognitive Development

The child's physical and motor development are closely related; the acquisition of many skills depends on development of the required musculature and on control of these muscles. The relationship of physical development to other areas of development is sometimes not so obvious, although no less real. For example, a child's play, particularly with peers, is often influenced by motor skills because various aptitudes are called for in different games. A child who is still incapable of jumping with both feet is not likely to be invited by older children to join in a game of jump rope; a child who cannot grasp marbles skillfully may be left out of the traditional spring marble games. Conversely, the child who is precocious in physical and motor development is likely to be the first one asked to participate in games — indeed, may be the one to initiate them. Clearly, then, physical and motor development may have an influence on the general social development of the child; game playing is one important means of socialization (more about this in Chapter 8).

As we have seen, the relationship between motor and intellectual development in the early years is one of the most fundamental aspects of Piaget's theory. The infant's world of the "here and now" is a world that has meaning only in action. The object exists only when the infant looks at it; its meaning is what can be done with it *now.*

But as the infant gains control over fine- and gross-motor movements, it eventually becomes possible to go *to* an object, to look *behind* it, to pick it up, to *explore* it. These seemingly simple but initially impossible acts open up an entirely new world of cognitions.

So it continues throughout early childhood. The child's increasing refinement of control over motor movements, and a consequent ever-growing store of experiences with real objects, leads gradually to an intellectual (cognitive) understanding of some of the properties of things. It leads as well to an understanding of abstractions such as the principles that govern the use of numbers, the formation of classes, or the abstraction of a host of other concepts. These are some of the subjects we look at next. (See Table 7.2 for a summary of some physical and motor achievements of early childhood.)

COGNITIVE DEVELOPMENT

We do not expect our preschool children, much less our infants, to be completely logical. We are seldom surprised when our 3-year-olds insist loudly that a small cat, identical to their small cat, must surely be theirs; we are not shocked by the 4-year-old's apparent failure to realize that there really aren't more candies in his sister's dish when they are all spread out; we express little dismay when our 2½-year-old calls a duck a chicken. For some reason, these instances of *prelogical* thinking simply amuse us; that is what we expect of young children.

But we *would* be surprised if our older children continued to insist on calling all reasonably shaggy-looking pigs "doggie"; if they refused to believe that 6 ounces of soft drink in a glass is the same amount as 6 ounces in a bottle; or if they thought that they could increase the mass of a wad of gum simply by stringing it out and wrapping it around their ears. These illustrate some of the intellectual (cognitive) differences that we expect between our preschoolers and older children.

Table 7.2
Physical Characteristics of the Child from 2 to 5 Years Old

At 2 Years Begins to	At 3 Years Begins to	At 4 Years Begins to	At 5 Years Begins to
Walk	Jump and hop on one foot	Run, jump, and climb with close adult supervision	Gain good body control
Run			Throw and catch a ball, climb, jump, skip with good coordination
Actively explore his environment	Climb stairs by alternating feet on each stair	Dress self using buttons, zippers, laces, and so on	Coordinate movements to music
Sit in a chair without support	Dress and undress self somewhat	Use more sophisticated eating utensils such as knives to cut meat or spread butter	Put on snowpants, boots, and tie shoes
Climb stairs with help (two feet on each stair)	Walk a reasonably straight path on floor		Skip
Build block towers	Walk on balance beam	Walk balance beam with ease	Jump rope, walk in a straight line
Feed self with fork and spoon	Ride a tricycle	Walk down stairs alone	Ride a two-wheel bike
Stand on balance beam	Stand on one foot for a short time	Bounce and catch ball	Roller skate
Throw ball	Catch large balls	Push/pull wagon	Fold paper
Catch	Hop	Cut, following lines	Reproduce alphabet and numbers
Jump	Gallop	Copy figure ×	Trace
Push and pull	Kick ball	Print first name	
Hang on bar	Hit ball		
Slide	Paste		
	String beads		
	Cut paper with scissors		
	Copy figures ○ and +		

Source: From G. W. Maxim (1989). *The very young* (3rd ed.). Columbus, Ohio: Merrill, p. 399. Reprinted by permission of Merrill, an imprint of Macmillan Publishing Company. © 1989 by Merrill Publishing.

This section looks at the cognitive development of the preschool child. We begin with a look at the preschooler's memory, summarize Piaget's view of cognitive development, and move to some other findings that present a more positive and optimistic view of the preschooler's intellectual capabilities.

The Preschooler's Memory

Between birth and the end of the early childhood period (around age 6), children are exposed to, learn, and remember an overwhelming assortment of things: the identities of people and animals; the locations of things; numbers, letters, and songs; thousands of words and all sorts of complex rules for putting them together.

From the very beginning, we clearly have some ability to learn and to remember. But, as we saw in Chapter 5, the neonate's memory is very brief. The effects of simple conditioning procedures sometimes last only hours or perhaps a day. Still, the infant is not long confused about whether this is his mother's voice or her face. Recognition of things like voices and faces is a certain sign of memory. But there are some important differences between the memories of infants and those of adults. Chief among them is the fact that the infant does not deliberately and systematically organize, group, or elaborate material in order to remember it—and these three activities are generally recognized as the most important memory strategies of adults and older children.

Incidental mnemonics. They are probably also not the most important memory strategies of preschoolers. In fact, a number of researchers have argued that the preschooler rarely uses systematic strategies for remembering. Most of what the preschooler remembers is the result of what Wellman (1988) calls *incidental* mnemonics. Incidental mnemonics are not deliberate; hence they are not strategies. They are, in a sense, accidental. They are what happens when someone pays attention, for whatever reason, and later remembers, or what happens when someone is exposed to the same thing often enough that it becomes familiar and known. Remembering, in these cases, is not the result of a deliberate and systematic attempt to elaborate or to rehearse but is, in a sense, involuntary.

We don't know a great deal about these incidental mnemonics. But we suspect they underlie much of the preschooler's learning of language and people and places and things. And because incidental and involuntary processes account for most of the learning we observe in the preschooler, and because we have not been able to find much evidence of adultlike strategies such as deliberately rehearsing or organizing, we have assumed that memory strategies develop only in later childhood. The evidence suggests that this is wrong. Preschoolers do use deliberate strategies to help them remember. But two things are noteworthy about these strategies: First, they seldom involve deliberate reorganization, elaboration, or even rehearsal; second, many of the preschooler's mnemonic strategies are faulty in the sense that they are misused and often do not lead to an improvement in memory.

Preschool strategies. That preschoolers deliberately use memory strategies seems clear from a number of different studies. For example, Wellman (1988) asked 3-year-olds to bury a toy in a sandbox. Once they had done so, they left the room with the experimenter to get more toys. Some of the children were asked to remember where they had buried the toy; others were asked if there was anything they would like to do before leaving but were given no instructions about remembering.

Strikingly, half the children who had been instructed to remember the toy's location *marked* it by marking the sand, placing a mound over the object, or sometimes by placing another toy on top of it; only 20 percent of the no-instruction group did likewise.

Marking the toy's location is an intelligent and effective strategy. As we noted, however, many of the preschooler's memory strategies are not so effective. Heisel and Retter (1981) asked 3- and 5-year-old youngsters to hide an object in one of the 196 separate containers arranged in a large 14-by-14 matrix and instructed some of them to remember where they had hidden the object. Significantly, many of the children in both age groups used memory strategies when they had been instructed to remember. The strategies used by the 5-year-olds were often very effective — namely, hiding the object in one of the corner locations, since these could be remembered and relocated very easily. But what is perhaps most striking is that the 3-year-olds' strategies, while every bit as consistent as those of the older children, were often very ineffective. Almost half of these 3-year-olds tried to hide the object in the same location on every trial, thus demonstrating that they were using a systematic strategy; but the location was typically somewhere near the center of the array. As a result, when they were later asked to find the object, these children fared almost as poorly as those who had not used strategies.

The overuse of an inappropriate memory strategy is among the most common of the mistakes made by young children trying to remember, says Wellman (1988). And one of the important developmental changes in memory strategies is a gradual reduction in the use of faulty strategies and a corresponding increase in more effective strategies. Effective strategies increase dramatically in elementary school.

Although much is still unknown about the development of memory strategies in the preschool period, it seems clear that these children are deliberate and often systematic in attempts to learn and remember; but they are not always totally effective.

Development of strategies. Ornstein, Baker-Ward, and Naus (1988) summarize the progression of children's development of memory strategies in five stages:

1. In the beginning, the young child doesn't deliberately use strategies to remember.

2. The preschooler may occasionally use strategies, but these don't always result in memory improvement.

3. In the early elementary school years, children use somewhat more effective strategies but are often distracted by irrelevant information.

4. Later, strategies become increasingly effective and are applied to a variety of settings.

5. Finally, as a result of repeated practice with memory strategies, their use becomes habitual and automatic.

In summary, our preschoolers are clearly able to remember. But in most cases, memory results not from the deliberate use of memory strategies, but

Between the ages of 2 and 4, children begin to classify objects they encounter by noting their characteristics. Long snouts, curly tails, and grunt-like noises will help this boy identify this mud-covered creature as a pig rather than a cat.

from *incidental mnemonics* — for example, paying attention to something or being exposed to it more than once. In contrast, the elementary school child often deliberately uses memory strategies.

One of the important differences between the older memorizer and the preschooler is that older children have acquired some understanding of the processes involved in learning and remembering. They have developed intuitive notions of themselves as information processors, capable of applying strategies and of monitoring and changing them as required. In the current jargon, they have developed some of the skills involved in **metamemory,** which is defined as the knowledge that children have about the processes involved in remembering (Borkowski, Milstead, & Hale, 1988). (There is more about the memories of older children in Chapter 9.)

PIAGET'S VIEW

In Chapter 5 we looked at the *sensorimotor* intelligence of the infant — Piaget's label for the first major stage of intellectual development, so called because the infant's intelligence involves immediate sensation and perception. The next major stage, spanning the preschool years, is the *preoperational*.

In Piaget's theory, an operation is a thought characterized by some specific logical properties — a logical thought. The child who believes that he has more

Table 7.3
Piaget's Stages of Cognitive Development

Stage	Approximate Age	Some Major Characteristics
Sensorimotor	0–2 years	Motoric intelligence World of the here and now No language, no thought in early stages No notion of objective reality
Preoperational Preconceptual Intuitive	2–7 years 2–4 years 4–7 years	Egocentric thought Reason dominated by perception Intuitive rather than logical solutions Inability to conserve
Concrete operations	7–11 or 12 years	Ability to conserve Logic of classes and relations Understanding of number Thinking bound to concrete Development of reversibility in thought
Formal operations	11 or 12–14 or 15 years	Complete generality of thought Propositional thinking Ability to deal with the hypothetical Development of strong idealism

gum when he rolls it into a fat ball and less when he spreads it out like a thin pancake on his sister's pillow is demonstrating preoperational (or prelogical) thinking.

Piaget divides the preoperational period (ages 2 to about 7 years) into two sub-periods: the first, lasting from 2 to 4, is termed *preconceptual;* the second, from 4 to 7, is called *intuitive* (Table 7.3).

Preconceptual Thinking

The major intellectual difference between the sensorimeter child and the preoperational child is in the means each has of representing the world and reasoning about it. The young infant's intelligence is initially rooted in sensation and action; but toward the end of the second year, and especially with the advent of language, infants begin to symbolize. They begin to represent their actions mentally, to anticipate consequences before the action actually occurs, and to develop some notion of causes — of actions as means to ends.

Preconcepts. As children begin to symbolize they develop the ability to internalize objects and events in the environment and to relate them by their common properties — in other words to develop **concepts.** But these concepts are not as complete and logical as an adult's and are therefore referred to as **preconcepts.** Despite their incompleteness, they are nevertheless sufficient to permit the child to make the simple classifications necessary for identifying some of the objects of the world. Thus children recognize a man because they have a building concept that tells them that a *man* is whatever walks on two legs, has hair, wears pants, and speaks in a gruff voice. By noting their characteristics, children can identify dogs, birds, elephants, and houses. What they frequently cannot do, however, is distinguish among different individuals belonging to the same species. Piaget (1951) illustrates this with his son, Laurent, who pointed out a snail to his father as they were walking. "Regardez l'escargot," he allegedly said in the polite manner of a Swiss child of the early 1920s. It is not certain what Piaget's reply to this observation was, but he reports that several minutes later they came upon another snail, and the child exclaimed that here again was the snail. The child apparently fails to recognize that similar objects can belong to the same class and still be different objects — that is, they can retain an identity of their own. This overclassification is an example of a *preconcept*. A related example is the preschooler who steadfastly continues to believe in Santa Claus, even after seeing 10 different Santas on the same day. For the child they are all identical (Lefrançois, 1967).

There are two other striking features of the child's reasoning processes during the preconceptual period, evident in **transductive reasoning** and **syncretic reasoning**.

Transductive reasoning. *Transduction* can be contrasted with the two broad types of logical reasoning: *deduction* and *induction*. To deduce is to go from the general to the particular. For example, from my knowledge that mammals give birth to live young, I might deduce that a specific mammal such as a three-toed sloth gives birth to tiny live sloths. In contrast, to induce is to go from specific examples to a broader generalization. After observing a number of barn swallows build nests of a mixture of mud and a cementlike type of saliva, I might generalize that all (or most) barn swallows build similar nests.

Transductive reasoning makes inferences from one particular to another — that is, from one instance to another, often because of superficial similarities. It is very much like inductive reasoning except that it is based on a single case rather than many. If I find that one red-headed person has a particularly charming personality, I might transduce that all red-headed persons will also be charming. Transductive reasoning can occasionally — and somewhat accidentally — lead to a correct inference; it can also lead to totally incorrect conclusions. Consider the following example:

> *A* flies.
>
> *B* flies.
>
> Therefore *B* is *A*.

Clearly if *A* is a bird and *B* is also a bird, then *A* is a *B* and vice versa. If *A* is a plane and *B* is a bird, the same reasoning process leads to an incorrect conclusion. Thus it is that a young preschooler can unashamedly insist that cats are dogs and chickens, turkeys.

Syncretic reasoning. The preschooler's classification behavior is also marked by the use of syncretic reasoning in which different objects are grouped according to the child's limited and frequently changing rules. For example, a 2-year-old child who is placed in front of a table bearing a number of objects of different kinds and colors and who is asked to group those objects that go together might proceed something like this: The blue truck goes with the red truck because they both are trucks, and this thing goes with them because it is blue and that truck is blue. Here is a ball and here is a marble and they go together, and here is a crayon that is yellow like the ball so it goes with them too. The important point is that the child's rules change; children see little reason to use the same rule consistently. We adults, whose thinking is not so magical, do not have the same luxury.

Intuitive Thinking

The period of **intuitive thinking** begins at about age 4 and ends at approximately 7. It is labeled *intuitive* because much of the child's thought is based on immediate comprehension rather than logical processes. Children solve many problems correctly, but they do not always do so using logic. Piaget refers to a problem in which a child is shown three balls that are then inserted into a hollow cardboard tube so that the child can no longer see them. The balls are blue, red, and yellow. At first when the tube is held vertically, the child knows clearly which ball is on top. Then the tube is turned a half rotation (180 degrees), and the subject is asked which ball is now at the top. Alternatively, it may be turned a full rotation, one and one-half turns, two turns, and so on. Piaget found that as long as subjects could continue to *imagine* the position of the balls inside the tube, they could answer correctly. But they could not arrive at a rule about the relationship between odd and even numbers of turns or half turns and the location of the balls. The solution to the problem was achieved through intuitive mental images rather than logical reasoning.

Intuitive thinking is also characterized by difficulties in knowing what things to include in a class, or category; *egocentricity* (an inability to adopt another's point of view); and a marked reliance on perception. We will look at each of these qualities.

Classification. The preschooler's difficulties with class *inclusion* are easily demonstrated in experiments that present the child with a collection of objects made up of two subclasses. For example, the objects may consist of wooden beads of which 15 are brown and 5 are blue. The subject is asked what the objects are. "They are wooden beads," the child answers. The experimenter then divides the beads into the subclasses, brown and blue, and asks whether there are more brown beads or more wooden beads. The trick is obvious, you say? Not to the child at this stage of development. The common reply is "There are more brown beads." The answer reflects the child's incomplete understanding of classes. It is as though breaking down a class into its subparts destroys the parent class.

Egocentricity. An experiment in which a girl doll and a boy doll are placed side by side on a piece of string illustrates the *egocentric* nature of the preschool child's thought. The experimenter holds the ends of the string in both hands and stands behind a screen that hides the dolls from the child's view. The child is asked to predict which of the dolls will appear first if the experimenter moves the string toward the right. Let us assume that the boy doll appears first. The experimenter then returns the dolls to their original position and repeats the same question, "Which of the dolls will now appear first if they are moved to the same side?" The procedure is repeated several times regardless of whether the child answers correctly. A normally intelligent child will answer correctly for every early trial. What happens in later trials is striking: The child eventually makes the opposite and clearly incorrect prediction! If asked why, one of the more common answers is that it is not fair that the same doll comes out first every time; now it is the other doll's turn. Children inject their own values, their own sense of justice, into the experimental situation, demonstrating their egocentric thought processes. The term *egocentric* is not derogatory but simply points out an excessive reliance on the thinker's individual point of view coupled with a corresponding inability to be objective.

Egocentric thought is further demonstrated by the preschooler's inability to imagine what a mountain looks like when seen from another point of view — for example, the top or bottom or another side. It is apparent too in what Piaget terms **egocentric speech,** the characteristic self-talk of the budding young linguist who repeats words and sounds to himself — much as a young prelingual infant might babble — but using real words. Egocentricity abounds as well in the conversation of young children where speakers pay little attention to their listeners or to other speakers, except that they sometimes take turns in delivering their little pronouncements:

> Geoff: It's a black one.
>
> Jason: I have to go home soon.
>
> Geoff: I'm going to find a red one.
>
> Jason: I'm thirsty.
>
> Geoff: I don't like black ones.

A conversation? No: More a *collective monologue,* Piaget tells us. But real conversations, which require the nonegocentric ability to adopt another's point of view, are not far behind (discussed later in this chapter).

Reliance on perception. The preschooler's *perception* also dominates thinking, as is easily shown in Piaget's conservation problems (see Chapter 9). In a typical conservation of mass problem, for example, a child is shown two identical balls of modeling clay ("Play-Doh" or similar substance) and acknowledges that there is the same amount of clay in each. One of the balls is then flattened into a thin pancake, broken into small pieces, rolled into a long snake, or otherwise deformed. The child now believes that the ball of clay that has

Egocentrism is evident in the behavior of the 4-year-old who, when she speaks on the phone, nods and shakes her head and smiles and makes other gestures that totally bewilder the grandmother on the other end.

been altered contains either more or less clay, depending on its appearance. The preoperational child relies on actual perception of the object rather than on any of the logical rules that will later govern thinking (for example, nothing has been added to or taken away from the clay, and so it must still contain an identical amount). Figure 7.5 illustrates simple tasks that can be used to demonstrate some of the important prelogical characteristics of the preschooler's thought processes.

THE NEO-PIAGETIANS

An increasing number of researchers, sometimes referred to as *neo-Piagetians*, no longer consider it appropriate to refer to preschool children as "prelogical." Their logic may not be as advanced as yours or mine, and there may be something to be learned by contrasting it with a more advanced logic; it is, nevertheless, a logic that is worthy of study in its own right.

The term *neo-Piagetian* is a collective word for developmental theorists whose research stems from a Piagetian tradition, but who have gone beyond where Piaget stopped. In a loose sense, it includes all those who continue to replicate his work and to ponder his questions and his answers.

Replications of Piaget's Work

Literally hundreds of studies have been conducted to investigate Piaget's view of the child's progression through stages of cognitive development. With a few exceptions, most have found that the sequence described by Piaget is valid, not only in European and North American countries, but in many other parts of

Figure 7.5

Tasks and experiments in preoperational thought.

Preoperational thought may be:

Preconceptual		Similar objects are assumed to be identical.
Transductive	A dog	Reasoning is from particular to particular.
Syncretic	"Put those that go together on the table."	Groupings are made according to idiosyncratic and changing criteria.

Preconceptual period: 2–4 years

Intuitive		Tube is rotated; child must predict order of balls.
Perception dominated	A. B 1 2 1 2	Child admits two balls of modeling clay are "the same" in A. In B, where one has been flattened, child thinks amount has changed.
Egocentric		Boy and girl dolls are behind screen. They are always brought out on the same side so that boy always appears first. Child eventually predicts the other doll should be first: "It's her turn."
Prone to errors of classification		Child realizes some flowers are daisies, fewer are tulips, but answers "Daisies" to the question "Are there more flowers or more daisies?"

Intuitive period: 4–7 years

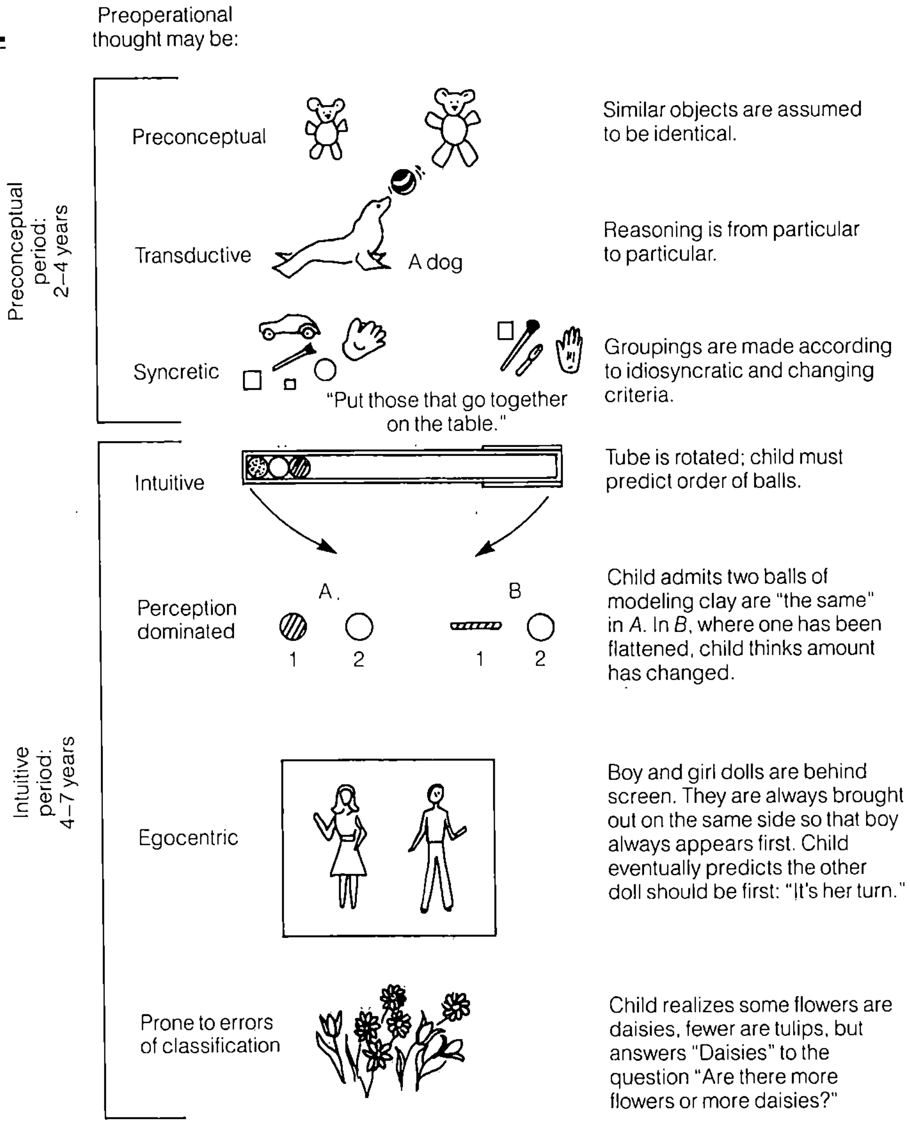

the world as well. For example, when Opper (1977) looked at the classification abilities of preoperational children in Thailand and Malaysia, she found that they, like Piaget's subjects, believed that a bouquet consisting of seven roses and two orchids contained more roses than flowers. Other cross-cultural research is in general agreement that the sequence described by Piaget is cross-culturally valid (Dasen, 1977). However, some evidence shows that Piaget's estimates of the ages of attainment are, in effect, underestimates for some North American and European children on specific tasks. This evidence typi-

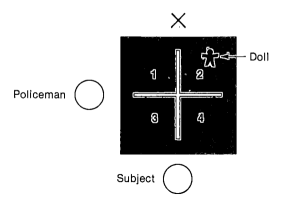

Figure 7.6

Arrangement for the Hughes experiment. Subjects had to determine whether a doll hidden in 1, 2, 3, or 4 could be seen by the policeman. In a later part of the experiment, a second policeman was placed at X. The child now had to decide where the doll would have to be hidden so as not to be seen by either policeman. Preschoolers had little trouble answering correctly.

cally comes from experiments that attempt to make it simpler for children to demonstrate knowledge of the concept or ability in question. Some of these studies, for example, concern Piaget's "mountain" problems which illustrates the child's egocentricity (inability to adopt someone else's point of view).

In Piaget's original demonstration of egocentricity, children observed three mountains of unequal height set on top of a table. They were allowed to walk around the display, becoming familiar with all sides of the mountains. Later they sat on one side of the table, a doll was placed on the other side, and they were asked to select photographs representing the doll's point of view. Piaget found that children in the preoperational period usually indicated that the doll would see the same things they themselves saw, a finding that he interprets as evidence of egocentricity.

When Piaget's mountain task is made simpler, the child sometimes responds quite differently. Liben (1975) asked preschoolers to describe what a white card would look like from their point of view and from the experimenter's point of view under a number of different conditions involving the wearing of colored glasses. In one condition, for example, the experimenter would wear green-tinted glasses and the children, no glasses. A correct, nonegocentric response in this case would be that the card would look green to the experimenter. Liben found that almost half the 3-year-olds answered correctly, and most of the older children had no difficulty with the questions. Similarly, when Hughes (reported in Donaldson, 1978) presented preschoolers with a situation where they had to determine whether a "policeman" could see a "boy" doll from a vantage point quite different from the child's, subjects had little difficulty determining what the policeman's point of view would actually be (Figure 7.6).

Do these studies mean that Piaget's conclusions about the preoperational child's egocentricity are invalid? The answer is no. Donaldson (1978) points out that all these studies present the child with problems that are really very different from the problem of the mountains. The child who can accurately predict whether a policeman can see into an area when the policeman is on the opposite side of the table from the child should not be expected to be able to describe what the physical array would look like to the policeman. Among other things, doing so would require that the child be able to reverse left and right (in other words, that the child realize the policeman's left is the child's right) — a task that is sometimes difficult even for adults, as those of us who have occasionally been surprised by our movements in mirrors can testify.

What these and related studies most clearly point out is that egocentricity and other characteristics of child-thinking are far more complex than had been suspected. Indeed, they are far more complex than Piaget himself had suspected, and it is only recently that the neo-Piagetians have begun to explore that complexity. The most striking thing about these recent investigations is their emphasis on what preoperational children *can* rather than what they *cannot* do. As Flavell (1985) notes, it is now inappropriate and misleading to think of the preschool child's mind as *pre*operational or *pre*conceptual.

Cognitive Achievements of the Preschooler

What then are the most significant cognitive advances that occur during the period between infancy and ages 6 or 7?

Symbolic representation. First, there are monumental advances in the child's ability to represent the world symbolically. According to Fischer and Silvern's (1985) summary of neo-Piagetian research, this level, which they label *representations*, first emerges between the ages of 18 and 24 months. Accordingly, the ability to represent has its roots in sensorimotor development and is probably most evident in language.

Classifying. A second major class of achievements during this period falls under the level described by Fischer and Silvern (1985) as *relations of a few representations*. These capabilities are thought to emerge around the age of 4 to 5 years and are evident in the child's ability to solve problems that require understanding relationships among different ideas. For example, when Smith (1979) asked 4-year-olds questions of the type, "A basenji is a kind of dog but not a poodle. Is a basenji an animal?" many answered correctly. Similarly, many had no difficulty with questions of the form, "An abalone is a kind of food but not a plant. Is an abalone a vegetable?" These are class-inclusion questions; they require at least some knowledge of class membership (animals include dogs; nonplants are not included among vegetables). They depend on the child's ability to relate concepts.

Number concepts. Also included among abilities that fall within the level *relations of a few representations* is the preschooler's remarkable understanding of number. There are few preschoolers who cannot count objects and who do not understand that six jellybeans is more than four. Indeed, the great majority will tell you without prompting that six is exactly two more than four or that if you had six jellybeans to begin with and your little brother ate four of them, you would have only two left.

Gelman (1982; Gelman & Gallistel, 1978) identifies two kinds of knowledge about numbers that appear during the preschool period. First there are the number abstraction skills that give the child an understanding of *numerosity* — of how many things there are in a collection of, say, snails in one's pockets. Second, there are *numerical reasoning* principles that allow the child to reason about or predict the outcome of certain simple numerical operations such as adding to or taking from.

Gelman, a neo-Piagetian concerned with the achievements rather than the cognitive weaknesses of the preschool period, describes the principles that underlie number abstraction. These are the principles that govern counting, because counting is the way in which the young child establishes numerosity. There are five such principles. We take them completely for granted in spite of the fact that they are remarkably complex and wonderfully logical — far more logical than we had expected the preschool child to be.

The *one-on-one principle* says that if you are to count something, you must assign a single number to each item; you must include every item in your assignment, but no item must be assigned more than one number. The *stable order principle* requires that the assignment of numbers to items be sequential, successive, and nonarbitrary. That is, the correct order for counting is always one, two, three, and never one, three, two. Of course, the neophyte counter may indulge in certain idiosyncrasies, may distort the conventional sequence or invent a brand new one such as in, "One, two, free, eleben, twenty!" What is remarkable, however, is that the child who invents such a sequence will often use it repeatedly, *in stable order.*

The *cardinal principle* says that the last number assigned to the last item in a collection describes the numerosity of that collection. Gelman (1982) points out that many children as young as 2½ or 3 years old appear to understand this principle even when they are still incapable of verbalizing it. For example, some children will successfully count five objects such as flamingos, but will then be uncertain about what to answer when the examiner asks, "How many pink flamingos are there in the pail?" But when a puppet subsequently counts out the flamingos, "One flamingo, two flamingos, three . . . , four . . . , five flamingos!" and then announces, "There are four flamingos!" the child may spot the error immediately.

The three counting principles just described explain *how* to count. A fourth, *the abstraction principle,* relates to *what* can be counted; it says, in effect, that anything can be counted: yuppies, puppies, and guppies; ponies and

Most preschoolers can tell you without hesitation that if you had seven jellybeans to begin with and your little brother ate five of them, you would have only two left.

baloneys; hops, skips, and jumps. Four-year-olds behave as though they are completely aware of this. If you ask them how many things there are in the car, they may count people and books, dogs and steering wheels, ignition keys, and various other gidgets and gadgets. They know, intuitively and brilliantly, that objects do not have to belong to the same class to be countable — that countability is an abstraction that belongs to everything.

Finally, the *order irrelevance principle* states that the order in which items are counted does not matter, that to successfully count the three animals in the garage requires only the assignment of a number, in correct sequence, once to each of the items. The horse can be one, the hedgehog two, and the toad three; or the toad can be one, the horse two, the hedgehog three. In one of Gelman's studies, a puppet leads the child to count objects in different orders, and then exclaims, "I tricked you. I made you make them all number one!" But the child is seldom confused by this procedure. It is as though, with the understanding of the counting principles, there comes an understanding that numbers do not belong to objects or events — that they are abstractions that can be applied to all events, subject only to the logical rules that give them meaning.

Number abstraction and numerical reasoning skills are important and complex cognitive abilities that illustrate dramatically some of the achievements of the preschooler. These achievements stand in sharp contrast to Piaget's view of the deficits in *pre*operational thought (Gold, 1986).

As Gelman (1978) notes, our preoccupation with what preschool children cannot do has blinded us to their achievements. Research has only recently begun to pay attention to the fact that preschoolers are not egocentric in all situations, do have considerable understanding of numbers, and can classify and make logical inferences under a variety of circumstances. Also, as we have known for some time but have not always emphasized, their language development is nothing short of phenomenal. In short, preschoolers are a tremendous cognitive distance from sensorimotor children. The extent to which their capabilities can be influenced through preschool education is examined in the next section.

PRESCHOOL EDUCATION

There are many different forms of preschool education programs. Some are distinct; they are describable in terms of specific principles and procedures. The majority, however, are thoroughly eclectic. They are variously known as kindergartens, nurseries, preschools, playschools, intervention programs, compensatory education — even daycare centers (which are discussed in Chapter 8). They are found in schools and homes, in church basements and community centers, in parks and shopping malls, in universities and technical schools, even in office buildings. Their offerings are a varied mixture dictated in part by the ages of their charges, the resources available, the wishes of parents, the restrictions and mandates of local laws and regulations, and the inclinations and capabilities of instructors and caregivers. The following sections present very brief summaries of some forms of preschool education.

Nursery Schools

For many years, nursery schools were among the most prevalent form of preschool education. They typically take in very young preschoolers and emphasize social and emotional development. Their principal activities consist of games, dancing, singing, listening to stories, and so on — many of the functions that are also performed by good daycare facilities. Clarke-Stewart (1984) reports that children who attend nursery schools are, on the average, more self-reliant, more outgoing, more spontaneous, and more confident than comparable children who do not attend nursery school.

Compensatory Programs

Compensatory preschool programs are designed to make up for initial deficits in children. The best-known and most massive compensatory education program ever undertaken in the United States was Project Head Start, which began in 1964, and which was conceived as part of the American war on poverty. The program allocated large amounts of funds to the creation of eight-week summer programs for children from disadvantaged backgrounds. Later, a second, related project, *Project Follow Through,* was set up to continue the efforts of Project Head Start.

Because of the great variety of approaches employed in these projects, it proved extremely difficult to assess their effectiveness. However, many early studies indicated that children enrolled in Head Start programs continued to be inferior to more advantaged children who had not been exposed to compensatory preschool programs, and critics were quick to conclude that huge amounts of money had been squandered in poorly planned, poorly executed, and basically ineffective programs (Bronfenbrenner, 1977). However, more recent research has sometimes found quite dramatic improvements resulting from Head Start programs — and has also found a simple explanation for the often negative findings of other research. As Lee, Brooks-Gunn, and Schnur (1988) point out, most of the early research did not look at initial differences between groups exposed to Head Start and comparison groups, but simply looked at differences *after* the programs. When Lee and her associates looked at initial differences among a sample of 969 subjects, they found tremendous differences between groups who were to attend Head Start Programs and the other children on virtually every measure of cognitive functioning. And although at the conclusion of the program, there were still significant differences between these groups on most measures, the Head Start children had improved dramatically during the program.

In summarizing a large number of studies that have looked at the effectiveness of Head Start programs, Haskins (1989) concludes that there is no doubt that such programs have an immediate, positive impact on children, although the long-term effects are not as pronounced or as clear. However, the *best* forms of preschool education may produce detectable long-term benefits in "life success measures" — such as, for example, reductions in teenage pregnancy, delinquency, unemployment, and reliance on welfare assistance.

What are these *best* forms of preschool intervention? We are not yet completely certain, but research that has looked at differences among the dozens of different approaches to compensatory preschool education reports that the most effective forms of intervention are highly specific, "model" approaches (Haskins, 1989). These are usually based on identifiable theories and characterized by well-formulated approaches and carefully developed materials.

Among the better known model approaches that have sometimes been used as Head Start programs (or in other nursery school or kindergarten programs) are the *Direct Instruction Approach* and the *Montessori Method.* The Direct Instruction Approach was initiated by Bereiter and Engelmann (1966). It offers a sharp contrast to the traditional approach of most kindergartens and nursery schools. Instead of being primarily child-centered and emphasizing social and emotional development, it is instructor-centered and emphasizes the teaching of skills and concepts. Instructional methods are highly structured and involve *telling* the children and *asking* them to repeat, alone or in unison. It teaches reading, language, and arithmetic. Not surprisingly, it has shown some marked positive results in these areas (see Figure 7.7).

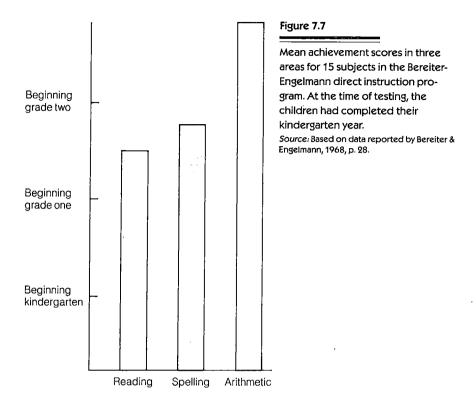

Figure 7.7

Mean achievement scores in three areas for 15 subjects in the Bereiter-Engelmann direct instruction program. At the time of testing, the children had completed their kindergarten year.

Source: Based on data reported by Bereiter & Engelmann, 1968, p. 28.

Direct Instruction has its critics, however. Some fear that such approaches place too much emphasis on learning basics, on repetition, on drill, on success. They argue that the high-pressure, achievement-oriented principles that underlie Direct Instruction violate our fundamental belief in the rights of children to play, to enjoy, to dream, to make magical, nonrealistic things.

The Montessori method, which dates back to the turn of the century (Montessori, 1912), is another very structured approach to preschool education. It was initially developed for use with mentally retarded children, but has proven highly effective and popular as a general program. Unlike most preschool programs, however, it is designed for use in elementary and high school as well.

One of the distinctive features of the Montessori approach is the use of a variety of specially developed materials for teaching sense discriminations. Montessori believed that all learning stems from sense perception and can therefore be improved by training the senses. Perhaps the best-known of her materials are large letters of the alphabet covered with sandpaper. These are used to teach the child to read. The prescribed teaching method requires not only that children look at the letters, but also that they trace their shapes with their fingertips, saying the sound of the letter and getting a tactile sensation of it at the same time (see Figure 7.8 for examples of some Montessori materials).

Evaluations of Montessori programs have generally been quite positive, in spite of the criticism that such programs, given their highly structured nature, might stifle the child's creativity. For example, a study of the long-term effects of preschool programs found that the highest achievers in grades six, seven, and eight were males who had been exposed to a preschool Montessori program (Miller & Bizzell, 1983).

Kindergartens

Not very many years ago, kindergartens were typically considered an optional preschool program. Now, however, a majority of North American children attend kindergartens, most housed in regular schools, funded in the same manner as schools, and staffed by teachers whose certification requirements are typically the same as those who teach at more advanced levels. In many ways, then, kindergartens are part of regular school. Many no longer simply prepare the child for the first-grade tasks of learning to read and write and count; they actually engage in the business of teaching these things (if the children don't already know them). One of the big differences between kindergarten and regular schools, in most (but no longer all) jurisdictions is that kindergarteners can run home at lunch time and stay there the rest of the afternoon; or they can stay home all morning and go to school only in the afternoon.

But perhaps we are *hurrying* our children too much, Elkind (1981a) warns. Perhaps we should let them slow down and be children, and play and dream, and do magical things that don't require knowing how to read and write and count real numbers in perfect sequence.

Not only are we hurrying our children, says Elkind (1987), but many parents are also *miseducating* them. These are "Gold Medal" parents whose burning ambition is to produce a star basketball or hockey player, a world-class gymnast, a violin prodigy. Or they are "College Degree" parents whose babies are destined for Harvard or MIT. For these parents, children have become symbols of parental ambitions and proof of parental success.

We have to strike a balance, Elkind (1981a) urges, between the *spoiled* child, who remains a child too long, and the *hurried* child, who does not remain a child long enough and whose life might be plagued by "a fear of failure — of not achieving fast enough or high enough" (p. xii).

Effective Intervention: The Family Context

Our discussion of preschool education has focused on only a few of the many distinct approaches that have been employed, with emphasis on distinctive intervention (remedial) preschool programs and several other programs that are equally striking but not geared solely or specifically toward intervention. A large number of other preschool programs could also have been included.

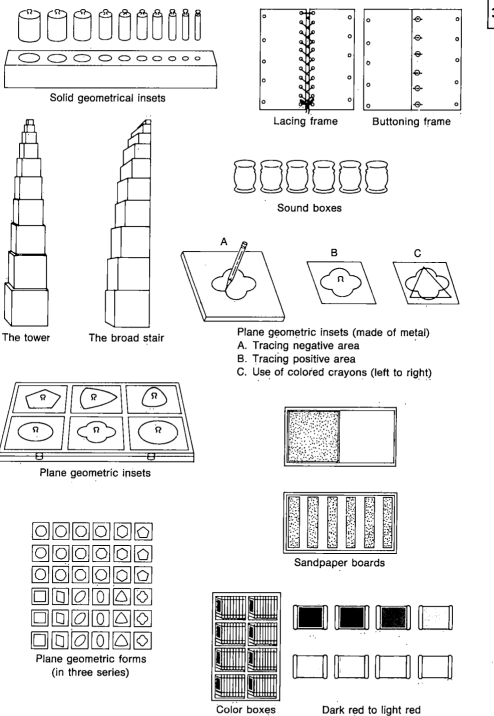

Solid geometrical insets

Lacing frame

Buttoning frame

Sound boxes

The tower

The broad stair

A

B

C

Plane geometric insets (made of metal)
A. Tracing negative area
B. Tracing positive area
C. Use of colored crayons (left to right)

Plane geometric insets

Sandpaper boards

Plane geometric forms
(in three series)

Color boxes

Dark red to light red

Figure 7.8

Some traditional Montessori materials.

Working Mothers and Preschool Children

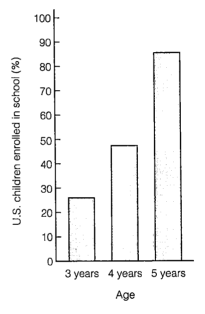

Figure 7.9   Preprimary school enrollment, 1988, for U.S. children age 3 to 5. *Source:* Adapted from U.S. Bureau of the Census (1990), p. 166.

In 1988, 58 percent of U.S. children between the ages of 3 and 5 (a total of 5.6 million children) had mothers who were employed. Of these, 3.7 million had mothers employed full time and 1.9 million had mothers employed part time. Another one-half million had unemployed mothers, and 4.3 million had mothers who were not in the labor force. Of the nearly 11 million U.S. children age 3 to 5 in 1988, nearly 6 million were in nursery schools and kindergartens. Only 14 percent of the 5-year-olds were not enrolled in preprimary schools.

Bronfenbrenner (1977b), following review of major intervention programs, suggests a sequential strategy that might be used for the most effective type of intervention with disadvantaged children. This strategy is based on the fundamental assumption that the essential requirement for an effective intervention program is to take into account the family as a childrearing unit and to provide conditions that will ameliorate a negative home environment. In brief, he suggests that health, nutrition, housing, and employment need to be raised to an adequate level for intervention programs to be effective.

The sequential strategy for intervention described by Bronfenbrenner occurs in five stages. It begins before parenthood (Stage 1: preparation for parenthood) and its goal is to give schoolchildren adequate information about the care of children and the nutritional and health requirements of pregnant women. The second stage (Stage 2: before children come) involves taking steps to ensure that the family into which the child will be born will provide adequate shelter, food, and economic security. The third stage (Stage 3: the first three years of life) is concerned with the establishment of emotional bonds between parents and children through caregiving activities and other interactions. Not until the fourth stage does intervention in the form of a preschool program begin (Stage 4: ages 4 through 6). Bronfenbrenner suggests this program be cognitively oriented and that it involve the parents directly. Nor does intervention cease when the child enters first grade. In the fifth stage (Stage 5: ages 6 through 12), parents are encouraged to become highly involved in school activities.

There is little doubt that the first six years of a child's life are tremendously important for later development. There is also little doubt that not all parents are sufficiently well equipped, or indeed have the required time, to give their children the experiences that would be most beneficial for them. It is up to the psychologist and the expert in early childhood education to provide better information about the nature of these experiences, the best way in which they can be provided, and the optimal time for doing so.

LANGUAGE AND THE PRESCHOOLER

More than three decades ago, psychologist Hayes and his wife tried to teach a chimpanzee to speak (Hayes & Hayes, 1951). They had reasoned that if any animal other than the human one were ever to succeed in learning a language, a close biological relative like the chimpanzee would be the most likely candidate. But they failed miserably. It seems that the chimpanzee's vocal apparatus simply does not lend itself to speaking a language.

Some years later, a succession of individuals undertook to teach chimpanzees a different form of language: American Sign Language. Its big advantage is that it would not require chimpanzees (or gorillas in at least one case) to make sounds, but simply to make gestures. A number of these individuals

Certain things are difficult to communicate without language.

reported what seemed like remarkable success (for example, Premack & Premack, 1972; Fouts, 1987). However, critics quickly insisted that none of the chimpanzees in question had actually learned a language. Detailed examinations of videotapes of "sign-speaking" chimpanzees indicated that what they had learned was simply to imitate, to associate a symbol or gesture with food, or to use some movement or gesture to make some demand associated with reinforcement (for example, Terrace, 1985).

Language, *the use of arbitrary sounds with established and accepted referents, either real or abstract, that can be arranged in sequence to convey different meanings*, is still, as far as we know, uniquely human.

In Chapter 5 we looked at the roots of language in infancy. We noted that infants seem remarkably well prepared to learn language. And parents, for their part, fulfill the essential role of teacher, unconsciously "fine-tuning" their verbal interactions to a level appropriate for their infant.

The sequence of language development from infancy through childhood can be described in terms of six sequential stages (see Table 7.4). The *prespeech* stage lasts until around age 1 and is characterized by a transition from crying, gurgling, cooing, and babbling to the utterance of meaningful speech sounds and then to the sentencelike word. The next stage, that of two-word sentences (duos), is evident by the age of 18 months (see Chapter 5 for more details).

The story continues here with a discussion of the remaining three stages.

Table 7.4
Stages in Children's Development of Grammar

Stage of Development	Nature of Development	Sample Utterances
1. Prespeech (before age 1)	Crying, cooing, babbling.	"Waaah," "dadadada."
2. Sentencelike word (holophrase) (by 12 months)	The word is combined with nonverbal cues (gestures and inflections).	"Mommy." (meaning: "Would you please come here, mother.")
3. Two-word sentences (duos) (by 18 months)	Modifiers are joined to topic words to form declarative, question, negative, and imperative structures.	"Pretty baby." (declarative) "Where Daddy?" (question) "No play." (negative) "More milk!" (imperative)
4. Multiple-word sentences (by 2 to 2½ years)	Both a subject and predicate are included in the sentence types. Grammatical morphemes are used to change meanings ("ing" or "ed," for example).	"She's a pretty baby." (declarative) "Where Daddy is?" (question) "I no can play." (negative) "I want more milk!" (imperative) "I running." "I runned."
5. More complex grammatical changes and word categories (between 2½ and 4 years)	Elements are added; embedded, and permuted within sentences. Word classes (nouns, verbs, and prepositions) are subdivided. Clauses are put together.	"Read it, my book." (conjunction) "Where is Daddy?" (embedding) "I can't play." (permutation) "I would like *some* milk." (use of "some" with mass noun) "Take me *to* the store." (use of preposition of place)
6. Adultlike structures (after 4 years)	Complex structural distinctions made, as with "ask-tell" and "promise."	"Ask what time it is." "He promised to help her."

Source: Based in part on Barbara S. Wood, *Children and communication: Verbal and nonverbal language development* (2nd ed.), © 1981, p. 142. Reprinted by permission of Prentice-Hall, Inc., Englewood Cliffs, New Jersey.

Multiple-Word Sentences

In time, children move from two-word combinations to multiple-word sentences. This typically occurs around the age of 2 to 2½. "Allgone dog" becomes "Dog is gone" and eventually "The dog is gone" or "My dog is gone." The significance of this transition from a linguistic point of view is that it requires the use of complete subjects and predicates. The grammatical sophistication of multiword combinations as they are employed at this stage far outdoes that of earlier two-word combinations.

Although the child's speech continues to be somewhat telegraphic after the stage of two-word sentences, children now make increasing use of morphemes to express meaning (Brown, 1973). Recall that these are the smallest units of meaning in language. They include all words, as well as grammatical endings such as *ed* and *ing*, suffixes, prefixes, articles, and so on. The use of grammatical morphemes, for example, is what allows the child to transform the verbs *go* to *going*, *jump* to *jumped*, *eat* to *eated*, and *do* to *doed.*

There is evidence of inventiveness as well in the child's use of speech at this stage. Carlson and Anisfeld (1969) report the case of a 29-month-old boy who manipulated phonemes in songs and rhymes. To the tune "The bear went over the mountain," he sang "Da de de doder da doundin"; and for "I've been working on the railroad," he sang 'I pin purkin' on a pail poad." Indeed, examples of inventiveness abound in the speech of many children, as in that of one of my young linguists who, having learned that "pitch black" was very black, insisted that other things can be "pitch clean," "pitch empty," or "pitch big."

More Complex Changes

Between the ages of 2½ and 3 or 4, children begin to acquire some of the more complex aspects of syntax. In particular, they develop the ability to make meaningful *transformations*. These typically take one of three forms: *conjunction, embedding,* and *permutation* (Wood, 1981). Simple conjunction is illustrated by the addition or combination of the two sentences "Where?" and "We go" to form a third sentence, "Where we go?" Embedding is inserting. For example, the word "no" may be embedded in the sentence "I eat" to form a sentence with quite a different meaning: "I no eat." Permutation is altering the order of words in sentences to change their meaning. Initially, children make use of intonation rather than permutation. For example, the sentence "I can go" may be a simple declaration when the "I" or the "can" is emphasized but becomes a question when "go" is emphasized. A simple permutation from "I can go" to "Can I go?" achieves the same meaning with much less ambiguity.

As children begin to show an understanding of various adult-accepted rules for transforming sentences, they also behave as though they had an implicit understanding of the grammatical function of various words and phrases. They employ nouns as nouns and not as verbs; adjectives are no longer treated as verbs; and nouns are further categorized as plural or singular. Evidence of children's understanding of this type of categorization is evident in their appropriate use of verbs and of such determiners as *that, the, those,* and *these.* For example, the child will now say "That box is empty"; an earlier error might have taken the form of "This boxes is empty" (see Table 7.5).

Adultlike Structures

The further refinement and elaboration of speech requires mastery of countless subtle and intricate grammatical rules that we all employ unconsciously (termed **phrase structure** and **transformational rules**). Phrase structure rules govern the arrangement of words in meaningful expressions; they specify what is and is not grammatically acceptable and meaningful. They tell us that "the

Speech at Age 4 Years, 6 Months

Table 7.5
Age at Which Children Demonstrate a Given Language Capability*

Achievement	Age (years)	
	50 percent of children	90 percent of children
Combines 2 different words	1.6	2.3
Names 1 picture	1.7	2.5
Uses plurals	2.3	3.2
Gives first and last name	2.7	3.8
Comprehends cold, tired, hungry	2.9	4.1
Recognizes 3 colors	3.0	4.9
Defines 6 words	4.8	6.3

Source: From Denver Developmental Screening Test Reference Manual: Revised 1975 Edition by W. K. Frankenburg, J. B. Dodds, A. W. Fandal, E. Kazuk, M. Cohrs, 1975, Denver, CO: University of Colorado Medical Center.

*Based on norms from Denver Developmental Screening Test.

Language development in the preschool period is almost explosive, so rapidly do children's vocabularies grow and the sophistication of their grammar improve (Table 7.5). Rémi's story at 4½ — with accompanying art — displays imagination and verbal skills far in advance of a 2-year-old's.

The Story of the Gas Station (as told by Rémi with his Legos: 4 Years, 6 Months)

I'm going to fill up with regular. Vrooooom.

Thanks. Vrr-rrr-rrr.

I'm coming up to fill it with regular. Whtttt-taah.

Smash!!

Broken car now. They crashed into each other.

I want to oil my car.

Oh. Oh. I have a flat tire. I need some air.

Phhh. Phhh. Phhh.

Tchuuu.

I'm stuck. He broke the house down. He needs a new tire.

Neeowrr. Neeowrr.

Wowee! He got a flat tire.

I need unleaded gas.

Tchuu. Schewww.

The end.

fat mosquito" is a correctly structured phrase, but "Fat the mosquito" is not (although "Fat, the mosquito" might be). Transformational rules are the grammatical rules that permit us to transform the structure of phrases, to combine them, and to make a variety of meaningful statements. A transformational rule allows us to transform a passive sentence into an active one ("The dog was bitten by the man" to "The man bit the dog") or a negative to a positive ("I did not go" to "I went"). Much of this learning occurs in the first elementary grades.

EXPLANATIONS OF LANGUAGE DEVELOPMENT

Each of us uses language as though we had a complete, although unconscious, understanding of a great variety of phrase structure and transformational rules. Initially, children have no understanding of these rules and speak as though they had none. But in an amazingly short time, they acquire functional knowledge of an incredibly complex grammar. We have been able to describe some of the details of the sequence of language acquisition; but can we explain how and why children learn language?

There are two principal classes of explanations for the development of language. One emphasizes the role of experience (learning); the other emphasizes the importance of biology (hereditary predispositions), of what the child brings to the learning situation (Rice, 1989).

The Role of Early Experience

There is an overwhelming amount of learning involved in making the transition from the first meaningful sound to the fluent conversations of the 6-year-old. Yet most children accomplish this learning apparently effortlessly and in much the same sequence across different cultures (Rice, 1989). "Children learn language," says Rice (1989), "as a means of talking about what they know so they can accomplish social goals important to them" (p. 153).

Strangely, however, adults who are initially without language (because of isolation, for example) do not fare as well. Recall Genie, the abandoned child described in Chapter 3. As a child, she had been exposed to almost no language models (her father barked and growled at her); and although she was rescued at the age of 13½, attempts to teach her to speak were not very successful. Similarly, adult learners who try to acquire a second language usually experience more difficulty doing so than do young children; and even if they are successful, their pronunciation will typically be characterized by a variety of errors that would not be found among those who learned the language at a younger age. There appears to be a *sensitive* period early in life when learning one or more languages will be easiest.

Parents as Teachers

The observation that children acquire the speech patterns, idioms, accents, and other language characteristics of those around them lends strong support to the belief that learning is centrally involved in language acquisition. Parents and other caregivers play an important role as language models: They provide the child with models of correct language, as well as with models of the subtle rules governing conversations and the communication of messages, in nonverbal as well as verbal ways. Put another way, they provide models of the *pragmatics* as well as of the semantics, syntax, and phonology of language. In addition, parents also serve as important dispensers of reinforcement for the child's verbalizations.

In Chapter 5 we spoke of the bidirectionality of parent-child influence, noting that what a caregiver does influences the infant and, no less true, what the infant does influences the caregiver. We see evidence of bidirectionality of influence in the development of language as well (Bruner, 1977, 1978; Stern et al., 1983). The infant's level of language comprehension and use appears to have subtle but marked effects on the behavior of parents. Bruner (1978) refers to a *fine-tuning theory* of mother-infant interaction — "mother" because she is more often the principal caregiver than is the father. His observations of mothers and their children lead him to conclude that virtually all mothers alter their speech patterns according to the understanding of their children. It is as though the mother becomes a teacher, not because she consciously intends to be, but because she "fine-tunes" her responses and behaviors to the immediate demands of her child. Furthermore, there is a consistency and regularity in the mother's altered speech patterns. One mother typically employed four sequential types of statements when "reading" to her young son. First she would say "Look": an attention-getting utterance. Next she would pose a standard question — "What is that?" — pause, and provide a label: "It's an X." Finally, following the child's response, she would say, "That's right." Additional evidence of "fine-tuning" occurred whenever the child responded earlier in the sequence. If, for example, he said "Truck" as the page turned, the mother would go immediately to her final response: "That's right."

Motherese. In later stages of language development, the role of the mother as sensitive, fine-tuned teacher becomes even more apparent. Boyd (1976) notes that the language mothers employ when talking to their children — sometimes called *motherese* — is quite different from what they would normally use when speaking with adults. Motherese is a good example of pragmatics in language; the mother adjusts her speech to the requirements of the situation. Thus, mothers tend to use simpler, shorter, and more repetitive utterances. In other words, they *reduce* (by simplifying and repeating). On other occasions, mothers *expand* the child's expressions. A child might say, "Daddy gone," to which the mother might reply, "Yes, Daddy is gone."

There are other, perhaps more subtle, ways in which the speech of the mother (or other caregivers, as well as siblings) is influenced by the presence of infants. Moskowitz (1978) describes typical caregiver speech as simpler, higher pitched, characterized by exaggerated intonation, made up of shorter sentences, and consisting of a higher than normal percentage of questions. In addition, the speech of caregivers vis-à-vis their infants is almost always centered on the present and only seldom on the past or future, almost as though they knew, with Piaget, that the young infant's world is a world of the here and now. Accordingly, as Goodwin (1980) suggests, we would expect that most of the child's first words would deal with things that are immediate, directly perceivable, and important to the child — an expectation that is confirmed by research (Rice, 1989).

Studies that have examined the relationship between specific aspects of motherese and children's language development tend to support the view that the shorter sentences, uncomplicated grammars, and absence of pronouns and complex verb tenses of motherese contribute positively to language development (Furrow, Nelson, & Benedict, 1979).

In summary, there is growing evidence that the mother (or father) plays a crucial role in the development of language and that this role goes well beyond providing a suitable model of the family's language. Unconsciously, parents modify their speech and become teachers — perhaps far better teachers than they could possibly be trained to be. As Moskowitz observes, the level of a mother's language usage appears to remain relatively constant at a stage very close to six months in advance of where the child is. From birth, there is an "interpersonal synchrony" between mother and infant (Schaffer, Collis, & Parsons, 1977); research has scarcely begun to explore the nature and dimensions of this synchrony.

Maltreated children. Additional evidence of the importance of parent-infant interaction is found in studies of the language development of abused and neglected children. Early evidence seemed to indicate that as many as 20 percent of abused children were delayed in language development (for example, Johnson & Morse, 1968). The finding is somewhat difficult to explain. Why should abuse, in and of itself, impede the normal development of language? However, more recent research reveals that it is not so much *abuse* as *neglect* that is the important factor (Allen & Wasserman, 1985). Now the explanation is simpler. Abuse is typically defined as involving such actions as attacking, hitting, shoving, beating; neglect involves disregard of safety, inadequate nutrition, inattention to health needs. In other words, the abusive parent physically hurts the child; the neglecting parent ignores the child. Physical abuse, because it does not also involve absence of verbal interaction with a caregiver, would not be expected to be manifested in retarded language development. In contrast, neglect, which would typically include the absence of frequent and sustained caregiver-infant interaction, would be expected to affect the acquisition of language skills.

Allen and Oliver (1982) looked at the relationship of language development to abuse and neglect in a group of 79 preschool children. As expected, they found that neglected children were significantly retarded in language development; abused children were not.

Sadly, however, many abused children are also neglected. And vice versa. In the Allen and Oliver study, of the 51 maltreated children studied, a mere 17 were neglected only; another 13 were abused but not neglected. The remaining 31 children were both abused and neglected.

The Role of Biology

In spite of the important role that experience plays in the development of language, it does not offer a complete explanation for many aspects of language learning. For example, it does not explain why children of deaf parents babble like other children (Lenneberg, 1960). Lenneberg's observations suggest that the earliest appearances of speech sounds seem to occur relatively independently of the environment, almost as though biology preprograms humans for language acquisition. However, as we saw in Chapter 5, by 10 months the babbling of deaf infants is not as clear, systematic, or repetitive as that of hearing children (Eilers & Oller, 1988).

Additional evidence that experience is not a complete explanation of language acquisition is the observation that many of the errors children make when they are learning a language are not errors they could have learned through imitation. Indeed, as Chomsky (1972) notes, many of these errors are not only completely novel but are also highly predictable. These errors furnish far more impressive evidence of the child's linguistic capabilities than they would if they were based entirely on imitation.

Children may say, for example, "It doos" for "It does," because, clever little linguists that they are, they have invented a rule that says adding the sound *s* to any verb makes it appropriate for a third-person subject — and the children's syntactical rule admits of no exceptions; hence the term *overregulation* for this type of error. There are many examples: "I sayed" for "I said"; "It goed" for "It went"; and "I runned" for "I ran." In many ways, these young linguists are more consistent than the language. "Mistakes" are logical errors resulting from irregularities in the language rather than from the misapplication of rules (Slobin, 1972).

One additional line of evidence linking biology with language learning is the parallels that exist between motor and language development. These parallels are illustrated in Table 7.6, which depicts the normal course of language and motor development to age 4. Lenneberg (1967) deliberately juxtaposes the two to convey their close relationship. Lenneberg, Nichols, and Rosenberger (1964) found evidence for this parallel when they examined the language and motor development of 61 Down syndrome children aged 2 to 22 years. One of their striking observations was that when the children were still crawling, regardless of age, they were usually at the babbling stage in their language

Table 7.6
Milestones in Motor and Language Development

At the Completion of	Motor Development	Vocalization and Language
12 weeks	Supports head when in prone position; weight is on elbows; hands mostly open; no grasp reflex.	Markedly less crying than at 8 weeks; when talked to and nodded at, smiles, followed by squealing gurgling sounds usually called *cooing,* which is vowel-like in character and pitch modulated; sustains cooing for 15–20 seconds.
16 weeks	Plays with a rattle placed in hands (by shaking it and staring at it); head self-supported; tonic neck reflex subsiding.	Responds to human sounds more definitely; turns head; eyes seem to search for speaker; occasionally some chuckling sounds.
20 weeks	Sits with props.	The vowel-like cooing sounds begin to be interspersed with more consonantal sounds; labial fricatives, spirants, and nasals are common; acoustically, all vocalizations are very different from the sounds of the mature language of the environment.
6 months	Sitting: bends forward and uses hands for support; can bear weight when put into standing position, but cannot yet stand without holding on; reaching: unilateral; grasp: no thumb apposition yet; releases cube when given another.	Cooing changing into babbling resembling one-syllable utterances; neither vowels nor consonants have very fixed recurrences; most common utterances sound somewhat like *ma, mu, da,* or *di.*
8 months	Stands holding on; graps with thumb apposition; picks up pellet with thumb and fingertips.	Reduplication (or more continuous repetitions) becomes frequent; intonation patterns become distinct; utterances can signal emphasis and emotions.
10 months	Creeps efficiently; takes side-steps, holding on; pulls to standing position.	Vocalizations are mixed with sound play such as gurgling or bubble blowing; appears to wish to imitate sounds, but the imitations are never quite successful; beginning to differentiate among words heard by making differential adjustment.
12 months	Walks when held by one hand; walks on feet and hands — knees in air; mouthing of objects almost stopped; seats self on floor.	Identical sound sequences are replicated with higher relative frequency of occurrence, and words (*mama* or *dada*) are emerging; definite signs of understanding some words and simple commands.

Table 7.6
Milestones in Motor and Language Development (*continued*)

At the Completion of	Motor Development	Vocalization and Language
18 months	Grasp, prehension, and release fully developed; gait stiff, propulsive and precipitated; sits on child's chair with only fair aim; creeps downstairs backward; has difficulty building tower of three cubes.	Has a definite repertoire of words — more than 3, but less than 50; still much babbling but now of several syllables with intricate intonation pattern; no attempt at communicating information and no frustration for not being understood; words may include items such as *thank you* or *come here,* but there is little ability to join any of the lexical items into spontaneous two-item phrases; understanding is progressing rapidly.
24 months	Runs, but falls in sudden turns; can quickly alternate between sitting and standing; walks stairs up or down, one foot forward only.	Vocabulary of more than 50 items (some children seem to be able to name everything in environment); begins spontaneously to join vocabulary items into two-word phrases; all phrases appear to be own creations; definite increase in communicative behavior and interest in language.
30 months	Jumps up into air with both feet; stands on one foot for about two seconds; takes few steps on tiptoe; jumps from chair; good hand and finger coordination; can move digits independently; manipulation of objects much improved; builds tower of six cubes.	Fastest increase in vocabulary with many new additions every day; no babblings at all; utterances have communicative intent; frustrated if not understood by adults; utterances consist of at least two words, many have three or even five words; sentences and phrases have characteristic child grammar — that is, they are rarely verbatim repetitions of an adult utterance; intelligibility is not very good yet, though there is great variation among children; seems to understand everything that is said to him or her.
3 years	Tiptoes 3 yards; runs smoothly with acceleration and deceleration; negotiates sharp and fast curves without difficulty; walks stairs by alternating feet; jumps 12 inches; can operate a tricycle.	Vocabulary of some 1,000 words; about 80 percent of utterances are intelligible even to strangers; grammatical complexity of utterances is roughly that of colloquial adult language, although mistakes still occur.
4 years	Jumps over rope; hops on right foot; catches ball in arms; walks line.	Language is well established; deviations from the adult norm tend to be more in style than in grammar.

Source: From Eric H. Lenneberg, *Biological foundations of language.* Copyright 1967 by John Wiley & Sons, Inc., New York. Used by permission of John Wiley & Sons, Inc.

development; and when they had begun to walk, they had also begun to talk. For these children, as for normal children, simple motor development and language development seem closely allied.

In summary, evidence of a biological influence on language learning may be found in the similarities among the earliest speech sounds of infants from very different backgrounds; in the ease and rapidity with which children learn language; in the fact that children make only a fraction of the mistakes they might be expected to make if they were learning primarily through reinforcement, imitation, and trial and error; and in the observation that many of the mistakes children do make are not imitative but appear to result from the overregulation of rules that are themselves correct and useful.

A number of biological theories of language learning attempt to explain the child's incredibly rapid acquisition of grammatical rules, particularly during the third and fourth years — for example, Chomsky's (1957; 1965) theory of LAD (or *Language Acquisition Device*) or Nelson's (1989) RELM (the *rare event learning mechanism*). What LAD and RELM have in common is that they attempt to account for the infant's apparent predisposition for acquiring language by making the assumption that we are born with some special language-learning capacity. Children behave as though they were prewired for grammar, says Chomsky. How else are we to explain the fact that they make so few errors while learning syntax?

But LAD and RELM are really not explanations at all; they are simply metaphors. Infants behave *as though* they have at their command a range of cognitive skills, of language-related predispositions. And from this observation, we might infer that there must be some innate neurological prewiring at birth. But as Rice (1989) observes, there is no satisfactory explanation of how these things work. Metaphors are not machines; they are simply comparisons.

A CHANGING LANGUAGE CONTEXT

In 1982, almost 75 percent of schoolchildren in the United States were white; approximately 10 percent were Hispanic; and the remainder included a varied mixture of ethnic groups.

By the year 2020, projections are that the percentage of white school-age Americans will have dropped to about 50 percent and the Hispanic group will have increased to around 25 percent. The remainder will be blacks (about 16.5 percent) and other races (Pallas, Natriello, & McDill, 1989).

The educational implications of these dramatic demographic changes are considerable. In 1982, most schoolchildren spoke English, the dominant, standard, majority language. Will that still be the case in 2020? (See Figure 7-10.)

Two Views of Bilingualism

For most children whose early environment includes two languages, learning a second language does not appear to be much more complicated than learning to ride a bicycle. In the end, however, for most individuals there is a dominant

In 1982, nearly 75 percent of U.S. schoolchildren were white, and the dominant language was clearly standard English. Demographers project that within the next several decades, fewer than half of all schoolchildren in major urban schools will speak English as a first language – a situation that will have important implications for education. Part of the reason for these changing demographics is a much lower birthrate among white families (17.2 per 1,000 population in 1970; 14.8 in 1988) than among blacks (25.2 per 1,000 in 1970; 21.5 in 1988) and other races (26.1, per 1,000 in 1970; 21.3 in 1988). In addition, net immigration rate continues to be much higher for races other than white.

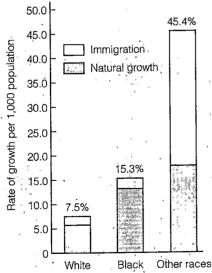

Figure 7.10   Rate of annual population growth from natural increases and immigration for three U.S. groups, 1988. *Source:* Adapted from U.S. Bureau of the Census (1990), p. 14.

or preferred language. Few individuals become what Diaz (1983) calls *balanced bilinguals* — people who are equally fluent and equally comfortable in both languages.

There are two points of view with respect to the psychological effects of bilingualism. One maintains that there is a limited amount of cognitive space available for language and that learning two or more languages places such a strain on cognitive capacity that the individual suffers. According to this view, it is as though the second language competes with the first and, in the end, the individual is not as proficient in either language as the monolingual individual. This competitive view is based in part on early studies of bilingualism, which often concluded that bilingual children were handicapped. Not only did they perform less well on measures of ability (such as intelligence tests), but they also tended to do less well in either language.

The second view maintains that there is no competition among languages and no clear limitation of cognitive resources necessary for language learning. This view is based on research which indicates that "all other things being equal, higher degrees of bilingualism are associated with higher levels of cognitive attainment" (Hakuta & Garcia, 1989, p. 375).

Which view is correct?

The simple answer is that either may be at least partly correct depending on the individual and the context. *Subtractive bilingualism* is the term coined by Lambert (1975) to describe the negative influence of a second language. *Additive bilingualism* describes those situations where learning a second language has a positive influence on the first.

Subtractive bilingualism. Research indicates that for some minority group children (whose first language is a minority language), learning a second language may be a *subtractive* experience. But for those whose first language is the dominant, majority language, learning a second language is more often an *additive* experience (Cummins & Swain, 1986).

Learning a second language for children who are members of a distinct minority group (such as the French-speaking in Canada and the Spanish-speaking in the United States) may be *subtractive* in the sense that they become progressively less functional and fluent in their first language as their language skills improve in the second. This does not happen because learning the second language actually interferes with learning or remembering the first, but for one of several other reasons. One is that the majority language (the second language in this case) is usually the dominant language in the media and in the community. As a result, the minority language receives little support and reinforcement outside the home. Consequently, it tends to be used in less valued social roles and milieus (Landry, 1987).

A second explanation for the occasionally negative (subtractive) effect of learning the dominant language as a second language is that use of the minority language in the home is sometimes discouraged by parents or by the children themselves. And third, the minority language employed in the home is sometimes not a very good model of that language. It is often characterized by idiom and colloquialism, by vocabulary impoverishment, by improper grammar, and by idiosyncratic pronunciation (Carey, 1987). And if it is not part of the children's schooling, they are unlikely to read or write in it. Thus they may develop a relatively high level of oral proficiency in the minority language while developing little competency in reading or writing it. For all of these reasons, competence in the minority language suffers; and the bilingual experience becomes subtractive.

Additive bilingualism. As we've noted, learning a second language for children whose first language is the majority language appears to be largely an *additive* experience. Such is the case, for example, for many English-speaking children enrolled in French immersion programs in Canada and in Spanish immersion programs in the United States. The evidence seems clear that these programs can be very successful in developing linguistic skills, as well as in contributing to general academic achievement (Cummins & Swain, 1986). Although most students who go through immersion schooling don't develop as high a level of proficiency as native speakers, their language deficiencies don't seem to interfere with their use of the second language. In addition, these students typically achieve at least as well as comparable students in conventional English programs in academic subjects and on measures of social and cognitive development. And within one year of receiving English instruction, their performance on measures of English literacy is as good as that of monolingual English students (Genesee, 1985).

The question that opens this section is: Which view is correct? The one which maintains that languages compete and therefore that learning two languages is a subtractive experience? Or the view which holds that learning a second language has a generally positive influence?

The answer is that although one language may suffer as a second is being learned, *it is not because of competition between the two*, but more often because of social conditions that reduce the value of one language and that provide a poor model of the language or even actively discourage its use. The current view is that a second language does not interfere with the first; in fact, level of proficiency and rate of learning of the second language is closely related to proficiency in the first (Hakuta & Garcia, 1989).

ESL: English as a Second Language

There is currently some debate about the best way of teaching English as a second language. One position holds that it is better to teach and strengthen the native language first in order to develop a high level of proficiency in it before teaching English. The other position recommends immersing students in an English environment from the very beginning with as little use as possible of the native language. Analyses of the many studies that have attempted to compare these two approaches have not resulted in any very simple conclusions (Willig, 1985). Both approaches clearly work; which is better depends largely on circumstances having to do with the learner's native language and social context.

Bilingual education, argue Cummins and Swain (1986), can be a positive experience both for minority and majority group children. Not only does a *good* bilingual program develop functional proficiency in a second language, but it can also strengthen the first language. Immersion programs are likely to provide an additive experience for children whose first language is the majority language. These are children who already have a high level of proficiency in their native language. However, for minority-group children, instruction should occur primarily in the minority language, and the majority language should be learned as a second language. French minority-group children whose schooling is primarily in French, with English as a second language, not only maintain and improve their French far more than those schooled primarily in English, but they also perform as well in English (Cummins, 1986).

Nonstandard Languages

Some of the issues relevant to bilingualism are also relevant to what are termed **nonstandard languages**. The language that most of us understand, read, and speak is the **standard language**. It is viewed as correct and acceptable; it serves as a *standard* against which to judge less appropriate forms of the language — dialects such as those spoken by some members of minority-language groups. The varieties of English that might be spoken by some American blacks (sometimes called black English), by Americans of Hispanic origin, or by French Canadians are examples. We often assume that the frequent schooling problems of those less proficient in standard English has to do with their language.

Bernstein (1958, 1961) argues that the reason for this is that language and thought are closely linked. He suggests that nonstandard forms of English, which he labels **restricted language codes,** are in many ways inferior to standard forms, labeled **elaborated language codes.** Elaborated language is grammatically correct, complex, and precise. Restricted language is simple, grammatically incorrect, uses a limited vocabulary, and often resorts to gestures to make a point (Table 7.7). It is little wonder, Bernstein argues, that children whose homes are characterized by restricted language codes are often at a disadvantage in school. For the first time in their lives, they are required to use increasingly precise and grammatically correct language. They inevitably begin by performing less well than those who have been more fortunate in their early language experiences. Before they have had a chance to catch up, they will find themselves so far behind that they may feel it is hardly worth trying.

There is evidence to suggest, however, that Bernstein's view might not be the best explanation for the poorer performance of those who don't speak the standard form of the majority language. It is not so much because the nonstandard language is less complex, less sophisticated, and less grammatical that the child does less well in school. Rather, it is because the language is *different*.

Table 7.7
Hypothetical Examples of Restricted and Elaborated Language Codes

Restricted	Mother	Clean your feet.
	Child	Why?
	Mother	Because.
	Child	Because why?
	Mother	I said so, that's why.
	Child	But why?
Elaborated	Mother	Blow your nose, Henry. It is about to drip on the carpet.
	Child	Why don't you want it to drip on the carpet, Mom? Why, Mom? Why . . . ?
	Mother	Because it's messy, Henry, and we must keep the carpet clean for when Daddy comes home, because Dad doesn't like to have nose drips all over the carpet.

Since instruction in school occurs in the standard language and since achievement is measured in that language, these children are clearly at a disadvantage, no matter how sophisticated their nonstandard language (Baratz, 1969).

What can be done to enhance the child's sophistication in the standard language? What should be done? Or should anything be done?

Here, as elsewhere, the questions are simpler than the answers. Cummins (1986) argues that minority-group children should be instructed in their minority language, with the majority language presented as a second language. Seymour (1971) makes the same recommendations vis-à-vis black children who use a nonstandard dialect. He suggests that at least part of the time, schools should encourage the use of the nonstandard dialect.

Another argument, however, says that since most commerce outside school takes place in the majority language, those who know only other dialects of that language will be at the same disadvantage outside school as they are in it.

So the questions remain unanswered.

SPEECH AND LANGUAGE PROBLEMS

We assume that by the time children reach school age, their language skills will be sufficient for them to understand and follow instructions, express interests and wants, tell stories, ask questions, carry on conversations — in short, communicate. Sadly, that is not always the case.

There are a number of different language and speech problems, each of which can vary tremendously in seriousness (see, for example, Schiefelbusch & McCormick, 1981). At one extreme are children who, because of severe mental retardation, neurological damage or disease, mental disorders such as autism or childhood schizophrenia, or deafness, are essentially nonverbal. Their communication might consist of a few gestures or signs.

There are others whose speech is largely incomprehensible, sometimes because conceptual development is so poor that thought sequences seem illogical and speech becomes largely nonsensical and sometimes because of speech production problems like those reflected in poor articulation, voice control problems, and stuttering.

And there are those whose language development is less advanced that normal, perhaps because of mild mental retardation or because of a learning disability reflected in language deficits. The predominant view is that these children don't learn different language forms or acquire language differently; their skills simply develop more slowly. Some of these children are of normal or above-normal intelligence and have no deficits other than their problems with language. However, because of our schools' predominantly verbal teaching and testing methods, many of these children are viewed as intellectually handicapped, and their language problems may be interpreted as the result of inferior ability rather than as the cause of poor achievement.

It is not clear what causes language problems in the absence of other handicaps. Although an impoverished and unstimulating home context may sometimes be implicated, in some cases children of apparently normal intelligence from advantaged backgrounds experience significant developmental delays or language impairments (Rice, 1989).

Speech problems and delayed language development are most common among children who have some other handicap — that is, retarded children and others suffering from motor, neurological, or mental disorder. They are relatively uncommon among the majority of children.

LANGUAGE AND THOUGHT

The significance of language acquisition for children is in many ways obvious. Not only does language allow children to direct the behavior of others according to their wishes (as when children ask for something) but it also provides a means for acquiring information that would otherwise be inaccessible (as when children ask questions, listen to stories, or watch television). In addition, there is considerable evidence that language is closely involved in logical thought processes, although the exact relationship between thinking and language remains uncertain. One extreme position, first elaborated by Whorf (1941, 1956)(and therefore labeled the *Whorfian hypothesis*), maintains that language is essential for thinking. This position is based on the assumption that all thinking is verbal and that thought is therefore limited to what is made possible by language.

Whereas an extreme Whorfian position maintains that language is necessary for thought, psychologists such as Piaget and Vygotsky argue that thought often precedes language. Piaget (1923), for example, points out that the development of certain logical concepts often precedes the learning of words and phrases corresponding to those concepts. Words such as *bigger, smaller, farther,* and so on do not appear to be understood until the concepts they represent are themselves understood.

Vygotsky's (1962) position is similar to Piaget's. Both argue that language and thought first develop independently. Thus, there is considerable evidence of what we consider to be thought among preverbal children and nonhuman animals. But after the age of two, language and thought become more closely related. After that age, thought becomes increasingly verbal, and language acquires the capacity to control behavior.

Vygotsky's view, described in Chapter 2, holds that speech has three separate forms, each with different functions: Social speech is directed toward others to control their behavior or to express simple thoughts and emotions. Egocentric speech (common between 3 and 7) is a form of self-talk spoken out loud that serves to control the child's own behavior. And inner speech is self-talk that provides a means for directing our thinking and our behavior. (See Table 5.5 Chapter 5.) It is, according to Vygotsky, the source of all our higher mental functioning (Vygotsky, 1986; Wertsch, 1985).

An Experiment

Pyles (1932) presented 80 children, aged 2 to 7, with the task of learning to differentiate among five objects. All the children had to do was to select the correct object to obtain the toy hidden under it. In one situation the stimuli were five familiar animal forms, each labeled appropriately by the experimenter. The second variation employed five unnamed and unfamiliar forms. In the third variation, the objects were also unfamiliar but were given names. The subjects were shown each of the three variations until they chose the correct object four consecutive times, showing that they had learned, or until 25 trials were completed.

The results of the experiment demonstrate clearly that learning is much easier with familiar objects whose names are already well known by the subjects (Figure 7.11). Also, giving names to unfamiliar objects greatly increases how easily they can be distinguished from one another. Only 54 percent of the sample successfully solved the unfamiliar-object–no-name condition, whereas 72 percent of the subjects chose correctly when the objects were given names. This strongly suggests that language improves learning.

A Conclusion

It is difficult to argue, as did Benjamin Whorf, that thought depends on language and that it will not occur in its absence. To accept that position would be to deny that those who are prelinguistically deaf and who have not learned an alternate communication system can think. We would also have to believe that

Figure 7.11

The median number of incorrect trials before choosing the correct stimulus four consecutive times. The results illustrate that verbalization facilitates learning.

Source: Based on data provided by Marjorie Pyles Honzik, Verbalization as a factor in learning, *Child Development, 3,* 1932, 108–113. Copyright 1932 by The Society for Research in Child Development. Used by permission of The Society for Research in Child Development and the author.

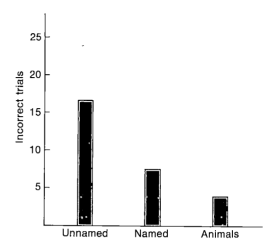

our prelinguistic infants cannot think and that, among those who have begun to develop language, thought is restricted to subjects and ideas for which the thinker has pertinent language symbols. And we would have to believe that the cats I have known cannot think. Edgar can think, I think.

We don't believe all these things (though not everyone would accept that Edgar and his relatives can think). So we accept that thought can occur in the absence of language. At the same time, however, research and good sense inform us that our sophisticated thought processes are inextricably bound with language — as are our belief systems, our values, our world views. So convinced are we of this that attempts to bring about difficult social changes often begin with attempts to change language. Antiracist and antisexist movements are a case in point. In the first edition of this text, it was acceptable to use masculine pronouns as though all children, all psychologists, and, indeed, all significant people, were male. Speaking of one of Blaise Pascal's *Pensées,* for example, I wrote: "one of the paradoxes of human existence is that despite man's great intelligence it is impossible for him to know where he came from or where he is going" (Lefrançois, 1973, p. 351).

That this type of chauvinistic sexism is no longer acceptable in our language may eventually be reflected in its eradication from our thoughts and those of our children.

COMMUNICATING AND CONVERSING

Language is more than a collection of sounds whose combinations refer to objects and actions and whose expression conveys our meanings; and it is more than a means for thinking and expressing our thoughts. Language is the means by which we draw information from past generations, record our own small contributions, and pass them on to generations that will come later. It is the great binding force of all cultures.

But infants, newly learning language, are not concerned with its great cultural contributions. Their first interest is in communicating — and the first communications are simple assertions ("that dog"; "see daddy"; "my ball") or requests ("milk!"; "more candy"). The second concern is with conversation.

A conversation is an exchange typically involving two or more people, although some people do talk to themselves — and answer. It is generally verbal, although it can consist of a combination of gestures and verbalization, or it can consist entirely of gestures as in the case of ASL (American Sign Language). Genuine conversational exchanges begin around age 2. Initially, they are highly telegraphic, as is the child's speech; there aren't a great many variations possible when your sentences are limited to a single word. A short excerpt from an intelligent conversation with one of my own illustrates this:

Him: Fish.

Me: Fish?

Him: Fish!

Me: Fish? Fish swim.

Him: Fish! Fish! (*The conversation becomes more complex.*)

Me: There are fish in the lake. (*An original thought, meant to stimulate creativity.*)

Him: Fish. (*Pointing, this time, in the general direction of the lake, I think.*)

From this primitive, repetitive conversation, children progress to more complex expressions and begin to learn the importance of subtle cues of intonation, accentuation of words, rhythm of sentences, tone, and accompanying gestures. They learn, as well, about the implicit agreements that govern our conversations — the well-accepted rules that determine who shall speak and when, whether interruptions are permissible and how they should occur, what information must be included in our conversations if we are to be understood, and what we can assume is already known.

Thus, more or less, does the infant progress from a sound to a word, from one word to two, from an expression to a conversation, from a conversation to a book. . . .

MAIN POINTS

1. There is a gradual slowing of physical growth after infancy. In addition, different parts of the body grow at different rates (the head grows more slowly, for example), so that a typical 6-year-old looks more like an adult (and less like an infant) than a 2-year-old.

2. Among significant motor achievements of infancy are learning how to walk and to coordinate other motor activities, including those involved in copying and tracing geometric designs — a task that involves perceptual, cognitive, and fine-motor skills. At birth, motor development may be assessed by means of scales such as the Apgar; later assessments use scales such as the Denver Developmental Screening Test.

3. Preschoolers' memories result largely from *incidental* mnemonics (paying attention; repeated exposure) rather than from the deliberate use of strategies (such as organizing or rehearsing). However, older preschoolers will deliberately use strategies when instructed to remember something, although these are sometimes inappropriate.

4. Piaget's preoperational period has two substages: *Preconceptual thinking* (2 to 4) is marked by errors of classification (for example, similar objects may be reacted to as though they were identical); is transductive (conclusions are based on superficial particulars); and uses syncretic reasoning (objects are grouped on the basis of personal and changing criteria). *Intuitive thinking* is characterized by egocentricity (difficulty adopting another's point of view), by errors of class inclusion (believing, for example, that a bouquet of 10 roses and 2 daffodils contains more roses than flowers), and by a marked reliance on perception.

5. Replications of many of Piaget's experiments have typically found a developmental sequence very similar to the one that he described, although some of the capabilities may be acquired at ages younger than those he reported for his subjects. The neo-Piagetians present a somewhat more optimistic view of the preschool child, emphasizing that one of the major achievements of this period is the ability to relate one or more ideas or concepts.

6. As a result of their ability to relate concepts, preschoolers can classify and solve simple class-inclusion problems. In addition, they have a remarkable understanding of number, which reflects both number abstraction skills (understanding of numerosity based on universal counting principles) and numerical reasoning (understanding of some of the effects of transformations).

7. Preschool education programs include nurseries, daycare centers, and a variety of other facilities. Children who attend nursery schools are sometimes more confident, more outgoing, and more self-reliant than children who don't. In general, compensatory preschool programs (Head Start, for example) have measurably positive effects on cognitive and social development.

8. The Direct Instruction Approach (Bereiter and Engelmann) stresses the three R's and uses drill and repetition with reinforcement. Montessori's approach emphasizes sense training and makes use of specially designed materials. Kindergartens, which are now typically part of the regular school program, may use either of these approaches or any of a variety of others, although most are simply eclectic.

9. Language — the use of arbitrary sounds with established and accepted referents, either real or abstract, that can be arranged in sequence to convey meaning — appears to be unique to humans.

10. The child goes from one-word sentences (holophrases) to two-word sentences (duos), and then to multiple-word sentences (rather than simply to three-word sentences). Multiple-word sentences appear by age 2 to 2½ and make extensive use of grammatical morphemes such as *ing* and *ed* to convey meaning. More complex sentences and adultlike grammatical structures are typically present in the fourth year.

11. Experience clearly affects language learning. In particular, the mother (and other caregivers) plays an important role as language teacher, her speech patterns (*motherese*) being strongly influenced, sometimes in subtle ways, by the presence of an infant. Motherese is characterized by shorter sentences, more repetition, simpler and more concrete concepts, and exaggerated intonation. It is, in a sense, fine tuned to a level about six months in advance of the child's current language development.

12. Neglected children are sometimes retarded in their language development, presumably because of lack of sustained language interaction with a caregiver. This finding has sometimes led to the conclusion that abused children may be language retarded because many neglected children are also abused.

13. Imitation and reinforcement are not complete explanations for the observation that the earliest speech sounds of infants are highly similar and that infants make few directly imitative mistakes as they learn language. Chomsky describes the role of biology in language learning in terms of a metaphor — language acquisition device (LAD) — which suggests that children learn language as if they were neurologically predisposed to do so. The metaphor is useful in explaining the ease and rapidity with which children learn overwhelmingly complex grammars.

14. Learning two languages is not a particularly difficult task for children who are exposed to both languages from infancy. Learning a second language later is more difficult and may be a *subtractive* (negative) or an *additive* (positive) experience. In general, *good* bilingual education enhances performance in both languages and has a positive effect on general intellectual functioning. When learning a second language has a negative effect on the first, it is often because of a context that devalues the first language, presents a poor model of it, or discourages its use.

15. The *standard* language (majority dialect) is the language form that is viewed as grammatically correct and acceptable and against which other forms of the language (*nonstandard*) are judged. Children who speak nonstandard dialects (for example, black English or French Canadian) are often at a disadvantage in school — not so much because their language is less sophisticated but simply because it is different.

16. The language sophistication of most school-age children is sufficient for them to ask and answer questions, tell stories, follow instructions, engage in conversations, and so on. However, some children experience language and speech problems ranging from complete absence of speech and comprehension to minor articulation and voice problems. These problems are often related to mental retardation, neurological damage or disease, mental disorders such as autism, or deafness.

17. The Whorfian hypothesis maintains that language precedes and is necessary for thought. Piaget notes there is considerable evidence of thought before language (and in nonhuman animals). Vygotsky suggests that language and thought initially develop independently but become more closely linked after age 2.

18. Vygotsky describes three stages in the development of speech: *social (external) speech* (to age 3; speech used to control others and to express simple thoughts); *egocentric speech* (3 to 7; speech used to control own behavior, but spoken out loud); *inner speech* (7 to adulthood; self-verbalizations silent, used to direct own thought and behavior).

19. Evidence suggests that language sophistication can contribute importantly to higher mental thought processes.

Further Readings

A good summary of Piaget's theory is provided by:

Wadsworth, B. J. (1989). *Piaget's theory of cognitive and affective development* (4th ed.). New York: Longman.

The following are excellent sources of information concerning the current state of affairs in cognitive development research. They are highly representative of the neo-Piagetians:

Flavell, J. H. (1985). *Cognitive development* (2nd ed.). Englewood Cliffs, N.J.: Prentice-Hall.

Case, R. (1985). *Cognitive development: A systematic reinterpretation.* New York: Academic Press.

Shulmann, V. L., Restaino-Baumann, L. C. R., & Butler, L. (Eds.). (1985). *The future of Piagetian theory: The neo-Piagetians.* New York: Plenum Press.

Three comprehensive and practical guides for those concerned with the education of preschoolers are the following:

Lundsteen, S. W., & Tarrow, N. B. (1981). *Guiding young children's learning: A comprehensive approach to early childhood education.* New York: McGraw-Hill.

Hendrick, J. (1930). *The whole child: New trends in early education* (2nd ed.). St. Louis: C. V. Mosby.

Read, K., & Patterson, J. (1980). *The nursery school and kindergarten: Human relationships and learning* (7th ed.). New York: Holt, Rinehart & Winston.

A highly readable paper that summarizes and analyzes research on ape-language studies and that also provides a very useful account of current knowledge and beliefs about human language learning is:

Terrace, H. S. (1985). In the beginning was the name. *American Psychologist, 40,* 1011–1028.

The early development of language in infants is described in more detail in:

Wood, B. S. (1981). *Children and communication: Verbal and nonverbal language development* (2nd ed.). Englewood Cliffs, N.J.: Prentice-Hall.

Carroll, D. W. (1986). *Psychology of language.* Monterey, Calif.: Brooks/Cole.

For an analysis of the relationship between thought and language, see:

Greene, J. (1975). *Thinking and language.* London: Methuen.

The Greenberg and Tobach book is a fascinating collection of papers dealing with language and thinking both in animals and in humans:

Greenberg, G., & Tobach, E. (1987). *Cognition, language, and consciousness: Integrative levels.* Hillsdale, N.J.: Lawrence Erlbaum.

The book by Cummins and Swain provides a current account of bilingual education programs and their effects:

Cummins, J., & Swain, M. (1986). *Bilingualism in education: Aspects of theory, research and practice.* London: Taylor & Fry.

Whoever is delighted in solitude is either a Wilde Beast, or a God.
Francis Bacon, *Essays 27: Of Friendship*

Social Development

R onald is one of my little nephews. He had his third birthday a short while ago. I visited him on his birthday, and I made him cry. Twice.

The first time he cried was when I gave him a model of a yellow Volkswagen Beetle as a birthday present, nicely wrapped in purple paper covered with tiny pictures of pink ponies. Ronald loves horses, and I had briefly considered getting him one for his birthday; but I didn't think my sister would be especially happy with that idea, since she does not like horses in her parlor. So I just gave Ronald the paper instead; and as he was ripping it off the Beetle, I said, "It's a horse. I got you a tiny baby horse!"

It was a joke and some of the adults laughed, and Ronald got terribly excited.

But when he saw the yellow Volkswagen, his lip began to quiver and his eyes filled with tears.

"Your uncle didn't mean a real horse," his mother explained, but it wasn't the right thing to say; he ran to her and buried his face in her lap, sobbing. I would rather have been somewhere else.

He recovered quickly, and I tried to make it up to him when I left. "Uncle Guy's going to Alaska," I said. "Do you want to come?" He nodded solemnly. We all laughed. Nice joke, huh?

"You want to come, huh?" He nodded again and reached out for me to pick him up, which I did.

"Let's go," I said. He nodded vigorously. I held him for a while longer. "Heh, heh," I said. Pretty funny.

"Let's go," he said.

"Heh, heh," I repeated. "You can't *really* come. When you're older."

He looked at me for a long moment, as if trying to understand. Then his lip began to quiver again.

When I left, he was sobbing in his mother's arms.

SOCIALIZING EMOTIONS

I wished I had bought him a horse, because if I had bought him a horse, he would not have cried (although his mother might have).

You see, young children do not always know what is real and what is not; they cannot always tell the difference between a jest and a promise. Nor, of course, can we; but we are much better at it than they are. In addition, young children do not have the fine control adults have over their emotions or over the expression of those emotions. Put another way, their emotions are not completely socialized.

The socialization of emotions involves at least three things: learning to interpret emotions; achieving some control over them; and learning when, where, and how displaying them is appropriate and expected.

Interpreting Emotions

One important thing that happens during infancy is that children gradually discover that they are *selves* — that they are separate and individual and that they are capable of feelings (Olson, 1981). Along with the recognition of the self as separate comes the realization that others, too, are separate and permanent and also capable of feelings.

Initially the infant does not know how to interpret the feelings of others. Facial expressions of joy or sadness, for example, are meaningless for the 1-month-old infant. But sometime between the ages of 3 and 6 months, there appears a growing recognition not only that others are capable of emotional reactions, but also that these can be inferred from expressions and from behavior (Oster et al; 1989). By the age of 9 months to a year, infants in ambiguous situations actively search other people's faces as though looking for a clue that might guide their own behavior. When they see others crying, they are likely to feel sad — perhaps even to cry. And if others laugh and are happy, they too are more likely to be joyful (Termine & Izard, 1988).

During the preschool years, children's ability to make inferences about other people's emotions and to interpret their own emotions appears to be global and relatively imprecise. If specifically asked to describe what they think someone else is feeling, they might infer that someone feels "good" or "bad" because they are crying or laughing. Not until later childhood or even adolescence do children spontaneously analyze others' emotions, trying to sort them out and understand their causes (Hughes, Tingle, & Sawin, 1981).

Early in the preschool period, children cannot readily tell the difference between emotions that are real and those that are a pretense. Thus, if someone falls but jumps up and "laughs it off" in embarrassment, the 2-year-old is likely to conclude that the person is happy. In contrast, in the same situation the 5-year-old is likely to interpret the situation more accurately, realizing that the person who has fallen is, in fact, pretending. Harris and Gross (1988) speculate that children probably discover that some expressions of emotion are false when they begin to realize that they are themselves able to mislead others about their own emotions. This realization usually appears sometime between the ages of 4 and 6.

Regulating Emotions

We saw in Chapter 6 that even very young infants are capable of simple behaviors whose effect is to control the emotions they feel. For example, a frightened infant might close his eyes, suck his thumb, or snuggle his face in his mother's lap — an example of what Gianino and Tronick (1988) call *self-directed* regulatory behaviors. Alternately, the infant might push away the object that is frightening him — an example of *other-directed* regulatory behaviors.

Preschoolers, with their ever-expanding mobility and rapidly developing cognitive and social skills, become increasingly adept at avoiding situations that lead to negative emotions and at seeking out and maintaining those associated with good feelings — which is perhaps why my nephew Ronald has been avoiding me so completely.

Emotional Expression

It has begun to embarrass Ronald to cry in front of me — and even more to cry in front of strangers. But it doesn't bother him very much to cry in front of his mother or his sister. Ronald has begun to learn what researchers refer to as *display rules.*

Display rules have several aspects: One has to do with learning when and how it is appropriate to display certain emotions; another deals with understanding the emotional expressions (emotional displays) of others. For example, as we saw earlier, part of display-rule learning involves discovering that the expression of emotion does not always correspond with the underlying emotion. Even young children are able to smile when they lie or pretend it doesn't hurt when it would be embarrassing to cry.

It is not clear how preschoolers learn simple display rules such as, for example, the rule saying that if you are disappointed with a gift, you should not cry in front of the giver. Ronald had not learned this rule yet. But when Cole (1986) filmed 3- to 4-year-old girls opening a disappointing gift either alone or in front of the giver, she found highly noticeable differences between the facial displays in the two situations. Although the girls' disappointment was clear when they opened the gift alone, most of them covered their feelings with smiles when the giver was present. What is interesting, however, was that these girls were unaware of their deception. It seems that preschoolers learn to control their emotional expression before they realize the effects of their behavior on others.

Lewis, Sullivan, and Vasen (1987) report that although older preschoolers attempt to control their emotional displays, they are successful with only a limited number of emotions. Even we adults are not always able to hide our feelings. If someone gives us a horse when we fully expected a car, we might find it very difficult to smile — even though our socialization is far more advanced than that of children.

THEORIES OF SOCIAL DEVELOPMENT

Socialization is the process by which children learn behaviors that are appropriate for people of their sex and age. It is the means by which they acquire the traditions, the beliefs, the values, and the customs of their people; it is the means by which they learn the rules of membership in a group — rules like how and when to display emotion.

Socialization is clearly a culture-bound process, defined and determined by context. North American audiences clap their hands, cheer, and whistle when they are pleased; European audiences whistle when they are displeased. The content of what is learned might vary a great deal depending on the context — a fact that makes our average child even more of a myth. But the processes by which socialization occurs might be highly similar in different cultural groups.

Erik Erikson

As we saw in Chapter 2, one of the important theories of social development is that advanced by Erik Erikson. It describes the child's development in terms of a series of stages, each of which is characterized by conflicting tendencies or desires, and each of which requires the attainment of some new competence. The theory's emphasis is clearly on *social* development (hence the label *psychosocial* development).

The first three of Erikson's psychosocial stages span the years from birth to around the end of the preschool period. To review briefly, the first, *trust versus mistrust*, lasts through most of infancy. The task here is to develop sufficient trust in the world to be able to go out and begin exploring it actively. Throughout this period, the most important influence in the infant's life is clearly the principal caretaker(s) — often, though by no means always, the mother.

The second stage, *autonomy versus shame and doubt*, spans the first year or so of the preschool period. At this time, children begin to discover that they are authors of their own actions — a discovery that is intimately tied with the development of intentionality.

The third stage, *initiative verus guilt*, spans the remaining preschool years. The new sense of competence required of the child involves a sense of initiative — a sense of personal agency. But there still lingers a desire to retain the comfort and security that come from leaving responsibility with other people — especially parents.

According to Erikson's theory, then, much of "growing up" during the preschool period involves developing a sense of an autonomous self — a self that is capable of forming intentions and of behaving in ways that are effective. The underlying competencies are greatly facilitated by the infant's physical exploration of the environment, as well as by mushrooming language skills that make it possible to explore in other ways — as, for example, when the 4-year-old bombards caretakers with questions. The development of social competence through the preschool period also requires achieving progressive independence from parents. The overprotective parent who does not easily permit independence may make the child's progression through Erikson's stages more difficult. (See Chapter 2 for more details; see also Table 8.1.)

Social Imitation

Erikson (1968) believed that one of the important mechanisms by which preschool children become socialized is *imitation* — especially in the first two or three years of life. Later, *identification* (a process whereby children do not merely imitate models, but adopt their values and beliefs — in a sense, becoming *like* them) becomes more important.

As we saw in Chapter 2, an important theory of social learning based on imitation has been advanced by Albert Bandura. To summarize briefly: Bandura's theory stems from a behavioristic tradition. It attempts to explain the complex effects of modeling partly in terms of rewards and punishments, whether these are actual or imagined. But it is also a cognitive theory: It gives a fundamentally important role to the *informative* function of models and to the observers' understanding and interpretation of that information. It is what the observer imagines and expects that is important in learning through imitation.

Bandura describes three separate effects of imitation. There is the modeling effect, evident in learning new behavior; the inhibitory and disinhibitory effects, in which the rewards or punishment a model receives serve to bring about *(disinhibit)* some previously suppressed behavior or, alternately, to *inhibit* current behavior; and the eliciting effect, where the model's behavior serves to evoke a related behavior in the observer.

Cooperation and competition. Imitation-based theories of social learning are especially useful for explaining how children in nontechnological societies learn how to do such things as set snares and traps or wield brooms and corn-grinding stones. But most of us no longer need to learn how to operate a corn-grinding stone or lay out a trap. So what do we learn from social imitation?

Among other things, perhaps we learn important social tendencies such as cooperation and competition. In fact, there is considerable research to support the belief that children are *socialized* to be cooperative or competitive by the predominant way of life, the mores, the traditions, of their immediate social

Table 8.1
Erikson's Psychosocial Stages of Preschool Development

Stage	Approximate Age	Principal Development Task
Autonomy vs. shame and doubt	18 months to 2 or 3 years	Developing a sense of control and mastery over actions; learning that one is autonomous, that intentions can be realized; overcoming the urge to return to the comfort of trusting parents, and especially the mother, to do all important things
Initiative vs. guilt	2 or 3 to 6 years	Developing a sense of self, largely through identifying with parents; developing a greater sense of responsibility for own actions; achieving progressive independence from parents

environment (Madsen, 1971). Children from different ethnic groups can be remarkably different in terms of cooperation and competition.

Studies of cooperation and competition often use the four-person *cooperation board,* an 18-inch paper square covered with a piece of paper that may be marked with target circles as in Figure 8.1 (page 391) (Madsen, 1971). Near the center of the paper a heavy Plexiglas cone serves as a pen holder. It is moved over the paper by means of four strings that pass through eyelets at each of the four corners of the board. As it moves, the pen traces a line on the paper. In a typical experiment, subjects may be asked to draw a line through each of the targets in numbered sequence, or they may be required to draw a line through *their* assigned circle (the one to the left or right of their particular corner). Note that this can be accomplished only if subjects cooperate. That is, no one subject, by pulling his or her string alone, can cause the pen to pass over an assigned circle.

In a variation of this procedure, target circles might be drawn under the strings at each of the four corners. Now it is possible for a subject to draw a line through a corner circle simply by pulling harder than anybody else — that is, by competing and winning. Of course, if one subject is strong enough to win by competing, it is also possible for that subject to prevent all the others from drawing lines through their circles.

Madsen and Lancy (1981) used the cooperation board to look at competition and cooperation among two groups of Papua New Guinea children. The first

During the preschool years, parents and family are important influences in the child's development of a sense of autonomy and initiative.

group, the Imbonggu, are described as a highly intact tribal group whose traditional way of life is based on cooperation. The second, the Kila-Kila, are a more heterogeneous group, heavily influenced by rapid modernization and living in an urbanized setting characterized by violence and crime.

In the first part of the study, children, in groups of four, were simply instructed to draw a line through the numbered circles, in order, and were rewarded *as a group* for being successful (each child was given a coin). The objective here was simply to determine whether children were *able* to cooperate when so instructed and when rewarded for doing so. Following three one-minute trials under this "group reward" condition, subjects were then asked to write their names next to one of the circles (either to their right or left) and were told they would receive a coin each time the line passed through *their* circle. Now, in order to be successful, subjects must cooperate. If they did not, the most competitive and aggressive subject would simply succeed in pulling the pen over to a corner. Subjects were then given three additional one-minute trials.

The results of the study are striking. There were no differences between the Imbonggu and Kila-Kila on the first three trials. Each of the groups improved on every trial, and by the third trial, each succeeded in crossing an average of slightly more than 12 circles. But the results on the fourth, fifth, and

Both developing and industrialized societies transmit important aspects of culture through a process of social imitation. Although our children no longer need to learn how to grind corn or set traps, imitation can contribute to the development of important tendencies such as cooperation.

sixth trials, where subjects were being rewarded individually rather than as a group, are intriguing. Whereas the Imbonggu continued to improve on each of the trials — a clear sign that they continued to cooperate — the performance of the Kila-Kila foursomes deteriorated dramatically. In fact, two-thirds of the Kila-Kila groups did not cross a single circle on the fourth trial; in contrast, the Imbonggu group that cooperated the least still managed to cross six circles (see Figure 8.2).

There appears to be little doubt that competitive and cooperative tendencies are markedly different among these groups. Madsen and Lancy (1981) attribute this difference to their "primary group" affiliations — that is, to the cultural groups in which the children have been socialized. Similar research has found the same sorts of patterns among various other groups where the cultures are different in terms of cooperation and competition. Thus rural Mexican children have been found to be more cooperative, less competitive, than urban Mexican children — as have kibbutz Israeli children compared with urban Israeli children; Blackfoot Indians compared with urban Caucasians in

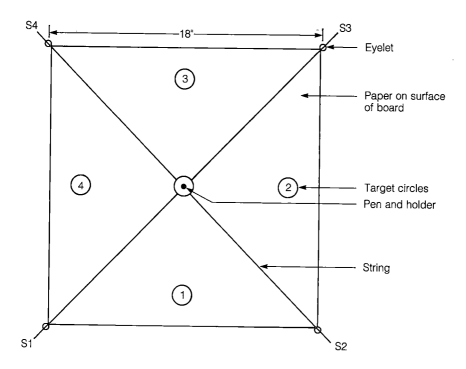

Figure 8.1

Cooperation board.
Source: Madsen & Lancy
(1981), p. 397.

Canada; urban and rural Colombians; urban and rural Maoris in New Zealand, and various other groups (Madsen & Lancy, 1981).

Observational learning in our society. It seems reasonable to suppose that observational learning — social imitation — is somehow involved in the acquisition of important cultural values and tendencies (reflected, for example, in competition and cooperation), even in such diverse and heterogeneous societies as ours. Perhaps most of the Imbonggu are cooperative because their primary groups — their immediate families and friends — are mostly cooperative. And perhaps the majority of the Kila-Kila are associated with more competitive primary groups. We, on the other hand, are not so homogeneous. Some of us are gentle and cooperative, and some are fiercely competitive. And others, of course, are both, depending on the situation.

But we too are socialized. Observational learning is also prevalent in our culture. Our models are perhaps not as simple, not as obvious, as they might be in a more homogeneous society. You see, a model need not be a real person whose behavior is copied by another. Anything that serves as a pattern for behavior may be considered a model: characters in literature, movies, television programs; verbal and written instructions; religious beliefs; or folk heroes (such as musicians or athletes). Frequently, models are symbolic rather than

Figure 8.2

Differences in coop-
eration and compe-
tition between
Imbonggu and Kila-
Kila children.
Source: Adapted from
Madsen & Lancy (1981),
p. 399.

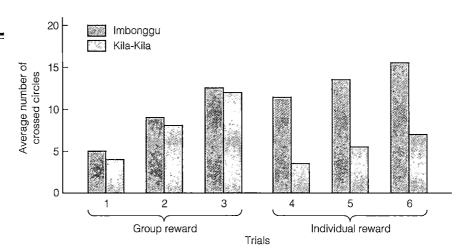

living people; indeed, these are the most common models in a technological society. Their effects are displayed in a variety of ways in the behavior of adults as well as children — and one of the most powerful transmitters of these symbolic models may well be your television set (about which we say more in Chapter 10).

Another very powerful source of social influence is the young child's playmates. For in play there is both competition and cooperation.

PLAY

The games that children play, unlike the games that adults play, are fun games. They are not designed to impress, to persuade, to deceive, or to annoy; they are played for the playing. That, in a nutshell, is the difference between work and play: **Play** is designed for no end but its own enjoyment. Though **work** may consist of exactly the same activities as play, it is engaged in not for the sake of pleasure but for what may be gained as a result.

Pretend Pretend and Real Pretend

Little children are sometimes uncertain about the difference between reality and fantasy. Three-year-old Mollie wants to play a pretend game with the other nursery school children, but she knows some *pretend* bad thing is going to happen. But, as Paley (1986) puts it, "what if the bad thing doesn't know it's pretend?" (p. 45).

"Go to sleep, Mollie," Libbie orders. "There might be something dangerous. You won't like it."

"I know it," Mollie says. "But I got a bunk bed at home and I sleep there."

"Bunk beds are too scary," Amelia says.

"Why are they?" Mollie looks worried.

"It's a monster, Mollie. Hide!" (Paley, 1986, p. 45)

But Mollie protests that there are no monsters in her house today. Still, she is unwilling to take any chances: "I'm going to be a statue," Mollie whispers. "So he won't see me." (p. 45)

Now Frederick comes roaring in on all fours. "I'm a lion. I'm roaring," he says.

"Is he scaring you, Mollie?"

"No."

"Is anyone scaring you?"

"The bunk bed," she answers solemnly. (p. 45)

Mollie, like many other 3-year-olds, can create her own ghosts and monsters; and she has developed her own ways of dealing with them. If they threaten too frighteningly, she can become a statue so they won't see her, or she can hide by the teacher — or she can, ultimately, resort to her knowledge that the monsters are pretend monsters.

But when others create monsters, Mollie can never be quite certain that they are truly *pretend pretend*. Perhaps, just perhaps, one of them might be *real pretend*.

We, of course, do not suffer from the same limitations as does Mollie (nor do most of us enjoy quite as boundless an imagination). We have somehow learned to tell the difference between fantasy and reality; we can dismiss our monsters if they frighten us. Can't we?

DiLalla and Watson (1988) looked at the progression of the child's ability to differentiate between fantasy and reality by having children play monster and superhero pretend games with an experimenter. They found that at the youngest ages (3 and 4 years in this study), subjects did not readily differentiate between fantasy and reality. If, while playing, they were brought back to *reality* by some interruption, they could not easily return to the fantasy after the interruption. Older subjects, however (5 and 6 year olds), could go in and out of a fantasy character, invent new characters, or transform old ones at will. When younger subjects were asked about the meaning of *pretend*, they could not answer but typically simply ignored the question. In contrast, older subjects were able to discuss the meanings of *real* and *pretend*.

Types of Play

Pretend play (sometimes called *imaginative* play) is only one of the two broad forms of play in which young children engage; the other is *practice* play (also called sensorimotor play). The principal characteristic of practice play is physical activity. It is the type of play that is evident among the young of many animals: for example, a kitten chasing a ball (Vandenberg, 1987).

Table 8.2
Types of Play

Type	Example
Practice (Sensorimotor)	
Solitary	Bouncing a ball, up, down, up, down ...
Social	Playing baseball
Pretend (Imaginative)	
Solitary	Giving a doll pretend tea
Social	Dramatizing monsters in a group

Both practice and pretend play can be solitary or social. Solitary play requires a single player; social play requires at least two children (see Table 8.2).

Note that these simple categories of play are by no means mutually exclusive. A single "game" or play session might involve elements of practice and pretend games and might be solitary in some respects and social in others. And, as we shall see, there are a number of different forms of social play.

Functions of Play

Ethologists argue that practice play among animals is useful in developing and exercising physical skills that might be important in hunting prey or escaping predators (Aldis, 1975). In addition, play might also serve to establish social position and to teach acceptable behaviors such as in the mock-fighting, rough-and-tumble play of lion cubs.

Some of the functions of practice play among children are, in some respects, not very different from those of play among animals. Practice play is useful in developing and exercising physical skills; and it may contribute significantly to social adaptation.

But practice play is only one form of play; pretend or imaginative play is the other. Pretend play may have quite different functions. Pretending involves important cognitive abilities related to symbolizing, imitating, and imagining. Not surprisingly, research reports positive correlations between play and level of cognitive development (Trawick-Smith, 1989). Erikson believes that play is one of the means by which children learn to master reality (Hrncir, 1989). Similarly, Johnson and Yawkey (1988) argue that one of the most important functions of play is to help the child relate and understand different events.

And quite apart from whatever larger purpose play might serve, much of it is simply fun. Why else play?

For children the world of make-believe is almost real — all they need do is pretend.

Practice Play

Practice *play* involves the manipulation of objects or the performance of activities simply for the sensations that result. It is often the only type of play that infants are capable of during the early stages of development. Sensorimotor play may consist of motor activities such as creeping, crawling, walking, running, skipping, hopping, or waving a hand, a foot, or any other part of the anatomy that is wavable. It also includes manipulating objects, people, parts of one's own anatomy, or anything else that is manipulatable. We see it in countless solitary games of young children, such as moving the hand along the steep precipice of the table edge and roaring "rrrrrrrr" deep in the throat in the manner of a well-tuned motorcycle; running around a room with arms spread wide, sputtering like a badly tuned airplane "ahrahrahrahrahr"; or jumping up and down on the bed repeating rhythmically "upupupupupupupup . . ." But these last activities are not simply sensorimotor; they are also pretend play.

Pretend Play

Pretend play includes the multitude of make-believe games that are made possible when, around the age of 2, the child can make objects, people, and activities be things they actually are not. Fenson (1987) reports that children as young as 1 year can pretend. At that age, pretending most often takes the form of simulating common activities — for example, pretending to eat or pretending to sleep.

Pretend play becomes increasingly prevalent throughout the preschool years. Children who run about the room frightening their grandmothers with the sound of an airplane motor are engaging not only in a sensorimotor game but in one that is imaginative as well. They are no longer themselves, they are airplanes. Their voices are no longer simply voices but the roar of incredibly powerful airplane engines. The worn carpet has been transformed into fluffy clouds, and the bread crumbs on it are tiny houses and people far below our heroic aviators.

For children the world of make-believe is almost real. It is so close and so easily accessible; all they need do is pretend. Unhappily, it is an art that is lost somewhere during the process of becoming an adult; an art that is sadly lacking among adults who pride themselves on a hard-nosed awareness of what is real and what is imaginary — who have a troubling fear of one day mistaking the imaginary for the real. But children who run about screaming like banshees, transforming their world into the dense and terrifying jungles of an equatorial coast to be prowled in search of enemies, have no such fear; they are simply children.

The child's pretend play includes a variety of related activities. There is play in which children imagine they are someone or something else: Boys are often superheroes such as Superman (or super antiheroes such as dragons or monsters); girls are often mothers or nurses (Paley, 1984). There are related games in which children imagine that the activities they undertake are something other than what they really are or that the objects they play with are something different (like the airplane).

One type of imaginative play becomes increasingly prevalent as the preschooler ages: daydreaming. Unlike other types of imaginative play in which the child actively engages in fantasy, daydreaming is imagining without the activity. Greenacre (1959) reports that daydreaming increases when children reach school age. Before that time their activity-oriented behavior does not lend itself to unlimited daydreaming.

Another type of imaginative play, related to daydreaming, makes use of the imaginary playmate — constant companion and friend to approximately half of all preschool children (Pines, 1978). These imaginary friends, complete with names and relatively stable personality characteristics, are spoken to, played with, loved, and hated by their creators. They are given names, forms, and places; and the young preschooler will seldom admit their imaginary nature.

The Implications of Imagination

In the play behavior of young children we find the first manifestations of imagination — manifestations that occur largely in the realm of the fantastic, the unreal. Fantasy has not always been encouraged by students of childhood or by grandparents. In a less enlightened age, daydreaming might have been feared as an indication of lack of contact with reality. Imaginary playmates would have been feared even more. Wertham (1954) included fairy tales among those aspects of fantasy that are harmful to young children, and Hurlock (1964) cautioned against the possibly negative effects of daydreaming, claiming that children who daydream excessively suffer physically from the resulting inactivity and also suffer psychologically from an eventual overreliance on daydreams to romanticize a self with which they are not happy.

Research and theory should do a great deal to relieve any leftover fears of imagining and pretending that we might have. Contemporary theorists believe that pretend play has a very constructive role in the development of cognitive and social skills. Piaget (1951), for example, views symbolic (pretend) play as one of the means by which the child progresses to more advanced forms of thought. Pretend play, along with deferred imitation and language, is one of the surest signs of mental representation.

Pretend play, says Leslie (1988), contributes to one of the cognitive capacities that sets us apart from other species: Specifically, it eventually enables us to think about ourselves and about others as thinkers — as organisms capable of having different states of mind. When mother puts a banana in her ear and says "Hello," 4-year-old Nancy recognizes at once that the banana is a pretend telephone. But there is no confusion here between reality and fantasy; she still knows very clearly that this is a banana. What is also clear to Nancy, however, is that mother can have different states of mind — and that she can too. Nancy has begun to develop a "theory of mind," says Leslie. And one important aspect of this theory is the recognition of others and of self as thinkers capable of deliberately selecting and manipulating ideas — even pretend ideas. Here, in the preschool period, is the dawning of what psychologists label *metacognition* — knowing about knowing.

If pretending, daydreaming, and creating imaginary playmates served as some sort of compensation for an unhappy or disturbed childhood, as Freud believed, then we might expect pretend play to be more common among unhappy, disturbed, and perhaps lonely children. In fact, however, imaginative play is more common among children whose biological and psychological needs are reasonably well satisfied (Freyberg, 1973). In societies where children have to assume work responsibilities at very early ages, there is far less childhood play — an observation that is also often true of children who are economically and socially disadvantaged (Schwartzman, 1987).

One of the few variables that successfully predicts later creativity is the presence of an imaginary playmate in childhood (Schaefer, 1969). College students who recall an imaginary playmate tend to be more creative than those who do not. The imaginary playmate is associated with other characteristics as well. In a study of 141 3- and 4-year-olds, approximately half of whom had imaginary playmates, Singer (1973) and his associates found that children with imaginary playmates watched less television (and selected fewer violent programs when they did), were less aggressive, smiled more, were less bored, and were more advanced in their language development. Other studies show a relationship between very low predispositions to fantasy play and antisocial behavior or susceptibility to delinquency (see Singer, 1973).

We are, Vandenberg (1987) explains, myth-making creatures — not in the sense that a myth is a lie or a mistake, but in the sense that a myth is a useful invention. "Humans," he says, "are myth-making beings who create reality through belief in stories they have constructed about reality" (p. 4). In this sense, our realities are nothing more than "trusted fantasy."

Perhaps, but there is certainly a great deal more that can be said about reality and myths. Still, what is fundamentally important to us as human beings is that we *can* pretend. We can imagine all sorts of things and yet know that what we imagine is not necessarily so — or, alternately, that it just might be so, that perhaps we or someone else can make it so.

There is surely a profound reality among our pretensions and our fantasies — just as there is also something quite *fantastic* and nonreal about them. Cobb (1977) describes the "genius of childhood" in terms of its imagination. He says it is "the imagination of childhood from which all later creative activities evolve" (p. 18).

Social Play

The child's developing motor skills owe a great deal to sensorimotor play; and cognitive development owes much to imaginative play. By the same token, some of the roots of the child's personality and interpersonal skills lie in social play.

Social play is any type of play that involves interaction among two or more children. Accordingly, either practice or pretend play is social when it involves more than one child. Skipping rope alone in the darkness of one's basement is a solitary sensorimotor activity; skipping rope out on the playground with others turning the rope, "pepper, pepper, salt and . . . ," is a cooperative or social activity. Similarly, creating elaborate and fantastic daydreams in the solitude

Calvin and Hobbes

by Bill Watterson

of one's bedroom is private imaginative play; but playing "let's pretend" — "you be the veterinamen and I'll be the dog" — is social imaginative play.

In the early part of this century, Parten (1932) observed the play behavior of groups of nursery school children, and identified five different manifestations of social play describable in terms of the type and amount of peer interaction involved. Although these develop sequentially, they also overlap (see Table 8.3).

Solitary play. In *solitary play,* the child takes little notice of others, preferring instead to play alone with toys or to engage in some solitary motor activity. Much of the child's play before the age of 2 appears to be solitary. Indeed, many researchers, including Piaget (1923), believe the infant's play is almost exclusively solitary. More recently, however, researchers have identified primitive forms of social play that sometimes occur before the age of 6 months (Brenner & Mueller, 1982). "Peek-a-boo" games, as well as games that include tickling, tossing, and related activities, are good examples, although these typically occur with parents or older children, rather than with peers. But there are examples of nonsolitary play among peers prior to the age of 2 (Ross, 1982). Such play usually involves what Brenner and Mueller refer to as *shared meaning* (rather than shared rules) and is illustrated in the "chase" games of toddlers or in the "touch me and I'll touch you" game.

Onlooker play. As the label implies, *onlooker play* consists of a child simply watching others play, but not participating actively. Onlooker play is not uncommon throughout childhood. Frequently, the onlooker may talk with the players, perhaps even giving them advice or asking questions.

Parallel play. In a third type of play, *parallel play,* children play side by side, often with similar toys, but do not interact, do not share the activities involved

> The presence of an imaginary playmate in childhood can predict creativity in later life. College students who recall an imaginary playmate tend to be more creative than those who don't.

Table 8.3

Parten's Classifications of Children's Social Play

Classification	Possible Activity
Primitive social	"Peek-a-boo."
Solitary play	Child plays alone with blocks; other children in same room play independently with other toys.
Onlooker play	Child watches others play "tag" but does not join in.
Parallel play	Two children play with trucks in sandbox, but do not interact. They play beside each other, but not together.
Associative play	Two children play with dolls, talk with each other about their dolls, lend each other diapers and dishes, but play independently, sharing neither purpose nor rules.
Cooperative play	"Let's pretend. You be a monster and I'll be the guy with the magic sword and . . ."

in the game, and do not use any mutually accepted rules. Parallel play is never-theless social play of a primitive sort because it involves two or more children who apparently prefer to play together even if they do not interact. Some re-search indicates that the presence of toys often detracts from social interaction and leads to a parallel or perhaps solitary play, particularly among very young children (Vandell, Wilson, & Buchanan, 1980). Not surprisingly, in the absence of toys, children are more likely to interact with each other.

Bakeman and Brownlee (1980), following an examination of videotapes of 32- and 42-month-old infants at play, suggest that parallel play often serves as a bridge to other forms of play. That is, even when children are capable of more advanced forms of play, they will often engage in parallel play first and then, in the same play session, make a smooth transition to a form of group play (such as *associative* or *cooperative*).

Associative play. With advancing age, children become more interested in interacting with peers and are more likely to include toys in what is termed *associative play.* This type of play involves interaction among children, even though they continue to play separately. In associative play, children some-times share toys, but each child plays independently without mutually ac-cepted goals or rules.

Cooperative play. Children who play *cooperatively* help one another in activ-ities that require shared goals and perhaps even a division of roles. Although most research on the preschooler's play behavior indicates that associative and cooperative play are not common before the age of 4 or 5, there is sometimes evidence of cooperation in the play of much younger children. Rubin and col-

Social play is more than just fun. It provides a valuable opportunity for acquiring interpersonal skills, for learning how to resolve conflict, and for developing cooperative behavior.

leagues (1976) report that preschoolers who have had considerable experience with similar-aged peers (in daycare facilities, for example) are far more likely to play cooperatively whenever they can than are children reared in more solitary circumstances (see Figure 8.3 for a description of children's favorite play places).

A particularly important example of cooperative social play is found in the drama that children sometimes enact in their pretend play.

"You be the baby."
"I be the baby."
"I be the mother."
"You be the mother. I be the baby."
"If you're bad . . . if you wee-wee your diaper, well, you know . . ." (*making an abrupt spanking gesture, but smiling broadly all the while*).

Garvey (1977) found that the most common roles in dramatic play were mother-infant, mother-child, or mother-father. She found too that children often reveal their fears and worries, their hopes and aspirations, in their dramatic play. Social play of this kind is more than just fun; it provides an important opportunity for acquiring and practicing behaviors involved in social interaction, for developing cooperative behaviors, for learning how to resolve conflict, and for fostering imagination and creativity.

Also, as Paley (1984) points out, in the roles that children adopt for their pretend dramas — monster or mother, baby or father, superhero or witch — they reveal much about the gender roles with which they are comfortable.

Figure 8.3

A map of children's favorite places. When 9- to 12-year-olds, 48 boys and 48 girls, were asked to draw their favorite places, these are the places shown most often in their drawings. Figures indicate the percentage of children including a given item on their list.

Source: Moore (1986).

LAWNS .71
PLAYGROUNDS
PLAY EQUIPMENT
SCHOOLYARDS .65
CHILD'S OWN HOME .51
LOCAL PARKS .40
SINGLE TREES .36
THROUGH STREETS .34
PAVEMENTS .30
OTHER DWELLINGS .29
FENCES .28
FRIEND'S HOMES .25
FOOTPATHS .24
SWIMMING POOLS .19
SPORTS FIELDS .18
FLOWERS/MISC. STRUCTURES .17
PONDS & LAKES .16
SHRUBS .15
CHILD'S SCHOOL/CHILD'S FRIENDS .13
TRAFFIC/BRIDGES .11
SELF PORTRAIT/TOPOGRAPHY/DIRT & SAND .10

★   ★   ★   ★   ★   ★

TREE CLUSTERS/YARDS & GARDENS .09
HILLS/ASPHALT & CONCRETE/CLIMATIC CONDITIONS .08
CAR PARKS/CLIMBING TREES/WOODLAND/ABANDONED BUILDINGS .06
WILD BIRDS & INSECTS/CUL DE SACS/CULVERTED STREAMS/LOCAL SHOPS/TALL
GRASS, LEAVES & WEEDS/CATS & DOGS/BUILDING INTERIORS/SHOPPING CENTERS/COMMUNITY
BUILDINGS/VEGETABLE GARDENS/ROCKS/STREAMS/WILD ANIMALS/CHILD'S RELATIVES & OTHER
ADULTS/RAILWAY LINES/BUS STOPS/FORTS, CLUBHOUSES & CAMPS/SPORTS COURTS/VACANT BUILDING
SITES/FRUITING TREES/NEIGHBOR'S & BABYSITTER'S HOUSES/SECRET, HIDING PLACES/TREE
HOUSES/TREE SWINGS/FISH & AQUATIC LIFE/CHILD'S SIBLINGS/CHURCHES—.05 and less.

GENDER ROLES IN EARLY CHILDHOOD

All cultures may be defined in terms of the various behaviors and attitudes that are considered normal for boys and girls — or men and women. In a few cultures, there is little difference in these behaviors and attitudes; boys and girls are expected to think and behave in similar ways. In most cultures, however (ours is no exception), there are, on the average, quite profound differences between the ways in which males and females are expected to think, act, and feel.

The range of behaviors that are considered appropriate for males and females — in other words, that are considered masculine or feminine — together with the attitudes and personality characteristics associated with each, are what define **gender roles** (also referred to as *sex* roles). The learning of sex-appropriate behavior is referred to as **gender typing.**

In Chapter 6, we saw that gender typing begins from the very earliest moment when the mere fact that the child is male or female *determines* much of what a parent's reactions to the infant will be. Thus parents unabashedly describe their newborn sons as strong, lusty, vigorous, and alert and their newborn daughters as fine-featured, delicate, and pretty (Rubin, Provenzano, & Luria, 1974).

Determinants of Gender Roles

Like most other aspects of human development, gender differences involve the interaction of biological, family-based, and cultural forces. Although the processes involved are not completely understood, it seems likely that family-based and cultural forces are influential at least partly through a process of imitation and identification. Boys learn to behave as "boys" and girls as "girls" at least partly through identifying with their parents and with other males and females.

A more cognitive explanation suggests that gender typing results from the infant's intellectual understanding of the meaning of gender. Kohlberg (1966) describes three stages — three levels of understanding — that reflect the child's increasing awareness of gender:

1. *Basic gender identity* describes the initial stage where the infant recognizes simply that he is a boy or she is a girl.
2. *Gender stability* refers to the realization that gender is permanent and unchangeable.
3. *Gender constancy* reflects the child's eventual understanding that superficial changes (in ways of behaving or dressing, for example) are irrelevant to one's basic gender.

Kohlberg argues that once children become aware of their gender identity and its meaning, they actively participate in organizing their behaviors as well

The past few decades have witnessed great strides in reducing gender-role stereotypes in books, movies, and in our attitudes, although we still have a long way to go.

as their environments to conform with sex-appropriate patterns. Thus having decided that she is a female, a girl selects feminine toys and behaviors. And having decided that he is a male, the boy leaves the doll corner except when he raids it with his phasers and missiles or haunts it as a pretend monster.

Genetic Influences

Genetic influences are an important factor in determining some gender-role differences. Lynn (1974) presents the following argument: If a difference is genetically based, it would (1) be displayed at a very young age before the time that other environmental forces could have influenced it; (2) be evident in a wide variety of cultures; (3) be seen among subhuman primates; and (4) be related to the effects of hormones on masculinity and femininity. All these criteria appear to be satisfied in the observed greater aggressiveness of males than females. Males are more aggressive than females at an early age (Maccoby & Jacklin, 1980); this finding is consistent in most cultures and also for non-human primates (Mitchell, Arling, & Moller, 1967); and the injection of male hormones into pregnant mothers affects the subsequent aggressiveness of female children who are in utero at the time (Money & Ehrhardt, 1968).

Other Influences

We should not conclude, however, that the greater aggressiveness of males in our culture is inevitable given probable genetic differences in aggression. The influence of cultural and family-based factors cannot be discounted. Parents treat displays of aggression in children differently according to their sex; they are likely to encourage it in boys and punish it in girls. In addition, many occupations requiring physical aggression and strength have traditionally been restricted to males, whereas those requiring nonaggressive, passive, nurturant behavior have been considered more appropriate for women. Hence the models provided for children are clear. And, as Connell (1985) notes, almost all the soldiers, police officers, wardens, admirals, bureaucrats, and politicians who control the machinery of collective violence are men — as are most murderers, rapists, muggers, and scoundrels.

Are these sociocultural facts a result of innate biological differences, or do sociocultural expectations simply exaggerate these differences? In other words, do basic, genetic sex differences cause societies to ascribe different roles to the sexes, or do these different roles cause the sex differences? Is this a chicken-and-egg problem?

Parental attitudes are also very important in determining gender-role behavior of children. Parents typically reinforce daughters less for independence, aggression, and problem solving and are more protective of daughters than of sons (Block, 1983). In addition, daughters are less likely than sons to be permitted the kinds of independent explorations that are closely related to the development of spatial-visual abilities (Russell & Ward, 1982). When mothers are asked at what ages they would allow their children to play alone outside, to cut with scissors, and so on, ages are almost always higher for girls than for boys. It appears that gender-role training begins very early in life.

Subsequently, cultural models on television, in books, and in most of society tend to reinforce children's developing notions of behaviors, attitudes, and interests that are most clearly appropriate for their sex (Askew & Ross, 1988). Studies of the role of television in sex typing, for example, have found that children who are exposed to conventional, stereotyped portrayals of male-female roles tend to have more stereotyped conceptions of what these roles are and should be (Tan, 1976). By the same token, when researchers have presented children with programs designed to reduce gender-role stereotypes, results have been encouraging (Roberts & Bachan, 1981). Tremendous strides have been made in the past several decades in removing sexual biases in books, films, television, and also in our attitudes — which is not to say that we have yet gone as far as we should.

Sex Differences in Play

When they are only 3, boys will gladly pretend to be babies, mothers, fathers, or monsters. Most are as comfortable wearing the discarded apron and the nursery school teacher's high-heeled shoes as the fire fighter's hat or the ranch hand's boots. They play in the "doll corner" as easily as do the girls.

But when they are 5, Paley (1984) informs us, the atmosphere in the doll corner changes dramatically. Now when there are pretend games, the boys are monsters and superheroes; and in the pretend games of the girls, there are princesses and sisters. But these are not the only changes that come with age. In Paley's (1984) words:

> In the class described in this book, for example, [a kindergarten class] you hop to get your milk if you are a boy and skip to the paper shelf if you are a girl. Boys clap out the rhythm of certain songs; girls sing louder. Boys draw furniture inside four-story haunted houses; girls put flowers in the doorways of cottages. Boys get tired of drawing pictures and begin to poke and shove; girls continue to draw. (p. xi)

Several consistent findings have emerged from studies that have looked at sex differences in play behavior. To begin with, there is little evidence of any greater predisposition toward fantasy (imaginative play) in either girls or boys (Singer, 1973). But there is repeated evidence of sex typing, not only in the toys that boys and girls are given but also in the toys they choose. Rheingold and Cook (1975) looked at the rooms of 96 children and found, not surprisingly, that boys are given what we consider to be male-typed toys: trucks, airplanes, boats, soldiers, and guns. Girls are given dolls, plastic dishes, cooking utensils, and doll houses.

Additional sex differences in play behavior are that boys employ more physical space in their play, play outdoors more and are more interested in "rough and tumble," noisy play. Girls are more interested in "nurturant" play (helping, caring for). Boys tease, wrestle, push, run, and engage in sex-typed role-playing games where they are fire fighters, builders, warriors, and so on; girls often play house, cooking, cleaning, looking after children, and helping each other with aprons, hats, and other items of clothing (Pitcher & Schultz, 1983).

These sex differences are less apparent among 2-year-olds, where there is a great deal of cross-sex play, than among 5-year-olds, where boys tend to play more often with other boys and girls with girls. Pitcher and Schultz note that societies, and consequently parents, have traditionally attempted to maximize sex differences in the play (and other interests) of young children — sometimes even punishing and ridiculing children whose games seemed less appropriate for their sex. More recently, there have been concerted social efforts toward understanding and reducing these differences. As Christopherson (1988) puts it, "the learning of gender roles . . . reflects one of the earliest and most profound focuses in the family socialization process" (p. 129). We look at the family in more detail next.

THE CONTEMPORARY FAMILY

The **nuclear family** was once North America's most prevalent family; only a few years ago, more than 85 percent of all children lived in families consisting of a mother, a father, and approximately half of one sibling, this latter phenomenon made possible solely through those statistical manipulations that revealed the average family size to be around 3.19 — and dropping (U.S. Bureau of the Census, 1988). In contrast, a majority of the world's societies have traditionally been characterized by **extended families** — parents, immediate children, grand-parents, uncles, aunts, cousins, and various other assorted relatives.

Our vision of the "typical" North American family is most often that of a nuclear family — mother, father, and one or two children — with father as bread-winner, although mother, too, might work. This view is a myth, argue Lamanna and Riedmann (1988). They point out that at present, fewer than 30 percent of all families conform to this vision. Of the remainder, a large and growing proportion are single-parent families. Almost 90 percent of one-parent families are headed by a mother (U.S. Bureau of the Census, 1990).

The decline in the proportion of nuclear families, with the corresponding increase in one-parent families, is due to a number of factors. Although the number of unmarried women having babies and keeping them has increased and the number of widowed parents has also increased, neither of these facts accounts for a very large number of one-parent families. The most important contributing cause is clearly a dramatic rise in divorce rates — a rise of more than 700 percent during the current century (Pfeffer, 1981).

Although the family can easily be described in terms of its composition (mother, father, children), it is not at all easily described as a unit of social influence. To begin with, it is a dynamic rather than a static unit: dynamic not only because it changes with the addition of new members (and sometimes the loss of old ones) but also because it changes in response both to external and to internal pressures. That is, the family exists as a relatively isolated unit within society, but at the same time it responds to pressures from its social, political, religious, and educational environment. This is evident in changes that have occurred in childrearing styles through history, many of these changes being reflected in the advice given parents by society's experts (to breast-feed or not, to be permissive or controlling, to spank or not to spank, to toilet train early or late).

In addition to being responsive to outside influences, the family functions as a network of dyadic (paired) relationships: mother-child, father-child, mother-father, child-child. And, as we saw in Chapter 6, it includes more com-plex relationships that define family systems (marital relationships, parenting styles, and their interrelationships in the triadic system of mother-father-child) (Belsky, 1981). These relationships change constantly as parents and children grow, and the nature of influence in these relationships is mutual and interac-tive. Parents change as a function of their children, even as children change as a function of their parents, a fact that we have frequently and understandably overlooked.

Given the highly dynamic nature of the family as a social unit, it has proven extremely difficult to isolate particular characteristics of parents and to assess their influence on specific characteristics of children. In addition, because the family has traditionally been a highly private unit, researchers have only infrequently had access to the most intimate aspects of its function-ing except occasionally in cases of pathology or crime. Most of the research data have therefore been limited to what could be obtained from interviews or observation by a third party. Unfortunately, each of these methods has drawbacks. Data from interviews are subject to errors resulting from intentional or accidental distortion, the weaknesses of human memory, the inadequacy of questions asked, and the occasional reticence of interviewees. Observation by a third party, even when it is accomplished through an impersonal camera, must always take into account the possibility (and sometimes the probability) that the presence of the observer will influence the behavior of the observed.

Vertical and Horizontal Relationships

Whoever is delighted in solitude is either a wilde beast or a God, Francis Bacon informs us. That may not be entirely true, but the point is nevertheless important: Social interaction and social competence are fundamental to human happiness.

How does the infant become a socially competent child? And eventually a socially competent adolescent and adult? Mainly as a result of experience in close relationships, claims Hartup (1989). Growing children develop two kinds of relationships, the quality of which may affect them for the rest of their lives: *vertical* relationships and *horizontal* relationships.

Vertical relationships exist between two individuals who have different amounts of status or social power. The first kinds of relationships that infants develop — specifically the caregiver-infant relationship — is a clear example of a vertical relationship. Relationships with older relatives, with teachers, perhaps with employers, are also examples of vertical relationships.

The principal function of vertical relationships in childhood is to provide security; in addition, vertical relationships serve an important instructional function. It is largely within the caregiver-infant relationship that basic social skills begin to emerge.

Horizontal relationships are relationships between equals — for example, peer friendships. Horizontal relationships, says Hartup (1989), are the contexts within which the basic skills that emerge in the caregiver-infant relationship are elaborated. And the "construction of well-functioning relationships," he asserts, "may be the most significant achievement in the child's socialization" (p. 125).

The importance of parenting in establishing the child's first and most important vertical relationships can hardly be overemphasized.

Parenting in Early Childhood

In Chapter 6 we reviewed some of the important dimensions of parenting from the infant's point of view. We saw that the most important features of caregiving for the infant are *attentiveness, physical contact, verbal stimulation, material stimulation, responsive care,* and *absence of restrictiveness.* As Belsky, Lerner, and Spanier (1984) point out, infants who stand the best chance of optimal intellectual development are those whose parents provide the greatest sources of stimulation (speaking, holding, touching, responding to, providing toys, and so on); those who limit the amount of stimulation to which the infant is exposed are likely to have an opposite effect.

As infants age and as their verbal, motor, and intellectual abilities blossom, important dimensions of parenting begin to change. But parenting is no less important for older children than it is for preschoolers.

Baumrind (1967) investigated the effects of parenting by looking at pre-school children identified as belonging to one of three personality groups: The first group consisted of buoyant, friendly, self-controlled, and self-reliant children; the second group, of discontented and withdrawn children; and the third group, of children who lacked self-reliance and self-control.

When Baumrind then looked at the parenting styles of the mothers and fathers of these children, she found some consistent differences. Parents of children in the first group were significantly more controlling, demanding, and loving than parents of either of the other groups. Interestingly, parents of the discontented and withdrawn children also exercised much control but were detached rather than warm and loving. And parents of the children who lacked self-reliance (had low self-esteem) were warm but highly permissive. This study is representative of a number of other studies demonstrating that children of relatively demanding but loving parents tend to be better adjusted, more independent, and more self-reliant.

On the basis of studies such as these, Baumrind identifies three differ-ent styles of parenting, each of which is characterized by different types of pa-rental control (Baumrind, 1966, 1971, 1977): **permissive, authoritarian,** and **authoritative.**

Permissive parenting is a nonpunitive, nondirective, and nondemanding form of parental control. Permissive parents allow children to make their own decisions and to govern their own activities. They do not try to control through the exercise of the power that comes from authority, physical strength, status, or the ability to grant or withhold rewards; but they might, on occasion, try to appeal to the child's reason.

Authoritarian parenting is grounded on firm and usually clearly identified standards of conduct. These are often based on religious or political beliefs. The authoritarian parent values obedience above all, and exercises whatever power is necessary to make the child conform. Children in authoritarian homes are given no responsibility for personal decisions; nor are they involved in rational discussion of the family's standards.

Authoritative parenting falls somewhere between permissive and author-itarian control. It uses firm control, but allows for rational discussion of stan-dards and expectations; it values obedience, but tries to promote independence. Authoritative parents, in contrast with authoritarian parents, are those whose standards derive more from reason than from religious or political beliefs (Ta-ble 8.4).

Table 8.4
Parenting Styles

Style	Characteristics	Examples
Permissive	Laissez-faire; nonpunitive; child responsible for own actions and decisions; autonomy more important than obedience; nondemanding.	"Okay. I mean sure. Whatever you want. You decide."
Authoritarian	Dogmatic; very controlling; obedience highly valued; self-control and autonomy limited; little recourse to reasoning.	"You're going to darn well study for 40 minutes right now. Then you say your prayers and go right to bed. Or else!"
Authoritative	Based on reason; permits independence but values obedience; imposes regulations, but allows discussion.	"Don't you think you should study for a while before you go to bed? We'd like you to get good grades. But you know we can't let you stay up that late. It isn't good for you."

Source: Based on Baumrind (1966, 1971, 1977).

Do Parents Make
a Measurable Difference?

Which of these parenting styles is best? And will it be best under all circumstances? How much do parents really matter?

Two models have dominated most of our thinking about the importance of parents in the development of the child (Skolnick, 1978). Both stress the malleability and vulnerability of the child. On the one hand, there is the Freudian model, which asserts that children are extremely sensitive to the emotional experiences of their early lives and especially to their relationships with their parents. On the other, the behavioristic model emphasizes the plasticity of children in response to the rewards and punishments of their environments (see Chapter 2).

If these models are accurate, they are useful mainly for the advice that relevant research might give about specific experiences that children should have or for whatever cautions such research might provide about experiences to which they should not be exposed. In fact, a great deal of the parent-child research of the last 50 years may be viewed as an attempt to provide information of this type. How successful have we been as dispensers of childcare advice?

Perhaps not very. Although *retrospective* studies with delinquent and otherwise disturbed adolescents and adults have generally found that their childhoods were marked by a variety of traumas sometimes associated with alcoholic or abusive parents, poverty, authoritarianism, rejection, and a variety of other factors, *nonretrospective* studies have not always corroborated these findings. A retrospective study is essentially a study that looks backward. The most common retrospective studies identify a group of people who have something in common at the present time and then use interviews, questionnaires, and other data (sometimes from school or medical records, for example) to explain this commonality.

When researchers used information from retrospective studies in an attempt to predict which of a group of children would be maladjusted and which would be happy and well-adjusted, they were unsuccessful two-thirds of the time (Skolnick, 1978). Indeed, some very successful, well-adjusted individuals had home environments that should have placed them at high risk. It seems that predicting the effects of childrearing practices is far more difficult than explaining these effects after the fact. What this indicates most clearly is that our after-the-fact explanations might have been entirely wrong in the first place.

One of the most painstaking studies of parent-child influences was conducted in the early 1950s by Sears and his associates (Sears, Maccoby, & Lewin, 1957; Sears, 1984). They interviewed 379 mothers of kindergarten children, rated each on more than 100 childrearing practices, and looked at the relationships between these practices and the personalities of their children. In general, the observed relationships were unimpressive and the findings ambiguous.

McClelland and his associates (1978) later tracked down 78 subjects from the original Sears study — subjects who had been children at the time of the original interviews but who were now 31 years of age. These subjects were interviewed in depth, and 47 of them were brought into a clinical setting for a battery of psychological tests. The conclusion of McClelland and his associates is particularly striking when considered in relation to our predominant model of child vulnerability and plasticity: "Wide variations in the way parents reared their children didn't seem to matter much in the long run. Adult interests and beliefs were by and large not determined by the duration of breast-feeding, the age and severity of toilet-training, strictness about bedtimes, or indeed any of these things" (p. 46).

Following extensive investigations of the relationships between behavior and characteristics of parents and the personalities of their children Baumrind (1977) concludes that there is no *one* best way of rearing children. Like McClelland, she argues that there are no specific childrearing practices that should be advocated rather than others (about breast-feeding, toilet training, and coloring with oils, for example); but there are some general characteristics of parents, reflected in their behaviors and attitudes toward their children, that might have highly positive effects — and negative ones, too. She found, for example, that parents who were firm and directive were more likely to have children who would be responsible (as opposed to socially disruptive and intolerant of others) and active (as opposed to passive). But what she advocates is not *authoritarian* but authoritative parenting — parenting that is firm, but reasonable; demanding, but warm, nurturing, and loving.

Baumrind also argues against the permissiveness that was ushered in by what is sometimes termed the *Spock era* of childrearing (in reference to Dr. Benjamin Spock, not Mr. Spock of "Star Trek"). She suggests that permissiveness is based on a number of false assumptions, especially that firm feeding habits, toilet training, spanking, and other forms of punishment are unquestionably bad and that unconditional love is good. She points out that punishment is effective and does not rupture attachment bonds between parents and children, provided it is reasonable punishment by an authoritative and loving parent; that unconditional love is likely to lead to the development of selfish and obnoxious children; and that there is virtually no good research evidence to support a belief that toilet training or insisting on regular feeding habits is inadvisable.

Childcare Advice

How do parents learn to care for children? In many close-knit and allegedly "primitive" societies, there are always older members around to show the young ones what must be done. And when the young ones have themselves become old, they in turn will teach the next generation.

But it is not so simple in our more complex and perhaps more impersonal societies. There are many parents who have had little exposure to parenting and who do not have ready access to the wisdom of the older advisors. Who will teach them?

As we saw in the preceding section, childcare advice is sometimes implicit, or even explicit, in the results of developmental research. However, most parents do not have access to this research and might not derive much immediately practical advice from it if they had. Some of these parents simply rely on their own intuition, common sense, and intelligence. But many others turn to one or more of three major groups of commercial childcare advisors: the medical profession, books, and parenting courses.

Physicians and nurses have long served as one of the major sources of advice about rearing children. Similarly, ministers, priests, and other religious authorities have traditionally been (and often continue to be) an important source of childrearing advice.

Childcare books are another important source of advice for parents. Clarke-Stewart (1978) found in one survey that most parents had read at least one childcare book; some had read as many as five or more. In fact, Abram and Dowling (1979) report that reading is the most preferred method of obtaining childcare advice for the majority of parents. Not surprisingly, mothers are more likely than fathers to read such books; so too are younger and less experienced parents (Hough & Stevens, 1981).

Of the hundreds of childcare books now available, many present overly simplistic, recipelike approaches to the problems of childrearing. Unfortunately, the problems encountered in raising children are often complex and will not always respond to simple solutions (Griffore, 1980). In spite of this, however, these books offer advice that is generally based on widely accepted cultural values; and their general effect will be positive more often than negative. Classic childcare books include Ginott (1965, 1969), Dodson (1970, 1974), and Spock (1976).

Parent training courses are a third source of commercial childcare advice. There are a handful of well-known and widely established courses including Gordon's parent effectiveness training (PET), Adler's systematic training for effective parenting (STEP), and Berne's transactional analysis (TA) (Gordon, 1975, 1976; Dinkmeyer & McKay, 1976; Harris, 1973; Berne, 1964). Parent training courses are almost invariably based on a recognition of the rights of children and take into consideration their needs and desires. That is, they treat children as important human beings and tend to discourage the more punitive approaches to parental control. Accordingly, shouting, threatening, physical punishment, and anger-based behaviors are strongly discouraged; reasoning and encouragement are encouraged (Brooks, 1981). The ultimate aim is to foster a warm, loving, and nurturant relationship between parent and child. And the principal method by which each of the various techniques operates involves communication. Put another way, what most parent education programs have in common is: (1) They encourage parents to be authoritative (firm, democratic, reasonable, respectful) rather than authoritarian (harsh, controlling, demanding, dogmatic, powerful) or permissive (laissez-faire, noncontrolling, weak); and (2) they teach specific techniques to help parents become authoritative.

The parent education programs also share some major weaknesses: The solutions they provide are frequently too simple for the complexity of the problems with which parents must occasionally deal. In addition, they typically do not take into account important differences among children of different ages and of different sex. And finally, they sometimes mislead parents into thinking that all answers are to be found in a single method (Brooks, 1981).

A Summary

In summary, there appears to be reason to question the assumption that all children are highly fragile and that the development of their personalities and their consequent social adjustment and happiness are entirely in the hands of their parents. As we saw, general categories of parenting styles do not predict future adjustment very well; and there appears to be little concrete evidence that such specifics of childrearing as when to toilet train or whether or not to breast-feed matter very much in the long run.

Still, it would be foolish to maintain that parents do not make a difference. First, because our measures of parenting style are crude and inexact, we might be overlooking some truly important dimensions of the child-parent relationship in our studies. We should also note that Baumrind did find important relationships between some aspects of parenting styles and children's

Table 8.5
Christopherson's Seven Guidelines for Childrearing

- Behavior and relationships with others depend on the extent to which the child's basic needs are met.
- Parents need to recognize each child as a unique individual.
- The faith, honesty, confidence, and affection between the parent and child affects the quality of the parent-child relationship.
- Parents should separate the worth of a child from the behavior.
- The child should be allowed as much freedom as possible to make mistakes and discoveries, but to do so with safety and respect for the rights of others and for the social convention.
- Parents should arrange the environment to encourage prosocial behavior.
- Parents should be ready to lend support directly or indirectly through physical or verbal guidance.

Source: Compiled from Christopherson (1988), pp. 133–136.

characteristics. Specifically, parents who were controlling but warm and loving rather than detached tended to have children who were more independent, better adjusted, and more self-reliant. Similarly, Moran and O'Brien (1984) found that democratic (authoritative) parenting styles fostered the development of higher levels of moral reasoning, and Getzels and Jackson (1962) found a close relationship between loving but authoritative parenting and high creativity.

As McCartney and Jordan (1990) note, the conclusions from this research have not always been clear because of the complexity of the interactions involved. Researchers have tended to use simple models that were not adequate for this complexity. If the conclusions are to be valid and useful, they argue, researchers must adopt ecological models such as that proposed by Bronfenbrenner (see Chapter 2). That is, they must look at parenting or childcare effects in light of characteristics of the child's face-to-face interactions (microsystem) as well as other interactions that impinge more indirectly on children (meso-, exo-, and macrosystems). Furthermore, they have to take into consideration the interconnectedness of these systems — that is, the entire complex of interactive relationships — and how children's individual characteristics modify, and are modified by, their ecologies.

Parents do make a difference, but our recommendations concerning the best parenting styles must be tentative. "At the most simple level," says Christopherson (1988), "if the children are basically happy, the parents are probably not doing too much that is wrong" (p. 133). At a more detailed level, he offers seven guidelines for childrearing practices (see Table 8.5). The equations are more complex than we had thought; parts are still missing. And our new ecological systems models suggest that finding these parts will require considering the possibility that parenting styles that are excellent for certain kinds of children under a given set of circumstances would be quite disastrous for other children — or under different circumstances.

FAMILY COMPOSITION

The ecological model suggests as well that we need to look at a variety of family variables and their interactions — variables such as birth order and family size.

Birth Order

Galton (1896) was among the first to note the effects of **birth order** when he observed that among the great scientists that Britain had produced there was a preponderance of firstborn children. Since then, research has attributed a number of advantages to being firstborn (or an only child). Among them are more rapid and more articulate language development, higher scores on measures of intellectual performance, higher scores on measures of achievement motivation, better academic performance, more curiosity, and a higher probability of going to college (see Melican & Feldt, 1980; Page & Grandon, 1979; Ernst & Angst, 1983). And, for what it's worth, the probability of a firstborn child going into space seems considerably higher than that of a laterborn child. *Newsweek* (1969) reported that of the seven original astronauts, two were only children and the remaining five were firstborns; of the first 23 astronauts to travel in space, 21 were either only children or firstborns. Of the remaining men, one had an older brother who died as an infant; the other was 13 years younger than his older brother.

Many of the characteristics associated with being firstborn are also shared by children who have no siblings (Velandia, Grandon, & Page, 1978). An only child is not only the first child born but also remains the first child throughout life. Interestingly, twins and triplets, even when they are firstborn in a family, do not display the same advantages, especially in language development.

There are a number of plausible explanations for the observed effects of birth order. Certainly, these effects are due not simply to being firstborn, a middle child, or lastborn but more likely to the fact that the interactions and relationships to which the child is exposed are, at least to some extent, determined by position in the family (Grotevant, Scarr, & Weinberg, 1977). As Zajonc and Markus (1975) point out, a firstborn child enjoys a close relationship with two adult models. It is hardly surprising that language development should be more accelerated under these conditions than it might be if the child had been born later or had been one member of a multiple birth. In these latter cases, not only do the parents have less time to interact with the child but also other, nonadult models are now an important part of the family environment.

Before we go running off bragging that we're firstborns or only children — or complaining that we're not — we should note that the contribution of birth order to intelligence and academic achievement may, after all, be quite negligible. Following a massive investigation of 9,000 high school students and their brothers and sisters (a total of more than 30,000 subjects), Hauser and Sewell (1985) found that the importance of birth order was quite trivial. What appears to be important is not whether you are first- or laterborn, but the size of your family.

Family Size

In general, although things may be cheaper by the dozen, the larger the family, the more limited the advantages to the children. In the Hauser and Sewell (1985) study, large family size had a significantly negative impact on schooling. In addition, a number of investigators have found consistent evidence of lower intelligence test scores among members of larger families (Grotevant, Scarr, & Weinberg, 1977; Zajonc, 1976). In explaining these findings, Zajonc has argued that the intellectual climate in homes with large families is, on the average, less conducive to cognitive development than the climate characteristic of homes with smaller families. However, here as elsewhere, we cannot easily separate the effect of family size from social class, religion, or rural verus urban environment. Unfortunately, as Page and Grandon (1979) observe, much of the research on family size has not considered the fact that large families are far more common among the poor, the culturally deprived, and certain ethnic minorities. When these factors are taken into account, it becomes clear that socioeconomic status is a more important predictor of intelligence and academic achievement than family size or birth order (Page & Grandon, 1979; Doby, 1980).

In summary, birth order and family size appear to be related to intellectual development. But the relationships are not very high and seem to be due primarily to socioeconomic factors associated with large and small families (larger families are more common among lower socioeconomic groups).

We should always bear in mind that the conclusions of social sciences are usually based on the average performance of large groups of individuals. Within these groups, there are those whose behavior does not even come close to matching the predictions that social sciences might make. Thus there are saints and geniuses whose siblings numbered in the tens and twenties; and there are poltroons and oafs who were the firstborn in tiny little families.

Life is not that simple.

ONE-PARENT FAMILIES

As we saw earlier, close to half of all American children are spending (or will spend) an average of six years in a family with only one parent; and in more than 90 percent of these families, the single parent is the mother (see Figure 5.4). The majority of these one-parent families result from separation or divorce; a smaller number result from death of the mother or father or bearing children out of wedlock.

Family Living Arrangements of U.S. and Canadian Children

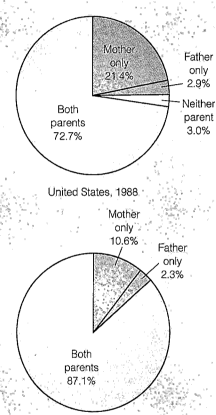

United States, 1988

Mother only 21.4%
Father only 2.9%
Neither parent 3.0%
Both parents 72.7%

Mother only 10.6%
Father only 2.3%
Both parents 87.1%

Canada, 1987

In 1970, more than 85 percent of American children lived in a family with both parents present, and 10 percent lived with only their mothers. Between 1970 and 1988, divorce rates increased dramatically, and the percentage of children living only with mothers approximately doubled. During the same period, however, the percentage living with fathers almost tripled — although percentage of children living with fathers only is still less than one-sixth that living with mothers. The percentage of children living with neither parent has remained constant at about 3. In Canada, 12.9 percent of all families were one-parent families in 1987.

Figure 8.4 Living arrangements of U.S. and Canadian children. *Source:* Adapted from U.S. Bureau of the Census (1990), p. 53; Minister of Supply and Services Canada (1989), pp. 2–31.

How Crucial Is Father Absence?

The impact of the one-parent family on the social and emotional welfare of children has recently received a lot of attention (see Kurdek, 1983). Much of this research has focused on the significance of the father's absence, and observed effects have often been attributed to this lack. Unfortunately, the situation is not so simple. Some of the effects of one-parent families can at times be attributed to changes that occur in the family itself after the father has left rather than to the lack of a father as a source of psychological influence. The child has to cope not only with the absence of the father but also with a husbandless mother. In addition, the economic conditions of the one-parent home are, on the average, considerably less advantageous than those of the two-parent family. In one investigation Ferri and Robinson (1976) found that more than half of 168 divorced mothers relied primarily on various forms of social assistance for their livelihood — a condition that had not changed substantially eight years after the divorce. Similarly, the average income in mother-headed homes is less than half that of father-headed homes (Weiss, 1984) — a phenomenon that has led to the *feminization of poverty* (Friedan, 1983). (Figures 8.5 and 8.6).

In summary, we might expect that father absence could have an effect on children, either because the roles traditionally fulfilled by the father would no longer be fulfilled (or might be fulfilled less adequately by the mother, who must also continue to carry out her own roles) or because the absence of the father has an effect on the mother, who then interacts with her children in a different way. These traditional fatherly roles are, on the one hand, economic and, on the other, psychological. Freudian theory suggests, for example, that the presence of both parents is especially crucial during the phallic phase of development (ages 4 to 6), when children resolve their Oedipus or Electra complexes, identify with the like-sexed parent, and begin to develop appropriate sex roles. Accordingly, the presence of a father is especially important for young boys. But it is also highly important for girls, not only because a father's behavior indicates to a daughter what men should be like when she begins to date but also because of the role a loving and accepting father plays in the development of a daughter's self-esteem. Similarly, the absence of a mother, an increasingly common situation, might be expected to have different effects on boys than on girls.

In addition to the economic impact of divorce or separation and the psychological impact of the loss of a male or a female model are the immediate (and sometimes long-term) effects of rupturing or altering the emotional bonds that link parent and child.

There is considerable evidence that separation and divorce, or the death of one parent, is a difficult — sometimes traumatic — experience for most children. Allison and Furstenberg's (1989) investigation of 1,197 children found that marital breakup had widespread and lasting effects evident in higher incidence of problem behavior, psychological distress, and poorer academic performance. These effects vary considerably, depending on such factors as the child's age, the relationship of the child to the departed as well as to the remaining parent, and parental relationships following breakup of the marriage. We look at each of these factors in the following sections.

Developmental Effects of Divorce

In a comprehensive series of ongoing studies, Wallerstein and Kelly (1974, 1975, 1976; Wallerstein, Corbin, & Lewis, 1988) have examined the relationship of age to children's reactions to divorce. The study sample consists of 60 middle-class, relatively affluent families in which divorces occurred and in which the mothers retained custody of the children. A team of researchers studied each child during a six-week period shortly after the divorce and again a year later and, in addition, obtained access to school records. Results are summarized for children divided into groups according to ages. (Interviews were also conducted 10 and even 15 years later with some of the children.)

The early effects of parental separation for the youngest group (2- to 3-year-olds) included regression displayed in loss of toilet habits, bewilderment, and clinging behavior in the presence of strangers. In some cases, development still appeared to be retarded one year later. Three- and 4-year-old preschoolers exhibited loss of confidence and self-esteem and were prone to blame themselves for the departure of the father. As Neal (1983) observes, preschoolers typically understand divorce as a question of one parent leaving *them*, rather than of parents leaving each other. They are likely to think they have done something "bad" to cause the parent to leave.

The next age group (5- and 6-year-olds) was less affected developmentally, although there was a tendency for some of the daughters to deny the reality of the situation and to continue expecting that their fathers would return. The 7- and 8-year-olds were understandably frightened by the divorce and intensely saddened, many of them missing their fathers constantly. Many of these children also lived in fear of making their mothers angry, perhaps imagining that she too might leave them.

Nine- and 10-year-olds initially reacted with apparent acceptance, many of them trying to understand why the divorce had occurred. But their outward calm covered feelings of anger, sometimes intense hostility toward one or the other parent (or both), and shame (Wallerstein & Kelly, 1976). A year later, half of these children seemed to have adjusted, with resignation and some lingering sadness, to their new situation. Significantly, however, half suffered from varying degrees of depression, low self-esteem, poorer school performance, and poorer relationships with peers.

Interviews of young adolescents (aged 12 to 14) revealed a much deeper understanding of their parents' divorce (Springer & Wallerstein, 1983). Most of these adolescents had become keen observers and analyzers of interactions

AT A GLANCE

Economic Characteristics of Mother-Only Families

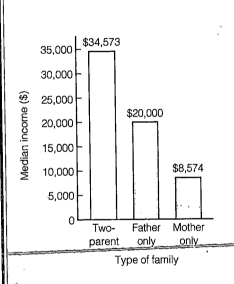

Figure 8.5   Median income of mother-only, father-only, and two-parent U.S. families, 1988. The median is the midpoint; half the families in each category earn more than the median and half earn less. *Source:* Adapted from U.S. Bureau of the Census (1990), p. 52.

In 1988, nearly three-fourths of U.S. children under 18 lived with both parents. Of these nearly 46 million children, 72.8 percent lived in families that owned rather than rented their homes. Of the 1.8 million children who lived with their fathers only, more than half (54 percent) lived in owned homes. In contrast, only about one-third (33.9 percent) of the 13.5 mil-

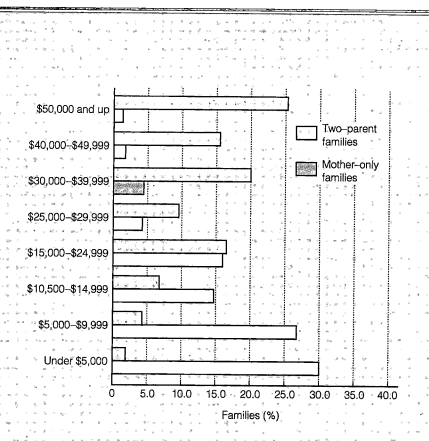

Figure 8.6   Percentage of two-parent and mother-only U.S. families in various income brackets, 1988.

Source: Adapted from U.S. Bureau of the Census (1990), p. 52.

lion children living with mothers only were living in owned homes. Moreover, income in these mother-only homes was dramatically lower than in two-parent or father-only homes.

between their parents, and many were able to evaluate the situation objectively and arrive at plausible psychological explanations for their parents' divorce. Unlike younger children, they were much less likely to harbor feelings of guilt about the divorce or hostility toward their parents. However, some of these children, who initially seemed to have coped well with the divorce, later manifested varying degrees of anger, resentment, and maladjustment. These children are examples of what Wallerstein (1989) labeled the "sleeper" effect.

In this study, as in Allison and Furstenberg's (1989) investigation, marriage dissolution has its most profound effects on younger children. In addition, children who have previously had emotional or adjustment problems, or who have recently been subjected to other stresses such as serious illness, are most likely to be adversely affected.

Sex differences in adjustment to divorce are also striking, boys being more adversely affected than girls (Hetherington, Cox, & Cox, 1979; Guidubaldi & Cleminshaw, 1985). Whereas emotional and adjustment problems suffered by girls have typically disappeared within two years, those experienced by boys are often manifested in adjustment problems (truancy, delinquency, and so on) considerably later (Mitchell, 1985).

A Summary

Marital disruption and its effect on children is a complex and difficult subject. There are too many variables involved for us to grab them easily, lay them flat on the tables of our reason, see their interrelatedness, and understand them clearly. Even our simplest summaries remain in need of further summarizing and simplification.

Peterson, Leigh, and Day (1984) provide a possibility — an approach that separates the variables involved and underlines their interaction. They present what they refer to as a "middle range theory of the potential impact of divorce." It is a theory that deals with two principal variables. The independent variable is the degree of *parental disengagement.* (Recall from Chapter 1 that an independent variable is a variable that, in an experiment, is manipulated by the experimenter; it is the variable that is expected to have an effect on outcomes.) The dependent variable is the child's *social competence.* (A dependent variable is that which is presumably affected by the independent variable.)

Degree of parental disengagement (which ranges from varying levels of marital discord through temporary separation, long-term separation, divorce, and death) may affect the child's social competence, which is manifested in the child's ability "to engage in social relationships and possess adaptive psychological qualities" (Peterson, Leigh, & Day, 1984, p. 4).

In examining the relationship of these two variables — parental disengagement and the child's social competence — Peterson and colleagues (1984) take into account much of the wealth of research in this area and reduce its conclusions to a series of propositions (statements). The most important of these are summarized here.

1. The higher the degree of disengagement, the greater the impact on the child. In other words, divorce would generally be more stressful than temporary separation. By the same token, a situation where one of the parents breaks all ties with the child would be more stressful than one where both parents continue to maintain close ties with the child.

2. The severity of the *immediate crisis* brought about by the divorce is closely related to the negative impact of divorce. Children who have been abused or neglected by a parent are less likely to view the divorce as a very serious calamity and are likely to experience a lower degree of stress.

3. The more accurate the child's perception of the parents' relationship prior to marital breakup, the less negative the consequences. Those who incorrectly view their parents' relationship as "happy" immediately prior to separation or divorce suffer the highest stress.

4. The more positive and amicable the parents' relationship following the marriage breakup, the less negative the effect on the child.

5. The closer the relationship between the leaving parent and the child prior to marital breakup, the more serious the effect on the child.

6. Age is related to the severity of consequences in a curvilinear fashion with the most serious consequences occurring for children between the ages of 3 and 9, and the least severe occurring before and after those ages.

7. When fathers are the ones who disengage (move out of the home), consequences are usually more serious for boys than for girls.

There are several dangers in interpreting research on marital dissolution. One is that we might inadvertently stress the negative aspects of divorce. Although divorce is almost invariably a trying time for children, living in conflict (and sometimes with physical and mental abuse) can also be very trying. Lowery and Settle (1985) review several studies that suggest that there is a point at which family conflict in the intact home has greater negative effects on children than the potentially negative effects of divorce. When that point is reached, divorce *is* the best solution, both for parents and for their children. We have to be careful not to mistakenly assume that what might be generally true for groups must also be true for all individuals. We might erroneously conclude, for example, that divorce is always detrimental to the welfare of children and that intact families are always good. This is clearly not the case. It bears repeating that there are expert and loving single parents who can effectively overcome whatever trauma might be associated with the loss of one parent and that there are countless two-parent families where parenting is inadequate and where love is seldom if ever shown.

Following a review of research on children's reactions to divorce, Hetherington, Stanley-Hagan, and Anderson (1989) conclude that most children (and parents) adapt to life in a single-parent home within two or three years of the initial disruption. However, remarriage often occurs at about the time that adjustment seems almost complete, and the period of adjustment to the remarriage is often longer than the period of adjustment to the divorce — especially for older children.

CHILDREN IN STEPFAMILIES

Although close to half of all American children spend at least some time in a one-parent family, many of these also eventually become members of stepfamilies (also called blended families). A stepfamily is the family grouping that results from the remarriage of a widowed or divorced parent and where, consequently, only one of the two married adults in the family is the child's biological parent. Almost one in every five American families with children under 18 is a stepfamily (Glick, 1989); and projections are that this proportion may reach 50 percent by the year 2000.

It is revealing to note that stepfamilies are not as enduring as first marriages — remarriages have a 50 percent higher probability of ending within five years (Pill, 1990). In addition, remarriages in which there are stepchildren are more likely to dissolve than if there are no children, especially if the children are older — above 9 (Visher & Visher, 1988).

Research on stepfamilies and stepchildren is still somewhat limited, perhaps because stepfamilies are less common than nuclear or one-parent families and also because of the number and complexity of relationships that can exist within a stepfamily. For example, the marriage of a man and woman who have both been married previously and who both have children can create an overwhelming number of new relationships involving the biological relatives of each of the stepparents, not to mention previous spouses and their parents, siblings, uncles, aunts, and cousins.

Loss of a parent through separation, divorce, or death is, as we have seen, usually a difficult and sometimes a traumatic experience for children. Unfortunately, the remarriage of the parent in a one-parent family does not automatically do away with the difficulties or the trauma. Indeed, it often brings a whole new set of problems. The child who has had to cope with the initial disruption of the family through death or divorce must now cope with another reorganization of the family. And whereas remarriage is almost invariably seen as a highly positive gain for the child's parent because it reestablishes an important relationship, it is often seen as a loss by the child because it implies a change in the relationship between the child and the natural parent. As Visher and Visher (1982) point out, many children experience feelings of abandonment following the remarriage of a parent. Much of the time and attention that the parent had previously given them is now given to the stepparent.

In addition to the loss, real or imagined, of some of the biological parent's attention and perhaps affection, the stepchild must now also deal with the establishing of new relationships with the stepparent, with stepsiblings if there are any, and perhaps with a new set of grandparents and other relatives. Furthermore, the stepchild's role in the family often changes. This can be particularly difficult for adolescent children. Their newly developed adult roles, sometimes accelerated by the absence of the parent (for example, the boy has become "man of the house" following his biological father's departure), can be severely disrupted by the appearance of a new stepparent (Duberman, 1975). Similarly, the creation of a new stepfamily can disrupt established patterns of control and discipline and sometimes lead to serious problems ("You're not my dad! I don't have to listen to you!").

Other problems sometimes associated with the stepfamily include sexual fantasies and inclinations between stepsiblings as well as between children and their stepparents (and resulting feelings of guilt and confusion); stepsibling rivalry and competition; ambivalence about the stepchild's role in the family; confusion over whether and how the departed parent should continue to fit into the child's life; and the need for the child to abandon the fantasy or wish that the natural parents might one day be reunited (Chilman, 1983).

Fortunately, the effects of stepfamilies on children are seldom inevitably and entirely negative. The fairy-tale stereotype of the stepfather or stepmother as the wicked wielder of terrible powers is, in fact, a fairy tale. Clearly, most stepparents are kind and considerate people who want to love and be loved by their stepchildren. When the initial adjustments have been made, the stepchild might, in a great many cases, be as fortunate as many in intact nuclear families.

DAYCARE

In the old days, most North American children spent their preschool years in intimate contact with their mothers, a situation that Bowlby (1982), Klaus and Kennell (1983), and others would consider an ideal childrearing arrangement. Today an increasing number of children are cared for during the day by others. In fact, daycare is now the norm for more than 50 percent of all American preschool children — a percentage that is climbing (Browne Miller, 1990). Almost 75 percent of mothers of preschoolers now work, and it is becoming increasingly common for many mothers to go back to work within weeks of childbirth. Gamble and Zigler (1986) report that *infant* daycare is the fastest growing type of supplemental care in the United States. It is small wonder that questions concerning the effects of daycare should be of such immediate practical concern.

General Effects of Daycare

The growing number of children in daycare facilities is due not only to an increase in the number of one-parent families where the parent must work but also to the large number of families where both parents work — sometimes because of financial need, often for other reasons (Hoffman, 1989).

Daycare takes a variety of forms ranging from situations where families can afford to hire a private caregiver to substitute for the mother during her absence, with the caregiver spending the working time in the child's home, to institutionalized centers for large numbers of children with many caregivers, or to private homes that look after perhaps a half dozen youngsters — referred to as family daycare. Although family daycare is the most common form of early childcare, most of the research in this area has focused on institutional centers (Goelman, Shapiro, & Pence, 1990).

Bronfenbrenner, Belsky, and Steinberg (1977) reviewed several dozen studies, most of which attempted to compare daycare and home-care children in social, intellectual, and motor development. Cognitive differences were seldom significant. A number of studies found a slightly greater tendency for daycare children to interact with others (both peers and adults), and a number reported somewhat more aggressiveness among daycare children. Kagan, Kearsley, and Zelazo (1977) found few important differences between a group of 33 infants who attended a daycare center and comparable children who were kept at home by their mothers. On a battery of measures administered on eight occasions — including assessments of attentiveness, language development, confidence, memory, and maternal attachment — daycare and home-care infants performed equally well.

Unfortunately, studies such as these do not permit us to make a final evaluation of the social, cognitive, and emotional effects of daycare in general. There are several reasons for this: First, much of the research has looked at children from middle- or upper-class backgrounds where daycare is often provided by university-affiliated centers. For example, the Kagan, Kearsley, and Zelazo study was conducted in a Harvard University daycare center. Centers such as this are typically more development-oriented, both in cognitive and social areas, than are the larger and often more custodial institutions to which a great many parents take their children.

Second, early investigations of the effects of daycare were concerned primarily with comparing daycare with home care. Accordingly, the questions asked were global questions: Are daycare children as advanced socially? As advanced cognitively? As well adjusted?

In general, the available evidence suggests that the answers to each of these questions is yes: Daycare has no detrimental effects on young children. In fact, it is quite possible that competent daycare might have noticeably beneficial effects on certain children (those from less-advantaged backgrounds, for example).

Quality of Daycare

The most important conclusion is that any negative effects of childcare will be associated with *bad* childcare. But the research is quite unanimous that high-quality care typically has positive effects.

Quality of the care provided in daycare facilities is closely related to children's social development, to the quality of parent-child interaction, and to the child's general cognitive development (Phillips, McCartney, & Scarr, 1987; Peterson & Peterson, 1986). In the Phillips, McCartney, and Scarr study, which involved 166 daycare children, a significant relationship was found between indicators of daycare quality (such as staff-child ratio, caregiver-child interaction, equipment and supplies, and so on) and the child's social development as revealed in measures of intelligence, considerateness, sociability, task orientation, and dependence. In the Peterson and Peterson study, daycare quality was assessed in terms of three components: variety of equipment available; degree of caregiver involvement with children; and evaluation of the setting, activities, curriculum, and teacher behavior. The study looked at the relationship between quality of daycare and parent-infant interaction. Children from lower-quality centers had more difficulty following instructions and had less-sustained dialogues with their mothers; they tended to use more single-statement utterances. In contrast, children who attended higher-quality centers tended to engage in sustained dialogues with their mothers and to display more maturity in following instructions. The authors suggest that children learn patterns of adult-infant interaction in daycare facilities. In lower-quality centers that are characterized by a high ratio of children per caregiver, interactions tend to be briefer and less frequent.

Finding Quality Daycare

Working parents make a variety of arrangements for the care of their young children. A few, mostly the very wealthy, hire private "nannies" and tutors; many parents leave children in their own homes with relatives, friends, or neighbors; and an increasing number turn to daycare facilities. Too, there are some children who are simply not cared for — who are left alone; sometimes on the street and sometimes at home and in school. Among these are the *latchkey children* — so called because their parents sometimes hang keys around their necks so they can let themselves into their empty homes when the schools discharge them (Long & Long, 1983).

Of those children who are placed in daycare facilities, most are to be found in what is termed *family daycare* — that is, in private homes where one or more adults look after a number of children. Parents often select family daycare when they have a choice because they assume this arrangement is more likely to offer the type of experiences and care for their children that they would themselves provide in their own homes. In addition, family daycare is generally more convenient and less expensive than what is termed *center daycare*.

Although research indicates that daycare in general does not usually have detrimental effects on young children, there is evidence that high-quality daycare might have decidedly beneficial effects; conversely, bad daycare might have the opposite effects. How can parents determine what is likely to be good or bad daycare?

In a highly practical book, Endsley and Bradbard (1981) try to advise parents on this question. They suggest that although it is difficult to evaluate different daycare programs, those that are very bad may have a number of characteristics in common, and those that are excellent might also. Among characteristics of poor programs are the following:

1. Unsanitary and unhealth physical surroundings
2. Obvious physical hazards
3. Excessive overcrowding both in terms of the available space and too many young children for the available supervising adults (for example, adult-child ratios that exceed 1 to 20 or, in the case of infants, 1 to 10)
4. Lack of activities and materials that are interesting and challenging to young children
5. Staff, usually untrained, who are at best thoughtless and insensitive and at worst reject and abuse young children
6. Disregard for parent's feelings about childrearing (p. 32)

In contrast, characteristics associated with high-quality programs include:

1. The financial resources to design and equip a special environment for their children
2. The time, freedom, motivation, and physical energy to work only with their children for 6 to 10 hours each day
3. The training necessary to organize experiences and activities to develop optimally their children's understanding of themselves and the world about them (p. 33)

Kagan (1978) too stresses that what appears to be important in daycare is that the ratio of staff to children be kept high, that staff be reasonably knowledgeable about child development, and that children be given ample opportunity to exercise social, cognitive, and language skills.

Licensing requirements for establishing daycare facilities vary tremendously throughout North America (Young & Zigler, 1986). As a result, although there are many high-quality facilities available, there are others whose environments are of far lower quality.

How can a parent assess the quality of daycare facilities? Endsley and Bradbard (1981) suggest that parents should obtain personal references and, perhaps most important, visit the centers, observe them in operation, and talk with the people in charge. To facilitate the evaluation process, they provide detailed checklists of what to look for and what questions to ask. Sadly, however, most of us are likely to spend more time looking, comparing, and obtaining references when buying a car than we are when finding someone to care for our children.

Quality of childcare is just as important in family daycare as it is in institutional centers — and, as mentioned earlier, family daycare is currently the most common childcare option in North America. Many of the guidelines mentioned earlier might be employed to evaluate family childcare, although they are intended primarily for center care. In addition, research conducted by

Goelman et al. (1990) indicates that it may be possible to assess the quality of a family care center on the basis of the nature of the interactions that characterize members of the family providing the care. Specifically, highest-quality care is associated with home environments where children are offered a high level of cognitive stimulation; where family life is well-organized; where family members have a sense of independence and self-sufficiency; and where the family spends time on intellectual, cultural, and recreational activities (p. 18).

Some Conclusions

At least five tentative conclusions are suggested by the research on the effects of daycare on children and infants. Bear in mind, however, that there are tremendous individual differences in the ways in which different children respond to out-of-home care.

1. The use of daycare facilities is growing rapidly as a result of increases in the number of single-parent families and mothers who work.

2. In general, daycare does not have detrimental effects on the social, emotional, and intellectual development of children. There are exceptions. These are most often related to quality of daycare and to the age of the children.

3. There is no evidence that daycare in infancy prevents the formation of parent-infant attachment bonds, disrupts them, or serves to displace the attachment person.

4. Daycare in early infancy may lead to the development of insecurely or anxiously attached children. This is more likely to happen to young boys than to young girls.

5. Positive and negative effects of daycare are closely related to the quality of daycare.

The most important of these conclusions, from the parent's point of view, is the last. The key factor is clearly quality of the care provided.

MAIN POINTS

1. Socializing emotions requires learning how to interpret feelings, achieving some control over them, and learning rules concerning when and how to display them (display rules). By the age of 9 months, infants can interpret emotions in others and are capable of self- and other-directed behaviors to regulate their emotions. Later in the preschool period, they attempt to control their emotional displays, but not always very successfully.

2. Erikson's stage theory of social development describes the resolution of psychosocial conflicts through the development of competence. Stage 3, *initiative versus guilt*, spans the preschool period and involves developing a sense of personal agency and accepting responsibility for one's actions.

3. Bandura suggests that much social learning takes place through observational learning (imitation), including acquiring such socially important characteristics as the tendency to cooperate or to compete, which are highly influenced by the individual's immediate culture.

4. There are two broad categories of children's play: practice (or sensorimotor) play, which is mainly physical activity; pretend (or imaginative) play, which consists of acting as though the actor, the actions, or the objects acted with or on are something other than what they really are. These can be social, in which two or more children interact, or solitary.

5. Practice play among both humans and other animals may be useful in developing and exercising important physical skills, as well as for establishing social position and teaching acceptable forms of behavior. Pretend play is importantly related to cognitive development. Social play underlies personality development and the development of social skills.

6. Infants as young as 1 year of age are often capable of pretend play (for example, pretending to be asleep or pretending to eat). Later during the preschool period, boys' pretend play often involves monsters or superheroes; girls' pretend play is often more concerned with home-related or nurturant themes.

7. Social play, which involves interaction among two or more children, may be onlooker play where the interaction involves nothing more than looking without joining in; parallel play where two children play side by side but not together; associative play where children play together physically but do not share rules or goals; and cooperative play where children share rules and roles.

8. Gender roles, the range of behaviors that are considered appropriate for males and females, together with the personality characteristics common to what we think of as *masculinity* and *femininity*, appear to result from an interaction of genetic, family-based, and cultural forces.

9. A cognitive explanation for gender typing (the learning of gender roles) describes three stages in the child's understanding of gender: recognizing basic gender identity — that is, maleness or femaleness; second, realizing that gender is stable, permanent, and unchangeable; and third, realizing that superficial changes, in dress or behavior, for example, do not alter gender.

10. Genetic influences on gender differences are especially evident in the greater aggressiveness of males. Family-based influences are reflected in the fact that most parents treat boys and girls differently, rewarding aggression, independence, and boisterousness in boys and rewarding nurturant, affective, compliant behavior in girls.

11. Sex differences in play include the tendency of boys to play more physically, are apparent in the toys they are given — and choose — and are evident in the roles they assume in their pretend games (boys are monsters, villains, superheroes; girls are cooks, mothers, babies). These differences are more apparent later than earlier in the preschool period.

12. A nuclear family consists of mother, father, and children. Extended families also include a variety of other blood relatives. The family is a highly dynamic

social unit; it changes as a function of external pressures and as a result of internal events. Here, as elsewhere, influence is bidirectional.

13. Baumrind describes parenting styles as *permissive* (nonpunitive, noncontrolling, nondemanding); *authoritarian* (dogmatic, controlling, obedience-oriented); or *authoritative* (firm but based on reason, nondogmatic, geared toward promoting independence but encouraging adherence to standards).

14. It is difficult to predict future adjustment and personality characteristics of children on the basis of what might be known about the childrearing practices of their parents.

15. Three important sources of childcare advice are the medical profession, books, and parenting courses. Although they may offer valuable advice, they sometimes present overly simple solutions for very complex problems.

16. Evidence suggests that firstborn and only children are more achievement-oriented than their siblings; in addition, they are more likely to go to college, to achieve eminence, to score higher on tests of intellectual performance, and to develop language facility sooner. As a group, they also tend to be less independent and more anxious. Children from larger families on the average do less well than children from smaller families on measures of intellectual performance, a fact that might be due as much to other social variables as to family size itself.

17. Some of the effects of one-parent families on children may be due to the lack of a father; they may also be due to altered economic conditions or to the children having to cope with a husbandless mother.

18. Preschool children often view divorce as having a parent leave *them* (rather than having parents leave each other) and think the divorce has occurred because they have been "bad." Older children often experience considerable anger and hostility, mixed with sadness. Adolescents view the situation more realistically and often become highly analytical about their parents' relationship and the reasons for divorce.

19. Divorce appears to affect the *child's social competence* (degree of adjustment and ability to engage in positive social relationships). The severity of the effect relates to the child's sex (more severe for males); age (more severe between ages 3 and 9 than before and after that period); the accuracy of the child's perception of the parent's previous relationship; the severity of the immediate crisis (for example, for abused children, parental separation may not be as serious a crisis as for children who have a very close relationship with the departing parent); and the parent's relationship following marital breakup (the more positive the relationship, the less serious the consequences).

20. Stepfamilies result from the remarriage of a widowed or divorced parent. Stepchildren sometimes face problems relating to loss (real or imagined) of some of the biological parent's time and affection; establishing new relationships with the stepparent, stepsiblings, and perhaps new sets of grandparents and other relatives; coping with stepsibling rivalry; dealing with new sexual

inclinations and fantasies; and abandoning the fantasy that the biological parents might one day be reunited. In many cases, these potential problems are insignificant and the stepchildren adjust easily to their new family.

21. As many as 50 percent of North American preschoolers spend time in daycare facilities; an increasing number of infants are included in that group. In general, daycare does not have detrimental effects on the social, emotional, and intellectual development of children. Exceptions to this general rule are typically related to *quality* of daycare.

22. Quality of daycare is uneven across jurisdictions, partly because licensing requirements vary a great deal. Parents would be wise to devote as much time, care, and intelligence to selecting daycare as they might spend in the selection of a new car.

Further Readings

Paley's books offer a fascinating, often delightful, description of life in the preschool. The first of these short books follows 3-year-old Mollie through a year of nursery school, revealing her excitement and her fears in the little dramas that are an intrinsic part of Paley's classes. The second follows the lives of a kindergarten class, providing insights into how they struggle to arrive at their own understanding of what it means to be a boy or a girl.

Paley, V. G. (1986). *Mollie is three: Growing up in school.* Chicago: University of Chicago Press.

Paley, V. G. (1984). *Boys and girls: Superheroes in the doll corner.* Chicago: University of Chicago Press.

In recent years, the number of one-parent, father-headed homes has increased even more rapidly than single-parent, mother-headed homes — although the latter is still far more common than the former. Greif's book presents a detailed look at the implications of single-fatherhood. Nofsinger's book is an annotated bibliography of books, articles, and video material relating to the impact of divorce on children.

Greif, G. L. (1985). *Single fathers.* Lexington, Mass.: D. C. Heath.

Nofsinger, M. M. (1990). *Children and adjustment to divorce: An annotated bibliography.* New York: Garland.

For an intelligent discussion of sexism in education, as well as in everyday life, and suggestions about measures that can be taken to counter it, see:

Askew, S., & Ross, C. (1988). *Boys don't cry: Boys and sexism in education.* Philadelphia: Open University Press.

In the following book, Cataldo describes and evaluates a great many parent education programs and gives numerous sources of childcare information for parents.

Cataldo, C. Z. (1987). *Parent education for early childhood: Child-rearing concepts and program content for the student and practicing professional.* New York: Teachers College Press.

Endsley and Bradbard provide a useful guide for parents attempting to evaluate daycare facilities:

Endsley, R. C., & Bradbard, M. R. (1981). *Quality day care: A handbook of choices for parents and caregivers.* Englewood Cliffs, N.J.: Prentice-Hall.

In the following book, Stein presents an intriguing look at how childrearing practices contribute to gender-role differences:

Stein, S. B. (1983). *Girls and boys: The limits of nonsexist childrearing.* New York: Charles Scribner's.

Sweet childish days, that were as long

As twenty days are now.

William Wordsworth, *To a Butterfly*

V
Middle Childhood

Do you remember them, those sweet childish days? Do you remember how summer vacation stretched so far you could not see its end? Do you remember too that in those childish days, trees were magnificent and gigantic and butterflies wore shimmering coats of dazzling iridescence in the sunlight and birds warbled startling songs that our more mature senses can no longer see or hear?

It is a sadness to see the days shrink so, to discover that hours are only minutes, to find the seasons whirling mindlessly on each other's heels as though they can hardly wait to get it over with. To think that there once was time to kill.

"Time to kill." Such a senseless phrase. Even children, who have so much more time than we have, have much better things to do with their time than to try to kill it — things like learning about the fine, concrete logic that controls and explains the world, about strategies for remem-

bering important things (they also work for things grown-ups think are trivial), or about the value of the self and the importance of friends. If there is any time still left, there is little need to kill it; it can always be spent watching television.

These are the subjects of the next two chapters. As you read them, it might be worthwhile to stop and wonder whether the trees that crowd the 12-year-old's forests are as tall as those that tower in the forests of the 6-year-old. And is there some way we too, like the child, can put 20 days between the coming and the going of our suns?

Give me a firm place to stand, and I will move the earth.
Archimedes, *Collectio, Papus Alexander*

Physical and Cognitive Development

t was an X-rated movie. Of course, I didn't see it; I was told about it afterward. The plot is irrelevant; the behavior of the viewers is not.

In one apparently moving scene, the camera panned on the upper portions of several actors engaged in what were presumed to be important activities some distance below the camera's lower limit. It was at that point that my friend had to stand on his seat to look over the heads of those in front of him who had risen in an attempt to peer down below the heads of the actors. My friend was able to rise high enough to see over the heads in front of him. But he could not see the action below the camera.

In this sense, and in one other, studying the child is very much like watching a movie. In writing this text, I find myself vainly stretching my intellectual and intuitive neck in an attempt to see below and beyond the work of Piaget, Skinner, Freud, Bronfenbrenner, and a thousand others. At the same time, I can sometimes sense you peering over my shoulder trying to understand what might be in my computer that is not on my screen — and I want to say to you, "Can you see?" It's a frustrating business because we both know there is much more there than is now apparent. Within the limitations of words on printed pages, it is absolutely impossible to convey the complete story of children and childhood — just as it was impossible for my friend to see below the screen. We can only imagine and hope that our imagination is not too desperately far from the truth.

There is yet another sense in which studying children is like watching a motion picture and, at the same time, quite unlike it. A movie gives the illusion of continual motion; yet it can be halted at any point to reveal that it actually consists of isolated pictures — static representations. The development of a child can also be stopped and examined in much the same way as it is possible to examine the individual pictures that make up a movie. That is really what happens when we attempt to discuss children by reference to stages, ages, and phases. There is, nevertheless, a fundamental difference between the development of a child and the progression of a movie. The static pictures that define a motion picture are its reality and their movement is an illusion. The static stages that define child development are illusory; the reality of human development is its continuous movement.

MIDDLE CHILDHOOD

The movement that concerns us in this chapter occurs during the years referred to as **middle childhood.** The boundaries are somewhat arbitrary: It begins near the age of 6, a convenient age because the preschool period ends there, and it ends at approximately age 12.* Because this stage terminates with the onset of pubescence, and pubescence occurs at different ages for males and females and for different individuals of the same sex, its upper boundary is more indefinite.

PHYSICAL DEVELOPMENT

There are tremendous changes through middle childhood. This chapter covers some of the major physical and intellectual changes; social changes are discussed in Chapter 10.

The physical development of many of the world's children is neither normal nor optimal — sometimes because of inadequate diet and sometimes simply because of lack of exercise. Current estimates are that as many as 30 percent of all North American children may be obese (Cusack, 1984); and as we saw in Chapter 1, vast numbers of the third world's children are undernourished. These observations underline the importance of knowledge about the normal course of physical development and about the contributions of nutrition and exercise to physical and mental well-being.

Growth

Although girls tended to be slightly shorter and lighter than boys from birth to the end of the preschool period, the growth curves for each were almost identical; that is, both gained at approximately the same rate. This pattern changes in middle childhood. Figure 9.1 summarizes height and weight data for boys and girls from the ages of 6 to 12. An examination of these norms reveals that although the average girl is three-quarters of an inch (2 cm) shorter at age 6, she has caught up with and surpassed the average boy by the age of 11 and is still slightly taller than the boy at the age of 12. In weight, girls are close to 2 pounds (1 kg) lighter at age 6 and do not catch up with boys until the age of 11. Between 11 and 12, however, there is a sudden spurt of weight gain for girls that puts them 3 pounds (1.4 kg) ahead of boys in the course of a single year. Chapter 12 points out that not until the age of 14½ do boys overtake girls in weight, and not until 14 do they exceed girls in height. The weight and height of average men exceeds that of women.

---

* Some authors end middle childhood at age 10 and insert another period between there and adolescence, labeled *late childhood* or *preadolescence.*

Figure 9.1

Height and weight at 50th percentile for U.S. children.

Source: Health Department, Milwaukee, Wisconsin; based on data by H. C. Stuart and H. V. Meredith, prepared for use in Children's Medical Center, Boston. Used by permission of the Milwaukee Health Department.

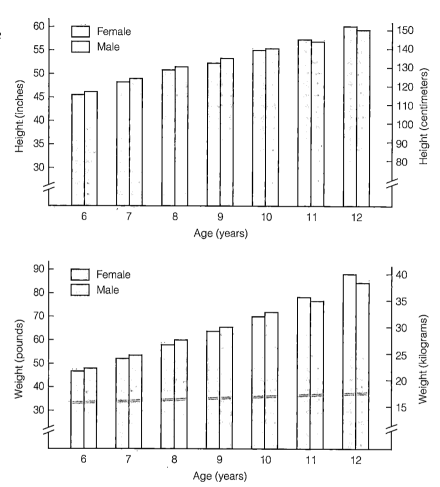

Another trend of physical growth that continues throughout middle childhood is a gradual decrease in the growth of fatty tissue, coupled with increased bone and muscle development. Muscle development is generally more rapid in boys, whereas girls tend to retain a higher percentage of body fat (Smoll & Schutz, 1990).

The growth spurt in height and weight during this period occurs approximately two years earlier for girls than for boys. The physical differences that exist not only between the sexes but also among members of the same sex are sometimes a source of acute embarrassment for children. At a time when peer approval has become among the most important things in life, it may be a great misfortune — or sometimes a great fortune — to be either precocious or retarded in physical development. It may be humiliating for a boy to suddenly find that his younger sister has become taller than he. It can be equally uncomfortable

Increased locomotor skills result in more sophisticated kinds of play.

to be the tallest boy or the tallest girl in the class and to live with the secret fear of being a tall, skinny freak.

Nature sometimes compensates for initial discrepancies. The tall girl finds that she was an early bloomer; she ceases to grow at the time when her peers begin their growth spurts, and in a short time she finds herself surrounded by equals. The short boy discovers that he was merely a slow starter; when his friends have nearly reached their adult heights, he suddenly stretches skyward.

But nature does not always make up for early differences. The early bloomer does not invariably stop growing while later developers catch up; we are not all destined to reach the same end. Clearly, some end up short and others tall; some are light and others heavy. Our hypothetical average child hides these individual differences.*

Nutrition, Health, and Growth

If they are well nourished, between the ages of 6 and 12, children grow 2 to 3 inches (4.4 to 6.6 cm) and gain about 5 to 7 pounds (roughly between 2 and 2.75 kg) each year. Normal gains in height are a better indicator of the long-term adequacy of the child's nutrition than are weight gains; gains in weight often reflect the shorter-term effects of nutrition (Pipes, Bumbals, & Pritkin,

---

*See Chapter 12 for a discussion of the psychological effects of early and late maturation.

1985). During middle childhood, there is a high need for protein in the child's diet, as well as a high need for vitamins and minerals (especially calcium, because of the rapid development of the skeleton).

Unfortunately, many of the world's children are not well nourished, and many millions die of starvation each year (see Chapter 1). Although starvation is uncommon in North America, malnutrition is not. Malnutrition takes one of two forms: overnutrition, often leading to obesity; and undernutrition, often reflected in the intake of foods low in protein and essential vitamins and minerals.

Obesity. The most common nutritional problem among children in North America is obesity. As we saw, estimates of its prevalence vary, ranging as high as 30 percent of all children (Cusack, 1984). Obesity is a serious condition that is difficult to rectify. Its relationship to cardiovascular and other health problems is well known; its implications for the child's social and emotional well-being are perhaps less obvious but no less real. Not only does the severely obese child often find it difficult to participate in the games and activities that are a fundamental part of the lives of many children, but such a child may also be subjected to the ridicule and ostracism that is reflected in the countless derogatory nicknames children invent (Tubs, Piggy, Fatslop, and others less kind).

Obesity in children is linked to a number of factors. Overeating is clearly the most important: Children simply take in more than they expend in growth and activity. This, of course, does not mean that the obese child eats excessively all the time. In fact, many obese children might only eat slightly more than they require each day; the cumulative long-term effect is obesity.

Also important is the child's genetic background. Some children are clearly more susceptible to obesity than others. Those whose parents are themselves obese are far more likely to also become obese than are children of slim parents (Brownell & Wadden, 1984).

A third very important factor in childhood obesity is inactivity. Children who lead sedentary lives, who spend much of their day watching television, are more likely to gain excess weight. Watching television is especially important in contributing to weight gain, not only because it is physically passive, but also because it encourages indulging in a variety of high-calorie snacks and drinks.

Although obesity is difficult to reverse, it can be prevented in most children even where genetic background predisposes the child to gaining weight. Two factors need to be controlled: diet and exercise. Children need to be encouraged to develop good eating habits. Care has to be taken to ensure that they consume adequate amounts of proteins, vitamins, minerals, and fibers — and also that they resist the ever-present temptation of the junk foods. Meals should be leisurely — not a bite on the run. And food should not be a reward — or a punishment.

Diseases and infections. Although the development of vaccines has drastically reduced the incidence of diseases and infections among children, most nevertheless suffer occasionally from a variety of problems. Most common are respiratory infections such as colds. Less common are communicable diseases such as chicken pox, mumps, mononucleosis, measles. Very uncommon are such vaccine-preventable diseases as tetanus, poliomyelitis, pertussis (whooping cough), and smallpox. Rabies, too, is uncommon.

Motor Development

Children's muscular control continues to develop during the years from 6 to 12. Early in this period, their control of large muscles is considerably better than their control over smaller muscles (an explanation for the inelegant writing of first- and second-grade children). By the end of middle childhood, control of the large muscles has become nearly perfect and control over the small muscles is much improved.

Changes in locomotor skills, agility, coordination, and physical strength are particularly interesting, not only because they demonstrate consistent differences between sexes, but also because they may be significant in explaining some of the child's interests. For example, throughout middle childhood the boy's physical strength (measured in terms of grip strength) is superior to the girl's, even though the average girl is taller and heavier than the boy (Corbin, 1980). Similarly, boys consistently outjump girls after the age of 7, presumably because boys' leg power and arm-leg coordination for jumping are better than girls' (Figure 9.2). Johnson (1962) also found that boys did better than girls in tests of kicking, throwing, catching, running, broad jumping, and batting. Girls surpass boys in a number of motor skills during middle childhood, particularly when the skills require muscular flexibility, balance, or rhythmic movements, such as those in hopscotch and rope skipping and some forms of gymnastics (Cratty, 1978).

Not surprisingly, these differences are consistent with the gender typing of these activities. That is, rope skipping and hopscotch have traditionally been more feminine than masculine; throwing balls, catching, running, and jumping are considered more masculine. In addition, the differences between boys and girls, where there are differences, are seldom very great. There is typically a great deal of overlap so that in activities where boys are better than girls, some girls are better than some boys; conversely, where girls are, on the average, better than boys, some boys are better than some girls (Lockhart, 1980).

It is important to note that although sex differences in motor skills are typically very small during middle childhood, after adolescence, the disparity increases dramatically, generally in favor of the males (Smoll & Schutz, 1990). As noted, however, this is not the case for some skills, such as those requiring balance, where girls perform better than boys (Laszlo, 1986).

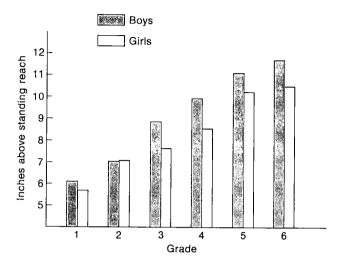

Figure 9.2

Number of inches above standing reach jumped by boys and girls from
grades one through six.

Source: Based on data from Robert D. Johnson, "Measurements of achievement in fundamental skills of elementary school children," *Research Quarterly,* 1962, *33,* 94–103, p. 97. Copyright 1962 by the American Association
for Health, Physical Education and Recreation. Used by permission of the American Association for Health,
Physical Education and Recreation.

What is not clear is the extent to which sex-related differences in motor
skills, both in childhood and later in adolescence, result from innate biological
differences between the sexes and the extent to which cultural norms, expectations, and experience are involved. We do know, however, that at least for
some activities, proportion of adipose (fatty) tissue is closely related to performance *for both boys and girls.* In a comparison of the motor performance of
more than two thousand children aged 9 to 17, Smoll and Schutz (1990) found
that fatness alone accounted for as much as 50 percent of the variance between
males and females. Since females *on average* retain significantly more adipose
tissue than boys from early childhood on, some of the observed male-female
differences in motor performance are probably related to this biological difference. We should note, however, that in this same investigation, with advancing
age, sex differences in motor performance were increasingly influenced by
environmental factors.

It bears repeating that sex differences in motor skills are often trivial. And
although some of these differences are a function of innate biological differences, at the same time social expectations and environmental opportunities
might have a great deal to do with determining the activities in which youngsters become interested and proficient.

Some Physical and Sensory Problems

As we saw in Chapter 4, not all children are born with normal sensory abilities or physical skills; nor do all have the same potential to develop these. Those who differ markedly from the average are termed *exceptional.*

Exceptionality may be seen in all areas of human development: physical and motor, intellectual, and social-emotional. In each of these areas, exceptionality may be positive; that is, it might be manifested in extraordinary talents and skills. Or it may be negative; it might be apparent in deficits and disorders. Later in this chapter, we look at both the positive and negative dimensions of exceptionality with respect to intellectual development in middle childhood. Here we look briefly at physical and sensory problems.

Prevalence. Estimates of the prevalance of physical disabilities vary a great deal. The U.S. Office of Education (1975) estimates that perhaps 5 children out of 1,000 are physically handicapped. However, this figure does not include visually handicapped or hearing-impaired children. The number of legally blind individuals in the population is estimated at between 1 and 5 per 1,000. But many of these are not functionally blind; that is, they are able to see well enough to be mobile and often to read large print with or without magnifying equipment. Estimates of hearing impairment indicate that approximately 16 out of 1,000 school-age children have hearing problems (Punch, 1983). Approximately 1 out of every 1,400 babies is born with a severe hearing loss (Jaffe & Luterman, 1980).

A number of other physical problems in middle childhood sometimes require special education or services. These include diseases and conditions such as muscular dystrophy, cancer, asthma, diabetes, and the absence of one or more limbs, as well as paralysis. Some are congenital (present at birth), some are caused by infections, and others result from accidents of various kinds. In many cases, serious emotional and social problems are associated with them; many of these problems are related to difficulties the child experiences in being accepted by others and in developing a positive self-concept. Hence, a great deal of what special education programs, parents, and therapists can do for physically exceptional children relates to their emotional and social well-being.

Visual impairment. Those who can see at 20 feet what a "normal" person can see at 20 feet are said to have 20/20 vision (or normal vision); those who can see at 20 feet what normal people see at 200 feet are said to have 20/200 vision and are classified as legally blind if their *corrected* vision in their better eye is no better than 20/200. Accordingly, a large majority of individuals who are classified as legally blind do, in fact, see, this being one reason why the term *visually impaired* is highly preferable to the term *blind.* Approximately half of

That deaf children lag behind "normal" children in academic achievement has less to do with actual intelligence than with language deficiencies. Accordingly, educational programs for the deaf emphasize language development.

all legally blind children can read large type or print with the help of magnification. For the special education teacher, it is especially important to determine whether a child will be able to learn to read visually or will have to learn to read by touch. For those who can read visually, the "special" qualities of education might not need to go beyond providing magnifying equipment or large type, unless there are other problems involved. Multiple handicaps are not uncommon (Donovan, 1980).

Special classrooms and special teachers for visually impaired children are much less common today than they once were. Many of these children are now educated in regular classrooms, a practice termed *mainstreaming*, about which more is said in a later section of this chapter. Those who must learn to read Braille, however, require special equipment and teachers (Donovan, 1980).

Hearing impairment. Although we can define deafness in several ways, the most useful for our purposes are those that distinguish between prelinguistic and postlinguistic deafness — in other words, between loss of hearing that occurs before learning a language and that which occurs later. Unfortunately, loss of hearing is most often congenital or occurs within the first two years of life, often from infections such as *otitis media*, an inflammation of the middle ear (Erickson, 1987). Fewer than 1 child in 10 who is deaf lost hearing after the age of 2. In effect, deafness is the inability to hear sounds clearly enough for the ordinary purposes of life. The hard of hearing are described as those who suffer from some hearing loss but who can function with a hearing aid and sometimes without.

In terms of cognitive development, deafness generally presents a far more serious handicap for the child than does visual impairment, largely because of the severe difficulties the child has learning to understand and to speak — hence the historical but no longer popular expression "deaf and dumb" or "deaf-mute." There is little evidence that the visually impaired are intellectually handicapped as a result of their blindness, but the same is not true of those who are hearing impaired. Although there is considerable controversy over whether deaf children are as intelligent as "normals" (see Berdine & Blackhurst, 1985), investigators generally agree that their academic achievement often lags behind, a fact that can be attributed largely to language deficiencies. Furth (1973) points out that only a very small percentage of deaf individuals ever progress far enough in their development of language skills that they can read a college-level text with understanding. This, of course, applies to the prelinguistically deaf and not to those whose loss of hearing occurred after they had already learned a language.

In addition to the academic problems often associated with deafness, there are often a number of emotional and social problems. The most frequent explanation for these problems is that deaf children are often highly isolated socially, because our predominant medium of interaction is language. Meadow (1975) also notes that in adults these emotional problems are frequently seen in difficulties in living (marital and occupational problems, for example) rather than in severe emotional disturbance.

The education of the deaf generally requires specially trained teachers and most often occurs in institutions. Understandably, the principal emphasis is on the acquisition of language — usually one or a combination of American Sign Language (ASL), finger spelling, and speechreading (lipreading).

The education of children with only a partial hearing loss may also require special instruction, especially if the loss is manifested in speech disorders. Although many children with partial hearing are able to follow conversations at close range or if they are sufficiently loud, they often have difficulty distinguishing among consonants for which there are no visual clues (for example, *p-b*, *t-d*, and *f-v*). Their speech may consequently be affected. Special education for these children can often be implemented without removing them from regular classrooms, simply by providing special instructional sessions for them. Itinerant teachers (who travel from class to class or school to school) are often used for this purpose.

The Physically Gifted

Our cultural, hence political and educational, emphases in the area of exceptionality have long focused on individuals whose exceptionalities have placed them at a disadvantage relative to normal children. But there are exceptional individuals at the other end of the spectrum as well. Although increasing attention is being paid to cognitive giftedness, particularly as it is displayed in

Third-graders begin to rely more on logic and less on intuition to solve problems.

intellectual and creative endeavors, much less attention has been focused on systematically identifying those who possess exceptional physical skills and on providing special education programs so that these children might "develop their full human potential." Indeed, there is an increasingly noticeable lack of research on the emotional, social, and intellectual characteristics of those so gifted and on the ways their development might be enhanced. One of the few ways that we recognize physical giftedness is to furnish scholarships for those who are inclined toward competitive athletics.

INTELLECTUAL DEVELOPMENT: PIAGET'S VIEW

When we left our discussion of children's minds early in Chapter 7, it was not because their minds had stopped growing while they continued to advance physically and socially, but because considering all aspects of development at once would be too complex and confusing. We pick up the thread of intellectual development once more, keeping in mind that as their intellect is developing, children are also growing in other ways. For the moment, our guide is Jean Piaget, and the period through which we are moving is **concrete operations.** The child approaches this period by way of the sensorimotor period (birth to 2 years) and two preoperational subperiods: preconceptual thought (2–4 years) and intuitive thinking (4–7 years) (see Table 9.1).

According to Piaget, the child's thinking toward the end of the intuitive stage is egocentric, perception-dominated, and intuitive. Consequently, it is

Table 9.1
Piaget's Stages of Cognitive Development

Stage	Approximate Age	Some Major Characteristics
Sensorimotor	0–2 years	Motoric intelligence World of the here and now No language, no thought in early stages No notion of objective reality
Preoperational Preconceptual Intuitive	2–7 years 2–4 years 4–7 years	Egocentric thought Reason dominated by perception Intuitive rather than logical solutions Inability to conserve
Concrete operations	7–11 or 12 years	Ability to conserve Logic of classes and relations Understanding of number Thinking bound to concrete Development of reversibility in thought
Formal operations	11 or 12–14 or 15 years	Complete generality of thought Propositional thinking Ability to deal with the hypothetical Development of strong idealism

marked by contradictions and errors of logic. With the beginning of the period of concrete thought, many of these deficiencies will disappear and be replaced by more logical thinking. Recall, however, that although Piaget's descriptions serve to highlight some of the important features of preschool thinking, they do not do justice to the child's cognitive achievements. It is worth noting as well that Piaget's concept of stages as major developmental milestones characteristic of most children, and occurring in predetermined sequence, no longer seems as useful as it once did. There are two main reasons for this. One is the discovery that there are tremendous individual variations in the performances of different children of the same ages on the various Piagetian tasks. The other reason is that very minor changes in the tasks can sometimes lead to very different responses. Accordingly, a number of the neo-Piagetians have

suggested different and usually less specific developmental milestones sometimes labeled *levels* rather than stages (Fischer & Silvern, 1985).

In spite of the recognition that Piaget's stages are not universal and that
they fail to account for some important features of development (such as aspects of *metacognition* and *social cognition* with which we deal later), they
serve to illustrate important differences between the thinking of the preschooler and that of the older child. These differences are most clearly illustrated in the conservations.

The Conservations

Conservation refers to the fact that the quantitative aspects of objects do not
change unless something has been added to or taken away from them, despite
other changes in the objects. In Chapter 7, for example, we described a situation
where a child is presented with two equal balls of modeling clay and asked
whether there is still as much clay in each after one has been rolled into
something like a snake. The preoperational child's belief that there is more clay
in the snake than in the ball (because it is now longer and therefore *looks* as
though it has more) is an example of the inability to *conserve*. The eventual
realization that the transformed object does not have more or less substance
than it previously had marks not only the acquisition of concepts of conservation but also the transition between preoperational thought and concrete
operations.

The significance of the acquisition of conservation is not so much that
children cease to be deceived by a problem but rather that they have now
developed certain fundamental logic rules, evident in much of their thinking.
That is, in the course of what Kuhn (1984) calls "meaning-making" (or what
Piaget called "constructing" knowledge), the child has discovered that there is
a logic that governs things and relationships — that the game of knowing has
rules. These rules make it possible for children to overcome many of the errors
that characterized their thinking during the preoperational period. In a sense,
they free the child from reliance on perception and intuition; like adults, children can now rely on logic. Put another way, they can rely on *operations*
(thought processes governed by rules of logic) rather than on *preoperations*.

That children attempt to use logic and "make meaning" does not mean
that they will always respond correctly. In fact, one of the clearest illustrations
of meaning-making occurs during the preoperational period and *leads to an
incorrect answer*. When a young child — say 3 or 4 years of age — is asked to
draw what the water would look like in a tilted jar, the most common response
is that shown on the left (A) in Figure 9.3 — rather than the correct response,
which is shown on the right (B). As Kuhn (1984) points out, the child has never
actually seen anything like the drawing on the left. It does not therefore reflect
actual experience with the world so much as the child's attempts to make
sense — to construct meaning — out of experience.

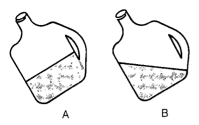

A   B

Figure 9.3

Young children typically draw fluid level in a tilted jar as shown in (A) rather than (B) — not because they have ever seen anything like (A) in the real world, but because the logic they use in their attempts to *make meaning* out of their experiences is not always appropriate.

Part of the meaning that the young schoolchild invents relates to a gradual recognition of the logic that governs things. Three rules of logic that are discovered (or invented) during this period are particularly important for the acquisition of conservation. They are **identity, reversibility,** and **compensation.** Each can be illustrated by the conservation of quantity problem just described. In this problem, children are presented with two identical clay balls that they recognize contain the same amount of modeling clay. One is then elongated whereas the other is left unchanged. Each subject is asked whether the deformed object still contains the same amount of clay as the unchanged object, or whether it has more or less. If they say that it has an equal amount (conservation), they may be reasoning in one of three ways. They may think that nothing has been added to or taken away from the elongated object and that it must therefore be identical to what it was (identity). Or, they might reason that the sausagelike shape can be reformed into the original ball, in which case the sausage and ball must contain the same amount (reversibility). A third assumption might be that the elongated object appears to have more material because it is longer but also appears to have less because it is thinner. The two dimensions therefore compensate each other and the changes are canceled (compensation).

To clarify, *identity* is the notion that for every operation (internalized act or thought) there is an operation that leaves the product unchanged. In other words, amount does not change if nothing is added or taken away. *Reversibility* means that every operation can be undone (reversed or unthought) and that certain logical consequences follow from this possibility. Thus, even a very ugly clay sausage can be made back into a ball resembling the original ball. *Compensation* specifies that several operations can be combined in different ways to yield the same result.

How general are these logical rules? That is, once the child has learned about identity, compensation, and reversibility, do these rules apply to all thinking? The answer is no. Consider, for example, that there are many different kinds of conservation — about as many as there are characteristics of objects that can vary in quantity. Thus, in addition to conservation of amount (or mass, involving liquids or solids, or discontinuous materials like beads, beans, or baubles), there is conservation of number, length, area, volume, and so on. If the rules of logic that make these conservations possible were completely general, they would all be acquired at the same time. That is, when children realize that the amount of clay does not change when a ball is flattened, they should also realize that the amount of water does not change when it is poured from a tall thin vase into a shallow wide bowl. But, as Figure 9.4 shows, approximate ages at which the various conservations are acquired span a number of years.

Additional evidence that the child's rules of logic at the concrete operations stage are not completely general is derived from a series of *extinction* studies (studies in which reinforcement is withdrawn to bring about the cessation of a response). In these studies, children who have already acquired a specific conservation are provided with actual evidence that their reasoning is incorrect. The argument is that if a conserver truly believes that conservation is a logical and necessary consequence, there should be strong resistance to extinction of that logic. To simplify, consider a typical extinction experiment in conservation of weight. First, subjects are presented with two identical clay balls. Each agrees that both weigh an equal amount and they continue to maintain that this is the case, even after one or both of the balls have been deformed or broken into little pieces. At this point, however, the experimenter asks subjects to verify their conservation response by means of a balance scale. Alas, the scale is rigged so that one of the balls now seems to weigh more than the other.

Miller (1981) reviewed more than 25 extinction experiments. In a majority of them, subjects believed evidence that contradicted their original conservation response and that, by the same token, also contradicted the logical rules that led to that response. Thus, young conservers (and sometimes older ones) do not always behave as though they believe these rules of logic to be necessarily true in all relevant cases. However, further questioning of subjects in the extinction studies revealed that they did not doubt the certainty of the logical rule but that they were simply not always clear about when to apply the rule. Miller's (1981) research indicates that even young children realize that social rules, for example, are arbitrary and uncertain but that Piagetian rules of logic are more universal. However, the rigged balance scale presents a real-life problem rather than a problem in logic. In this situation the child is not deciding whether the logical rule is correct (she knows it is), but whether the scale is correct.

Acceleration of Conservation

American researchers and educators were fond of asking Piaget questions like this: "If we can accurately describe some of the important capabilities that children develop and the sequence in which these appear, might it not also be possible to accelerate their appearance by providing children with appropriate experiences? And could we not, by so doing, speed up the developmental pro-

1. Conservation of substance (6–7 years)

A

The experimenter presents two identical modeling clay balls. The subject admits that they have equal amounts of clay.

B

One of the balls is deformed. The subject is asked whether they still contain equal amounts.

2. Conservation of length (6–7 years)

A

Two sticks are aligned in front of the subject. The subject admits their equality.

B

One of the sticks is moved to the right. The subject is asked whether they are still the same length.

3. Conservation of number (6–7 years)

A

Two rows of counters are placed in one-to-one correspondence. Subject admits their equality.

B

One of the rows is elongated (or contracted). Subject is asked whether each row still has the same number.

4. Conservation of liquids (6–7 years)

A

Two beakers are filled to the same level with water. The subject sees that they are equal.

B

The liquid of one container is poured into a tall tube (or a flat dish). The subject is asked whether each still contains the same amount.

5. Conservation of area (9–10 years)

A

The subject and the experimenter each have identical sheets of cardboard. Wooden blocks are placed on these in identical positions. The subject agrees that each cardboard has the same amount of space remaining.

B

The experimenter scatters the blocks on one of the cardboards. The subject is asked whether each cardboard still has the same amount of space remaining.

Figure 9.4

Some simple tests for conservation with approximate ages of attainment.

cess, increase children's cognitive capabilities, and perhaps even make them more intelligent?" But Piaget did not have a direct answer for this question. His concerns had always been more with the description and explanation of cognitive development than with attempts to change its ordinary course. However, an impressive number of other researchers have attempted an answer. Many have looked at the possibility of accelerating the development of concepts of conservation — concepts that are simply defined, easy to measure, and highly significant for general cognitive development. The main assumption is that if the acquisition of concepts of conservation is truly important in the child's cognitive development and if it can be accelerated through training, then perhaps we can design school programs that would be far more beneficial for cognitive growth than those presently used.

Many of the early studies designed to teach conservation to young children before the time they would be expected to acquire it naturally were not successful or have reported mixed success. Investigators have used a variety of approaches. Siegler and Liebert (1972) accelerated acquisition of liquid conservation by giving children rules and information about the accuracy of their responses. Rosenthal and Zimmerman (1972) used a conserving child as a model. Many nonconserving subjects later demonstrated knowledge of conservation on related but not identical tasks. In contrast to these studies, Kuhn (1972), who also used a modeling procedure, failed to increase conservation behavior appreciably in subjects; and Rosenthal and Zimmerman, giving instruction in relevant rules, were also unsuccessful.

In summary, the conclusion that development can be altered easily and significantly through short-term training programs in specific areas is not warranted by the available evidence. Conservation can be accelerated, but training programs, especially if the children are still some distance from acquiring conservation naturally, need to be detailed and systematic (see Furth, 1980; Gelman & Gallistel, 1978). And whether such efforts, when successful, contribute significantly to intellectual development — or to happiness and self-esteem — remains unclear.

Seriation, Number, and Classes

In addition to acquiring various conservations, children gain or improve three other abilities as they enter concrete operations. First, they learn to deal with classes, achieving the capacity to understand class inclusion and to reason about the combination and the decomposition of classes. An 8-year-old, for example, would be unlikely to make a mistake when asked to decide whether there are more roses or more flowers in a bouquet consisting of 15 roses and 5 tulips. At this level, children typically understand that roses make up a subclass of the larger class of flowers. Similarly, they would have little difficulty multiplying two classes in this problem: If there are red balls and gray balls, and some are large whereas others are small, how many different kinds of balls are there? The classes to be multiplied are red and gray balls by large and small ones. The answer is illustrated in Figure 9.5. Recall from Chapter 7 that preschool children too have some ability to deal with class-inclusion problems. Many can correctly answer questions in the form: "A Siamese is a cat, but not an alley cat. Is a Siamese an animal?" However, they typically cannot respond correctly to the flowers problem.

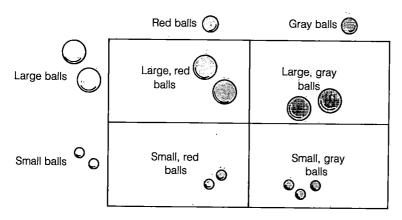

Figure 9.5

How many kinds of balls are there if there are red ones and gray ones and large ones and small ones? An illustration of the classification abilities of the child during the period of concrete operations.

Figure 9.6

A test of a child's understanding of seriation. The elements of the series are presented in random order and the child is asked to arrange them in sequence of height. The top row was arranged by a 3½-year-old; the bottom, by an 8-year-old.

A second achievement of the period of concrete operations is the ability to understand the concept of **seriation** — that is, the concept of ordering in sequence. One of Piaget's seriation tasks involves presenting the child with a series of objects (for example, dolls) each a different length so that the objects can easily be arranged from longest to shortest. The bottom row of Figure 9.6

illustrates the arrangement desired, quickly produced by the child in concrete operations even when the series is presented in random order. The child at the stage of intuitive thinking, however, is ordinarily incapable of responding correctly (top row). A typical response is to place several of the dolls in order while ignoring the fact that others may fit in between those that have already been positioned. If the next doll the child selects is too short to be placed where the child intended it to be (at the upper end), it is placed without hesitation at the other end, even though it might be taller or shorter than the doll that is already positioned there. The child fails to make an inference that signals complete understanding of seriation. This understanding is almost essential to the solution of the problem: If A is greater than B, and B is greater than C, then must A also be greater than C? Understanding this concept eliminates the necessity of making all the comparisons that would otherwise be necessary.

A third achievement of concrete operations is a more complete understanding of number — an achievement that depends on some of the logical rules involved in classification and seriation. The ordinal properties of number (their ordered sequence, first, second, third, . . .) depend on a knowledge of seriation; and their cardinal properties (their quantitative properties, the fact that they represent collections of different magnitude) depend on classification. As we saw in Chapter 7, however, many preschool children already have an impressive knowledge of number, a fact that Piaget largely overlooked as he searched for the limitations of preoperational versus operational thought.

Summary of Concrete Operations

An *operation* is a thought that is characterized by rules of logic. Because children acquire conservations early in this period and because these concepts are manifestations of operational thinking, the period is called *operational*. It is also termed *concrete* because children's thinking deals with real objects or those they can easily imagine. Children in the concrete operations stage are bound to the real world; they do not yet have the freedom made possible by the more advanced logic of the formal operations stage — freedom to contemplate the hypothetical, to compare the ideal with the actual, to be profoundly unhappy and concerned about the discrepancy between this world and that which they imagine possible.

THE CHILD AS INFORMATION-PROCESSOR

Piaget's view of the growth of mind is one approach to understanding the intellectual development of children; there are others. Some are concerned with exploring the accuracy and the usefulness of Piaget's system and with elaborating it. These approaches have informed us that Piaget's stages are perhaps not entirely universal, that transitions between them are not abrupt, and that there are sometimes marked variations in the responses of a single child to problems that appear to require the same underlying logical competence. These observations present problems for stage theories such as Piaget's and have led people like Fischer (1980), Case (1985), and Flavell (1985) to look for different stages or to suggest the use of terms such as *level* rather than stage. Still, Piaget's system continues to be the most widely known and widely researched of cognitive developmental theories.

But there is another current view of the cognitive development of the child — one that complements rather than contradicts Piaget's. It begins, as all views of the developing person must, with the observation that a newborn infant is, as my grandmother so poetically put it, "pretty dawgoned ignorant" (this is a tough translation of what might be viewed as somewhat impolite French). The expression is not at all derogatory when applied to an infant (although it was when she applied it to Frank). The difference, you see, is that the infant is supposed to be ignorant. Infants are not expected to know that day follows night, which itself follows day; that butterflies whisper to each other when they perch on buttercups in the sunshine; or that tigers have tails. In fact, they are strangers to their very own hands and feet, strangers to the world. These things are not *familiar* to them. And, as Rheingold (1985) points out, the process of development is a process of becoming familiar with the world.

The difference between the newborn — who is almost totally unfamiliar with everything around — and the older child — who has learned about tigers, tautologies, and tarantulas — can be described in a number of ways. We can say, with Piaget, that the developing child, through the processes of assimilation and accommodation, has *constructed* a sort of reality that conforms, more or less, to certain logical rules that, in turn, define a sequence of orderly stages.

Or we can say that the developing child begins with no knowledge base, few strategies for dealing with cognitive material, and no awareness of the self as a knower or as a processor of information. This approach permits us to view development as the business of acquiring a knowledge base, developing cognitive strategies, and gradually gaining an awareness of self as a knower. Put another way, this is an *information-processing approach* to cognitive development.

There are then three fundamental things that the information-processing approach looks at: the knowledge base and its creation; the processes and strategies by which information becomes part of the knowledge base or is retrieved from the base; and the emergence of the child's awareness of self as a player of what Flavell (1985) calls the "game of cognition." The first two of these relate to human memory. That is, the individual's knowledge base is made up of what is in memory; and the strategies that enable the child to develop and use a knowledge base are those that permit adding or retrieving things from memory. The third component of the information-processing approach — the recognition of self as a knower capable of using and evaluating strategies — involves what is termed *metacognition*. Literally, metacognition refers to knowing about knowing.

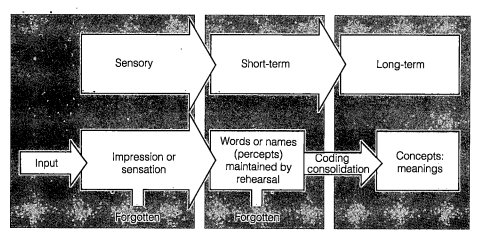

Figure 9.7

The three components of memory. The top row depicts three types of memory; the bottom row depicts the content of the memory process. Sensory information first enters sensory memory. From there it may go into short-term memory, where it is available as a name or word, for example, as long as it is rehearsed. Some of the material in short-term memory may then be coded for long-term storage, where it might take the form of meanings and concepts. It is important to note that these three components of memory do not refer to three different locations in the brain or other parts of the nervous system, but refer to how we remember — or, more precisely, how we study memory.

Source: Psychological Theories and Human Learning by Guy R. Lefrançois. Copyright 1982 by Wadsworth, Inc. Reprinted by permission of Brooks/Cole Publishing Company, Monterey, California.

Memory Components

Our information-processing model views the child as a consumer and processor of information — as a little organism that sheds its ignorance as it builds up a store of memories. The most common description of this model is based on the work of Atkinson and Shiffrin (1971), which describes the human information-processor in terms of three types of information storage: **sensory memory** (also called sensory register), **short-term memory,** and **long-term memory.** Each of these is distinguished primarily in terms of the amount and nature of processing that it involves. The term *processing* refers to such mental activities as sorting, analyzing, rehearsing, summarizing, and so on (see Figure 9.7).

Sensory memory. The first memory stage in this information-processing model requires virtually no cognitive processing. In one sense, it is nothing more elaborate than the momentary impressions associated with sensory stimulation. Our sensory systems (vision, hearing, taste, smell, touch) are sensitive to an overwhelming array of stimulation that constantly bombards them. Clearly, the bulk of this stimulation is not attended to. You cannot, at every moment, be aware of all the sights, sounds, tastes, smells, and feelings that are immediately possible — indeed, that require only that you pay attention. Hence most of the sensory stimulation that surrounds us is not processed at all, but has only a fleeting (less than one second) and unconscious effect on memory.

The most important characteristic of sensory memory from the information-processor's point of view is that although the stimulation is not attended to or processed, it is nevertheless available for processing. A series of experiments in which different messages are fed to each of a subject's ears by means of headphones serve to illustrate this. In some of these experiments subjects are instructed to pay attention to the message being broadcast into one ear while other unrelated messages are fed to the other ear (Cherry, 1953). Later questioning typically shows that subjects have no memory whatsoever of what has transpired in the unattended ear. In fact, they fail to notice changes from one language to another (Broadbent, 1952) and cannot recall the message even when it consists of only a single word repeated as many as 35 times (Moray, 1959). But when the subject's name is mentioned a *single* time in the unattended ear, attention shifts immediately. This phenomenon is sometimes called the *cocktail-party phenomenon* because it can often be observed in crowded rooms where individuals busily engaged in one conversation will turn immediately when their name is spoken by someone else across the room.

Short-term memory. Your ability to recall the beginning of a sentence as you read it illustrates short-term memory. And if you cannot remember the beginning of the sentence, it is usually because you are not paying *attention*. The consequence of not paying attention is that the stimulation being ignored (not being attended to) flits through sensory memory but never makes it to short-term memory.

Another way of looking at short-term memory is to say that it includes everything that is immediately conscious (everything that is now being attended to). In a sense, short-term memory is equivalent to attention span. It is also called "working" memory (Dempter, 1985). Or, as Calfee (1981) puts it, it is sort of a scratch pad for thinking. But this scratch pad has two important limitations: First, its capacity appears to be limited to around seven items (plus or minus two) (Miller, 1956); second, it seems to hold material only for seconds rather than minutes.

The storage limitations of short-term memory — of attention spans — are evident in the fact that we can typically consider only around seven discrete items at one time. We can glance carelessly at a flock of geese drifting through an autumn sky and *see*, without having to count one, two, three . . . , that there are exactly four or six or even seven geese. But if there were 13, our immediate estimate would be just that — an estimate or a guess. We cannot hold 13 separate geese simultaneously on the screens of our short-term memories. But these storage limitations are perhaps not as serious as they might seem. Whereas it is true that we seem to be able to attend to only about seven items at once, a process called **chunking** can be used to increase memory capacity significantly. Chunking is nothing more complex than grouping into related units — three

We are constantly bombarded by sensory stimulation — though perhaps not as dramatically as this girl. Fortunately for our sanity, we are unaware of most of this stimulation.

groups of four geese and a stubborn loner. Miller (1956) illustrates the process by reference to a change purse that can hold only seven coins. If you put seven pennies into this purse, then its full capacity is seven cents. If, however, you fill it with seven groupings (chunks) of pennies — such as nickels, dimes, or quarters — its total capacity increases dramatically.

Some people slip golden coins into the purses of their memories.

One common measure of short-term memory is to have subjects try to repeat a sequence of unrelated numbers they have just heard — a task that is used on a number of intelligence tests. Average adolescents and adults are able to repeat correctly six or seven (or sometimes even nine) digits. In contrast, 6-year-olds will typically succeed in repeating only two or so.

The child's limited *working* memory may be extremely important in explaining some aspects of cognitive development. Siegler (1989), for example, suggests that children are often unable to solve certain problems simply because they cannot keep in mind all relevant information simultaneously. Put another way, the ways in which they **encode** (represent in memory) information are different. And Case (Case et al; 1988), in his neo-Piagetian theory of cognitive development, claims that the most important constraint on the child's use of schemes to understand and to solve problems is simply a limitation on short-term storage space.

Sensory memory, as we saw, does not involve cognitive processing, but is simply a fleeting impression almost like an echo. In contrast, short-term memory is highly dependent upon *rehearsal* or repetition. Without this type of processing, the material quickly fades and is forgotten. When I look up a telephone number and dial it immediately, I need only repeat the number for as long as it takes to dial it. Typically, by the time I have finished dialing, I will no longer remember the number. It resided in short-term memory for only that brief period during which it was rehearsed, and then it disappeared again.

Long-term memory. But if I think I might need the number again tomorrow, there are several things I can do. One is simply to write it down so that I will not have to remember it. That would impose little cognitive strain. I would not have to use any of the strategies required to move material from short-term to long-term storage. Still, however, it would require the use of long-term memory; tomorrow I would have to remember not only that I made a note of the necessary number, but also where that note is. And I would have to remember a tremendous range of other information as well, including how to translate telephone numbers into the orderly and sequential act of dialing, how to speak and listen with a telephone, and so on. Put another way, even as habitual a behavior as using a telephone requires quite a large knowledge base. And our knowledge base is, in effect, our long-term memory. It includes everything we know — about ourselves, about the world, about knowing.

Our contemporary models or metaphors for long-term memory are almost invariably **associationistic.** That is, they are based on the fundamental notion that all items of information in our memories are associated or connected in a variety of ways. It is precisely because of these associations that we are able to remember so impressively — in many ways, far more impressively, in fact, than a computer (Wickelgren, 1981). Computer memories typically work on the basis of location; items have *addresses* that permit them to be found. In contrast, our human memories seem to be ordered by content (in other words, by meaning) rather than location. All we need to know is what to look for, and not where.

The associationistic view of human memory has led to a number of abstract models to describe what it is that is stored in long-term memory over periods of minutes, weeks, or years. These models are essentially cognitive; they relate to associations that are based on meaning, and they make use of a variety of terms including *nodes, schemas, scripts, frames, networks, categories, coding systems,* and others. These labels serve as metaphors and not as literal descriptions. They do not say long-term memory *is* such and such but, rather, long-term memory is *like* such and such or might be *compared* to such and such. These terms are, in effect, models of the structure of knowledge — models of our knowledge base. As Bransford (1979) suggests, they are models of the educated mind.

Schemata and Scripts

Historically, much of the research on memory has dealt with the ability to remember specific items (numbers, words). However, there may not be a very close relationship between the ability to remember a list of 12 items and memory in real-life situations. It seems intuitively clear that in most real-life situations, we remember meanings rather than specific instances (Smith & Graesser, 1981). When someone tells you a funny story, you remember its gist and perhaps the wording of the punch line, but seldom the exact wording of the entire story, the pauses, the intonations, and the facial expressions of the speaker. Put another way, what appears to be remembered are the cognitive beasties sometimes called **schemata.** Schemata are like clusters of knowledge that define concepts. They are what we know about this or that. Our schemata relating to aardvarks might include items of knowledge relating to size, color, characteristic sounds, general reputation, and their habit of dancing extravagant mazurkas. They might also include some affective (emotional) reactions having to do with the taste of these creatures or their smell. If someone tells me a story about aardvarks, what I remember of the story will be profoundly influenced by my aardvark schema.

One aspect of schemata that is particularly important in remembering real-life information like what goes with what, the gist of stories, or even such mundane things as whether desserts come before or after soups and salads is called a **script.** Scripts are the part of cognitive structure (of knowledge — hence of schemata) that deals with routines and sequences. We all know the script for going into a restaurant, eating, and ordering . . . which is why the first part of this sentence jars. Our scripts say ordering and then eating, not vice versa.

Current work on children's memories indicates that their story memories, like ours, are highly dependent on their relevant schemata and scripts. For example, when children are told script-based stories, they tend to fill in gaps according to their personal scripts. In one study, M. K. Johnson, Bransford, and Solomon (1973) presented subjects with the following short passage:

> John was trying to fix the birdhouse. He was pounding the nail when his father came out to watch him and to help him do the work.

When subjects were later shown these sentences along with others, one of which was

> John was using the hammer to fix the birdhouse when his father came out to watch and to help him do the work.

they overwhelmingly agreed that they had seen the last sentence rather than the two that they had actually seen. Note that the hammer was not even mentioned in the original text. It seems clear that subjects recalled the central ideas of the two sentences and "generated" the hammer because hammers are what we use to pound nails. Their birdhouse-building scripts, like yours and mine, use hammers.

One of the clear implications of the observation that we often "generate" on the basis of our understanding when attempting to remember is that understanding should facilitate memory. Paris and Lindauer (1976) asked children to remember the simple sentence "The workman dug a hole in the ground," adding "with a shovel" for half their subjects. One of the recall procedures was to present subjects with cue words (in this case, *shovel*). It is significant that the word *shovel* served equally well as a cue for those children who had not seen the word in the original sentence. It seems clear that the cue word would have been totally meaningless for children who did not initially understand that holes can be dug with shovels.

Memory Processes

There are three basic processes involved in remembering: rehearsal, organization, and elaboration. In addition, there are a number of specific strategies that can be employed with each of these processes (Horton & Mills, 1984).

Rehearsal, as we saw, involves repetition and is importantly involved in maintaining information in short-term memory as well as in transferring material from short- to long-term storage. The simplest rehearsal strategy is to name the material (five, five, five, one, two, one, two) over and over again until it seems unlikely that it will escape. More elaborate rehearsal strategies involve associating mental images with what is to be remembered (Higbee, 1977). Most children younger than 5 do not spontaneously rehearse and cannot easily be taught to do so (Wellman, 1988).

To *elaborate* is to extend material or add something to it in order to make it more memorable. For example, elaboration might consist of forming associations between new material and existing knowledge, or of creating mental images that go beyond (elaborate on) the actual material. Elaboration that relates to the meaning of what is being learned seems most effective. Bradshaw and Anderson (1982) had subjects try to recall sentences such as "The fat man read the sign." Those who elaborated this sentence to something like "The fat man read the sign warning of thin ice" significantly improved their ability to remember that the man in question was fat. Again, younger children do not spontaneously elaborate to improve recall. By age 12, memory strategies of this kind are more common (Justice, 1985).

Organization as a memory process refers to the act of grouping and relating material. Chunking material into related groups is one example of organization. Assume, for example, that you have been asked to memorize the following list as rapidly as you can: pencil, horse, pen, house, barn, cat, apartment building, bear, typewriter. Some of you will immediately notice that the list can easily be organized into three groups of related items (animals, dwellings, writing instruments) and will use this organization to help remember the items. Interestingly, however, young children will not organize material the way you would. Their use of strategies is more limited than yours; they know less about knowing (see Figure 9.8).

Figure 9.8

Three basic pro-
cesses involved in re-
membering. Before
age 5, children do
not spontaneously
use these strategies
for remembering and
cannot easily be
taught to do so.
After age 5, many will
have learned to re-
hearse when they
want to remember
something; but be-
fore age 12, most will
not elaborate and
organize as deliber-
ately and systemati-
cally as would an
adult.

Rehearsal   Elaboration   Organization

The Development of Memory

An information-processing model of memory is particularly useful for looking
at the development of memory because it leads to a number of predictions
about infant and child memory that can be tested directly. We would expect,
for example, that for the stages of memory that involve little cognitive processing, young children might not perform very differently from older children or
adults but that where processing strategies are necessary, there would be more
differences between younger and older children. In other words, there should
be a correspondence between the child's development of skills relating to rehearsing, organizing, and elaborating and the ability to recall material over a
longer period of time.

In general, the predictions derived from information-processing theories of
memory have been supported by research. That is, recall that does not depend
on processing strategies does not appear to change very much as the child
develops. For example, recognition memory, a task that does not ordinarily
involve complex strategies, is highly accurate from early childhood on (Paris &
Lindauer, 1982). Similarly, comparisons between adults and children with respect to sensory and short-term memories – neither of which requires any
strategy more elaborate than simple repetition – have found few significant
differences.

It appears that short-term and sensory memory change little from childhood to adulthood because they do not require the use of elaborate or cognitively demanding strategies. By the same token, recall that is highly dependent on the use of processing strategies should improve as the child's recognition and understanding of strategies improves. This prediction too is supported by the evidence. It appears that very young children do not rehearse and organize as systematically as older children (Gitomer & Pellegrino, 1985). Paris and Lindauer (1982) note that research has found significant developmental changes in memory under at least four sets of circumstances: when the memory tasks require intentional memorization, when the material is unfamiliar, when specific organizational strategies are required, and when the task requires a change in the learner's strategies.

Liberty and Ornstein (1973) presented fourth-graders and college students (average ages 10 and 19, respectively) with a list of 28 words, each printed on a separate card. Subjects were asked to sort the cards, face up, into bins on the table in front of them so they would be easier to learn. The sorting procedure was repeated six times or until the subject sorted consistently (always put the same cards together). At this point, subjects were tested for recall.

There are two important findings from this study. The first is that older subjects consistently remembered more words than did the younger subjects, which is not surprising given that the task is essentially one of long-term recall. The second finding is perhaps more revealing because it corroborates the hypothesis that processing strategies are less adequate in younger children. Whereas there were relatively few differences in the ways different college students chose to group the words, younger subjects were far more idiosyncratic.

It appears that the most important developmental changes in children's memories have to do with the use of the three basic processes involved in remembering — and especially in long-term memory: rehearsal, elaboration, and organization. Preschoolers apparently seldom use these strategies to learn and remember. Appel et al. (1972) showed 4-, 7-, and 11-year-olds pictures under two sets of instructions: "Look at these pictures" or "Remember these pictures." When the 7- and 11-year-olds were asked to remember, they deliberately employed strategies to aid their recall. In contrast, 4-year-olds behaved exactly the same way under both sets of instructions, relying on recognition rather than strategies.

METACOGNITION AND METAMEMORY

Not only are younger children less capable of organizing material but they also seem to be less aware of the importance of doing so. In other words, they seem to know less about knowing, to understand less about understanding (Flavell, 1982). They are not reflective about themselves as knowers and seem not to have recognized the special skills that allow them to know and remember. Put another way, they still lack in metacognitive skills.

Knowledge about knowing is termed **metacognition.** The skills of metacognition are what allow us to monitor our own progress, to estimate the effects of our efforts to learn, and to predict our likelihood of success in remembering. They tell us that there are ways in which to organize material so that it will be easier to learn and remember, that there are rehearsal and review strategies that are more effective for one kind of learning than another, and that some kinds of learning require the deliberate application of cognitive strategies whereas others do not. In other words, metacognition refers to knowing about knowing rather than simply to the content of what is known. And because memory is inseparably linked with cognition, it includes what is sometimes labeled **metamemory** — knowing about remembering.

Metacognitive skills seem to be largely absent in young children. This does not mean that they use no memory or learning strategies; it simply means that they are not aware of them, that they do not consciously apply them. When Moynahan (1973) asked young children whether it would be easier to learn a categorized list of words or a random list, children below third grade selected either list; children in third grade were more likely to select the categorized list. Paradoxically, even when children are capable of engaging in useful memory strategies, they often do not.

Borkowski, Milstead, and Hale (1988) point out that among children there is a greater spread between memory behavior and memory knowledge (metamemory) than there is among adults. They suggest that the explanation for this is that metamemory consists of different components, not all of which are learned and used at the same time. One of the components of metamemory is *knowledge of specific strategies* — knowing, for instance, that grouping items might facilitate recall. Specific strategies such as this are sometimes understood by young children or can be taught to them (Pressley, Forrest-Pressley, & Elliott-Faust, 1988). Another component has to do with knowing how and when to use a specific strategy — a component that Borkowski et al. (1988) label *metamemory acquisition procedures.* Teachers are often not very systematic about teaching memory skills, say Borkowski and associates. As a result, children are usually left to decide on their own whether a strategy should be used, what strategy, when, and how. It should come as little surprise, then, that they often know *about* a strategy but do not spontaneously use it.

Metamemory and Self-Efficacy

Knowing about strategies and their usefulness is only one of the factors involved in learning and remembering; **motivation** is another.

Motives are the *whys* of behavior. They are what account for the fact that behavior occurs in the first place. They also serve to direct it, and they explain its termination. At an oversimplified biological level, the need for food — what we understand as *hunger* — accounts for food-related behaviors such as going to a restaurant, ordering, and eating. And the eventual satisfaction of this need explains why we stop eating and leave the restaurant. As noted, however, this illustration is oversimplified. Other factors — such as the availability of a restaurant or of sufficient funds, or the wish to maintain a trim figure — also have a lot to do with directing this behavior. But perhaps most important, it is our *knowledge* about the relationship between restaurants, money, food, and hunger that drives our actions. We can *imagine* the succulent broccoli on a plate as we read "Vegetarian Delights," or the juicy drumstick as we decode "Chicken In Hurry." Ultimately, it is our anticipations, our cognitions, that move us.

Cognitions motivate our behaviors, says Bandura (1989a), in the sense that they allow us to preview the consequences of our actions and thus to establish goals. And this process is intimately linked with how competent and capable we think we are. As we saw in Chapter 2, those who have high estimates of personal competence — what Bandura labels high *self-efficacy* — are most likely to accept difficult challenges and set high goals. Those who see themselves as less effective — who lack confidence — set lower goals and give up rapidly when they begin to fail.

The best learners — hence those who are best at using memory strategies — are typically individuals who have positive beliefs about the efficacy of their memories. As we noted, simply knowing about memory strategies is not enough. When Rebok and Balcerak (1989) taught a specific memory strategy for remembering words, subjects later used the strategy only if they believed it made them better memorizers. Those whose perceived memory-efficacy was unaffected by the training did not spontaneously use the strategy. Bandura (1989) concludes: "Training in cognitive skills can produce more generalized and lasting effects if it raises self-beliefs of efficacy as well as imparts skills." In addition to awareness of specific strategies, children's metacognitive and metamemory skills need to include notions of themselves as competent, skillful knowers and rememberers.

Cultural Differences

Cognitive strategies are learned; accordingly, they reflect the effects of schooling and of culture. For example, memory strategies such as categorization appear to be more common among German children than among children in the United States (Schneider et al., 1986). Similarly, studies have demonstrated that in the absence of schooling, children (and adults) do not perform as well on many cognitive and memory tasks (Das & Dash, 1990). Not only does schooling add to the child's knowledge base, claim Das and Dash, but it also enhances cognitive skills. And the single factor that is perhaps most intimately involved in increasing cognitive skills and knowledge base is literacy. As Olson (1986) put it, "Language makes us human; literacy makes us civilized . . ." (p. 109).

Reading requires the exercising of what Kirby and Das (1990) describe as among the most important cognitive processes: planning, attending, and processing. It is inevitable that it should also lead to advances in other cognitive skills and strategies.

Metacognition and metamemory deal with our knowledge about how we know — our awareness of ourselves as players of what Flavell (1985) calls the "game of cognition." The object of the game of cognition is to pay attention, to learn, to remember, to retrieve from memory, and to do a variety of things such as sorting, analyzing, synthesizing, evaluating, creating, and so on.

There is more than one way to play the game of cognition. Some people play it very badly. They learn slowly, remember inaccurately, and seem lost and clumsy when faced with tasks requiring evaluations, synthesis, or creation. Others play it very well. Their responses are quick and accurate, their syntheses elegant, their creations startling.

One of the differences between those who play the game of cognition well and those who play less well — but by no means the only difference — is that the better players have better tools with which to play. Put another way, their **cognitive strategies** are better.

Simply defined, cognitive strategies are what control cognitive behavior. It is a cognitive strategy that tells one person to rehearse a list of the aardvark's characteristics and another person to create bizarre mental images of the creature. The strategy itself has nothing to do with the content of what is learned, remembered, or retrieved, but deals only with the processes involved in these activities. In Gagné and Briggs's (1983) words, it is "contentless." In this sense, cognitive strategies are related to what we call *intelligence.* And perhaps to *creativity* as well.

INTELLIGENCE

"Intelligence is what the tests test," Boring (1923, p. 35) informed us. This, perhaps the simplest available definition of what is not a simple concept, is a useful and not entirely tongue-in-cheek definition. *Weight* is not a simple concept either. Yet to say that weight is what a scale measures is, in fact, useful and accurate. A butcher need not understand or know the scientific definition of weight to make proper use of the scales. Perhaps a psychologist or a teacher need not know what intelligence is to make use of the results of intelligence tests.

And then again, perhaps we do need to know, because there is a fundamental difference between measuring weight and measuring intelligence. We agree about weight; we *know* what it is. We define it precisely and objectively. Our scales measure weight with marvelous accuracy. They measure exactly what they are supposed to measure, and nothing else (in measurement terms, they are **valid**). And they measure consistently, yielding the same measurements for the same weights over and over again (again in measurement terms, they are **reliable**).

What Is It?

But we do not know exactly what **intelligence** is. A number of theorists have assumed that it is a quality of human functioning that depends on some basic, general capacity or trait in the person — that if you have a lot of this general something (popularly referred to as *g*), your behavior will be intelligent in all areas. In other words, if this supposition is correct, those who are highly intelligent (have high *g*) should do well in all tasks: mathematical, verbal, spatial, reasoning, memory, and so on. **General factor theory,** as it is known, originated with Spearman (1927).

A second broad approach to the definition of intelligence is based on the assumption that rather than depend on a common underlying factor, intelligence consists of a number of separate abilities. One example of the **special abilities theory** is provided by Thurstone (1938), who identified seven "primary mental abilities" on the basis of test results and who defined intelligence in terms of these abilities:

S   *(space)* visualization of geometric figures from different angles

N   *(number)* speed of computational skills

P   *(perceptual speed)* speed of perceiving details

V   *(verbal meanings)* grasp of meanings of words

W   *(word fluency)* speed of manipulating single words

M   *(rote memory)* facility in memorizing simple material

I   *(induction)* logical reasoning ability

Gardner's Approach

Gardner (1983), like Thurstone, rejects the notion of a single, global capacity underlying intelligence. But unlike Thurstone, Gardner does not speak of separate intellectual abilities, but of separate and distinct intelligences — of, in his words, *multiple intelligences.* There are, Gardner informs us, six broad forms of these intelligences: linguistic, musical, logical-mathematical, spatial, bodily-kinesthetic, and personal (having to do with interpersonal skills and self-knowledge). In any given society, one or more of these intelligences will be considered more important than others. In ours, for example, linguistic and logico-mathematical skills are clearly most important. Accordingly, these are the skills that are taught in our schools. And they are also the skills that are most often measured by our intelligence tests.

Cattell's Approach

Cattell's approach to defining and measuring intelligence has important developmental implications. Cattell (1971) distinguishes between two kinds of intelligence. There are, on the one hand, certain abilities that seem to underlie much of our intelligent behavior. These abilities, labeled **fluid abilities** (or sometimes *fluid intelligence*) are not learned and are therefore relatively unaffected by cultural and environmental influences. Fluid abilities are manifested in the individual's ability to solve abstract problems, and are evident in measures of general reasoning, memory, attention span, and analysis of figures.

In contrast to these basic fluid abilities is a grouping of intellectual abilities that are primarily verbal and that are highly influenced by culture, experience, and education. These abilities, labeled **crystallized abilities** (or *crystallized intelligence*), are reflected in measures of vocabulary, general information, and arithmetic skills.

There are several developmental predictions that can be based on the notion of fluid and crystallized intelligence. First, because fluid intelligence is independent of experience, it should remain constant throughout most of development, increasing slightly perhaps as the nervous system matures through childhood and adolescence, and maybe decreasing somewhat in old age as the nervous system ages. Second, because crystallized intelligence is highly dependent on experience, it should grow with increasing age, perhaps right through old age.

These predictions have been extensively investigated by Horn and Donaldson (Horn, 1976; Horn & Donaldson, 1980), who report that crystallized abilities do increase, sometimes into very old age, and that fluid abilities show some slight declines during old age. Other researchers argue that decline with age has been exaggerated and is neither inevitable nor irreversible.

Sternberg's Approach

Intelligence, Sternberg (1984) informs us, is a *contextual* quality — that is, it is a quality of human functioning that is best defined in terms of the context in which it occurs. More simply, intelligence is what makes adaptation possible, and adaptation occurs in specific contexts. Thus certain behaviors may be highly intelligent in one context but quite unintelligent in others. In Sternberg's (1984) words, intelligence is the "purposive selection and shaping of and adaptation to real-world environments relevant to one's life" (p. 312).

How do we find out what intelligence is in a particular context? One way, according to Sternberg, is to ask people. If you ask enough people, you might arrive at a pretty clear definition. In North American cultures, that definition would include three broad groupings of abilities. Intelligent people are those who have high practical problem-solving ability, who have high verbal ability, and who are socially competent. Elsewhere, the definition might be somewhat different.

But there is more to intelligence than these abilities, Sternberg (1985) suggests: There are three major components that together lead to the **triarchic theory** of human intelligence. The three arches are *metacomponents, performance components*, and *knowledge-acquisition components*.

The metacomponents are the cognitive strategies of which we spoke earlier. Sternberg identifies a number of cognitive strategies including skills re-

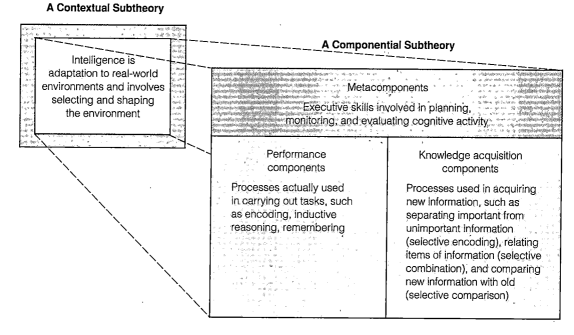

A Contextual Subtheory

Intelligence is adaptation to real-world environments and involves selecting and shaping the environment

A Componential Subtheory

Metacomponents

Executive skills involved in planning, monitoring, and evaluating cognitive activity.

Performance components

Processes actually used in carrying out tasks, such as encoding, inductive reasoning, remembering

Knowledge acquisition components

Processes used in acquiring new information, such as separating important from unimportant information (selective encoding), relating items of information (selective combination), and comparing new information with old (selective comparison)

Figure 9.9

Sternberg's information-processing view of intelligence consists of three related subtheories. The first two, the contextual and the componential, are represented here; the third relates intelligence to experience with different tasks.

lated to problem identification (skills involved in selecting a process for solving a problem); skills related to allocation of resources; and skills related to monitoring one's cognitive processes (being sensitive to feedback and changing strategies or modifying them). This component of intelligence includes what we have been discussing as metacognition or metamemory (Gardner, 1985).

Performance components relate to actually doing — in contrast to the metacomponents, which are involved in selecting problems and procedures, responding to feedback, changing procedures, and so on. Put another way, the metacomponents of intellectual functioning define its executive functions, its decision-making functions. Performance refers simply to the execution of decisions made at the metacomponent level.

Knowledge acquisition components are what is actually achieved in the process of learning. This component has to do with adaptation. Hence it relates directly to Sternberg's contextualist view of intelligence (see Figure 9.9).

Measuring Intelligence

The principal use of intelligence tests is for prediction. An intelligence test score is, in effect, a prediction that an individual will do well (or not do well) on tasks that require intelligence. It says, "so-and-so has an *aptitude* for doing well on things that require intelligence." But we have not reached complete agreement on what intelligence is — on what it is that so-and-so needs to do well. As a result, some people prefer to measure aptitude rather than intelligence. An aptitude is something more specific than intelligence; thus there is musical aptitude, numerical aptitude, reading aptitude, even scholastic aptitude. The term *aptitude,* being specific rather than general, does not have the same connotations as the term *intelligence.* Being told that you have low scholastic aptitude is not nearly as devastating as being told that you have low intelligence.

Among the most widely used and respected intelligence tests are the Stanford-Binet and the Wechsler. These are individual intelligence tests; that is, they can be administered to only one child at a time and only by a trained tester. They yield a richer picture of intellectual functioning than do group tests — tests that can be administered to a large group at one time and that are commonly of a paper-and-pencil variety.

The Stanford-Binet. The Stanford-Binet (4th edition; Thorndike, Hagen, & Saitler, 1985) consists of a wide range of different types of questions. At the youngest age levels, for example, it requires children to identify parts of the body on a large paper doll; to build a tower with blocks; to recognize objects in terms of their functions ("show me the one that we drink out of; can cut with; use to iron clothes"); to string beads; to copy simple geometric designs. At higher age levels, it asks subjects to repeat digits (in order and reversed); to answer questions based on a story; to define words; to name the days of the week; to identify synonyms and antonyms. And at adult levels, it requires the solution of arithmetic problems; the explanation of proverbs; discrimination between abstract words; and the solution of complex problems. And these are only a few of the more than 100 different *tests* that comprise the Stanford-Binet.

The Stanford-Binet yields scores in four separate areas: verbal reasoning, quantitative reasoning, abstract/visual reasoning, and short-term memory. It also provides a composite score that is described as a measure of "adaptive ability" and that can be interpreted as an **intelligence quotient (IQ).** The IQ derives its meaning from the fact that we know that the *average* IQ of large, unselected populations is around 100, and that it is distributed as shown in Figure 9.10. Note that approximately two-thirds of all individuals have measured IQs that range between 85 and 115. Fewer than 2.5 percent score above 130 or below 70.

The Stanford-Binet has traditionally been a highly verbal test that correlates relatively well with school success. Because it was highly verbal, however, it tended to penalize children whose language development was different from or slower than that of the "average" child. However, the fourth edition of the test is designed to reduce this limitation.

The Wechsler tests. The Wechsler tests yield a composite IQ score comparable to that obtained with the Stanford-Binet. The tests differ in several important respects, however. Most notably, the Wechsler scales also yield separate standardized scores for a variety of subjects, as well as a verbal IQ and a performance

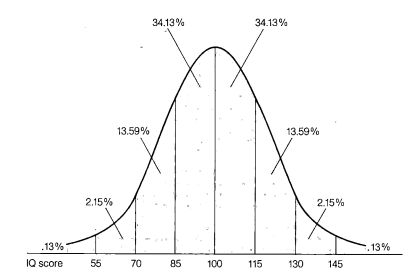

Figure 9.10

A normal curve depicting the theoretical distribution of IQ scores among humans. Note, for example, that the average score is 100 and that 68.26 percent of the population scores between 85 and 115. Only 2.28 percent scores above 130.

IQ (in addition to the composite IQ). Deficiencies in language background are frequently evident in disparities between verbal and performance scores.

Among the various forms of the Wechsler tests are the WAIS–R (Wechsler Adult Intelligence Scale Revised, ages 16 to 75), the WISC–R (Wechsler Intelligence Scale for Children Revised, ages 5 to 15), and the WPPSI (Wechsler Preschool and Primary Scale of Intelligence, ages 4 to 6½). The various subtests of the WISC–R are described in Table 9.2.

Developmental Changes in IQ

A normal 6-year-old child can correctly repeat two or three digits if they are given to him clearly and distinctly at a rate of approximately one per second, but would not be expected to repeat four digits in reverse order. An average 3-year-old can quickly identify legs, arms, hands, nose, and mouth on a doll, but might hesitate if asked to point to the infranasal depression. Clearly, there is a marked improvement in children's problem solving, remembering, language, reasoning, and so on. Does that mean that intelligence improves?

The answer, of course, depends on how intelligence is defined. If it is defined simply in terms of being able to *do* those things we consider to be examples of intelligent behavior (like remembering, reasoning accurately, and expressing oneself clearly), then the answer is yes, children become more intelligent with age. But if intelligence is defined *psychometrically* (that is, in terms of how we measure it), the answer is no. Measured IQ is not an absolute indicator of how much or what a child can do; instead, it is a measure of what a child can do *compared* with what other children of similar ages and experience can do. And because all comparable children improve at similar rates and in similar ways (on the average), then the *average* child's measured intelligence does not change from year to year. By definition, it stays right around 100.

Table 9.2
The Wechsler Intelligence Scale for Children Revised (WISC—R)

Verbal Scale	Performance Scale
1. **General information** Child is asked questions relating to information most children have the opportunity to acquire.	1. **Picture completion** Child indicates what is missing on pictures.
2. **General comprehension** Child is asked questions designed to assess understanding of why certain things are done as they are.	2. **Picture arrangement** Child arranges a series of pictures to tell a story.
3. **Arithmetic** Child is given oral arithmetic problems.	3. **Block design** Child is required to copy a design exactly with colored blocks.
4. **Similarities** Child indicates how certain things are alike.	4. **Object assembly** Child assembles puzzles.
5. **Vocabulary** Child gives meanings of words.	5. **Coding** Child pairs symbols with digits following a key.
6. **Digit span** Child repeats orally presented sequence of numbers, in order and reversed.	6. **Mazes** Child traces way out of mazes with pencil.

But, as we have said more than once, there is no average child; the average is merely a mathematical invention. What about the individual?

The individual, research informs us, may display a great variety of intellectual developmental patterns. As a result, measured differences between two individuals do not necessarily remain constant. For some children, measured IQ may increase over a period of years; or it may decrease; or it might go up and down like a bouncing ball (McCall, Applebaum & Hogarty, 1973). For the majority, however, measured IQ is relatively stable; it fluctuates within a range that would be expected given the imprecision of the tests.

As we noted earlier, intelligence tests given early in life (for example, before the age of 2) do not correlate very highly with those given in later childhood or adolescence. However, the correlation between tests given at later ages is generally quite high (in the order of .7 or more). Patterns of change in measured intelligence through the adult years and into old age have been the source of some controversy. It appears, however, that abilities that are influenced by schooling and culture such as general information, arithmetic skill, and verbal comprehension (Cattell's crystallized abilities) may increase well into old age. In contrast, abilities that are more independent of experience and perhaps more dependent on the smooth functioning of an unimpaired nervous system may show some decline in old age. These include some reasoning tasks and tests of perceptual speed (Cattell's fluid abilities). In general, however, barring injury or disease, observed declines are usually inconsequential until well into old age (Honzik, 1984).

There is still considerable conflict and disagreement about what constitutes intelligence. Special aptitudes—such as musical, numerical, verbal, or even scholastic—are easier to define and measure.

Misconceptions About and Misuses of IQ

We sometimes assume that all individuals have an "IQ," as though this IQ were a fixed something possessed in lesser or greater quantities by everyone. In fact, the IQ is simply a mathematical expression based largely on a person's ability to perform in prescribed circumstances. It does not reveal mystical, hidden qualities that would otherwise be known only by clever psychologists who have dedicated their lives to the pursuit of the hidden truth. Given the questionable validity and reliability of intelligence tests, even if intelligence were a fixed, detectable, and measurable quality of human performance, we have not yet developed the tools to detect and measure it accurately.

It is also widely believed that IQ is very highly related to success, especially in school. And it is, in fact, correct that measured intelligence correlates moderately highly with performance in school. But numerous studies have shown that previous success correlates even more highly with present or future success than does IQ (Cohen, 1972). Although IQ is important, it is perhaps not all that important.

Traditional measures of intelligence have two additional weaknesses. First, they typically do not measure a wide variety of interpersonal skills, athletic ability, creativity, and many personality variables that are very important to the individual (Weinberg, 1989). Second, many intelligence tests have been culturally biased; they penalized children whose backgrounds were different from the dominant white, middle-class majority. They were culturally biased because they were constructed with the middle-class child in mind and because they were usually standardized on samples comprising middle-class children. It was almost inevitable that children from minority groups would do less well on these tests than their like-aged, middle-class, white counterparts. However, the most recent revisions of the Wechsler and the Stanford-Binet have taken this weakness into account and have used more representative norming samples. Accordingly, they are much fairer to minorities.

Despite the many weaknesses of intelligence tests, they are extremely widely used, particularly in schools. Unfortunately, they are not at all widely understood. Psychologists, educators, and parents all too often behave as though IQ were fixed, measurable, and so important that it must be shrouded in secrecy, for some have more and others less, some are bright and others stupid — and would it not be thoroughly unfair and perhaps even a little undemocratic to make public such important knowledge?

The important point is that the knowledge may not be nearly so valid or important as we have assumed it to be (Gould, 1981). We are still measuring something that we cannot define, and not measuring it very accurately in any case. Furthermore, our tests are often unfair, not only because they are intrinsically unfair for certain children (they are not **culture-fair**) but also because we use them unfairly. We base some of our most important educational decisions on numbers that represent an unknown, that bear a moderate and sometimes unimpressive relationship to school success, and that are widely known to be highly variable (unreliable).

This is not an argument for abandoning intelligence testing, although it has been abandoned in a number of jurisdictions — usually at the insistence of parent groups. Rather, the argument is for the restrained and intelligent use of information derived from tests. This means that no important decisions should be based on a single test and that considerable additional information about the individuals concerned should affect our decisions. And perhaps nowhere is this more true than when dealing with exceptional children.

INTELLECTUAL EXCEPTIONALITY

Exceptionality refers to mental, physical, or social/emotional functioning that departs significantly from the norm in *either* direction. Thus there are those who are exceptionally gifted, who possess extraordinary talents; and there are those to whom nature and nurture have been less kind. In the remaining pages of this chapter, we speak of both dimensions of intellectual exceptionality: mental retardation on the one hand and intellectual giftedness or very high creativity on the other.

Mental Retardation

Definition. The most obvious feature of **mental retardation** is a general depression in ability to learn, a feature that is not so obvious as a concomitant depression in adaptive behavior. These two characteristics make up the widely accepted definition of retardation presented by the American Association on Mental Deficiency (AAMD): "Mental retardation refers to significantly sub-average general intellectual functioning existing concurrently with deficits in adaptive behavior, and manifested during the developmental period" (Grossman, 1983). The AAMD definition of mental retardation is essentially the definition now adopted by the American Psychiatric Association (1980) as well.

The meaning of *mental retardation* within the context of this definition is clarified by Grossman's (1983) analysis of the key terms involved. First "general intellectual functioning" is defined in terms of test scores on one or more of the well-known individual intelligence tests — for example, the Stanford-Binet or the Wechsler Scales. An IQ of 70 is the accepted (and admittedly inexact) cutoff between normalcy and mental retardation.

Second, impairments in adaptive behavior are described as significant maturational deficits, most often manifested in inability to learn and/or inability to reach the levels of independence, social responsibility, or social effectiveness that would normally be expected. Failure to learn to dress oneself during the preschool period might be one indication of an impairment in adaptive behavior; failure to toilet train would be another.

Finally, the definition specifies that the deficits must be manifested during the developmental period — a period that extends from conception to age 18.

Identification. In practice, mental retardation is most often identifed and defined by performance on intelligence tests, with some occasional, though limited, attention to adaptive behavior, a characteristic that is difficult to measure or define (Landesman & Ramey, 1989). In an important departure from this traditional approach, Feuerstein (1979) suggests that the most useful assessments of mental retardation should not be based on static measures of intelligence. They should not simply reflect how the child has benefited from experience until now, but rather should give some indication of the child's capacities for benefiting from experience in the future. Feuerstein argues that what is needed is a dynamic assessment of intellectual potential. To this end he developed a *Learning Potential Assessment Device (LPAD)*, which focuses on intellectual functioning — on intellectual processes — rather than simply on whether or not the child is capable of responding correctly. The instrument (actually a modification of several existing tests) permits the examiner to teach the child — to offer hints and clues, to direct and aid. In the end, it may give a much more useful picture of the child's potential, as well as of possible remediation.

Prevalence and causes. Estimates of the prevalence of mental retardation vary. The normal distribution of intelligence in the general population suggests that between 2 and 3 percent of the population are retarded (Scheiner & McNabb, 1980). If level of adaptation is taken into account, only 1 percent is actually retarded (Mercer, 1973) — thus the importance of considering this factor as well as measured intelligence.

The causes of mental retardation are also varied. They may be related to brain damage or to hereditary and environmental influences. Chromosomal aberrations and defects like those seen in Down syndrome (see Chapter 3) or maternal conditions such as rubella, drugs, radiation, infections, malnutrition, and other factors may be implicated (MacMillan, 1982). Although identifying causes may be very important, particularly for medicine and genetics, it is much less important for special educators and clinicians. Hence mentally retarded children are ordinarily described in terms of degree rather than cause of exceptionality.

Categories and characteristics. Important distinctions are made among four categories of retardation: mild, moderate, severe, and profound. These categories are defined in terms of scores on intelligence tests (Figure 9.11). Overlapping categories that are of more practical use for special educators distinguish among educable, trainable, and custodial retardation.

The largest proportion of retarded children (approximately 75 percent) are only mildly retarded. Most of these children are not identified as being retarded until they enter school. Before this time, they ordinarily develop social and language skills and experience relatively normal motor development. In school, most are capable of academic achievement at approximately the sixth-grade level, although they do not normally reach this level until their teens. These are the group described as *educable mentally retarded* (EMR).

Children classified as moderately retarded compose another 20 percent of the retarded group and, along with some of the severely retarded, are often described as *trainable*. These children are capable of learning to talk during the preschool period; most will also learn to walk, although their verbal and motor skills are generally markedly inferior to those of normal children. A large number of mildly retarded children are mainstreamed — that is, educated in regular schools though often with special teachers and equipment.

Severe mental retardation is usually associated with poor motor development, few communication skills (although these sometimes develop slightly later in life), and a high degree of dependence throughout life.

Profound mental retardation generally requires special care. Children who are profoundly mentally retarded may not learn toilet or dressing habits; in addition, many do not learn to walk.

The mildly retarded. The largest group of mentally retarded children, the mildly retarded, are of special importance to the regular classroom teacher,

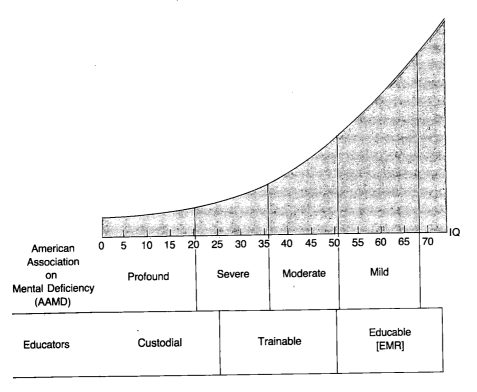

Figure 9.11

Two common classification schemes for mental retardation. Note that these classifications are based entirely on measured IQ. In practice, adaptive skills would also be taken into account. The AAMD classifications shown here are based on the Stanford-Binet or Cattell tests. The Wechsler Scales have a different distribution and therefore different "cutoff" points: 55–69 (mild); 40–54 (moderate); 25–39 (severe); below 25 (profound).

particularly because mainstreaming requirements make it likely that many regular classrooms will also include a number of exceptional children.

Many mildly retarded children are not noticeably different from other children in their social and personality characteristics or in their needs. But they do experience more difficulty in learning and sometimes as a result develop less positive self-concepts and other personality problems. There is little evidence to support the once prevalent notion that they learn differently than do normal children. Present evidence indicates that they go through much the same developmental and learning sequences but at a slower rate (see Haywood, Meyers, & Switzky, 1982). The most consistent differences between mildly mentally retarded and normal children are in memory and attention span. In

Many exceptional children are not noticeably different from other children in their social and personality characteristics or in their needs.

general, these children are less able to attend and can attend for shorter periods of time (Mercer & Snell, 1977). They also appear to be inferior in short-term memory skills. In other words, they have difficulty remembering items that have just been presented to them. Once they have learned, however, their long-term memories do not appear to be different from those of normal children (Robinson & Robinson, 1976). Their poorer short-term memories are most frequently explained in terms of an inability to make use of processing strategies such as organizing and rehearsing.

In addition to attentional and memory problems, mildly retarded children sometimes show language deficits and inferior motor development. Contrary to popular opinion, they are not stronger, faster, or in other ways physically gifted as though nature or nurture were compensating for a deficiency in one area by endowing the individual in another (see, for example, Bruininks, 1977).

One of the most important goals in educating the mildly retarded is to develop healthy social and emotional characteristics. Unfortunately, our cultural prejudices have placed such value on excellence and such a stigma on mental retardation that the emotional well-being of those who are intellectually disadvantaged is often unfairly threatened.

Learning Disabilities

There are a significant number of children in schools who, in the absence of perceptible emotional or physical disturbances and without being mentally retarded, experience serious learning difficulties in one or more areas. Such children have sometimes been described as suffering from hyperactivity, learning dysfunction, cerebral dysfunction, minimal brain damage, perceptual handicaps, dyslexia, perceptual disability, or simply as being slow learners. Each of these terms is relatively nonspecific, often confusing, and sometimes meaningless. In 1963, Samuel Kirk proposed a new term that would, in effect, include all the conditions previously described by these and other labels: **learning disability.** It does not carry the stigma attached to such terms as *brain damage* or *cerebral dysfunction,* nor does it complicate our understanding with excessive categorization (see Kirk, 1979).

Definition. The term *learning disability* is now widely used to describe a large variety of conditions. Unfortunately, these conditions are not always easily defined or identified. U.S. Public Law 94-142, which provides funding programs for special education, includes a definition of learning disabilities that serves as a guideline for the allocation of funds. However, the definition is open to a number of interpretations and has led to considerable controversy. Consequently, various jurisdictions have modified existing definitions and established their own criteria for learning disabilities. As a result, different states and provinces define learning disabilities in different ways.

In spite of the considerable disagreement that still exists concerning what learning disabilities are — and what they are not — most definitions concur with respect to four general characteristics of any condition so labeled (Morsink, 1985):

1. *Discrepancy.* There is a marked discrepancy between the child's actual and expected behavior. This discrepancy is most often evident in an uneven pattern of academic achievement.
2. *Deficit.* The learning disabled child has a specific performance deficit. Such a child may do reasonably well in most subjects, but will be unable to do certain things that other children do easily.
3. *Focus.* The learning disabled child's deficits typically center on one of the basic psychological processes involved in language and sometimes on arithmetic. Hence the condition is often manifested in disorders of listening, thinking, talking, reading, writing, spelling, or arithmetic.
4. *Exclusions.* The problems associated with learning disabilities are not the result of other problems relating to hearing, vision, or general mental retardation.

Symptoms and identification. Initial indications of learning disabilities are typically tentative and probabilistic. Perhaps the most overt characteristic — the one most likely to be noticed by parents and teachers — is general academic retardation. Note, however, that academic retardation does not define a learning disability, although it often occurs as a result of the child's problems with reading, writing, and other aspects of the language arts.

Other general symptoms that are sometimes associated with learning disability include inattentiveness, mood shifts, hyperactivity, and impulsiveness (see Table 9.3).

Table 9.3
Some Symptoms Associated with Learning Disabilities

Inattentiveness (short attention span)
Impulsiveness
Hyperactivity
Frequent shifts in emotional mood
Impaired visual memory (difficulty in recalling shapes or words)
Motor problems (difficulty in running, hitting a ball, cutting, writing)
Disorders of speech and hearing
Specific academic difficulties (reading, writing, spelling, arithmetic)

Source: Based in part on Clements (1966) and the Edmonton Public School Board (1978).

A variety of tests are used in identifying the learning disabled. These are designed to provide information concerning three aspects of the student's characteristics and functioning (Morsink, 1985). They measure general intelligence, examine basic psychological processes involved in learning and remembering, and look at the possibility that other factors — such as visual problems, hearing deficits, physical or health handicaps, low intelligence, or environmental disadvantages — might be involved. Whereas the first and third of these (measuring intelligence and eliminating other deficits) are relatively straightforward, the second (assessing basic psychological processes) is not. One of the problems is that there is no general agreement on what these processes are. Certain tests, such as the Detroit Tests of Learning Aptitude, attempt to look at processes involved in activities such as reading and are sometimes useful for identifying specific weaknesses.

Given these problems of definition and identification, it is not surprising that faulty categorization is highly common in this area. Following a survey of 800 children classified as "learning disabled," Shepard, Smith, and Vojir (1983) found that more than half of this sample had characteristics that did not conform to government regulations for meeting the definition criteria. Many had emotional disorders, mild retardation, or specific language problems.

Faulty categorization of this kind might partly account for the fact that the number of children classed as learning disabled more than doubled between 1978 and 1983 (Kavale & Forness, 1985). Now more than two of every five students receiving special education in the United States is classified "learning disabled" — a total of almost 4 percent of the school population (Chalfant, 1989).

Although a number of standardized tests are useful for diagnosing the nature of specific disabilities and sometimes for suggesting appropriate remedial procedures, initial identification, which must always be highly tentative, is difficult. In addition, final identification, diagnosis of the specific problem (or problems), and remedial suggestions are ordinarily beyond the expertise of the regular classroom teacher. These activities should involve a person specially trained in learning disabilities. Here perhaps more than anywhere else, given problems of definition and identification, teachers and others must be careful not to mislabel children.

Categories of learning disabilities. Relatively little is known about the origins and causes of specific learning disabilities — although brain damage or some other neurological impairment is suspected in many cases (Held, 1984). Various diseases and infections, malnutrition, and other environmental or genetic factors might also be involved.

Learning disabilities are most often classified according to the specific area of disability and are labeled according to whether they involve oral or written speech, comprehension or production of speech, or particular problems in spelling or arithmetic. By far the most frequently diagnosed learning disabilities are those that have to do with language, and more specifically, with reading.

A general term for a learning disability manifested in reading problems is **dyslexia.** Dyslexia is usually first manifested in problems associated with learning to read and may later be evident in spelling difficulties (erratic rather than consistent errors) (Hargrove & Poteet, 1984). Dyslexic individuals are typically of average measured intelligence but, in spite of ample opportunity to learn to read, are usually several years behind in reading skills. Remedial teaching can sometimes be highly effective in overcoming some of the effects of dyslexia.

There is some evidence that dyslexia is a developmental disorder related to a maturational defect and that it often becomes less severe as the child ages (Critchley & Critchley, 1978). Nevertheless, there are a number of adults who suffer from various degrees of dyslexia.

Other reading-related learning disabilities are sometimes evident in any of the following problems (Morsink, 1985): attention difficulty, perceptual problems, poor motivation or attitude, poor sound-symbol association, memory problems, language deficits, and transfer difficulties. Learning disabilities associated with arithmetic may be of two kinds: those having to do with computation (difficulties in adding, subtracting, multiplying, or dividing) and those relating to processing visual or auditory information. Accordingly, reading problems are sometimes associated with arithmetic disabilities.

In addition to reading and arithmetic disorders, learning disabilities also include what are referred to as *process disorders* — that is, they are sometimes labeled in terms of a deficit in a basic psychological process. Thus there are deficits relating to perception (some students are confused by words that sound or look alike); memory (sometimes evident in problems associated with remembering and generalizing what has been learned); and attention (a condition labeled "attention deficit disorder" is sometimes associated with restlessness, hyperactivity, low frustration tolerance, and distractibility). In practice, however, it is often difficult to separate a basic process disorder from a disorder that is manifested in a specific subject area.

Learning disabilities, as they are presently defined, are usually treated in the regular classroom. Alternately, learning disability specialists, many of whom specialize in reading or writing skills, may work with these children in the regular classroom. In a declining number of cases, they are given no "special" treatment.

Intellectual Giftedness

There are two related manifestations of giftedness in cognitive functioning: high intelligence and high creativity. Recall that mental retardation is typically defined not only in terms of performance on an intelligence test but also in terms of adaptive behavior. In much the same way, intellectual giftedness cannot easily be identified solely on the basis of scores on measures of intelligence or creativity; motivational and personality factors that are associated with the full development of apparent potential must also be taken into account. For this reason, Hallahan and Kauffman (1986) suggest that "gifted" individuals be defined in terms of a combination of three criteria: high ability (often measured by intelligence tests), high creativity, and high task commitment (defined in terms of motivation and persistence). They suggest, further, that to be truly gifted, individuals must surpass 85 percent of their peers on all three measures and 98 percent on at least one. In this connection, the classic studies of giftedness by Terman et al. (1925) indicate that, in the same way as disadvantaged children are often handicapped in more than one area, the gifted are often exceptional in many respects.

U.S. Public Law 91-230, defines giftedness as follows:

> Gifted and talented children are those identified by professionally qualified persons who by virtue of outstanding abilities, are capable of high performance. These are children who require differentiated educational programs and/or services beyond those normally provided by the regular school programs in order to realize their contribution to society.

The law goes on to state that capacity for high performance may involve demonstrated achievement or the potential for high achievement in one or more of the following areas:

1. General intellectual ability
2. Specific academic aptitude
3. Creative thinking
4. Leadership ability
5. Visual and performing arts
6. Psychomotor ability

Marland (1972) estimates that somewhere between 3 and 5 percent of the school population might be considered gifted. However, special education programs are provided for nowhere near this number. This is especially true of the gifted who are culturally disadvantaged (Patton, Prillaman, & Tassel-Baska, 1990). An observation made by Terman (1925) more than half a century ago might still be true today: When comparing potential and achievement, we find that the most "retarded" group in our schools is the highly gifted.

Among these highly gifted are the creative, a group that we look at next.

Creativity

Stephen Winsten (1949), George Bernard Shaw's biographer, alluding to the "hair's breadth" separating genius and madness, said to Shaw one day: "The matter-of-fact man prefers to think of the creative man as defective, or at least akin to madness." And Shaw quickly replied, "Most of them are, most of them are. I am probably the only sane exception" (p. 103).

Not so. There are other exceptions. Indeed, we have little evidence that many of the highly creative are mad — or vice versa. Like intelligence, creativity is a quality of human behavior and personality that is possessed by everyone. Even as some people are highly intelligent, others are very stupid. Similarly, some are highly creative; others are very ordinary.

Some definitions. Psychology offers us a wealth of definitions for *creativity.* Guilford (1959) assures us that it involves responses or behaviors characterized by "fluency, flexibility, and originality." Parnes and Harding (1962) define creativity as a behavior that results in "a novel work that is accepted as tenable or useful or satisfying by a significant group of others at some point in time" (p. 86). Mednick (1962) argues that creativity is "the forming of associative elements into new combinations which either meet specified requirements or are in some ways useful. The more mutually remote the elements of the new combination, the more creative the process of solution" (p. 221).

Do these definitions mean anything clear and simple? Hoge (1988) suggests that perhaps they don't. One of the major problems in the area of giftedness, he asserts, has to do precisely with the definition of the qualities in question. In practice, these qualities are most often defined in terms of scores on tests: intellectual giftedness is defined as a very high measured IQ; high creativity is defined in terms of an extraordinarily high score on a test designed to measure creativity. And the school administrator who must make a decision about who will be labeled "gifted" (and who, at least by implication, will be labeled "not gifted") also looks at test scores and perhaps asks teachers for their nominations. There are serious problems with this approach, claims Hoge. First, there is considerable ambiguity about the meaning of high IQ or high creativity scores; second, what is represented by these tests is often quite different from the definitions that government agencies or school jurisdictions have adopted;

and third, the programs that are provided for children identified as gifted are not often matched to the specific strengths revealed by tests (nor are they designed to eliminate any of the relative weaknesses that might have been uncovered).

Measuring creativity. Creativity is most frequently measured by means of open-ended tests — tests that require subjects to produce a variety of different responses. The intellectual ability called on is defined as *divergent thinking.* Individuals think divergently when they produce a number of different solutions for a single problem. In contrast, measures of intelligence typically present items that require *convergent thinking* — the production of a single correct response.

Most measures of creativity are based on Guilford's (1950) work, elaborated by Yamamoto (1964) and Torrance (1966, 1974). The Torrance Tests of Creative Thinking continue to be widely used in research (see Diaz, 1983). These tests are based on Guilford's assumption that the most important factors involved in creative ability are *fluency, flexibility,* and *originality.* Accordingly, the open-ended tasks that are used to measure creativity allow the student to produce a variety of different responses that can then be scored in terms of these factors. For example, one item asks subjects to think of as many uses as they can for a brick. Counting the total number of responses gives a measure of fluency. Flexibility is revealed in the number of shifts from one class of uses to another (for example, shifting from responses where bricks are used for building purposes to ones where they are used for holding objects down). Originality is revealed in the number of unusual or rare responses. Table 9.4 gives one example of a creativity item and how it might be scored.

You might want to test your creativity with the problems that appear on page 489. Their solutions are given on page 490.

Interestingly, when children are given tests of divergent (creative) thinking and told to be creative, their scores typically increase (Runco, 1986a). This finding has sometimes been used as a basis for arguing that children who normally score high on creativity tests simply perceive the test differently. It is significant, however, that children who improve most on measures of originality when they are asked to be creative are those who score highest on measures of giftedness in the first place.

Runco (1986b) makes the important point that while measures of creativity reflect creative *potential,* they do not reflect creative performance. The greatest achievers — those who eventually attain eminence in the world — are characterized by more than just high scores on measures of intelligence and creativity. We'll say more about eminence shortly.

Some characteristics of creative children. Creativity appears to be a relatively stable personality characteristic. That is, children who are creative as preschoolers tend to continue to be creative throughout their childhood and into adulthood. We see evidence for this in studies that have found relatively high

Creative Problems

Problems vary considerably in difficulty as well as in the strategies that might be used to solve them. Greene (1975), for example, describes six levels of problems:

Level 1: The solver already knows the solution. The problem is therefore simply one of retrieving from memory. (Example: What is the second last phone number you had?)

Level 2: The solution is unknown, but rules and procedures that will lead to the solution are known (finding the square root of 1,244).

Level 3: The solution is learned in the course of dealing with the problem (finding a way out of a forest — or a city).

Level 4: Different possible solutions must be selected and evaluated (doing a crossword puzzle).

Level 5: Problem needs to be reformulated and analyzed, and the required solution will be a novel one (inventing something).

Level 6: Solver first needs to realize that a problem exists and is then required to generate new solutions or new procedures for arriving at solutions (inventing a new fuel-saving carburation device).

It is probably true that the lives of ordinary people are filled largely with lower-level problems. Indeed, the lives of most people might involve very few problems of the kind we are considering here. But you, whose life is more extraordinary, might want to consider the following "creative" problems (answers appear on the following page):

1. Let us suppose that one day you walk from Pascal to Shell River. You leave at eight o'clock in the morning, stop four or five times to rest, fish off the bridge for almost an hour at lunch time, and finally arrive at Shell River at four in the afternoon. Having spent the night in Shell River, you return to Pascal the next day following exactly the same route, again leaving at eight o'clock in the morning. But this time you walk faster and reach Pascal by noon. Is it true that at some point on your return trip, you will necessarily be at one place at exactly the same time that you were at that place the day before?

2. Using only six matches of equal length, make four equal-sized triangles where the length of each side is equal to the length of one match.

3. Two fathers and two sons went fishing and caught only three trout. Each took one home. How can that be?

4. Two trains hurtle toward each other, one traveling 100 miles per hour, the other going a mere 50 miles an hour. When the trains are only 75 miles apart, a deranged hummingbird flies from the front of one train directly toward the other at an incredible speed of 90 miles an hour. And when it reaches the other train, it turns immediately and flies back to the first again. Again it turns . . . and again . . . and again — flying back and forth between the two trains, always at 90 miles an hour, slowing down not a whit every time it turns. How far will this deranged hummingbird have flown by the time the two trains collide?

Solutions to "Creative Problems"

1. You will, indeed, be at exactly the same place and time once on your way back from Shell River. This is easy to explain (and understand) if you consider what would happen if one person left Shell River and the other Pascal at the same time and on the same day. It makes no difference how fast each goes; providing they follow the same route, they must meet (that is, they must be at the same place and time on one occasion). The problem is identical to this situation; you are simply "meeting" yourself on a different day.

2. If you had trouble with this one, it is probably because of "set" — the predisposition to respond in certain ways. You likely tried to lay the matches flat on some horizontal surface. The solution (top of next column) requires a shift from horizontal to vertical.

3. The problem is a bit of a "trick." Two fathers and two sons need not be four people; they might, as in this case, be only three: a grandfather with his son and grandson. Hence two fathers and two sons!

4. The problem sounds far more complex than it is. The two trains, because their speeds are constant, will collide in exactly 30 minutes. That is because they cover 150 miles in one hour (one travels 100 miles, and the other, 50), and they start out 75 miles apart. The crazed hummingbird, no matter that it turns back and forth faster and faster as the trains approach each other, can only travel 45 miles in 30 minutes because it is always going 90 miles an hour.

Table 9.4

Sample Answers and Scoring Procedure for One Item from a Creativity Test

Item:	How many uses can you think of for a nylon stocking?
Answers:	* Wear on feet
	§* Wear over face
	* Wear on hands when it's cold
	†* Make rugs
	* Make clothes
	§†* Make upholstery
	†* Hang flower pots
	* Hang mobiles
	§†* Make Christmas decorations
	†* Use as a sling
	†* Tie up robbers
	§†* Cover broken window panes
	§†* Use as ballast in a dirigible
	†* Make a fishing net
Scoring:	* Fluency: 14 (total number of different responses)
	† Flexibility: 9 (number of shifts from one class to another)
	§ Originality: 5 (number of unusual responses — responses that occurred less than 5 percent of the time in the entire sample)

correlations between measures of creativity taken at younger and at older ages (for example, Kogan & Pankove, 1972; Magnusson & Backteman, 1978). Note, however, that these correlations are typically considerably lower than those obtained under similar circumstances for measures of intelligence (Kogan, 1983). It is not clear to what extent this is due to the greater unreliability of measures of creativity and to what extent it might be due to greater fluctuations in creativity itself.

A number of studies have looked at the relationship between creativity and intelligence. For example, Getzels and Jackson (1962), examining children in a private Chicago high school, found that the most creative students were often not the most intelligent. Interestingly, although many of the highly creative students achieved as well as those with higher measured intelligence (but lower measured creativity), they were typically not liked as well by teachers. Getzels and Jackson suggest this might be due to the highly creative individual's greater independence and lower willingness to conform.

Another study of creativity and intelligence attempted to discover whether the personality characteristics of children representing the highest and lowest extremes of these variables were consistently different (Wallach & Kogan, 1965). Results of this study, summarized in Figure 9.12, indicate that highly intelligent but less creative students tend to be addicted to school and are well

Figure 9.12

Characteristics of
children identified as
high and low on
measures of intelli-
gence and of diver-
gent thinking.
Source: Based on studies
reported by Wallach &
Kogan (1965).

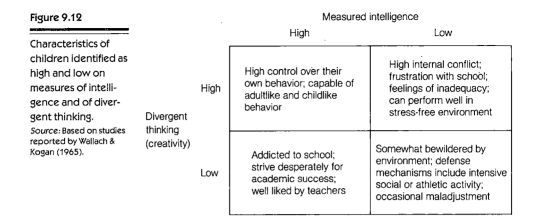

	Measured intelligence	
	High	Low
Divergent thinking (creativity) — High	High control over their own behavior; capable of adultlike and childlike behavior	High internal conflict; frustration with school; feelings of inadequacy; can perform well in stress-free environment
Divergent thinking (creativity) — Low	Addicted to school; strive desperately for academic success; well liked by teachers	Somewhat bewildered by environment; defense mechanisms include intensive social or athletic activity; occasional maladjustment

liked by teachers. In contrast, highly creative but less intelligent students are most frustrated with school and suffer most from feelings of inadequacy. The most favored group, not surprisingly, comprises those who are high on both intelligence and creativity. Wallach and Kogan report that these students were most in control of their behaviors and were capable of adultlike as well as childlike behaviors. Related to this, other studies have found a close relationship among playfulness, fantasy, and creativity (see, for example, Dansky, 1980; Kogan, 1983).

Eminence. For practical purposes, there is seldom a need to separate high intelligence and high creativity. Not only is there a close relationship between the two, but also programs for gifted and talented children are not tailored for one or the other. And studies of eminent individuals — that is, of those who have achieved fame and recognition on the basis of outstanding performance in any area — typically find that these individuals are both highly intelligent and specially gifted in a creative sense (Albert & Runco, 1986).

But eminent individuals are something other than simply highly intelligent and specially gifted. There are countless individuals who score extremely high on all our measures of giftedness and intelligence, but who never approach eminence. A follow-up of the Terman studies of genius, for example, found that very few of the original sample ever attained eminence (Oden, 1968).

What is special about those few gifted individuals who achieve eminence? Perhaps a number of personality characteristics — things like high motivation and persistence and, perhaps most important, the right *family context*. It is no accident that there is a high correlation between parent's measures of divergent thinking and those of their children (Runco & Albert, 1986). Family background seems to have been an important factor in the lives of a majority of those who have achieved eminence.

Albert and Runco (1986) warn that perhaps we have taken too simple and too cognitive a view of giftedness and that, as a result, we have been guilty of neglecting important personality and family variables. They suggest that there are seven important factors involved in the development of eminence. First, if children are to become eminent in later life, they must be both intelligent and creative; second, they must develop the values, motivation, and abilities that allow them to undertake important or highly unusual work; third, their family context must be such that it encourages the development of these values and drives; fourth, there must be a proper "fit" between talents and career demands, such that the demands of the career are sufficiently challenging to lead to eminence; fifth, the family must provide the right combination of experiences (that is, musical, athletic, academic, and so on); sixth, the family history must be consistent with appropriate experiences and values (that is, grandparents, who were influenced by their parents, also influenced their children, who now influence the children of whom we speak); and seventh, the immediate direction provided by the family should also be consistent with the development of the gifted child's talents (rather than unrealistic, overly demanding, or uncaring).

Among these factors, there are important implications for the nurturing of giftedness.

Trends and Controversies in Special Education

There are a number of related trends in implementing special services for exceptional children; also, there are a number of controversies associated with these trends. Some of these are apparent in the preceding pages of this chapter and are summarized briefly here.

One notable trend in special education is a gradual shifting of the responsibility for exceptional children from organizations and institutions established specifically to deliver special services to the public school systems. This trend, in part, reflects a growing recognition that children who are exceptional in a disadvantaged sense should have an opportunity whenever possible to lead lives as nearly "normal" as possible. Deinstitutionalization and nonsegregation are the natural consequences of this trend; and perhaps nowhere is this more obvious than in the mainstreaming movement.

In effect, to mainstream is to place in regular classrooms children who might once have been placed in "special" classrooms or even in institutions. The mainstreaming movement followed the passage of U.S. Public Law 94-142 in 1975 in the United States. Specifically, this law requires, among other things, that school jurisdictions provide special services for exceptional children in "the least restrictive environment" possible (Macmillan & Meyers, 1979). Subsequently, various court decisions interpreted "the least restrictive environment" to mean the regular classroom. In California, for example, between 14,000 and 22,000 children previously classified as educable mentally retarded were moved into regular classrooms following the implementation of new legislation (Bancroft, 1976). Among other things, the effectiveness of special classrooms for mildly retarded children had been called into question and a consensus seemed to be growing that mildly retarded children would do better in regular classrooms.

Other studies have not always confirmed earlier findings. Some children fare better academically in regular classrooms; some fare better in special classrooms with other retarded children. Some mildly retarded children develop more positive self-concepts in regular classrooms; others develop better self-concepts in segregated classrooms. The controversy has not been entirely resolved (for a critical review of related research see, for example, O'Neill, 1984).

A second controversy concerns the use of labels. Critics of the use of labels argue that they are unfair because (1) a disproportionate number of minority-group children are labeled (and perhaps mislabeled, owing to the biased nature of many of our tests); (2) the imposition of a label changes the child's environment by affecting the child's self-concept; and (3) there is a growing tendency to view exceptional children as being quantitatively rather than qualitatively different from normal children. In spite of these objections, labeling has definitely not been abandoned, although there has been a concerted attempt to use more euphemistic (less stigmatizing) labels, to use them more judiciously, and to avoid making labels serve as explanations. It has never been very useful to label Johnny *dyslexic* and then to say that he can't read because he's dyslexic. Here, as elsewhere, labels name and classify; they do not explain.

THE MAGICAL CHILD

"The parents of the magical child lead him into the world by example," Pearce (1977, p. 213) tells us. "At seven, he is open to suggestion, able to construct the abstractions needed for moving into the world . . . he is fascinated with the world and becomes analytic. He wants to take the world apart and see what makes it tick."

In Piaget's terms, the child of which we have spoken in this chapter is ready to construct a knowledge system that will lead to a mounting understanding of the world.

Or, in the language of information-processing theory, the child seeks to develop a knowledge base, to discover processes and strategies for dealing with knowledge, and to develop a sense of self as perceiver, knower, and rememberer.

As we noted, infants are not expected to know that day follows night; that butterflies whisper to each other when they perch on buttercups in the sunshine; and that there is a smooth, cold logic that can be invented to explain the mysteries of numbers and classes and series, though perhaps not the whispers of butterflies. Those are among the discoveries of later childhood.

But happily, the grand mysteries of cognition are not all solved through middle childhood. There is yet a concreteness to the child's logic, a limit to the reaches of imagination. We continue the story in Chapter 11.

MAIN POINTS

1. Middle childhood spans the ages from 6 to 12. Although boys are normally heavier and taller than girls throughout their lives, there is a brief period late in middle childhood when girls become heavier and taller than boys because they undergo their adolescent growth spurt approximately two years earlier than boys. Boys surpass girls in many motor activities but not in those involving rhythmic movements and balance, such as playing hopscotch. Boys can usually reach higher, jump farther, and run faster than girls.

2. A child's height is a good indicator of the long-term effects of nutrition; weight sometimes reflects effects that are more short term. Obesity is the most common childhood nutritional problem. It is linked to overeating and underexercising, as well as to genetic background.

3. Sex differences in motor abilities are usually very small during childhood and are consistent with the gender typing of the skills measured. After childhood, many of these differences increase.

4. Physical and motor problems that sometimes cause children to require special services include cerebral palsy, epilepsy, a variety of diseases, congenital physical problems, and physical problems resulting from accidents.

5. The majority of children who are classified as legally blind (corrected vision poorer than 20/200 in the better eye) can nevertheless see well enough to read large print with or without magnification and to function normally in society. Hearing impairments often have more socioemotional and academic problems associated with them than do visual impairments because of the crucial role that hearing plays in the acquisition of language.

6. Piaget describes middle childhood in terms of concrete operations. An important example of concrete operations relates to conservation — the realization that certain transformations do not change the quantitative features of objects. Three important rules of logic in conservation are *identity* (some operations — such as adding zero or multiplying by 1 — result in no change); *reversibility* (operations can be undone — for example, if 2 is subtracted from the sum of 6 + 2, the result is again 6); and *compensation* (several operations can be combined in different ways to yield the same result — for example, 6 + 2 is equal to 2 + 6).

7. In addition to the conservations, children acquire abilities relating to classification, seriation, and number during the period of concrete operations.

8. The developing child begins with no knowledge base, few strategies for dealing with cognitive material, and no awareness of the self as a knower or as a processor of information. Information-processing approaches to cognition look at these three aspects of cognition.

9. A basic information-processing model (attributed to Atkinson and Shiffrin) describes memory in terms of three components: *sensory memory* describes the momentary effect of sense impressions, involves no cognitive processing, and lasts for a second or less; *short-term memory,* similar to attention span, describes the retention of material for a few seconds but no more than a

minute and involves rehearsing; *long-term memory* describes retention for an indefinite period of time and appears to be related to cognitive processing.

10. The three basic processes involved in remembering are *rehearsal* (repetition), *elaboration* (extending or adding something to material — for example, using mental images or embedding in longer sentences), and *organizing* (grouping and relating material; forming associations).

11. Sensory and short-term memory do not appear to be substantially different in younger children and adults, but long-term memory is much superior in older children and adults. Developmental changes in long-term memory are generally attributed to the development of processing abilities in children, to their eventual recognition of themselves as active processors, and to their increasing knowledge about knowing (*metacognition* and *metamemory*).

12. *Metacognition* refers in part to our awareness of ourselves as players of the game of cognition. We play this game with rules called cognitive strategies and are influenced by our estimates of how good we are (how optimistic our estimates of self-efficacy).

13. *Intelligence* has sometimes been defined as "what the tests test." The *general factor theory* of intelligence (Spearman) suggests that intelligence is a broad underlying ability that determines performance in all areas. *Special abilities theory* suggests that intelligence consists of a number of separate and distinct abilities.

14. Gardner suggests we have multiple intelligences, not one, but that our culture only emphasizes (and measures) one or two of these: linguistic, musical, logical-mathematical, spatial, bodily knowledge, and personal knowledge.

15. Cattell describes two classes of mental abilities that make up intelligence: *Fluid abilities* are not learned, are unaffected by culture, and are evident in the ability to solve abstract problems, to reason, to remember, and to analyze figures; *crystallized abilities* are learned, are highly influenced by culture, and are reflected in measures of vocabulary, general information, and arithmetic skills.

16. Sternberg's *contextual theory* defines intelligence in terms of how well people adapt and function in the environments that they have selected — that is, in context. Sternberg's *triarchic theory* identifies three components of intelligence: the *metacomponents* (include cognitive strategies; defined by metacognition and metamemory — awareness of self as a knower); the *performance component* (includes whatever is involved in doing — relates to such intellectual skills as analyzing, sorting, elaborating); and the *knowledge-acquisition component* (relates to what is achieved in the process of learning — has to do with adaptation and therefore includes the contextualist aspects of the theory).

17. Two widely used *individual* (can only be given to one person at a time) intelligence tests are: the Stanford-Binet (ages 2 to adulthood, widely used with young children, highly verbal) and the Wechsler tests (different forms available for ages 4½ to adult; yield separate performance and verbal scores, as well as a composite IQ).

18. Defined psychometrically (in terms of its measurement), *average* IQ does not change from year to year; however, the measured intelligence of any given individual may increase or decrease, sometimes unpredictably. Intelligence tests given before the age of 2 do not predict later intelligence very well; tests given later correlate quite highly with measures in adolescence or adulthood.

19. Measured IQ is not a mystical, fixed, unchanging, and unmodifiable something. Intelligence tests often do not measure a variety of important things (interpersonal skills, motivation, creativity, athletic and musical ability) and were often culturally biased.

20. Mental retardation is characterized by a general depression in ability to learn and is defined in terms of subnormal performance on measures of intelligence *and* depression in adaptive behavior. Feuerstein's Learning Potential Assessment Device (LPAD) attempts to measure potential for future learning rather than simply the effects of past experience.

21. Mental retardation is currently classified by severity of retardation, regardless of cause: mild, moderate, severe, and profound. Educationally relevant labels, also corresponding to degree of retardation, are educable, trainable, and custodial. Learning processes do not appear to be very different in mildly retarded and normal children. The attention span and short-term memories of the mildly retarded are inferior, however.

22. The term *learning disability* is currently employed to include a wide range of specific learning problems that are not associated with mental retardation or other physical or emotional disturbance. Learning disabilities are often manifested in language-related problems and are often evident in difficulties associated with learning to read or to do arithmetic.

23. Intellectual giftedness is manifested in exceptional intelligence, exceptional creativity, and high motivation. Creativity is often defined in terms of innovation or originality and may involve intellectual characteristics not ordinarily measured by intelligence tests. The Torrance Tests of Creative Thinking, based on Guilford's work, are widely used in research on creativity.

24. Creativity appears to be a relatively stable personality characteristic that is quite highly related to intelligence. Some evidence suggest that highly creative children may be less well liked by teachers than others who are highly intelligent but less creative.

25. Recent trends in special education include deinstitutionalization, mainstreaming, and an antilabeling movement.

Further Readings

The following is a highly readable and excellent analysis of cognitive development. It looks in detail both at Piaget's theory and at current work in information processing and metacognition:

Flavell, J. H. (1985). *Cognitive development.* Englewood Cliffs, N.J.: Prentice-Hall.

Those interested in more technically detailed research in these areas might consult:

Dillon, R. F. (1985). *Individual differences in cognition* (Vol. 2). New York: Academic Press.

The following two books by Sternberg present some of the flavor of current interest in cognitive strategies and metacognition as they relate to intelligence. The first presents his theory of intelligence; the second summarizes beliefs about intelligence and provides some practical advice for improving intellectual functioning:

Sternberg, R. J. (1985). *Beyond IQ: A triarchic theory of human intelligence.* New York: Cambridge University Press.

Sternberg, R. J. (1986). *Intelligence applied: Understanding and increasing your intellectual skills.* New York: Harcourt Brace Jovanovich.

The following two collections present accounts of research and theory on memory development in childhood:

Brainerd, C. J., & Pressley, M. (Eds.). (1985). *Basic processes in memory development: Progress in cognitive development research.* New York: Springer-Verlag.

Weinert, F. E., & Perlmutter, M. (Eds.). *Memory development: Universal changes and individual differences.* Hillsdale, N.J.: Lawrence Erlbaum.

A provocative and practical book dealing with the development of creativity, critical thinking, and problem-solving skills is:

Fisher, R. (1990). *Teaching children to think.* Oxford: Basil Blackwell.

For a sensitive look at giftedness and numerous practical suggestions for fostering excellence in the home and in the school, see:

Clark, B. (1983). *Growing up gifted: Developing the potential of children at home and at school* (2nd ed.). Columbus, Ohio: Charles E. Merrill.

There are numerous outstanding sources of information regarding different methods of increasing or encouraging creativity. The books by de Bono are captivating accounts of some novel approaches to thinking and creative problem solving. Osborn's book is one of the classics in this area:

de Bono, E. (1970). *Lateral thinking: A textbook of creativity.* London: Ward Lock Educational.

de Bono, E. (1976). *Teaching thinking.* London: Temple Smith.

Osborn, A. (1957). *Applied imagination.* New York: Charles Scribner's.

You should not take a fellow eight years old
And make him swear to never kiss the girls.
Robert Browning, *Fra Lippo Lippi*

Social Development

My young daughter's imaginary playmate, Horton, began to live with us when she was 4. We paid little attention at first; he didn't take much room at the dinner table, usually just wanting to sit on her lap. And he ate only small tidbits from his mistress's plate. Later he sometimes required his own chair. And one night it was necessary to place a large turkey drumstick on his plate. There it sat, sadly becoming colder while we ate our meal. "He doesn't really like turkey," our daughter informed us, "and I don't either."

But generally Horton was no great bother. He spent most of his time sitting in a chair, always close to his mistress where she could talk to him — which she did at great length and with sometimes breathless intimacy. And whenever we went anywhere, he always came with us. Often we had to wait for him; he had the annoying habit of not being ready on time. Whenever this happened, his mistress would rush back to get him from her bedroom or sometimes from the bathroom, for he too occasionally needed to use that facility. She would drag him out then, complaining and scolding so severely that I sometimes felt sorry to see him so humiliated in front of his family.

Near her seventh birthday I asked her about Horton. "What do you mean?" she said. I told her what I thought I meant. "He likes chocolate and he wears different clothes," she answered. "Is he real?" I inquired. She looked up rather sadly. "No, he isn't. He's imaginary."

I have not seen Horton for some years now.

THE DEVELOPMENT
OF SOCIAL COGNITION

My daughter's sense of reality had changed; the line between fantasy and reality had become clearer. Still, at age 6 or 7, life has not yet drawn the thick, black line that we adults see so clearly between the real and the unreal. Our frames of reference are quite different from those of childhood. Our world views are more scientific, more reasonable. And our cognitions do not so readily admit magic.

Cognition refers to knowing; *metacognition* is defined in terms of knowing about knowing; and *social cognition* refers to an awareness of others as selves that, like our own selves, are also capable of feelings, motives, intentions, and so on. Put another way, metacognition implies an awareness of the self as a processor of information. It also implies a capacity to select, monitor, evaluate, and direct activities involved in information processing. Social cognition implies an awareness of self and others — an awareness of people and their behaviors. As Showers and Cantor (1985) note, social cognitions help us make sense of situations.

The development of social cognitions begins in early infancy and is thought to be closely linked with the development of the self-concept. Most developmental psychologists believe that the child is not born with a notion of self — that a newborn cannot differentiate between the self and the nonself (Olson, 1981). One of the important things that happens during infancy is that the child gradually begins to differentiate the self — to separate it from what is out there. At the same time as the self is being differentiated, the infant begins to recognize that there are things out there that are persons and others that are nonpersons. Perhaps even more important, infants begin to form attachments to one or more of the person-things. Thus begins the process of socialization.

But the infant's social cognitions unfold slowly and reflect many of the limitations that characterize nonsocial cognitions. Recall how young infants and even preschoolers have difficulty adopting another person's point of view, as is illustrated by Piaget's mountains problem (in which children view a three-dimensional "mountain" display from one angle and are asked to describe what it would look like from a different angle). These children also have trouble with social cognitions — they cannot easily make inferences about what other people are thinking or feeling. Indeed, to begin with, they are not even aware that other people exist and that they too have feelings and motives. The beginnings of the ability to interpret another person's socioemotional point of view — in other words, to empathize — is an essential first step in the development of social cognitions. Here too can be found the roots of caring.

Do We Really Care?

We are social animals, says Batson (1990). We live in society, and most of our behavior has to do with others. We spend extraordinary amounts of time trying to influence people, trying to get them to like us, trying to change their behavior.

But do we really care about others? Or, deep down, are we always motivated by purely selfish concerns? Is it only ourselves about which we really care?

In spite of its tremendous importance, psychology typically avoids this question. It is, after all, a difficult question. Besides, perhaps we share some unverbalized assumptions, some implicit answers. Psychology's implicit answer for these questions, says Batson, is simple: Basically, we are social egoists — The only person I really care about is *moi!* The other people I seem to value and love, I value for *instrumental* reasons — that is, because of what they do and are *for me.*

But psychology's implicit answer is incorrect, Batson reassures us. Not only do we genuinely care for others, but we are capable of a thoroughly selfless sort of empathy, where we care for others not for our sake, but solely for theirs.

Empathy, or the ability to share in another's point of view, can only come about as children realize that others have thoughts and feelings too.

Role-Taking and Empathy

Altruism and other forms of prosocial behavior imply caring and concern for the plights of others. They imply, as well, that those who care must be able to adopt the point of view of others. If not, they would not be able to care.

Investigations of cognitive role-taking have focused on the extent to which children are able to infer that other people may think differently than they do. Shantz (1975, 1983) summarizes this research in terms of four sequential stages that appear to characterize the development of cognitive role-taking skills. At the earliest stage, the child is unaware that another person is capable of having independent thoughts (or awareness). In a sense, the self and others are "fused" and indistinct (Hoffman, 1979). This realization seems to become general by the age of 6 and defines the second stage. During the third stage (around age 8), children realize that their own behavior may lead to inferences by others. The fourth stage, the ability to infer relatively accurately what other people are thinking, develops around the age of 10.

A close relationship exists between emotional and cognitive role-taking. Clearly, a child would be highly unlikely to make inferences concerning another's feelings prior to the realization that others are capable of independent and private thoughts. Studies of *empathy* (the ability to recognize and share the feelings of others) frequently ask children to recognize the emotion that would accurately reflect the reaction of a person in a story. One of the important and difficult problems with this type of research is that it is usually impossible to determine to what extent the child is accurately inferring emotional reaction and to what extent the emotion described is simply a projection of how the child would react in a similar situation.

Table 10.1
Selman's Developmental Progression in Social Cognition

Perspective-Taking Stages	Examples
0. Egocentric (to 6 years)	There is no perspective but mine. People feel the way I would in that situation.
1. Social-Informational (6–8)	Okay, so others have a point of view too, but they would feel the way I do if they had the same information.
2. Self-Reflective (8–10)	Actually, we can have different points of view. There's hers and there's mine. I can see mine; she can see hers.
3. Mutual (10–12)	Well, maybe I can see hers and she can see mine. We can even talk about our different points of view.
4. Social and conventional (12–15 +)	Actually, within the context of discombobulism, and taking into consideration the teachings of MUMU and the charter of personal delimitations, her point of view is totally philanthropic. On the other hand . . .

Hoffman (1975, 1978) suggests that the ability to empathize follows a developmental progression paralleling the development of cognitive role-taking skills. Accordingly, it is not until later childhood that the child will empathize to the extent that the inferences made about the emotional reactions of others will be related to *their* experiences and not those of the child. However, Hoffman believes that very young children are capable of a primitive sort of empathy before they can clearly separate themselves from others. That is, an infant can empathize with another who has been hurt and might even cry as a result. But as Flavell (1985) points out, the fact that a child cries in the presence of another crying child might have nothing to do with the ability to represent or understand what the other child is feeling.

Selman (1980, 1981) has conducted extensive investigations of the development of social cognitions in children. Many of these investigations have relied heavily on Piaget's interviewing techniques (the *méthode clinique*), and Selman often summarized their results in stages, much as Piaget did. For example, he describes the development of the child's ability to adopt and understand another person's point of view in five stages — labeled 0 to 4 (see Table 10.1). Adopting another's point of view is, in effect, similar to what we have been calling role-taking; Selman calls it perspective-taking. In his investigations of role-taking, he uses stories that present a moral dilemma (Selman, 1980):

Holly is an 8-year-old girl who likes the climb trees. She is the best tree climber in the neighborhood. One day while climbing down from a tall tree, she falls off the bottom branch but does not hurt herself. Her father sees her fall. He is upset and asks her to promise not to climb trees anymore. Holly promises.

Later that day, Holly and her friends meet Shawn. Shawn's kitten is caught up in a tree and can't get down. Something has to be done right away, or the kitten may fall. Holly is the only one who climbs trees well enough to reach the kitten and get it down, but she remembers her promise to her father. (p. 36)

The story is read to each child, who is then asked whether Holly knows how Shawn feels about the kitten; what Holly thinks her father will do if she climbs the tree; how Holly's father will feel if he knows she has climbed the tree; and what the child being questioned would do in the same situation.

Selman's role-taking stages, illustrated by reference to the kitten story, are as follow:

Stage 0: the egocentric viewpoint. Until perhaps the age of 6 or so, children are largely unaware of the existence of any perspective — of any role — other than their own, very personal view. When asked how someone else is likely to feel in a certain situation, their responses almost invariably reflect the feelings they would themselves experience: "Her daddy will be happy 'cause he likes the kitten."

Stage 1: social-informational role-taking. Between ages 6 and 8, children become aware that others have different points of view — different perspectives. But they have little understanding of the reasons for these different points of view and are likely to assume that anybody who knew what they know would think and feel as they do: "He'd let her climb if he understood how she felt!"

Stage 2: self-reflective role-taking. Eight- to 10-year-old children have gradually become aware that the feelings and thoughts of others, as well as their own personal feelings, can be inferred by others. But they respond only in terms of one or the other of the individuals involved: "He'll be mad 'cause he doesn't want her to climb trees."

Stage 3: mutual role-taking. Between 10 and 12, children can switch effortlessly from one point of view to another and can interpret and respond as might an objective onlooker: "Holly and her father can talk to each other. They will understand each other. They can work it out."

Stage 4: social and conventional role-taking. From ages 12 to 15 and beyond, adolescents can use the principles and ideals of their social systems, political ideologies, or religions to analyze and evaluate their perspectives as well as those of others: "It depends on whether her father thinks the cat's life or Shawn's feelings are more important than obedience . . . Besides, . . ."

SELF-WORTH

Social cognition, as we saw, implies an awareness of self and of others as distinct selves. Put another way, it implies a concept of the self – a **self-concept.**

Concepts such as self-worth, self-esteem, or self-concept are all aspects of what we refer to in Chapter 2 as *self-referent* thought – thought that has to do with our selves. In that chapter, we dealt at some length with Bandura's concept of self-efficacy. Self-efficacy means competence in dealing with the environment. The most efficacious people are those who can deal most effectively with a variety of situations. Bandura (1986) identifies two components of self-efficacy: One includes the skills that are required for effective performance; the other consists of the individual's own estimates of personal effectiveness. This component (estimate of effectiveness) is the most important from a psychological point of view, not only because of the implications our judgments of self-efficacy have for behaving, but also because of their relationship to our notions of self-worth.

Some Definitions

In common usage, the term *self-concept* is often an evaluative term that refers primarily to what we think of ourselves – how we evaluate ourselves. Thus, people are described as having *positive* self-concepts when they think well of themselves, and *negative* self-concepts when they do not think much of themselves. In fact, these meanings are better captured by expressions such as *self-esteem* and *self-worth*, which are clearly evaluative. Notions of self-worth are clearly part of self-concept. But just as clearly, there are aspects of the self-concept that are not evaluative, that have to do with abstract, cognitive notions of what the self is rather than with whether the self is good or bad, worthwhile or worthless, lovable or detestable, moral or immoral.

Theoretical Approaches to Self-Worth

There are two major, and very old, theoretical approaches to explaining self-worth – or self-esteem (see Table 10.2). One, advanced by William James (1892) – the man most often accused of being the father of psychology – says essentially: My self-worth is a direct function of the difference between what I would like to be and what I think I am. Thus, the closer my actual self (as I perceive my *self*) to my ideal self (the way I would personally like to be), the more I will like myself, and, hence, the higher my self-esteem.

The second approach, described by Cooley (1902), is quite distinct from James's approach. It says, in effect, my self-worth is a direct function of what I think others think of me. My worth is, in a real sense, reflected in their behavior toward me – hence Cooley's expression *looking-glass self.* If people avoid me,

Table 10.2
Two Theories of the Basis of Self-Worth

Theory	Example of Reasoning Process
Cooley: Looking-glass self (What I think important others think of me)	"Willie asked me out. Billy asked me out. Sam looks at me as if he wants to ask me out, and he could go out with anybody in the school. I must be pretty attractive."
James: Discrepancy between actual and ideal self (What I would like to be versus what I think I am)	"I'm a blonde, which is what I would want to be if I had a choice. My skin is clear, and I like my eyes— nice blue. Physically, I know I'm well, pretty attractive. But I've just been pulling off C's in school, which is the pits. I want at least B's."

that is clear evidence that I am not very worthy; if they appear to seek me out, then the evidence is more positive. Note, however, that these "others" who serve as mirrors in whose behavior I can view my *self* do not consist of just anybody, but only of people who are important to me, of people who, in Mead's (1967) phrase, are *significant others* — or, in Bronfenbrenner's words, people who are part of the child's microsystem. For a preschooler, the microsystem is defined primarily by face-to-face interactions with parents and, to some extent, siblings. For the elementary school child, the microsystem will come to include peers and teachers as well — and perhaps coaches, mentors, tutors, religious leaders, and so on.

Harter (1985a, 1985b, 1987, 1988) has developed ways of measuring self-worth that are based directly on these approaches. Using these measurements, she has investigated the theories as well as the development and importance of self-worth in the lives of elementary school children.

Measuring and Investigating Self-Worth

Harter's studies typically use a test called the *Self-Perception Profile for Children*. It asks children questions relating to how well they think they do in each of the five areas considered important for developing notions of self-worth (namely athletic, scholastic, social, physical, and moral). In some studies, children are also asked how *important* they think it is to do well in these areas. This provides investigators with a basis for computing the difference between actual performance (competence) and the child's wishes and allows the determination of a measure relating to James's approach to self-worth.

In addition to answering questions relating to actual competence and to importance of competence, children might also be asked to what extent they feel their importance is recognized by others, how well others treat them, whether they think they are liked, admired, and respected. This line of questioning provides information relating to the regard in which others hold the child (Cooley's approach).

Finally, children might also be asked questions relating to a more global concept of self-worth — questions relating to how well they like themselves as people.

Use of questions such as these permits investigators to answer a number of important questions. For example: Are competence/aspiration-based estimates of self-worth (James's theory) actually related to global notions of self-worth? Are "looking-glass" estimates (Cooley's theory) related to general concepts of self-worth? Are discrepancies between competence and the ideal more important in one area than another (for example, are athletics more important than scholastics)? Are there developmental changes in areas of importance? Is the source of approval and social regard important?

Harter (1987) provides answers for a number of these questions based on her investigations of children in grades 3 through 8 (approximately 8 to 13 years of age). Prior to the age of 8, children do not seem to have a single, clearly defined, and measurable notion of self-worth; accordingly, younger children are not included in Harter's samples.

Some Important Findings

First, although one aspect of self-worth may be described as a single, global concept (that is, in terms of a general estimate of personal worth), it seems clear that children make individual estimates of self-worth in at least five important and separate areas: scholastic competence, athletic competence, social acceptance, physical appearance, and behavioral conduct (Table 10.3). In other words, some children may see themselves as athletically competent (good and worthwhile); but these same children may have decided that they were not "good" in a moral sense — or that they are not as worthwhile scholastically.

Second, Harter's studies indicate that the child's global judgments of self-worth reflect both major sources described by James and Cooley. That is, the difference between a child's competencies (in each of the five important areas) and the child's aspirations and desires is reflected in estimates of self-worth. At the same time, how others regard the child also has a direct and very important influence on self-esteem.

Third, it is revealing, though not particularly surprising, that not all five areas are equally important to every child. Consequently, high or low competence in some areas will have little effect on self-concept whereas competence in very important areas will exercise a very powerful influence. For example, if athletics are more important than being good (behavior conduct), not being a good athlete will be more damaging to self-esteem than behaving immorally. In Harter's studies physical appearance is clearly the most important area in determining self-worth, both for the younger (grades 3 to 6) and the older (grades 6 to 8) children. That is, children who see themselves as attractive are

Table 10.3
Areas in Which Children Evaluate Their Self-Worth

Area	Description
1. Scholastic competence	How competent, smart, the child feels with regard to schoolwork
2. Athletic competence	How competent the child feels at sports and games requiring physical skill, athletic ability
3. Social acceptance	How popular or socially accepted the child feels with peers
4. Behavioral conduct	How adequate the child feels with regard to behaving in the way one is supposed to behave
5. Physical appearance	How good-looking the child feels, how much the child likes such characteristics as height, weight, face, hair

Source: From "The Determinants and Mediational Role of Global Self-Worth in Children," by S. Harter, 1987.

Note: Children's estimates of self-worth are based on (1) what significant other people (the microsystem) think of the child's capabilities and worth (Cooley's *looking-glass theory*) and (2) the extent to which the child lives up to personal ideals and aspirations (James's *discrepancy between aspirations and competence theory*). Both kinds of evaluations occur in the five areas described here.

most likely to like themselves. For both these age groups, behavioral conduct (goodness of behavior in a moral sense) was least important (see Table 10.4).

Fourth, as we have already noted, some sources of social regard and support are more important than others. For example, it might not matter very much that some nameless fan yells disparaging remarks while 10-year-old Willie stands at the plate waiting for the pitch; but it might matter a great deal if his coach later makes the same remarks. In Harter's (1987) studies, the most important sources of support in determining self-worth, for both the younger and the older children, are parents and classmates, rather than friends or teachers. It is noteworthy that parents retain their importance through these years, since this contradicts a popular belief that as peers become more important, parents must become less important. It is also significant that classmates are typically more important than are friends. This may well be because classmates' opinions may be seen as more objective evaluations; the evaluation of friends, on the other hand, may be more biased.

Fifth, estimates of self-worth are closely linked with affect (emotion or mood), which, in turn, has a great deal to do with motivation. As Harter (1988) comments, elementary school children who like themselves (that is, who have highly positive notions of self-worth) are the happiest; in contrast, those who do not think very highly of themselves are more likely to feel sad or even

Table 10.4
Correlations Between Children's Self-Worth and Perceived Inadequacies in Specific Areas

	Grades 3–6	Grades 6–8
Physical appearance	.66	.57
Social acceptance	.36	.45
Scholastic competence	.35	.36
Athletic competence	.33	.24
Behavioral conduct	.30	.26

Source: "The Determinants and Mediational Role of Global Self-Worth in Children" by S. Harter, 1987. In *Contemporary Topics in Developmental Psychology* (p. 229), N. Eisenberg (Ed.), New York: John Wiley. © 1987 John Wiley & Sons, Inc. Used by permission of the publisher.

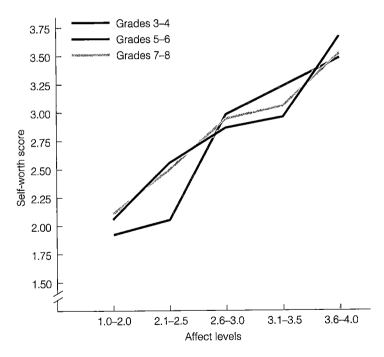

Figure 10.1

The relationship between mood and self-concept. In Harter's study, children who were sad (low affect level) had the lowest opinions of themselves.

depressed. Also, children who are happy are most likely to feel motivated to do things; those who are sad are least likely to want to do things. Figure 10.1 depicts the relationship between mood and self-worth scores for three groups of children from grades 3 through 8. Note that for all three groups, very low

Strong, positive feelings that we are worthwhile contribute to mental health, happiness, confidence, and high achievement. What we think of ourselves is related to two things: how competent we think we are in important areas (James's competence/aspiration theory) and what we think important others think of us (Cooley's looking-glass theory). Having the very best goose is the boy's proof that he is competent and that others think so too. It's almost enough to make him smile.

affect scores (sadness bordering on depression) are associated with very low self-worth scores; conversely, high affect is associated with high measures of self-worth.

Some of the practical implications of self-worth are clear. To the extent that positive self-esteem is closely related to happiness and to high motivation — and, by the same token, to social adjustment and general well-being — parents, teachers, and others who share responsibility for rearing youngsters must be concerned with far more than their cognitive development or their physical well-being. They must also attend to the development of the self; they must do what they can to ensure that the evaluation that every child places on the *self* is a positive judgment, as far as possible.

Unfortunately, as we saw, the causes of self-worth are not simple. They include factors over which we have limited control — things like the child's scholastic competence or physical appearance. But they also include things over which we have more control — things like our personal estimates of them, our communication of love and support.

We are not alone in determining children's self-worth. Friends, classmates, teachers, parents are all important. Not only do they provide explicit or implicit judgments of the children's worth, but they also serve as models of competence — and perhaps of incompetence as well — against which children can measure their own worth. Television, too, provides children with models of competence, some of which might seem hopelessly impossible. As well, it provides tremendously powerful models of violence and aggression. These topics consume the remainder of this chapter.

FRIENDS AND PEERS

The development of friendships through childhood is highly dependent upon the child's social cognitions. Clearly, the infant whose social cognition does not admit the possibility that others also have feelings, motives, and intentions will have more limited and more one-sided relationships than might an older child.

Children's Views of Friendship

Selman (1976, 1980, 1981) describes the child's views of friendship in terms of two broad stages. In the first, characteristic of perhaps a 3- to 5-year-old, a friend is merely a playmate. Friendship is seen as nothing more complex than "playing together." Hence a friend is someone who happens to be physically present and who plays with the child. At this stage, children have no concept of friendship as an enduring kind of relationship. And if they are asked how friendships are formed, they are likely to say, "By playing together." If asked to describe a friend, they will speak of activities, but not of traits or characteristics ("He plays with me" or "He doesn't hit me").

In the second stage, generally by the age of 11 or 12, children have developed the notion of friends as individuals involved in some type of mutual sharing. Their conceptions of friendship have now expanded to include the notion that friendships develop over time and that they involve a reciprocal sharing of thoughts and feelings and a high degree of mutual trust. When asked to describe friends, children at this stage are likely to speak of qualities ("She understands people; she's so sincere") and of mutual interests ("We like a lot of the same things"). Whereas younger children assume that the best friends are those who live close by and who want to play, older children realize that the best friends are those who share interests, who are mutually supportive, who *like* each other. A 5-year-old assumes that to become friends it is only necessary to play together; a 12-year-old believes that to become friends it is necessary to get to know one another.

The pattern in the development of friendships is highly similar to that which characterizes the development of role-taking skills, or the ability to empathize — which is not surprising because these are all aspects of social cognition. It is a pattern that begins with an undifferentiated state — a state in which the infant does not separate self from world or even people from non-people — and that progresses through intermediate stages marked by an increasing ability to adopt the emotional and cognitive perspective of others. It entails a growing tendency to view others as social beings rather than as physical entities. And ultimately, it requires a shift from the view that social interaction consists only of momentary encounters to an appreciation of the lasting and mutual nature of relationships.

Dimensions of Childhood Friendships

Friendships are of paramount importance in the life of the child. Not only do they provide intimacy, encouragement, and support, but they might also help the child develop the capacity to form meaningful and lasting emotional relationships in adulthood. Friendships are extremely important factors in the socialization of children (Hartup, 1989).

Best friends. Strictly speaking, only *one* of our friends can be *best* friend; none of the others can be more than second best. However, in common usage *best friend* does not refer to the one very best friend, but to a particularly close type of friendship in which several people can be best friends all at the same time.

It seems that most 6- to 12-year-old youngsters have more than one best friend, although that is not always apparent in the research. Berndt (1988) points out that if children are asked to name their best friend, they will obligingly name only one person. But if they are asked to name their best *friends*, they gladly name a number of people. And if the question is changed only slightly, and they are asked instead to indicate whether each child in their class is a best friend, a friend, or not a friend, some children will name most of the class as best friends.

For children, there is not as clear and important a distinction between best friends and other friends. But by adulthood, says Berndt (1988), we have learned to make fine distinctions between a best friend, close friends, good friends, and other friends.

Most children have a number of close friends rather than only one best friend. Friends are usually of the same age and most often of the same race and grade. Not surprisingly, friends usually share common interests. And childhood friendships are almost invariably among members of the same sex.

Berndt's investigations of friendship and helping among schoolchildren found that girls tended to have slightly fewer friendships than boys but these were generally more intimate — that is, they included more self-revelation and more close sharing. Even among girls, however, very few children have only one best friend; most have two or three. Also, for the large majority of children from kindergarten to eighth grade, friendship patterns appear to be highly mutual. If one child indicates that a second is a best friend, the second child

Sharing and compe-
tition—seemingly
contradictory ten-
dencies—are both
seen in close child-
hood friendships.
These friends might
be happy to trade
sandwiches with
each other and just
as eager to see who
finishes first.

will very likely also have chosen the first as a best friend. As Hartup (1983)
notes, reciprocity is a prominent characteristic of all childhood friendships.

Cooperation and competition among friends. Friendships are typically cooperative socializing contexts, says Hartup (1989). In many situations, friends are
more likely to cooperate and help each other than to compete. Strangely, however, there are situations in which friends are more competitive than one might
expect. In one of Berndt's experiments, for example, pairs of friends were given
a timed coloring task where each would be rewarded on the basis of the number
of squares colored correctly on a pattern but where only one crayon of the
appropriate color was provided. In one experimental condition, the child who
first has the crayon does not have to share with the friend but may do so.
Although experiments such as these tend to show that friends will compete
under these circumstances (some "friends" never share the crayon), there is
generally less competition (more cooperation) among girls than boys – a finding
that probably reflects the effects of social learning.

Berndt (1988) suggests that one possible explanation for the fact that children sometimes compete rather than cooperate has to do with the implicit

understanding that friends should be equal. Thus children may not cooperate if cooperating means that the friend will be more successful and more rewarded, but may choose to compete instead.

Importance of friends. There is little doubt that having friends is extremely important to all normal children. And it should come as no surprise that more than half the children referred for emotional or behavioral problems are described as having no friends or as having difficulty in peer interactions (see Oden, 1988).

Rubin (1980) suggests that, among other things, friendships contribute significantly to the development of social skills (such as being sensitive to other people's points of view; learning the rules of conversation; learning sex- and age-appropriate behaviors). In addition, interactions with friends are importantly involved in developing notions of self and, especially important, in developing notions of self-worth. Friendships may also foster feelings of belonging to a group and may therefore play an important role in the development of notions of cultural identity.

In addition to these general functions served by friendships, there is strong evidence that friends have powerful influences on each other. Berndt (1988) summarizes research that has found that a child's academic performance can be positively or negatively influenced by choice of friends. Similarly, friends may serve to encourage or discourage deviant behaviors (such as delinquency or drug use).

Close friends are only one source of influence on the developing child; peers are another.

Peer Groups

A *peer group* is a group of equals. Most individuals in our society have a peer group, excluding hermits — whose peers, by definition, are also isolated and therefore of little consequence to their development. Actually, most people have a number of peer groups: individuals whose occupations bring them into frequent contact with one another, individuals who are related by virtue of common causes, similar ambitions, identical avocations, geographic accident, or the whims of fortune. Each of these groups elicits specific behavior from its members more or less different from that elicited by other groups, and each is influential in determining a person's values, beliefs, goals, and ideals.

The peer group is both a product of culture and one of its major transmitters, particularly during middle childhood and adolescence. During the years of middle childhood (Freud's latency period), the peer group typically consists of like-sexed children. In addition, because of the different abilities, capacity for understanding, and varied interests among the different ages spanning this period, the peer group usually consists of peers close in age. During adolescence the peer group may be enlarged to include members of both sexes and a wider range of ages (Hartup, 1983).

Parents and Peers

Peer groups are relatively unimportant to most infants. Many remain dependent on their immediate families during their early years and are not brought into extensive or prolonged contact with other children until later in the preschool period. During these years, the family is the primary socializing force in their lives — the source of positive reinforcement or the source of punishment. Later, however, children turn increasingly toward peer groups and the immediate family gradually diminishes in importance as a socializing force. With increasing numbers of children in daycare facilities, the importance of peer groups during the preschool period has increased significantly in recent decades.

As peer groups become more important, and families less, some important changes occur in the ways in which children conform to parents and to peers. These changes have been investigated in Berndt's studies of children's responses to peer and parental pressure. In one study, 251 children in grades 3, 6, 9, and 11–12 were asked to respond to hypothetical situations in which parents or peers urged them to do something antisocial, something prosocial, or something neutral (Berndt, 1979). Two findings from this study are especially important. First, as expected, conformity to parents decreased steadily with age. Second, as conformity to parents decreased, conformity to peers increased. Significantly, however, the increase in peer conformity is curvilinear rather than simply linear. That is, peer conformity does not increase forever, although conformity to parents probably continues to decrease even into our adult lives. Instead, peer conformity increases from early childhood until it reaches its peak at around the sixth or ninth grade (roughly ages 11 through 14); it then begins to decline again.

Unfortunately, the Berndt study does not directly compare degree of children's conformity to peers with conformity to parents (it included no situations in which parents urged children to perform antisocial acts). In addition, because the situations were hypothetical ("What would you do if . . . ?"), there is no way of determining how children would actually behave under similar circumstances in real life. Nevertheless, the results (summarized in Figure 10.2) confirm the observation that parental influence is initially relatively high, but declines, whereas peer influence increases at least until the upper end of middle childhood.

Research conducted by Prado (1958) illustrates the shift in allegiance from family to peers during late childhood and adolescence. Prado selected two groups of boys, all of whom had indicated that their father was their favorite parent. One group consisted of boys between 8 and 11 years of age; the second of boys between 14 and 17. For the experiment boys and their fathers were brought to a laboratory, along with the boy's best friend — a boy of similar age who had been selected as the "best friend" on the basis of interviews and questionnaires. The friends and the fathers were asked to throw darts at a target. The target was arranged so that the boy could not see the exact scores made by his father or his friend. His task was to estimate their performance.

Figure 10.2

Changes in average conformity scores as a function of age and source of pressure.

Source: From T. J. Berndt, "Developmental changes in conformity to peers and parents." *Developmental Psychology,* 1979, *15,* 608–616. © 1979 by the American Psychological Association. Reprinted by permission of the author.

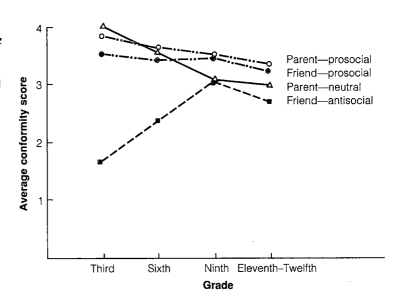

The results of the study reveal that both the younger boys and the adolescents were almost equally accurate in their estimates. However, the younger boys consistently overestimated the scores made by their fathers and underestimated those made by their friends. In contrast, adolescents tended to underestimate their fathers' scores and overestimate their friends' scores. The evidence strongly suggests that from middle childhood to adolescence there is a marked decline in the importance of parents and a corresponding increase in the importance of peers.

We should be cautious in interpreting studies such as these, however. That children now conform more to peers and somewhat less to parents or that they overestimate how peers will perform in a trivial task does not mean that peers are more important than parents in the life of children. That is clearly not the case, as forcing children to select between parents and peers would quickly prove. Furthermore, as we saw earlier, the approval and regard of parents continues to be as important as that of peers and more important than that of friends in influencing self-worth.

Here, as in other areas of human development, relationships and interactions are complex and influence each other. Accordingly, it is misleading and overly simplified to consider parent-child relations on the one hand, and child-peer relations on the other, and to compare and contrast them as though they were completely isolated and unrelated. There is evidence, for example, that the kind of relationship a child has with parents is very closely related to later relationships with peers (Elicker & Sroufe, 1989). Securely attached infants (see Chapter 6) are more likely to later have good relationships with peers. Similarly, the most social competent preschool children are often those who have the most positive and playful relationships with parents (Parke et al., 1989).

Peer Acceptance

One technique for assessing peer acceptance or rejection is called **sociometry.** It involves the use of a questionnaire or an interview to determine patterns of likes and dislikes in a group. For example, the investigator might present each of the children with the pictures or names of all the other children in their class and ask them to sort them according to the ones they would most like to be with or those whom they like the best. The investigator might also ask children to select those children whom they like the least and would least like to be with. Alternative methods include asking children to select the most popular boy or girl in the room, the smartest child or the dumbest one (see, for example, Hartup, 1975). The data gathered in this way may be interpreted through pictorial or graphic representations in a **sociogram** (Figure 10.3). Information of this kind is sometimes useful in research that looks at the qualities that make children popular or that lead to social isolation.

The characteristics of children most likely to be accepted as peers and friends vary depending on age and sex. In general, children who are friendly and sociable are more easily accepted than those who are hostile, unsociable, withdrawn, or indifferent (Putallaz & Gottman, 1981). Similarly, children who are intelligent and creative are more acceptable than those who are slow learners or retarded (Green et al., 1980). Size, strength, athletic prowess, and daring are particularly important characteristics for membership in boys' peer groups; maturity and social skills are more important for girls, especially as they approach adolescence (Langlois & Stephan, 1981). Attractiveness is important for both (Hartup, 1983).

The observation that friendly, socially competent children have more friends (have higher *status* as the sociologists put it) raises an interesting and important question: Are these observed differences between high-status (accepted) and low-status (rejected) children the cause or the result of their status? Does a friendly child have many friends because she is friendly, or is she friendly because she has many friends? Similarly, does social rejection lead to socially incompetent behavior, or is the socially incompetent behavior present to begin with, and lead to social rejection?

Current research strongly suggests that popular children are popular because they are more competent socially and that unpopular children lack social skills (Asher & Renshaw, 1981). In other words, how a child interacts with others is a primary cause of social status. Of course, social status also influences how a child interacts.

In support of the view that social competence is an important influence on social status, Asher (1983) reports studies where children are observed in situations with unfamiliar peers. Strikingly, after only a handful of play sessions, these children have achieved a status remarkably similar to that which characterizes their interaction with familiar peers. Perhaps even more important, certain characteristics of the interaction styles of the high-status children are readily apparent. According to Asher, these reflect three important qualities of social competence. First, socially competent children quickly sense what is

Figure 10.3

A sociogram of a fourth-grade class-room. The popular children are Scott, Matthew, Tracy, and Marie. The unpopular are Rose and Craig.

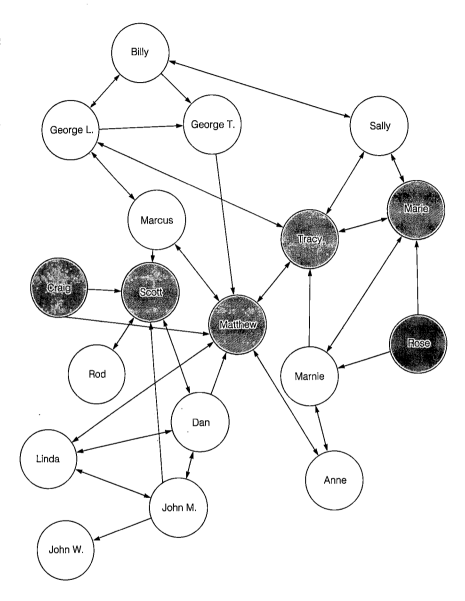

happening in an unfamiliar social situation and are able to modify their behaviors accordingly. They are less likely to engage in behaviors that are inappropriate or unexpected than socially incompetent children. Second, socially competent children are able to respond to what others initiate, rather than always initiating. Third, the socially competent are more patient with social relationships. They realize that relationships develop slowly over time; they do not insist on becoming leaders or best friends immediately.

Table 10.5
Five Categories of Social Status

Category	Characteristics
Sociometric stars	Especially well liked by most.
Mixers	High peer interaction. Some well liked; others not.
Teacher negatives	Typically in conflict with teachers. Some are liked; others not.
Tuned out	Not involved; are ignored rather than rejected.
Sociometric rejectees	Not liked very much. Rejected rather than simply ignored.

Source: Based on Gottman, 1977.

Social Isolation

We are not all equally loved and sought after by our friends. Indeed, not all of us have friends. Some of us are *social isolates.*

There are two separate definitions of social isolation that are often used in studies of this phenomenon. The first looks at frequency of interaction among peers and defines social isolation in terms of scarcity of interaction; the socially isolated are those who do not often interact with peers or others. The second looks at nature and extent of peer acceptance and defines the socially isolated as those who are seldom selected as "best friend" by anyone but who might often be chosen as "someone I don't really like very much." Evidence suggests that these two measures are, in fact, different (Gottman, 1977). Some individuals are liked and accepted but do not interact a great deal with their peers; others are very low on everybody's list of "my best friends" or "who I would most like to be with" or "who I would most like to be like" but nevertheless interact frequently with peers.

In an attempt to investigate these definitions and to arrive at a clearer description of social isolation, Gottman conducted a study of 113 preschool children enrolled in Head Start classrooms. Each child was observed at length by three different observers who used a time-sampling procedure and detailed recordings of peer-peer and peer-teacher interaction as well as observations of the child alone. Time samples consisted of 12 separate three-minute observations for each child. In addition, a "picture" sociometric technique (described by Hartup, Glazer, & Charlesworth, 1967) was used. Each child was presented with a random arrangement of classmate photographs, making sure the child recognized each of the photographs, and was asked for three positive choices (find someone you especially like at school) and three negative choices (now find someone you don't like as much).

From his data, Gottman described five distinct categories of children (Table 10.5). *Sociometric stars* include those who are consistently "especially liked." *Sociometric rejectees* are consistently "not liked very much." A third group, the *teacher negatives,* were typically in conflict with teachers. These might or might not be low on measures of peer acceptance. *Mixers* were observed to interact most with peers. These children too might be high or low on measures of acceptance. Finally, the *tuned out* are children who are frequently not involved with what is going on.

Rejectees are those who are not liked very much by any of their peers; they are actively rejected by everyone. These are the children who, in childhood, are the butts of all the cruel jokes and taunts. There is evidence that rejected children may be more likely to initiate conflict and are poor at resolving it (Hartup, 1989).

The tuned out, rather than being strongly rejected by their peers, are simply ignored. This group includes the abnormally shy and withdrawn; it also includes those whose behavior might be described as immature. Thus, in this preschool group, many among the tuned out (the ignored) were more likely to pout, cry, have their eyes shut, suck their fingers, shuffle, fall, flinch, be chased, crawl, whine, or use baby talk.

Gottman suggests that it might be important for parents and teachers to know more about socially isolated children. How do they become that way? What are the implications of social isolation? What can be done to help social isolates?

It is important to note that there are wide individual differences in the sociability of different children. Not all are outgoing, talkative, expansive; many appear withdrawn and shy. We should not make the mistake, however, of assuming that children who appear shy are also unfriendly and are likely to be rejected by their peers or socially tuned out. In fact, countless children — and adults — who are not socially outgoing are nevertheless extraordinarily socially competent. Such children may have a large number of close friendships and might, in fact, be among Gottman's "sociometric stars."

There is some evidence that sociability is partly genetic. Identical twins are highly similar to each other, even at very young ages, prior to the time that personality would have been greatly affected by environmental influences (Goldsmith, 1983). That environmental influences are also involved is clear as well. Ainsworth's research (reviewed in Chapter 6) provides evidence that the nature of the attachment between caregiver and child influences the child's relationships with others. Specifically, securely attached infants are more likely to be highly sociable. Similarly, Baumrind's research (reviewed in Chapter 8) indicates that warm, supportive, and authoritative parents are more likely to raise well-adjusted, sociable children.

Functions of Peers

During the first years of school, children's peer groups have several important functions, some of which have already been mentioned. First, the child's need for acceptance and approval is satisfied mostly by the peer group (with the gradual reduction of parental influence). Children also need to develop a favorable self-concept — to achieve self-worth — and the concept of the self is directly related to how children think others perceive them. As we saw, if you believe others think highly of you, you are more likely to think highly of yourself (develop a positive self-concept) than if you feel others do not think much of you.

A second function of peer groups is what is termed *normative*. What this means is that the peer group serves to teach and reinforce important cultural norms. Thus, peer groups are important for the formation of values and attitudes. In one study, for example, Lamb, Easterbrooks, and Holden (1980) found that children as young as 3 reinforce their peers for sex-appropriate behavior, but are quick to criticize what they perceive to be inappropriate cross-sex behavior. Not surprisingly, children who are reinforced tend to continue the behavior for which they received reinforcement. In contrast, most of those who are not reinforced, or who are criticized, abandon their old behavior and go to some new activity within a minute or less.

In connection with the importance of peer groups for the child, studies have shown the harmful effects that the absence of contact with peers seems to have on the young of other species. Harlow and Zimmerman (1959) report that infant monkeys reared in isolation are often unable to achieve mature social relations when finally brought into contact with their peers. Such monkeys, particularly males isolated for a prolonged period, are typically incapable of normal sexual activities. The females fare better because their sexual role is passive rather than active; consequently they occasionally become pregnant and bear young. But it is both striking and potentially significant that these monkey mothers are unable to display the maternal attachment typical of mothers reared under more normal conditions. In fact, some monkey mothers raised without peers will torture their own offspring (Harlow, Harlow, & Suomi, 1971).

For humans, there is little doubt that peers are extremely powerful sources of punishment and reinforcement. In addition, they are an important source of information about sex- and age-appropriate and inappropriate behaviors as well as about how to do things, what one should look and sound like, what music is good and bad, and on and on.

But peers are not the only source of influence on the child. The family, as we saw in Chapter 8, is another. So is the school.

THE SCHOOL

Outside of the family, say Asp and Garbarino (1988), the school is the most pervasive socializing influence in the life of the child. When children leave home and enter school, they leave behind much of their "play" and begin the serious "work" of childhood. Now the process of socializing for adulthood takes on a new urgency — a new seriousness. The child is now called upon to learn new rules and to adopt new roles.

In Bronfenbrenner's terms, the transition from home to school is a transition from one microsystem (the family in face-to-face interaction) to another (teachers and peers in immediate interaction). The implications for the continued development of social, cognitive, and physical competence, as well as for the development of the child's sense of self and of worth, can hardly be overestimated.

Schools are centrally involved in teaching children much that is necessary for their effective interaction in our increasingly complex world. They are our fundamentally important, formal, monolithic disseminators of culture. To simplify greatly, children acquire essential language and cognitive skills in schools. Here too children develop the social skills and public personality that will characterize them throughout life.

It is not easy to separate the influence of schools from that of other powerful socializing forces (such as the family or television, for example). Each of these is influential not only in the face-to-face interaction that defines the child's microsystem, but also in the more remote interactions that define the mesosystem (or the exo- and macrosystems; see Chapter 2). That is, families influence schools even as democratic consensus, political decisions, the exercise of judicial power — and so on — may influence the systems with which the child interacts.

Teacher Expectations

One illustration of how schools can affect children is found in studies of the influence of teacher expectations, first systematically investigated by Rosenthal and Jacobson (1968a, 1968b). The study involved administering an intelligence test in the spring of the school year, telling teachers this was a test designed to identify academic "bloomers" (students *expected* to blossom next year) and later "accidentally" allowing teachers to see a list of likely bloomers. In fact, these bloomers were a randomly chosen group of about 20 percent of the school's population. No other treatment was undertaken.

Significantly, most teachers observed exactly what they expected. The experimental group not only scored higher on measures of achievement than a comparable control group, but also scored higher on a general measure of intelligence.

The Rosenthal and Jacobson study and others like it have been criticized extensively. In particular, Barber and Silver (1969a, 1969b) have examined many of the studies with which Rosenthal and Jacobson support their hypothesis and contend that few of them clearly demonstrate the effects of teachers' expectations. Rosenthal's (1969) replies to these criticisms are equally adamant in maintaining that the studies do indeed support his conclusions.

Many replication studies have been undertaken in an effort to resolve the controversy (Meyer, 1985). Brophy and Good (1974) reviewed 60 of these and concluded that many are confusing and inconclusive. However, many of these

Schools play a vital role in helping children develop a public personality that will characterize them throughout life.

studies do show patterns of teacher expectations that appear to be linked with student self-concept as well as achievement. Similarly, Braun's (1976) review of the teacher-expectation literature supports the conclusion that many teachers develop predictable patterns of expectations. Specifically, teachers often develop more positive expectations for children from more advantaged socioeconomic backgrounds, as well as for students who are more attractive, more articulate, and who sit close to the teacher and speak clearly. Teachers also develop more positive expectations for those given more positive labels: "learning disabled" rather than "mentally retarded" (Rolison & Medway, 1985); "excellent" rather than "weak" (Babad, 1985). Thus the effects of teacher expectations have sometimes been invoked as a partial explanation for the poorer school performance of some minority-group children.

Unfortunately, a cursory overview of the results of studies such as these makes them seem far more dramatic and important than they actually are. In addition, there is a tendency to assume that negative expectations are more potent and more pervasive than are positive expectations. That is not the case.

Self-Expectations

We have known for some time that teacher expectations might have an effect on the performance of some students. We might also have suspected, had we thought about it, that the individual's personal expectations might have an even more profound influence on performance.

Research in this area has recently focused on what is generally called **attribution theory.** An attribution is an assignment of cause (or blame or origin). If I think my stupidity is due to my having hit my head on a low branch, then I *attribute* my stupidity to that event. Attribution theories look for predictable regularities in the ways we attribute causes to the things that happen around us (or to us) (see Weiner, 1979, 1980a, 1980b).

As we saw in Chapter 2, children appear to be very different in the ways in which they typically assign responsibility for their successes or failures. In general, there are two orientations (with many falling between these two classifications). Some accept personal responsibility for the consequences of their behavior. They are *internally oriented* (Weiner, 1980a) or *mastery-oriented* or *persistent* (Dweck, 1986). Others are more likely to attribute successes and failures to circumstances or events over which they have no control; these are *externally oriented* individuals (Weiner, 1980a). In Dweck's terms, these individuals are characterized by *helplessness* rather than by persistence.

Differences between mastery-oriented and helpless children are often highly apparent. Mastery-oriented children are most likely to attribute their successes to ability or effort (factors that are personal or over which they at least have personal control); in contrast, helpless children are more likely to attribute their successes or failures to luck or the difficulty of the task (it was too hard or too easy), factors over which they have no personal control — in the face of which they are helpless (Table 10.6)

Investigators have found several important differences between children who can be classed as helpless and those described as mastery-oriented. First, mastery-oriented children tend to be much more highly achievement-oriented (Thomas, 1980). Second, mastery-oriented and helpless children react very differently to successes and failures. When Diener and Dweck (1980) arranged a problem situation so that all children would experience an unbroken sequence of eight successes, helpless children still predicted they would not do very well if they had to repeat the eight tasks. In contrast, mastery-oriented children were confident they would continue to perform as well. In other words, children who see themselves as being helpless find it difficult to interpret success as indicating they are capable. Even after succeeding, they not only continue to underestimate the number of likely future successes but they also overestimate the number of likely future failures. In contrast, when mastery-oriented children were given a series of failure experiences, they continued to see themselves as capable and to predict future success experiences. They have higher expectations of themselves.

Changing expectations and attributions. Can expectations and attributions be changed, and will these changes be reflected in behavior? Perhaps. In one study, Dweck and Reppucci (1973) identified a group of children whom they described as *learned helpless*. These were children who reacted extremely strongly to failure — who seemed to attribute failure to lack of ability or other factors they could not control. They typically gave up following a single failure, even though they had both the motivation and the ability to succeed. Dweck

Table 10.6
Why Did You Fail or Succeed? Internally Oriented
Versus Externally Oriented Attributions

External	Internal
Difficulty (task easy or too difficult)	Ability (intelligence, skill, or the lack thereof)
Luck (bad or good)	Effort (hard work, industriousness, self-discipline, or laziness, distractions, lack of time)

If this boy is *internally* oriented, he is likely to attribute his performance to his ability and effort (or lack thereof). If he is *externally* oriented, he is more likely to think he was lucky (or unlucky) or that the task was too easy (or too difficult).

(1975) later demonstrated that it is possible to train such children to take personal responsibility for failure and to attribute it to insufficient effort rather than to lack of ability. Subsequently, contrary to their earlier behavior, many of these children began to persist following failure.

A related study conducted by De Charms (1972) involves what the author terms "personal causation training." De Charms describes two broad categories of people: pawns, who characteristically see themselves as "pushed around," and origins, who see themselves as the *originators* of their own behaviors. In Dweck's terms, *pawns* are the learned helpless; *origins* are characterized by feelings of control — they are mastery-oriented and persistent. The study attempted to make pawns more like origins. To this end, teachers were given training in "personal causation" — training designed to encourage self-study, to foster the evaluation of personal motives, to bring about an understanding of the value of realistic goals and proper planning, and to highlight the importance of the distinction between origins and pawns. Subsequently, teachers helped develop a series of classroom exercises for their grades six and seven classes. The purpose of these exercises was to achieve the same general goals as those of their own personal causation training. Final results showed an increase both in teacher and student motivation, as well as a significant increase in the academic achievement of students.

What attribution-change programs have in common, Wittrock (1986) notes, is that they attempt to move the student in the direction of *effort* attributions. That is, they are designed to lead the student to the understanding that success and failure ought to be attributed to personal efforts. And there is increasing evidence that they can be successful, at least in the short term. Still, a number of crucial questions remain to be answered. Perhaps the most important of these concerns the origins of helplessness. Although most researchers think it is learned (Tzuriel, 1989) and that it can therefore be unlearned, the issue is still not clear. In addition, helplessness has been implicated in physical and psychological disorders, as well as in achievement and adjustment problems, but its precise contribution to these is not clear (Seligman, 1975).

In summary, the influence of the school clearly goes well beyond simply imparting intellectual skills. It provides the child's first opportunity for meaningful and prolonged interaction with other significant adults and peers. It is a continuous source of information about the worth of self, as well as a large source of models illustrating more or less acceptable behaviors. The media, too, are a source of models.

TELEVISION

There is a fear in the hearts of grandparents that the mass media will taint their still tender and highly corruptible young. First they feared **fairy tales,** few of which have happy endings and even fewer of which are without violence. But the force of attacks on the Brothers Grimm and on Hans Christian Andersen never reached the passionate intensity with which the finger waggers went after the **comic book,** whose primary characteristics have been described as "violence in content, ugliness in form and deception in presentation" (Wertham, 1954, p. 90). In a stinging indictment documented with numerous case studies, Wertham ascribes many of the ills that beset young children to their

TV—a beneficial force increasing literacy, language sophistication, and moral reasoning? Or an antisocial agent robbing children of imagination, creativity, and social skills?

addiction to comics, which, he maintains, are replete with unexplained, unjustified, and often unpunished violence, sadism, and other forms of criminal perversion. He claims that comics qualify neither as art nor as literature, that they are antieducational, and that they demonstrate that the greatest evil is not crime but the stupidity that allows the criminal to be apprehended. His book is aptly titled *Seduction of the Innocent.*

Arnold (1969) presents an equally scathing indictment of comic books, objecting to the models of violence they present to young readers. But comics are only one of the mass exponents (and proponents) of violence; there are also books, toys, and television — the latter being the most widespread and the most powerful medium.

By the early 1970s, more than 99 percent of homes with young children had television sets (Murray, 1973); now many have two or even more. A 1984 Nielsen report (Nielsen Television Index, 1984) indicates that preschool children spend an average of 27.9 hours per week watching television. Figures for the 6- to 11-year-old group are very similar: 24.5 hours per week. A conservative estimate, Winn (1985) tells us, is that preschoolers spend more than a third of their waking time watching television. By the age of 18, only sleeping will have taken more of American children's time than watching television (Huston et al., 1990). By the age of 65, the average male viewer will have watched television for almost nine full years of his life! Many young children spend more time watching television than they spend in conversation with adults or siblings; and most spend more time watching television than they spend in school (Singer & Singer, 1983). Given these inordinate amounts of time spent in front of television sets, it seems critical to consider the influence of television on children.

For some time now, prophets of doom have been predicting that television will have highly negative effects on children. Their primary claims, based on personal opinion rather than experimental data, are that television is producing a generation of passive people or, alternatively, that the violence pervading many television programs will produce a generation of violent people. Furthermore, claim the critics, television transmits the message that immorality is often rewarded; thus it exercises a corrupting influence. And, given the amount of the child's time it consumes, it has a harmful effect on family relationships, on the social development of children, and on sports, reading, and playing bingo. Although the research evidence is incomplete, we have enough answers to partially respond to these criticisms and to present a more balanced impression of the actual influence of television on the lives of children.

Viewing Patterns and Comprehension

Viewing patterns are relatively clear-cut. Young children spend the greatest amount of time in front of their television sets followed by young adults and elderly people. Preschoolers tend to prefer cartoons. As they get older, preferences shift to situation comedies and to action/adventure programs. And although young children do not understand all they view, they tend to watch those parts of television programs that are understandable for them (Anderson, 1979). During the school years boys tend to prefer "mechanical" themes (science and action); nurturant themes (mothering, caring for) appeal more to girls (Mielke, 1983). These sex differences are not apparent in the preschool years (Anderson & Bryant, 1983).

What children see and understand from television might be quite different from what you or I might see. First, as Winn (1985) points out, children do not have the same backlog of experiences and understanding that we do — their conceptual bases are more fragmented, less complete. We can evaluate television in terms of things we know and have experienced. Television, in a very real sense, reminds us of life. In contrast, children are less able to relate television offerings to their knowledge about the world. Perhaps when this television-reared generation has finally grown up, real life will occasionally remind them of television. They might be a little like Kozinski's character in the novel and movie *Being There* — a man who had spent all his life in front of a television set and who, when he was finally forced into the real world, thought he would really rather watch. It was somehow better than being there.

What do children understand of television? Collins et al. (1978) report that the preschooler understands very little of motives, characters, or plots — hardly surprising given the preschooler's social cognitions. They are still barely aware of the possibility that others have private emotions, motives, and traits. Accordingly, the preschooler responds to the most salient features of what is actually happening — the sights, the sounds, the action. In contrast, elementary school children become progressively more sensitive to motives and more attentive to implications of actions for the characters involved. They pay attention to *why* things happen and to the consequences of their happening rather than simply to *what* happened. Accordingly, commercial programs for young children seem to be based on the assumption that the best way of capturing and holding the viewer's attention is through rapid action, constant change, high noise level, and slapstick violence (Huston & Wright, 1983). One very important question concerns the effects of this violence on children.

Aggression and Antisocial Influences

In the great body of literature that looks at the influence of television on children, the terms *violence* and *aggression* are used not only as though they mean exactly the same thing but also as though it is clear that everybody knows exactly what it is that they do mean. Not so. They mean slightly different things, they are manifested in rather different behaviors, and they are not understood in the same way by everybody.

Aggression. The more general of these two terms is *aggression*. It may be defined as "hostile or forceful action intended to dominate or violate" (Lefrançois, 1983, p. 504). It includes a wide range of behaviors beginning with insistence, assertiveness, or perhaps intrusion and culminating in anger and violence. Thus *violence* is simply an extreme form of aggressiveness. Violence implies physical action or movement and possible or actual harm to people or objects. It is well illustrated in television episodes where people are kicked, beaten, shot, or knifed, or where rocks and other objects are dropped on their heads from great heights. It is also evident in situations where dogs are kicked or cars are smashed.

Clearly, aggression is not always undesirable; the totally nonaggressive are unlikely to achieve many of their desires, as the more aggressive might. Indeed, our survival as a species, as well as that of many other animals, is very likely related to our aggressiveness. That, of course, does not necessarily mean that we still need to be as aggressive as many of us now are.

It seems clear that many — perhaps most — television programs contain violence in one form or another: sometimes verbal, frequently physical, and occasionally symbolic. The Surgeon General's report on television concludes that violence, defined as "the overt expression of physical force against others or self, or the compelling of action against one's will on pain of being hurt or killed," is the dominant theme of television and especially of children's television. One study reports that over 98 percent of all cartoons contain violent episodes, the frequency of violence in children's programs being six times greater than that in adult programs (Gerbner, 1972). The critical question concerns the effects of this violence on children.

The research. In an early series of studies, Bandura and his associates (Bandura, Ross, & Ross, 1963; Bandura, 1969) exposed children to violent models that were either live actors, films of real people, or films of cartoon characters.

AT A GLANCE

Aggression and Gender Differences in Criminal Behavior

Moyer (1976) describes six forms of aggression that can be observed among animals: *predatory*, linked with hunger rather than anger; *intermale*, often associated with mating or territory among animals; *sex-related*, evident in species where males become aggressive when sexually aroused; *fear-induced*, sometimes evident in cornered animals; *maternal*, evident in a mother's tendency to protect her young; and *irritable*, which occurs as a reaction to frustration. All of these can also be seen among humans, and most appear to be more common among males than females (even including maternal aggression, which — among humans — could be seen as *paternal* aggression.) It comes as no surprise that of 29 categories of crime tracked by the U.S. Federal Bureau of Investigation, there were only two for which there were more females than males arrested in 1988: (1) prostitution and commercialized vice and (2) juvenile running away (both "nonserious crimes"; see Figure 10.4).

Following exposure to a violent model (typically, the model was aggressive toward an inflated rubber clown), children were given objects similar to those toward which the model had been aggressive and were observed at play through a one-way mirror. In most studies of this kind, a majority of the children who have been exposed to models of violence behave aggressively; in contrast, those who have not been exposed to violent models most often respond nonaggressively.

Although these studies have been widely interpreted as evidence that violence on television would lead to violence in real life, this kind of generalization

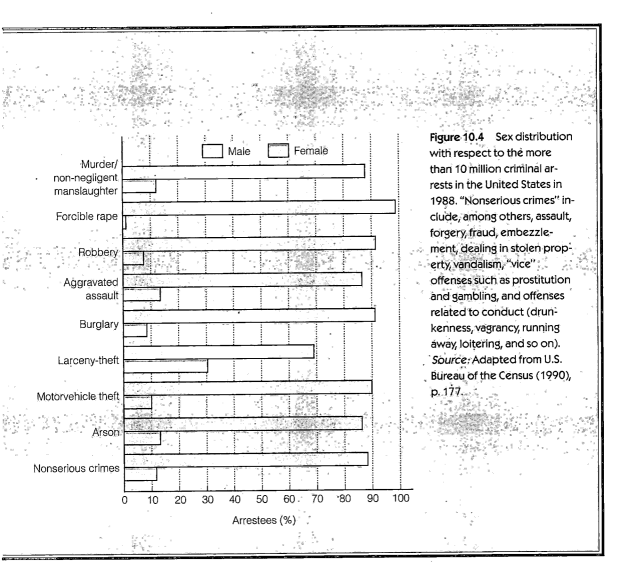

Figure 10.4 Sex distribution with respect to the more than 10 million criminal arrests in the United States in 1988. "Nonserious crimes" include, among others, assault, forgery, fraud, embezzlement, dealing in stolen property, vandalism, "vice" offenses such as prostitution and gambling, and offenses related to conduct (drunkenness, vagrancy, running away, loitering, and so on). *Source:* Adapted from U.S. Bureau of the Census (1990), p. 177.

is probably unrealistic. First, the aggression displayed in an ordinary television program is directed against people rather than against inanimate objects, and children learn early in life, through socialization, that aggression against people is normally punished. Next, the experimental situation generally requires that the child be exposed to the same objects that were used by the model immediately after observing the model or very shortly afterward. A child who watches a violent scene on television is rarely presented immediately with an object (or person) similar to the one on whom the televised violence was inflicted. Finally, striking a rubber clown with a mallet, kicking it, or punching it after seeing a model do so may not be a manifestation of aggression at all. The child has simply learned that these are appropriate behaviors with this inanimate object.

Studies of television viewing under less contrived circumstances are more likely to provide clearer information about its impact. Unfortunately, researchers have had great difficulty locating children who have not been exposed to television and who can therefore serve as control groups for these studies.

One study that does not suffer from this limitation is one conducted by Joy, Kimball, and Zabrack (1977), which spanned a two-year period and involved several small towns where television-viewing history was well known. When the study began, television was just being introduced in one of the towns whereas another still remained without television. Residents of these towns were highly comparable socially, educationally, and economically. And children in each of these towns appeared to be equally aggressive at the beginning of the study. Two years later, however, children in the town where television had been brought in manifested a significant increase in aggressive behavior.

Lefkowitz et al. (1972) report a longitudinal study that examined children's preferences for violent television programs and their aggressive behavior; the study attempted to relate these variables to the same children's preferences and manifest aggressive behavior 10 years later. Results indicate that preferences for violent programs are significantly related to aggressive and delinquent behavior 10 years later (at age 18), particularly for boys. Similar results have also been reported in Sweden where researchers found high positive correlations between television viewing and aggressiveness (Rosengren & Windahl, 1989). Note, however, that these studies do not prove that viewing violent television programs causes aggression. It may be that children who initially preferred violent programs would have been more aggressive and more prone to delinquency than other children even if they had not been exposed to these programs.

An important series of studies conducted in a number of countries (described as a *cross-national* study) looked at the effects of television violence on aggressiveness in children from five countries: the United States, Finland, Israel, Poland, and Australia (Huesmann & Eron, 1986a, 1986b). Not only are some of these cultures very different, but television accessibility and the nature of television programming also varied tremendously. For example, in the Israeli kibbutz, children watched TV for only one or two hours a week and were almost never exposed to television violence. In contrast, American children watched 20 or more hours of television, most of it characterized by violent themes and violent acts.

Some Conclusions

The main conclusion advanced by Huesmann and Eron is essentially the same as the conclusion reached by the Surgeon General's Report on Television and Social Behavior more than a decade earlier: television violence does have an adverse effect on some children. Second, the relationship between television viewing and aggression appears to be interdependent. That is, the most aggressive children tend to select the more violent television programs and to view more of them; at the same time, those who watch more violent programs tend to be more aggressive.

Finally, although some of the research linking television violence with aggressiveness in children has dealt with what might appear to be short-term and perhaps trivial manifestations of aggressiveness, there is now evidence of a link between aggressiveness in childhood and criminality. A study conducted by Huesmann and his associates (1984) found significant correlations between measures of aggression at the age of 8 and indications of antisocial aggression at the age of 30 (for example, spouse abuse, criminal convictions, physical punishment of children, and self-ratings of physical aggression).

Most summaries of research that has looked at the relationship between aggression and television viewing reach similar conclusions. As Rosenkoetter, Huston, and Wright (1990) put it, "Most professional reviews . . . have concluded that the weight of evidence indicates that television violence does increase viewer aggression" (p. 125).

It may be that the negative effects of television have less to do with violence and aggression on television than with some of its more general influences. As Singer (1982) suggests, "the problem with heavy television viewing is not so much that it may or may not stimulate aggression, but that it may interfere with the development of the social skills and mental capacities that children need to acquire the socially approved, successful behaviors they need to get what they want without resorting to aggression" (p. 60). He also points out that television viewing robs many children of what would otherwise be "play" time and may do a great deal to impede creativity (Singer & Singer, 1983). For example, some studies have found a high negative relationship between watching fantasy and violence, and enthusiasm for school work (Zuckerman, Singer, & Singer, 1980). Similarly, Meline (1976) reports that television may have a negative influence on the amount of imagination and creativity that children display in their problem-solving behavior. And Winn (1985), whose criticism of television is extensive, argues that it serves as a narcotic — that parents deliberately use it to pacify and control their children.

Why Is Television Influential?

Most explanations of the effects of television have relied on one or more of several explanations. Theories of imitation (observational learning) suggest that children learn aggressive behaviors from observing television models performing aggressive acts (Bandura & Walters, 1963). An attitude-change model suggests that constant exposure to violence might serve to desensitize children, leaving them with the impression that the aggressive acts so common on television are, in fact, trivial and socially acceptable.

Another explanation that contradicts these two is a *cathartic* model, based on Freudian theory. A *catharsis* is a behavior or event that serves as a release for pent-up emotions. For some individuals, painting might be a catharsis for aggressive impulses that cannot be acted on for moral reasons; others might try to kick their cats. Accordingly, the cathartic model of television influence maintains that exposure to television violence may be a release for pent-up hostility, aggressive urges, and other antisocial tendencies. To the extent that this model is valid, it would follow that television violence might result in a decrease in violent behavior. Similarly, prosocial themes on television might occasionally result in a decrease in prosocial behavior. Huesmann and Eron (1986a) suggest there is no evidence whatsoever that viewing violence prevents aggression by serving as a catharsis.

An important explanation of the effects of television violence is the cognitive, information-processing theory advanced by Huesmann and Eron. The theory is based on the notion that much of our social behavior is controlled by schemas (also called schemata) and scripts (these are described in Chapter 9). Schemata are metaphors for mental representations of what we know. Scripts are one aspect of schemata. They are metaphors for our knowledge of sequences and routines — of what should follow what.

According to this model, learning aggression from television violence requires that the child *encode* this violence — that there be some sort of mental representation of the violence. As we saw in Chapter 9, encoding or representing (putting in memory, in other words) involves processes such as rehearsing and elaborating. Huesmann and Eron suggest that whenever a child fantasizes a violent sequence, rehearsing occurs. And whenever violence is seen in a new context, or whenever a slightly different form of violence is seen in an old context, elaboration may be occurring. The result is that the imaginative and aggressive child who views a great deal of television violence ends up with a wealth of *violence* schemata. In addition, such a child also learns and rehearses a variety of scripts that detail when violence is appropriate and the precise sequence in which it is to be manifested. All that is left is for the child to retrieve these schemata and their related scripts as required.

A pair of spectators sitting close to me at a hockey game I recently attended engaged in a very brief discussion about the maternal origin of one of the players. One of these individuals, anxious to settle this important question, kept urging his reluctant adversary by using a not very original, but widely known script: "Go ahead! Hit me you #$%**! Come on! *Make my day!*"

Rock Videos and VCRs

Close to the very cutting edge of television technology, and sometimes very close as well to the edge of what society's evolving tastes and morals find acceptable, are rock videos. Basically, they are very simple: Take a popular, avant-garde, rock-type song; create images to accompany the lyrics; and combine the two in a frenetic, jarring, surprising, evocative, and sometimes bizarre way. The result? A dazzling, seductive, intriguing, audiovisual experience that has rapidly transformed the music industry — and that has alarmed some parents and educators as well. Why? Because, as one commentator put it, "some of them are sending messages that are questionable, to say the least: anti-work, anti-marriage, anti-family, pro-violence, pro–casual sex, pro–woman-as-victim" (*Television & your children*, 1985, p. 52).

Although research on the effects of rock videos as such is still rare, it seems reasonable to assume that they will be no less influential than the more ordinary television programs. Indeed, they might even be more influential given their technological slickness, the addictive quality of their lyrics and their rhythms, and their popularity with a teen and preteen generation that has increasingly easy access to home videocassette recorders (VCRs).

The rapid proliferation of VCRs brings an additional worry for those concerned with the potentially harmful effects of television. Rosengren and Windahl (1989) point out that parents and society either do not have, or often don't exercise, significant control over children's selections of the video recordings that they rent for home viewing. In most areas, it is possible for children to rent videos that depict aggression and standards of morality that would not be considered acceptable on public television. Similarly, the increasing availability of quasi-private channels through home satellite systems means that increasing numbers of children may be exposed to extreme forms of violence and pornography at very young ages. There is clearly a need for more research to ascertain the probable effects of this exposure and to identify the parameters that might interact to make some children more vulnerable than others.

Prosocial Effects

Fortunately, the messages of rock videos, private channels, and rented cassettes are not all sexist, antisocial, violent, and pornographic; nor are the effects of television all negative. Among the good things that television brings our children are the following (*Television & your children*, 1985):

1. Exposure to greatness
2. Access to the classics
3. Dramatic enlargement of experiences
4. Participation in history
5. Strengthening of sense of community
6. Entertainment

In the same way that television might be instrumental in undermining such values as nonviolence, family stability, cooperation, altruism, and gender equality, so too might it serve to bring about and strengthen these values.

Unfortunately, the most popular area of television research, particularly in the early 1970s when such research was at its height, has been concerned primarily with television's potential antisocial effects, especially with its contribution to aggression. At present, there are still only a relatively small number of studies concerned with the benefits of television. Their results are mostly encouraging.

Baran, Chase, and Courtright (1979) found that cooperation could be increased in young children after exposure to an episode of "The Waltons," which dealt with cooperation in problem solving. Similarly, research with episodes from "Mister Rogers' Neighborhood" and with a number of other deliberately prosocial programs indicates strongly that prosocial behavior can be positively affected (Ahammer & Murray, 1979). Among prosocial behaviors that have improved following television exposure are friendliness, generosity, cooperation, creativity, empathy, racial tolerance, and others (Rosenkoetter, Huston, & Wright, 1990).

The impact of "Sesame Street" on the cognitive development of children has been assessed through a series of independent investigations, as well as by studies conducted by the Educational Testing Service. In general, most of these studies report highly positive findings, which can be summarized as follows: (1) Most viewers gain significantly on a variety of measures including recognizing and naming letters, sorting different objects, naming body parts, and recognizing and labeling geometric forms. (2) Those who view more programs make the highest gains. (3) Adult supervision and encouragement of viewing, although helpful, are not necessary (Lesser, 1977). As Cook et al. (1975) observe, these findings strongly suggest that "Sesame Street" does lead to positive cognitive changes. The research does not show, however, that the difference in cognitive functioning between the advantaged and the disadvantaged at the preschool level has been reduced by "Sesame Street." In fact, some evidence indicates that middle-class children might have benefited more from educational television than less advantaged children, perhaps because they appear to watch more of it (Cook et al., 1975). Nevertheless, the beneficial effects of "Sesame Street" on intellectual development seem clear.

A Summary

There is little doubt that television can have both beneficial and harmful effects. That it has had more of one than the other is still uncertain and will be difficult to determine. Further clarification depends on longitudinal, carefully controlled studies where the characteristics of viewers as well as the characteristics of programs are carefully identified and where adequate control groups are available. We already have some indication that not all portrayals of violence have the same effects. Collins (1983), for example, suggests that comedies with slapstick violence and violent cartoons are too unrealistic to serve as powerful models of violence. In contrast, realistic portrayals of violence, violence perpetrated by "good guys" in their attacks upon "bad guys," and violence that appears in random fashion unrelated to the plot produce more real-life violence among viewers (Singer, 1982). Furthermore, the effects of violence on television are not solely a function of its realism but depend as well on the individual viewer. Collins (1983) presents a strong argument that the viewer's understanding of the program's content, previous social learning, and the circumstances that follow viewing interact to determine whether a television experience will have a discernible effect.

The Surgeon General's report makes a clear appeal for an increase in prosocial programming. And an increasing number of researchers are now arguing that schools should teach children the basic skills of television literacy — skills relating to distinguishing between reality and fantasy, making wise choices among available programming, and limiting viewing and engaging in other important social and intellectual activities such as conversation, reading, and playing (see Anderson, 1983).

Following a review of television and its effects on children, Huston, Watkins, and Kunkel (1989) recommend federal guidelines that would ensure a minimum amount of quality children's programming and that would protect children from commercial exploitation. The long-range goal, these authors argue, should be to eliminate advertising for children. This, they believe, would have a significant impact on programming. And ultimately, it might serve to reduce violence in the contemporary family.

VIOLENCE IN THE FAMILY

Even very conservative estimates of child abuse, spouse abuse, and child sex abuse are startling, says Emery (1989). He quotes surveys that have found that: 20 percent of all murderers are members of the victim's family; nearly a million instances of child abuse are *reported* each year in the United States; and between 2 and 3 percent of a random sample of women had been coerced into having sex with a father, stepfather, or brother before the age of 18.

Some argue that much of the violence in our society begins with violence in the home; and much of the violence in the home begins with cultural values that, at least implicitly, have maintained that it is acceptable for parents to use physical force to control and to punish their children.

Punishment: The Case Against

In addition to humanitarian and ethical objections to punishment, particularly of a physical nature, there are a number of other reasons for discouraging its use. In the first place, it does not always work. Second, because it does not ordinarily illustrate desirable behavior but rather draws attention to that which is undesirable, it contributes little if anything to learning socially acceptable behavior. Third, it is often accompanied by undesirable emotional side effects — negative reactions that can become associated with the punisher perhaps as easily as with the behavior for which the child is punished (Clarizio & Yelon, 1974). And fourth, punishment sometimes has effects opposite to those intended. Children whose parents punish them for aggressive behavior are more likely to be aggressive; children whose mothers are punitive when attempting to toilet train them are more likely to wet their beds later (Sears, Maccoby, & Lewin, 1957). Similarly, habitual mischief-makers whose misbehavior earn them an otherwise preoccupied parent's or teachers' punishment may misbehave even more. The attention that accompanies the act of punishing sometimes serves as reinforcement for the behavior punished.

Punishment: The Case For

There is a case to be made for the use of punishment, however, particularly when the punished behavior is dangerous to the child or to others. Lighting candles, burning holes in paper, and playing with wall sockets are frequently considered punishable offenses. And punishment can be effective in suppressing undesirable behavior under certain circumstances (Parke, 1970). The important variables in the administration of punishment appear to be timing, intensity, consistency, and the relationship between the punisher and punishee. Both with humans and with animals, delayed punishment is considerably less effective than punishment that immediately follows a transgression. Also very intense physical punishment is considerably more effective than mild punishment when effectiveness is determined in terms of number of reoccurrences of the punished behavior. In fact, intense punishment appears to be very effective even when it is delayed.

Punishment by a parent who is ordinarily warm and loving is significantly more effective than punishment by a usually cold and distant parent (Aronfreed, 1968). Parental consistency is also an important variable, with inconsistent parents being less effective than consistent parents. Reassuringly, there is no evidence that punishment administered by a loving parent decreases the affection between parent and child (Walters & Grusec, 1977). However, in considering the effects of physical punishment on children we should realize that any desirable changes that occur in children's behavior as a result reinforce the parents' punitive behavior and may lead to child abuse (Mulhern & Passman, 1979).

Kinds of Punishment

This discussion of the effects of punishment applies mainly to situations in which punishment involves doing something *negative* to the child — as opposed to removing something positive. Furthermore, many of the most valid objections to the use of punishment apply to physical punishment and much less to other forms of punishment.

Punishment may have effects opposite to those intended. Children whose parents punish them for aggressive behavior are more likely to become aggressive.

There are at least three different classes of punishment that are often used by parents and teachers and that are not as open to the objections just noted. These include *reprimands* and the use of *time-out* and *response-cost* procedures.

Reprimands are simply verbal or nonverbal indications of disapproval. They can be mild (a gentle headshake) or harsh (a shout). They are, in a sense, the opposite of praise. Praise says "I like . . ."; reprimands say "I do not like . . ."

Research indicates clearly that reprimands can be very effective in suppressing undesirable behavior and in bringing about more desirable responses. It also points out that the most effective reprimands not only identify the undesirable behavior but also provide specific rationales for doing something (or for not doing the opposite) (Van Houten & Doleys, 1983). Studies of the use of reprimands in the classroom also suggest that reprimands that are given at a closer distance are often more effective than those that are given from farther away (Van Houten et al., 1982).

In a time-out procedure children are removed from a situation in which they would ordinarily expect reinforcement. If students like being in a classroom (the classroom presents them with positive reinforcement), then removing them from the classroom (time out) is a form of punishment. Brantner and Doherty (1983) distinguish among several different time-out procedures that can be used in a classroom. One is *isolation*. It involves removing a student from the classroom. A less severe time-out procedure is *exclusion*, where the student is not sent out of the classroom but is simply prevented from participating in ongoing activities.

Response-cost is a form of punishment where the penalty for bad behavior is the loss of rewards that have been awarded for good behavior. Token-reinforcement programs in schools often make use of response-cost; not only can children earn tokens for certain behaviors but they also run the risk of losing them for misbehaviors. Research reported by Pazulinec, Meyerrose, and Sajwaj (1983) supports the finding that response-cost procedures can bring about significant increases in classroom achievement and marked reductions in disruptive behavior. One of the advantages they have over time-out procedures is that they do not remove the child from ongoing activities. In addition, they are usually combined with reinforcement programs, making it easier for parents and teachers to use them to bring about desirable behavior as well as to eliminate that which is less desirable.

Child Abuse and Neglect

Most of our social and psychological objections to the use of punishment relate to physical punishment and not to other forms of punishment and methods of control. The line between acceptable physical punishment — if, indeed, any form of physical punishment is acceptable — and physical abuse is thin. Yet physical punishment is still very much a part of contemporary childrearing. Indeed, physical violence, often an outgrowth of a parent's attempt to punish physically, is appallingly prevalent. A shocking one out of every seven murder victims is a child (Henderson & Henderson 1984).

Physical violence is only one form of child maltreatment; sexual abuse, emotional abuse, and neglect are others. *Reported* cases of child maltreatment have increased by about 10 percent a year since the 1970s (American Humane Association, 1983). However, as Straus and Gelles (1986) point out, it is not clear whether this means that child maltreatment is actually increasing or whether reporting and detection are more thorough. A large-scale survey of 2,143 families in 1975 and 3,520 families in 1985 found, in fact, that child and wife abuse *declined* appreciably in that 10-year period. While incidence of the

Table 10.7
Violence Against Children in the United States, 1975 to 1985 (Rate per 1,000 children aged 3 through 17)*

Type of Violence	$(n = 1,146)^{\dagger}$	$(n = 1,428)^{\ddagger}$
Minor violence acts		
Threw something	54	27
Pushed, grabbed, shoved	318	307
Slapped or spanked	582	549
Severe violence acts		
Kicked, bit, hit with fist	32	13
Hit, tried to hit with something	134	97
Beat up	13	6
Threatened with gun or knife	1	2
Used gun or knife	1	2
Violence indexes (cases)		
Overall violence	630	620
Severe violence	140	107
Very severe violence	36	19

Source: Adapted from "Societal Change and Change in Family Violence from 1975 to 1985 as Revealed by Two National Surveys" by M. A. Straus and R. Gelles, 1986, *Journal of Marriage and the Family, 48,* 465–479. Copyright 1986 by the National Council on Family Relations, 3989 Central Ave., N.E., Suite 550, Minneapolis, MN 55421. Reprinted by permission.

*For two-caretaker households with at least one child 3 to 17 years of age at home.

†A few respondents were omitted because of missing data on some items but *n* is never less than 1,140.

‡A few respondents were omitted because of missing data on some items but *n* is never less than 1,418.

more minor forms of child abuse had not changed appreciably, the more severe forms of abuse (kicking, beating up, using a knife or a gun), which conform to the public's general understanding of what abuse is, had declined by 47 percent (Table 10.7). Still, estimates are that close to 2 million children are sufficiently abused and neglected in the United States each year to require the help of protective agencies (American Association for Protecting Children, 1987). Given the difficulty of obtaining information from parents and even from doctors in cases of child abuse, this figure probably represents a very conservative estimate. In a survey of child abuse in the United States, Gelles (1979) found that 58 percent of a sample of 1,146 parents had used some form of physical violence on a child at least once during the past year. An astounding 2.9 percent admitted to having used a knife or a gun on one of their children at least once in their lifetimes — small wonder that one out of every five murders in the United States is committed among immediate family members in their own home (Figures 10.5 and 10.6).

Nature of child abuse and neglect. The term *child abuse* includes a tremendous variety of behaviors carried out against children. Chase (1975) categorizes these behaviors as follows:

Physical abuse generally involves physical injury to the child. It is described, perhaps overly dramatically but effectively, by Bakan (1971, p. 4):

> Children have been brought into hospitals with skulls fractured and bodies covered with lacerations. One parent disciplined a child for presumptive misbehavior with the buckle end of a belt, perforating an intestine and killing the child. Children have been whipped, beaten, starved, drowned, smashed against walls and floors, held in ice water baths, exposed to extremes of outdoor temperatures, burned with hot irons and steam pipes. Children have been tied and kept in upright positions for long periods. They have been systematically exposed to electric shock; forced to swallow pepper, soil, feces, urine, vinegar, alcohol, and other odious materials; buried alive; had scalding water poured over their genitals, had their limbs held in an open fire; placed in roadways where automobiles would run over them; placed on roofs and fire escapes in such a manner as to fall off; bitten, knifed, and shot; had their eyes gouged out.

More representative perhaps is Gil's (1970) finding that the majority of children who were reported victims of abuse suffered from bruises and welts (67.1 percent); abrasions, contusions, and lacerations (32.3 percent); bone fractures and skull fractures (10.4 and 4.6 percent, respectively); burns and scaldings (10.1 percent); and wounds, cuts, and punctures (7.9 percent).

Physical neglect consists of acts of omission rather than commission and generally involves parents' failure to ensure that children have adequate nourishment, shelter, clothing, and health care. Physical neglect is somewhat more difficult to detect than physical abuse, but nevertheless makes up a relatively large proportion of reported abuse cases.

Emotional abuse refers to parental behaviors that cause emotional and psychological harm to the child, but that are not instances of physical abuse or neglect — for example, continually shaming or ridiculing children, isolating them, depriving them of emotional contact and comfort, blaming, yelling, and other behaviors that might be classified as involving mental cruelty. The effects of emotional abuse, unlike those of physical abuse or neglect, are often invisible. Consequently, instances of emotional abuse are seldom reported. However, the long-term effects of emotional abuse and neglect are sometimes more serious than those of physical abuse. They may come to light years later, and often involve serious adjustment and emotional problems (Wolock & Horowitz, 1984).

Sexual abuse. *Sexual abuse* is a form of child abuse where sexual behaviors are forced upon a child. Victims of sexual abuse are primarily female and are often very young — in fact, they are sometimes still infants. Incest is often but not always involved in the sexual abuse of children.

Estimates of the prevalence of sexual abuse vary considerably. There are two reasons for this. One has to do with problems of definition. Sexual abuse may be defined as an unwanted sexual act involving physical contact; it may also be defined as any of a number of actions that *do not* involve physical contact (for example, a proposition or suggestion; verbal enticements; exhibitionism). Estimates will, of course, vary depending on the researcher's definition.

A second problem in arriving at accurate estimates has to do with the extreme social taboos that surround all forms of incest and especially father-daughter incest. Estimates of these acts have typically been based on cases reported to courts or other legal jurisdictions or that come to light in the course of mental health treatment and are probably gross underestimates.

Because of these problems, estimates of sexual abuse are largely meaningless, although they're extremely common. Finkelhor's (1986) survey of 10 recent studies found prevalence rates ranging from a low of 6 percent of the sample to 62 percent.

Research on father-daughter incest (and on other forms of incest as well) is scarce; it consists largely of psychiatric case studies or collections of informal reports. In one study, a group of 40 psychiatric patients who had had incestuous relationships with their fathers were compared with 20 other psychiatric patients whose fathers behaved seductively but who had not had directly incestuous relationships with them (Herman & Hirschman, 1981). In this study, *incest* was defined as any physical contact between father and daughter that has to be kept a secret. Genital fondling, masturbation, and oral-genital contact as well as actual intercourse were the most common forms of incest. Other behaviors such as showing a daughter pornography, describing sexual conquests, or asking for detailed descriptions of the daughter's sexual behavior were classified as seductive rather than incestuous, provided they did not involve physical contact.

This study and a review by Finkelhor (1986) indicate that there are some broad characteristics that might serve to identify situations where the risk of sexual abuse is higher than normal. To begin with, girls are at considerably higher risk than are boys, although boys too are at some risk. Those who live at home with their natural fathers are at higher risk, as are those whose mothers are employed outside the home or who are ill, disabled, alcoholic, or battered.

Abused Children

Reported instances of child abuse and neglect have risen dramatically in recent decades — from 10.1 cases per thousand children in 1976 to 32.8 cases in 1986. A total of slightly over 2 million children were victims of reported maltreatment in 1986. Of these children, 47.5 percent were male; 52.5 percent, female. Those perpetrating the maltreatment were male in 44.1 percent of cases and female in the other 55.9 percent. It is unclear to what extent rising rates represent an actual increase in maltreatment and to what extent they reflect increased awareness and reporting on the part of people such as teachers, physicians, relatives, and family acquaintances.

Changing our society's attitude toward corporal punishment may be the only truly effective means of preventing child abuse.

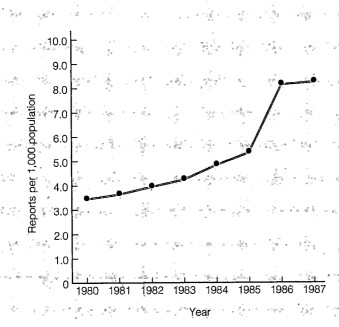

Figure 10.5 Reported cases of child neglect and abuse per 1,000 population, 1980 to 1987 (note that these figures would be much higher per 1,000 *children*). *Source:* Adapted from U.S. Bureau of the Census (1990), p. 176.

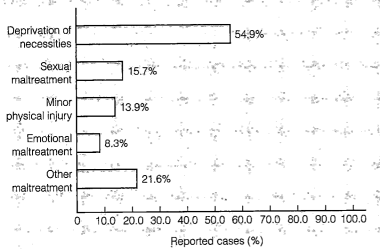

Figure 10.6 Child maltreatment cases, with type of maltreatment as a percentage of the nearly 2.1 million cases reported in the United States in 1986. (Note that some children are classified more than one way; hence percentages total more than 100). *Source:* Adapted from U.S. Bureau of the Census (1990), p. 176.

Girls living with a stepfather are also at higher risk. Note, however, that these are extremely broad categories that include so many individuals that their predictive value is severely limited.

The Consequences of Maltreatment

Quite apart from the physical consequences of child abuse — which may even include death — there are serious emotional and psychological consequences. These can result perhaps as readily from physical abuse and neglect as from emotional or sexual abuse. Abused children are often frightened; their behaviors may range from complete social withdrawal, uncontrolled aggression, and regression to behaviors characteristic of younger children: crying, truancy, and delinquency.

Emery (1989) makes the point that the long-term effects of child abuse are highly varied and often unpredictable. They include an increased probability of higher aggression, problems with peer relationships, impaired social development, lack of empathy, depression, and poorer performance on cognitive tasks. Studies of adults with behavioral and emotional problems (delinquency and criminality or mental disorders, for example) have often found that these adults were abused as children. Fischer and Pipp (1984) report, for instance, that child abuse seems to be related to the development of *multiple personality* — a mental disorder where the patient develops two or more highly distinct personalities (the classical "split" personality, often confused with schizophrenia, which is actually a different disorder). They found that most individuals suffering from this disorder seem to have been subjected to severe abuse as young children.

Among adolescents who have been victims of sexual abuse, there is a higher than normal incidence of running away, attempted suicides, emotional disorder, and adolescent pregnancies — particularly if the father was the abuser. One investigation of 41 rural mothers who had been pregnant as teenagers found that an astounding 54 percent had been sexually abused before the age of 18 (Butler & Burton, 1990).

Theories such as Bronfenbrenner's emphasize the importance of looking at the ecology — that is, at the interactions — within which the abused child and parent find themselves. From this perspective, child abuse may be seen as a symptom of a dysfunctional family. Membership in this family system would be expected to have negative effects not only on the victims of abuse, but on other family members as well. Accordingly, it is perhaps not surprising that when Jean-Gilles and Crittenden (1990) compared reported abuse victims to their siblings, they found remarkable similarities between the two. Siblings were also frequently subjected to abuse (often not reported) and manifested similar behavior problems. The common view that one child in a family serves as a scapegoat and that the others are spared abuse is largely inaccurate and misleading, claim Jean-Gilles and Crittenden. Hence attempts to understand, to prevent, and to treat child abuse and neglect need to take into consideration the entire family as a dynamic, functioning system.

Who Is Maltreated?

As might be expected, infants are often victims of child abuse. Hamner and Turner (1985) report that some 25 percent of all bone fractures in the United States occur in the first two years of life; many of these are related to physical abuse. In fact, between 10 and 15 percent of all injuries caused by child abuse occurs in infants. Among the factors that contribute to the likelihood of an infant's being abused are prematurity, the presence of deformities, being a twin, being born to a mother who has often been pregnant, and being born to a very busy or depressed mother (Klein & Stern, 1971; Carey, Miller, & Widlak, 1975).

Among young children, more of those abused are boys than girls; this is no longer true in early adolescence. Parents appear to punish young male children more violently than older male children. In contrast, young girls receive physical punishment less frequently than older girls. Gil (1970) suggests that parental anxieties about their daughter's sexual behavior may be a contributing factor. Probably because they carry the major responsibility of childcare, mothers tend to abuse more often than fathers, although they are not often as extreme in their abuse (Blumberg, 1974; Gelles, 1979).

In the United States, there is an overrepresentation of nonwhite children among those abused. This higher incidence appears to be related to a variety of socioeconomic factors, including poverty and lower educational levels of parents (Garbarino & Crouter, 1977). Father absence from the home or the presence of a father substitute is related to child abuse; and children from larger families (four or more children) are more likely to be victims of abuse than children from smaller families.

It would be misleading to suggest that the probability of being an abused child is linked solely to social and economic characteristics of the home, sex of the child, and personality characteristics of the parents. There is some evidence that certain children are much more likely than others to be victims of abuse (Martin, 1976). Such children are frequently the products of difficult births or cesarean delivery, are often premature, and often suffer from postnatal complications, facts that might contribute to the absence of a strong parent-infant bond, particularly if the child is hospitalized for some time following birth. In addition, children who are abused are sometimes characterized by extreme irritability, feeding problems, excessive crying, and other behaviors that are annoying to parents. Sadly, many of these children are abused in their homes, although none of their siblings are, and continue to be abused when placed in foster homes.

The Abusive Family Context

Child maltreatment sometimes appears to be a lower-class phenomenon. Parents of abused children tend to be from lower socioeconomic levels and have lower educational achievements; they also are more likely to be unemployed and to be recipients of social aid. However, higher-class parents may simply be better at hiding child maltreatment. It is largely true that when the poor and uneducated need help, they go to the police; when the more affluent and better educated need help, they go to professional counselors.

Many abusive parents have themselves suffered abuse as children (Kempe & Kempe, 1984). But only a small number of child abusers may be classified as psychotic or as suffering from some other personality disorder (Boisvert, 1972). As Emery (1989) notes, one of the most conclusive things that can be said about research in this area is that the majority of abusive parents are not psychopathic. However, many abusive parents share one or more of the following traits: limited knowledge of childrearing; low tolerance for common infant behaviors such as crying; and misinterpretations of children's motivations for crying (Emery, 1989).

Although the vast majority of parents are nonabusive, research indicates that most parents might become abusive under the right circumstances. In a series of investigations, Passman and his associates have systematically studied how parental punishment and rewards are affected by their children's behavior and gender. In one study, Mulhern and Passman (1979) found that when punishing a child leads to increases in desirable behavior, parents might subsequently tend to use even more punishment. Mothers tend to be more punitive than fathers and to punish boys more than girls (Mulhern & Passman, 1981). And with increasing stress, mothers become even more punitive (Passman & Mulhern, 1977).

These findings support two hypotheses: First, in some cases, it may be that children's responses to parental punishment influence parents' behavior, leading to even more punishment and perhaps even to physical abuse; second, the findings provide experimental corroboration for the hypothesis that parental stress is sometimes directly implicated in child abuse (see, for example, Knutson, 1978; Parke & Collmer, 1975).

An investigation of 28 abusive families found that parents in these families were less satisfied with their children, found childrearing difficult and unsatisfying, lived with more anger and conflict, and were less likely to reason with their children than simply to forbid certain behaviors (Trickett & Sussman, 1988).

In an effort to clarify some of the factors involved in child maltreatment, Belsky (1980) presents an ecological model that takes into consideration the entire family system. He suggests that certain influences on interactions in this system contribute to the likelihood of family dysfunction and child maltreatment. These include characteristics of the abused child (as we saw, some children are far more likely than others to be the victims of abuse); discord between husband and wife; economic problems sometimes associated with unemployment; social isolation; alcohol and drug abuse; and a macrosystem that condones the use of physical violence in the family and that, in addition, is reluctant to question the autonomy of the family or to invade its privacy.

What Can Be Done?

Although it is unlikely that child abuse can be completely eliminated, particularly because physical force is a widely accepted childrearing technique in contemporary societies, a number of things can be done. Gil (1970) suggests three separate approaches that might reduce the frequency and seriousness of child abuse. First, systematic educational efforts should be directed toward changing our contemporary permissive attitudes toward the use of physical punishment. Second, because poverty and its related ills appear to be related to the incidence of child abuse, efforts to relieve poverty should be greatly increased. Finally, preventive and therapeutic agencies should address themselves directly to problems of child abuse.

What can be done and what is actually being done are not the same. As Starr (1979) notes, most child abuse programs have focused on treating parents who abuse as well as on protecting victims of abuse; relatively few have been concerned with prevention. And estimates of the effectiveness of child abuse treatments vary considerably, ranging from a high of 80 percent improvement to a low somewhere around 40 percent (Kempe & Kempe, 1978).

Some prevention strategies have attempted to discover ways of predicting which parents or children are most likely to be involved in child abuse so that corrective action can be undertaken before the problem surfaces. But although several large-scale and well-controlled investigations have identified a number of characteristics that abused children have in common, many of these characteristics are also found among nonabused children. Consequently, we do not yet have any very good method for identifying children who are most likely to be abused and those less likely (Starr, Dietrich, & Fischhoff, 1981). Similarly, a systematic investigation of abusive and nonabusive parents also found that although abusive parents had much in common with other abusive parents, many nonabusive parents also shared these characteristics (Starr, 1982). Thus although we know that certain racial, economic, and social factors are involved in child abuse, we cannot reliably predict who is most likely to be abused (or abusive). Prevention based on prediction remains difficult, costly, and susceptible to the error of false identification.

Other preventive strategies that might be highly effective in the long term include Gil's (1970) suggestion that we change contemporary society's attitudes toward corporal punishment and Starr's (1979) suggestion that we make wider use of parent training programs. However, dramatic changes in parental attitudes are likely to be difficult to achieve. Nor can social agencies attempt to identify and label potential abusers without running the risk of unfair and discriminatory practices and invasion of privacy.

Emery (1989) describes two types of intervention currently used. The first is apprehension and punishment of abusers; the second includes social programs and therapy, often involving the entire family. Baxter and Beer (1990) suggest that school personnel also need to be involved. In particular, they need assistance in dealing with immediate problems relating to child maltreatment; and they need training in identifying instances of abuse and neglect and in understanding the legal and psychological implications of their involvement. There is a need too, argues Moriarty (1990) for screening procedures and preemployment testing to ensure that potential child molesters and abusers are not employed in situations where children are easy victims. Unfortunately, this is very difficult since there is no clear personality profile that easily identifies potential child maltreaters — other than perhaps criminal conviction or psychiatric diagnosis in the case of pedophiles.

Neither the problem nor its solution is simple.

SOCIAL-EMOTIONAL EXCEPTIONALITY

Among the possible consequences of child maltreatment, as we have seen, are a variety of adjustment and behavioral problems. Many of these problems, however, result from the interactions of a variety of other factors.

Problems associated with socioemotional exceptionality are both varied and highly individualistic; they are not easily classified or even defined. Terms that are frequently used synonymously to refer to children with problems in this area are *behavior disordered, emotionally disturbed*, and *socially maladjusted*. What each of these has in common is that they describe children who are troubled and who may also cause trouble for parents, teachers, peers, and others (Kovacs, 1989).

The labels describing social and emotional problems are only descriptions, not explanations. Children who are diagnosed as autistic are so labeled because they display a common set of behavioral and emotional symptoms; but the term *autism* serves in no way to explain these behaviors and symptoms.

The problems of identifying socioemotional maladjustment are far more difficult than those relating to physical exceptionality. Whereas reasonably competent individuals can usually arrive at an agreed-on diagnosis of visual or hearing impairments, the same does not hold for the common socioemotional problems (for example, autism, childhood depression and anxiety disorders, and attention disorders such as hyperactivity).

Prevalence, Nature, and Causes

Estimates of the prevalence of emotional or behavior disorders (the terms are used interchangeably in this section) vary considerably depending on the criteria used for identification and on whether estimates include mild as well as severe instances of disturbance. Balow (1980) reports that these estimates range from 0.5 to 40 percent of the school population. Tuma (1989) reports data indicating that about 15 to 19 percent of U.S. children and adolescents suffer from problems requiring some form of mental health services.

The causes of emotional disorders vary a great deal as well. These are often classified in one of two ways: predisposing versus precipitating, or biogenic as opposed to psychogenic. *Predisposing* factors are conditions that increase the risk that a child will develop and display emotional disturbances. Genetic factors, poverty, parental abuse, parental rejection, physical handicaps, age, sex, and racial and religious discrimination have been implicated as predisposing factors (Kazdin, 1989).

Precipitating factors in emotional disturbance are limited to events or situations that lead directly to the disturbance. Specific childhood traumas such as might be associated with the death of a parent, divorce, or an accident to the child might precipitate emotional disorders.

Classifying emotional disturbances in childhood presents a number of difficulties. Kazdin (1989) points out that because of some important characteristics of childhood behaviors, models of adult affective disorders are not always appropriate. First, a number of behaviors that might be problematic in adults and that could be interpreted as symptoms of underlying disorders are relatively common in younger children. For example, excessive emotional reactions to situations such as are manifested in temper tantrums or uncontrollable laughter might seem bizarre in adults and might be a symptom of some underlying disorder. In children, however, such behaviors are common and expected.

Second, there are often developmental changes in problem behaviors that have to be taken into account. The most common pattern is one where apparent problems become less frequent and less serious with increasing maturity. Lying, for example, is quite common among 6-year-old boys, but becomes far more infrequent by adolescence.

Third, over the course of development, some behavioral and emotional problems may be manifested in different symptoms. Kazdin (1989) illustrates this by reference to the youngster who initially threatens and shoves other children who are in his way, but whose aggressive behavior will later take other forms more appropriate for his age — for example, fighting or using weapons.

Finally, there are disorders that are primarily childhood problems; others are more common in adulthood. For example, hyperactivity (discussed in the next section) appears to be primarily a childhood disorder, although there is now evidence that many children do not "outgrow" it (Henker & Whalen, 1989).

In contrast, serious affective (emotional) disorders such as depression and mania were long thought to be adult rather than childhood disorders. We now know, however, that although children rarely suffer the manic disorders, they do suffer depression (Kovacs, 1989).

Given adequate knowledge of the child's biological history and environment, it is sometimes possible to identify children who may be described as being greater psychiatric risks than others. Anthony and his associates (1975; Anthony & Koupernik, 1974) have undertaken longitudinal research designed not only to identify factors that might be useful for predicting the probability of emotional disturbance in later childhood or even in adulthood but to prevent disorders as well. If we can accurately identify predisposing and precipitating factors, then it might also be possible to modify the environment in such a way as to reduce the incidence of emotional disturbance. However, we need considerably more research to identify the forces that are associated with emotional disorders and those that might be associated with healthy development as well.

Attention-Deficit Hyperactivity Disorder

Estimates are that as many as 3 percent of current elementary schoolchildren suffer from varying degrees of hyperactivity (APA, 1980). Some of these children experience considerable difficulty adjusting to school and home; many are considered to be relatively serious problems. The syndrome itself is frequently characterized by restlessness, inability to sit still, nonpurposive and disorderly behavior, impulsiveness, short attention span, and poor performance in school even when the children are of average intelligence. Small wonder that hyperactive children are treated as psychological and medical problems.

Diagnoses of hyperactivity (or hyperkinesis) are sometimes — perhaps even often — made inappropriately by parents and teachers who are confronted by children who are restless and who find it difficult to do the quiet things that adults sometimes demand. Strictly speaking, *attention deficit* hyperactivity disorder as defined by the American Psychiatric Association (1987) requires the presence of at least 8 of the 14 criteria presented in Table 10.8. The onset of the disorder needs to be before the age of 7 to differentiate it from disorders that might arise as reactions to stressful events or illness.

In general, hyperactivity is marked by *excessive* general activity for the child's age (often taking the form of incessant and haphazard climbing, crawling, or running); difficulty in sustaining attention and apparent forgetfulness; and impulsivity (tendency to react quickly; difficulty taking turns; low frustration tolerance). The criteria described by the APA also stipulate that the duration of the child's hyperactivity be at least six months.

Clearly, not all children suffering from this disorder will display the same combination and seriousness of symptoms. However, given the fact that the condition appears easy to diagnose (it is defined largely in terms of observable

Table 10.8
DSM-III-R Diagnostic Criteria for Attention-Deficit Hyperactivity Disorder

A. A disturbance of at least six months during which at least eight of the following are present:

1. Often fidgets with hands or feet or squirms in seat (in adolescents, may be limited to subjective feelings of restlessness)
2. Has difficulty remaining seated when required to do so
3. Is easily distracted by extraneous stimuli
4. Has difficulty awaiting turn in games or group situations
5. Often blurts out answers to questions before they have been completed
6. Has difficulty following through on instructions from others (not due to oppositional behavior or failure of comprehension), for example, fails to finish chores
7. Has difficulty sustaining attention in tasks or play activities
8. Often shifts from one uncompleted activity to another
9. Has difficulty playing quietly
10. Often talks excessively
11. Often interrupts or intrudes on others; for example, butts into other children's games
12. Often does not seem to listen to what is being said to him or her
13. Often loses things necessary for tasks or activities at school or at home (such as toys, pencils, books, assignments)
14. Often engages in physically dangerous activities without considering possible consequences (not for the purpose of thrill-seeking); for example, runs into street without looking

B. Onset before the age of 7.

C. Does not meet the criteria for a Pervasive Developmental Disorder.

Source: Adapted from *Diagnostic and Statistical Manual of Mental Disorders* (3rd ed., revised) (pp. 53–54), 1987. Copyright © 1987 American Psychiatric Association. Reprinted with permission.

Note: A criterion is considered to be met only if the behavior is considerably more frequent than that of most people of the same mental age. The items are listed in descending order of discriminating power based on data from a national field trial of the *DSM-III-R* criteria for Disruptive Behavior Disorders.

behaviors) and that it can therefore easily be *over*diagnosed, extreme caution should be exercised before applying the label to any child.

The most common treatment for a child diagnosed as having an attention deficit disorder with hyperactivity involves the use of stimulant drugs such as dextroamphetamine and methylphenidate (Ritalin). This might seem strange given that stimulants ordinarily increase activity and the hyperactive child already suffers from excessive activity. However, these drugs appear to have what is termed a *paradoxical effect* on children. That is, they appear to sedate rather than stimulate (Campbell & Randall, 1977). However, longer-term studies indicate that the effect may not be entirely "paradoxical" (O'Leary, 1984). In addition, stimulant drugs can have some negative side effects such as weight loss, growth retardation, and mood changes (Roche et al., 1979). Henker and Whalen (1989) note that the use of stimulants with hyperactive children is the most prevalent and the most controversial of child therapies. At present, several drug misuse suits are pending.

The causes of hyperactivity are unclear although research using twins indicates that it has a genetic component. Willerman (1973) found that if one member of a pair of identical twins was hyperactive, the other was much more likely to be. Similarly, Morrison and Stewart (1973) found that hyperactive children had more biological relatives who had also been hyperactive than did children who were not hyperactive. Also, far more males than females are hyperactive (between 80 and 90 percent more) (Wesley & Wesley, 1977), which supports the genetic hypothesis.

Other evidence suggests that hyperactivity is to a large extent a maturational problem involving the central nervous system. Many hyperactive children tend not to display the same symptoms of hyperactivity after adolescence, and the activity level of hyperactive children is frequently similar to that typical of children four or five years younger. However, not all children outgrow this hyperactivity at adolescence (Henker & Whalen, 1989).

Other explanations for hyperactivity have sometimes implicated neurological impairment or brain damage and dietary or vitamin-linked causes. However, there appears to be little evidence that neurological impairment or brain damage is involved in the majority of cases diagnosed as hyperactive, and the conclusion is the same for dietary factors. Whereas Feingold (1975a, 1975b) believes that certain food additives contribute to hyperactivity, carefully controlled research has not found this to be the case, at least for most children (see Hallahan & Heins, 1976). We have some reason to believe, however, that between 5 and 10 percent of hyperactive children react badly to certain food dyes and that these children might therefore be helped through dietary means (Ross, 1980).

Conduct and Personality Disorders

A number of sometimes serious behavior disorders of childhood and adolescence cannot easily be classified. Many of these are problems of socialization, seen in aggressive, hostile, and essentially antisocial behavior; alternatively, conduct disorders might be evident in withdrawal, social isolation, or extreme shyness. Not surprisingly, aggressive and hostile behaviors (delinquency, vandalism, and so on) are likely to be dealt with — or at least punished. Social isolation and extreme shyness are much more likely to be ignored.

Other social disorders may be seen in lying, stealing, inability to form close relationships with others, temper tantrums, disobedience and insolence, extremely negative self-concepts, and related behaviors and attitudes.

Anorexia nervosa is another disorder that might be classified as a conduct or behavior disorder. It involves drastic changes in eating habits, leading to serious — sometimes fatal — weight loss. Because it affects adolescents far more often than any other age group, it is discussed in more detail in Chapter 11.

Treatment of children exhibiting conduct and personality disorders depends largely on the severity of the disturbance. In cases of moderate or mild disturbance, teachers and parents can often cope adequately; with the occasional help of professional personnel, they can sometimes do much more than cope. More severe disturbances may require therapeutic and sometimes judicial intervention.

Stress in Childhood

Many of the emotional and behavioral problems of childhood, and perhaps a number of the physical problems as well, are related to something we call stress — a difficult concept that everybody understands at least intuitively.

In the physical sciences, stress refers to a force that is exerted on a body, sometimes causing deformation or breakage. In psychology, stress may be defined as a nonphysical force that is exerted on an individual, sometimes causing negative change. Johnson (1986) suggests that there are two approaches to defining stress. One is concerned with *stimuli*; the other with *responses*. Stimuli are said to be stressful when they make excessive demands on the individual; responses are stressful when they are accompanied by the physiological changes of high arousal such as increased heartrate, perspiration, trembling, and so on.

Stress is clearly not always negative. In fact, it is an essentially adaptive physiological response (Selye, 1974). It prepares the individual for action. Under appropriate circumstances, the sudden shot of adrenaline and the acceleration of heartrate increase the effectiveness of our running, our fighting, or our speechmaking. But under other circumstances, we may have an overload of stress. The implications of this overload vary from one individual to another, but are clearly not limited to adults. As we saw in Chapter 6, infants and preschoolers can suffer profound distress at the loss of a parent or sometimes even as a result of temporary separation from a parent. The effects are sometimes apparent in sleeping or eating disturbances, as well as in a general listlessness sometimes bordering on depression (Field, 1987).

Among children, the effects of stress might include physical complaints (such as stomach pains, sometimes caused by ulcers, or asthma) or emotional problems (such as persistent fears, high anxiety, or even depression) (Johnson, 1986).

Elkind (1981a) describes a number of sources of childhood stress, some of which are more common to this generation of children than they were to earlier generations. These sources of stress are easily described in terms of stimulus or demand overloads. There is, for example, *responsibility overload*, where young children with working parents are given responsibility for a variety of tasks that might include looking after younger siblings, buying groceries, preparing meals, cleaning the house, and so on. There may also be *change overload*, where children from mobile families are shunted rapidly from home to home, often in different neighborhoods, transferred from school to school, and left with a sequence of caregivers. *Emotional overload* may result when children are exposed to emotion-laden situations that impact directly on their lives, but over which they have little control (parents quarrelling, for example). Finally, there is *information overload* resulting largely from the tremendous amount of information to which television exposes the child. Add to all these potential sources of stress the sometimes exorbitant achievement demands that are placed on the child by school, parents, and society. "Hurry," they all say to Elkind's (1981a) *hurried child.* "Hurry! Grow up! There isn't much time!"

Clearly, not all children are exposed to the same stressful situations; nor will all react the same way. Some children remain unperturbed in the face of events that might prove disastrous for others. Nevertheless, psychology provides a number of ways of assessing stress in the lives of children or at least of determining potential for stress. Many of these are based on the assumption that all major changes in a person's life are potentially stressful and that, although most individuals can cope with a limited number of changes, there eventually comes a breaking point. Accordingly, these stress scales simply ask individuals to identify all major changes in their lives. Some changes are clearly more important than others (the death of a parent compared with changing schools, for example). Values are assigned accordingly (Holmes & Rahe, 1967).

Social-Emotional Giftedness

Here, as elsewhere, exceptionality has two dimensions: the disadvantaged, among whom are the autistic, the depressed, the hyperactive, and those exhibiting personality and conduct disorders; and the advantaged, to whom we have paid little special attention. Nevertheless, it is possible to identify two groups of gifted children in recent literature. One group, variously labeled "superkids" or "invulnerables" (see Pines, 1975, 1979), has been identified in research originally designed to investigate psychiatric risk among children. One of the observations that intrigued researchers was that a significant number of children whose biological and environmental histories were such that the likelihood of emotional disorder was extremely high did not become psychological casualties. Quite the contrary: Not only did some of these children appear to be invulnerable to the emotional disorders that would surely claim a large number of other children in the same circumstances but also they seemed to thrive on early adversity and to emerge unscathed and in some ways superior (Werner & Smith, 1982). Garmezy (1976) describes these invulnerables as exceptionally competent and at ease in social situations, highly capable in social interaction with adults, characterized by feelings of personal powerfulness (as opposed to helplessness or powerlessness), highly autonomous, and achievement-oriented.

The importance of understanding why some children survive and even thrive in high-risk situations and why others do not is related directly to the possibility of "inoculating" children against risk or of ameliorating risk for those who are most vulnerable. Anthony (1975) suggests, for example, that exposure to a certain amount of adversity may be crucial for the development of resistance to disturbance. At the same time, exposure to too many stresses may have just the opposite effect. It may be that there is a particular combination of personality characteristics or genetic predispositions that, in interaction with a stressful environment, produces a highly adjusted healthy person. The critical problem is to identify this combination of characteristics and environment in an effort to maximize the development of human potential. The emphasis is dramatically different from that which focuses on identifying and treating disorders.

Exceptional social and emotional competence may be seen not only in those who survive high risk but also in exceptional individuals whose early lives and biological history present no unusual psychological threats. Walker (1978) suggests that among the socially gifted may well be found the leaders of tomorrow, and perhaps the leaders of today were yesterday's socially gifted children.

Should we provide "special" education for the socially gifted?

MAIN POINTS

1. Social cognition refers to an awareness of ourselves and of others as being capable of feelings, motives, intentions. In infancy, it requires a gradual differentiation of the self from the environment and a recognition of people as persons. Later, it entails the ability to adopt other perspectives.

2. According to Shantz, cognitive role-taking progresses from an original stage in which the infant is unaware that another person is capable of independent thoughts or awareness. That awareness (around age 6) is followed by the knowledge that the child's own behavior can lead to inferences on the part of others (around 8) and is later followed by the ability to make relatively accurate inferences about other people's thoughts and feelings (around 10 or 12).

3. Selman's five stages of perspective-taking, in order, are egocentric (to age 6: I see everything from my point of view; I don't realize there might be others); social-informational (6–8: I realize that there are other points of view, but that is only because others do not know what I know); self-reflective (8–10: I recognize the existence of different points of view, but think everybody is aware only of theirs); mutual (10–12: We can recognize and talk about each other's points of view); social and conventional (12–15 + : I can analyze various perspectives in the light of abstract value and belief systems).

4. The term *self-worth* refers to how positive or negative our personal evaluations of our *selves* are. James defined self-worth in terms of the discrepancy between the individual's competence or actual performance and ideal or desired competence. Cooley believed we arrive at evaluations of our selves on the basis of how we think others evaluate us — hence the expression *looking-glass self.*

5. After the age of 8, children can make global assessments of their self-worth. They also make separate evaluations of their worth in five areas: scholastic, athletic, physical appearance, social acceptance, and morality. Through the elementary grades, physical appearance is most important. The most important sources of social regard in determining the child's self-worth are from parents and classmates (rather than from friends or teachers).

6. Children's concepts of self-worth are closely tied to their moods. High self-worth is associated with happiness; low self-worth, with sadness and depression. In turn, these moods are linked with motivation.

7. During the preschool period, children see friendship as a matter of playing together, but have no concept of enduring relationships. During elementary school, children arrive at the realization that friendships involve enduring and reciprocal relationships and that they are based more on similarities, trust, and affection than on simple physical proximity.

8. Most children tend to have more than one "best friend," to want positive outcomes for their friends, but to compete with them at the same time. Girls are slightly more likely than boys to have fewer best friends but to share a deeper intimacy; they are also less likely to compete than are boys.

9. A peer group is a group of equals. Conformity to peers increases through childhood, peaking at around ages 11 through 14, and declining somewhat after that. At the same time, conformity to parents tends to decrease through the school years.

10. Social competence appears to be one of the important factors contributing to high status; social incompetence contributes to lower status. High social competence is reflected in the child's ability to sense what is happening in social groups, in a high degree of responsiveness to others, and in an understanding that relationships develop slowly over time.

11. Social isolates are those who do not interact much with others or who are socially rejected. Gottman describes five categories of social status: sociometric stars (especially well liked); mixers (high interaction); teacher negatives (conflict with teachers; some high status, others not); tuned out (uninvolved; ignored rather than rejected); and sociometric rejectees (not liked).

12. Peer groups are important in developing positive self-concepts. They are also an important source of reinforcement (or the lack thereof) and thus serve an important normative function in the transmission of values and attitudes.

13. The school is a powerful socializing influence, centrally involved in teaching children much that is necessary for their effective interaction with our increasingly complex world.

14. Research on the effects of teacher expectations may provide an additional basis for understanding the performance of minority-group children, as well as of children who are labeled for other reasons. Student self-expectations are also important. Some children appear to be *mastery-oriented*; they accept personal responsibility for the outcomes of their behaviors (attributing it to intelligence or effort, for example) and are encouraged by success but not overly discouraged by failure. Others are *helpless*; they attribute their suc-

cesses and failures to factors over which they have no control (luck or task difficulty, for example) and tend not to change their estimates of their capabilities when presented with success.

15. Young children spend approximately one-third of their waking hours watching television. Initially, they prefer cartoons; as they become older, their preferences shift to situation comedies and action/adventure programs. Preschoolers pay little attention to characters, motives, and plots, but respond instead to action — to *what* is happening. Older children become more sensitive to motives, more attuned to *why* things happen and to the consequences of program events.

16. There is some evidence of a relationship between television viewing and aggression. The harmful effects television might have may be due as much to the activities it prevents or discourages (reading, socializing, playing, interacting with family members, developing hobbies) as to any direct influence. There are also fears that the anti-work, anti-family, pro-violence, pro–casual sex, anti-establishment messages of rock videos may have negative influences on children.

17. There is evidence that some forms of television can have prosocial effects, sometimes evident in greater friendliness, cooperation, creativity, empathy, and racial tolerance — depending on the nature of the programs viewed.

18. A cognitive information-processing explanation for the effects of television explains its imitation-related effects. It maintains that children encode violence (represent it mentally; the metaphor for the representation is *schema*), rehearse and elaborate it in fantasy and as a result of seeing variations of it in different television programs, and then retrieve it along with relevant scripts (routines detailing the sequence in which the violence is to be perpetrated) when they are moved to aggression. There is also a cathartic hypothesis (violence on television provides release of aggressive urges).

19. Violence in the family and instances of emotional abuse and neglect as well as of sexual abuse are frighteningly common. They may be related in part to cultural values that safeguard the privacy of the family and that condone parental use of physical punishment. Child abuse is not often linked with parent psychopathology, but is linked with a dysfunctional family context.

20. Punishment is not as effective in changing behavior as is reinforcement. Other objections to it include humanitarian and ethical considerations, the fact that it does not ordinarily provide a model of desirable behavior, that it is sometimes accompanied by negative emotional side effects, and that it sometimes has effects opposite to those intended.

21. Many of the objections to punishment apply primarily to physical punishment and not to *reprimands* (expressions of disapproval), *time-out* procedures (in which children are removed from situations where they would ordinarily expect reinforcement), and *response-cost* procedures (in which reinforcers that have already been earned are given up for misbehaviors).

22. Child abuse may be physical abuse (punching, kicking, beating), physical neglect (failure to provide food, clothing, shelter, health care), emotional abuse

(habitual ridicule, scolding, ostracism), or sexual abuse (sexual behaviors forced upon the child). Any of these forms of abuse can have serious and long-lasting physical and psychological consequences.

23. Infants are particularly likely to be among abused children (more probable if the infant is premature, deformed, irritable, or if the mother is overworked, often pregnant, or depressed). Nonwhites are overrepresented among this group in the United States. Abusers are sometimes disturbed in a clinical sense, although they often are not; many of those who abuse their children were themselves abused as children.

24. Among the suggestions for preventing child abuse are that society's attitudes toward the use of physical punishment be changed (an extremely difficult and long-term project) and that parents make wider use of parent education and parent training programs.

25. Causes of emotional disorders are sometimes described as predisposing (genetics and environmental conditions such as poverty, parental abuse, rejection, physical handicaps, ethnic discrimination) and precipitating (a specific environmental event leading to the onset of the disturbance, such as death of a parent, serious illness, or accident).

26. *Attention deficit disorder with hyperactivity,* often simply called hyperactivity or hyperkinesis, is characterized by excessive activity and deficits in attention span without evidence of brain damage or neurological dysfunction. Hyperactive children frequently present behavior problems for teachers and are sometimes treated with stimulant drugs (Ritalin).

27. Conduct and personality disorders are typically manifested in misbehaviors such as lying, stealing, delinquency, and aggression or social withdrawal and excessive shyness. These behaviors are usually extreme and persistent and should not be confused with misbehaviors that are not symptomatic of a disorder.

28. Stress among children can result from many sources, including responsibility overload, change overload, emotional overload, school-related stress, and information overload. Scales that look at major events in children's lives are sometimes useful in identifying the possibility of stress-related problems.

29. Children who run a higher than average risk of emotional disorder but who not only survive but also apparently thrive to become healthy, well-adjusted, bright children and adults are sometimes labeled "invulnerables."

Further Readings

Two good sources of information on the development of social cognition are:

Selman, R. L. (1980). *The growth of interpersonal understanding.* New York: Academic Press.

Shantz, C. U. (1983). Social cognition. In J. H. Flavell & E. M. Markman (Eds.), *Handbook of child psychology: Cognitive development* (Vol. 3). New York: John Wiley.

Comprehensive reviews of research on peer groups and the significance of peer interaction are provided by the following two references. The first is more general and somewhat simpler; the second is far more detailed and research oriented:

Shaffer, D. R. (1988). *Social and personality development* (2nd ed.). Monterey, Calif.: Brooks/Cole.

Hartup, W. W. (1983). Peer relations. In P. H. Mussen (Ed.), *Handbook of child psychology* (4th ed.). *Vol IV: Socialization, personality, and social development.* Edited by E. M. Hetherington. New York: John Wiley, 103–196.

A simple but insightful account of children's friendships is given in:

Rubin, Z. *Children's friendships.* Cambridge, Mass.: Harvard University Press, 1980.

The powerful effects of social pressure are dramatized in Golding's fictional account of the lives of a group of school boys marooned on an island. Is fact stranger than fiction?

Golding, W. (1962). *Lord of the flies.* New York: Coward, McCann & Geoghegan.

The following books are important sources of information on child abuse. Both are practical guides for parents and others who have some responsibility for abused and neglected children:

Finkelhor, D., and associates (Eds.). (1986). *A sourcebook on child sexual abuse.* Beverly Hills: Sage.

Henderson, G., & Henderson, B. B. (1984). *Mending broken children: A parent's manual.* Springfield, Ill.: Charles C. Thomas.

A thoughtful and often disturbing analysis of the harmful effects of television is detailed in the following highly readable and aptly titled book:

Winn, M. (1985). *The plug-in drug* (rev. ed.). New York: Viking, 1985.

The Huesmann and Eron book is a good summary of some of the major issues and conclusions in television violence research. It also presents detailed account of some cross-cultural investigations of the effects of television. The Rosengren and Windahl book is an examination of the impact of television on Swedish children.

Huesmann, L. R., & Eron, L. D. (Eds.). (1986). *Television and the aggressive child: A cross-national comparison.* Hillsdale, N.J.: Lawrence Erlbaum.

Rosengren, K. E., & Windahl, S. (1989). *Media matter: TV use in childhood and adolescence.* Norwood, N.J.: Ablex.

The following books are useful sources of information on stress. The first is a detailed collection of articles that look at the physiology of stress and at its effects at all age levels; the second is a short book concerned specifically with the effects of major changes in the lives of children and adolescents; and the third deals in a simple way with a variety of issues important to the lives of elementary school children.

Johnson, J. H. (1986). *Life events as stressors in childhood and adolescence.* Beverly Hills, Calif.: Sage.

Field, T. M., McCabe, P. M., & Schneiderman, N. (Eds.). (1987). *Stress and coping.* Hillsdale, N.J.: Lawrence Erlbaum.

Humphrey, J. N., & Humphrey, J. H. (1989). *Child development during the elementary school years.* Springfield, Ill.: Charles C. Thomas.

An excellent collection premised on an ecological view of the family is:

Moncrieff, C., Larner, M., Riley, D., Gunnarsson, L., & Henderson, C. R., Jr. (Eds.). (1990). *Extending families: The social networks of parents and their children.* New York: Cambridge University Press.

Life can only be understood backwards;

But it must be lived forwards.

Sören Kierkegaard, *Life*

Vi
Adolescence

Infants do not look backward. They would see little, in any case, in the gloom from which they came.

Older children could look backward; but for most, the living of life fills the days too full to leave much time for peering into the past. Besides, in the cemented-in-reality period of what Piaget calls "concrete operations," the grand questions that drive us to seek the meaning of life do not suggest themselves.

But they *do* suggest themselves to the adolescent. "What is the meaning of life?" they ask. What is the purpose? What is being? What ought? What should? What if? Why? Why?

Of course, the living of life continues forward; adolescents aren't spared the peculiar linearity of time. But they can occasionally look backward, see themselves against the backdrop of their pasts, dream their futures, fill their lives with fantasies of love and power and poetry.

In this section, we look at the changes that bridge the gulf between childhood and adulthood: physiological changes that lead to sexual maturity; intellectual changes that result in a more ideal logic; social changes that reflect new needs and sometimes new economic responsibilities. We look, too, at some of the more turbulent and the more negative aspects of the adolescent experience.

led and the
If, by chance, the a fight, thi
e possibility of your sister
when you see in, close th
your room, go the click of
so she hears you are u
knocks, tell her you are u
to see or that you are
ntration, or any
send

Look backward to your own adolescence — if you have finished it. Try to remember what it was like. Looking backwards, Kierkegaard insists, is the way to understand life.

Miss Nancy Ellicot smoked
And danced all the modern dances;
And her aunts were not quite sure how they felt about it.
But they knew that it was modern.

Thomas Stearns Eliot, *Cousin Nancy*

Physical and Cognitive Development

The sun had just begun to set when my father and our parish priest, Father Paradis, arrived. Father Paradis stood in front of me, just a little to the side, not quite facing me but close enough that there would be no mistake about whom he was addressing if he chose to speak. He shuffled his foot absently in the dust, as if uncertain where to begin.

We stood in the black dirt of my uncle's field where I had been working all day, pulling the cultivator back and forth with the ancient, knock-kneed John Deere. When I first saw my father and the priest standing in the newly turned dirt, I had shut off the tractor. The silence now seemed painful, and I wished for a moment that I had pretended not to see them, that I had continued, "chug . . . chug . . . chuck a chuck . . ." through the sunset and beyond.

"You know why we're here." My father's flat tone made it a statement, not a question.

"No," I said, trying to smile, trying to think of something clever and disarming to say.

"What is your . . . How . . . What kind of explanation . . ." I couldn't be certain whether it was anger, humiliation, or great disappointment that made my father struggle so with his questions.

"Let me . . ." the priest offered, sweeping his left arm out in the awesome gesture that always punctuated his sermons on the Great Sins. "Perhaps he can just confess quietly and you can take him home, away from temptation."

"Home? Confess?" I blurted, hardly eloquent in my confusion.

"Maybe he doesn't know!" the priest said; but his tone suggested this would be highly unlikely.

"Know what? What don't I know?"

"You know why your uncle has fired you," my dad said. Again a flat statement with only a slight quiver of anger and embarrassment in his voice.

Fired! My uncle liked me! How could he possibly fire me?

"Fired?" I said.

"Fired," the priest said.

"Fired," my dad echoed.

"Fired? Me?"

"Fired. You know why. You and Syl . . . You and Sylvia."

"We didn't do anything! We never did anything!"

"Perhaps a short confession," Father Paradis offered again.

"There's nothing to confess," I insisted. My father looked terribly discouraged.

"Your uncle saw you," he said. "He's seen you talking and he noticed you always sit next to each other and . . . Well, she's your cousin."

"Your cousin," Father Paradis repeated. "Dangerous," he added by way of explanation.

"So he thought it would be better if you left now before you got too carried away. And I brought Father Paradis in case you . . . well . . ."

"I didn't. I don't."

"A confession . . ." Father Paradis seemed disappointed. "Just take a minute. Right here. Get it over with right now."

"But I didn't," I insisted. "I never did."

"Well, maybe . . . did you think about it?" the priest suggested helpfully. "Were you tempted? That's where it starts."

"And she's your cousin too," my father added significantly. "And neither of you is even grown up yet!"

PRIMITIVE PASSAGES

Would it have been different if I had been grown up? Or was I grown up and the world simply didn't know it yet?

Growing up in Western cultures is rarely a simple, clear-cut matter. But in a number of other societies, sometimes labeled "primitive" by anthropologists, passage from childhood to adulthood is clearly marked by ritual and ceremony, collectively termed **rites of passage**. Interestingly, even in totally unrelated societies, these rites often share some common features. For example, in most societies rites of passage involve four steps. First, *separation* — the child is removed from the group. Among some tribes (the Navaho and Pueblo Indians, for instance) young boys are sent to live in buildings constructed for this purpose (Cohen, 1964). A common **taboo** (socially forbidden behavior) during this period is that of brother-sister or mother-son contact.

Second, prior to induction into adulthood, children are trained. The *training* typically leaves little doubt about the sorts of behaviors expected of adults — and the sorts of childish behaviors adults are expected to leave behind.

The third step is that of the *initiation* itself: the actual rituals that mark passage from childhood to adulthood. They are a time of celebration, but they are also usually a time of pain and suffering. Thus, many initiation ceremonies include one or more of the following: fasting, scarification (the inflicting of wounds with resulting scars), and circumcision (Bloch & Niederhoffer, 1958).

The final step of the passage rite is *induction* (absorption into the tribe). Inductees now know, without any doubt, that they are full-fledged, adult members of their social group.

Rites of passage can serve a number of useful functions. They impart a sense of adult responsibility to children, and they lessen the ambiguity that might otherwise exist between childhood and adulthood. In addition, many primitive rites reinforce certain important taboos such as those having to do with incest. Bloch and Niederhoffer (1958) suggest this may be the main reason for separating boys and girls, as well as parents and their opposite-sexed children, prior to initiation.

Another important function of a passage rite is that it creates a strong psychological bond between the initiate and the tribe, as well as among initiates. At the same time, it helps to weaken bonds that might otherwise exist between the child and the immediate family. It is as though initiates are being told that they belong to the tribe and not the family, that they can look to the tribe for support and strength, but that they must also defend and protect it.

CONTEMPORARY PASSAGES

These "primitive" societies have no adolescence as we commonly know it. There is only childhood, the passage, and adulthood.

We, on the other hand, have no rites of passage. Our young ones are exempted from the *separation*, the *training*, the *initiation*, and the *induction*. Instead, they are put through a period labeled **adolescence** — a period of life sometimes described as the most troubled, the most stressful, and the most difficult of all stages of development. The individual most responsible for this description of adolescence is G. Stanley Hall (1916), who is often referred to as the "father" of adolescence (mother unknown). Strongly influenced by Darwin's evolutionary theories, Hall advanced a profoundly biological theory of human development — a theory that maintains that in their development, all children go through a series of biologically ordained stages that parallel the evolution of the human race. The theory is known as the doctrine of recapitulation and is summarized in the phrase "ontogeny recapitulates phylogeny."

According to Hall's theory, all adolescents go through a period marked primarily by *Sturm und Drang* (storm and stress). He believed that because this period of upheaval and turmoil is biologically based, it is therefore largely inevitable, and it must also be common to all cultures. We now know that this view is fundamentally incorrect and misleading, that adolescence is not tumultuous for the majority of adolescents — although it is for some (Petersen, 1988). The interest in Hall's theory is primarily historical, although it profoundly influenced research and theory in adolescence throughout the century. Even today, we have not yet rid ourselves completely of the suspicion that

Like initiation rituals in some aboriginal societies, senior proms are a time of celebration and feasting; however, they do not mark a clear-cut passage from childhood to adulthood.

"storm and stress" is a predominant characteristic of the adolescent experience, although we know that it is not characteristic of adolescents in societies that provide rites of passage.

But in contemporary Western culture, there are no formal rites of passage (excluding perhaps the Bar or Bat Mitzvah in which the Jewish boy or girl becomes an adult at the age of 13 through a religious ceremony — and the "coming-out" or debutant party in certain social groups). No one tells the child, "Today you are an adult although yesterday you were a child." Our "rites" of passage are less definite — more confusing. They vary from one place to another — and from one decade to the next. They might include, among other things, getting a driver's license, being old enough to vote or to drink, loss of virginity, beginning work, growing (or trying to grow) a mustache, starting to date, graduating from high school, and so on. These events can span a wide range of ages, and none of them alone is certain evidence that adulthood has been reached. In this sense, our society is continuous (rather than discontinuous); it does not clearly demarcate passage from one stage to the next. Accordingly, there is no easy way to determine the end of adolescence; but its beginnings are somewhat more definite.

There are writers who claim that secondary schools now serve as *rites de passage* very similar to the traditional rites of many nonindustrialized societies. They have all the same characteristics, Fasick (1988) claims. They exemplify *separation* (children are segregated into schools) and *training* (the adolescent is formally socialized for the responsibilities of adult life); and there is something like *initiation* and *induction* in the high school graduation ceremony. Fasick suggests that this ceremony is almost universal for much of the middle and working class; for many adolescents, it clearly marks passage from the world of childhood to a world of adult responsibilities.

PHYSICAL DEVELOPMENT

Clear, predictable biological change is the one universal feature of adolescence in all cultures (Montemayor & Flannery, 1990). Biologically, adolescence is the period from the onset of puberty to adulthood, although it occasionally designates the period beginning with pubescence and terminating with adulthood. Alternately, it might simply indicate the span of the teen years (13 to 19). Puberty signifies sexual maturity; *pubescence* refers to the changes that result in sexual maturity. These changes occur in late childhood or early adolescence. Adulthood cannot easily be defined but may arbitrarily be considered to begin at the age of 20. It would be convenient to say that adolescence begins at 12, because we have included the earlier ages in preceding developmental periods. But the beginning of adolescence is variable, and age 12 simply serves as a general orientation.

Age of Puberty

Puberty defines sexual maturity — the ability to make babies — and is sometimes called *nubility* (Malmquist, 1978). As Jersild (1963) has observed, before puberty individuals *are* children; afterward they can *have* children. The problem in defining puberty this way is that it is almost impossible to determine exactly when a person becomes fertile. Past research has relied on information about the girl's first menstrual period (termed *menarche*) to discover the age at which puberty begins. Actually, however, a girl is frequently infertile for about a year after her first menstruation, so that the menarche is not an accurate index of puberty (Tanner, 1970); nevertheless it is a useful indication of impending sexual maturity (Malina, 1990). It is almost impossible to arrive at a clear index for boys, although first ejaculation is sometimes taken as a sign comparable to menarche. However, the probability that a boy can become a father immediately after first ejaculation is low — although not zero. The reason for this is that the concentration of sperm in the semen remains very low for the first year or so.

The average age for sexual maturity in North America is about 12 for girls and 14 for boys, immediately following the period of most rapid growth (the growth spurt). Consequently, the age of puberty may be established by determining the period during which the person grew rapidly. The period of rapid growth may begin as young as 8.7 for girls compared with 10.3 for boys (Malina,

1990). However, there is a wide age range. Some girls may not reach sexual maturity until age 16; some boys, not until age 18 (Tanner, 1975).

There have been some interesting historical trends in the age of menarche (first menstrual period) in different cultures and in different generations. In Western cultures, girls have been maturing earlier by as much as one-third or one-half year per decade since 1850 (Tanner, 1955). Thus, age of menarche has dropped from an average close to 17 to an average closer to 12 in the past hundred or so years. In addition, adolescents are often taller and heavier than they were several generations ago. This trend is labeled the *secular trend.* There is evidence that it has slowed or stopped in most developed countries (Frisch & Revelle, 1970).

Reasons for the secular trend are unknown. However, it is not evident in a number of less developed parts of the world. For example, in New Guinea, menarche still occurs at ages ranging from an average of 15.5 to 18.4 (Eveleth & Tanner, 1976). This observation, coupled with the fact that the secular trend seems to be a phenomenon of the last century or so, suggests that improved health care, improved nutrition, and generally improved living conditions may be part of the explanation (Chumlea, 1982).

Pubescence

Pubescence refers to all the changes that lead to sexual maturity. These changes, which are universal, are linked to a dramatic increase in hormones (Inoff-Germain et al., 1988). Most signs of pubescence are well known. Among the first in both boys and girls is the appearance of pigmented pubic hair, which is straight initially but becomes characteristically kinky during the later stages of pubescence. At about the same time as pubic hair begins to appear, the boy's testes begin to enlarge, as do the girl's breasts. The girl then experiences rapid physical growth, her first menstrual period, the growth of axillary (armpit) hair, the continued enlargement of her breasts, and a slight lowering of her voice. The boy's voice changes much more dramatically; he too grows rapidly, particularly in height and length of limbs; he acquires the capacity to ejaculate semen; he grows axillary hair; he eventually develops a beard, and if blessed by the gods who determine (cultural) signs of masculinity, he begins to grow a matting of hair on his chest.

The changes of pubescence that relate directly to the production of off-spring involve **primary sexual characteristics.** These include changes in the ovaries (organs that produce ova in the girl) and the testes (organs that produce sperm in the boy) so that these organs are now capable of producing mature ova and sperm. Changes that accompany the maturation of the sex organs but that are not directly related to reproduction involve **secondary sexual characteristics.** The appearance of facial hair in the boy and the development of breasts in the girl, voice changes, and the growth of axillary and pubic hair are all secondary sexual characteristics.

Table 11.1
Normal Sequence of Sexual Maturation for North American Girls

Sequence	Event
1	Beginning of adolescent growth spurt
2	Appearance of unpigmented pubic down
3	Breast elevation ("bud" stage)
4	Appearance of pigmented, kinky pubic hair
5	Increase in size of vagina, clitoris, and uterus
6	Decline in rate of physical growth
7	Menarche
8	Development of axillary (armpit) hair; continued enlargement of breasts; slight lowering of the voice
9	Increase in production of oil; increased perspiration; possible acne

Note: The first of these changes may occur as young as age 7¼; the last may not be completed before age 16. Average age of menarche is 12.

Although, as we have seen, the age at which primary and secondary sexual characteristics develop varies a great deal, the sequence of their appearance is more predictable — though not entirely fixed. Tables 11.1 and 11.2 summarize that sequence.

Physical Changes

The rapid changes in height and weight characteristic of pubescence begin before the age of 12 and are shown in Chapter 9 (Figure 9.1). Figure 11.1 shows average height and weight data for boys and girls from 12 to 18. By the age of 11½ girls often surpass boys in height and maintain a slight advantage until 13½. Girls outweigh boys at approximately 11, but by 14½ boys catch up to and surpass girls. An additional physical change, of particular significance to boys, is a rapid increase in the length of limbs. It is not uncommon for a boy to discover that his legs are suddenly several inches longer than they were a scant year ago and that he can reach an additional 4 or 5 inches. As a result of this growth he acquires the gangling appearance so frequently associated with early adolescence, exaggerated by the fact that his rate of purchasing clothes is often considerably behind the rate at which he outgrows them.

The body composition of boys and girls is different throughout childhood, with boys having relatively more of what is termed *fat-free mass* and less *fat mass*; the two, taken together, determine body weight (Malina & Bouchard, 1988). During the adolescent growth spurt, boy's proportion of fat decreases even more since fat-free mass grows at a faster rate than does fat mass. This is

Table 11.2
Normal Sequence of Sexual Maturation for North American Boys

Sequence	Event
1	Appearance of unpigmented pubic down; growth of testes and scrotum (sac containing testes)
2	Beginning of adolescent growth spurt
3	Enlargement of penis
4	Appearance of pigmented, kinky pubic hair
5	Lowering of voice; appearance of "down" on upper lip
6	First ejaculations occur
7	Decline in rate of physical growth
8	Development of axillary (armpit) hair; growth of facial hair
9	Increase in production of oil; increased perspiration; possible acne
10	Growth of chest hair

Note: The first of these changes may occur as young as age 9½; the last may not be completed before age 18. Average age of first ejaculation is 13 to 14.

not the case for girls, however, so that average sex differences in proportion of body weight due to fat mass are magnified.

Changes in muscular strength, aerobic performance, and motor capacity also reflect the physical growth spurt, especially in boys. As a result, sex differences in many areas of motor performance increase in favor of males (Beunen & Malina, 1988). This is especially evident in competitive athletics, where male records almost invariably surpass those of girls.

Early and Late Maturation

The average adolescent is no more real than the average child; both are abstractions, inventions designed to bring some semblance of order to our understanding of a very complex subject. Hence, although the average adolescent matures at 12 or 14 depending on sex, some mature considerably earlier and some considerably later. Given that maturity tends to be judged in terms of physical appearance, the age at which the physical changes of adolescence take place may be very psychologically important to the child.

In general, early-maturing boys suffer fewer psychological problems than those who mature later, probably largely because they frequently excel in activities and abilities that are highly prized in the adolescent peer culture. Not only are they larger and stronger and therefore more likely to excel in athletic activities but they are also more socially mature and hence more likely to serve as leaders in heterosexual activities. Detailed longitudinal studies of early and

Figure 11.1

Height and weight at 50th percentile for U.S. children.

Source: From the Health Department, Milwaukee, Wisconsin; based on data by H. C. Stuart and H. V. Meredith, prepared for use in Children's Medical Center, Boston. Used by permission of the Milwaukee Health Department.

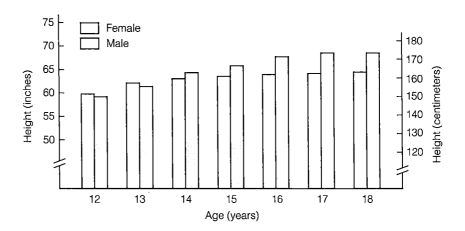

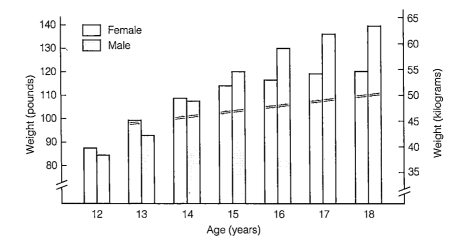

late maturation in boys have provided consistent findings (M. C. Jones, 1957, 1965; Crockett & Petersen, 1987). Early-maturing boys are typically better adjusted, more popular, more confident, more aggressive, and more successful in heterosexual relationships. In addition, they appear to have more positive self-concepts (about which more is said in the next chapter). In contrast, adolescent boys who mature later than average are, as a group, more restless, more attention-seeking, less confident, and have less positive self-concepts.

Note that the apparent advantages of early maturation among boys are most evident *during* adolescence and apply primarily to social areas (adjust-

These five young men are about the same age, but their levels of physical and sexual maturation differ. Such differences can have both short-term and lasting effects on their social
development as well.

ment, popularity, and leadership). In later life the advantages of early maturation are not nearly so apparent (Clausen, 1975; Peskin, 1973).

Findings are less clear and consistent for girls. Siegel (1982) reviews studies
that indicate that early-maturing girls are initially at a disadvantage, a finding
that directly contradicts the results of similar studies conducted with boys. In
later adolescence, however, these disadvantages have often disappeared. Thus,
it appears that the effects of early and late maturation in girls depends on their
ages. Early maturation is a disadvantage in the very early grades, when most
girls have not yet begun to mature and when the early-maturing girl is likely to
find herself excluded from peer group activities. Given the fact also that girls
are on the average two years in advance of boys in physical maturation, the
early-maturing girl may well be four or more years in advance of like-aged boys,
a fact that would not contribute positively to her social life. At a later age,
however, when most of her age-grade mates have also begun to mature, the

early-maturing girl may suddenly find herself in a more advantageous position. Her greater maturity is now something to be admired.

In summary, the effects of early and late maturation appear to be different for males and females. As Petersen (1988) notes, pubertal change is most stressful when it puts the adolescent out of step with peers, especially if the change is not interpreted as desirable. And the consequences of maturational timing are most clearly understood in terms of their effects on relationships and interactions that are important to the adolescent. Thus, early maturation may enhance peer relations for boys but is less likely to do so for girls. Furthermore, evidence suggests that relations with parents are better for early-maturing boys and for *late*-maturing girls (Savin-Williams & Small, 1986).

From an ecological perspective, what we know of the implications of maturational timetables presents an excellent example of child characteristics interacting with each other (specifically, degree of sexual maturity interacting with age) to determine important elements of the child's ecology (namely, the nature of interaction with parents and peers). But we should note that the child's ecology is individualistic, that every child–other interaction creates a unique microsystem. Thus, although there may be some general advantages or disadvantages associated with the timing of pubescence, there are many individual exceptions to our generalizations. Not all early-maturing boys and girls are characterized by the same advantages or disadvantages of early maturation; nor are all those who mature later affected in the same way.

Physical Concerns of Adolescents

Frazier and Lisonbee (1950) asked tenth-grade adolescents to indicate problems that concerned them and the degree to which they were worried about each. Items most frequently listed as the greatest worry for boys included the presence of blackheads or pimples, irregular teeth, oily skin, glasses, and other slight physical abnormalities such as noses that were too thin or too long, skin too dark, heavy lips, protruding chins, and so on.

Girls, like boys, were most concerned about the presence of blackheads or pimples ("zits"). In addition, they were particularly concerned about freckles. Scars, birthmarks, and moles are also a source of worry, as are the dangers of being too homely, having oily skin, and wearing glasses.

The evidence suggests that these physical concerns are just as real for today's adolescent as they were three decades ago. In a survey of 3,600 Canadian adolescents from 150 different schools, almost half indicated that their physical appearance is a matter of considerable concern, and almost the same number were worried about their height or weight (Bibby & Posterski, 1985). In this survey, the adolescent's greatest worry concerned life beyond graduation — "What am I going to do after high school?" — a problem that affected approximately two-thirds of all respondents. Other important concerns had to do with

Table 11.3
Personal Concerns of Contemporary Adolescents

Concern	Percentage Indicating "a Great Deal" or "Quite a Bit" of Concern
What am I going to do when I finish school?	68
Finances*	54
School concerns†	50
Time (not enough time to do the things they want)	48
Appearance	44
What is the purpose of life?	44
Boredom	43
Height or weight	43
Loneliness	35
Feelings of inferiority (poor self-image)	29
Sex	28
Parents' marriage	20

Source: Adapted from Bibby & Posterski, *The emerging generation: An inside look at Canada's teenagers,* Table 4.1, p. 60. Toronto: Irwin Publishing, 1985. Reprinted with permission of Stoddart Publishing Co., Ltd.

*40 percent of respondents worked part time

†Relating to fact that many do not find school enjoyable and to concerns over grades

such things as money, achievement in school, boredom, loneliness, and the parents' marriage (see Table 11.3).

Interestingly, the adolescent's worries about physical changes typically do not include concerns about menarche or spermarche (first ejaculation), *providing* the child has been prepared for these events. Gaddis and Brooks-Gunn (1985) interviewed 13 young adolescent boys and found that of the 11 who had experienced ejaculation, most had strong positive feelings about the event and none had been upset or ashamed. However, two of the boys had been unprepared for the event (usually nocturnal upon first occurrence, and referred to as a "wet dream") and had been very frightened. Girls' recollections of their menarche are often not as positive, perhaps because of the lingering remnants of cultural attitudes that led to menstruation being labeled "the curse" (Morrison et al., 1980). However, menstruation is not a source of worry for most girls.

The adolescent's concern with the body is to be expected given the importance of physical appearance to psychological adjustment — an importance related not only to the role that appearance plays in peer acceptance but also to the way perception of the body affects self-concept. In fact, physical appearance is generally recognized as probably the most important influence on the adolescent's self-worth (Harter, 1990). Accordingly, it is not surprising that the preferred body type for adolescent males is athletic — neither obese nor thin (Lerner & Korn, 1972). Nor is it surprising to find that the desire of some young adolescent girls to be slim is sometimes so overwhelming that it can be reflected in serious eating disorders.

NUTRITION

Most adolescents, especially if they are very active physically, expend a large number of calories each day. In addition, during the rapid skeletal and muscular growth of pubescence — the growth spurt — their bodies require a high intake of protein and minerals, and especially of calcium, for normal growth. Calcium deficiencies, especially in women, sometimes become apparent in later life in the form of osteoporosis (a weakening and thinning of the bones). As a result, we should not be alarmed to see our adolescents consuming great mounds of hamburgers, devouring bowls of spinach and lentils and wonderful lettuces, and drinking gallons of milk.

But we should be concerned if they eat snacks of mostly empty calories and sugar-laden drinks, or if they eat too little of anything at all, or if they eat only in binges. Because any of these might be a sign of a serious problem.

Obesity

As we saw in Chapter 9, obesity is the most common nutritional problem among children; not surprisingly, it is also the most common nutritional problem among adolescents, affecting somewhere up to a quarter of all North American teenagers (Whitney & Hamilton, 1984). Unfortunately, obese children often grow up to be obese adolescents; and they, in turn, have a high probability of growing up to be obese adults. The negative consequences of obesity for health, for estimates of self-worth, and for happiness are clear.

At a superficial level, the causes and cures of obesity seem simple. Other than for rare glandular and metabolic problems, and in spite of genetic contributions, obesity in adolescents — and others — is caused by taking in more calories than are expended. Weight reduction can therefore be achieved by consuming fewer calories (eating less or eating differently) and by expending more (exercising, being more active physically).

Unfortunately, the problem is not so simple. Its alleviation requires nutritional information that not all adolescents have or are willing and interested enough to accept; and it requires changing habits that are not only self-rewarding but also encouraged by the media and that are consequently

Anorexia nervosa often begins with a desire to be thin and ends in a condition in which the adolescent seems unwilling or unable to eat.

extraordinarily persistent. As a result, obesity continues to be a very significant North American problem, and its alleviation, a major industry.

Strangely, in spite of the prevalence of obesity, contemporary Western societies place tremendous emphasis on physical attractiveness which, especially among girls, is clearly defined as *thin*.

Anorexia Nervosa

Karen Carpenter, a well-known pop singer, died at the age of 32. Cause of death: heart failure due to a chemical imbalance that, in turn, was probably related to a medical condition for which the singer had been undergoing treatment. The medical condition? **Anorexia nervosa.**

Prevalence. Translated literally, *anorexia nervosa* means loss of appetite as a result of nerves. It describes a complex and only partially understood condition that, although still relatively rare, appears to be increasing in frequency. Crisp (1980) estimates that as many as 1 percent of girls aged 16 to 18 are anorexic (also termed *anorectic*); other estimates have sometimes been much higher.

Pope and associates (1984) conducted a survey of 544 female college and secondary school students and found that the percentage that could be described as anorexic was somewhere between 1 and 4.2, depending on the definitions used. Similarly, using very strict criteria for diagnosis of anorexia, Crisp, Palmer, and Kalucy (1976) found that 1 percent of the girls in nine London schools were severely anorexic.

In a study of more than 1,250 13- to 19-year-old adolescents, Lachenmeyer and Muni-Brander (1988) found that a full 13 percent of the girls reported significantly restricting their diets. These were girls who scored very high on a test designed to measure eating attitudes and behaviors that are known to be associated with anorexia. Although not every one of these "restricters" (see At a Glance, p. 584) meets strict criteria for a diagnosis of anorexia, each is at risk.

Although anorexia continues to be far more common among girls than boys, there are indications that eating disorders are now much more frequent among adolescent boys than had previously been suspected. Significantly, in this comprehensive survey, 6.3 percent of the males in a lower-socioeconomic (SES) sample (primarily black and Hispanic students) and 3.4 percent of a higher SES sample (primarily white) were also restricters. These rates for males are much higher than have traditionally been reported.

Definition. Anorexia nervosa is defined medically as involving a loss of at least 15 to 25 percent of "ideal" body weight, this loss not being due to any detectable illness (Yager, 1982). The American Psychiatric Association (1980) definition also includes disturbance of body image, refusal to maintain normal body weight, and significant weight loss as criteria of anorexia. It almost always begins with a deliberate desire to be thin and consequent dieting, and ends in a condition where the patient seems unwilling or unable to eat normally. Many affected females cease menstruating relatively early following initial dieting and many become excessively active and continue to engage in strenuous exercise programs even after their physical conditions have deteriorated significantly. In the absence of medical intervention, anorexia nervosa is sometimes fatal. Baker and Lyen (1982) report that estimates of anorexia-related death range from 0 to 19 percent.

Causes. The causes of anorexia nervosa are neither simple, nor well understood. As Walsh (1982) notes: "In anorexia nervosa, there are multiple psychological, behavioral, and physiological aberrations, suggesting that the central regulatory mechanisms which govern an individual's emotional and physical equilibrium are grossly disturbed" (p. 85). Although there is some evidence of endocrine imbalances in anorexia (Walsh, 1982), as well as some indication that the disease may be genetically linked (Holland et al., 1984), the condition is acknowledged as being primarily psychological. Some speculate that anorexic individuals are typically those who do not feel that they are in control of their lives, but who discover that they *can* control their body weight; in the end, control becomes an obsession. Others suggest that lack of positive self-image coupled with the emphasis that society places on thinness (particularly among females) may be manifested in anorexia in those cases where the person attempts to obtain parental and societal approval by dieting.

Another interesting hypothesis concerning a possible cause of anorexia suggests that *activity* may be implicated in as many as 38 to 75 percent of all cases (Epling, Pierce, & Stefan, 1983). One of the common observations about anorexics is that many of them continue to engage in strenuous physical activity even after they have become grossly emaciated. In this connection, it is interesting to note that mice and rats who are exposed to restricted feeding (unlimited food, but only for 60 minutes per day) and unlimited exercise (free access to a "running wheel") will sometimes starve themselves to death (Epling, Pierce, & Stefan, 1983). It seems that it is possible to develop something like anorexia among these animals through exercise and dieting. However, when rats and mice are exposed only to the diet (60 minutes per day of food access) but not to the exercise wheel, their body weight stabilizes and is maintained.

Are some anorexics like these rats? Epling and associates suggest that yes, at least part of the time, anorexia is related to activity. They cite evidence that indicates that under some circumstances humans, like rats, eat less when they exercise.

Treatment. Anorexia nervosa is a particularly frightening and baffling condition for parents. It is frightening because it can be fatal; and it is baffling and frustrating because it may seem to parents that the anorexic adolescent *deliberately* and totally unreasonably refuses to eat. And neither pleas nor threats are likely to work. What is?

Because anorexia nervosa is not, in most instances, primarily a biological or organic disorder, its treatment is often complex and difficult. There are no drugs or simple surgical procedures that can easily cure it. In some instances, patients respond favorably to antidepressant drugs such as chlorpromazine (Walsh, 1982); and, as we noted earlier, it is sometimes necessary to force-feed anorexic individuals to save their lives. In the main, however, successful treatments have typically involved one of several forms of psychotherapy. Among these, behavior therapy — the use of reinforcement and/or punishment in attempts to change behavior — has sometimes been dramatically effective, as have approaches that treat the entire family as a *system* that affects each of its individual members (Griffin, 1985). In addition, group therapies have sometimes been effective (Kline, 1985).

Bulimia

Whereas anorexia nervosa is characterized by not eating (in spite of the fact that some anorexics occasionally do go on infrequent eating binges), **bulimia** involves recurrent episodes of binge eating. The American Psychiatric Association (1980) in the *Diagnostic and Statistical Manual (DSM-III)* defines bulimia in terms of *recurrent* episodes of binge eating, where the patient is aware that the eating pattern is not normal and where depression or at least self-deprecation follows the eating binge. In addition, to diagnose an individual as bulimic, at least three of the following five conditions must be present: (1) consumption of high-calorie foods during a binge; (2) inconspicuous eating; (3) abdominal pain, sleep, or self-induced vomiting immediately following the

Eating Disorders Among Adolescents

An investigation by Penner, Thompson, and Coovert (1991) indicates that very thin, anorexic women consistently overestimate their body size; average-size, nonanorexic women do not. Anorexia, severely restricted eating, is just one of the eating disorders that relates to our current cultural emphasis on being thin. Bulimia, alternating food binges with severe dieting and self-induced vomiting and diarrhea, is perhaps three or four times more common than anorexia (Figure 11.2).

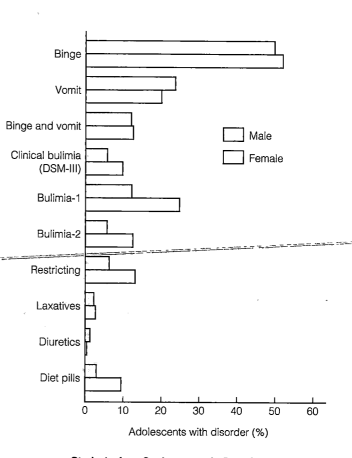

Study 1—Low Socioeconomic Sample

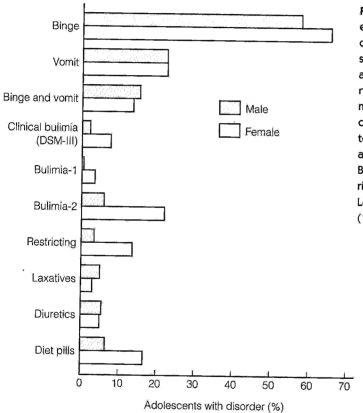

Figure 11.2   Prevalence rates for eating disorders among adolescents. The low-socioeconomic sample consisted of 328 females and 384 males; the high-socioeconomic sample consisted of 314 females and 235 males. Note that clinical bulimics meet all DSM-III criteria for bulimia; Bulimia-1 individuals meet all criteria except one; and Bulimia-2 individuals meet all criteria except two. *Source:* Data from Lachenmeyer and Muni-Brander (1988).

Study 2—High Socioeconomic Sample

Table 11.4
Possible Medical Consequences of Bulimia and Bulimarexia

Excessive weight fluctuations.

Dehydration and fluid shifts, sometimes resulting in headaches and fainting. Problem more serious if diuretics are used or if bulimia or bulimarexia follow prolonged fasting.

Electrolyte imbalance, aggravated by laxative or diuretic use as well as by repeated vomiting.

Hypoglycemic symptoms.

Malnutrition-related problems (might include cardiovascular, kidney, gastrointestinal, or blood problems as well as insomnia).

Dental/oral problems sometimes associated with loss of enamel as a result of frequent exposure to stomach acidity during vomiting episodes. Other possible gum, salivary duct, and tongue problems associated with emesis (vomiting).

Specific gastrointestinal difficulties, sometimes associated with ipecac abuse. Prolonged use can lead to cardiac problems and death.

Laxative-related problems, which vary depending on the nature of the laxative abused.

Insomnia resulting from malnutrition, nocturnal binges, or underlying depression.

Various neurological and endocrine problems.

Source: Based on Goode (1985).

eating binge; (4) repeated attempts to lose weight through stringent diets, cathartics, diuretics, or self-induced vomiting; and (5) frequent weight fluctuations. *Bulimarexia* is the term sometimes employed to describe a pattern of binge eating followed by a self-induced purge.

Unlike anorexia, bulimia does not usually present an immediate threat to life — although its eventual medical consequences, together with those of bulimarexia, can be quite serious, as shown in Table 11.4. Whereas anorexics are almost invariably dangerously thin, bulimics are only occasionally obese. The weight of many bulimics fluctuates widely from one episode to another. Often, however, they are neither fat nor thin, the reason being that many follow their eating binges with self-induced vomiting, diuretics, or extreme diets.

Prevalence. Bulimia is a more common eating disorder than anorexia. In the Pope et al. (1984) study of 544 female college students, between 1 and 4.2 percent of the sample could be classified as anorexic; a frightening 6.5 to 18 percent were bulimic. In another study, this one of a sample of 500 students who had gone to a university psychiatric clinic, 4.4 percent met all the criteria for a DSM-III classification of an eating disorder (Strangler & Printz, 1980). Of these, an astounding 86.4 percent were bulimic. Similarly, in the Lachenmeyer and Muni-Brander survey mentioned earlier, 7.6 percent of the total *nonclinical* lower-SES sample, and 4.7 percent of the higher-SES sample met *all* the criteria for a clinical diagnosis of bulimia! The proportion of males who are clinically bulimic is higher than expected: 5.7 percent of the males in the lower-SES group, compared with 9.7 percent of the females; and 2.1 percent of the males in the higher-SES group compared with 7.6 percent of the females. Percentages of the sample who occasionally binged or induced vomiting, or both, and who used laxatives, diuretics, and diet pills were also very high.

Causes. The characteristics that most clearly differentiate bulimic girls from those who are nonbulimic included a greater desire to be thin, a higher degree of dissatisfaction with their bodies, and chronic dieting. In addition, bulimic females were more likely to see themselves as being overweight, and were far more concerned with being thin. They tended to be significantly more depressed (Post & Crowther, 1985). Marston et al. (1988) report that adolescents who are most at risk are those whose parents have the highest frequency of addictive problems (alcoholism, drug use, overeating, and gambling).

Although bulimia has long been considered a rare disorder, there is evidence that a substantial number of overweight individuals who are not bulimic according to DSM-III criteria nevertheless engage in binge eating (over 50 percent in one study reported by Loro & Orleans, 1981). Furthermore, as many as 50 percent of anorexic patients also engage in binge eating followed by laxatives, vomiting, or fasting. Polivy and Herman (1985) refer to these individuals as *bulimic anorexics.* They suggest that part of the explanation for this condition may lie in the fact that dieting promotes the adoption of cognitive rather than physiological controls over eating. Put another way, whereas food intake would normally be regulated by the physiological mechanisms that have to do with hunger, the dieter deliberately takes conscious control of food intake and ignores physiological indicators of hunger. And perhaps the binges that follow dieting are partly facilitated by the awareness (cognition) that the individual can control the effects of the binge through a purge and through continued dieting, as well as by the fact that the individual has learned to ignore the physiological signals that ordinarily control food intake.

Treatment. As Schumer (1983) notes, the precise causes of bulimia, like those of anorexia nervosa, remain unknown, although the incidence of both conditions appears to be rising. Nor is there a simple and universally effective cure for either condition. Bulimia, like anorexia, is sometimes responsive to group therapies as well as to various individual psychotherapies (Kline, 1985). And there are those, like Polivy and Herman (1985), who argue that one of bulimia's main causes is dieting, and that to treat it effectively, it is necessary to treat dieting. And perhaps to treat dieting, it is necessary to change the social and cultural conditions that have placed such a tremendous value on thinness.

INTELLECTUAL DEVELOPMENT

We have traced, sketchily to be sure, the development of the child's mind from birth to the beginning of adolescence, using as our guides the theory of Jean Piaget as well as information-processing theories. Through Piaget's eyes, we saw the infant assimilating aspects of the environment, accommodating to others, equilibrating (balancing) the two processes, and constructing progressively more advanced views of reality. In time the infant succeeded in separating self from world, in representing aspects of the world symbolically, and in dealing with knowledge in increasingly logical ways. By the time we left the child's mind at the end of the concrete operations period, we had described a mind that understood the logical necessity of conservation when nothing has been added to or taken from a situation, and that could classify, seriate, and deal with number at a surprisingly sophisticated level.

Through the eyes of some of the neo-Piagetian theorists, we examined information-processing theories that did not always agree with Piaget's notion of a stage-bound developmental progression and that often described a more capable child than the one described by Piaget. Thus we saw that the preschooler is not always *prelogical* or *preconceptual*, but possesses impressive classification and number skills. And information-processing descriptions of the school-aged child describe a person with a rapidly expanding knowledge base, increasingly sophisticated and appropriate strategies for processing information, and a mounting awareness of the dimensions and processes of knowing, as well as of the characteristics of the self as a knower (metacognition).

In the following sections, we continue our examination of intellectual development, looking first at Piaget's contributions (see Table 11.5) and then at the more current offerings of the neo-Piagetians.

Piaget's View: Formal Operations

Some of the important distinctions between concrete and formal operations are illustrated in children's responses to the following Inhelder and Piaget (1958) problem: Subjects are presented with five test tubes that contain different unidentified chemicals; a combination of these chemicals will result in a yellow liquid. This phenomenon is demonstrated for subjects so they know that one special tube, which is kept apart, is the catalyst for the desired reaction. What they do not know is which combination of the other four tubes is the correct one. They are asked to discover this for themselves and are allowed to experiment as necessary to solve the problem.

Typical 10-year-olds begin by combining two of the chemicals. Assuming this combination does not provide any positive information, they then combine another two chemicals or perhaps they combine one of the first two test tubes with a third. They continue in this manner until, by chance, they arrive at a correct solution, whereupon they exclaim, "There, those two! That's the

Table 11.5
Piaget's Stages of Cognitive Development

Stage	Approximate Age	Some Major Characteristics
Sensorimotor	0–2 years	Motoric intelligence World of the here and now No language, no thought in early stages No notion of objective reality

Preoperational
  Preconceptual
  Intuitive
	2–7 years
	2–4 years
	4–7 years
		Egocentric thought
		Reason dominated by perception
		Intuitive rather than logical solutions
		Inability to conserve

Concrete operations	7–11 or 12 years	Ability to conserve Logic of classes and relations Understanding of number Thinking bound to concrete Development of reversibility in thought
Formal operations	11 or 12–14 or 15 years	Complete generality of thought Propositional thinking Ability to deal with the hypothetical Development of strong idealism

solution." If the experimenter then says, "Are there any other solutions — any other combinations that will also make a yellow liquid?" subjects will be forced to admit they do not know yet but that they can try to find out. Their strategy changes little. They continue to combine pairs of liquids; they may even combine several groups of three or perhaps all four, and to these they add liquid from the fifth tube. In the end they assert that they have tried them all and there is but one solution. If they are less fortunate and less persistent, they may be incapable of discovering even one correct combination.

Intelligent 14-year-olds behave in quite a different manner. As illustrated in Figure 11.3, they solve the problem by systematically combining the tubes by twos, threes, and finally all four, yielding 15 possible combinations (16 including the combination in which nothing is combined). There is no doubt in their mind about whether they have found the only correct solution or whether there are others.

This experiment illustrates several of the principal differences between the child's thinking during the stage of concrete operations and thinking characterized by formal operations. First, 10-year-olds begin their solution by attempting actual combinations; their hypotheses are real behaviors. The bright 14-year-old, however, begins by imagining all the possibilities and then tries them. There is a fundamental difference in the orientations. The first reflects

Figure 11.3

All possible combinations of the four test tubes to which the fifth can be added. The experiment requires the subject to discover the combination(s) that yields a yellow liquid when potassium iodide is added. The correct solutions are circled.

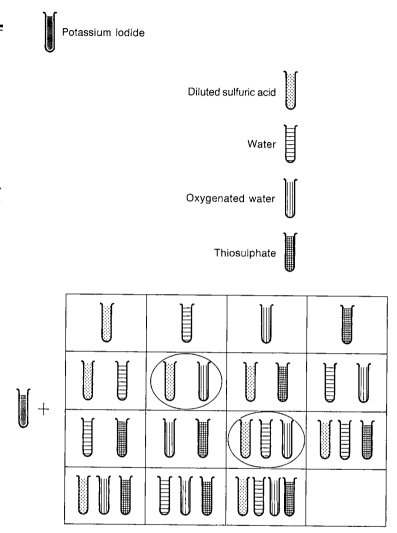

the concrete nature of the child's thought; the second reflects the *hypothetical* and *deductive* capacities of adolescent thinking.

Second, the experiment illustrates the *combinatorial* capacity of the adolescent's thinking. Because 10-year-olds consider every combination as a separate and unrelated hypothesis and because they arrive at these combinations in a haphazard fashion, they are likely to overlook several possibilities in the process. In contrast, the adolescent first considers the range of possible combinations. The concrete logic that was sufficient to deal with classes and seriation is replaced by what Piaget terms the "logic of propositions." This form of logic is a much more powerful tool for dealing with the hypothetical — with state-

Science fair projects involve proposing a hypothesis, researching the chosen topic, and generalizing solutions. Formal operations makes all these steps possible.

ments that need not relate to reality but are simply characterized by the possibility that they can be true or untrue (in fact, this is the definition of a **proposition:** a verbal statement that can be true or false).

Note that the changes in adolescent thinking described by Piaget's formal operations are potential but by no means always actual. Indeed, a great many individuals do not display formal thought between the ages of 12 and 15 – or even later (Fischer & Silvern, 1985). In light of a number of studies that have not found formal operations among older adolescents and even adults, Piaget (1972) has conceded that this stage of thinking is not so general as was previously thought and that social influences, particularly as they are manifested in different cultures, and individual interests and aptitudes are very important in acquiring formal operations (Furth, 1980).

The adolescent's newly acquired capability to deal with the hypothetical might not be very obvious, or perhaps even very important, if it were manifested only in problems of chemistry and physics. But formal operations extend well beyond the realms of science. They are apparent in new preoccupations with understanding the self as an abstraction (Harter, 1990), in an egocentric reliance on logic (Lapsley, 1990), and in an intense new idealism. Children can now contemplate states of affairs that do not exist; they can compare the ideal to the actual; they can become profoundly distressed at the failure of preceding generations to avoid the confusion that they now observe around them; and they can be puzzled by some of the profound questions that have always tormented philosophers. It is precisely the adolescent's ability to deal with the hypothetical that made it possible for 44 percent of the subjects in Bibby and Posterski's (1985) study to claim that they were very concerned about the

The ability to imagine and want a better world is often a characteristic of adolescence.

purpose and meaning of life. Such questions do not often suggest themselves to the 10-year-old.

With the idealism of formal operations, there also comes a belief in the omnipotence of thought. The egocentrism of adolescence (which we discuss later in this chapter) can be seen in the belief that reason and logic provide all the answers and in an apparent inability to adopt the point of view that admits that we do not have all the answers, and that even if we did, social, political, and other human realities sometimes oppose their implementation. It is this unshakable belief in the power of thought that may underlie the adolescent's absolutely insistent political, social, and religious arguments with parents and others.

An Information-Processing View

As we noted earlier, Piaget's stage-bound description of intellectual development, although it provides many important insights into cognitive functioning, is not always an accurate description of the child's capabilities. There is evidence, for example, that the abstract and logical thinking defined by formal operations is not ordinarily present at the beginning of formal operations (at age 11 or 12), and is sometimes not even present among adults. Fischer and Silvern (1985) report that only the easiest Piagetian tasks can be solved at the beginning of formal operations; the ability to solve problems requiring the manipulation of different abstractions does not appear for another three or four years. And some neo-Piagetian theorists suggest that there might be additional stages of cognitive development in adulthood (for example, Arlin, 1975; Basseches, 1984).

A complementary approach to understanding intellectual development falls under the general heading of information processing. As we saw in Chapter 9, information-processing theories are concerned with three important aspects of cognition: the acquisition of what Chi and Glaser (1980) label a *knowledge base*; the development of information-processing strategies; and the development of metacognitive skills.

To review briefly, the knowledge base consists of concepts, ideas, information, and so on. Infants begin life with very little knowledge base. The knowledge base derives from the individual's experiences; schools do a great deal to expand and organize the knowledge base. Information-processing strategies are the procedures involved in learning and remembering. Metacognitive skills relate to information the knower has about knowing and remembering, and to a personal awareness of the self as an information processor and, consequently, as a player of Flavell's (1985) game of cognition. As metacognitive skills increase, so too does the child's ability to analyze performance, to predict the likelihood of success, to change strategies, to evaluate and to monitor.

An information-processing view of development describes how each of these three aspects of information processing (knowledge base, processing skills, and metacognitive skills) change with age and experience.

First, it seems clear that knowledge base grows with increasing experience and exposure to schooling. Anderson (1980) describes how children progress from being *novices* in all areas to being *experts* in at least some areas — most especially in certain games, in aspects of social interaction, in certain levels and classes of school subjects, and perhaps in hobby-related or cultural pursuits. One of the important differences between experts and novices has to do with knowledge base. But the difference is not simply that experts know more (have more content in their knowledge structures), but also that they have formed more associations among the things they know. Their knowledge is richer in the sense that it suggests more relationships. The artist who is an expert in color does not understand the color blue in the same way as a novice such as I might. My pitiful understanding permits me to relate blue to robin eggs, morning skies, and koronian babies; the expert might relate it to these as well, but might also break it down into a dozen hues whose subtlety and associations have no meaning for me. More than this, the expert might well understand blue as a wavelength, might understand its relationships to other waves of different lengths, and might have a sense of its crispness or fragility that quite escapes me.

If development is a process of shedding some of the novice's ignorance and acquiring increasing expertise, then it follows that expertise involves more than changes in knowledge base — that it must also involve changes in information-processing capacity. Among other things, information-processing ca-

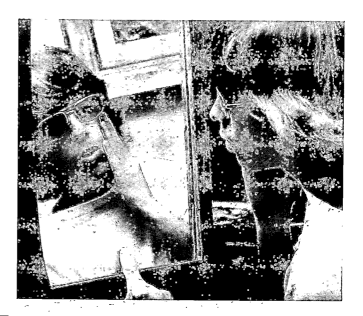

Surveys of adolescents indicate that future work and career is a predominant concern, as are more immediate problems relating to finances and to school. In addition, almost half of all adolescents express concern over their physical appearance and their height and weight. Among their physical worries are skin problems, irregular teeth, eyeglasses, and what they see as physical imperfections (noses too long, teeth too large, eyebrows too thin, and so on). The appearance of facial hair that needs to be shaved—or the lack thereof—can also be a source of concern.

pacity depends on the availability of appropriate strategies; and it depends on attention span.

That attention span increases with age is clear. Intelligence tests such as the Stanford-Binet, for example, require that subjects try to recall sequences of digits presented at one-second intervals. Whereas a preschool child might correctly recall a string of two or three digits, an adolescent might easily recall six or seven.

Changes in the availability of appropriate strategies are not as easily investigated, partly because it is not always simple to identify a strategy and determine whether or not it is present. However, Piaget's investigations of concrete and formal operations suggest that the strategies available to older adolescents are substantially different, and considerably more powerful, than those available to the younger child. First, the adolescent is more systematic, plans more carefully, considers more options. Second, the adolescent has more ready-made solutions. For example, there are many Piagetian tasks that present real problems for a younger child, but that can be solved almost from memory by an older child. A 6-year-old might need to "figure out" whether there is still the same amount of material in a deformed object; the adolescent need not "figure."

One additional important area of developmental change in information processing involves the child's understanding of the self as a processor of information and an increasing understanding of the processes of cognition. As we saw in Chapter 9, metacognitive skills seem to be largely absent in young children, but are clearly present in older children and adolescents.

In summary, information-processing views of cognitive development describe changes in three areas: content (knowledge base increases in terms of specific knowledge as well as in terms of relations and associations among items of information); processing capacities (increases in memory and attention capacities and increases in the availability of more sophisticated strategies); and metacognitive changes (increasing awareness of self as information-processor and increasing ability to monitor, evaluate, and control ongoing cognitive activities). These changes make more of an expert of the adolescent. But they do not eliminate the adolescent's egocentrism.

ADOLESCENT EGOCENTRISM

In Piagetian theory, *egocentrism* is not a derogatory term as it might be in ordinary usage. It refers less to a selfishness than to a cognitive and emotional self-centeredness and is apparent in children's inability to be completely objective in their understanding of the world and in their interactions with others. Recall, for example, that during sensorimotor development, egocentrism marks the infant's ability to differentiate between self and the physical world: Objects exist only when they are being looked at, tasted, felt, or smelled – a rather extreme egocentrism.

The egocentrism of the adolescent is perhaps not as extreme and certainly not nearly as naive as that of the infant. It is characterized by an inability to differentiate between objects and events of concern to others and those of concern to the adolescent. This egocentrism is sometimes apparent in behaviors that seem to be motivated by the adolescent's belief that everybody is watching and is terribly concerned.

Elkind (1967) clarifies the concept of adolescent egocentrism by examining two separate notions that the adolescent creates through egocentrism. These notions, the *imaginary audience* and the *personal fable*, may be extremely useful in understanding some aspects of adolescent behavior and experience.

Imaginary Audience

The adolescent's **imaginary audience** is a collection of all who might be concerned with the adolescent's self and behavior. It is the *they* in expressions such as "they say . . ." or "they predict . . ." Social psychologists inform us that each of us behaves as though "they" are watching and care. But the imaginary audiences of adults are much smaller, much less pervasive, and far less important than those of adolescents. According to Elkind, it is because of this imaginary audience to which the adolescent is continually reacting that young adolescents are often very self-conscious. It is also because of this same audience that many become so concerned with their hair, clothing, and other aspects of their physical appearance. It is as though adolescents believe that others are as deeply concerned about them as they themselves are and that these others constantly judge them.

How does research investigate beliefs such as these? How can psychology locate an imaginary audience?

With an instrument. Elkind and Bowen (1979) have developed such an instrument. It is appropriately called the *Imaginary Audience Scale (IAS)* and is based on the assumption that individuals will be self-conscious to the extent that their behaviors are subject to examination by an imaginary audience. The scale attempts to measure two aspects of self-consciousness: those that are abiding or relatively permanent (labeled AS for *abiding self*) and those that are temporary or transient (labeled TS for *transient self*). One example of an abiding aspect of self is intelligence; a more transient characteristic is hairstyle or clothing.

Items for the IAS scale were selected from a pool of suggestions given by students who were asked to describe situations they might find embarrassing. The final scale consists of 12 items, the first 4 of which are reproduced in Table 11.6.

Elkind and Bowen administered the IAS to 697 students in grades four, six, eight, and twelve. Several findings from this study are especially noteworthy. First, young adolescents (eighth-grade students) were significantly more reluctant to reveal themselves to an audience than younger children or older adolescents, which supports earlier beliefs about the imaginary audience and its relationship to the egocentrism of the adolescent. A second finding was that girls obtained higher scores than boys on the test. It seems that adolescent girls are perhaps more concerned with imaginary audiences than are adolescent boys and that both are more responsive to these audiences than younger or older subjects. We should note that these findings have not always been replicated. A number of investigations using Elkind and Bowen's IAS or the Adolescent Egocentrism Scale (Enright et al., 1980) found considerable variability in the ages at which children become egocentric — and in some instances, found little evidence of egocentrism (Buis & Thompson, 1989). Lapsley (1990) concludes that more often than not, egocentrism is manifested in adolescence. But we don't yet understand its origins, and our instruments for measuring it need improvement.

Clarification of adolescent egocentrism might have a number of practical implications, quite apart from what it might contribute to the elaboration of theory. In the first place, it might do a great deal to clarify the adolescent experience for us. Second, as Elkind (1981b) suggests, it might contribute in

Table 11.6
The Imaginary Audience Scale (IAS)

Instructions: Please read the following stories carefully and assume that the events actually happened to you. Place a check next to the answer that best describes what you would do or feel in the real situation.

TS scale   1. You have looked forward to the most exciting dress-up party of the year. You arrive after an hour's drive from home. Just as the party is beginning, you notice a grease spot on your trousers or skirt. (There is no way to borrow clothes from anyone.) Would you stay or go home?
_____ Go home.
_____ Stay, even though I'd feel uncomfortable.
_____ Stay, because the grease spot wouldn't bother me.

AS scale   2. Let's say some adult visitors came to your school and you were asked to tell them a little bit about yourself.
_____ I would like that.
_____ I would not like that.
_____ I wouldn't care.

TS scale   3. It is Friday afternoon and you have just had your hair cut in preparation for the wedding of a relative that weekend. The barber or hairdresser did a terrible job and your hair looks awful. To make it worse, that night is the most important basketball game of the season and you really want to see it, but there is no way you can keep your head covered without people asking questions. Would you stay home or go to the game anyway?
_____ Go to the game and not worry about my hair.
_____ Go to the game and sit where people won't notice me very much.
_____ Stay home.

AS scale   4. If you went to a party where you did not know most of the kids, would you wonder what they were thinking about you?
_____ I wouldn't think about it.
_____ I would wonder about that a lot.
_____ I would wonder about that a little.

Source: From D. Elkind and R. Bowen, Imaginary audience behavior in children and adolescents, *Developmental Psychology,* 1979, *15*(1), 38–44, p. 40. Copyright 1979 by the American Psychological Association. Reprinted by permission of the author.

important ways to our understanding of vandalism, teenage pregnancy, drug abuse, and other related behaviors. One of the important motives that might underly these behaviors may relate directly to what the adolescent expects the reaction of the imaginary audience to be. Teachers, parents, counselors, and friends are all members of that audience.

Mine is made up mainly of popes and presidents.

Personal Fable

Adolescent egocentrism is reflected not only in the creation of an imaginary audience but also in the elaboration of fantasies, the hero of which is, not surprisingly, the adolescent. These fantasies, labeled **personal fables,** have a number of identifying themes, the most common of which are "I am *special.*" "Eagles and gods do not do untidy things upon me." "I will not get pregnant." "I will not become addicted to these drugs I take only for recreation." "Mom, you just don't understand what real love is." "Nor do you, dad!"

One of the characteristics of the personal fable is a sense of invulnerability. Unfortunately, it is often sadly inappropriate as is evident in the fact that adolescents — especially males — have the highest accident rate of all age groups except those over 65 (U.S. Bureau of the Census, 1988).

Elements of the personal fable run through the lives of most of us. Most of us believe that we are somewhat unique — just a little special. But these beliefs appear to be greatly exaggerated in adolescence and may account in part for the casualness with which adolescents will take risks that they know cognitively to be horrendous (see Table 11.7).

MORAL DEVELOPMENT

With the conviction that frequently accompanies intuition, all of us believe implicitly that people are good or bad in differing degrees, that goodness or evil is an intrinsic part of what we are — of our selves. Are we really good or bad, or do we simply behave well some of the time and badly at other times? If we are really good or bad, are we born that way, or do we become one or the other later? Further, is being good in a moral sense the same thing as conforming to accepted social rules, or are the two separate?

Kohlberg (1964) discusses three aspects of morality. (We most often use the first two when judging the relative "goodness" of people.) The first is the behavioral aspect of morality, reflected in a person's ability to resist temptation; the second relates to the amount of guilt that accompanies failure to resist temptation; the third is the individual's estimate of the morality of a given act based on some personal standard of good or evil. Obviously, these dimensions of morality are not necessarily very closely related. A person may repeatedly violate some accepted code of conduct — behave immorally, in other words — and yet feel a great deal of guilt. A second may engage in exactly the same behavior and feel no guilt. Despite these differences, both may judge the act equally evil. Who is most moral?

Behaving Morally

Carroll and Rest (1982) suggest that there are four separate components involved in behaving morally: First, it requires recognizing a moral problem and being sensitive to the fact that someone's welfare is involved. Second is the

AT A GLANCE

Adolescent Risks and Violent Death

Table 11.7
1986 U.S. Death Rates (per 100,000 Population) by Age for Accidents

	White		Black	
Age	Male	Female	Male	Female
15–24	118.8	34.3	147.6	31.8
25–34	102.5	25.9	207.6	44.8
35–44	80.6	25.2	179.9	35.7
45–54	78.6	26.9	148.9	30.9
55–64	82.1	29.9	133.8	41.4
65 and older	155.4	81.7	187.1	81.2

Source: U.S. Bureau of the Census (1990).

The risk-taking behavior of adolescents, especially of adolescent males, may be due in part to what Elkind labels the *personal fable* – the feeling that the adolescent is special and somehow invulnerable, that bad things happen only to other people. Risk-taking behavior is manifested in drug abuse, dangerous hobbies, and automobile and other accidents and is especially evident in the incidence of violent death among white adolescent males. Violent death among blacks is more common than among whites and does not reveal the same pattern of higher incidence in adolescence, perhaps because it involves a higher proportion of homicides, which continue at a high rate after adolescence, and perhaps because of more limited access to automobiles. For both blacks and whites, violent death is considerably lower for females than for males.

need to make a judgment about what is right and wrong – about what ought to be done in a given situation. Third, the individual needs to make a plan of action that takes into account relevant ideals and values. Finally, the plan must be put into action.

It is entirely possible, Carroll and Rest argue, to fail to act morally because of a deficiency in only one of these components. Research on bystander intervention, stimulated by the now-famous murder of Kitty Genovese, is a case in point. Kitty was a New Yorker who, returning home from work at three o'clock one morning, was set upon by a maniac. At least 38 of her neighbors in fashionable Kew Gardens were awakened by her screams and came to their windows.

And watched. No one tried to help her; no one yelled at the murderer; no one even called the police. They simply watched for a full half hour as Kitty was being slowly murdered below them.

How can their behavior be interpreted in light of Carroll and Rest's analysis of what is required for moral behavior? It is possible that some of the bystanders who failed to respond might not have initially recognized the seriousness of the situation (it's only a lover's quarrel). Others might have been unable to devise a plan of behavior compatible with their ideals and values (how can I save her life without endangering mine?). Still others might have felt incapable of implementing the plan they might have devised (I should restrain the attacker physically, but I am not strong enough). Finally, there is the chilling possibility that some among the spectators might have developed values that run counter to helping someone in this situation (If he wants to kill her, hey, it's up to him).

These four components of moral behavior have been described using a number of different labels. For example:

1. Moral sensitivity (recognition of a moral problem)
2. Moral judgment (deciding what *ought* to be done)
3. Moral values (conscience; ideals; that which guides moral action)
4. Moral action (moral or immoral behavior)

Two of these four components, moral values (conscience) and the development of moral judgment, are especially important in psychology and have been extensively researched.

Conscience

What is a strong conscience? There are two historical approaches to answering this question. The psychoanalytic approach is based on the belief that the strength of the superego is the strength of conscience. It asserts that the stronger people's beliefs are about the immorality of an act, the less likely they are to engage in that act. Interestingly, the evidence has not always supported this position. Several studies and reports (for example, Hendry, 1960) indicate a low relationship between the strength of people's beliefs and actual behavior. Under some circumstances, it seems that the probability of behaving morally has more to do with the anticipation of reward and the probability of getting caught than with conscience.

The second approach, a more religious one, is based on the belief that a good conscience is a manifestation of strength of character and good habits that have been inculcated in the individual, usually through religious training. Kohlberg (1964) summarizes several studies that did not find a high relationship between religious training and overt behavior. Here too, available evidence suggests that beliefs about right or wrong have less to do with children's actual behavior than do the likelihood of their being caught or the gains to be derived from transgression. Other related factors are the individual's intelligence, ability to delay gratification (to choose long-range goals over short-range objectives), and self-esteem. It appears that children who have favorable self-concepts are less likely to engage in immoral behavior, presumably because they are more likely to feel guilty if they do.

Morality as a Cognitive Phenomenon

Based on these findings, Kohlberg argues that moral behavior does not reflect a fixed behavioral trait but rather a decision-making capacity. Furthermore, as Nucci and Turiel (1978) argue, morality is probably different from social convention. Learning social conventions involves learning behaviors that are accepted or not accepted but that are essentially arbitrary. Thus in Western cultures, conventions relating to eating tell us we should use knives and forks, sit at tables, eat off plates and bowls, and try to refrain from belching and doing other things unmentionable in polite textbooks. Elsewhere, we might learn to eat with sticks, squatting on the ground, lapping food off rocks, belching and making other fine noises with great gusto. Because these behaviors are arbitrary, if different behaviors are substituted for them we are not likely to be judged evil — foolish and disgusting, perhaps, but not truly evil. **Morality**, in contrast, is far less arbitrary. It refers to behaviors and judgments relating to broad issues of human justice such as the value of human life, the ethics of causing harm to others or to their property, and the place of trust and responsibility.

Darley and Schultz (1990) speak of three different kinds of justice that might be considered when investigating moral development. *Retributive justice* relates to punishment; *distributive justice* has to do with fairness in the allocation of rewards; and *procedural* justice relates to the impartiality and fairness of the methods by which moral decisions are reached.

Since morality is viewed primarily as a decision-making capacity, it has been investigated mainly as a cognitive phenomenon. Not surprisingly, the models that have guided most of the research have been based closely on Piaget's work and, more recently, on information-processing theories. Clearly, however, morality includes not only thought but also emotion and behavior (Walker, 1988).

Most of the research on moral development has dealt with what Eisenberg (1990) refers to as prohibition- or justice-oriented moral reasoning rather than with *prosocial* morality. With some exceptions, researchers have not been especially concerned with changes in children's prosocial behavior or with their motives for and understanding of this behavior. Instead, they have looked at children's understanding of right and wrong primarily as this understanding is reflected in their awareness that "wrong" things are prohibited and in their awareness that certain outcomes and punishments are fair — therefore moral — and others less fair.

Morality, Rules, and Games

There is a close relationship between playing games that have rules and the development of morality. Morality may be defined as the internalization of rules. Whereas the rules that govern game playing relate specifically to each game, the rules of morality govern all of life. And that too may be considered a game — not play, but a game nevertheless.

Children's understanding of the rules of games follows two frequently contradictory paths: their verbalized belief about the nature, the origins, and the permanence of rules; and their understanding of rules as reflected in their actual behavior. Piaget (1932) reports that the actual play behavior of children reveals an initial stage during which there is no adherence to rules (until approximately age 3). This stage is followed by an intermediate period during which children imitate rules but do not really understand them and consequently change them to conform to their interpretation of the game (ages 3 to 5). By the time children are 7 or 8 years old, they have begun to play in a genuinely social manner, with rules that are mutually accepted by all players and that are rigidly adhered to. Not until the age of 11 or 12 is the true nature of rules understood — when children realize that rules exist to make games possible and that they can be altered by mutual agreement.

Parallel to children's demonstrated understanding of rules is their verbalization of this understanding. Piaget questioned a number of children about the origins of rules and their characteristics. Their responses suggested the existence of three stages. The first lasts until the age of 3 and is characterized by no understanding of rules, which is reflected in their actual behavior as well. This initial stage is followed by a longer period during which children believe that rules emanate from some external source (such as God); rules are timeless and permanent; and above all, children should not take it upon themselves to change them. This stage corresponds to the period in children's lives when their actual behavior in games is characterized by constantly changing rules. During the next stage of their actual games behavior, they do not change rules but gradually come to accept that rules are made by people and that they can be changed by the players if they so wish. Note the clear contradiction between their beliefs and their overt behavior (Table 11.8).

Piaget (1932) also investigated children's notions of morality by telling them stories and asking them to make judgments about the goodness or evil of the characters. For example, he told a story of a child who accidentally breaks 15 cups, asking the subject to compare this behavior to that of a child who deliberately breaks a single cup. From the children's responses to these stories, Piaget reached the general conclusion that there are two broad stages in the evolution of beliefs about guilt. In the first, the child judges guilt by the apparent consequences of the act: The child who has broken the largest number of cups or who has stolen the greatest quantity of goods or the largest amount of money is considered more evil than the one who deliberately broke only one cup, stole just a few things, or just a little money. Following this stage, children's

Table 11.8
Piaget's Description of Children's Understanding and Use of Rules

Approximate Age	Degree of Understanding	Adherence to Rules
Before 3	No understanding of rules	Do not play according to rules
To 7 or 8	Believe rules come from God (or some other high authority) and cannot be changed	Break and change rules constantly
To 11 or 12	Understand social nature of rules and that they can be changed	Do not change rules; adhere to them rigidly
After 11 or 12	Complete understanding of rules	Change rules by mutual consent

judgment becomes more adultlike — they are more likely to consider the intentions and motives behind the act.

Put another way, what Piaget found was that very young children do not respond in terms of abstract conceptions of right and wrong as might an adolescent. Instead, they respond in terms of the immediate consequences of behavior. Thus, a young child's morality is governed by the principles of pain and pleasure. Good behaviors are those that have pleasant consequences; bad actions have unpleasant consequences. Piaget's label for this first stage of moral development is *heteronomy.* During this stage, the child responds primarily to outside authority, since authority is the main source of reinforcement and punishment. In the second stage, morality comes to be governed more and more by principles and ideals. Moral judgments become more individual and more autonomous; hence Piaget's label, *autonomy,* for the second stage.

Piaget thought that the transition between heteronomy and autonomy likely happened by the age of 9 or 10. However, subsequent research indicates that children as young as 6 or 7 are likely to consider the actor's intentions in judging the severity of an act (Darley & Shultz, 1990). Thus children will judge an act more harshly if it *intentionally* causes harm than if the harm is unintentional. Similarly, they will judge an actor more punishable if the harm should have been foreseen even if it was unintentional (Darley & Zanna, 1982). Also, children at this age have begun to consider other mitigating circumstances in their judgments of culpability. Thus various justifications such as necessity, provocation, or the fact that the transgressor has attempted restitution serve to reduce the degree to which children think a transgressor should be punished.

In some ways, then, the moral judgments of children are somewhat similar to those of adolescents and adults. But, as Kohlberg's (1980) research shows, in other ways they think quite differently.

Kohlberg's Stages

Kohlberg (1969, 1980) describes three levels in the development of moral judgments, each consisting of two stages of moral orientation (shown in Table 11.9). The three levels are sequential, although succeeding levels never entirely replace preceding ones, making it almost impossible to assign ages to them. However, children normally progress from an initial preconventional stage, in which they respond primarily to punishment or reward, to a rule-based, highly conventional morality. The final postconventional level, in which individuals respond to principles rather than to rules or to personal consequences, appears to be reached by only a handful of individuals. A reanalysis of Kohlberg's original data suggests, in fact, that only approximately one-eighth of subjects in their twenties operate at a Stage 5 level (Colby & Kohlberg, 1984). And evidence of Stage 6 judgments (based on universal ethical principles) could not be found in that sample. Accordingly, although Stage 6 is still included in Table 11.9, it exists as a "potential" stage rather than as one that has been discovered in behavior.

At the preconventional level, the child's judgment of right and wrong takes one of two orientations. In the first, the child believes that evil behavior is that which is likely to be punished, and good behavior is based on obedience or the avoidance of the evil of disobedience. Thus, the child does not evaluate right or wrong in terms of the objective consequences of the behavior or the intentions of the actor; judgment is based solely on the consequences to the child. The second preconventional moral orientation (Stage 2) is a hedonistic one, in which the child interprets good as that which is pleasant, and evil as that which has undesirable consequences. At this level begins the reciprocity that characterizes morality at the second level; but it is a practical reciprocity. Children will go out of their way to do something good for someone if they themselves will gain by the deed.

The second level, a morality of conventional role conformity, reflects the increasing importance of peer and social relations to the developing child. Stage 3, for example, is defined as morality designed to maintain good relations. Hence moral behavior is behavior that receives wide approval from significant people — parents, teachers, peers, and society at large. Stage 4, conformity to rules and laws, is also related to the child's desire to maintain a friendly status quo. Thus conforming to law becomes important for maintaining adults' approval.

At the highest level, postconventional, the individual begins to view morality in terms of individual rights (Stage 5) and as ideals and principles that have value as rules or laws, apart from their influence on approval. As we noted, however, Stage 5 moral judgments are rare even among adults; and Stage 6 judgments, based on fundamental ethical principles, even rarer. Colby and Kohlberg (1984) suggest that there is some doubt as to whether or not Stage 6 should even be included as a stage in moral development.

Table 11.9
Kohlberg's Levels of Morality

Kohlberg identified levels of moral judgment in children by describing to them situations involving a moral dilemma. One example is the story of a man whose wife is dying but who might be saved if given a drug that was discovered by a local pharmacist, who charges such an exorbitant price that the husband can't pay. Should he steal the drug?

Level I Preconventional	Stage 1: Punishment and obedience orientation	"If he steals the drug, he might go to jail." (Punishment.)
	Stage 2: Naive instrumental hedonism	"He can steal the drug and save his wife, and he'll be with her when he gets out of jail." (Act motivated by its hedonistic consequences for the actor.)
Level II Conventional	Stage 3: "Good-boy, nice-girl" morality	"People will understand if you steal the drug to save your wife, but they'll think you're cruel and a coward if you don't." (Reactions of others and the effects of the act on social relationships become important.)
	Stage 4: Law-and-order orientation	"It is the husband's duty to save his wife even if he feels guilty afterwards for stealing the drug." (Institutions, law, duty, honor, and guilt motivate behavior.)
Level III Postconventional	Stage 5: Morality of social contract	"The husband has a right to the drug even if he can't pay now. If the druggist won't charge it, the government should look after it." (Democratic laws guarantee individual rights; contracts are mutually beneficial.)
	Stage 6: Universal ethical*	"Although it is legally wrong to steal, the husband would be morally wrong not to steal to save his wife. A life is more precious than financial gain." (Conscience is individual. Laws are socially useful but not sacrosanct.)

Source: Based on Kohlberg (1969, 1980).

*Stage 6 is no longer included among Kohlberg's stages because none of his sample reached it. However, it is still described as a "potential" stage.

Generality of Kohlberg's Stages

Kohlberg's early research suggests that children progress through the stages of moral development in predictable sequence and at roughly the same ages. Theoretically, this makes a lot of sense, because moral judgments are essentially *cognitive* and would therefore be expected to reflect level of cognitive development. Specifically, as Walker (1988) explains, preoperational thought parallels Stage 1 moral reasoning (physical consequences and authority determine morality); concrete operations makes Stage 2 morality possible (morality is instrumental and self-serving); and the beginning of formal operations is necessary for Stage 3 morality (emphasis on being a "good" person; what is approved of is moral). Successively higher stages of moral judgment are made possible by the elaboration and consolidation of formal operations.

Note that the higher stages of moral development do not necessarily accompany advances in intellectual development. What Kohlberg and his followers maintain is that certain levels of cognitive performance are *essential* for corresponding levels of moral reasoning, but are not *sufficient*. This is, in fact, the principle that underlies the relationship between intellectual and moral development.

A number of researchers have criticized Kohlberg's concept of stages of moral development, and have contradicted his belief that these stages parallel cognitive development and that they are universal. For example, Holstein (1976) found that many subjects skipped stages, reverted to earlier levels of moral reasoning, or were so inconsistent in their responses to moral dilemmas that they could not easily be classified in any stage. Similarly, Kurtines and Grief (1974) and Fishkin, Keniston, and Mackinnon (1973) found few advances in moral reasoning among older children and found that subjects often operated at different stages depending on the specifics of the moral questions to which they were responding.

Following these criticisms, Kohlberg (1980) eliminated the sixth stage (no one ever reached it) and revised the scoring methods for the moral dilemma questions. He then reanalyzed his original data using the new scoring procedures (Colby & Kohlberg, 1984). What the reanalysis indicated was that progression through the stages takes much longer than had at first been thought and that postconventional morality is the exception rather than the rule even among adults. Specifically, 10-year-olds were typically either in Stage 2 or still in transition between Stages 1 and 2; young adolescents (ages 13–14) were primarily still in transition between Stages 2 and 3; and late adolescents as well as early adults, mainly in Stage 3. As we noted earlier, only one of every eight adults in this sample operated at a postconventional level.

Although Kohlberg's reanalysis indicates that the stages span wide age spreads, it also strengthens his contention that these are legitimate stages in that they conform to the three common criteria for stages: (1) progression is upward (not backward); (2) there is no skipping of stages; and (3) the thinking characteristic of a stage is generally applied to all content areas while the individual is at that stage.

Walker (1988) subsequently analyzed and summarized a large number of studies that have examined Kohlberg's findings. He also concludes that there is little skipping of stages or regression to earlier stages.

Most of the research agrees, however, that although progress through the higher stages may be possible with the development of formal operational thinking in adolescence, it typically remains potential rather than actual. As Lapsley (1990) notes, adolescence is not marked by principled moral reasoning, as we might expect given the adolescent's newly developed ability to deal with abstractions and principles. Most young adolescents reason at a preconventional, Stage 2 level (a self-serving, hedonistic morality) or at a conventional, Stage 3 level (emphasis on conforming, being good, doing the expected). In fact, Stage 3 reasoning is not very general until the age of 16 to 18 and is common into adulthood.

Researchers who are concerned with the information-processing, rule-governed aspects of moral development, rather than with Kohlberg-type stages, suggest that Kohlberg's moral dilemmas are perhaps too verbal and too abstract for children. They demand that the child understand and keep in mind very complex situations involving a number of actors; and they require the manipulation of a variety of factors and circumstances. Frequently, they do not provide sufficient information; but if they did, they would be even more complex. As a result, it is possible that the Kohlberg dilemmas underestimate children's moral reasoning. When questions are made simpler, or when children and adolescents are observed in naturalistic settings, researchers sometimes find evidence of very sophisticated moral reasoning at very young ages (see Darley & Shultz, 1990; Lapsley, 1990).

There is now mounting evidence that moral judgments are related not only to the age of subjects but also to a host of other variables, including the intentions of the transgressor; personal characteristics such as kindness and cruelty; social, material, or personal consequences; and interpersonal relationships (see, for example, Damon & Colby, 1987; Eisenberg, 1987). In short, moral development is probably far more complex than our presentation of Kohlberg's stages would suggest.

Gilligan's Approach

In addition to the criticism that progression through Kohlberg's stages may not be quite as predictable or systematic as Kohlberg had thought, Gilligan (1982) suggests that Kohlberg's research suffered from at least two other important weaknesses. One is that all his subjects were male — and there is evidence of important male-female differences in morality. The other is that the moral dilemmas that he employed in his investigations were typically totally irrelevant to the lives of his subjects. A person's response to an abstract or hypothetical moral dilemma ("What would you do if you had to choose between letting your partner die or spending the rest of your life in jail?") might be quite different from that person's actual behavior in the case of a real, rather than hypothetical, dilemma.

Gilligan reasoned that subjects' apparent stages of moral reasoning might seem *higher* in the case of an abstract and impersonal moral dilemma like that described in Table 11.9 than they would be in the case of a more immediate and perhaps more realistic dilemma. Accordingly, she and her associates developed three sexual dilemmas for use with adolescents. One of these dilemmas, for example, describes a situation where a high school girl's parents are away for the weekend, her boyfriend unexpectedly comes over, and after a while, they begin to neck and pet. Among the accompanying questions were the following:

1. Is this right or wrong? Are there any circumstances that would make it right — or wrong?
2. What if they had sexual intercourse? Is that right or wrong? Why?
3. (If applicable) Why do you think petting is OK but sexual intercourse is wrong?
4. Are there any circumstances that would make sexual intercourse right — or wrong? (Gilligan et al., 1971).

When Gilligan and her associates administered the sexual dilemmas, along with Kohlberg's standard moral dilemmas, to 50 high school students (25 males and 25 females), they found, as expected, that average scores on the standard dilemmas were significantly higher than scores on the sexual dilemmas. On the standard dilemmas, students scored between Stages 3 and 4; on the sexual dilemmas, they scored at Stage 3. Recall that Stage 3 judgments are profoundly influenced by a desire to maintain good relations, to gain the approval of parents and peers. Accordingly, adolescent judgments on the sexual dilemmas reflect a desire to do what is accepted and expected — what others would approve.

If moral judgments are significantly different in response to dilemmas with which subjects can identify but which are nevertheless abstract, they might be even more different if the dilemmas were real rather than abstract.

Following this line of reasoning, Gilligan examined morality in women by interviewing them while they were caught up in an actual moral dilemma. Her subjects were 29 women who had been referred to a counseling clinic for pregnant women and who were currently facing the decision concerning having an abortion.

Following an analysis of the women's reasons for having or not having an abortion, Gilligan identified three stages in female moral development. Briefly, in the first stage, the woman is moved primarily by selfish concerns ("This is what I want . . . what I need . . . what I should do . . . what would be best for me"). In the second stage, the woman progresses through a period of increasing recognition of responsibility to others. And the final stage reflects a morality of "nonviolence." At this stage, the woman's decision is based on her desire to do the greatest good both for self and for others.

If Gilligan's description of female moral development is accurate, it reflects a number of important differences between male and female morality. In contrast with Kohlberg's description of male moral progression from what are initially hedonistic (pain-pleasure) concerns toward a conventional, rule-regulated morality, Gilligan describes female morality as a progression from initial selfishness toward a recognition of social responsibility. Boys are perhaps more concerned with law and order than the personally meaningful dimensions of morality.

Gilligan suggests that female morality is more concerned with empathy than is male morality, that it responds more to social responsibility.

Muss (1988), following a review of a number of studies that have looked at sex differences in moral judgment, cautions that the distinctions between male and female morality are not as clear as Gilligan's conclusions might lead us to believe. He reasons that if Gilligan's descriptions are correct, it follows that females should, on the average, be more altruistic, more empathetic, more concerned with human relations; in contrast, males should be less altruistic. But research on altruism, cooperation, and other forms of prosocial behavior has not found these differences. Note, however, that these findings do not invalidate Gilligan's basic conclusions. It may well be that males and females are equally altruistic, but their altruism might stem from fundamentally different orientations, reflecting very different moralities. Females may, as Gilligan suggests, be altruistic because of their concern for humanity; males may be just as altruistic because of their adherence to principles and ideals that stress caring for each other.

One of the important contributions of Gilligan's approach is that it underlines the need to be aware of the possibility that many of our theories and conclusions in human development are not equally applicable to males and females. In Gilligan's (1982) words, the sexes speak *in a different voice*. Neither voice is louder or better; they are simply different.

Implications of Research on Moral Development

Some of the most important implications of our current knowledge and beliefs about morality relate to the observation that individuals who operate at the lowest levels (hedonistic) are more likely to be delinquent than those who operate at higher levels. As Gibbs (1987) notes, the delinquent's behavior generally reflects immature moral reasoning and egocentricity. Individuals who operate at higher levels of morality are more likely to be honest and to behave in a generally moral way (Kohlberg & Candee, 1984). By the same token, altruism in children is highly related to level of moral development. Children who are still at a hedonistic level (good things are those that lead to pleasant consequences) typically engage in less prosocial behavior (in this case, share less) than children at more advanced stages (Eisenberg-Berg & Hand, 1979). To the extent that these observations are accurate, anything that schools, families, and other socializing influences can do to increase levels of moral orientation would apparently be beneficial.

What can schools and parents do? Although the suggestions offered are still relatively abstract, research designed to increase levels of moral judgment or behavior in adolescents indicates that this is possible. Kohlberg (1978) reports that simply discussing moral dilemmas in the classroom typically leads to an increase in levels of moral judgment (approximately one-third of a stage). Also, Arbuthnot (1975) found that older adolescents displayed higher levels of moral reasoning after role-playing situations involving specific moral dilemmas. In the Arbuthnot investigation, subjects role-played with a partner (opponent) who used arguments at a level higher than that at which the subject had been assessed. Modeling procedures have also been employed to increase morality (Damon & Colby, 1987).

Clearly, the development of morality is an important social and family responsibility. Hoffman (1976) suggests four different types of activity that might be conducive to the development of altruistic, caring behavior:

1. Situations in which children are allowed to experience unpleasantness rather than being overprotected

2. Role-taking experiences in which children are responsible for the care of others

3. Role-playing experiences in which children imagine themselves in the plight of others

4. Exposure to altruistic models

One additional approach seems especially effective in fostering moral growth in adolescents: sociomoral discourse. Berkowitz, Oser, and Althof (1987) provide evidence that discussing moral problems and evaluating the ethical implications of behavior in groups can do much to elevate moral judgment and behavior.

In addition to what schools and educators might attempt to do, the values and behaviors of parents are highly instrumental in determining those of their children. Indeed, the values of adolescents typically resemble their parents' values rather than those of their peers (Reiss, 1966). Also, parents' social class, as well as their specific behaviors, are closely related to children's understanding of rules and social conventions (Johnson & McGillicuddy-Delisi, 1983).

Research reveals a clear relationship between parenting styles and children's morality. Specifically, the internalization of moral rules is fostered by two things: (1) the frequent use of discipline that points out the harmful consequences of the child's behavior for others; and (2) frequent expression of parental affection (Hoffman, 1979). Most forms of parental discipline, Hoffman argues, contain elements of "power assertion" and "love-withdrawal." That is, discipline usually involves at least the suggestion of the possibility of loss of parental love as well as something like deprivation of privileges, threats, or physical punishment. The main purpose of this "power assertion," according to Hoffman, is to get the child to stop misbehaving and pay attention. From the point of view of the child's developing morality, however, what is most important is that there now be an accompanying verbal component. The purpose of this verbal component is to influence the child cognitively and emotionally — perhaps by bringing about feelings of guilt or of empathy, and by enabling the child to foresee consequences. The verbal component might simply admonish ("Don't do that"); ideally, however, it should go beyond simply admonishing ("Don't do that because . . ." or "If you do that, the cat might . . .").

MAIN POINTS

1. In many "primitive" societies, termed *discontinuous*, progress from childhood to adulthood is marked by ritual and ceremony collectively known as *rites of passage.* Four common steps in these rites are separation, training, initiation, and induction. Initiation procedures sometimes involve scarification and circumcision.

2. Contemporary societies do not clearly demarcate passage from childhood to adulthood. Some writers claim that in our society, secondary schools serve as rites of passage in that they exemplify separation from society, training in terms of skills and knowledge, and initiation and induction into adult society through the high school graduation ceremony.

3. Puberty is sexual maturity. It results from pubescence. The changes of pubescence that make reproduction possible involve *primary* sexual characteristics (menstruation and the capacity to ejaculate semen). Other changes that are not directly linked to reproducing involve *secondary* sexual characteristics (axillary hair, breasts, and voice changes, for example).

4. For a time in late childhood and early adolescence, girls are taller and heavier than boys; but at about age 14, boys surpass girls. From childhood through adulthood, boys have relatively more fat-free mass than girls.

5. Early maturation appears to be advantageous for boys but less so for girls. Pubertal change is most stressful when it puts the adolescent out of step with peers, especially if the change is not seen as an advantage.

6. Common adolescent concerns include worries about the future, finances, school, appearance, feelings of inferiority, loneliness, the purpose of life, sex, the stability of the parents' marriage, and lack of time.

7. Although obesity is the most common nutritional problem of adolescence, concerns over appearance and weight are sometimes apparent in eating disorders such as anorexia nervosa (loss of appetite and, occasionally, eventual starvation) and bulimia (binge eating).

8. Anorexia involves significant weight loss, refusal to maintain weight, and distorted body image and is most common among adolescent girls (10 times as many girls afflicted as boys). Bulimia is defined in terms of recurrent episodes of binge eating that are accompanied by the realization that the behavior is not normal and by feelings of guilt or self-deprecation.

9. The intellectual development of the adolescent may culminate in thought that is potentially completely logical, that is inferential, that deals with the hypothetical as well as with the concrete, that is systematic, and that results in the potential for being idealistic. Then again, it may not. Among other things, formal operations make possible a type of intense idealism that may be reflected in adolescent frustration or rebellion, as well as in more advanced levels of moral orientation.

10. Information-processing views of development can be seen as complementary to Piaget's descriptions. These views are concerned with three aspects of cognition: the acquisition of a knowledge base; the development of information-processing strategies; and the development of metacognitive skills.

11. Cognitive-processing abilities develop by (1) increasing capacity (memory span increases significantly between early childhood and early adolescence) and (2) through the acquisition of better and more appropriate processing strategies.

12. Adolescent egocentrism describes a self-centeredness that often leads adolescents to believe that all others in the immediate vicinity are highly concerned with their thoughts and behaviors.

13. Egocentrism in adolescence may be manifested in the creation of the *imaginary audience* (an imagined collection of people assumed to be highly concerned about the adolescent's immediate behavior) and the *personal fable* (a type of fantasy whose themes stress the individual's invulnerability and uniqueness).

14. Carroll and Rest describe four components of moral behavior: recognizing a moral problem (moral sensitivity); deciding what ought to be done (moral judgment); devising a plan of action according to ideals (moral values); and implementing the plan (moral action). Failure to act morally may be due to a deficiency in any one of these four components. Moral judgments are viewed as mainly cognitive.

15. Piaget draws a parallel between the development of understanding rules governing games and moral development. Both proceed from an initial stage, where there is no understanding of rules, to a final stage, where rules are understood as being arbitrary, socially useful, and changeable.

16. Kohlberg describes the development of morality in terms of sequential progression through three levels — *preconventional* (concerned with self — pain, pleasure, obedience, punishment), *conventional* (concerned with the group, with being liked, with conforming to law), and *postconventional* (concerned with abstract principles, ethics, social contracts). Each level consists of two stages.

17. The evidence indicates that cognitive advances are *necessary* for advances in moral judgment, but are not *sufficient.* Most young adolescents reason at a preconventional Stage 2 level (concerned with self); Stage 3 morality (emphasis on conforming, on the group, on being good by doing what is expected and approved) does not become common until age 16 to 18. Principled morality (based on abstract ideals) is rare even among adults.

18. Gilligan's work suggests that men and women differ in their moral development. Whereas males become progressively more concerned with law and order, women respond more to social relationships and to the social consequences of behavior. However, these sex differences are not always very clear or very significant in other research.

19. Various programs using indoctrination, role playing, and modeling have been successful in increasing levels of moral judgment and sometimes behavior in subjects. Also two parenting-style variables are especially important in the internalization of moral rules: the use of discipline that points out the harmful consequences of the child's behavior for others; and the frequent expression of parental affection.

Further Readings

An excellent account of contemporary adolescence, viewed against the backdrop of historical changes in adolescence, is provided by:

Kett, J. F. (1977). *Rites of passage: Adolescence in America, 1790 to the present.* New York: Basic Books.

Eating disorders are a subject of considerable current interest and research. An entire issue of the following journal is devoted to examining their nature and treatment:

Transactional Analysis Journal, 1985, Vol. 15.

For a comprehensive collection of sometimes complex, though often fascinating, articles dealing with current approaches to cognition, see:

Chipman, S. F., Segal, J. W., & Glaser, R. (Eds.). (1985). *Thinking and learning skills* (Vol. 2) *Research and open questions.* Hillsdale, N.J.: Lawrence Erlbaum.

For contemporary research on the role of social interaction in the development of morality, see:

Kurtines, W. M., & Gewirtz, J. L. (Eds.), *Moral development through social interaction.* New York: John Wiley.

The following are two good sources of information on moral development. The first describes some of Kohlberg's recent revisions to his stage theory; the second is a collection of articles dealing with various aspects of moral development and its relationship to behavior:

Kohlberg, L. (1980). *The meaning and measurement of moral development.* Worcester, Mass.: Clark University Press.

Kurtines, W. M., & Gewirtz, J. L. (Eds.). (1984). *Morality, moral behavior, and moral development.* New York: John Wiley.

The following is an excellent collection of chapters dealing with the transition from childhood to early adolescence. Especially pertinent to this chapter are Malina's chapter on physical growth and performance, Eisenberg's chapter on morality and prosocial development, and Lapsley's account of social/cognitive development.

Montemayor, R., Adams, G. R., & Gullotta, T. P. (Eds.). (1990). *From childhood to adolescence: A transitional period? (Advances in adolescent development,* Vol 2). Newbury Park, Calif.: Sage.

Never throw stones at your mother,
You'll be sorry for it when she's dead,
Never throw stones at your mother,
Throw bricks at your father instead.

Brendan Behan, *The Hostage*

Social Development

I had thought to write about myself in these paragraphs. I thought I might describe for you the course of a marginally exemplary adolescence. But as my grandmother observed on more than one occasion, some things are damnably boring.

It occurred to me that I might describe my adolescent children for you — that I might pique your curiosity with tales of their debaucheries, their substance abuse, their flagrant and thoroughly unplanned pregnancies, their unbridled rebelliousness and delinquency.

But they are not at all like that, my adolescent offspring. And I cannot easily tell lies about them.

I might have written, instead, of adolescents raised by various of my colleagues, for there are among them a number whose sins are horribly fascinating. But those of their parents who read might be offended.

Instead I write of Debbie, Pat, and Linda; later we will speak again of the mythical average, and sadly nameless, adolescent.

Debbie, Pat, and Linda were among the hundred or so 16-year-old girls interviewed in depth by Sue Lees (1986) in a sociological study of the lives, the expectations, the hopes, the fears of British schoolgirls. The lives of these girls are largely wrapped up in their reputations; and their reputations are based on their assumed sexual availability. Reputations, how they can be ruined, how little can be done about it, and the powerlessness and inequities of their gender roles dominate their discussions and conversations.

"One thing I noticed," Debbie says, "is that there are not many names you can call a boy. But if you call a girl a name, there's a load of them. You might make a dictionary of names you can call a girl." (Lees, 1986, p. 32).

"Tight bitch, you tight bitch. That sort of word," Pat says in answer to a question about what a boy might call a girl who doesn't want to go out with him.

"That's a terrible thing to say to someone — 'you're too tight,'" Linda says.

"It's a vicious circle," Pat continues. "If you don't like them, then they'll call you a tight bitch. If you go with them they'll call you a slag afterwards." (p. 37).

There are other names too: "dog," "cow," "slut," "prostitute," "whore," "old dog," "tart," and "blind bitch."

What do names such as these mean in the lives of people like Debbie and her friends? Lees argues that they are strong evidence that the old double standard of sexual morality still pervades British adolescent society — that the sexual revolution has left that society largely untouched. As a result, girls continue to face profound social, economic, and intellectual disadvantages.

Are these observations true of all or most adolescents in Britain? Are they true in America and elsewhere? Are conditions changing? Is the revolution still underway?

More about this shortly; first some brief sections on socialization and the self.

SOCIAL DEVELOPMENT

Hodapp and Mueller (1982) observe that infancy is perhaps the least lonely period of the entire life span. At no other time are individuals more likely to be surrounded by others intimately concerned with their comfort and well-being: mothers, fathers, sisters and brothers, grandparents, medical personnel, and assorted relatives.

In contrast, adolescence is perhaps the beginning of the loneliest period of our lives, for it is then, Sartre insists, that we first begin to sense our terrible aloneness, our abandonment (see Chapter 13). As we are cast adrift from our parents, there is a fear that we will find nothing else upon which to anchor.

Maybe it is this realization, this fear, that drives us so strongly to seek the company of others — this and one other thing: Among the most important aspects of social adaptation are those that are directed by the hormonal changes of adolescence, those that have to do with the mounting urges of sexual maturation. Recognition of our aloneness and of our sexuality: these two, taken together, might do much to clarify our understanding of adolescence and of humanity.

Lerner and Shea (1982) argue that all human behavior is basically social. Even biological adaptation requires adjusting to a world filled with others of our own species. In their words, "biological adaptation is, in essence, social behavior" (p. 503). The social adaptation that occurs during adolescence has much to do with the continued discovery and invention of self.

SELF AND IDENTITY

The self is crucially important to a study of adolescence. In one sense, personality is the external manifestation of self; the self is the nebulous essence of an individual — nebulous not because it is unreal but because it cannot be seen or even understood very well. C rl Rogers (1951) and other humanistic psychologists maintain strongly that an individual's self can only be understood from the individual's unique point of view; because a self is necessarily private and alone, it can never be completely known by any outsider. And perhaps it cannot be known very well by the individual either.

Some Definitions

As we saw in Chapter 10, *self* is not an easy term to define. It includes evaluative aspects sometimes referred to as self-worth or self-esteem. In a global sense, self-worth (and self-esteem) is a reflection of how well I like myself. Recall, however, that self-evaluation is possible in a variety of areas, each of which is more or less important in determining evaluations of self-worth. For example, Harter (1983) studied children's evaluations of self-worth in five areas: athletic, scholastic, social, physical, and behavioral. And Marsh and Holmes (1990) have a self-description questionnaire that looks at the individual's assessments of physical ability and appearance, peer relations, academic performance, and specific school subjects. For those who think being a good athlete is most important for being liked, evaluations of their worth as athletes contributes significantly in determining global self-worth.

Another aspect of the self that is very important in understanding the adolescent experience is more cognitive and less evaluative. It has to do with a more objective (rather than emotional) understanding of who and what the self is — rather than with how well adolescents like themselves or how competent they think they are in important areas. Byrne and Shavelson (1987) suggest that it is useful to view this aspect of the self in terms of a multitude of facets that are hierarchically arranged. According to this model, childrens' global self-concepts result from a sequence of inferences and evaluations. The process begins with children perceiving their behavior. These perceptions lead to inferences about the *self* in different specific activities (playing ball; writing English compositions; solving arithmetic problems; playing the harpsichord; carrying on conversations). Inferences in specific areas lead, in turn, to inferences about the self in general areas (for example, athletics or academics). And all these inferences lead ultimately to a general self-concept. Clearly, however, the separation between the evaluative and the more cognitive aspects of self is artificial. In practice, it is difficult to make judgments about what the self is without also at least implicitly deciding whether that is good or bad, desirable or undesirable.

One indication of how difficult and complex notions of self are is found in the tremendous variety of expressions that are employed by different researchers and writers. We have discussed only a few of them (for example, self-concept, self-esteem, and self-worth). Two others are important here: identity and self-image. As we saw in Chapter 2, the term *identity* is a central concept in Erikson's description of adolescence; we discuss it in a later section of this chapter. Next, we look at self-image.

Self-Image

The term *self-image* is used extensively in adolescent research. It is essentially an evaluative concept; as such, it means something very much like what we have taken self-esteem or self-worth to mean. Thus, the *Offer Self-Image Questionnaire*, a widely used instrument for assessing self-image, has teenagers report on their attitudes and feelings about themselves in a number of different areas (Offer, Ostrov, & Howard, 1981). The questionnaire is based on the assumption that the adolescent has a multiplicity of selves that can be considered and evaluated separately: the *psychological* self, the *social* self, the *familial* self, the *coping* self, and the *sexual* self (see Table 12.1). Note that this assumption is identical to the assumption underlying Harter's investigations of self-worth in children, although the areas that each identifies are somewhat different.

The Offer questionnaire investigates each of these five facets of self by presenting adolescents with a series of statements (for example, *Being together with other people gives me a good feeling*) and having them select one of six alternatives relating to how well the statement describes the respondent (ranging from *describes me very well* to *does not describe me at all*).

The *psychological* self is composed of the adolescent's concerns, feelings, wishes, and fantasies. This self reflects adolescents' emotions, their conceptions of their bodies, their ability to control impulses. Examples of items relating to this facet of self are *I am proud of my body* or *I frequently feel ugly and unattractive.* (Each descriptor in the Offer questionnaire is worded both positively and negatively).

The *social* self consists of adolescents' perceptions of their relationships with others, their morals, their goals and aspirations. An item related to the social self is *I prefer being alone to being with kids my age.*

The *sexual* self reflects attitudes and feelings about sexual experiences and behavior: for example, *Sexual experiences give me pleasure* or *Thinking or talking about sex frightens me.*

The *familial* self consists of adolescents' feelings and attitudes toward parents and other members of their family: for example, *I can count on my parents most of the time* or *I try to stay away from home most of the time.*

Finally, the *coping* self mirrors psychological adjustment and emotional well-being and taps, as well, how effectively the adolescent functions in the outside world. Items designed to assess this aspect of the self deal with mastery of the external world (for example, *When I decide to do something, I do it*), psychopathology (*I am confused most of the time*), as well as indications of superior adjustment (*Dealing with new intellectual subjects is a challenge for me*).

The Offer questionnaire was developed more than 20 years ago (scoring procedures have changed since then) and has now been given to tens of thousands of adolescents. Results of the many studies that have used this questionnaire are especially useful for our purposes. They not only reflect self-image,

Table 12.1
Facets of Self in the Offer Self-Image Questionnaire

Important Aspects of Self	Relevant Self-Evaluative Questions
Psychological self	Do I like my body? Am I in control of myself? What are my wishes? My feelings? My fantasies?
Social self	Am I friendly? Outgoing? Do people like me? What kind of morals do I have? What are my aspirations? Am I a loner?
Sexual self	How do I feel about sex? What do I think of pornography? Am I sexually attracted to others? Sexually attractive to them? Comfortable with my sexuality?
Familial self	How do I feel about my parents? Home? Siblings? Other relatives? Do I prefer to stay home? Do people at home like me? Need me? Want me?
Coping self	How effective am I? How well do I cope with what others demand? What school demands? What I demand? Am I well adjusted? Reasonably happy? How decisive am I?

Note: What the adolescent feels about each of these *multiple selves* has important implications for adjustment and happiness.

but also provide important data concerning adolescent relationships with parents and peers, attitudes toward sexual matters, changes in values and morals, aspirations and goals, and so on. Thus there is a great deal in these studies that can clarify the nature of the adolescent experience for us.

In one important study, the *Offer Self-Image Questionnaire* was administered to 5,938 adolescents in 10 different countries (Offer et al., 1988). One objective of this study was to compare adolescents' self-images in each of these countries and perhaps to arrive at a closer understanding of what is universal about adolescence in today's world as well as what might be specific to given cultural contexts. The 10 countries participating in the study were Australia, Bangladesh, Hungary, Israel, Italy, Japan, Taiwan, Turkey, the United States, and West Germany. Translations of the Offer questionnaire were available for each of these countries so that all subjects could be questioned in their native language. Adolescents included in the study were classified into two age groups: younger (ages 13 to 15) and older (ages 16 to 19). Both males and females were included.

The Universal Adolescent

What is similar about adolescence in these 10 countries? Perhaps a surprising number of things. The "universal adolescent," to use Offer et al.'s phrase, resembles most other adolescents in some ways with respect to each of the major facets of self-image: (1) *Psychological* — These adolescents are usually happy and optimistic. They enjoy being alive. (2) *Social* — They also enjoy the company of others. They are caring and compassionate. They place great value on school, education, and preparation for adult work. (3) *Sexual* — The universal adolescent is confident about the sexual self and willing to talk and think about sex. (4) *Familial* — A great majority of adolescents in all 10 cultures express strongly positive feelings toward parents, a high degree of satisfaction with their home lives, and good feelings about their relationships at home. (5) *Coping* — Finally, adolescents across these cultures express confidence in their ability to deal with life. They feel talented and able to make decisions.

The Context-Bound Adolescent

But there are differences, too, across these cultures. Adolescents from Bangladesh were consistently lower on impulse control. Forty-two percent of the Bengali (Bangladesh) adolescents reported they were constantly afraid; many admitted feeling inferior to other people; they felt sadder, more lonely, more vulnerable. Why? Context seems the most plausible explanation. This was the poorest of the countries sampled. Lack of economic opportunities and of adequate medical care, coupled with widespread disease and starvation, might well lead to feelings of vulnerability and fear.

Other cross-national differences included the very high value placed on vocational and educational goals by American adolescents and the very low value placed on them by Hungarian and Israeli teenagers — probably because vocational choice is a complex and important developmental task for American adolescents. For most Israeli and Hungarian adolescents, choices are more limited or are largely predetermined by society.

Not surprisingly, there were marked differences in the sexual attitudes of adolescents from some countries. In particular, Turkish and Taiwanese adolescents reported extremely conservative sexual attitudes and behaviors (see Table 12.2) — clear evidence of the extent to which such attitudes are influenced by cultures. Similarly, Israeli adolescents reported the most positive family relationships, again not very surprising given the emphasis on family and community.

Sturm und Drang?

If the Offer et al. (1988) cross-national study, as well as the many similar North American surveys were to be summarized in a single paragraph, it might read something like this: Contrary to what has been a popular view of adolescence since G. Stanley Hall's pronouncements about the storm and stress of this period, adolescence throughout the world is predominantly a positive, nonturbulent, energetic, growth-filled period.

At the same time, we should note that approximately 15 percent of North American adolescents describe themselves as anxious, depressed, confused,

Table 12.2

Sexual Self: Sample Items Showing Consistent Intercountry Differences Across Age and Gender

Item	Percent endorsement								
	Australia	Bangladesh	Hungary	Israel	Italy	Taiwan	Turkey	United States	West Germany
Dirty jokes are fun at times.	82	33	39	78	69	43	19	78	69
I think that girls/ boys find me attractive.	53	63	58	68	55	41	59	73	63
Sexually I am way behind.	20	26	11	10	7	33	19	24	11
Thinking or talking about sex scares me.	7	50	13	6	7	27	22	10	6
Sexual experiences give me pleasure.	67	44	65	72	67	22	49	74	67
Having a girl-/ boyfriend is important to me.	69	77	68	75	76	52	74	73	82

Source: From *The Teenage World: Adolescents' Self-Image in Ten Countries* by D. Offer, E. Ostrov, K. Howard, and R. Atkinson, 1988, New York: Plenum. Reprinted by permission of the author and publisher.

Note: Items presented (1) were on a scale on which at least one country was consistently high (or low) in all four age-by-gender cells and (2) were consistently high (or low) for that country for that scale. Consistently high (or low) was defined in terms of being in the upper (or lower) third of nine countries in all four age-by-gender cells. Percentages shown are the average percent endorsement for that item for the country across four age-by-gender cells.

and emotionally empty (Offer, Ostrov, & Howard, 1984). True, this is a minority; but it is a relatively large one – and a very significant one. It includes adolescents whose notions of self-worth are largely negative but whose lives are only moderately unhappy; it includes, as well, those who are profoundly unhappy, who are delinquents and criminals, who seeks out and instigate violence, who abuse drugs, who are depressed and prone to suicide. We speak again of these turmoil topics in the final section of this chapter.

Developmental Changes in Notions of Self

My self is me. It includes what I think of me, what I think I am capable of, what I think others think of me. My notions of what I am – in other words, my *self-concept* – are not the same today as they were when I stole molasses cookies in Aunt Lucy's kitchen. The self-concept develops, as does the rest of the child. In

general, it becomes more abstract — less concrete. When Montemayor and Eisen (1977) had 262 boys and girls from grades four, six, eight, ten, and twelve
give 20 answers to the question "Who am I?" they found a progressive increase
in the number of responses relating to basic beliefs, values, personal style, self-
determination, and other abstract personal qualities. At the same time, there
was a dramatic reduction in the number of responses relating to geographic
area, citizenship, possessions, and physical attributes. For example, a typical 9-
year-old boy's responses included: "I have brown eyes; I have brown hair; I have
seven people in my family; I live on 1923 Pinecrest Drive." An 11½-year-old
girl offers somewhat less concrete notions of self: "I'm a human being; I'm a
girl; I'm a truthful person; I'm a very good pianist," and a 17-year-old girl
presents a highly abstract self-concept, based largely on interpersonal style and
emotional states: "I am a human being; I am an individual; I don't know who I
am; I am a loner; I am an indecisive person; I am an atheist" (pp. 317, 318).

Indications of other changes that occur in self-concepts with advancing age
are found in the Offer et al. (1988) survey of self-image in 10 countries. Among
other things, this study found that older adolescents (ages 16 to 19) compared
with the younger group (ages 13 to 15) were typically more self-confident, more
expressive, and more open to the opinions of others. Younger adolescents also
report more self-consciousness — a feeling that is probably closely linked with
their lower self-confidence. Not surprisingly, more of the younger than the
older group reported that thinking or talking about sex frightened them.

Some Origins of Self-Worth

It has been observed that children spend the first seven years of their lives
trying to determine *where* they are, the following seven wondering *who* they
are, and the next seven pondering the question of *why* they are. We might add
that throughout these 21 years and far beyond, an equally important question
is not where, who, or why, but simply whether the self — my *me* — is worthwhile, lovable, and other good things that most of us want to believe we are.
What I think of me — my self-worth or **self-esteem** — is fundamentally important to my behavior and to my happiness.

Psychological research on the development and importance of self-esteem
reveals some interesting and important findings. The classic study in this area
is Coopersmith's (1967) intensive investigation of self-esteem among 85 boys.
These boys were divided into groups according to their self-esteem, a concept
defined in Coopersmith's words as the "extent to which the individual believes
himself to be capable, significant, successful, and worthy. In short, self-esteem
is a *personal* judgment of worthiness that is expressed in attitudes the individual holds toward himself" (p. 5).* In other words, the term *self-esteem* is essentially synonymous with self-worth (see Chapter 10).

---

*Or, of course, "herself."

Among Coopersmith's most important findings were that individuals with higher self-esteem were more likely to be selected as friends; found it easier to make friends; were more likely to assume an active rather than a listening role in group discussions; were less likely to be highly conformist; scored higher on measures of creativity; were more outspoken, less sensitive to criticism, and less self-conscious. Supporting this, Elliott (1982) reports that adolescents low on self-esteem are more likely to present a false front (lie or deceive to make themselves look good).

The major portion of Coopersmith's investigation, however, attempted to identify factors related to the development of high or low self-esteem. Especially interesting is his finding of significant relationships between parental characteristics and childrearing modes and their children's self-esteem. Parents with high self-esteem tend to have children who also think highly of themselves; mothers with low emotional stability are more likely to have children with low self-esteem. Mothers of high self-esteem boys tended to have closer rapport with their sons and greater affection for them. High self-esteem boys tended to disagree less with their families than those characterized by lower self-esteem and to have more friends who were well known by parents, indicating a generally closer family relationship. Families of these boys were significantly more democratic in terms of decision making. Perhaps most striking, families of boys high in self-esteem were significantly less permissive, more demanding, stricter, more consistent in the enforcement of rules, but more prone to reinforcing good behavior. In Baumrind's (1977) terms, they were more authoritative than authoritarian, permissive, or laissez-faire (see Chapter 8).

Other interesting findings from this study are that boys high in self-esteem tend to be more intelligent, to appear happier to their mothers, to develop more rapidly in locomotor areas, and to achieve better in school.

In summary, the Coopersmith study indicates that self-esteem is closely related to adjustment and behavior, that an individual's chances for success as it is commonly defined increase with self-esteem. What is not clear is the extent to which high self-esteem determines success and happiness and the extent to which happiness and success contribute to the development of self-esteem. But perhaps it is unimportant to decide between the chicken and the egg. What does appear clear is that parental attitudes and behaviors are closely implicated in the development of self-esteem.

Identity

The notion that one of the most fundamental aspects of all development is the development of self-esteem (self-worth) is shared by a large number of psychologists, not all of whom have made their beliefs equally explicit and not all of whom have used the same language. Erikson's (1968) work is probably the best example of a theoretical position devoted to clarifying the importance of self (see Chapter 2). The expression he uses, essentially synonymous with the term *self*, is *identity.*

By the term *identity*, Erikson (1968) means a sort of *wholeness* that derives from the past but that also includes future goals and plans. Waterman (1984) defines identity more usefully in terms of:

> having a clearly delineated self-definition comprised of those goals, values, and beliefs to which the person is unequivocally committed. These commitments evolve over time and are made because the chosen goals, values and beliefs are judged worthy of giving a direction, purpose, and meaning to life. (p. 331)

For Erikson, the development of strong feelings of identity — of clear feelings of who one is — is the most important developmental task facing the adolescent. Accordingly, the primary developmental crisis facing the adolescent is the conflict between accepting, choosing, or discovering an identity and the diffusion of the adolescent's energies resulting from conflict and doubt about choice of identities. Recall that the fifth of Erikson's eight developmental stages is labeled *identity versus role diffusion.*

Resolution of adolescents' identity crises can take a variety of forms, the most common of which is the selection of an identity that conforms to societal norms and to the individuals' expectations of themselves. Erikson points out that one of the major social functions of prolonged adolescence is simply to serve as a period during which adolescents can experiment with a variety of roles in their quest for identity. He is not particularly alarmed that some of these roles constitute negative identities (delinquency and other forms of rebellion, for example) because in most cases they are temporary, eventually giving way to more acceptable and happier identities.

As Waterman (1988) points out, even when the adolescent appears to have achieved an identity — that is, to have made firm commitments to career and life-style plans — further changes often occur. He notes that some college students move in and out of identity crises before finally achieving a final commitment. And there are those among us who, like James Barrie's Peter Pan, never really do grow up.

Erikson's description of this developmental stage has been clarified by Marcia's investigations of the development of identity in adolescence (Marcia, 1966; Marcia & Friedman, 1970). Marcia describes the adolescent in terms of the extent to which he or she has achieved a positive, stable identity — what is called *identity status.* Using Erikson's concepts, Marcia has identified four distinct types of identity status based on whether the adolescent has undergone (or is currently undergoing) a crisis and on whether a commitment has been made to a specific identity.

Identity diffusion. Adolescents in this state are characterized by a total lack of commitment, nor have they experienced an identity crisis. These are individuals whose political, social, and religious beliefs are ambiguous or perhaps nonexistent and who have no vocational aspirations. Muuss (1975) suggests that whereas identity diffusion is common and normal in early adolescence, it is less normal in late adolescence. Individuals who have not developed a mature sense of identity by late adolescence are sometimes recognizable as what Marcia calls playboys or as disturbed individuals characterized by high anxiety, low self-esteem, and lack of self-confidence (Marcia, 1980). Waterman (1988) also reports that these individuals are likely to be at the preconventional level of moral reasoning and are often social isolates.

Foreclosure. A second identity status is defined by the adolescent's strong commitment to an identity without having experienced a crisis. Foreclosure is most clearly illustrated in those instances where political, religious, and vocational decisions have effectively been made for the adolescent and are accepted without question. This is frequently the case, for example, in close-knit religious or political communities where the roles of each individual (as well as their beliefs) are determined by others. It is also the case where adolescents simply allow parents or sometimes peers to make important identity-related decisions for them. These adolescents do not go through an identity crisis. Their most striking characteristics appear to be high adherence to authoritarian values (obedience, respect for authority) (Marcia, 1980).

Côté and Levine (1988) point out that the negative aspects of adopting a "ready-made" identity have been unfairly emphasized. On the positive side, some of the "foreclosed" choices that adolescents adopt are admirable. In addition, such individuals often manifest better adjustment, lower anxiety, and better relations with their parents.

Moratorium individuals. A large group of adolescents actively explore a variety of roles and experiment with different commitments for varying periods of time. These periods are termed *moratoria.* According to Erikson, one of the important functions of adolescence is to serve as a period during which it is not essential to be fully committed to one life-style, one vocation, one set of beliefs — a period when the adolescent can explore the tremendous variety of alternatives that might be available. During the moratorium stage, adolescents have vague, changing commitments. In this sense, they are in crisis. But it is a useful crisis for most adolescents, for in the absence of a moratorium during which they can explore, they are in danger of premature commitment (as in the case of foreclosure) or of continuing lack of commitment (as in identity diffusion).

Identity achieved. Adolescents who have experienced the moratorium (have, in other words, experienced a crisis of lesser or greater severity) and who have arrived at a choice — a commitment — may be described as *identity achieved.* Marcia reports that these adolescents are more independent, respond better to stress, have more realistic goals, and have higher self-esteem than adolescents

Table 12.3
Marcia's Descriptions of Identity Status in Terms of Crisis and Commitment

Status	Characteristics
Identity diffusion	No crisis; no commitment (ambiguous belief systems; no vocational commitment)
Foreclosure	No crisis; strong commitment (commitment predetermined by political, social, or religious affiliation)
Moratorium	Crisis; no commitment (period of exploration of alternatives)
Identity achieved	Crisis finished; commitment made

Note: A *crisis* is defined as a period of active and conscious decision making during which various alternatives are examined and evaluated. *Commitment* is acceptance of a combination of political, social, religious, or vocational alternatives.

in any of the other three categories. However, he also emphasizes that identities are never completely static and absolutely permanent.

In summary, the development of identity requires making a selection among the various alternatives in social, political, religious, and vocational commitments that present themselves to the adolescent. In short, it means determining who and what one is and will be. Adolescence may be described in terms of four different states relating to the development of identity. In the first, the adolescent does not know or care who he or she is (identity diffusion); in the second, identity has been imposed on the adolescent by parents, peers, or membership in a religious or political group (foreclosure); in the third, the adolescent is trying to select from among a number of identities and may experiment with a variety of changing commitments (moratorium); and in the last, the adolescent has gone through a period of experimentation and change, often described as a crisis, and has made a commitment to some positive identity (identity achieved) (see Table 12.3).

These categories also include those of us who remain adolescent throughout life.

SOCIAL DEVELOPMENT IN CONTEXT

The development of self does not occur in a vacuum — as our cross-cultural research so dramatically underlines. It occurs in a specific ecological context — a niche describable in terms of a wealth of interactions and influences. In Bronfenbrenner's (1989) terms, face-to-face interactions define the adolescent's microsystem — perhaps the single most important source of influence on the developing person. As we saw earlier, at every age through childhood, peers and parents are a fundamental part of the microsystem.

Table 12.4
Three Stages of Socialization

Stages	Time Frame	Conflict
High dependence on parents	Early childhood	Low
Decreasing dependence on parents Increasing independence	Late childhood Early adolescence	Increasing Increasing
High independence	Late adolescence Early adulthood	Decreasing Decreasing

Parent-Adolescent Conflict

At the risk of oversimplifying, we can describe the socialization of the adolescent in terms of three general stages based on the changing roles of friends and parents. (Table 12.4 indicates the general time frame of these stages.) Early in adolescence, parents continue to be of considerable importance, socially, emotionally, and physically. Young adolescents are dependent on the family not only for physical necessities, but also for the psychological support it provides. Clearly, however, the extent of this dependency is not nearly so great as it was in earlier periods of development.

Shortly after the onset of adolescence, children begin to move more rapidly toward greater independence. This progress defines the second stage in adolescent socialization — a period of conflict for both parents and children. Children find themselves torn between two forces: On the one hand is their former allegiance to their parents, their continued love for them, and their economic dependence on them; on the other hand is a newfound allegiance to friends and a need to be accepted by peers. Conflict between adolescents and their parents stems not only from their desire to associate more frequently and closely with peer groups but also from a variety of other sources. Adolescents often list such causes of strife as parental interference with social life, lack of adequate financial assistance, parental interference with school work or criticism of grades, and parental criticism of friends (Sebald, 1984.)

From a stage of high dependence on parents, the adolescent progresses through the intermediate stage of conflict just described and finally achieves the third stage — relative independence from parents. Independence does not imply that children break all bonds with their family and tie themselves irrevocably to groups of peers. In fact, as the Offer et al. (1988) study of adolescent self-image showed, the majority of teenagers have very good relations with their parents. Nevertheless, in adolescence individuals begin to achieve an independence allowing them to function in the milieu of peers that has become so important — an independence that, particularly in the second stage (early

The moratorium, says Erikson, provides an opportunity to experiment with different identities. Some, like those pictured here, come complete with costumes and hairstyles.

adolescence), frequently implies parental conflict. The **generation gap** is a cliché that describes the conflict between the reigning generation (the "Establishment") and the contemporary crop of adolescents from high schools to colleges, unemployed, employed, in love, out of love, or otherwise dead or alive. This gap is examined in more detail in a later section of this chapter.

The preceding discussion does not mean that parents and teenagers are always in conflict. In an ambitious examination of the parent-child relationships of 1,278 high school boys, Meissner (1965) found that changes in parent-child interaction included both positive and negative aspects. Subjects felt that as they became older they were given more opportunity for socializing; consequently, they became more tolerant of parental authority and more grateful for parental guidance. At the same time, however, a number of adolescents reported increased unhappiness in the home, greater misunderstandings between parents and children, and increasing conflicts with parents over religion. Boys reported spending less leisure time at home than previously. Meissner concludes that although the pattern is clearly one of "gradual **alienation**" (feeling of separation) from parental control and a corresponding increase in rebelliousness, the data do not wholly justify "rebelliousness" as a general description of adolescent-parent interaction.

Still, as Kaplan (1984) puts it, "the irrevocable giving-up of the love relationships of childhood entails an extended and painful emotional struggle" (p. 141). And although most writers no longer see this period as inevitably involving the turbulence, the *Sturm und Drang* described by G. Stanley Hall, the majority recognize that the emotional struggles involved in growing up are often manifested in varying degrees of parent-child conflict. As Bibby and Posterski (1985) describe it, there is still "turbulence on the home front" —

Figure 12.1

Percentage of ado-
lescents selecting
each value as "very
important." Values
were presented as
"terminal" or "end-
state"—as something
desirable and worth
striving for, for the
future.

Source: Based on R. W.
Bibby and D. C. Posterski,
*The emerging generation:
An inside look at Cana-
da's teenagers,* Toronto:
Irwin Publishing, 1985, Ta-
ble 2.1, p. 17. Reprinted
by permission of Stoddart
Publishing Co., Ltd.

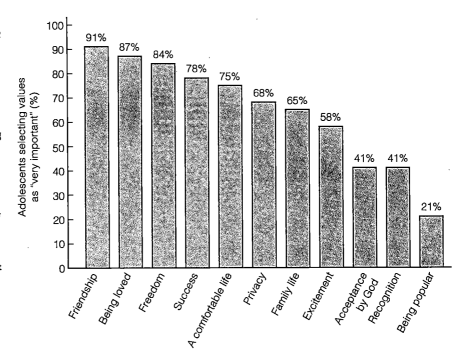

small wonder, perhaps, given that the 3,600 adolescents in their survey ranked friendship first in terms of importance to them; family life ranked eighth among 11 values (see Figure 12.1).

The contemporary view is that conflict typically arises because the changing needs and interests of the adolescent require a readjustment in the family system. Accordingly, it is not surprising to find that conflict is greatest during early adolescence — presumably prior to changes in the family — but declines in later adolescence. Petersen (1988) reports that areas of conflict have apparently not changed appreciably in the last 50 years, that they still concern the more "mundane" things in life — chores, curfews, and so on. Potentially more explosive matters such as those relating to sex and drugs are not usually discussed.

Peer Groups

Adolescent peer groups vary in size, interests, social backgrounds, and structure. They might consist of two or three like-sexed persons (buddies, pals, best friends), larger groups of like-sexed individuals, or couples, usually of opposite sexes, who currently find themselves in the throes of romantic love. Yet another type of peer group comprises persons of both sexes who "hang out" together. In addition, there are *gangs* about which we say more in a later section.

Adolescent peer groups, which are of tremendous importance to social development, tend to consist of individuals of similar ages.

Most adolescents belong to several groups at the same time. Indeed, friends (who are typically part of the peer group) are the adolescent's most common source of enjoyment (Bibby & Posterski, 1985).

Research indicates that peer groups change in predictable ways through adolescence, becoming both larger and more complex (Crockett et al., 1984). At the same time, adolescents spend increasing amounts of time with peers whom they have chosen as friends, rather than simply with classmates. The intimacy of friendships also increases, with adolescents sharing more thoughts and feelings, rather than simply engaging in activities together (Gottman & Mettetal, 1987).

Figure 12.2 illustrates the development of groups in adolescence as they progress from small groups of like-sexed members to interaction between groups of different sexes, leading eventually to the formation of what Dunphy (1963) calls the "crowd" — a large heterosexual group that has evolved from the smaller single-sex groups. In later stages of adolescence, there is a gradual disintegration of the earlier cohesiveness of the groups, brought about by the pairing of boys and girls into couples.

One of Dunphy's important observations is that adolescent peer groups tend to consist of individuals of relatively similar ages. Hartup (1978) suggests that age segregation is pervasive throughout development. When children have a choice, they are most likely to select friends similar to them in age (as well as ability and interests, both of which are related to age). He suggests as well that

Figure 12.2

Developing stages of peer groups during adolescence.

Source: After Dexter C. Dunphy, "The social structure of urban adolescent peer groups," *Sociometry,* 1963, 26, 230–246, p. 236. Copyright 1963 by the American Sociological Association. Used by permission of the American Sociological Association and the author.

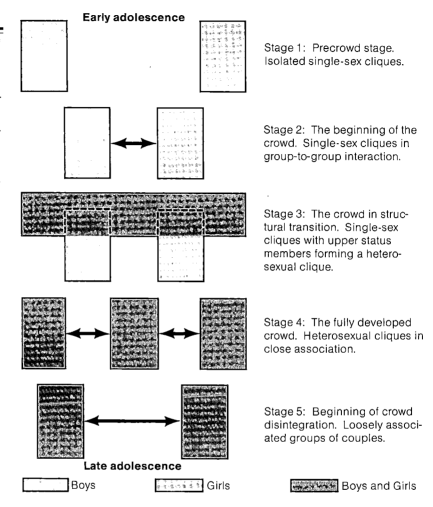

Early adolescence

Stage 1: Precrowd stage. Isolated single-sex cliques.

Stage 2: The beginning of the crowd. Single-sex cliques in group-to-group interaction.

Stage 3: The crowd in structural transition. Single-sex cliques with upper status members forming a heterosexual clique.

Stage 4: The fully developed crowd. Heterosexual cliques in close association.

Stage 5: Beginning of crowd disintegration. Loosely associated groups of couples.

Late adolescence

☐ Boys   ▦ Girls   ▦ Boys and Girls

age segregation is not necessarily a good thing, a point also argued by Bronfenbrenner (1970) and others. These researchers maintain that it is extremely important for children to have contact with individuals of a variety of ages. Contact with young children might help prepare adolescents for parenthood; by the same token, contact with older people is important for the socialization of children and adolescents.

The extent to which adolescent groups are segregated by age has been investigated by Montemayor and Van Komen (1980). They observed a total of 513 subjects, of whom 403 were adolescents. Observations took place in natural settings (parks, shopping centers, schools, playgrounds, and so on), where the investigators simply approached groups of people containing adolescents and questioned them about the relationship of the people in the group (for example,

parents, friends, relatives). These researchers found considerable evidence of age segregation, particularly in schools. Older adolescents were most likely to be found with same-sex, same-age peers; younger adolescents were sometimes found with people of different ages, most of these being relatives. In general, adolescents were found most often with other adolescents, rarely with younger children, and also rarely with parents (especially fathers).

Teenagers who are sociable, cheerful, and active are typically those who are most liked by their peers.

The characteristics of adolescents who are well liked by their peers are similar to the qualities of well-liked school-aged children described in Chapter 10. Children who are friendly, sociable, and outgoing as opposed to hostile, withdrawn, and unsociable are most liked by their peers. In addition, adolescents tend to stress personality characteristics associated with happiness. The person who is sociable, cheerful, active, and fun loving is typically the most popular.

The importance of being accepted by peers is highlighted in a large-scale study reported by Gronlund and Holmlund (1958). A group of 1,073 sixth-grade children were asked to select five people with whom they would like to sit, work, or play. Based on these sociometric data, the investigators divided the entire sample into two groups designated the *high-status* group and the *low-status* group. The high-status children were those selected more often — 27 or more times; low-status children were those selected fewer than 3 times. Seven years later the records of some of the children in these groups were examined to determine how many had graduated from high school. It is significant that 82 percent of the high-status group compared with 45 percent of the low-status group had graduated, particularly because observed differences in intelligence between the two groups were too small to account for the higher dropout rate of the low-status children. Such studies, however, are not certain evidence that peer rejection is the causal factor in school dropouts, delinquency, or other forms of social maladjustment. It is equally plausible to suppose that those factors responsible for maladjustment are the very factors that cause the child to be rejected by peers in the first place.

GENDER ROLES

In Chapter 8 we pointed out some of the typical differences in the play behavior of young boys and girls. Not only is the play of boys frequently more boisterous, more aggressive, and more physical than that of girls, but the toys they select (and that parents select for them) tend also to be "sex-typed."

But differences between the sexes go far beyond the toys with which they play and their physical movements while playing. They include as well the sometimes dramatic, and sometimes very subtle, differences in attitudes, in behaviors, in expectations, even in personality, that distinguish male from female. The differences are evident in the language used to describe each — terms such as *tight bitch* and *slag* illustrated in the introduction to this chapter; terms such as *darling* and *honey* and *sweetheart* as well. Labels such as these belittle by dehumanizing, by generalizing as though the persons labeled were collections of identical objects, by emphasizing superficial qualities, by propagating untruths and stereotypes.

Differences between the sexes, together with the attitudes and personality characteristics associated with them, are what define *gender roles*, or what are sometimes called *sex roles. Gender* refers specifically to the psychological characteristics typically associated with biological sex. Thus there are two sexes, male and female, and two corresponding genders, masculine and feminine. Bem (1974) also argues that there are individuals who share relatively equally the characteristics of both genders, and labels these individuals "androgynous." The learning of sex-appropriate behavior (of gender roles) is referred to as gender-typing. Explanations of gender-typing are presented in Chapter 8.

Gender-Role Stereotypes

Very early in life, children begin to learn about the behaviors their culture finds acceptable and desirable for their sex. What do they learn in North America? Traditionally, males learn that it is masculine to walk without excessive buttock movement, to run fiercely with arms swinging free, to sit with legs sprawled, to throw a ball with a full swing and a flexed wrist, to wrestle and fight (or at least to be playfully aggressive), to love sports, and to be interested in science and mathematics. Females learn that it is feminine to walk with a more exaggerated buttock movement, to run with elbows tucked into the rib cage and with limp-wristed hands, to sit with legs crossed properly at the knee and hands held neatly in the lap, to throw a ball with a stiff-wristed motion, to sit quietly and demurely, to play the piano, to be interested in arts and books, and to learn to cook and sew.

These sexual stereotypes are in some cases superficial and trivial; in others, they are more fundamental. Some might reflect basic anatomical differences; others are influenced more by context. In general, North American gender roles associate the male figure with active, work-oriented, and positively evaluated activities and the female figure with more passive, home-oriented, and less positively evaluated roles. Boys and girls still have little difficulty in identifying personality characteristics that are stereotypically masculine or feminine. In fact, not only do they agree as to what boys and girls should be like, but also they agree that masculine characteristics are more desirable (Shepherd-Look, 1982).

"If you woke up tomorrow and discovered that you were a *girl*, how would your life be different?" Tavris and Baumgartner (1983) asked a group of American boys. "Terrible . . . ," "a catastrophe . . . ," "I would immediately commit suicide . . . ," were some typical answers. But when girls were posed the same question — that is, what would happen if you discovered you had become a boy? — they responded quite differently: "Great . . . ," "now I can do what I want . . . ," "now I can be happy. . . ."

Patterns of responses were clear: Girls often responded positively to the "change-sex" question; boys did so extremely rarely. And this difference was evident in children as young as age 8 and as old as age 17. These sexual stereotypes appeared to be learned very young and to be very pervasive in 1983. Are they different today?

Intons-Peterson (1988) asked the same question of 11-, 14-, and 18-year-old Swedish and American adolescents in an effort to answer this question. Other measurements were also used to uncover predominant beliefs about differences between males and females. She selected Sweden because, since 1968, the Swedish government has had an explicit, family-based social program aimed at the equalization of the sexes. As a result, Intons-Peterson expected that gender stereotypes would not be as marked in Sweden as in the United States and that male and female reactions to the sex-change question would not reflect as decided a preference for the male sex.

Part of her predictions are borne out by the results of the study. As expected, personality characteristics thought to be most descriptive of males in the United States reflect the "hard-driving, macho image of lore" (Intons-Peterson, 1988); females are seen as less aggressive, gentler. And although these differences are also apparent in the Swedish samples, they are not as extreme. Swedish samples were more likely to see women as capable and effective and men as being emotional and tender.

Responses to the sex-change question are interesting and informative. First, patterns of responses were essentially identical to what they had been in 1983. Most males still responded very negatively to the thought of becoming female; and although a majority of females were content with their gender, most responded by writing stories describing the positive aspects of becoming male. A second, important finding is that this asymmetry is more apparent for the 18-year-olds than for the younger group, especially in Sweden. This might be evidence that attempts to eradicate sex stereotypes and to achieve greater gender equality are beginning to have an effect.

Third, there was strong evidence of very similar gender stereotypes in each country. When confronted with the possibility of becoming male, girls wrote that they would now enjoy athletics more, that they would travel and stay out later at night, that they would study less but think more about a career. They also felt they would be more aggressive and less emotional, that they would be less concerned about their appearance, and that they would need to become interested in fighting and in "showing off." Boys faced with the possibility of becoming female saw themselves becoming burdened by menstruation and more concerned with contraception and becoming pregnant. They expected to be more passive, weaker, and restricted more to indoor activities. They thought, too, that they would become more interested in permanent sexual relationships and more emotional.

In summary, the value placed on male and female roles seemed not to have changed since Tavris and Baumgartner (1983) reported how males were often horrified at the thought of becoming female — but females were often delighted at the thought of becoming male. In the Intons-Peterson (1988) study, the pattern is essentially the same: The male role is generally evaluated far more positively than the female.

These evaluations reflect some of our culture's widely held beliefs about gender — in other words, they reveal our prevalent sexual stereotypes. Stereotypes are sometimes partly valid; sometimes not. Rarely are they entirely one or the other. Gender stereotypes are no exception. What *are* some of the real differences between males and females?

Gender Differences

There are obvious biological and physical differences related to anatomical sex. Thus male infants weigh more than female infants and continue to do so throughout life except for a brief period in late childhood. Females, on the other hand, mature approximately two years earlier than males. Other differences are less readily apparent but no less real. Beginning from puberty, male blood pressure is higher than that of females; female heartrate is between two and six beats higher than that of males; metabolic rate of males is higher than that of females, physical energy is greater, recuperative time is less, and muscle fatigue is slower (Shepherd-Look, 1982).

In many ways, however, males are the weaker sex — and they are so from the very beginning. Recall that men produce perhaps 50 percent more sperm bearing the male (Y) sex chromosome than the female sex chromosome. But there are not 150 male infants born for every 100 females. Even prior to conception, the male sperm is more fragile. And thus it continues throughout life. At birth, there are perhaps 105 males for every 100 females. But males are more vulnerable to most infections and diseases so that, by adolescence, numbers of males and females surviving are approximately equal; by the age of 65, there are almost 150 females living for every 100 males!

Not only are males more fragile and less long-lived, but they are also more prone to learning, speech, and behavior disorders, greatly overrepresented among the retarded and the mentally disordered, and more prone to bed-wetting, night-terrors, and hyperactivity (Shepherd-Look, 1982).

Apart from these primarily physiological differences between the sexes, are there real psychological differences?

The answer is yes, but it is not a simple yes; and it is not without controversy.

In an earlier review and summary of much of the important research in this area, Maccoby and Jacklin (1974) concluded that there are relatively clear differences between the sexes in four areas: verbal ability (favoring females); visual/spatial ability (favoring males); mathematical ability (favoring males); and aggressiveness (less among females).

But at least some of these gender differences no longer seem as clear in the early 1990s as they did in 1974 — evidence perhaps that because they resulted primarily from socialization processes, they reflected a cultural context that has changed dramatically in the last several decades. Let's look briefly at research in each of these four areas.

Verbal ability. The research Maccoby and Jacklin (1974) summarized indicates that females have greater verbal ability than males. However, subsequent research has found that while the difference sometimes exists, it is not very general, it is usually very small, and it is not apparent at early ages (Shepherd-Look, 1982). In a large-scale survey of performance in high school (and beyond), Marsh (1989) found no significant differences between boys and girls on measures of verbal performance. Girls in this sample were somewhat more likely than boys to take further English courses, but they were no less likely to take mathematics courses.

Visual/spatial ability. Males often do better than females in tests of visual-spatial ability after early adolescence (see Hyde & Linn, 1986). Tests of spatial ability often require that the subject visualize three-dimensional objects and be able to rotate or otherwise manipulate them mentally. As Chipman (1988) notes, there isn't a great deal of information about the importance of spatial ability although some researchers argue that this gender difference may be related to differences in mathematics achievement (Pearson & Ferguson, 1989).

Mathematics. There is some evidence that males perform better than females in mathematical skills *from adolescence onward,* primarily at the highest levels of mathematics achievement where males outnumber females more than 17 to 1 (Benbow & Stanley, 1983). However, gender differences in mathematics are negligible in the earlier years. That females do not continue to do as well in mathematics may be explained by culturally determined interest and motivational factors. Eccles and Jacobs (1986) found, for example, that student anxiety about math, its perceived value for the student, and parents' stereotyped views of how boys and girls typically perform in math — especially mothers' beliefs about how difficult math is — account for most of the observed gender differences in mathematics achievement.

Significantly, in the same way as gender differences in verbal performance have declined and, in many instances, completely disappeared, so too have differences in mathematics performance. Hyde, Fennema, and Lamon (1990) did a meta-analysis of 100 studies in this area. A meta-analysis is a statistical summary of separate studies that have looked at the same questions. Ideally, it leads to the sort of answers that might have been provided by a single research study combining all the subjects — hence, all the data — from all the studies involved. The Hyde et al. (1990) meta-analysis, for example, involved more than 3 million subjects. Their conclusion? Girls actually show a slight superiority in mathematical computation in elementary and junior high school; but differences in favor of males emerge in high school and are most evident in problem solving. Becker (1990) reports very similar findings based on student performance on the SAT (Scholastic Aptitude Test). Only at the higher age levels do differences favor males. And, as Friedman (1989) concludes following a meta-analysis of research done between 1974 and 1987, differences in both mathematics and verbal ability are nonexistent or very small and are declining.

Aggression. As we saw in Chapter 8, males are *generally* more aggressive than females. Following yet another meta-analysis (there has been a great deal of interest and, consequently, of research in this area), Hyde and Linn (1986) conclude that males are, *on average,* more aggressive both physically and verbally. This gender difference is assumed to have a biological as well as a cultural basis. But even if aggressiveness is related to anatomy and to hormones (hence to genes), it does not follow that observed gender differences would continue to exist in the same form in different sociocultural contexts.

A conclusion. Studies of gender differences reveal very small *average* differences — where there are any differences at all. They do not provide data that would be sufficient for making inferences about specific individuals. As Linn and Hyde (1989) point out, gender differences in height and strength are far more significant and far more stable. Interestingly, so are gender differences in career accessibility and in earning power. Other than perhaps for aggressiveness, not only are psychological gender differences very small, but they have been declining (Jacklin, 1989; Friedman, 1989). It is likely that important social changes are involved here; gender differences may become even smaller in coming decades and may even disappear completely in some areas. And perhaps, as Chipman (1989) argues, these small average sex differences are not very important in any case. Perhaps it would be far more useful to try to understand how interests and abilities develop and interact.

SEX

This section deals with an area of profound preoccupation for many adolescents — an area that consumes a great deal of their time and energy and to which they sometimes devote themselves with rarely equaled ardor. I speak of Sex.

To begin with, sex is simply a category — male or female — that is rather easily defined by some obvious biological differences between members of the sexes named above.

Sex is also a psychoanalytic term referring to thumb sucking, defecation, masturbation, fantasies, repressions, and indeed, to all of living. According to Freud, sex is the source of energy that motivates all of us from birth to death, whether by way of the "normal" psychosexual stages or through the labyrinth of neuroses and psychoses springing from the constant warring between our ids and superegos. Needless to say, not all theorists agree with this Freudian notion.

Sex is also more than a psychoanalytic term or a biological dichotomy. It can mean (as it does in this section) nothing more or less complicated than the physical union between male and female, or variations thereof, or the wish thereto, or the fantasy thereof.

Sexual Beliefs and Behavior

Researchers have gathered data that indicate a marked change in sexual beliefs and behavior of the adolescent in recent generations. Some interpret this change as a movement toward promiscuity and shallow, meaningless relationships between casual acquaintances. Cobliner (1988) shares this view. Basing his arguments on "converging evidence from a variety of reliable sources . . . including personal interviews by the author," he writes:

> sexual involvement between partners of the opposite sex has been sporadic, episodic, without commitment, and accompanied by a deliberate effort of both partners to suppress tender, romantic feelings and intimacy. . . . It is suggested that the prevailing sexual conventions of college-age youth clash with the fundamental urge to form human attachments; diminish and often shut out the experience of passion in sexual unions; and bring about inner turmoil that weakens self-confidence. (p. 127)

Others have a different interpretation and see change in sexual behaviors and attitudes as a significant and long-overdue recognition of the desirability of what is regarded as the highest form of communication between humans. Fortunately, my role is not to judge but to report. You may judge if you wish.

Kinsey and his associates (1948, 1953) provided the first major source of information about sexual behavior in the United States. The Kinsey data reveal that although most children have engaged in some form of sexual play before adolescence, not until puberty do they become capable of an adult sexual response. There is also evidence in the Kinsey data that immediately following puberty, boys experience sexual arousal in response to a wider range of stimuli than girls. Arousal gives rise to an urgent desire for orgasm. In the Kinsey surveys, virtually all male adolescents reported experiencing orgasm by the time of marriage; only 30 percent of the females reported doing so. Similarly, far more males than females reported engaging in premarital sexual intercourse.

By the middle 1960s, incidence of premarital sexual intercourse for females was approaching that reported for males (40 and 60 percent, respectively; Packard, 1968); by 1970 the figures had increased again (Athanasiou, 1973); and by the 1980s, they were almost identical for men and women (Brooks-Gunn & Furstenberg, 1989).

Other research, using erotic slides, films, and stories, has generally found that the sexual responsiveness of men and women is not significantly different and that both sexes are aroused by much the same sorts of stimuli (Fisher & Byrne, 1978).

The Kinsey finding that fewer girls than boys engaged in premarital sexual behaviors prior to 1950, besides reflecting the social context of the time, might have been due in part to women's reluctance to admit having had intercourse — even in a questionnaire. At the same time, it is not unlikely that men might have exaggerated their exploits. It is no secret that male society actively reinforces its members for the frequency and range of their sexual experiences. Female society is much quieter about its reinforcement, although there is evidence of impending change with the emergence of the newly liberated woman. Note too that the majority of studies of adolescent sexual behavior are conducted with college or high school students and might therefore not represent what things are like in the general population.

Adolescent Sexual Practices

The so-called sexual revolution is manifested in two trends in the behavior of adolescents and young adults. First, as we noted, there has been a significant increase in the number of young people reporting intercourse; and second, the number of women represented in this group has increased far more dramatically than the number of men. Darling, Kallen, and Van Dusen (1984) reviewed 35 studies of sexual behavior spanning the years 1903 to 1980. They report that prior to 1970, the number of men reporting premarital intercourse was approximately double that of women; currently, the numbers are nearly equal.

The Alan Guttmacher Institute (*Teenage pregnancy*, 1981) reports that by age 19, 8 out of every 10 men and 7 out of every 10 women are sexually active. However, these figures do not seem to mean that sex has become totally casual and matter of fact among today's adolescents contrary to Cobliner's (1988) analysis presented at the beginning of this section. In fact, the majority (almost 90 percent) do not think it is appropriate to have intercourse on the first date; but almost half believe it is quite appropriate after a few dates (Bibby & Posterski, 1985). For the majority of male and female adolescents, the critical determining factor is whether the partners have a caring and committed relationship. As Reiss (1966) put it, the old double standard that maintained that premarital sexual intercourse was all right for boys ("boys will be boys and all that"), but not for girls ("girls are . . . well, you know, different") has been replaced by a new standard that holds that sexual activity is permitted for both sexes providing there is affection between partners (see Table 12.5).

Brooks-Gunn and Furstenberg (1989) report that one of the major changes in sexual behavior in recent decades is a lowering of the age of first intercourse for girls. They note, however, that it is not uncommon for teenagers to have sex at age 14 or 15 and then not to repeat the activity for another year or more.

Among the most obvious antecedents of sexual activity are the biological changes of pubescence. Changes in hormone levels affect sexual arousal directly. In addition, changes in secondary sexual characteristics, such as breast enlargement in the girl or lowering of the boy's voice, may serve as important sexually linked stimuli. Parental influences are also considered important factors in the sexual behavior of adolescents, although there is not a great deal of research on the link between the two (Brooks-Gunn & Furstenberg, 1989). Similarly, peers probably influence whether or not an adolescent is likely to engage in sexual intercourse. In this connection, it is perhaps significant that adolescents often overestimate the amount of sexual activity engaged in by their peers and underestimate the age of first intercourse.

Masturbation

The most common form of sexual outlet for adolescent males and females is masturbation. Sorensen (1973) reports that 49 percent of all adolescents age 13 to 19 have masturbated at least once. Males masturbate more frequently than females, reaching their peak sexual activity (*peak* is defined as frequency of orgasm, regardless of its cause) between their sixteenth and seventeenth years. Among some adolescents, the practice may still be accompanied by totally unfounded fears of impotence, mental retardation, or some other dire consequences. Early writers such as G. Stanley Hall (1916) treated masturbation as abnormal, debilitating, and sinful and provided parents with a number of suggestions for its avoidance or cure.

Table 12.5
Appropriate Dating Behavior:
The Adolescent View

"If two people on a date like each other, do you think it is all right for them to . . . ?"

	Male (%)	Female (%)	Total (%)
Hold hands			
Yes, first date	92	91	92
Yes, after a few dates	7	9	8
No	1	0	0
Kiss			
Yes, first date	84	80	82
Yes, after a few dates	16	19	18
No	0	1	0
Neck			
Yes, first date	59	42	50
Yes, after a few dates	38	52	45
No	3	6	5
Pet			
Yes, first date	42	16	28
Yes, after a few dates	50	63	56
No	8	20	15
Have sexual relations			
Yes, first date	19	3	11
Yes, after a few dates	51	33	42
No	29	59	44
If they love each other	1	5	3

Source: Based on Bibby & Posterski, *The emerging generation: An inside look at Canada's teenagers,* Table 5.1, p. 76. Toronto: Irwin Publishing, 1985. Reprinted by permission of Stoddart Publishing Co., Ltd.

Note: Based on a survey of 3,600 high school students, aged 15 to 19.

Although contemporary attitudes toward masturbation are that it is normal, pleasurable, and harmless, some adolescents continue to feel guilty and ashamed about masturbating, this being more the case among younger than older adolescents (Hass, 1979).

Adolescent Pregnancy

Estimates suggest that there are as many as 12 million sexually active teenagers in the United States — 7 million male and 5 million female. Of the 5 million or so sexually active females, approximately 1 million become pregnant each year (see Figures 12.3 and 12.4). The teenage birthrate in the United States accounts for 16 percent of all births (Brooks-Gunn & Furstenberg, 1986). It is now among the highest in the world — approximately 17 times higher than in Japan and 3 times higher than in the Soviet Union and about twice as high as that in Canada (Jones and associates, 1986). Who gets pregnant? Why? What are the outcomes and implications of teenage pregnancy?

Who gets pregnant. Teenage pregnancies are not restricted to any particular social, economic, religious, or ethnic group. However, in the United States, pregnancies are more common among black than white teenagers (Zelnik, Kantner, & Ford, 1981).

Why? The vast majority of teenage pregnancies are unplanned. Black and DeBlassie (1985) suggest that there are a number of plausible reasons for increasing rates of teenage pregnancy. First, social attitudes toward sexual activity and toward pregnancy have changed dramatically in recent decades. Pregnancy no longer brings with it shame and humiliation. Accordingly, there is less pressure, both on boys and girls, to prevent conception.

Second, there are a raft of psychological factors that might motivate pregnancy, or at least sexual intercourse. These might include the loneliness and alienation that are often part of life in socially and economically depressed surroundings and that might sometimes lead the girl to grant sexual favors in an attempt to obtain commitment and friendship. They might also include the girl's wish to "get back" at overprotective parents or the boy's wish to establish the "macho" image that some male societies still reinforce. There is some evidence, for example, that teenagers from more rigid, authoritarian families are more likely to become pregnant (Romig & Bakken, 1990). And at times, teenagers may be motivated by a genuine desire to have a baby — someone to love.

Third, there is the adolescent's egocentrism, the *personal fable* that stresses the special invulnerability of the teenager and that is premised on the belief that "It won't happen to me." Arnett (1990) found a close relationship between contraception use among high school students and two measures often highly descriptive of the adolescent experience. One was a measure of adolescent egocentrism; the other, not surprisingly, a measure of *sensation-seeking* — of the urge to confront danger and take risks.

Fourth, and perhaps most important, the majority of pregnancies occur accidentally and as a consequence of ignorance or misinformation concerning

Births to Unmarried Teenagers

Kids deserve a better teacher than experience.

In the United States, the number of infants being born to unmarried women is steadily increasing. In 1970, about 1 in 10 births (10.7 percent) was to an unmarried mother; by 1987 the proportion was nearly 1 in 4 (24.5 percent), with unmarried teen mothers (ages 15–19) accounting for nearly a third of such births. The birthrate among unmarried women of all ages is likewise going up. In 1987, there were 36.1 births per 1,000 unmarried women, up from 26.4 in 1970. For young women age 15–19, the birthrate per 1,000 unmarried women increased by more than half, from 22.4 in 1970 to 34.1 in 1987.

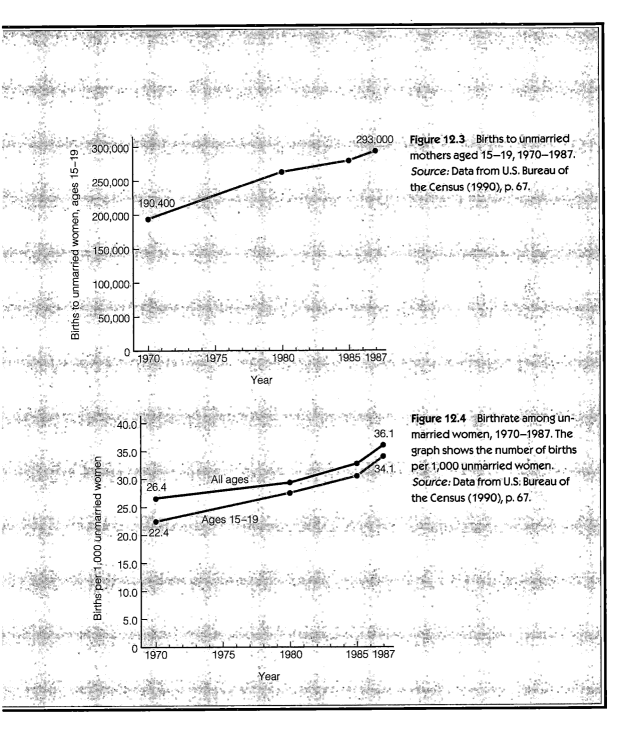

Figure 12.3 Births to unmarried mothers aged 15–19, 1970–1987. *Source:* Data from U.S. Bureau of the Census (1990), p. 67.

Figure 12.4 Birthrate among unmarried women, 1970–1987. The graph shows the number of births per 1,000 unmarried women. *Source:* Data from U.S. Bureau of the Census (1990), p. 67.

sex and contraception. More than half of all teenagers do not use contraception at the time of first intercourse, and perhaps a third continue to use none later (Arnett, 1990). Significantly, approximately half of all pregnancies occur within six months of first intercourse. Many teenagers do not know where to get birth control information. And of those who have adequate information, many are only intermittently sexually active. For them, the cost of the safest birth control methods makes their use prohibitive. In addition, use of an IUD (intrauterine device), oral contraceptives, or of a diaphragm requires the cooperation of a physician. As a result, of those who do employ contraception, many are forced to use the least reliable methods: withdrawal, rhythm (attempting to time intercourse to coincide with the woman's cyclical periods of infertility), and rubber condoms. Brooks-Gunn and Furstenberg (1989) argue that we need to know much more about teenage sexual activity and attitudes toward condoms in order to encourage their use.

Interestingly, a survey of 329 adolescents found that those whose parents were sexually liberal were more likely to use contraception (Baker, Thalberg, & Morrison, 1988). However, they were not more likely to be sexually active.

Implications. The effects of teenage pregnancies, the majority of which are unplanned and unwanted, often include a dramatic disruption in the mother's educational and career plans. There are also much higher health risks with teenage pregnancy and delivery, both for mother and infant (Anastasiow, 1984) — risks that seem to be worse for the second or third teenage pregnancy than for the first (Smith, Weinman, & Malinak, 1984). Moreover, the economic and social conditions under which the majority of teenage mothers are forced to live, and the emotional stresses associated with these conditions, as well as with childrearing, can be a heavy burden. Grindstaff (1988) surveyed a group of 30-year-old women, almost a third of whom had borne children in adolescence. Not surprisingly, he found that those who had no children or who had waited until the age of 25 before having them were better off educationally and economically.

Although the economic disadvantages of teenage childbearing often disappear over time, as Furstenberg, Brooks-Gunn, and Chase-Lansdale (1989) put it, "The children of teenage mothers however, are distinctly worse off throughout childhood than the offspring of older childbearers" (p. 313).

The implications of teenage parenthood are clearly more direct and more applicable for mothers and children than for fathers, a great many of whom are not involved in any pregnancy-related decisions or in childrearing later. However, school dropout rates are higher for teenage fathers, even when they do not marry the mother (Marsiglio, 1986). A survey by Redmond (1985) involving 74 white males indicates that most unwed fathers would like to be told if a pregnancy occurs. Most would also like to be involved, along with the girl and their parents, in making decisions relating to the outcome of the pregnancy. Interestingly, however, they are unlikely to involve peers in this process.

Divorce rates for teenage marriages are much higher than for marriages that occur later. In addition, some research indicates that these marriages are sometimes associated with suicide, depression, and child mortality. Following a three-year investigation of 48 teenage couples between 15 and 19 years of age, DeLissovoy (1973) concluded:

> In general, I found the young parents in this study to be, with a few notable exceptions, an intolerant group — impatient, insensitive, irritable and prone to use physical punishment with their children. (p. 22)

Clearly, however, these observations and conclusions do not apply to all teenage parents. Many are sensitive, caring, and competent parents. Sadly, however, the probability that this will be the case, given their relative immaturity and lack of experience and information, is not overwhelmingly high.

What to do? There are no simple solutions for complex social problems. Black and DeBlassie (1985) suggest that what is needed is a safe, inexpensive, and effective contraceptive device for those who are intermittently sexually active. Failing that, or perhaps in addition to it, Brooks-Gunn and Furstenberg (1989) list a number of preventive strategies. These include offering free access to contraception, providing information about sexuality and contraception, influencing sexual attitudes, and expanding adolescents' life options. Various school-based family life and sex education programs, public television programs, and government family planning services are also important strategies. And, given the current epidemic of serious, sexually transmitted diseases (STDs), there is renewed interest in advocating sexual abstinence as well (Hess, 1990). (STDs are discussed in detail shortly.)

Sex education in schools remains controversial; even more controversial is the move by a number of school jurisdictions to provide condom dispensers for students. Some parents fear that sex education and easy access to contraception may serve to increase adolescent sexual behavior and to foster values that run counter to those of the family and the community. As a result, there are some who advocate sexual-abstinence programs or who, at the very least, encourage delaying first intercourse. However, adolescents are not always highly motivated to participate in such courses, especially when what the programs teach contradicts their values and their behaviors. When Christopher and Roosa (1990) investigated the effects of an adolescent pregnancy prevention program that focused on self-esteem and resisting peer pressure and that taught that sex should occur only in marriage, program dropout rates were very high. Nor was there any evidence that the program was effective in reducing sexual activity. However, Christopher and Roosa point out that the most successful programs are typically not based on abstinence alone, but also provide the alternative of effective contraception.

Brooks-Gunn and Furstenberg (1989) report that sex education programs are rare in elementary school, although the vast majority of parents and school jurisdictions support them in high school. They report, as well, that the fear that these programs might increase sexual activity does not appear to be warranted. And where systematic research has been conducted on the effects of these programs, dramatic reductions in rates of unwanted pregnancies have been found for many of them (Edwards et al., 1980; Zabin et al., 1988).

Homosexuality

Homosexual experiences during adolescence do not appear to be highly common. Evidence suggests that approximately 1 out of every 10 adolescent boys, and perhaps half that number of girls, have isolated sexual experiences with someone of the same sex, usually during early adolescence (Dreyer, 1982). Estimates of the number of these who subsequently adopt a homosexual or bisexual life-style are extremely unreliable, but are probably considerably less than the 8 or 9 percent who have had adolescent homosexual experiences. That homosexual groups have become more visible and more outspoken in recent decades may account for the popular perception that their numbers have increased. Hyde (1986) reviews evidence suggesting that numbers have remained stable and that incidence of homosexuality is very similar in a number of cultures.

Causes of homosexuality are not known, although there are a variety of theories: genetic, social learning, hormonal. And it is extremely difficult – in most cases, impossible – to alter sexual preference.

STDs: Sexually Transmitted Diseases

There are more than two dozen known **sexually transmitted** (or *veneral*) **diseases.** Among the most common of these are chlamydia, gonorrhea, and herpes. Less common are syphilis and AIDS.

Chlamydia is currently the most common of the **STDs.** It was rarely seen until very recent years and still goes largely undetected. Estimates are that as many as 1 of every 10 sexually active women has chlamydia – twice as many as have gonorrhea. It is now one of the leading causes of infertility among women and is especially widespread in North Africa, the Far East, Britain, and the Scandinavian countries (*Chlamydia – more common than gonorrhea,* 1988). In the majority of women, chlamydia presents no symptoms in its early stages (approximately 80 percent); this is also the case for about 20 percent of infected men. In later stages, abdominal pain may send the victim for medical help, but by then the woman is often infertile. Chlamydia can be treated easily and effectively with antibiotics.

Gonorrhea. Gonorrhea is transmitted through sexual intercourse. Symptoms in the male usually include a discharge from the penis and pain during urina-

Courtship in most industrialized societies is a long-lasting process without a lot of explicit rules.

tion. Symptoms in the female are more subtle and often go unnoticed. The disease can usually be treated simply and effectively with penicillin and related drugs. Like some other sexually transmitted diseases, it can sometimes be prevented through the use of a condom or simply by washing the genitals thoroughly after intercourse.

Herpes. Herpes is caused by a virus and remains incurable, although the virus can remain inactive for long periods of time. The disease is contagious only when lesions are present (like tiny cold sores, commonly found on the penis and scrotum in males, and on the vulva, vagina, and cervix in females).

AIDS. AIDS (Acquired Immune Deficiency Syndrome) is a sexually transmitted disease caused by the human immunodeficiency virus (HIV) — an organism that appears to mutate rapidly, thereby increasing the difficulty of treating it (AIDS virus strains beat pill, 1989). At present it is incurable and fatal. It is transmitted through the exchange of body fluids, principally blood and semen. Largely for that reason, AIDS has been found primarily among four high-risk groups: intravenous drug users who often share needles; homosexual males who engage in anal intercourse; hemophiliacs who have been exposed to the virus through blood transfusions; and certain groups of Haitians who engage in rituals involving blood exchange. As of October 1986, total reported cases in the United States included 24,424 males, 1,775 women, and an additional 350 children (Long, 1987). By November 1988, cases of pediatric (child) AIDS had risen to 1,230 in the United States, and more than 130,000 cases had been reported to the World Health Organization. The AIDS death toll in the United States has now surpassed total Vietnam War casualties (Morin, 1988). There is mounting evidence that numbers are increasing in North America, Africa, Latin America, Western Europe, Australia, and parts of the Caribbean (*Increase expected in AIDS*, 1988). AIDS among American children is expected to total 10,000 cases by 1991 (Task Force on Pediatric AIDS, 1989). Close to 80 percent of current pediatric AIDS cases resulted from infection transmitted from the mother at birth; almost all the remainder resulted from blood transfusion.

The fact that total numbers suffering from the disease seem relatively small, coupled with the observation that AIDS is relatively uncommon outside the four high-risk groups, has been a source of reassurance for many. However, there are indications that our complacency may be misplaced and that numbers are higher than expected (*The AIDS threat*, 1988). What is perhaps even more alarming is Masters, Johnson, and Kolodny's (1988) assertion that AIDS is spreading rapidly in the heterosexual community. They argue that far more individuals are currently infected than official reports indicate; that transmission can occur from male to female or female to male in either vaginal or anal intercourse, and even through oral sex; and that because of a time lag of up to 7 months between exposure to the AIDS virus and the ability to detect antibodies, some of the blood supply used for transfusions is contaminated. These conclusions are based on projections derived from testing samples of 400 apparently monogamous men and women and 400 nonmonogamous persons. Nonmonogamous subjects were those who had had six or more sexual partners in the past year, *but who did not belong to any of the traditional high-risk groups*. Whereas only 1 of the 400 monogamous subjects had been infected with the AIDS virus, a startling 7 percent of the women and 5 percent of the men in the nonmonogamous group had been exposed! The majority of these were found in the higher-incidence geographic areas — specifically New York and Los Angeles. New tests for the AIDS virus itself (HIV) rather than for its antibodies are now being developed and may be especially useful in early treatment (AIDS fears subside . . . , 1989).

Masters, Johnson, and Kolodny insist that there is no completely reliable way of preventing transmission of the AIDS virus during intercourse or oral sex. However, use of condoms does provide a much higher degree of protection than sex without condoms; and a chemical component of some spermicides (nonoxynol-9) appears to kill the AIDS virus.

There has been some speculation that incidence of casual and extramarital sexual encounters and sexual activity among homosexual males would decline significantly or change in other ways in the wake of widespread accounts of increases in the incidence of AIDS and other STDs. Stall, Coates, and Hoff (1988) and Morin (1988) report that a number of programs aimed at homosexual males have resulted in dramatic declines in casual sexual encounters and especially in unprotected sexual activity among this group.

Adolescents appear to be well informed about AIDS and how it is transmitted, say Roscoe and Kruger (1990); and as many as one-third claim they have changed their sexual behavior because of fear of AIDS. That means, however, that two-thirds have not.

THE TURMOIL TOPICS

Adolescence is undoubtedly a time of turmoil for many; at the same time, it is quite the opposite for a number of adolescents who pass exuberantly through their teen years. These individuals discover the joys of their increased powers of mind and body and are successful in overcoming or avoiding the turmoil that besets their less fortunate peers.

Offer and Offer (1975), following extensive analysis of data derived from administering their self-image questionnaire to groups of adolescent boys, describe three routes male adolescent development can take. *Continuous* growth describes a positive pattern of steady growth; *surgent* growth describes a pattern where positive growth alternates with brief periods of turmoil and strife; and *tumultuous* growth is characterized by the turmoil that Hall claimed was the major characteristic of this period. Interestingly, fewer than one quarter of these samples could be classified as tumultuous. And as we saw earlier, typically, only 15 percent of all adolescents describe themselves as anxious or confused or depressed (Offer, Ostrov, & Howard, 1984). Clearly, then, the turmoil topics — delinquency, drugs, suicide — relate only to the minority.

But they are an important minority. And these are important topics.

Sources of Adolescent Frustration

There are a number of possible sources of **frustration** for adolescents: their inability to define their role — to achieve a sense of identity; their sense of the depressing distance between the utopia of which they dream and the world as they see it; sexual unemployment at a time when they are not only capable of being in love, of having intercourse, and of producing offspring but also actively desire to do so; and economic unemployment brought about by increasing demands for schooling.

Adolescents may also feel frustrated by ambivalence about where childhood ends and adult status begins. The responsibilities that are occasionally placed on their shoulders — as in time of war, for example — are adult responsibilities. At the same time, the privileges granted them are often those of children. Until recently, and even now in many places, they could not drink publicly, could not vote, and could not run for public office, although they could go out and get shot for their country. This, at least in their view, was unfair and consequently frustrating.

Additional frustration comes from conflicting cultural pressures. Adolescents have been led to believe that kindness, generosity, modesty, and affection are among the highest virtues; yet they observe cruelty, selfishness, ambition, and the cold impersonality of existence in large cities (and sometimes in small homes as well). They are taught that people should be individuals, that they should "do their own thing," yet the advertising media constantly urge them to conform. Indeed, most adult culture urges conformity. These conflicts are powerful sources of frustration.

All the frustration that stems from adolescents' ambivalence about their role and from conflicting demands that are made of them may be less important than the perceived distance between the ideals they envisage and espouse and the reality they observe. Some of them will have begun to question and examine established social and religious rules and to struggle with new principles. Implicit in these principles are beliefs about desirable states of affairs — about what ought to be — in short, about the ethical aspects of human existence. There are people starving, people in pain, people dying needlessly, people fighting, people destroying their environments. There is injustice, greed, anger, rape, murder, dishonesty, and a thousand forms of hypocrisy. There is a callous disregard for the humanity of persons in the depersonalized movements of technology. Some adolescents are acutely aware of these realities and of other evils of greater or lesser magnitude; as a result they may drop out in some way, or they may rebel quietly or violently.

Delinquency

Delinquency is a legal rather than a scientific category. Its definition varies from one legal jurisdiction to another depending on the particular laws of that jurisdiction. Most simply, a delinquent is a juvenile who has been apprehended and convicted for transgression of established legal rather than moral laws. Adults in similar situations are criminals rather than delinquents.

When delinquency is defined in this manner, we can quite accurately base surveys of its prevalence on police and legal records. These records indicate a tremendous increase in the delinquency rate in recent decades. There are now more crimes committed by adolescents and younger children than by people over 25 (U.S. Bureau of the Census, 1981). However, many of the offenses for which juveniles are apprehended and brought to court are status offenses such as truancy, running away, sexual promiscuity, under-age drinking, or driving without a license (see Table 12.6).

When delinquency is defined simply in terms of transgression rather than in terms of transgression, apprehension, and conviction, the picture changes dramatically. In self-report questionnaires, approximately 80 percent of all adolescents admit to having broken one or more laws (Hindelang, 1981). But fewer than 10 percent are ever arrested.

An analysis of surveys of delinquency reports that as many as 16 percent of all adolescents engage in sufficiently serious antisocial behavior (armed robbery, burglary, theft, rape, drug addiction) to be considered delinquent (Cavan & Ferdinand, 1981). Clearly, however, not all of these will be apprehended and convicted. As Vaz and Lodhi (1979) note, the majority of crimes are never reported.

A number of factors appear to be related to delinquency, but because most of the studies that have investigated delinquency simply indicate correlations, it is impossible to identify its specific causes. Age, for example, is related to delinquency; we have no evidence that it causes delinquency. Other related but not necessarily causal factors include social class, intelligence, peers, parents, personality, and sex.

Social class. Literature on the relationship between social class and delinquency is ambiguous and inconclusive. Although the lower classes, as well as some racial subgroups, are greatly overrepresented among delinquent groups, it is by no means clear that there are, in fact, many more delinquents among these groups. Because of the nature of the present law-enforcement systems, the often unconscious prejudices of the systems, and their consequently greater likelihood of recognizing and apprehending delinquents among minority and lower-class groups, it is hardly surprising that more of these adolescents are classified as delinquents. At the same time, to the extent that delinquency is a form of rebellion that is sometimes motivated by the desire for material possession, it is reasonable to expect that more of the poorer adolescents would be delinquent. Furthermore, lower-class parents tend to look to the police for help with their children; middle-class parents go to therapists (Chambliss, 1974).

Intelligence. There is a large body of evidence linking delinquency with lower than average measured intelligence (see Binder, 1988, for a review of some of these studies). The evidence indicates, in fact, that the difference between average IQs of delinquent and nondelinquent groups may be in the order of approximately eight IQ points (Quay, 1987). However, this should not be taken as direct evidence that lower intelligence *causes* delinquency. Quay notes that much of this difference in measured intelligence may be accounted for in terms of lower verbal ability. This puts children at a disadvantage in social interaction as well as in school. Consequently, they are more likely to get into trouble with teachers, school administrators, parents, and perhaps friends as well.

About 60 percent of all admissions to juvenile detention centers are readmissions. Males outnumber females 4 to 1.

Peers. The influence of peer groups is related to delinquent behavior and has been extensively investigated particularly in the study of gangs (for example, Cartwright, Tomson, & Schwartz, 1975). Like other peer groups, the delinquent gang reinforces its dominant values and serves as well as a model for translating these values into actual behaviors. Examples of the importance of peer groups in establishing values and in encouraging certain kinds of behavior are prevalent in television programs. They are also prevalent in various detention centers and other correctional institutions. Because correctional institutions comprise primarily delinquent peer groups, it is not particularly surprising that some 60 percent of all admissions are, in fact, readmissions (Stuart, 1969). The same observation could be made about adult correctional institutions. (The term *correctional* is a euphemism. Indeed, some writers claim that "nothing works" in this area; see Binder, 1988).

Parents. The father is perhaps the most influential parent with respect to delinquency (Biller, 1982). Fathers of delinquent boys are, on the average, more severe, more punitive, more prone to alcoholism, more rejecting, and more likely to have engaged in delinquent behavior themselves. Herzog and Sudia

Juvenile Delinquency and Violence

Table 12.6
Number (in 1,000s) and Types of Delinquency Cases Disposed of by American Juvenile Courts in 1985

Reason for Referral	Cases (thousands)		
	Male	Female	Total
All delinquency offenses	912	205	1,117
Violent offenses	61	9	70
Criminal homicide	1	—	1
Forcible rape	4	—	4
Robbery	23	2	25
Aggravated assault	33	8	41
Property offenses	380	91	471
Burglary	124	9	133
Larceny	220	77	297
Motor vehicle theft	30	5	35
Arson	6	1	7
Delinquency offenses	472	105	577
Simple assault	62	22	84
Vandalism	74	8	82
Drug law violations	62	13	75
Obstruction of justice	48	16	64
Other*	226	48	274

— indicates fewer than 500 cases

*Includes such offenses as stolen property offenses, trespassing, weapons offenses, other sex offenses, liquor law violations, disorderly conduct, and miscellaneous offenses.

Source: Adapted from U.S. Bureau of the Census (1990), p. 186.

Random and unprovoked violence, sometimes perpetrated by gangs and sometimes by individuals, is as frightening as it is unpredictable. Violence that is not random, but that is based on allegiance to ideology and on hatred of identifiable groups (as is the case for some racist groups) is no less terrifying. Although the number of delinquency cases dealt with by American courts has not changed very much in recent years (in the United States, 1.050 million cases in 1975 and 1.117 million in 1985; in Canada, 77,350 cases in 1987), incidence of violent offenses in the United States increased from 57,000 cases in 1982 to 70,000 cases in 1985. Male juvenile delinquents still outnumber females by a factor of more than 4 to 1; with respect to violent offenses, males outnumber females by approximately 7 to 1.

(1970) report as well a higher probability of delinquency among boys from fatherless homes. They speculate that father absence may contribute to delinquency in sons, perhaps by failure to provide adequate male models, perhaps as a function of protest against female domination, or simply because of inadequate supervision. Girls too appear to be more prone to delinquency in father-absent homes (Lynn, 1979) or where the mother is viewed as cold and rejecting (Kroupa, 1988). Friedman (1969) suggests that delinquency in such cases may result in part from the girls' sexual "acting-out" in retaliation against mothers who deprecate absent fathers.

Personality. A large number of studies have looked at the possibility that delinquency is at least partly a function of the individual's personality characteristics. In one study, for example, Monachesi and Hathaway (1969) administered the MMPI (Minnesota Multiphasic Personality Inventory — a widely used, very detailed, and comprehensive personality test) to more than 15,000 ninth-grade students. In later years, police and court records were checked routinely for the names of these students. Like a number of other researchers, Monachesi and Hathaway reported that several personality variables appeared to correlate most highly with later delinquency: namely those having to do with psychopathic tendencies (evident in amorality and rebelliousness) and emotional instability (high scores on what is labeled "neuroticism," manifested in high anxiety and mood fluctuations).

There is evidence as well, that high impulsivity (low impulse control), high need for stimulation (danger-seeking orientation), and low self-esteem are related to delinquency (Binder, 1988). With respect to low self-esteem, we noted earlier that delinquents typically think less well of themselves than do nondelinquent adolescents (Ahlstrom & Havighurst, 1971).

Sex. The adolescent's sex, too, is related to incidence of delinquency. Approximately four times more boys than girls are apprehended and convicted. This observation may be partly explained by the male's greater aggressiveness. Traditionally, delinquency among males has involved more aggressive transgressions, whereas girls were apprehended more often for sexually promiscuous behavior, shoplifting, and related activities. Evidence indicates this pattern is now changing, as more girls become involved in aggressive delinquent acts, including breaking and entering, car theft, and even assault (Vaz & Lodhi, 1979). Drug-related offenses also account for an increasing number of detentions.

In summary, it appears that a complex of psychological and social forces impinges on the potential delinquent, although no single factor can reliably predict delinquent behavior. Social class, age, sex, home background, intelligence, personality, relationship with the father, and peer influences are all implicated, but these, alone or in combination, cannot give a complete picture. Clearly, many adolescents from the most deprived of backgrounds are not delinquents, and many from apparently superior environments are.

Adolescent Activists

It would be impossible to provide a complete analysis of the "turmoil topics" selected for this discussion. We not only have insufficient space but also insufficient knowledge. Nevertheless, knowledge has progressed some distance beyond some of our favorite stereotypes and several of these can now be discounted.

To begin with, popular belief maintains that the adolescent activist is a malcontent, a social misfit, a disturbed individual, a potential criminal, a lower-class complainer, or some other form of undesirable individual. Interestingly, when adolescent rebellion is defined by student activism, a somewhat different picture of adolescents-as-rebels emerges: They are, in fact, typically well-adjusted, middle-class individuals — social malcontents to be sure, but no more potential criminals than you or I.

A second stereotype, no longer as common as it once was, asserts that most college kids are radicals — that the main reason they go to college is to join demonstrations, to sit in hallways of administration buildings, to burn anyone in effigy, to protest their country's attitude toward internal and external problems, to agitate against the stupidity of all people. This venerable folk belief is only partly correct. There are cerainly some students whose social consciences demand that they express their dissatisfaction and concern, but the total number of students involved in this demonstrative behavior even at the height of student activism in the 1960s was seldom more than 15 percent of the student body, and usually much lower than that (Trent & Crais, 1967). One of the traditional weaknesses of stereotypes is that they are applied to all individuals who have superficially similar appearances.

Adolescent Gangs

Sociologists define a gang as a group that forms spontaneously, that interacts on a face-to-face basis, and that becomes aware of its group membership through conflict with some other group or, perhaps more often, with some representatives of established society (Cartwright, Tomson, & Schwartz, 1975). A gang may consist of different numbers of individuals from a wide variety of backgrounds and locales, although it typically includes a fairly homogeneous group of people who at least live close to one another and who often attend the same school. But most important, a group does not become a gang until it comes into conflict with something external. It is hardly surprising, then, that the word *gang* has always been closely associated with juvenile delinquency, truancy, rebelliousness, and other disturbing behaviors.

Of special current interest are gangs whose members engage in violent behaviors — sometimes simply because of an apparent taste for violence and mayhem. Some British soccer riots and the occasional school-holiday violence seen in some North American resort areas are examples of this kind of violence. At other times, gang violence is premised on fundamental beliefs and principles that express themselves in strong feelings against certain groups or institutions. In my home city, for example, two members of a group identifying themselves as *neo-Nazi skinheads* recently beat up and blinded a 60-year-old man who had, more than a decade earlier, expressed anti-Nazi views (The "scene" and the skinheads, 1990). Their admitted philosophy is clearly racist; their dream is of an all-white society; their music is counterculture, frenetic, anarchist; their dress, hairstyles, and make-up intended to shock and outrage; and violence is their modus operandi.

But they are only one faction of one subgroup; there are many other gangs, most of them small. Some of them are determinedly nonviolent; others are anything but. In my city, they call themselves by such names as skaters, punks, thrashers, headbangers, and death rockers. In California, where the neo-Nazi skinhead movement originated, there are other groups, other labels (for example, SHARP, a counterculture group that claims to be antiracist and that has also been involved in violent incidents).

Fagan, Piper, and Moore (1986) argue that violence among delinquent gangs is often an expression of a new identity that gang members adopt. Adolescents who join small, highly cohesive, counterculture groups are provided with a set of beliefs and principles that are sometimes very well articulated. Their allegiance to the gang is not only a rejection of family, school, and larger cultural values, but is also an embracing of the values and of the individuals in a new community.

But not all adolescents who are dissatisfied, disillusioned, or in need of the community of groups join them in protest. A significant number of the severely dissatisfied drop out of society. Lest another stereotype be fostered, we must point out that the methods of dropping out described here are undertaken by the adventurous and the timid; by the weak and the strong; by the deluded and the rational — and frequently they are not attempts to drop out but merely attempts to intensify the experience of living.

Drugs

Drug use is a fact of life. Drugs are with us constantly in the guise of coffee, tea, headache tablets, cocktails, and in thousands of other forms. People have been familiar with drugs for centuries, although they have not always known the chemical components of the substances that they ate, drank, chewed, applied to wounds, inhaled, put in ears, or otherwise used on their persons. But the label is much less important than the effect and sometimes the availability.

For adolescents, the discovery of drugs is considerably simpler than it might have been some centuries or even decades ago. One need no longer go about testing brews made from plant leaves or chewing on roots and seeds. The communications media have discovered drugs for today's youth. It takes only nominal intelligence for a teenager to be aware of the availability of drugs. Not only do the media serve as a source of information but they also convey an often misleading image of adolescents and drugs. There is little doubt that the frequency of drug use among teenagers increased dramatically in the past three decades, just as alcohol consumption increased drastically several generations ago. At the same time, however, reports of the seriousness of the problem and of the extent of drug use are seldom based on more than conjecture and opinion.

Table 12.7
Classification of the Most Frequently Abused Drugs

Class	Examples
Narcotics	Opium Morphine Heroin Codeine Methadone
Sedatives (downers)	Barbiturates (Phenobarbital, Seconal, Nembutal) Tranquilizers (Valium, Librium, Vivol) Alcohol
Stimulants (uppers)	Cocaine Crack Amphetamines (Benzedrine, Dexedrine, Methedrine)
Hallucinogens (psychoactive, psychotropic, psychedelic, psychomimetic)	LSD PCP Mescaline Psilocybin Marijuana
Inhalants	Glue Paint thinner Aerosol sprays Solvents
Unclassified (or sometimes classified as stimulant)	Nicotine
"Designer" Drugs	Any of a combination of chemicals and drugs, often manufactured by amateur chemists

Bell and Battjes (1985) report significant declines between 1979 and 1984 in use of hallucinogens, tranquilizers, marijuana, opiates, and even cigarettes. However, there are some indications that alcohol use and abuse has increased during the last three decades (Franklin, 1985) and evidence, as well, that use of cocaine has increased (Newcomb & Bentler, 1988). The United States has the highest rates of illegal drug use among industrialized nations (Newcomb & Bentler, 1989; see Table 12.8).

Some Definitions. The American Psychiatric Association (1980) distinguishes among a number of drug-use terms. **Drug abuse** refers primarily to the *recreational* use of drugs and is not considered a disorder unless it impairs social or

Table 12.8

Percentage of High School Seniors Who Used the Indicated Drug During the Preceding 12 Months

Graduating class of	1975	1980	1985
Number of students in sample	(9,400)	(15,900)	(16,000)
Marijuana	40	49	41
LSD	7	7	4
PCP*	NA	4	3
Cocaine	6	12	13
Heroin	1	0.5	0.6
Stimulants *includes prescription drugs*	16	21	NA
Stimulants *excluding prescription drugs*	NA	NA	16
Barbiturates	11	7	5
Tranquilizers	11	9	6
Alcohol	85	88	86

Source: Based on L. D. Johnston, P. M. O'Malley, & J. G. Bachman (1986).
NA indicates data not available.
*Number of students in sample is one-fifth indicated.

occupational functioning. **Drug dependence** is a disorder ordinarily resulting from the repeated use of drugs and manifested in a strong desire to continue taking the drug — either for the pleasant sensations that might result or to escape feelings of withdrawal.

The APA distinguishes between **physiological dependence,** commonly called *addiction,* where the desire to continue taking the drug is at least partly organically based (for example, not taking it will lead to unpleasant physiological reactions), and **psychological dependence,** sometimes called *habituation,* where the desire to continue taking the drug has to do mainly with its psychological rather than its physiological effects. **Drug tolerance,** another important term, refers to changes that occur in the user so that with the passage of time, more and more of the drug is required to produce the desired effect.

Newcomb and Bentler (1989) make the important point that whether or not drug use is *abuse* depends on the drug, the organism, and the context. Thus, use of certain drugs that are toxic or that are likely to have serious adverse consequences is probably abuse; use of drugs by young children or adolescents may be abuse because of the possibility that drug use will interfere with important aspects of development and adjustment; and use of drugs in inappropriate contexts (at work; in school) is also more likely to be abuse.

Researchers have sometimes assumed that there is a drug-use continuum that reflects psychological health and adjustment. At the most positive extreme is the drug abstainer; at the most negative extreme, the frequent drug user or the addict. In between are those who experiment with drugs, but who are not frequent users. However, a longitudinal study conducted by Shedler and Block (1990) indicates that the assumption is inaccurate. The study looked at psychological characteristics of children from preschool through age 18. At age 18, children were identified as drug abstainers, drug experimenters, and drug users. As expected, drug users were found to be the least well-adjusted, the most impulsive, and the most likely to suffer from emotional problems. But the abstainers were not the best adjusted of the three groups; the drug-experimenters were. In Shedler and Block's (1990) words, "the picture of the abstainer that emerges is of a relatively tense, overcontrolled, emotionally constricted individual who is somewhat socially isolated and lacking in interpersonal skills" (p. 618).

Reasons for drug use. In the Shedler and Block study, children who later became frequent drug users were often identifiable by a complex of common characteristics even as young as age 7. These children typically did not get along as well with their peers, were less advanced in moral judgments, were more impulsive, displayed less self-reliance, had lower self-esteem, and were more prone to emotional distress. At age 11, these children continued to be more emotional, less attentive, and less cooperative, and reacted poorly to stressful situations. In short, frequent drug users frequently appear to be relatively maladjusted as children.

However, as Franklin (1985) notes, the reasons for drug use are many and complex and are not to be found solely in the personality characteristics of the frequent drug user. Also, the reasons why drug use becomes drug dependence or abuse in some cases, but not in others, are many. Among the variables most often identified in the literature are genetic factors, personality characteristics (which are also genetically influenced), and social/environmental factors. Marlatt et al. (1988) review a number of studies which indicate, for example, that children of alcoholics may be as much as four times more likely to become alcoholics than children of nonalcoholics. Other studies report a more modest relationship. However, what these studies mean isn't entirely clear. They might mean that there are genetically determined physiological (chemical-hormonal-metabolic) characteristics that make one person more susceptible than another to alcoholism. They might also mean that the social and economic implications of being raised in the home of an alcoholic parent are conducive to alcoholism. Or both.

Research reveals a number of variables that are relatively good predictors of the likelihood of drug abuse. As we saw in the Shedler and Block (1990) study, these include early maladjustment and related personality characteristics. In addition, drug use among peers, drug use among parents, delinquency, stressful life changes (death of a parent or divorce, for example), and low self-esteem are all implicated (Marlatt et al., 1988). Interestingly, low self-esteem is perhaps the single personality variable most often implicated in drug abuse (Franklin, 1985).

Reasons for first *using* (and not necessarily eventually *abusing*) drugs often have to do with a simple urge to experiment and perhaps with peer pressure as well (Pearl, Bryan, & Herzog, 1990). Newcomb and Bentler (1989) argue that there is little evidence to support the belief that experimentation with drugs presents a significant danger to later health and psychological well-being. In fact, research indicates that the majority of adolescents who drink heavily will moderate their use of alcohol as adults (Kandel & Logan, 1984).

Use of drugs is most likely to become misuse, Franklin (1985) suggests, among individuals with poor self-esteem who also experience the strong pressures of a peer drug culture and who are not reared in a growth-fostering environment (parental neglect, abuse, alcoholism; poverty; inadequate schooling; and so on). The type of drug experimented with is also very important. Some drugs have a higher potential for physiological and psychological dependence than others (heroin and freebase cocaine, or crack, for example). In addition, genetics may well be involved in the nature and intensity of the individual's reaction.

The fact that there are genetic, social, and personality variables that appear to be related to the likelihood of drug use and abuse should be interpreted with caution. The evidence does not warrant the conclusion that these inevitably *cause* drug abuse. Nor, as experience clearly shows, does the apparent absence of these factors guarantee that a given adolescent is safe. As Polson and Newton (1984) point out, one of the most common refrains heard when parents are first confronted with the fact of their child's drug use is: "Not my kid, couldn't happen to my kid."

Sadly, perhaps, it could.

Implications of teenage drug use. It is clearly unrealistic to expect that adolescents will not experiment with drugs. As Newcomb and Bentler (1989) note, the vast majority will have puffed on a cigarette or sipped somebody's alcoholic drink well before adolescence. In adolescence, not to drink occasionally — and perhaps not to smoke cigarettes or try marijuana — would, in many instances, not be socially *normal*. Society's focus, these authors claim, should be on *delaying* drug experimentation as long as possible in order to allow for the development of social and intellectual adaptive skills. The emphasis should perhaps be less on preventing *use* as on preventing *abuse*.

The short-term implications of drug abuse among adolescents are sometimes painfully obvious. Alcohol, for example, is implicated in a staggering number of fatal, teenage automobile accidents. Less dramatic, but no less real, drug abuse may be reflected in poorer school achievement, dropping out of school, failure to adjust to the career and social demands required for transition to young adulthood, deviance, and criminality. Watts and Wright (1990) report very high correlations between use of alcohol, tobacco, marijuana, and other illegal drugs and delinquency. In their study of black, white, and Mexican-American adolescents, frequent drug use was the best predictor of both minor and violent delinquency.

The long-term implications of teenage drug abuse have been examined by Newcomb and Bentler (1988), who looked at seven different aspects of the lives of young adults (including family formation, stability, criminality, mental health, social integration). They found that teenagers who had used high levels of drugs were more likely to have left school early and to have consolidated family and career plans earlier. Those who had used a variety of drugs had often adopted adult roles less successfully; their attempted careers and marriages were more likely to have failed.

The long-term medical consequences of drugs such as nicotine and alcohol have also been extensively researched and are well known. In the following sections we look at these and at some other commonly used drugs.

Marijuana. **Marijuana** is derived from hemp, a tall annual plant appearing in male and female forms. It is from the flowering top of the female hemp plant and from leaves on both male and female plants that *Cannabis sativa* is derived. The specific chemical grouping that accounts for its effects is *tetrahydrocannabinol* (THC). It is variously known as dawamesc, hashish, bhang, grass, ganja, charas, marijuana, muta, grefa, muggles, pot, reefer, guage, stick, Acapulco Gold, Panama Red, Panama Gold, Thai stick, jive, Indian, Jamaican, and tea.

Marijuana is ordinarily smoked although it can also be eaten or drunk. Its primary psychological effect is inducement of a pleasant emotional state. There is also evidence that if taken in sufficient doses and in sufficiently pure forms, it may evoke the same types of hallucinogenic reactions that are sometimes associated with stronger drugs like LSD (Cox et al., 1983).

Marijuana does not appear to be physically addictive, although there is a possibility that regular use might be associated with psychological dependence. There is evidence, as well, of apathy and loss of motivation following prolonged abuse (see *Cannabis,* 1976).

The physiological effects of marijuana use depend largely on the dosages and the frequency of use. Cox et al. (1983) report that minor cardiovascular changes (increased heartrate, for example) are common even with very low doses. With prolonged use and heavier doses, evidence suggests that the respiratory system is adversely affected and that the seriousness of the effects are probably greater than those following prolonged smoking of tobacco (Panzica, 1983). Marijuana produces more tars than tobacco, and these contain a higher concentration of certain cancer-causing agents (Cox et al., 1983).

Another possible physiological effect of marijuana use involves memory. Studies using rats exposed to marijuana smoke have found significant loss of memory for recently learned tasks (Essman, 1984). In addition, 24 hours after exposure to marijuana smoke, high concentrations of THC were found in the part of the rat brain that is thought to be associated with memory (the hippocampus).

The widely held fear that marijuana is the first step toward heroin addiction has generally been discounted. There is no evidence that marijuana users develop tolerance to marijuana as users do to some of the so-called hard drugs. Hence the marijuana user does not need to go to more powerful drugs to continue to achieve the same "high." Nor is there any evidence that using marijuana leads to a psychological craving for heroin.

LSD. LSD-25 (**d-lysergic acid diethylamide tartrate**) is the most powerful hallucinogen known. Because it is a synthetic chemical, it can be made by anyone who has the materials, the equipment, and the knowledge. The most common street name for LSD-25 is acid; others are barrels, California sunshine, blotters, cubes, domes, flats, wedges, purple haze, jellybeans, bluecaps, frogs, microdots, and window panes. Its use appears to have declined recently (Bell & Battjes, 1985).

LSD-25 (ordinarily referred to simply as LSD) is usually taken orally, commonly in the form of a white, odorless, and tasteless powder. Its effects vary widely from one person to another, as well as from one occasion to another for the same person. The predominant characteristic of an LSD experience (called an "acid trip") is the augmented intensity of sensory perceptions. Color, sound, taste, and vision are particularly susceptible. On occasion, an acid trip is accompanied by hallucinations, some of which may be mild whereas others can be sufficiently frightening to lead to serious mental disturbance in the subject even after the immediate effects of the drug have worn off (Cox et al., 1983).

Alcohol. Alcohol, the most commonly used and abused drug in contemporary society, is a central nervous system depressant. In relatively moderate doses, its primary effect is to suppress inhibition, which is why many individuals who have consumed alcohol behave as though they had taken a stimulant. In less moderate doses, the individual progresses from being "high" or "tipsy" to intoxication. Literally, to be *intoxicated* is to be poisoned. Behavioral symptoms of varying degrees of intoxication may include impaired muscular control, delayed reflexive reactions, loss of coordination and balance, impaired vision, uncertain speech, faintness, nausea, amnesia (blackouts), and, in extreme cases, paralysis of heart and lung muscles sometimes leading to death.

Alcohol is physiologically addictive, although prolonged or excessive consumption is generally required before symptoms of physical addiction are present. Signs of psychological dependency (a strong desire to continue taking the drug) may appear considerably sooner (Cox et al., 1983). One of the major physiological effects of alcohol is its contribution to cirrhosis of the liver — one of the 10 leading causes of death in the United States. In addition, it is implicated in more than half of all motor vehicle deaths, a large number of which involve adolescents.

Alcohol consumption among adolescents is widespread. Most surveys report that extremely few teenagers have not tried alcohol at least once (Newcomb & Bentler, 1989). An estimated 9.3 million adolescents aged 14 to 17 are "problem drinkers" according to a special report to Congress (U.S. Department of Health, Education & Welfare, 1978). That translates to close to 20 percent of adolescents in that age group.

Why do adolescents drink? There are clearly a large number of reasons, including social pressure, experimentation, insecurity and other personal problems, as well as simply for the sensation of being "tipsy," "high," or "drunk." One U.S. government survey reports that as many as one-quarter of seventh-grade students claim to get drunk at least once a year—and an astounding 10 percent of twelfth-grade students get drunk an average of once a week (U.S. Department of Health & Human Services, 1974). Brown and Finn (1982) suggest that deliberately drinking to get drunk (as opposed to getting drunk as a result of foolishly having the proverbial "one too many") underlies a great deal of teenage drinking. In their sample of 1,269 teenagers, 36 percent of the 12-year-olds thought that getting drunk is the purpose of drinking. As in other studies, this number increases around ages 14 and 15 (59 and 64 percent, respectively), but drops subsequently (42 percent at age 17).

Why do adolescents want to get drunk? To feel good, have fun, celebrate, let off steam, cheer up, forget worries, feel less shy, and impress friends, they claim (Brown & Finn, 1982). But when they are asked what their actual behaviors and feelings are when they are drunk, although a large number do "feel good" and "laugh a lot," a significant number fall asleep, feel unhappy, cry, damage property, and get into fights—and approximately one-third at all age levels occasionally get sick.

When is alcohol consumption by adolescents deviant or a problem? Is it a problem only when the adolescent gets into trouble? Does it become a problem when alcohol consumption becomes habitual or excessive or when it interferes with normal social or physical functioning?—or is it always a problem, as the behavior is generally illegal? There are no easy answers.

Cocaine. **Cocaine** is ordinarily a white powder derived from coca leaves. Also known as coke, big "C," snow, gold dust, star dust, flake, Bernice, or Corine, it is most commonly inhaled vigorously through the nostrils, although it can also be injected. Cocaine is sometimes purified to produce "freebase" cocaine, which, when inhaled, has a more profound effect on the user. Some users mix it with heroin and inject it intravenously (called a "speedball").

In moderate doses, the primary effect of cocaine, like that of other stimulants, is one of euphoria and high energy. In higher doses, it can lead to hallucinations and sometimes convulsions. Although it does not appear to be physiologically addictive when used conventionally (that is, when "snorted"), psychological dependence often leads to habitual use (Krikstone & Levitt, 1975).

Pure cocaine is among the most expensive of drugs and, perhaps largely for this reason, has not been nearly as common among adolescents as many of the less expensive drugs. Nevertheless, Keyes and Block (1984) found that 18 percent of a sample of 100 young adolescents from the San Francisco East Bay Area had used cocaine at least once. Of this same group, 96 percent had used alcohol at least once, and 51 percent had used marijuana. In the larger national samples surveyed by Johnston et al. (1983), approximately 5 percent of high school seniors had used cocaine during the preceding 30 days.

There are now indications that cocaine use has increased very dramatically among high school populations where it is most often used not as a powder but as a solid substance somewhat similar to a small chunk of "rock" candy and most commonly called rock or crack. Crack is easily and quickly manufactured by cooking down ordinary powdered cocaine with bicarbonate of soda. Small pieces of the resulting solid are then smoked, usually in a waterpipe. The euphoric effect or "rush" occurs within 5 to 10 seconds and is far more intense than that associated with inhaling ordinary cocaine — the reason being that the concentrations of cocaine that reach the brain are many times higher than is the case with inhalation. Consequently, there is a far higher risk of overdosing with crack, of experiencing convulsions, or even of dying. In addition, although cocaine has not ordinarily been considered physiologically addictive, many users of crack experience an overwhelming compulsion to use it again as soon as possible, even after using it only once. It is now thought to be as addictive as heroin (Ringwalt & Palmer, 1989). The use of crack is also associated with psychological changes, the most common of which involve strong feelings of paranoia. Many users also become violent.

Crack appears to be particularly attractive to adolescents for several reasons. First, it is far cheaper than cocaine (25 dollars or less for a single "hit" — and in spite of the high cost of pure cocaine, even at these prices, dealers easily double their money when they buy cocaine, cook it down into crack, and resell it). Second, its effect is almost instantaneous and intensely euphoric. And third, so much glamour and misinformation has surrounded the so-called recreational use of cocaine that many adolescents think there is nothing to fear. Next to marijuana, it is now the most frequently used illegal drug among adolescents (Ringwalt & Palmer, 1989).

One survey estimated that there were over 1 million crack users in the United States in 1986 (ABC "Nightline," April 7, 1986). Of these, approximately 85 percent were expected to experience serious paranoia, and 38 percent could become violent. Two out of 5 were likely to become drug dealers to support their habit.

Other drugs employed by some adolescents include various other hallucinogens such as STP and MDA (methyl amphetamines), PCP (phencyclidene), inhalants, various barbiturates and other, milder tranquilizers, and a range of new molecular variations of these and other chemicals, sometimes collectively labeled "designer drugs." Of these, alcohol is still the drug of choice, both among adolescents and adults (see Table 12.9).

Suicide

Suicide, the deliberate taking of one's life, is final — an end that is sought when individuals can see only two choices: life as it is now or death. Evidently, they prefer to die. If an adolescent is a male, he will probably shoot himself; a female is more likely to use poisoning or asphyxiation (Ladame & Jeanneret, 1982). Obviously, many other methods are available, but some of these result in a death that appears accidental (drowning, a car accident) and is difficult to identify as a suicide unless the person has left a note, a letter, or a book that can be interpreted as a message to end it. Because a suicide note appears in only 15 percent of all reported suicides, there are probably many apparent accidents that are, in fact, unidentified suicides.

Suicide is not a pleasant topic — it so violently contradicts our implicit belief in the goodness of life. Consequently, a powerful social stigma is associated with the act, and the event is often covered over both by the information media and by the attending physician. As a result, people know only of suicides of people whom they have known (and sometimes not even then) or of particularly prominent persons (not always those either) or of people who commit the act so flagrantly that it compels attention. There are relatively few scientific investigations of suicide, its causes, and the personalities of those who deliberately choose their time and method of departure. Do children commit suicide? How often? How about adolescents, disillusioned idealists that they are, caught up in the stress and turmoil of the transition to adulthood? Here are some facts.

The suicide rate in the United States is about 12 per 100,000. Few children under the age of 15 commit suicide. Suicide rates increase slowly from adolescence, peaking at above age 65 for white males and at around ages 45 to 55 for white females; peaks are at younger ages for American blacks, and are also lower (U.S. Bureau of the Census, 1988). The most dramatic recent increase in suicide rates is among those aged 15 to 19, where suicide rates nearly doubled between 1970 and 1986 (U.S. Bureau of the Census, 1990; see Figure 12.5).

Among adolescents, far more girls than boys attempt suicide, but a higher percentage of the boys are successful. Some have argued that this is because the boys who attempt suicide are more serious about wanting to die than are the girls. It may also be because the more violent and instantaneous methods employed by males (a gun, for example) do not provide much opportunity for help. In contrast, the slower and more passive methods most often employed by females (such as pills) often allow time for rescue.

Table 12.9
Symptoms of Drug Use and/or Abuse

Drug	Signs and Early Symptoms	Long-Term Symptoms
Narcotics	Medicinal breath Traces of white powder around nostrils (heroin is sometimes inhaled) Red or raw nostrils Needle marks or scars on arms Long sleeves (or other clothing) at inappropriate times Physical evidence may include cough syrup bottles, syringes, cotton swabs, and spoon or cap for heating heroin	Loss of appetite Constipation
Sedatives	Symptoms of alcohol consumption with or without odor; poor coordination and speech, drowsiness, loss of interest in activity	Withdrawal symptoms when discontinued Possible convulsions
Stimulants	Excessive activity Irascibility Argumentativeness Nervousness Pupil dilation Dry mouth and nose with bad breath Chapped, dry lips Scratching or rubbing of nose Long periods without sleep Loss of appetite Mood shifts Changes in friends "Hangover" symptoms	Loss of appetite Possible hallucinations and psychotic reactions
Hallucinogens, marijuana	Odor on breath and clothing Animated behavior or its opposite	None definite
LSD, PCP, MDA, STP	Bizarre behavior Panic Disorientation	Possible contribution to psychoses Recurrence of experiences after immediate effects of drug
Inhalants	Odor of glue, solvent, or related substance Redness and watering of eyes Appearance of alcoholic intoxication Physical evidence of plastic bags, rags, glue, or solvent containers	Disorientation Brain damage

Suicide Rates

Adolescent suicide rates have risen dramatically in the past several decades. In the United States, the rise reflects an enormous increase for males but not for females. At all ages, U.S. rates are higher for males than females (24,226 male suicides in 1988; 6,678 female suicides) and for whites than blacks. Males typically use more violent and perhaps more final methods such as guns (64 percent of all male suicides compared with 39.5 percent of female suicides); female methods are more passive and protracted and sometimes less successful (for example, poison: 37.7 percent of female suicides compared with 14.5 percent of male suicides).

Figure 12.5 Changes in suicide rates for U.S. adolescents, 1970 to 1986. *Source:* Adapted from U.S. Bureau of the Census (1990), p. 86.

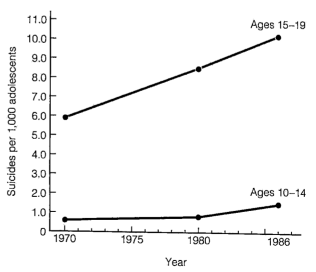

The reasons for adolescent suicide include concern over studies, health problems, and relationship problems. In addition, adolescent suicides are often precipitated by a single event such as the death of a parent or friend, fear of pregnancy, rejection by a close friend, or arrest.

Adolescent suicide, like most adult suicides, rarely occurs without advance warning. The most common warning is, simply, one or more unsuccessful attempts at suicide. Ladame and Jeanneret (1982) report that as many as four out of five adolescents who succeed in committing suicide have previously attempted to kill themselves at least once. Other warning signs include statements such as "I wish I were dead." "Nobody would miss me if I weren't here." "I wish I'd never been born."

Suicide is still the solution of an isolated few. Most of us choose to wait for death and hope that it will be a long time in coming.

ANOTHER NOTE

Suicide would not have been a very pleasant note upon which to end this chapter. Nor would it have been very realistic. Indeed, closing the chapter with the "turmoil topics," as we have, is misleading.

It bears repeating that the adolescents whose lives are described among these last pages are not our "average" adolescents. Our average adolescents are more joyful than sad, more exuberant than depressed, more confident than self-deprecating. They like order more than chaos, purpose more than dissipation — and junk food more than drugs.

And they laugh and smile a lot more than they cry.

That's a better note upon which to end.

MAIN POINTS

1. Global self-worth (or self-esteem) reflects an evaluation of the self — how well I like myself. Self-evaluations are possible in a number of different areas and activities (for example, scholastic or athletic; playing ball or playing poker). The Offer Self-Image Questionnaire asks teenagers to report their attitudes and feelings in a number of areas in an attempt to assess the most important of the *multiplicity* of selves that make up global self-concept: psychological; social; familial; coping; and sexual.

2. Among the characteristics shared by the majority of adolescents in a number of different countries (the universal adolescent) are: general happiness and optimism; caring and concern for others and the enjoyment of the company of others; confidence and openness about sexual matters; strongly positive feelings toward the family; and confidence in their ability to deal with life.

3. There are important, consistent differences among adolescents from different cultures (for example, lower confidence, more loneliness, greater feelings of vulnerability on the part of Bengali adolescents; very high values placed on educational and vocational goals by American adolescents and very low values placed on these values by Israeli and Hungarian teenagers; reltively conservative sexual attitudes among Turkish and Taiwanese adolescents). These differences reflect historical and immediate context.

4. Contrary to Hall's belief, adolescence is not a period of storm and stress for the majority of the world's adolescents. In North America, approximately 15 percent of adolescents describe their lives as turbulent, confused, unhappy.

5. High self-esteem is closely related to adjustment and happiness. Authoritative parenting appears to be conducive to the development of high self-esteem.

6. According to Erikson, the major developmental task of adolescence is to develop a sense of identity — that is, to select among the various choices of available roles. Marcia describes four possible identity statuses of the adolescent: *identity diffusion* (no commitment and no identity crisis — characteristic of early adolescence); *foreclosure* (strong commitment to an identity imposed on the adolescent sometimes by parents, sometimes by religious affiliation); *moratorium individuals* (adolescents actively exploring alternative identities, some of which may be negative; vague, changing commitments); and *identity achieved* (commitment following the crises of the moratorium).

7. Increasing allegiance to peers does not necessarily entail a high degree of parent-adolescent conflict. Most teenagers have good relations with their parents, although one of the developmental tasks of this period clearly involves increasing independence from parents.

8. Peer groups begin as small single-sex groups in early adolescence and progress through four additional stages: single-sex groups that interact as groups but remain intact; a stage when the "crowd" has begun to form but still consists of single-sex groups interacting in a closer fashion; large heterosexual groups form; the heterosexual crowd breaks into less cohesive groups of couples.

9. The adolescent's acceptance by peers is profoundly important for social and psychological well-being. Friendships tend to be highly age-segregated and to involve individuals who are more similar than dissimilar. High-status (well-liked) children tend to be happier, more cheerful, more active, and more successful.

10. The "sex-change question" — what if you were a boy (girl)? — reveals predominantly positive evaluations of the male role and negative evaluations of the female role by both males and females. Our gender stereotypes see the male role as more active, more aggressive, more rational, more powerful; the female role is seen as more passive, more emotional, more nurturant, less aggressive.

11. Males appear to be the more fragile sex, as is revealed in substantially higher mortality rates and much lower life expectancies. In our cultures, males have traditionally been more aggressive and females more submissive and nurturant.

12. Gender differences in verbal ability, once thought to favor females, now appear very small and are not usually apparent prior to adolescence except among some disadvantaged groups. Similarly, differences in mathematical ability, once thought to favor males, now appear trivial, are apparent only from adolescence onwards, and are better explained in terms of culturally determined interests and opportunities rather than in terms of basic genetically ordained differences.

13. The sexual revolution among adolescents has taken two directions: an absolute increase in the number of adolescents reporting sexual intercourse before marriage and a much greater increase in sexual activity among females than among males. Almost half of young adolescents consider sexual relations permissible if partners have been together a number of times and have developed a caring relationship. Masturbation is relatively common among adolescents and is practiced somewhat more frequently by males than by females.

14. Approximately 20 percent of sexually active teenage girls become pregnant each year. Most of these pregnancies are accidental and occur within six months of the first intercourse. Of those who do not miscarry, the majority choose abortion. Of those who do not choose abortion, 31 percent marry before the birth of the infant, and 69 percent have out-of-wedlock infants. Fewer than 4 percent of these infants are given up for adoption.

15. Evidence suggests that teenage parents are more likely to divorce than are people who marry later. In addition, their marriages are more likely to be associated with depression, suicide, infant mortality, child neglect, and other signs of inadequate parenting.

16. The most common sexually transmitted diseases (STDs) are gonorrhea, herpes, and chlamydia. Syphilis and AIDS are rarer. Gonorrhea, chlamydia, and syphilis can be cured with drugs; herpes can sometimes be controlled but not cured; AIDS, which is most common among homosexual males, intravenous drug users, and hemophiliacs, is fatal. There is some evidence that AIDS may now be spreading rapidly among the heterosexual population.

17. Adolescents may be frustrated by their inability to define their role and by the distance that they observe between the ideal world they contemplate and the one in which they live. Not all adolescents are frustrated, and some are less so than others.

18. Delinquency is a legal category defined by juvenile apprehension and conviction of a legal transgression; it appears to include more lower-class than middle-class adolescents. Other factors related to delinquency include sex, intelligence, self-esteem, family background, and peer influences.

19. Only about 15 percent of college students join demonstrations and other similar activist events; of those who do participate, many are pacific, very few are drug addicts, and some are sincere, well intentioned, and justified in their beliefs and demands. A small minority also become members of countercultural and sometimes violent gangs.

20. Incidence of drug use among adolescents appears to have leveled off in recent years following dramatic increases in the 1960s. In particular, use of tranquilizers and hallucinogens such as LSD seems to have declined. However, use of

cocaine may have increased. Alcohol is still the drug of choice, nicotine is second, and marijuana is third.

21. "Drug abuse" refers to the recreational use of drugs. "Drug dependence" is a disorder manifested in a strong desire to continue taking a drug. It may be physiological where the desire to take the drug is partly organically based (also termed *addiction*), and where not taking the drug may lead to unpleasant physiological reactions; or it may be psychological where the urge to continue taking the drug has to do more with its psychological effects than with physiological addiction (also termed *habituation*).

22. Reasons for drug abuse probably include a complex of genetic and social-environmental factors. Good predictors of the likelihood of drug abuse among teenagers include earlier maladjustment; drug use among peers or parents; delinquency; stressful life changes; parental neglect, abuse, or abandonment; and low self-esteem.

23. Marijuana does not appear to be physiologically addictive although it may lead to psychological dependence. Its effects on the respiratory system appear to be more harmful than those of tobacco. There is evidence that it might also affect recent memory.

24. LSD-25 (d-lysergic acid diethylamide tartrate) is the most powerful known synthetic hallucinogenic drug. Both LSD and marijuana are nonaddictive, but both can cause psychoticlike reactions, although these are less common with marijuana.

25. Alcohol is the most popular drug among adolescents. It is a highly addictive central nervous system depressant.

26. Cocaine is a relatively expensive stimulant that creates feelings of euphoria and relieves fatigue. It is not physiologically addictive, but frequently leads to psychological dependence. Crack or rock is less expensive, more potent, and highly addictive.

27. Suicide is an uncommon end, although its frequency among adolescents has more than doubled in recent decades. More girls than boys attempt suicide, but fewer are successful, perhaps because their most common methods allow time for help (poisons) whereas those of males do not (guns). Although adolescent suicides are often precipitated by a single event (such as the death of a friend, pregnancy, parental divorce, arrest), few occur without warning. The most common warning is a previous suicide attempt or indirect statements about suicide ("I wish I were dead").

28. For most adolescents, life is only occasionally turbulent and stressful; most of the time, it abounds with joy and excitement.

Further Readings

Offer and associates presented a self-image questionnaire to nearly 6,000 teenagers in 10 different countries. The result is a fascinating look at the thoughts and attitudes of teenagers around the world.

Offer, D. O., Ostrov, E., Howard, K., & Atkinson, R. (1988). *The teenage world: Adolescents' self-image in ten countries.* New York: Plenum Press.

Gender stereotypes are widely held beliefs about male-female characteristics and differences. The first of the following two references examines the typical stereotypes and prejudices of American and Swedish adolescents; the second presents a balanced view of the gender differences psychology has actually found.

Intons-Peterson, M. J. (1988). *Gender concepts of Swedish and American youth.* Hillsdale, N.J.: Lawrence Erlbaum.

Halpern, D. F. (1986). *Sex differences in cognitive abilities.* Hillsdale, N.J.: Lawrence Erlbaum.

Lees's book describes a blatantly sexist and unfair adolescent subculture; Stein's book describes how sexual stereotyping begins from birth and continues through life:

Lees, S. (1986). *Losing out: Sexuality and adolescent girls.* London: Hutchinson.

Stein, S. B. (1983). *Girls and boys: The limits of nonsexist childrearing.* New York: Charles Scribner's.

The Polson and Newton book presents a firsthand look at drug abuse and rehabilitation among adolescents. The UNESCO publication may be of particular value to parents, educators, and others concerned with *prevention* of drug abuse. Perkins and McMurtrie-Perkins present down-to-earth advice for parents concerned about drug use by their children.

Polson, B., & Newton, M. (1984). *Not my kid: A family's guide to kids and drugs.* New York: Arbor House.

Educating against drug abuse. (1987). UNESCO, 7 Place de Fontenoy, 75700, Paris.

Perkins, W. M., & McMurtrie-Perkins, N. (1986). *Raising drug-free kids in a drug-filled world.* Austin, Texas: Hazelden.

Jones, E. F., and associates. (1986). *Teenage pregnancy in industrialized countries.* New Haven, Conn.: Yale University Press.

The following collection presents a detailed look at adolescent parenting and particularly at various programs that are available for teenage parents:

Sugar, M. (Ed.). (1984). *Adolescent parenthood.* New York: SP Medical and Scientific Books.

The following two sources look at sexual behavior and pregnancy among adolescents. The first summarizes two major studies and looks at changes that have occurred in recent years; the second presents a detailed look at a controversial topic — abortion:

Zelnik, M., Kantner, J. F., & Ford, K. (1981). *Sex and pregnancy in adolescence.* Beverly Hills, Calif.: Sage.

Sachdev, P. (Ed.). (1985). *Perspectives on abortion.* Metuchen, N.J.: The Scarecrow Press.

"'Begin at the beginning,' the King said, very gravely,

'and go on till you come to the end: then stop.'"

Lewis Carroll, *Alice in Wonderland*

VII
Epilogue

"'Begin at the beginning,' the King said . . ."

We began close to the beginning and in the many pages between there and here, we probed and pulled and tugged at the secrets of the developing child's life as though we might unravel its fabric, uncover its mysteries, understand its profoundest truths.

We have seen much, understood much of the processes and products of development.

But if we have uncovered the profoundest truth of all, it is simply that we have recognized more clearly the wonderful complexity of the unfolding of a human being.

To recognize that complexity is not to understand it all.

Our painting of the child is not yet done. But, sadly, there are forms we have not yet learned to draw, colors we have still to invent.

". . . and go on till you come to the end: then stop."

But there is no end, no *real* end, until the picture we have tried to paint is complete.

One more short chapter; one more stroke of the brush.

We'll call it *The End.*

When I am dead, I hope it may be said
"His sins were scarlet, but his books were read."
Hilaire Belloc, *On His Books*

The End

A Summary

Other Views
Humanism
Existentialism

Had you been standing behind me these last months, looking over my shoulder, you would surely have thought I was writing this book. But it is not really so, for books are only partly from the minds and guts of their authors. A large part of them comes from somewhere else, and we, the authors, sit at our keyboards waiting for them to happen. Not until a book has set itself down on paper does it actually exist. Before that time it could have taken any number of forms. But from the moment it is recorded it has its own definite shape and substance.

The life of a child is something like a book. It too can take any number of shapes and directions, and no one knows precisely what that form will be until it happens. But quite unlike a book, as the life of a child unfolds and takes form and substance, it never irrevocably possesses that form. It changes constantly. That is the undeniable truth of human development.

Sometimes we forget that. Late last night as I staggered through a dimly lit hallway in our house, I met a tall stranger who, it seemed, grumbled something mean under his breath. I jumped back in sudden fright, curling my toes and raising my fingers in some unconscious and thoroughly primitive defensive gesture.

But it was only my 14-year-old son who had muttered a greeting and who now lurched toward his bedroom, all arms and legs and long, scrawny neck. I had forgotten that he has suddenly become almost as tall as I am, that most of the time his voice rumbles from hidden places in his chest.

He is not a stranger at all, this son. Nor are my other two children, but sometimes I wonder who they will become, even who they are.

It is easy for me to sit here in this booklined workplace and keyboard such humanistic phrases as "There is no average child," "It is whole infant with whom we are concerned," "A child is an incredibly complex little organism," "A child is qualified for the title of linguist extraordinaire." But it is something else to be faced with the living linguist, the whole infant, the nonaverage child, and the incredibly complex organism all at once and in the flesh — and not just for a brief passing glance but for an uninterrupted period of years.

As I look at my children, I cannot help thinking that they are what I have undertaken to describe in this book. And I now know so much more clearly than before that there is no average child — that I am in fact talking about the various layers that I have chosen to call chapters or chapter sections, and that the whole process of attempting to set down in static words a thing that is at once as dynamic and as elusive as a child in the process of becoming necessarily robs both the child and the process of their dynamism.

To repeat again that this is so makes it no less so. But perhaps it does make us more aware of what concerns us: that a child, like an adult, is never what will be but is always becoming. The small insight I have gained from trying to relate what I have written to my children is this: When all the layers that make up the chapters and sections of this book have been bound together and the painting of the child finally rendered, it will still bear only a faint resemblance to its subject. For the subject of the process of becoming does not stop and pose; by its very nature it continues to move forever.

A SUMMARY

The subject of this book is the movement of the child from the beginning through adolescence, divided into 12 chapters. Here is some of what each of those chapters said:

Chapter 1. Child development studies the progressive adaptation of mythical average children — although we know that children are neither average nor mythical; they are real and individual. Our beliefs about children reflect our social/cultural contexts; our methods are those of science.

Chapter 2. Theories direct our investigations and shape our beliefs about what is important. What *is* important, you ask? Early emotional experiences and especially child/parent relationships, says Freud. Social competence, insists Erikson. Consequences, the behaviorists inform us. The ability to symbolize and to anticipate the outcomes of our behavior, says Bandura. Language, culture, and social/historical context, Vygotsky asserts. The ecology of human interaction in open systems, thinks Bronfenbrenner.

Chapter 3. The fact that there is a you or a me is largely a matter of fortune. It could have been another ovum; it could have been any one of several million other sperm cells. In each case, the result would have been someone else. Or would it? What you and I are continually becoming is not solely a function of the intricate arrangement of DNA molecules that our parents passed on to us (that they, in turn, got from their parents, and so on, so that there exists in a remote sense a common pool of genes for all of us). What we are is also a matter of where we have been at different times in our lives, and of who the people around us have been — of our contexts, the ecologies of our micro-, meso-, exo-, and macrosystems.

Chapter 4. We begin as a microscopic speck in one of our mother's Fallopian tubes. Through the next 266 days, this indistinct glob of cells changes into the form and functions that make up the newborn. And although these changes are ordered, systematic, and highly predictable, they are nevertheless subject to external influences such as drugs, illnesses, malnutrition, and other stressors.

And then we are born. And just about everybody loves us!

Chapters 5 and 6. As infants, we discover our hands, our feet, and our parents; and we learn that blankets are to chew. Later, we are initiated into the wonderful secrets of language, and we learn that there are things to cry and laugh about of which we could never have dreamed. And if we continue to be lucky, just about everybody still loves us a lot. We *mean* something!

Chapters 7 and 8. In early childhood, we learn mystical, magical things that dazzle our senses and our minds. A new logic invades our thinking — egocentric, perception-dominated, and intuitive, but nevertheless the germ of a finer, more advanced logic. As preschoolers, our world enlarges; the microsystems of our ecology are no longer defined only by parents and siblings, but also include peers and playmates and caretakers and teachers. Sometimes we have to struggle a little to be loved. Some of us pretend we don't care all that much. But deep down, we do.

Chapters 9 and 10. Through middle childhood, we expand our powers of mind and body, refining our thinking, expanding our knowledge base, honing our language and our social skills. And perhaps as our construction of reality becomes more sophisticated, we begin to forget a little of the magic and the mystery that filled our younger lives. But not all of it, for we are still in those sweet childish days, when every day is like 20. Now our lives are filled with buddies, and love is a remote abstraction. Really being liked is enough.

Chapters 11 and 12. Finally we become adolescents, newly aware of the power of the logic that is now ours, egocentric and full of our *selves*, smitten with a sense of power and invulnerability, imbued with a wonderful conviction that we are somehow special. Then Bang! puberty strikes, sending hormones raging through our veins, and we are driven even further from our childish games as we struggle to invent the many meanings of love. We teeter uncertainly on the brink of adulthood — sometimes torn and confused, sometimes angry and rebellious, sometimes hungry to try everything that life has to offer before it is too late, desperate to gather our rosebuds while we may. And sometimes, as adolescents we just sleep in for a surprisingly long time.

At every step in the chronology that composes this text, something was said of the physical, the cognitive, and the social development of the average child. And at every step, you were urged to keep in mind that the average of which we spoke was an invention and that, further, we were dividing this invention into layers and pieces so that we could communicate clearly. Although we occasionally stopped to say things about children who are not entirely average in all ways, we were forced to treat these *exceptional* children as averages too. In the process, we have robbed children of their individuality and we have stripped much of the dynamism and the magic from the processes and the outcomes of development.

That part of the story has now been told. There remains only the attempt to bring the various layers and pieces into a cohesive whole to provide a richer, more accurate, more complete, and more *human* picture of the child in the process of becoming.

OTHER VIEWS

Who am I? Is the I who is sitting here thinking about who he is different from the I who questioned my grandmother's fertile theories? Was I the same me when, as an adolescent, I wondered about life, its purposes and goals, the reaches beyond its obvious limits, society and the predicaments that it had created for itself, and a thousand other questions of grave and immediate consequence? Was the I who went to school as a freshly scrubbed 6-year-old the same person who graduated from college many years later? Who is my self and what is it; how does it become what it is?

Perhaps we still can't answer the question of personal identity — a question that has plagued philosophers, psychologists, theologians, grandmothers, and all manner of thinkers since thinking began. But there are two useful answers that are often given, both intuitive, highly subjective, but no less meaningful. The first asserts there is an unidentifiable something about the self that continues from the dawning awareness of a personal identity until the oblivion of psychotic disorder, memory loss, or death destroys all sense of existence. The other answer does not contradict the first but simply extends it: The self is continually developing, despite the individual's feeling of a single and unique personal identity throughout life.

As we saw in Chapter 2, the self and its development have been a primary concern of humanistic psychology; it is also a major concern of existential philosophy. These two orientations can each add to our understanding and appreciation of the phenomena of development. A rigorous discussion of their contributions is beyond the scope of this text. Nevertheless, a summary of humanism and an introduction to existentialism are presented here, partly as an alternative to the somewhat unreal picture that results from attempting to examine the child in objective psychological detail and partly as a finishing touch for the painting that has been attempted in this text.

Humanism

Recall that humanism is a concern for humans, for humanity, for the development of humanness, and for its expression. It exalts the individual and glorifies the self. Thus the concepts of paramount concern to the humanistic psychologist include notions such as self-structure, self-concept, self-image, self-understanding, self-acceptance, self-enhancement, self-realization, and self-actualization. Humanism is concerned with that which is most clearly human; accordingly, it sees the development of self (self-actualization) as the goal toward which humans should strive.

The process of self-actualization is the act of becoming whatever one has the potential to become through one's own efforts; it is the process of actualizing — of making actual or real that potential. But it is not a static goal toward which individuals consciously or unconsciously strive; it is a process, an ongoing activity. Self-actualization is, in fact, the process of development. We could have substituted different terms in this text to make this relationship more apparent. For example, instead of speaking of development, we might have spoken of self-actualization or of the development of self; instead of referring to the frustrations of adolescents, who cannot easily determine whether they are child or adult, we could have referred to the difficulty of establishing the identity of the self during the transition from childhood to adulthood; and instead of discussing forces that impede or accelerate development, we could have discussed self-enhancement or changing self-structure or contributions to self-esteem. The picture that would have emerged might have been a more integrated one, for we would constantly have been speaking of the self. It would also have been a more realistic picture that dealt more with the real child than with the hypothetical average child — for the self belongs solely to the individual; there is no "average" self. To speak of the *average* self is to distort the concept miserably. At the same time, our portrait would probably have been a more global, less precise, and less informative study of the child.

Existentialism

To complete our description of the child, we might consider the concepts of **existential psychology,** which are similar to those of humanistic psychology. From Jean-Paul Sartre we borrow a description of the human condition — cynical and pessimistic, but one that enables us to understand better the direction of development, particularly in its nearly adult stages. From Martin Buber we borrow ideas from a philosopher of personalism, which is only a short distance from humanism.

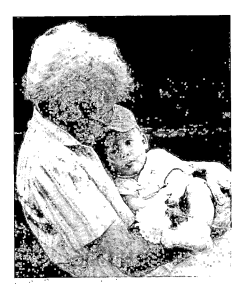

If the process of human development has a goal, then it may be a capacity to feel great love; the reward for having reached that state must be great happiness.

The existential picture of people and of the forces that move them, as presented by Jean-Paul Sartre, can be described by three words: *anguish, abandonment,* and *despair*. These words summarize the human condition—they are both the facts of existence and its consequences. We are forever in anguish because we are constantly forced to make decisions and yet have no guides for these decisions. There is no guarantee that anything we do is correct, for there is no God, Sartre informs us; and without a God all action must be justified in terms of its effects on others. Such resolution is a tremendous and terrible responsibility, and its consequence is deep and undying anguish.

We have also been abandoned, and **abandonment** is an indescribably lonely feeling. We have not been abandoned simply by others but abandoned in a general sense, without purpose and with no a priori values; abandoned to be free — *free* to make choices but also *required* to make them. So we despair because we are free but without hope, because to will something is not necessarily to achieve it and because when we die all our efforts may have been in vain.

This is atheistic existentialism, and we describe it here to give a perspective through contrast to the more optimistic reflections of Martin Buber. Buber (1958, 1965) tells us there are four main evils in the modern world and the effect of these evils is to highlight the importance of the human self. The first of these evils is our terrible loneliness, and loneliness has long been recognized by existentialists as a concept of extreme importance. Existence as a self is essentially a lonely experience, because the self always belongs only to the individual — it can never be shared completely. Therefore, we are always alone. Buber's second evil is the never-ending drive for technological progress, the individual's worth lessening with the increasing importance of machines and science. The third evil stems from human duality, the good-versus-evil dichotomy — the id warring with the superego. Finally, Buber contends that the individual is being degraded by the state; the conglomerate, impersonal, and faceless entities that define states are incompatible with the uniqueness and personal worth of the individual.

The result of these evils is summarized in a single existentialist (and humanistic) term: *alienation*. To be alienated is to be separated from — to be a stranger to. We are alienated from ourselves, from others, and from our environment. In short, we have been uprooted from the relationships that we should have with all three: our private self, those who surround us, and our environment. Accordingly, the greatest evil that besets us, social animals that we are, is alienation; and the greatest good is *love* — love of self and love of others. Buber's philosophy is seldom pessimistic, for it asserts strongly that our salvation, our happiness, and our consequent self-actualization can be achieved through love. Love is simply a question of relationships, what Buber terms the I-Thou relationship: In the I-Thou relationship the object or person being related to is not being used selfishly; the relationship is mutual; there is dialogue as opposed to monologue; and people say and do what they honestly mean rather than what is merely convenient or socially appropriate.

If the process of human development has a goal — if it ever ceases to be a process of becoming — then its goal must surely be a capacity to feel great love, and the reward for having reached that state must surely be great happiness.

Does self-actualization ever become self-realization? Does the adolescent ever know that the child has grown up? Does the adult? The old person?

Glossary

This glossary defines the most important terms and expressions used in this text. In each case the meaning given corresponds to the usage in the text. For more complete definitions, consult a standard psychological dictionary.*

Abandonment The existential dilemma. An atheistic-existential concept referring to an intense feeling that results from the realization that we have been abandoned on earth with no purpose, no knowledge of where we come from or where we are going. (See *alienation.*)

Abortion A miscarriage occurring usually before the twentieth week of pregnancy when the fetus ordinarily weighs less than 1 pound.

Accommodation The modification of an activity or an ability that the child has already learned, to conform to environmental demands. Piaget's description of development holds that assimilation and accommodation are the means by which an individual interacts with the world and adapts to it. (See *assimilation.*)

Acquired immune deficiency syndrome (AIDS) An incurable and fatal sexually transmitted disease, transmitted through the exchange of body fluids.

Adaptation The process whereby an organism changes in response to the environment. Such changes are assumed to facilitate interaction with that environment. Adaptation plays a central role in Piaget's theory. (See *accommodation, assimilation.*)

Adolescence A general term signifying the period from the onset of puberty to adulthood, typically including the teen years (13 to 19). (See *puberty.*)

AFP test A screening test designed to detect the likelihood of a fetal neural tube defect by revealing the presence of *alphafetoprotein* in the mother's blood.

Afterbirth The placenta and other membranes that are expelled from the uterus following the birth of a child.

Alienation In existential philosophy and psychology, an individual's feeling of separation from

---

*Some of these definitions are taken from the glossary in Guy R. Lefrançois, *Psychology for teaching: A bear . . .* (7th ed.). Belmont, Calif.: Wadsworth, 1991. Used by permission.

people and things that are important to that individual. (See *existential psychology.*)

Alzheimer's disease A disease associated with old age (but also occurring as young as 40), marked by progressive loss of memory and of brain function and eventual death.

Amniocentesis A procedure whereby amniotic fluid is removed from a pregnant woman by means of a hollow needle. Subsequent analysis of this fluid may reveal chromosomal aberrations (Down syndrome, for example) and other fetal problems.

Amniotic sac A sac filled with a dark fluid (amniotic fluid) in which the fetus develops in the uterus.

Anal stage The second of Freud's psychosexual stages of development, beginning at approximately 8 months and lasting until around 18 months. It is characterized by the child's preoccupation with physical anal activities.

Anorexia nervosa A medical condition not due to any detectable illness, primarily affecting adolescent girls and involving a loss of 15 to 25 percent of ideal body weight. It usually begins with dieting and ends when the patient is unwilling or unable to eat normally.

Anoxia A condition in which there is an insufficient supply of oxygen to the brain.

Artificial insemination An artificial breeding procedure often used in animal husbandry and sometimes with humans. This procedure eliminates the necessity for a physical union between a pair of opposite-sexed individuals.

Assimilation The act of incorporating objects or aspects of objects to previously learned activities. To assimilate is, in a sense, to ingest or to use for something that is previously learned; more simply, the exercising of previously learned responses. (See *accommodation.*)

Association Refers to links or bonds among stimuli and responses. (See *associationistic.*)

Associationistic A term often employed synonymously with stimulus-response explanations of learning. Also used to describe a memory model premised on the assumption that items of information in memory are *associated* in various ways in terms of their meanings.

Attribution theory Theories that look for regularities in the ways we attribute things that happen to certain causes, either internal or external.

Authoritarian A highly controlling, dogmatic, obedience-oriented parenting style in which there is little recourse to reasoning and no acceptance of the child's autonomy.

Authoritative A moderately controlling parenting style in which value is placed on independence and reasoning, but where parents impose some regulations and controls.

Autism A serious childhood mental disorder usually apparent by 30 months, characterized by social unresponsiveness, poor or nonexistent communication skills, and bizarre behavior.

Autosomes All chromosomes in mature sperm and ova other than the sex chromosome. Each of these cells therefore contains 22 autosomes.

Babbling The relatively meaningless, repetitious sounds that young infants repeat.

Babinski reflex A reflex present in the newborn child but disappearing later in life. The toes fan out as a result of being tickled in the center of the soles of the feet. Normal adults curl their toes inward rather than fanning them outward.

Basic needs Unlearned physiological requirements of the human organism; specifically, the needs for food, drink, and sex.

Behavior modification A general term for the application of behavioristic principles (primarily principles of operant conditioning) in systematic and deliberate attempts to change behavior.

Behavioristic theory A general term for those theories of learning concerned primarily with the observable components of behavior (stimuli and responses). Such theories are labeled *S-R learning theories* and are exemplified in classical and operant conditioning.

Birth The process whereby the fetus, the placenta, and other membranes are separated from the mother's body and expelled. (See *labor.*)

Birth order The position a child occupies in a family (for example, first, second, or third born).

Blind procedure An experimental procedure where subjects or experimenters are not aware of who are members of experimental and control group. When only one of these is unaware, the procedure is termed *single-blind*; when both are unaware, the procedure is *double-blind.*

Breech birth An abnormal presentation of the fetus at birth: buttocks first rather than head first.

Bulimia Recurrent episodes of binge eating where the patient, typically an adolescent girl, is aware that the eating pattern is not normal and where depression or self-deprecation follows the episode.

Canalization Waddington's term to describe the extent to which genetically determined characteristics are resistant to environmental influences. A highly canalized trait (such as hair color) remains unchanged in the face of most environmental influences; less highly canalized characteristics (such as manifested intelligence) are highly influenced by the environment.

Cephalocaudal Referring to the direction of development beginning with the head and proceeding outward toward the tail. Early infant development is cephalocaudal because children acquire control over their heads prior to acquiring control over their limbs.

Cervix The small circular opening to the womb (uterus) that dilates considerably during birth to permit passage of the baby.

Chorion biopsy A procedure where samples of the membrane lining the uterus are used to permit prenatal diagnosis of potential birth defects.

Chromosomal disorders Chromosomal errors sometimes evident in the presence or absence of extra chromosomes or portions thereof.

Chromosome A microscopic body in the nucleus of all human and plant cells containing the genes — the carriers of heredity. Each mature human sex cell (sperm or ovum) contains 23 chromosomes, each containing countless numbers of genes. (See *genes.*)

Chunking A memory strategy that involves grouping related items of information in an attempt to make them easier to remember.

Classical conditioning Also called learning through stimulus substitution because it involves the repeated pairing of two stimuli so that a previously neutral (conditioned) stimulus eventually comes to elicit the same response (conditioned response) that was previously evoked by the first stimulus (unconditioned stimulus). This type of conditioning was first described by Pavlov.

Cocaine A stimulant drug, ordinarily inhaled as a white powder, the primary effects of which are feelings of euphoria. Possible effects also include hallucinations. In some forms (freebase or as what is called "crack" or "rock"), its effects are more immediate and more intense, and its use leads more readily to psychological dependence.

Cognition Mental processes such as thinking, knowing, and remembering. Theories of cognition attempt to explain intellectual development and functioning.

Cognitive strategies Procedures, knowledge, and information that relate to the processes involved in learning and remembering rather than to the content of what is learned. Cognitive strategies have to do with identifying problems, selecting approaches to their solution, monitoring progress, and using feedback. They are closely related to metacognition and metamemory.

Cohort A group of individuals who have in common the fact that they were born within the same range of time.

Comic book A collection of cartoon stories, most of which are not comic and many of which are characterized by violence.

Communication The transmission of messages. Communication does not require language, although it is greatly facilitated by it. Lower animals communicate although they do not possess language.

Compensation A logical rule relating to the fact that certain changes can compensate for opposing changes, thereby negating their effect. For example, as a square object becomes longer, it also becomes thinner. Increases in length compensate for decreases in width. These changes combine to negate any actual changes in mass.

Concept A collection of perceptual experiences or ideas related by virtue of their possessing common properties.

Conceptualization The forming of concepts (ideas or meanings). An intellectual process leading to thinking and understanding.

Concrete operations The third of Piaget's four major developmental stages, lasting from age 7 or 8 to approximately 11 or 12, characterized primarily by the child's ability to deal with concrete problems and objects or objects and problems easily imagined in a concrete sense.

Conditioned response A response that is elicited by a conditioned stimulus. A conditioned response resembles its corresponding unconditioned response. The two are not identical, however.

Conditioned stimulus A stimulus that does not elicit any response or elicits a global response initially, but as a result of being paired with an unconditioned stimulus and its response acquires the capability of eliciting that same response. For example, a stimulus that is always present at the time of a fear reaction may become a conditioned stimulus for fear.

Conditioning A term used to describe a simple type of learning whereby certain behaviors are determined by the environment. (See also *classical conditioning, operant conditioning.*)

Conservation A Piagetian term implying that certain quantitative attributes of objects remain unchanged unless something is added to or taken away from them. Such characteristics of objects as mass, number, area, and volume are capable of being conserved.

Contextual model A developmental model that emphasizes the importance of the individual's interaction with environmental *context*. It looks at the historical period in which individuals are raised, as well as at the unique experiences they have.

Control group Consists of subjects who are not experimented with but who are used as comparisons to the experimental group to ascertain whether the outcomes were affected by the experimental procedure.

Correlation A mathematical measure of a relationship among variables. It is usually expressed as a number ranging from + 1.00 (a perfect positive relationship) through 0 (no relationship) to − 1.00 (a perfect inverse relationship).

Correlational studies Studies that attempt to determine the extent to which two or more variables covary. Correlational research cannot establish cause-and-effect relationships.

Critical period The period during which an appropriate stimulus must be presented to an organism for imprinting to occur.

Cross-sectional study A technique in the investigation of child development that involves observing and comparing different subjects at different age levels. A cross-sectional study would compare 4- and 6-year-olds by observing two groups of children at the same time, one group consisting of 6-year-old children and the other of 4-year-old children. A longitudinal study would require that the same children be examined at the age of 4 and again at age 6.

Crystallized abilities Cattell's term for intellectual abilities that are highly dependent on experience (verbal and computational skills and general information, for example). These abilities may continue to improve well into old age. (See *fluid abilities.*)

Culture-fair tests Psychological tests designed to measure accurately among individuals whose cultures are different. Although no test is absolutely free from cultural bias, some are more fair than others to disadvantaged groups.

Defense mechanism A relatively irrational and sometimes unhealthy method employed by people to compensate for their inability to satisfy their basic desires and to overcome the anxiety accompanying this inability.

Deferred imitation Imitating people or events in their absence. Deferred imitation is assumed by Piaget to be critical to developing language abilities.

Delivery The second stage of labor, beginning with the baby's head emerging (in a normal delivery) at the cervical opening and terminating with the birth of the child.

Deoxyribonucleic acid (DNA) A substance assumed to be the basis of all life, consisting of four chemical bases arranged in an extremely large number of combinations. The two strands of the DNA molecule that compose genes are arranged in the form of a double spiral (helix). These double strands are capable of replicating themselves as well as crossing over from one strand of the spiral to the other and forming new combinations of their genetic material. The nuclei of all cells contain DNA molecules.

Dependent variable The variable that may or may not be affected by manipulations of the independent variable in an experimental situation. (See *independent variable, variable.*)

Development The total process whereby individuals adapt to their environment. Development includes growth, maturation, and learning.

Developmental psychology That aspect of psychology concerned with the development of individuals.

Diabetes An insulin deficiency disease, some forms of which are associated with a recessive gene.

Diary description A method of child study that records sequential descriptions of a child's behavior at predetermined intervals (daily or weekly, for example). Sometimes useful for arriving at a better understanding of general developmental patterns.

Diethylstilbestrol (DES) A drug once widely prescribed to lessen the probability of miscarriages. It has been linked with medical problems in offspring.

Dilation and curettage (D&C) A surgical procedure that involves scraping the walls of the uterus. It is occasionally necessary after birth if all of the placenta has not been expelled.

Dominant gene The gene (carrier of heredity) that takes precedence over all other related genes in genetically determined traits. Because all genes in the fertilized egg occur in pairs (one from the male and one from the female), the presence of a dominant gene as one member of the pair of genes means that the hereditary characteristic that it controls will be present in the individual. (See *recessive gene.*)

Double-blind procedure An experimental method where neither subjects nor experimenters involved in data collection or analysis are aware of which subjects are members of experimental groups and which are not. Double-blind procedures are employed as a safeguard against experimenter and subject bias.

Double helix The natural state of DNA molecules. Essentially, two spiralling, intertwining chains of corresponding molecules.

Down syndrome The most common chromosomal birth defect, related to the presence of an extra twenty-first chromosome (technically labeled *trisomy 21*) and sometimes evident in mild to severe mental retardation.

Drug abuse The continued use of drugs in spite of persistent physical, social, psychological, or occupational problems that result.

Drug dependence Drug dependence is marked by a preoccupation with obtaining a drug, a compulsion to use it, and relapse following attempts to cease using it.

Drugs Chemical substances that have marked physiological effects on living organisms.

Drug tolerance Physiological changes following drug use that lead to higher doses of the drug being required to achieve the same effect.

Dyad A group of two people in interaction. A *triad* consists of three people.

Dyslexia A form of learning disability manifested in reading problems of varying severity. Dyslexia may be evident in spelling errors that are erratic rather than consistent.

Ecological validity An expression sometimes used to refer to the fact that psychological phenomena are highly dependent on environmental factors. For example, cultural, social, and other systems affect our behavior. More precisely, a generalization is said to be ecologically valid to the extent that it takes environmental circumstances into account.

Egg cell (See *ovum.*)

Ego The second stage of the human personality, according to Freud. It is the rational, reality-oriented level of human personality, which develops as the child becomes aware of what the environment makes possible and impossible and therefore serves as a damper to the id. The id tends toward immediate gratification of impulses as they are felt, whereas the ego imposes restrictions that are based on environmental reality. (See *id, superego.*)

Egocentric speech Vygotsky's intermediate stage of language development, common between ages 3 and 7, during which children often talk to themselves in an apparent effort to control their own behavior. (See *inner speech, social speech.*)

Elaborated language code A phrase employed by Bernstein to describe the language of middle- and upper-class children. Elaborated language codes are grammatically correct, complex, and precise. (See *restricted language code.*)

Electra complex A Freudian stage occurring around the age of 4 or 5 years, when a girl's sexual feelings lead her to desire her father and to become jealous of her mother. (See *Oedipus complex.*)

Elicited response A response brought about by a stimulus. The expression is synonymous with the term *respondent.*

Eliciting effect That type of imitative behavior in which the observer does not copy the model's responses but simply behaves in a related manner. (See *inhibitory-disinhibitory effect, modeling effect.*)

Embryo stage The second stage of prenatal development, beginning around the first week after conception and terminating at the end of the sixth week.

Emitted response A response not elicited by a known stimulus but simply emitted by the organism. An emitted response is an operant.

Encode Change into a form that can be represented in memory.

Environment The significant aspects of an individual's surroundings. Includes all experiences and events that influence the child's development.

Epigenesis The developmental unfolding of genetically influenced characteristics.

Episiotomy A small cut made in the vaginal opening to facilitate the birth of a child. An episiotomy prevents the tearing of membranes and ensures that once the cut has been sutured healing will be rapid and complete.

Equilibration A Piagetian term for the process by which we maintain a balance between assimilation (using old learning) and accommodation (changing behavior; learning new things). Equilibration is essential for adaptation and cognitive growth.

Ethology The science concerned with the study of behavior in natural settings.

Eugenics A form of genetic engineering that selects specific individuals for reproduction. Applying eugenics to humans raises a number of serious moral and ethical questions. It is widely accepted and practiced with animals, however.

Event sampling A method of child study in which specific behaviors are observed and recorded and unrelated behaviors are ignored.

Exceptionality A category used to describe physical, social, or intellectual abilities and performance that are significantly above or below average.

Existential psychology A philosophical-psychological movement characterized by a preoccupation with existence. Existential philosophers describe the human condition in such terms as abandonment, loneliness, despair, and alienation. These feelings are purported to result from individuals' lack of knowledge about their origin and eventual end. Hence the term *existentialism*, because the only knowable reality is existence.

Exosystem Interactions between a system in which the child is involved (microsystem) and another system that does not ordinarily include the child (father's relationships with employers, for example).

Experiment A procedure for scientific investigation requiring manipulation of some aspects of the environment to determine what the effects of this manipulation will be.

Experimental group A group of subjects who undergo experimental manipulation. The group to which something is done in order to observe its effects. (See *control group.*)

Extended family A large family group consisting of parents, children, grandparents, and occasionally uncles, aunts, cousins, and so on. (See *nuclear family.*)

Fairy tales Stories, many of which have very ancient origins, frequently told to young children. Fairy tales are only infrequently about fairies, although many end with "and they lived happily ever after."

Many are characterized by violence and by the description of fear-inducing situations.

Fallopian tube One of two tubes that link the ovaries and the uterus. Fertilization (conception) ordinarily occurs in the Fallopian tubes. From there the fertilized egg cell moves into the uterus and attaches to the uterine wall.

Fertilization The union of sperm and ovum; the beginning of life.

Fertilized ovum stage (also **germinal** stage) The first stage of prenatal development, beginning at fertilization and ending at approximately the second week.

Fetal alcohol syndrome A collection of symptoms in the newborn associated with maternal alcohol consumption during pregnancy and sometimes evident in varying degrees of neurological, mental, and physical problems.

Fetoscopy A surgical procedure that allows the physician to see the fetus while obtaining samples of tissue for determining its status.

Fetus An immature child in the uterus. Fetal development begins approximately six weeks after conception and lasts until the birth of the baby.

Fluid abilities Cattell's term for intellectual abilities that seem to underlie much of our intelligent behavior and that are not highly affected by experience (general reasoning, attention span, memory for numbers). Fluid abilities are more likely to decline in old age than are crystallized abilities. (See *crystallized abilities.*)

Forceps Clamplike instruments that sometimes assist in the delivery of a baby.

Formal operations The last of Piaget's four major developmental stages. It begins around the age of 11 or 12 and lasts until about 14 or 15. It is characterized by the child's increasing ability to use logical thought processes.

Fragile X syndrome A sex-linked primarily male disorder that increases with the mother's age and that is often manifested in mental retardation.

Fraternal twins Twins whose genetic origins are two different eggs. Such twins are as genetically dissimilar as average siblings. (See *identical twins.*)

Frustration An affective (emotional) reaction to the inability to gratify one's desires.

Gametes Mature sex cells. In humans, the egg cell (ovum) and the sperm cell.

Gender roles The particular combination of attitudes, behaviors, and personality characteristics that a culture considers appropriate for the individual's anatomical sex — what is considered masculine or feminine. Also termed *sex roles.*

Gender typing Learning behavior according to the sex of the individual. The term refers specifically to the acquisition of masculine behavior for a boy and feminine behavior for a girl.

General factor theory A theory of intelligence based on the assumption that there is a basic, underlying quality of intellectual functioning that determines *intelligence* in all areas. This quality is sometimes labeled g. (See *special abilities theory.*)

Generalizability The extent to which conclusions can be applied (generalized) from one situation to others. The generality of conclusions.

Generalized reinforcer A stimulus that, through learning, is reinforcing for a wide variety of behaviors. Such consequences of behavior as praise, social prestige, money, and power are important generalized reinforcers for human behavior.

Generation gap A cliché referring generally to the conflict that exists between the established generation and the one still growing.

Genes The carriers of heredity. Each of the 23 chromosomes contributed by the sperm cell and the ovum at conception is believed to contain between 40,000 and 60,000 genes. (See *dominant gene, recessive gene.*)

Genetics The science that studies heredity.

Genital stage The last of Freud's stages of psychosexual development, beginning around the age of 11 and lasting until around 18. It is characterized by involvement with normal adult modes of sexual gratification.

Genitalia A term referring generally to sex organs.

Genome The complete set of genetic instructions contained in our genes.

Genotype Our inherited chromosomal or genetic makeup.

Gestation period The period of time between conception and birth (typically 266 days for humans).

Growth Ordinarily, such physical changes as increasing height or weight.

Hawthorne effect The observation that members of experimental groups sometimes seem to improve their performance simply because they know they are participating in an experiment.

Head-turning reflex A reflex elicited in infants by stroking the cheek or the corner of the mouth. Infants turn their heads toward the side being stimulated.

Heredity The transmission of physical and personality characteristics and predispositions from parent to offspring.

Humanism A philosophical and psychological orientation primarily concerned with the worth of humans as individuals and processes that augment their human qualities.

Huntington's disease An inherited neurological disorder characterized by neural degeneration, typically beginning between the ages of 20 and 40 and usually leading to death.

Hypothesis An assumption, prediction, or tentative conclusion that may be tested through the application of the scientific method.

Id One of the three levels of the human personality, according to Freudian theory. The id is defined as all the instinctual urges to which humans are heir and is the source of all human motives. A newborn child's personality, according to Freud, is all id.

Identical twins Twins whose genetic origin is a single egg. Such twins are genetically identical (See *fraternal twins*).

Identification A general term referring to the process of assuming the goals, ambitions, mannerisms, and so on of another person — of identifying with that person. (See *imitation.*)

Identity A logical rule specifying that certain activities leave objects or situations unchanged. (See *reversibility.*)

Imaginary audience An expression of adolescent egocentrism; an imagined collection of all who might be concerned with the adolescent's self and behavior.

Imitation The complex process of learning through observation of a model.

Immature birth A miscarriage occuring sometime between the twentieth and the twenty-eighth weeks of pregnancy and resulting in the birth of a fetus weighing between 1 and 2 pounds.

Imprinting An instinctlike type of learning that occurs shortly after birth in certain species and that is seen in the "following" behavior of young ducks or geese.

In utero A common medical term meaning "in the uterus."

Independent variable The variable in an experiment that can be manipulated to observe its effect on other variables. (See *dependent variable, variable.*)

Individuation The recognition of one's own individuality.

Infancy A period of development that begins a few weeks after birth and lasts until approximately 2 years of age.

Infanticide The murder of a child.

Information-processing approach Psychological theories that attempt to explain cognitive processes such as remembering, decision making, or problem solving. They are concerned primarily with how information is processed (organized, rehearsed) and stored.

Inhibitory-disinhibitory effect The suppression (inhibition) or appearance (disinhibition) of previously acquired deviant behavior.

Inner speech Vygotsky's final stage in the development of speech, attained at around age 7, and characterized by silent "self-talk," the *stream-of-consciousness* flow of verbalizations that give direction and substance to our thinking and behavior. Inner speech is involved in all higher mental functioning. (See *egocentric speech, social speech.*)

Intelligence A property measured by intelligence tests. Seems to refer primarily to the capacity of individuals to adjust to their environment.

Intelligence Quotient (IQ) A way of describing intelligence by assigning it a number. May be arrived at by giving tests to estimate mental age, and then multiplying the ratio of mental to chronological age by 100. Average IQ is therefore 100.

Intrauterine Within the uterus.

Intuitive thinking Thought in children from ages 4 to 7 based on immediate comprehension rather than logical processes. Also characterized by difficulties in class inclusion, egocentricity, and marked reliance on perception.

Labor The process during which the fetus, the placenta, and other membranes are separated from the woman's body and expelled. The termination of labor is usually birth.

Language Complex arrangements of arbitrary sounds that have accepted referents and can therefore be used for communication among humans.

Lanugo Downy, soft hair that covers the fetus. Lanugo grows over most of the child's body sometime after the fifth month of pregnancy and is usually shed during the seventh month. However, some lanugo is often present at birth, especially on the infant's back.

Latency stage The fourth of Freud's stages of psychosexual development, characterized by the development of the superego (conscience) and by loss of interest in sexual gratification. This stage is assumed to last from the age of 6 to 11 years.

Learning Includes all changes in behavior that are due to experience. Does not include temporary changes brought about by drugs or fatigue or changes in behavior resulting simply from maturation or growth.

Learning disability Significant impairment in a specific skill or ability in the absence of a general depression in ability to learn (mental retardation).

Libido A general Freudian term denoting sexual urges. The libido is assumed to be the source of energy for sexual urges. Freud considered these urges the most important force in human motivation.

Longitudinal study A research technique in the study of child development that observes the same subjects over a long period of time. (See *cross-sectional study.*)

Long-term memory Memory that lasts from minutes to years and that involves rehearsal and organization.

LSD-25 (d-lysergic acid diethylamide tartrate) A particularly powerful hallucinogenic drug; an inexpensive, easily made, synthetic chemical that can sometimes have profound influences on human perception. In everyday parlance it is often referred to as "acid."

Macrosystem All interactive social systems that define a culture or subculture.

Marijuana A substance derived from the hemp plant. When smoked, it ordinarily induces a pleasant emotional state.

Marker genes Genes whose presence on a chromosome is associated with a known characteristic.

Maturation A developmental process defined by changes that are relatively independent of a child's environment. Although the nature and timing of maturational changes are assumed to result from genetic predispositions, their manifestation is at least partly a function of the environment.

Mature birth The birth of an infant between the thirty-seventh and the forty-second weeks of pregnancy.

Meaning A large term whose meaning is *meaning*. Relates to the significance or sense of a thing.

Mechanistic model A model in human developmental psychology based on the belief that it is useful to view human beings in terms of their reactive, *machinelike* characteristics.

Meiosis The division of a single sex cell into two separate cells, each consisting of 23 chromosomes rather than 23 pairs of chromosomes. Meiosis therefore results in cells that are completely different, whereas mitosis results in identical cells.

Menarche A girl's first menstrual period, an event that transpires during pubescence.

Menses A monthly discharge of blood and tissue from the womb of a mature female. The term refers to menstruation.

Mental retardation A global term referring to the mental state of individuals whose intellectual development is significantly slower than that of normal children and whose ability to adapt to their environment is consequently limited.

Mesosystem Interactions among two or more microsystems (for example, family and school).

Metacognition Knowledge about knowing. As we grow and learn, we develop notions of ourselves as learners. Accordingly, we develop strategies that recognize our limitations and that allow us to monitor our progress and to take advantage of our efforts.

Metamemory The knowledge that we develop about our own memory processes — knowledge about *how* to remember rather than simply about our memories.

Metaneeds Maslow's term for higher needs. In contrast to basic needs, metaneeds are concerned not with physiological but with psychological functions. They include the need to know truth, beauty, justice, and to self-actualize. Also termed *growth needs*.

Microsystem Defined by immediate, face-to-face interactions, where everybody affects everybody (for example, child and parent).

Middle childhood An arbitrary division in the sequence of development beginning somewhere near the age of 6 and ending at approximately 12.

Mitosis The division of a cell into two identical cells. Occurs in body cells as opposed to sex cells.

Model A pattern for behavior that can be copied by someone else.

Modeling effect Imitative behavior involving the learning of a novel response. (See *eliciting effect, inhibitory-disinhibitory effect.*)

Morality The ethical aspect of human behavior. Morality is intimately bound to the development of an awareness of acceptable and unacceptable behaviors. It is therefore linked to what is often called conscience.

Moro reflex The generalized startle reaction of a newborn infant. It characteristically involves throwing out the arms and feet symmetrically and then bringing them back in toward the center of the body.

Morphemes Combinations of phonemes that make up the meaningful units of a language. (See *phonology.*)

Mother-infant bonding The emotional bond that exists between mother and infant.

Motivation Our reasons for behaving. What initiates, directs, and accounts for the cessation of behavior.

Motor development The development of such physical capabilities as walking, climbing, creeping, grasping, and handling objects.

Muscular dystrophy A degenerative muscular disorder, most forms of which are genetic, usually manifested in an inability to walk and sometimes fatal.

Nature-nurture controversy A very old argument in psychology about whether genetics (nature) or environment (nurture) is more responsible for determining development. Also called *heredity-environment question.*

Need Ordinarily, a lack or deficiency in the organism. Needs may be unlearned (for example, the need for food and water) or learned (the need for money or prestige).

Negative reinforcement A stimulus that, when it is removed from the situation, increases the probability of occurrence of the response that precedes it. A negative reinforcer is usually an unpleasant or noxious stimulus that is removed when the desired response occurs.

Neonatal abstinence syndrome Neonatal symptoms associated with narcotics use by the mother that has resulted in the newborn also being addicted. Severe cases may be fatal.

Neonate A newborn infant. The neonatal period terminates when birthweight is regained.

Neural tube defects Spinal cord defects often linked with recessive genes, sometimes evident in failure of the spine to close (spina bifida) or in the absence of portions of the brain.

Nonstandard language A variation (different dialect) of the dominant *standard* language. Nonstandard dialects are often ungrammatical and local.

Norm An average or standard way of behaving. Cultural norms, for example, refer to the behaviors expected of individuals who are members of that culture.

Normal curve A mathematical function represented in the form of a symmetrical bell-shaped curve that illustrates how a large number of naturally occurring or chance events are distributed.

Nuclear family A family consisting of a mother, a father, and their offspring. (See *extended family.*)

Object concept Piaget's expression for the child's understanding that the world is composed of objects that continue to exist quite apart from the child's immediate perception of them.

Observational learning Learning through imitation.

Obstetrics A sophisticated medical term for midwifery; the medical art and science of assisting women who are pregnant, both during pregnancy and at birth.

Oedipus complex A Freudian concept denoting the developmental stage (around 4 years) when a boy's increasing awareness of sexual feelings leads him to desire his mother and envy his father. (See *Electra complex*.)

Open systems A theory that recognizes the interactive nature of biological, psychological, and social systems, and the impossibility of predicting final outcomes with absolute **confidence** (in contrast with a *closed* system, which is completely predictable).

Operant The label employed by Skinner to describe a response not elicited by any known or obvious stimulus. Most significant human behaviors appear to be operant. Such behaviors as writing a letter or going for a walk are operants, if no known specific stimulus elicits them.

Operant conditioning A type of learning in which the probability of a response changes as a result of reinforcement. Much of the experimental work of B. F. Skinner investigates the principles of operant conditioning.

Operational thought A Piagetian developmental stage beginning around the age of 7 or 8. Specifically, an operation is a thought that is governed by certain rules of logic.

Oral stage The first stage of psychosexual development, lasting from birth to approximately 8 months of age. The oral stage is characterized by preoccupation with the immediate gratification of desires. This is accomplished primarily through the oral regions, by sucking, biting, swallowing, playing with the lips, and so on.

Organismic model This model in human development assumes that people are active rather than simply reactive and that they are therefore more like biological organisms than like machines.

Orienting response The initial response of humans and other animals to novel stimulation. Also called the orienting reflex or orientation reaction. Components of the orienting response include changes in EEG patterns, respiration rate, heart-rate, and galvanic skin response.

Ovary A female organ (most women have two of them) that produces ova (egg cells).

Ovum (plural, **ova**) The sex cell produced by a mature female approximately once every 28 days. When mature it consists of 23 chromosomes as opposed to all other human body cells (somatoplasm), which consist of 23 pairs of chromosomes. It is often referred to as an egg cell. (See *sperm cell*.)

Palmar reflex The grasping reflex that newborn infants exhibit when an object is placed in their hand.

Perception Reaction to and interpretation of physical stimulation (sensation). A conceptual process, dependent on activity of the brain.

Permissive A parenting style that may be characterized as "laissez-faire." Permissive parents are nonpunitive and undemanding. Their children are autonomous rather than obedient and, as such, are responsible for their own decisions and actions.

Personal fable An expression of adolescent egocentrism marked by the elaboration of fantasies, the hero of which is the adolescent.

Phallic stage The third stage of Freud's theory of psychosexual development. It begins at about the age of 18 months and lasts to the age of approximately 6 years. During this stage children become concerned with their genitals and may show evidence of the much-discussed complexes labeled *Oedipus* and *Electra*. (See *Electra complex, Oedipus complex*.)

Phenotype Manifest characteristics related to genetic makeup.

Phenylketonuria (PKU) A genetic disorder associated with the presence of two recessive genes.

Phoneme The simplest unit of language, consisting of a single sound such as a vowel.

Phonology The phonemes or sounds of a language.

Phrase structure rules The implicit (or explicit) rules that govern the formation of correct phrases. For example, a phrase structure rule might specify that correct noun phrases may consist of a noun; an article and a noun; an article, an adjective, and a noun; a pronoun; and so on.

Physiological dependence Commonly called *addiction*; refers to physiological changes following drug use such that stopping use leads to withdrawal symptoms.

Placenta A flat, thick membrane attached to the inside of the uterus during pregnancy and to the developing fetus. The placenta connects the mother and the fetus by means of the umbilical cord, through which the fetus receives nourishment.

Play Activities that have no goal other than the enjoyment derived from them.

Populations Collections of individuals (or objects or situations) with similar characteristics.

Positive reinforcement A stimulus that increases the probability of a response recurring as a result of being added to a situation after the response has occurred. It usually takes the form of a pleasant stimulus (*reward*) that results from a specific response.

Positive symptoms Symptoms of pregnancy that determine positively that the woman is bearing a child. These include fetal heartbeat, the ability to feel the fetus by palpating the woman's stomach, X-rays, and ultrasound.

Postmature birth The birth of an infant after the forty-second week of pregnancy.

Pragmatics In reference to language development, implicit rules that tell children when and how to speak.

Preconcept The label given to the preconceptual child's incomplete understanding of concepts, resulting from an inability to reason correctly about related classes. (See *preconceptual thought.*)

Preconceptual thought The first substage of the period of preoperational thought, beginning around 2 and lasting until 4. It is so called because the child has not yet developed the ability to classify and therefore has an incomplete understanding of concepts. (See *preconcept.*)

Pregnancy The condition of a woman who has had an ovum (egg cell) fertilized and who, nature willing, will eventually give birth.

Premature birth The birth of a baby between the twenty-ninth and thirty-sixth weeks of pregnancy. A premature baby weighs somewhere between 2 and 5½ pounds and is seldom capable of surviving if less than 2 pounds.

Prenatal development The period of development beginning at conception and ending at birth. That period lasts approximately nine calendar months in the human female (266 days). Chickens develop considerably faster.

Preoperational thought The second of Piaget's four major stages, lasting from about 2 to 7 or 8 years. It consists of two substages: intuitive thinking and preconceptual thinking. (See *intuitive thinking, preconceptual thought.*)

Primary circular reaction An expression used by Piaget to describe a simple reflex activity (such as thumb-sucking) that serves as a stimulus for its own repetition. (See *secondary circular reaction, tertiary circular reaction.*)

Primary reinforcer A stimulus that is reinforcing in the absence of any learning. Such stimuli as food and drink are primary reinforcers because presumably an organism does not have to learn that they are pleasurable.

Primary sexual characteristics Changes of sexual maturation involved in the production of offspring (for example, the ability of the testes to produce sperm and of the ovaries to produce ova).

Productiveness The quality of language that allows its users to *produce* an almost unlimited range of meanings simply by combining words and using pauses, intonations, and so on, in different ways.

Prolapsed cord A condition that sometimes occurs during birth when the umbilical cord becomes lodged between the infant's body and the birth canal, cutting off the infant's supply of oxygen. The effect may be brain damage of varying severity, depending on the length of time until delivery following prolapsing of the cord.

Proteins A molecule made up of chains of one or more amino acids. In a sense, proteins are the basis of organic life.

Proximodistal Literally, from near to far. Refers to a developmental progression where central organs develop prior to external limbs and where the infant acquires control over muscles closer to the center of the body before acquiring control over those more peripheral.

Psycholinguistics A branch of study concerned with the relationship between language (linguistics) and development, thinking, learning, and behaving (psychology).

Psychological dependence Sometimes called *habituation*; refers to a strong desire to continue using a drug.

Psychology The science that examines human behavior (and that of animals as well).

Psychosexual development A Freudian term describing child development as a series of stages that are sexually based. (See *anal stage, genital stage, latency stage, oral stage, phallic stage.*)

Psychosocial development A term used by Erikson to describe human development as a sequence of stages involving the resolution of crises that are primarily social.

Puberty Sexual maturity following pubescence.

Pupillary reflex An involuntary change in the size of the pupil as a function of brightness or darkness. The pupillary reflex is present in the neonate.

Quickening The name given to the first movements of the fetus in utero. Quickening does not occur until after the fifth month of pregnancy.

Rabbit test A once-common test for pregnancy that required sacrificing a virgin rabbit or mouse. It has been replaced by highly reliable, inexpensive, easily performed chemical tests that can be conducted much earlier than could the rabbit test.

Reaction range All the possible outcomes for a particular characteristic given variations in the nature and timing of environmental influences.

Recessive gene A gene whose characteristics are not manifest in the offspring unless it happens to be paired with another recessive gene. When a recessive gene is paired with a dominant gene, the characteristics of the dominant gene will be manifest.

Reinforcement The effect of a reinforcer — an increase in the probability of a response recurring. (See *negative reinforcement, positive reinforcement, reinforcer, reward.*)

Reinforcer A reinforcing stimulus.

Reliable A measure is reliable to the extent that it measures accurately whatever it measures.

Replicability A crucial quality of valid scientific or experimental procedures. A procedure is said to be replicable when it can be repeated and the results of so doing are identical (or highly similar) with each repetition.

Respondent A term employed by Skinner in contrast to the term *operant* (also synonymous with *elicited response*). A respondent is a response elicited by a known specific stimulus. Unconditioned responses of the type referred to in classical conditioning are examples of respondents.

Restricted language code A term employed by Bernstein to describe the language typical of the lower-class child. Restricted language codes are characterized by short and simple sentences, general and relatively imprecise terms, idiom and colloquialism, and incorrect grammar. (See *elaborated language code.*)

Reversibility A logical property manifested in the ability to reverse or undo activity either empirically or conceptually. An idea is said to be reversible when a child can imagine its opposite, and realize that certain logical consequences follow from doing so.

Reward An object, stimulus, event, or outcome that is perceived as pleasant and may therefore be reinforcing.

Rite of passage Ritualistic ceremony marking the passage from childhood to adulthood in many primitive societies.

Schemata In information-processing theory, a global term used as a metaphor for concepts. Schemata are what we know about things.

Scheme (also **schema** or **schemata**) The label employed by Piaget to describe a unit in cognitive structure. A scheme is, in one sense, an activity together with its structural connotations. In another sense, scheme may be thought of as an idea or a concept. It usually labels a specific activity: the looking scheme, the grasping scheme, the sucking scheme.

Script A term used to describe our knowledge of what goes with what and in what sequence. Scripts are that part of cognitive structure which deals with the routine and the predictable.

Secondary circular reaction Infant responses that are circular in the sense that the response serves as a stimulus for its own repetition and secondary because the responses do not center on the child's body, as do primary circular reactions. (See *primary circular reaction, tertiary circular reaction.*)

Secondary sexual characteristics Changes of pubescence that accompany maturation of the sexual organs (for example, growth of facial hair, development of breasts, voice changes).

Self The concept that an individual has of himself or herself. Notions of the self are often closely allied with individuals' beliefs about how others perceive them.

Self-actualization The process or act of becoming oneself, developing one's potentiality, achieving an awareness of one's identity, fulfilling oneself. The term *actualization* is central to humanistic psychology.

Self-concept The ideas an individual has of him- or herself. Notions of the self reflect what we think others think of us, our own estimates of what we are relative to what we would like to be, and our estimates of our competence and "goodness" in various important areas.

Self-efficacy Describes our estimates of our personal effectiveness. The most *efficacious* individuals are those who deal most effectively with a variety of situations, especially those that are ambiguous or stressful.

Self-esteem The individuals opinion of his or her own behavior and person.

Self-referent Ideas or thoughts that have to do with the self and, specifically, with self-knowledge. Self-referent thoughts are often evaluative; they deal with our personal estimates of how effective we are in our dealings with the world and with others (see *self-efficacy*).

Semantics The component of language that relates to meaning or significance of sounds.

Sensation The physical effect of stimulation. A physiological process dependent on activity of the senses.

Sensitive period A period during which specific experiences have their most pronounced effects — for example, the first six months of life during which the infant forms strong attachment bonds to the mother or caregiver.

Sensorimotor period The first stage of development in Piaget's classification. It lasts from birth to approximately age 2 and is so called because children understand their world primarily through their activities toward it and sensations of it.

Sensory memory The simple sensory recognition of stimuli (also called short-term sensory memory). Sensory memory requires no cognitive processing and does not involve conscious awareness.

Seriation The ordering of objects according to one or more empirical properties. To seriate is essentially to place in order.

Sex chromosome A chromosome contained in sperm cells and ova responsible for determining the sex of the offspring. Sex chromosomes produced by the female are of one variety (X); those produced by the male may be either X or Y. At fertilization (the union of sperm and ovum), an XX pairing will result in a girl; an XY pairing will result in a boy. Hence the sperm cell is essentially responsible for determining the sex of the offspring.

Sexually transmitted disease (STD) Also called *venereal diseases;* any of several dozen diseases transmitted primarily through sexual intercourse (for example, gonorrhea, herpes, chlamydia, and AIDS).

Short-term memory Information that lasts from a few seconds to a minute, requiring limited cognitive processing.

Siblings Offspring whose parents are the same. Siblings simply are brothers and sisters.

Social speech In Vygotsky's theorizing, the most primitive stage of language development, evident before the age of 3, during which the child expresses simple thoughts and emotions out loud.

The function of social speech is to control the behavior of others. (See *egocentric speech, inner speech.*)

Socialization The complex process of learning those behaviors that are appropriate within a given culture as well as those that are less appropriate. The primary agents of socialization are home, school, and peer groups.

Sociobiology A science founded on the assumption that many social behaviors are genetically based.

Sociogram A pictorial or graphic representation of the social structure of a group.

Sociometry A measurement procedure employed extensively in sociological studies to determine patterns of likes and dislikes in groups and to plot group structure.

Special abilities theory A theory of intelligence based on the assumption that intelligence consists of a number of separate factors (for example, numerical, verbal, memory) rather than a single underlying factor common to performance in all areas. (See *general factor theory.*)

Specimen description A method of child study in which detailed specific instances of a child's behavior are recorded. Useful for in-depth studies of individual children.

Sperm cell The sex cell produced by a mature male. Like egg cells (ova), sperm cells consist of 23 chromosomes rather than 23 pairs of chromosomes.

Stages Identifiable phases in the development of human beings. Such devlopmental theories as Jean Piaget's are referred to as stage theories because they describe behavior at different developmental levels.

Standard language The correct (hence standard) form of a society's dominant language; the form that is taught in schools and against which other dialects are judged for correctness.

STD See *sexually transmitted disease.*

Sucking reflex The automatic sucking response of a newborn child when the oral regions are stimulated. Nipples are particularly appropriate for eliciting the sucking reflex.

Sudden infant death syndrome (SIDS) Unexplained and unexpected infant death. The leading cause of infant death between the ages of 1 month and 1 year (not really a *cause*, since the cause remains unknown; rather, a *label*).

Suicide The deliberate taking of one's life.

Superego The third level of personality according to Freud. It defines the moral or ethical aspects of personaltiy and is in constant conflict with the id. (See *ego, id.*)

Symbolic The final stage in the development of a child's representation of the world. The term is employed by Bruner to describe a representation of the world through arbitrary symbols. Symbolic representation includes language, as well as theoretical or hypothetical systems.

Syncretic reasoning A type of semilogical reasoning characteristic of the classification behavior of the very young preschooler. In syncretic reasoning, objects are grouped according to egocentric criteria, which are subject to change from one object to the next. In other words, children do not classify on the basis of a single dimension but change dimensions as they classify.

Syntax The grammar of a language, consisting of the set of implicit or explicit rules that govern the combinations of words composing a language.

Taboo A prohibition imposed by social custom. A behavior widely accepted as forbidden and inappropriate by a culture.

Tay-Sachs disease A fatal genetic enzyme disorder that can be detected before birth, but that cannot yet be prevented or cured.

Temperament The biological basis of personality — its hereditary components. The expression *infant temperament* refers to infants' characteristic emotional responses.

Teratogens Drugs and other substances that cause fetal defects.

Teratology The study of birth defects.

Tertiary circular reaction An infant's response is circular in the sense that the response serves as the stimulus for its own repetition, but the repeated response is not identical to the first response. This last characteristic, the altered response, distinguishes a tertiary circular reaction from a secondary circular reaction. (See *primary circular reaction, secondary circular reaction.*)

Time-lag study A developmental study in which subjects of one age are compared to other groups who are also the same age, but at a different point in time (for example, comparing 12-year-olds in 1995 with 12-year-olds in 1990 and in 1985).

Time sampling A method of child observation where behavior is observed during specific time intervals, frequently with the aim of recording instances or frequency of specific behaviors.

Toddler A label sometimes used to describe the child between the ages of 18 months and 2½ years.

Transductive reasoning The type of semilogical reasoning that proceeds from particular to particular, rather than from particular to general or from general to particular. One example of transductive reasoning is the following: (1) Cows give milk. (2) Goats give milk. (3) Therefore, goats are cows.

Transformational rules Implicit (or explicit) grammatical rules that govern the alteration of expressions and their resulting meanings. For example, there is a transformational rule specifying that a declarative sentence may be transformed into a question by altering the order of the words (as in transforming "I can go" to "Can I go?").

Transitional objects Blankets, teddy bears, or other objects that children focus affection and attention on while in transition between a state of high parental dependency and the development of a more independent self.

Transverse presentation A crosswise presentation of the fetus at birth.

Trauma An injury or nervous shock. Traumatic experiences are usually intense and unpleasant.

Triarchic theory Sternberg's label for his description of intelligence. The three *arches* of human intelligence are metacomponents (cognitive strategies that have to do with identifying problems, solving them, monitoring progress, and other aspects of metacognition and metamemory); performance components (the actual execution of procedures selected at the metacomponential level); and knowlege-acquisition components (what is actually achieved in the process of learning and behaving).

Ultrasound A diagnostic technique in medicine whereby high-frequency sound waves are employed to provide images of internal body structures. Ultrasound recordings are used extensively to evaluate the condition of the fetus.

Umbilical cord A long, thick cord attached to what will be the child's navel at one end and to the placenta at the other. It transmits nourishment and oxygen to the growing fetus from the mother.

Unconditioned response A response elicited by an unconditioned stimulus.

Unconditioned stimulus A stimulus that elicits a response before learning. All stimuli capable of eliciting reflexive behaviors are examples of unconditioned stimuli. For example, food is an unconditioned stimulus for the response of salivation.

Uterus A relatively sophisticated term for the womb.

Valid A measure is said to be valid to the extent that it measures what it is intended to measure. (See *reliable.*)

Values Judgments or beliefs about the desirability of certain behaviors or goals.

Variable A property, measurement, or characteristic that is susceptible to variation. In psychological experimentation such qualities of human beings as intelligence and creativity are referred to as variables. (See *dependent variable, independent variable.*)

Vegetative reflexes Reflexes pertaining to the intake of food (for example, swallowing and sucking).

Version Turning; in obstetrics, refers to turning the child in the uterus to facilitate birth.

Visual acuity Sharpness and clarity of vision. Visual acuity is often expressed in terms of Snellen ratings where 20/20 vision is considered average (the individual can see as well at 20 feet as individuals with normal vision). Vision can be poorer than 20/20 (for example, 20/40 where the individual sees as clearly at 20 feet as people with normal vision see at 40) or better (for example, 20/15 where the individual sees as well at 20 feet as average people do at 15).

Work Activities engaged in, not primarily for the pleasure derived from them, but rather for what may be gained as as a result of the activities. (See *play.*)

Zone of proximal growth Vygotsky's phrase for the individual's current potential for further intellectual development — a capacity not ordinarily measured by conventional intelligence tests. He suggests that hints and questions might help in assessing this *zone*.

Zygote A fertilized egg cell (ovum). A zygote is formed from the union of a sperm cell and an egg cell; it contains 46 chromosomes (a full complement).

References

Abel, E. L. (1984). *Fetal alcohol syndrome and fetal alcohol effects.* New York: Plenum Press.

Abram, M. J., & Dowling, W. D. (1979). How readable are parenting books? *The Family Coordinator, 28,* 365–368.

Abroms, I. F., & Panagakos, P. G. (1980). The child with significant developmental motor disability (cerebal palsy). In A. P. Scheiner & I. F. Abroms (Eds.), *The practical management of the developmentally disabled child.* St. Louis: C. V. Mosby, 145–166.

ACOG Technical Bulletin. (1988). *Human Immune Deficiency Virus Infections.* Number 123. Washington, D.C., December.

Acredolo, L. P. (1978). Development of spatial orientation in infancy. *Developmental Psychology, 14,* 224–234.

Acredolo, L. P., & Hake, J. L. (1982). Infant perception. In B. B. Wolman (Ed.), *Handbook of developmental psychology.* Englewood Cliffs, N.J.: Prentice-Hall.

Adair, J. G., Sharpe, D., & Huynh, C. (1989). Hawthorne control procedures in educational experiments: A reconsideration of their use and effectiveness. *Review of Educational Research, 59,* 215–228.

Adams, P. L., Milner, J. R., & Schrepf, N. A. (Eds.). (1984). *Fatherless children.* New York: John Wiley.

Adams, R. E., Jr., & Passman, R. H. (1979). Effects of visual and auditory aspects of mothers and strangers on the play and exploration of children. *Developmental Psychology, 15,* 269–274.

Adams, R. E., Jr., & Passman, R. H. (1981). The effects of preparing two-year-olds for brief separations from their mothers. *Child Development, 52,* 1068–1070.

Adams, R. E., Jr., & Passman, R. H. (1983). Explaining to young children about an upcoming separation from their mother: When do I tell them? *Journal of Applied Developmental Psychology, 4,* 35–42.

Ahammer, I. M., & Murray, J. P. (1979). Kindness in the kindergarten: The relative influence of role playing and prosocial television in facilitating altruism. *International Journal of Behavior Development, 2,* 133–157.

Ahlstrom, W. M., & Havighurst, R. J. (1971). *400 losers.* San Francisco: Jossey-Bass.

AIDS fears subside but the risk remains. (1989). *Edmonton Journal,* March 13, C1.

The AIDS threat: Who's at risk? (1988). *Newsweek,* March 14, pp. 42–52.

AIDS virus strain beats pill; scientists scramble for new cure. (1989). *Edmonton Journal,* March 15, A2.

Ainsworth, L. L. (1984). Contact comfort: A reconsideration of the original work. *Psychological Reports, 55,* 943–949.

Ainsworth, M. D. S. (1973). The development of infant-mother attachment. In B. M. Caldwell & H. N. Ricciuti (Eds.), *Review of child development research* (Vol. 3). Chicago: University of Chicago Press.

Ainsworth, M. D. S. (1979). Infant-mother attachment. *American Psychologist, 34,* 932–937.

Ainsworth, M. D. S., & Bell, S. M. (1969). Some contemporary patterns of mother-infant interaction in the feeding situation. In A. Ambrose (Ed.), *Stimulation in early infancy.* New York: Academic Press.

Ainsworth, M. D. S., Blehar, M. C., Waters, E., & Wall, S. (1978). *Patterns of attachment.* Hillsdale, N.J.: Lawrence Erlbaum.

Albert, R. S., & Runco, M. A. (1986). The achievement of eminence: A model based on a longitudinal study of exceptionally gifted boys and their families. In R. J. Sternberg & J. E. Davidson (Eds.), *Conceptions of giftedness.* New York: Cambridge University Press.

Alcock, J. (1984). *Animal behavior: An evolutionary approach* (3rd ed.). Sunderland, Mass.: Sinauer.

Aldis, O. (1975). *Play fighting.* New York: Academic Press.

Allen, M. C., & Jones, M. D. (1986). Medical complications of prematurity. *Obstetrical Gynecology, 67,* 427.

Allen, R. E., & Oliver, J. M. (1982). The effects of child maltreatment on language development. *Child Abuse and Neglect, 6,* 299–305.

Allen, R. E., & Wasserman, G. A. (1985). Origins of language delay in abused infants. *Child Abuse and Neglect, 9,* 335–340.

Allison, P. D., & Furstenberg, F. F., Jr. (1989). How marital dissolution affects children: Variations by age and sex. *Developmental Psychology, 25,* 540–549.

Als, H., Tronick, E., Lester, B. M., & Brazelton, T. B. (1979). Specific neonatal measures: The Brazelton Neonatal Behavior Assessment Scale. In J. D. Osofsky (Ed.), *Handbook of infant development.* New York: John Wiley.

American Association for Protecting Children. (1987). *National estimates of child abuse and neglect reports 1976–1986.* Denver: American Humane Association.

American Humane Association. (1983). *Highlights of official child neglect and abuse reporting.* Denver: American Humane Association.

American Psychiatric Association. (1980). *Diagnostic and statistical manual of mental disorders.* Washington, D.C.: American Psychiatric Association.

American Psychiatric Association. (1987). *Diagnostic and statistical manual of mental disorders* (3rd ed., revised). Washington, D.C.: American Psychiatric Association.

Anastasi, A. (1958). Heredity, environment, and the question "how?" *Psychological Review, 65,* 197–208.

Anastasiow, N. (1984). Preparing adolescents in child bearing: Before and after pregnancy. In M. Sugar (Ed.), *Adolescent parenthood.* New York: SP Medical and Scientific Books, 141–158.

Anderson, D. R. (1979). Active and passive processes in children's television viewing. Paper presented at the annual meeting of the American Psychological Association, New York, August.

Anderson, D. R., & Bryant, J. (1983). Research on children's television viewing: The state of the art. In J. Bryant & D. R. Anderson (Eds.), *Children's understanding of television: Research on attention and comprehension.* New York: Academic Press, 331–355.

Anderson, J. A. (1983). Television literacy and the critical viewer. In J. Bryant & D. R. Anderson (Eds.), *Children's understanding of television: Research on attention and comprehension.* New York: Academic Press, 297–327.

Anderson, J. R. (1980). *Cognitive psychology and its applications.* San Francisco: W. H. Freeman.

Anthony, E. J. (Ed.). (1975). *Exploration in child psychiatry.* New York: Plenum Press.

Anthony, E. J., & Koupernik, C. (Eds.). (1974). *The child in his family: Children at psychiatric risk* (Vol. 3). New York: John Wiley.

Appel, L. F., Cooper, R. G., McCarrell, N., Sims-Knight, J., Yussen, S. R., & Flavell, J. H. (1972). The development of the distinction between perceiving and memorizing. *Child Development, 43,* 1365–1381.

Arbuthnot, J. (1975). Modification of moral judgment through role playing. *Developmental Psychology, 11,* 319–324.

Aries, P. (1962). *Centuries of childhood: A social history of family life* (R. Baldick, trans.). New York: Alfred A. Knopf. (Originally published 1960.)

Arlin, P. K. (1975). Cognitive development in adulthood: A fifth stage? *Developmental Psychology, 11,* 602–606.

Arnett, J. (1990). Contraceptive use, sensation seeking, and adolescent egocentrism. *Journal of Youth and Adolescence, 19,* 171–182.

Arnold, A. (1969). *Violence and your child.* Chicago: Henry Regnery.

Aronfreed, J. (1968). *Conduct and conscience.* New York: Academic Press.

Asher, S. R. (1983). Social competence and peer status: Recent advances and future directions. *Child Development, 54,* 1427–1434.

Asher, S. R., & Renshaw, P. (1981). Children without friends: Social knowledge and social skill training. In S. R. Asher & J. M. Gottman (Eds.), *The development of children's friendships*. New York: Cambridge University Press.

Askew, S., & Ross, C. (1988). *Boys don't cry: Boys and sexism in education*. Philadelphia, Penn.: Open University Press.

Aslin, R. N., Pisoni, D. P., & Jusczyk, P. W. (1983). Auditory development and speech perception in infancy. In M. H. Haith & J. J. Campos (Eds.), *Handbook of child psychology* (2nd ed.): *Infancy and developmental psychology*. New York: John Wiley.

Aslin, R. N., & Smith, L. B. (1988). Perceptual development. *Annual Review of Psychology, 39*, 435–473.

Asp, E., & Garbarino, J. (1988). Integrative processes at school and in the community. In T. D. Yawkey & J. E. Johnson (Eds.), *Integrative processes and socialization: Early to middle childhood*. Hillsdale, N.J.: Lawrence Erlbaum.

Athanasiou, R. (1973). A review of public attitudes on sexual issues. In J. Zubin & J. Money (Eds.), *Contemporary sexual behavior: Critical issues in the 1970's*. Baltimore: Johns Hopkins University Press.

Atkinson, R. C., & Shiffrin, R. M. (1971). The control of short-term memory. *Scientific American, 225*, 82–90.

Babad, E. Y. (1985). Some correlates of teachers' expectancy bias. *American Educational Research Journal, 22*, 175–183.

Babson, S. G., Pernoll, M. L., Benda, G. I., & Simpson, K. (1980). *Diagnostics and management of the fetus and neonate at risk: A guide for team care* (4th ed.). St. Louis: C. V. Mosby.

Baillargeon, R. (1987). Object permanence in 3½- and 4½-month-old infants. *Developmental Psychology, 23*, 655–664.

Bakan, D. (1971). *Slaughter of the innocents*. Toronto: CBC Learning Systems.

Bakeman, R., & Brownlee, J. R. (1980). The strategic use of parallel play: A sequential analysis. *Child Development, 51*, 873–878.

Baker, L., & Lyen, K. (1982). Anorexia nervosa. *Current Concepts in Nutrition, 11*, 139–149.

Baker, R. L., & Mednick, B. R. (1984). *Influences on human development: A longitudinal perspective*. Boston: Kluwer-Nijhoff Publishing.

Baker, S. A., Thalberg, S. P., & Morrison, D. M. (1988). Parents' behavioral norms as predictors of adolescent sexual activity and contraceptive use. *Adolescence, 23*, 265–282.

Bakwin, H. (1949). Psychologic aspects of pediatrics. *Journal of Pediatrics, 35*, 512–521.

Balow, B. (1980). Definitional and prevalence problems in behavior discorders of children. *School Psychology, 8*, 348–354.

Bancroft, R. (1976). Special education: Legal aspects. In P. A. O'Donnell & R. H. Bradfield (Eds.), *Mainstreaming: Controversy and consensus*. San Rafael, Calif.: Academic Therapy Publications.

Bandura, A. (1969). *Principles of behavior modification*. New York: Holt, Rinehart & Winston.

Bandura, A. (1977). *Social learning theory*. Englewood Cliffs, N.J.: Prentice-Hall.

Bandura, A. (1981). Self-referent thought: A developmental analysis of self-efficacy. In J. H. Flavell & L. Ross (Eds.), *Social cognitive development: Frontiers and possible futures*. Cambridge: Cambridge University Press.

Bandura, A. (1986). *Social foundations of thought and action: A social cognitive theory*. Englewood Cliffs, N.J.: Prentice-Hall.

Bandura, A. (1989a). Regulation of cognitive processes through perceived self-efficacy. *Developmental Psychology, 25*, 729–735.

Bandura, A. (1989b). Social cognitive theory. In R. Vasta (Ed.), *Annals of child development* (Vol. 6). Greenwich, Conn.: JAI Press.

Bandura, A., Ross, D., & Ross, S. A. (1963). Vicarious reinforcement and imitative learning. *Journal of Abnormal and Social Psychology, 67*, 601–607.

Bandura, A., & Walters, R. (1963). *Social learning and personality development*. New York: Holt, Rinehart & Winston.

Banks, M. S. (1980). The development of visual accommodation during early infancy. *Child Development, 51*, 646–666.

Banks, M. S., & Salapatek, P. (1983). Infant visual perception. In P. H. Mussen (Ed.), *Handbook of child psychology* (4th ed.) (Vol. 2). *Infancy and developmental psychobiology*. (M. M. Haith and J. J. Campos, Eds.). New York: John Wiley, 435–572.

Baran, S. J., Chase, L. J., & Courtright, J. A. (1979). Television drama as a facilitator of prosocial behavior: "The Waltons." *Journal of Broadcasting, 23*, 277–285.

Baratz, J. D. (1969). Bi-dialectical task for determining language proficiency in economically disadvantaged Negro children. *Child Development, 40,* 889–901.

Barber, T. X., & Silver, M. J. (1969a). Fact, fiction, and the experimenter bias effect. *Psychological Bulletin Monographs Supplement, 70,* 1–29.

Barber, T. X., & Silver, M. J. (1969b). Pitfalls in data analysis and interpretation: A reply to Rosenthal. *Psychological Bulletin Monographs Supplement, 70,* 48–62. (b)

Baron, M., Risch, N., Hamburger, R., Mandel, B., Kushner, S., et al. (1978). Genetic linkage between X-chromosome markers and bipolar affective illness. *Nature, 326,* 289–292.

Barr, H. M., Streissguth, A. P., Darby, B. L., & Sampson, P. D. (1990). Prenatal exposure to alcohol, caffeine, tobacco, and aspirin: Effects on fine and gross motor performance in 4-year-old children. *Developmental Psychology, 26,* 339–348.

Barss, V. A. (1989). Obstetrical management. In J. W. Hare (Ed.), *Diabetes complicating pregnancy: The Joslin Clinic Method.* New York: Alan R. Liss.

Basseches, M. (1984). *Dialectical thinking and adult development.* Norwood, N. J.: Ablex.

Bates, E. (1976). *The emergence of symbols.* New York: Academic Press.

Bates, E., Bretherton, I., Shore, D., & McNew, S. (1981). Names, gestures, and objects: The role of context in the emergence of symbols. In K. E. Nelson (Ed.), *Children's language* (Vol. 3). New York: Gardner Press.

Bates, E., Thal, D., Whitesell, K., Fenson, L., & Oakes, L. (1989). Integrating language and gesture in infancy. *Developmental Psychology, 25,* 1004–1019.

Bates, J. E. (1980). The concept of difficult temperament. *Merrill-Palmer Quarterly, 26,* 299–319.

Batson, C. D. (1990). How social an animal? The human capacity for caring. *American Psychologist, 45,* 336–346.

Baumrind, D. (1966). Effects of authoritative parental control on child behavior. *Child Development, 37,* 887–907.

Baumrind, D. (1967). Child care practices anteceding three patterns of pre-school behavior. *Genetic Psychology Monographs, 75,* 43–88.

Baumrind, D. (1971). Current patterns of parental authority. *Developmental Psychology Monographs, 4,* 1.

Baumrind, D. (1977). Some thoughts about childrearing. In S. Cohen & T. J. Comiskey (Eds.), *Child develop-* ment: Contemporary perspectives. Itasca, Ill.: F. E. Peacock.

Baxter, G., & Beer, J. (1990). Educational needs of school personnel regarding child abuse and/or neglect. *Psychological Reports, 67,* 75–80.

Bayley, N. (1969). *Bayley scales of infant development.* New York: Psychological Corp.

Becker, B. J. (1990). Item characteristics and gender differences on the SAT-M for mathematically able youths. *American Educational Research Journal, 27,* 65–87.

Beilin, H. (1989). Piagetian theory. In R. Vasta (Ed.), *Annals of child development* (Vol. 6). Greenwich, Conn.: JAI Press.

Bell, C. S., & Battjes, R. (1985). *Prevention research: Deterring drug abuse among children and adolescents.* NIDA Research Monograph 63. Rockville, Md.: National Institute on Drug Abuse.

Bell, N. J., Avery, A. W., Jenkins, D., Feld, J., & Schoenrock, C. J. (1985). Family relationships and social competence during late adolescence. *Journal of Youth and Adolescence, 14,* 109–117.

Belmont, J. M. (1989). Cognitive strategies and strategic learning: The socio-instructional approach. *American Psychologist, 44,* 142–148.

Belsky, J. (1980). Child maltreatment: An ecological integration. *American Psychologist, 35,* 320–335.

Belsky, J. (1981). Early human experience: A family perspective. *Developmental Psychology, 17,* 3–23.

Belsky, J., Lerner, R. M., & Spanier, G. B. (1984). *The child in the family.* Reading, Mass.: Addison-Wesley.

Belsky, J., & Rovine, M. J. (1988). Nonmaternal care in the first year of life and the security of infant-parent attachment. *Child Development, 59,* 157–167.

Bem, S. L. (1974). The measurement of psychological androgyny. *Journal of Consulting and Clinical Psychology, 42,* 155–162.

Benbow, C. P., & Stanley, J. C. (1983). Sex differences in mathematical reasoning: More facts. *Science, 222,* 1029–1031.

Berdine, W. H., & Blackhurst, A. E. (Eds.). (1985). *An introduction to special education* (2nd ed.). Boston: Little, Brown.

Bereiter, C., & Engelmann, S. (1966). *Teaching disadvantaged children in the preschool.* Englewood Cliffs, N.J.: Prentice-Hall.

Bereiter, C., & Engelmann, S. (1968). An academically oriented pre-school for disadvantaged children: Results from the initial experimental group. In D. W.

Brison & J. Hill (Eds.), *Psychology and early childhood education*. Ontario Institute for Studies in Education, Monograph Series, No. 4, 17–36.

Berg, W. K., & Berg, K. M. (1979). Psychophysiological development in infancy: State, sensory function, and attention. In J. D. Osofsky (Ed.), *Handbook of infant development*. New York: John Wiley.

Berg, W. K., & Berg, K. M. (1987). Psychophysiological development in infancy: State, startle, and attention. In J. D. Osofsky (Ed.), *Handbook of infant development*. New York: John Wiley.

Berkowitz, M. W., Oser, F., & Althof, W. (1987). The development of sociomoral discourse. In W. M. Kurtines & J. L. Gewirtz (Eds.), *Moral development through social interaction*. New York: John Wiley.

Berndt, T. J. (1979). Developmental changes in conformity to peer and parents. *Developmental Psychology, 15*, 608–616.

Berndt, T. J. (1988). The nature and significance of children's relationships. In R. Vasta (Ed.), *Annals of child development* (Vol. 5). Greenwich, Conn.: JAI Press.

Berne, E. (1964). *Games people play*. New York: Grove Press.

Bernstein, B. (1958). Social class and linguistic development: A theory of social learning. *British Journal of Sociology, 9*, 159–174.

Bernstein, B. (1961). Language and social class. *British Journal of Sociology, 11*, 271–276.

Bertalanffy, L. von. (1950). The theory of open systems in physics and biology. *Science, 111*, 23–29.

Beunen, G., & Malina, R. M. (1988). Growth and physical performance relative to the timing of the adolescent spurt. *Exercise and Sport Sciences Review, 16*, 503–540.

Bibby, R. W., & Posterski, D. C. (1985). *The emerging generation: An inside look at Canada's teenagers*. Toronto: Irwin Publishing.

Bijou, S. W. (1989). Behavior analysis. In R. Vasta (Ed.), *Annals of child development* (Vol. 6). Greenwich, Conn.: JAI Press.

Bijou, S. W., & Sturges, P. S. (1959). Positive reinforcement for experimental studies with children — Consumables and manipulatables. *Child Development, 30*, 151–170.

Biller, H. B. (1982). Fatherhood: Implications for child and adult development. In B. B. Wolman and others (Eds.), *Handbook of developmental psychology*. Englewood Cliffs, N.J.: Prentice-Hall.

Binder, A. (1988). Juvenile delinquency. *Annual Review of Psychology, 39*, 253–282.

Black, C., & DeBlassie, R. R. (1985). Adolescent pregnancy: Contributing factors, consequences, treatment, and plausible solutions. *Adolescence, 78*, 281–290.

Bloch, H. A., & Niederhoffer, A. (1958). *The gang: A study in adolescent behavior*. New York: Philosophical Library.

Block, J. H. (1983). Differential premises arising from differential socialization of the sexes: Some conjectures. *Child Development, 54*, 1335–1354.

Bloom, B. S. (1964). *Stability and change in human characteristics*. New York: John Wiley.

Bloom, L. (1973). *One word at a time: The use of single word utterances before syntax*. The Hague: Mouton.

Blumberg, M. L. (1974). Psychopathology of the abusing parent. *American Journal of Psychotherapy, 28*, 21–29.

Boisvert, M. J. (1972). The battered child syndrome. *Social Casework*, 475–480.

Bolton, P. J. (1983). Drugs of abuse. In D. F. Hawkins (Ed.), *Drugs and pregnancy: Human teratogenesis and related problems*. London: Churchill Livingstone, 128–154.

Bookmiller, M. M., & Bowen, G. L. (1967). *Textbook of obstetrics and obstetric nursing* (5th ed.). Philadelphia: W. B. Saunders.

Boring, E. G. (1923). Intelligence as the tests test it. *New Republic, 35*, 35–37.

Borkowski, J. G., Milstead, M., & Hale, C. (1988). Components of children's metamemory: Implications for strategy generalization. In F. E. Weinert & M. Perlmutter (Eds.), *Memory development: Universal changes and individual differences*. Hillsdale, N.J.: Lawrence Erlbaum.

Bornstein, M. H. (1979). Effects of habituation experience on posthabituation behavior in young infants: Discrimination and generalization among colors. *Developmental Psychology, 15*, 348–349.

Bornstein, M. H., & Marks, L. E. (1982, January). Color revisionism. *Psychology Today*, 64–72.

Bouchard, T. J., Jr., & McGue, M. (1981). Familial studies of intelligence: A review. *Science, 212*, 1055–1059.

Bower, T. G. R. (1971). The object in the world of the infant. *Scientific American, 225*, 30–38.

Bower, T. G. R. (1977). *The perceptual world of the child*. Cambridge, Mass.: Harvard University Press.

Bowes, W. A., Jr., Brackbill, Y., Conway, E., & Steinschneider, A. (1970). The effects of obstetrical medication on fetus and infant. *Monographs of the Society for Research in Child Development, 35*(4).

Bowlby, J. (1940). The influence of early environment. *International Journal of Psychoanalysis, 21,* 154–178.

Bowlby, J. (1953). Some pathological processes set in train by early mother-child separation. *Journal of Mental Science, 99,* 265–272.

Bowlby, J. (1958). The nature of the child's tie to his mother. *International Journal of Psychoanalysis, 39,* 350–373.

Bowlby, J. (1969). *Attachment and loss: Vol. 1. Attachment.* New York: Basic Books.

Bowlby, J. (1979). *The making and breaking of affectional bonds.* London: Tavistock Publications.

Bowlby, J. (1980). *Attachment and loss: Vol. 3. Loss, sadness and depression.* New York: Basic Books.

Bowlby, J. (1982). *Attachment and loss: Vol. 1. Attachment* (2nd ed.). London: Hogarth Press.

Bowman, J. M. (1990). Maternal blood group immunization. In R. D. Eden, F. H. Boehm, & M. Haire (Eds.), *Assessment and care of the fetus: Physiological, clinical, and medicolegal principles.* Norwalk, Conn.: Appleton & Lange.

Boyd, G. A. (1976). *Developmental processes in the child's acquisition of syntax: Linguistics in the elementary school.* Itasca, Ill.: F. E. Peacock.

Brackbill, Y. (1979). Obstetrical medication and infant behavior. In J. D. Osofsky (Ed.). *Handbook of infant development.* New York: John Wiley.

Bradley, B. S. (1989). *Visions of infancy: A critical introduction to child psychology.* Cambridge: Polity Press.

Bradshaw, G. L., & Anderson, J. R. (1982). Elaborative encoding as an explanation of levels of processing. *Journal of Verbal Learning and Verbal Behavior, 21,* 165–174.

Bransford, J. D. (1979). *Human cognition: Learning, understanding and remembering.* Belmont, Calif.: Wadsworth.

Brantner, J. P., & Doherty, M. A. (1983). A review of timeout: A conceptual and methodological analysis. In S. Axelrod & J. Apsche (Eds.), *The effects of punishment on human behavior.* New York: Academic Press.

Braun, C. (1976). Teacher expectations: Sociopsychological dynamics. *Review of Educational Research, 46,* 185–213.

Brazelton, T. D. (1973). *Neonatal behavioral assessment scale.* Philadelphia: J. B. Lippincott.

Breast milk prevents disease. (1984). *Glimpse,* Vol. 6, No. 2.

Brendt, R. L., & Beckman, D. A. (1990). Teratology. In R. D. Eden, F. H. Boehm, & M. Haire (Eds.), *Assessment and care of the fetus: Physiological, clinical, and medicolegal principles.* Norwalk, Conn.: Appleton & Lange.

Brenner, J., & Mueller, E. (1982). Shared meaning in boy toddler's peer relations. *Child Development, 53,* 380–391.

Broadbent, D. E. (1952). Speaking and listening simultaneously. *Journal of Experimental Psychology, 43,* 267–273.

Brock, D. J. H. (1982). *Early diagnosis of fetal defects.* London: Churchill Livingstone.

Broderick, P. (1986). Perceptual motor development in children's drawing skill. In C. Pratt, A. F. Garton, W. E. Tunmer, & A. R. Nesdale (Eds.), *Research issues in child development.* Boston: Allen & Unwin.

Bronfenbrenner, U. (1970). *Two worlds of childhood: U.S. and U.S.S.R.* New York: Russell Sage Foundation.

Bronfenbrenner, U. (1977a, May). Nobody home: The erosion of the American family. *Psychology Today,* 41–47.

Bronfenbrenner, U. (1977b). Is early intervention effective? In S. Cohen & T. J. Comiskey (Eds.), *Child development: Contemporary perspectives.* Itasca, Ill.: F. E. Peacock.

Bronfenbrenner, U. (1979). *The ecology of human development.* Cambridge, Mass.: Harvard University Press.

Bronfenbrenner, U. (1989). Ecological systems theory. In R. Vasta (Ed.), *Annals of child development* (Vol. 6). Greenwich, Conn.: JAI Press.

Bronfenbrenner, U., Belsky, J., & Steinberg, L. (1977). Day care in context: An ecological perspective on research and public policy. In *Policy issues in daycare.* Washington, D.C.: U.S. Department of Health, Education, & Welfare.

Bronson, G. W. (1971). Fear of the unfamiliar in human infants. In H. R. Schaffer (Ed.), *The origins of human social relations.* London: Academic Press.

Bronson, G. W. (1972). Infants' reactions to unfamiliar persons and novel objects. *Monographs of the Society for Research in Child Development, 37,* No. 3.

Brooks, J. B. (1981). *The process of parenting.* Palo Alto, Calif.: Mayfield.

Brooks-Gunn, J., & Furstenberg, F. F., Jr. (1986). The children of adolescent mothers: Physical, academic, and psychological outcomes. *Developmental Review, 6,* 224–251.

Brooks-Gunn, J., & Furstenberg, F. F., Jr. (1989). Adolescent sexual behavior. *American Psychologist, 44,* 249–257.

Brophy, J. E., & Good, T. L. (1974). *Teacher-student relationships: Causes and consequences.* New York: Holt, Rinehart & Winston.

Brown, J., & Finn, P. (1982). Drinking to get drunk: Findings of a survey of junior and senior high school students. *Journal of Alcohol and Drug Education, 27,* 13–25.

Brown, J. L. (1964). States in newborn infants. *Merrill-Palmer Quarterly, 10,* 313–327.

Brown, R. (1973). *A first language: The early stages.* Cambridge, Mass.: Harvard University Press.

Browne Miller, A. (1990). *The day care dilemma: Critical concerns for American families.* New York: Plenum Press.

Brownell, K. D., & Wadden, T. A. (1984). Confronting obesity in children: Behavioral and psychological factors. *Pediatric Annals, 13,* 473–480.

Bruininks, R. H. (1977). *Manual for the Bruininks-Oseretsky Test of Motor Proficiency.* Circle Pines, Minn.: American Guidance Service.

Bruner, J. S. (1977). Early social interaction and language acquisition. In H. R. Schaffer (Ed.), *Studies in mother-infant interaction.* London: Academic Press.

Bruner, J. S. (1978). Learning the mother tongue. *Human Nature,* September, 43–49.

Bruner, J. S. (1983). *Child's talk.* New York: W. W. Norton.

Bruner, J. S. (1985). Models of the learner. *Educational Researcher, 14,* 5–8.

Buber, M. (1958). *I and thou.* New York: Charles Scribner's.

Buber, M. (1965). *The knowledge of man* (M. Friedman, Ed.). New York: Harper & Row.

Buis, J. M., & Thompson, D. N. (1989). Imaginary audience and personal fable: A brief review. *Adolescence, 24,* 773–781.

Bullinger, A. (1985). The sensorimotor nature of the infant visual system: Cognitive problems. In V. L. Shulman, L. C. R. Restaino-Baumann, & L. Butler (Eds.),

The future of Piagetian theory: The neo-Piagetians. New York: Plenum Press.

Buss, A. H., & Plomin, R. (1985). *Temperament: Early developing personality traits.* Hillsdale, N.J.: Lawrence Erlbaum.

Butler, J. R., & Burton, L. M. (1990). Rethinking teenage childbearing: Is sexual abuse a missing link? *Family Relations, 39,* 73–80.

Byrne, B. M., & Shavelson, R. J. (1987). Adolescent self-concept: Testing the assumption of equivalent structure across gender. *American Educational Research Journal, 24,* 365–385.

Cairns, R. B. (1983). The emergence of developmental psychology. In P. H. Mussen (Ed.), *Handbook of child psychology* (4th ed.) (Vol. 1): *History, theory, and methods* (W. Kessen, Ed.). New York: John Wiley, 41–102.

Cairns, R. B., Gariépy, J. L., & Hood, K. E. (1990). Development, microevolution, and social behavior. *Psychological Review, 97,* 49–65.

Cairns, R. B., & Valsiner, J. (1984). Child psychology. *Annual Review of Psychology, 35,* 553–577.

Caldwell, B. M. (1980). Balancing children's rights and parents' rights. In R. Haskins & J. J. Gallagher (Eds.), *Care and education of young children in America: Policy, politics and social science.* Norwood, N.J.: Ablex.

Caldwell, B. M. (1989). Achieving rights for children: Role of the early childhood profession. *Childhood Education, 66,* 4–7.

Caldwell, J. C. (1986). Routes to low mortality in poor countries. *Population and Development Review, 12,* 171–214.

Calfee, R. (1981). Cognitive psychology and educational practice. In D. C. Berliner (Ed.), *Review of Research in Education* (Vol. 9). Washington, D.C.: American Educational Research Association.

Campbell, B. A., & Randall, P. J. (1977). Paradoxical effects of amphetamine on preweanling and postweanling rats. *Science, 195,* 888–891.

Campos, J. J., Barrett, K. C., Lamb, M. E., Goldsmith, H. H., & Sternberg, C. (1983). Socioemotional development. In P. H. Mussen (Ed.), *Handbook of child psychology* (4th ed.) (Vol. 2): *Infancy and developmental psychobiology* (M. M. Haith & J. J. Campos, Eds.). New York: John Wiley, 783–916.

Campos, J. J., Langer, A., & Krowitz, A. (1970). Cardiac response on the visual cliff in prelocomotor human infants. *Science, 170,* 196–197.

Cannabis (marijuana and hashish). (1976). Edmonton, Alberta: Alberta Alcoholism & Drug Abuse Commission, Public Information Series.

Carey, E. J. B., Miller, C. L., & Widlak, F. W. (1975). Factors contributing to child abuse. *Nursing Research, 24*, 293–295.

Carey, S. T. (1987). Reading comprehension in first and second languages of immersion and Francophone students. *Canadian Journal for Exceptional Children, 3*, 103–108.

Carey, W. B. (1989). Introduction: Basic issues. In W. B. Carey & S. C. McDevitt (Eds.), *Clinical and educational applications of temperament research*. Berwyn, Penn.: Swets North America.

Carlson, P., & Anisfeld, M. (1969). Some observations on the linguistic competence of a two year old child. *Child Development, 40*, 572–574.

Carroll, D. W. (1986). *Psychology of language*. Monterey, Calif.: Brooks/Cole.

Carroll, J. L., & Rest, J. R. (1982). Moral development. In B. B. Wolman and others (Eds.), *Handbook of developmental psychology*. Englewood Cliffs, N.J.: Prentice-Hall.

Cartwright, D. S., Tomson, B., & Schwartz, H. (1975). *Gang delinquency*. Monterey, Calif.: Brooks/Cole.

Caruso, D. A. (1989). Quality of day care and home-reared infants' interaction patterns with mothers and day care providers. *Child and Youth Care Quarterly, 18*, 176–179.

Case, R. (1985). *Intellectual development: A systematic reinterpretation*. New York: Academic Press.

Case, R., Hayward, S., Lewis, M., & Hurst, P. (1988). Toward a Neo-Piagetian theory of cognitive and emotional development. *Developmental Review, 8*, 1–51.

Casler, L. (1961). Maternal deprivation: A critical review of the literature. *Monograph of the Society for Research in Child Development, 26*(2).

Cattell, R. B. (1971). *Abilities: Their structure, growth, and action*. Boston: Houghton Mifflin.

Cavan, R. S., & Ferdinand, T. N. (1981). *Juvenile delinquency* (4th ed.). New Yorker: Harper & Row.

Chalfant, J. C. (1989). Learning disabilities: Policy issues and promising approaches. *American Psychologist, 44*, 392–398.

Chambliss, W. J. (1974). The state, the law, and the definition of behavior as criminal or delinquent. In D. Glaser (Ed.), *Handbook of criminology*. Chicago: Rand McNally.

Chase, N. F. (1975). *A child is being beaten*. New York: Holt, Rinehart & Winston.

Chasnoff, I. J. (1986). Perinatal addiction: Consequences of intrauterine exposure to opiate and nonopiate drugs. In I. J. Chasnoff (Ed.), *Drug use in pregnancy: Mother and child*. Boston: MTP Press.

Chasnoff, I., Burns, W., Schnoll, S., & Burns, K. (1985). Cocaine use in pregnancy. *New England Journal of Medicine, 313*, 666–669.

Cherry, E. C. (1953). Some experiments on the recognition of speech with one and two ears. *Journal of the Acoustical Society of America, 25*, 975–979.

Chess, S., & Thomas, A. (1989a). Temperament and its functional significance. In S. I. Greenspan & G. H. Pollock (Eds.), *The course of life: Vol II. Early Childhood*. Madison, Conn.: International Universities Press.

Chess, S., & Thomas, A. (1989b). The practical application of temperament to psychiatry. In W. B. Carey & S. C. McDevitt (Eds.), *Clinical and educational applications of temperament research*. Berwyn, Penn.: Swets North America.

Chez, R. A., & Chervenak, J. L. (1990). Nutrition in pregnancy. In R. D. Eden, F. H. Boehm, & M. Haire (Eds.), *Assessment and care of the fetus: Physiological, clinical, and medicolegal principles*. Norwalk, Conn.: Appleton & Lange.

Chi, M. T. H., & Glaser, R. (1980). The measurement of expertise: Analysis of the development of knowledge and skill as a basis for assessing achievement. In E. L. Baker & E. S. Quellmalz (Eds.), *Educational testing and evaluation: Design, analysis and policy*. Beverly Hills, Calif.: Sage.

Chilman, C. S. (1983). Remarriage and stepfamilies: Research results and implications. In E. D. Macklin & R. H. Rubin (Eds.), *Contemporary families and alternative lifestyles: Handbook on research and theory*. Beverly Hills, Calif.: Sage.

China fears sexual imbalance. (1983). *Edmonton Journal*, March 14, p. D-4.

Chipman, S. F. (1988). Far too sexy a topic. *Educational Researcher, 17*, 46–49.

Chlamydia — More common than gonorrhea. (1988). *Folio*. Edmonton, Alberta: University of Alberta, Nov. 24., p. 6.

Chomsky, N. (1957). *Syntactic structures*. The Hague: Mouton.

Chomsky, N. (1965). *Aspects of the theory of syntax*. Cambridge, Mass.: M.I.T. Press.

Chomsky, N. (1972). *Language and mind* (Enl. ed.). New York: Harcourt Brace Jovanovich.

Christopher, F. S., & Roosa, M. W. (1990). An evaluation of an adolescent pregnancy prevention program: Is "Just say no" enough? *Family relations, 39,* 68–72.

Christopherson, V. A. (1988). The family as a socialization context. In T. D. Yawkey & J. E. Johnson (Eds.), *Integrative processes and socialization: Early to middle childhood.* Hillsdale, N.J.: Lawrence Erlbaum.

Chugani, H. T., & Phelps, M. E. (1986). Maturational changes in cerebral function in infants determined by FGG positron emission tomography. *Science, 231,* 840–843.

Chumlea, W. C. (1982). Physical growth in adolescence. In B. B. Wolman and others (Eds.), *Handbook of developmental psychology.* Englewood Cliffs, N.J.: Prentice-Hall.

Churchill, J. A. (1965). The relationship between intelligence and birth weight in twins. *Neurology, 15,* 341–347.

Clarizio, H. F., & Yelon, S. L. (1974). Learning theory approaches to classroom management: Rationale and intervention techniques. In A. R. Brown & C. Avery (Eds.), *Modifying children's behavior: A book of readings.* Springfield, Ill.: Charles C. Thomas.

Clark, H. H., & Clark, E. V. (1977). *Psychology and language: An introduction to psycholinguistics.* New York: Harcourt Brace Jovanovich.

Clarke-Stewart, K. A. (1978). Popular primer for parents. *American Psychologist, 9,* 175–179.

Clarke-Stewart, K. A. (1984). Day care: A new context for research and development. In M. Perlmutter (Ed.), *The Minnesota symposia on child psychology: Vol. 17. Parent-child interaction and parent-child relations in child development.* Hillsdale, N.J.: Lawrence Erlbaum.

Clarke-Stewart, K. A. (1989). Infant day care: Maligned or malignant. *American Psychologist, 44,* 266–273.

Clarkson, M. G., & Berg, W. K. (1983). Cardiac orienting and vowel discrimination in newborns: Crucial stimulus parameters. *Child Development, 54,* 162–171.

Clausen, J. A. (1975). The social meaning of differential physical and sexual maturation. In S. E. Ragastin & G. H. Elder (Eds.), *Adolescence in the life cycle: Psychological change and social context.* New York: John Wiley.

Clements, S. D. (1966). *Minimal brain dysfunction in children: Terminology and identification* (NINDB Monograph No. 3). Washington, D.C.: U.S. Department of Health, Education, & Welfare.

Cobb, E. (1977). *The ecology of imagination in childhood.* New York: Columbia University Press.

Cobliner, W. G. (1988). The exclusion of intimacy in the sexuality of the contemporary college-age population. *Adolescence, 23,* 127–136.

Cohen, D. K. (1972). Does IQ matter? *Current, 141,* 19–30.

Cohen, L. B. (1979). Our developing knowledge of infant perception and cognition. *American Psychologist, 34,* 894–899.

Cohen, Y. A. (1964). *The transition from childhood to adolescence.* Chicago: Aldine.

Colby, A., & Kohlberg, L. (1984). Invariant sequence and internal consistency in moral judgment stages. In W. M. Kertines & J. L. Gewirtz (Eds.), *Morality, moral behavior, and moral development.* New York: John Wiley.

Cole, P. M. (1986). Children's spontaneous control of facial expression. *Child Development, 57,* 1309–1321.

Collins, W. A. (1983). Interpretation and inference in children's television viewing. In J. Bryant & D. R. Anderson (Eds.), *Children's understanding of television: Research on attention and comprehension.* New York: Academic Press, 125–150.

Collins, W. A., & Gunnar, M. R. (1990). Social and personality development. *Annual Review of Psychology, 41,* 387–416.

Collins, W. A., Wellman, H., Keniston, A. H., & Westby, S. D. (1978). Age-related aspects of comprehension and inference from a televised dramatic narrative. *Child Development, 49,* 389–399.

Condon, W. S., & Sander, L. W. (1974). Neonate movement is synchronized with adult speech: Interactional participation and language acquisition. *Science, 183,* 99–101.

Connell, B. (1985). A new man. In *The English Curriculum,* ILEA. London: English Centre Publication.

Cook, T. D., Appleton, H., Conner, R. F., Shaffer, A., Tamkin, G., & Weber, S. J. (1975). *"Sesame Street" revisited.* New York: Russell Sage Foundation.

Cooley, C. H. (1902). *Human nature and the social order.* New York: Charles Scribner's.

Coopersmith, S. (1967). *The antecedents of self-esteem.* San Francisco: W. H. Freeman.

Corbin, C. B. (1980). The physical fitness of children: A discussion and point of view. In C. B. Corbin (Ed.), *A textbook of motor development.* Dubuque, Iowa: Wm. C. Brown.

Côté, J. E., & Levine, C. (1988). A critical examination of the ego identity status paradigm. *Developmental Review, 8,* 147–184.

Coustan, D. R. (1990). Diabetes mellitus. In R. D. Eden, F. H. Boehm, & M. Haire (Eds.). *Assessment and care of the fetus: Physiological, clinical, and medicolegal principles.* Norwalk, Conn.: Appleton & Lange.

Cox, T. C., Jacobs, M. R., Leblanc, A. E., & Marshman, J. A. (1983). *Drugs and drug abuse: A reference text.* Toronto: Addiction Research Foundation.

Cratty, B. J. (1978). *Perceptual and motor development in infants and children* (2nd ed.). Englewood Cliffs, N.J.: Prentice-Hall.

Creasy, R. K. (1988). Preterm labor and delivery. In R. K. Creasy & R. Resnik (Eds.), *Maternal-fetal medicine; Principles and practice.* Philadelphia: W. B. Saunders.

Creasy, R. K. (1990). Preterm labor. In R. D. Eden, F. H. Boehm, & M. Haire (Eds.), *Assessment and care of the fetus: Physiological, clinical, and medicolegal principles.* Norwalk, Conn.: Appleton & Lange.

Crisp, A. H. (1980). *Let me be.* New York: Grune & Stratton.

Crisp, A. H., Palmer, R. L., & Kalucy, R. S. (1976). How common is anorexia nervosa: A prevalence study. *British Journal of Psychiatry, 128,* 549–554.

Critchley, M., & Critchley, E. A. (1978). *Dyslexia defined.* Springfield, Ill.: Charles C. Thomas.

Crockett, L. J., Losoff, M., & Petersen, A. C. (1984). Perceptions of the peer group and friendship in early adolescence. *Journal of Early Adolescence, 4,* 155–181.

Crockett, L. J., & Petersen, A. C. (1987). Pubertal status and psychosocial development: Findings from the Early Adolescence Study. In R. M. Lerner & T. T. Foch (Eds.), *Biological-psychosocial interactions in early adolescence: A life-span perspective.* Hillsdale, N.J.: Lawrence Erlbaum.

Crowley, P. A. (1983). Premature labour. In D. F. Hawkins (Ed.), *Drugs and pregnancy: Human teratogenesis and related problems.* New York: Churchill Livingstone, 155–183.

Cummins, J. (1986). Empowering minority students: A framework for intervention. *Harvard Educational Review, 56,* 18–36.

Cummins, J., & Swain, M. (1986). *Bilingualism in education: Aspects of theory, research and practice.* London: Taylor & Fry.

Curtiss, S. (1977). *Genie: A psycholinguistic study of a modern-day wild child.* New York: Academic Press.

Cusack, R. (1984). Dietary management of obese children and adolescents. *Pediatric Annals, 13,* 455–464.

Damon, W., & Colby, A. (1987). Social influence and moral change. In W. M. Kurtines & J. L. Gewirtz (Eds.), *Moral development through social interaction.* New York: John Wiley.

Dansky, J. L. (1980). Make-believe: A mediator of the relationship between play and associative fluency. *Child Development, 51,* 576–579.

Darley, J. M., & Shultz, T. R. (1990). Moral rules: Their content and acquisition. *Annual Review of Psychology, 41,* 525–556.

Darley, J. M., & Zanna, M. P. (1982). Making moral judgments. *American Scientist, 70,* 515–521.

Darling, C. A., Kallen, D. J., & Van Dusen, J. E. (1984). Sex in transition, 1900–1980. *Journal of Youth and Adolescence, 13,* 385–394.

Darnell, J., Lodish, H., & Baltimore, D. (1986). *Molecular cell biology: Revised printing with expanded index.* New York: Scientific American Books.

Darwin, D. (1877). A biographical sketch of an infant. *Mind, 2,* 285–294.

Das, J. P., & Dash, U. N. (1990). Schooling, literacy and cognitive development: A study in rural India. In C. K. Leong & B. S. Randhawa (Eds.), *Understanding literacy and cognition: Theory, research, and application.* New York: Plenum Press.

Dasen, P. R. (Ed.). (1977). *Piagetian psychology: Cross-cultural contributions.* New York: Gardner Press.

David, C. B., & David, P. H. (1984). Bottle feeding and malnutrition in a developing country: The "bottle-starved" baby. *Journal of Tropical Pediatrics,* Vol. 30.

Davis, S. M., & Harris, M. B. (1982). Sexual knowledge, sexual interests, and sources of sexual information of rural and urban adolescents from three cultures. *Adolescence, 17,* 471–492.

Dawkins, R. (1976). *The selfish gene.* New York: Oxford University Press.

DeCasper, A. J., & Fifer, W. P. (1980). Of human bonding: Newborns prefer their mother's voices. *Science, 208,* 1174–1175.

De Charms, R. (1972). Personal causation training in the schools. *Journal of Applied Social Psychology, 2,* 95–113.

DeLissovoy, V. (1973). Child care by adolescent parents. *Children Today,* July, 22–25.

DeMause, L. (1975, April). Our forebears made childhood a nightmare. *Psychology Today*, 85–88.

Dement, W. C. (1974). *Some must watch while some must sleep*. San Francisco: Newman.

Dempter, F. N. (1985). Short-term memory development in childhood. In C. J. Brainerd & M. Pressley (Eds.), *Basic processes in memory development: Progress in cognitive development research*. New York: Springer-Verlag.

DeMyer, M. K., Barton, S., DeMyer, W. E., Norton, J., Allen, J., & Steele, R. (1973). Prognosis in autism: A follow-up study. *Journal of Autism and Childhood Schizophrenia, 3*, 199–246.

Dennis, W. (1941). The significance of feral man. *American Journal of Psychology, 54*, 425–432.

Dennis, W. (1951). A further analysis of reports of wild children. *Child Development, 22*, 153–158.

deRegt, R. H., Minkoff, H. L., Feldman, J., & Schwartz, R. H. (1986). Relation of private or clinic care to the Cesarean birth rate. *The New England Journal of Medicine, 315*, 619–625.

Desor, J. A., Maller, O., & Greene, L. S. (1978). Preference for sweet in humans: Infants, children and adults. In J. M. Weiffenbach (Ed.), *Taste and development: The genesis of sweet preference*. Bethesda, Md.: National Institute of Dental Research, DHEW Publication 77-1068.

deVries, M. W. (1989). Difficult temperament: A universal and culturally embedded concept. In W. B. Carey & S. C. McDevitt (Eds.), *Clinical and educational applications of temperament research*. Berwyn, Penn.: Swets North America.

deVries, M. W., & Sameroff, A. J. (1984). Culture and temperament: Influences on infant temperament in three East African societies. *American Journal of Orthopsychiatry, 54*, 83–96.

Diaz, R. M. (1983). Thought and two languages: The impact of bilingualism on cognitive development. In E. W. Gordon (Ed.), *Review of Research in Education* (Vol. 10). Washington, D.C.: American Educational Research Association.

Dick-Read, G. (1972). *Childbirth without fear: The original approach to natural childbirth* (4th ed.) (H. Wessel & H. F. Ellis, Eds.). New York: Harper & Row.

Diener, C. I., & Dweck, C. S. (1980). An analysis of learned helplessness: II. The processing of success. *Journal of Personality and Social Psychology, 39*, 940–952.

DiLalla, L. F., & Watson, M. W. (1988). Differentiation of fantasy and reality: Preschoolers' reactions to interruptions in their play. *Developmental Psychology, 24*, 286–291.

Dinkmeyer, D., & McKay, G. (1976). *Systematic training for effective parenting (S.T.E.P.)*. Circle Pines, Minn.: American Guidance Service.

Doby, J. (1980). Firstborn fallacies. *Science, 80*, 4–10.

Dodson, F. (1970). *How to parent*. New York: New American Library.

Dodson, F. (1974). *How to father*. New York: New American Library.

Donaldson, M. (1978). *Children's minds*. London: Fontana/Croom Helm.

Donate-Bartfield, E., & Passman, R. H. (1985). Attentiveness of mothers and fathers to their baby's cries. *Infant behavior and development, 8*, 385–393.

Donovan, C. M. (1980). Program planning for the visually impaired child. In A. P. Scheiner & I. F. Abroms (Eds.), *The practical management of the developmentally disabled child*. St. Louis: C. V. Mosby, 280–289.

Dreyer, P. H. (1982). Sexuality during adolescence. In B. B. Wolman (Ed.), *Handbook of developmental psychology*. Englewood Cliffs, N.J.: Prentice-Hall.

Drugan, A., Johnson, M. P., & Evans, M. I. (1990). Amniocentesis. In R. D. Eden, F. H. Boehm, & M. Haire (Eds.), *Assessment and care of the fetus: Physiological, clinical, and medicolegal principles*. Norwalk, Conn.: Appleton & Lange.

Duberman, L. (1975). *The reconstituted family: A study of remarried couples and their children*. Chicago: Nelson-Hall.

Duffty, P., & Bryan, M. H. (1982). Home apnea monitoring in "near-miss" Sudden Infant Death Syndrome (SIDS) and in siblings of SIDS victims. *Pediatrics, 70*, 69–74.

Duncan, S., & Fiske, D. W. (1977). *Face-to-face interaction: Research methods and theory*. Hillsdale, N.J.: Erlbaum.

Dunphy, D. C. (1963). The social structure of urban adolescent peer groups. *Sociometry, 26*, 230–246.

Dweck, C. S. (1975). The role of expectations and attributions in the alleviation of learned helplessness. *Journal of Personality and Social Psychology, 31*, 674–685.

Dweck, C. S. (1986). Motivational processes affecting learning. *American Psychologist, 41*, 1040–1048.

Dweck, C. S., & Reppucci, N. D. (1973). Learned helplessness and reinforcement responsibility in children.

Journal of Personality and Social Psychology 25, 109–116.

Eccles, J. S., & Jacobs, J. E. (1986). Social forces shape math attitudes and performance. *Signs, 11*, 367–389.

Eckardt, G., Bringman, W. G., & Sprung, L. (Eds.). (1985). *Contributions to a history of developmental pschology*. Berlin: Morton.

Eckerman, C. O., & Whatley, J. L. (1975). Infants' reactions to unfamiliar adults varying in novelty. *Developmental Psychology, 11*, 562–566.

Eckland B. K. (1977). Darwin rides again. *American Journal of Sociology, 82*, 693–697.

Eden, R. D., Blanco, J. D., Tomasi, A., & Gall, S. A. (1990). Maternal-fetal infection. In R. D. Eden, F. H. Boehm, & M. Haire (Eds.), *Assessment and care of the fetus: Physiological, clinical, and medicolegal principles*. Norwalk, Conn.: Appleton & Lange.

Edmonton (Alberta) Public School Board. (1978). *Learning disability*, Fall, No. 7.

Educating against drug abuse. (1987). UNESCO, 7 place de Fontenoy, 75700, Paris.

Edwards, L., Steinman, M., Arnold, K., & Hakanson, E. (1980). Adolescent pregnancy prevention services in high school clinics. *Family Planning Perspectives, 12*, 6–14.

Egeland, B., & Sroufe, L. (1981). Attachment and early maltreatment. *Child Development, 52*, 44–52.

Egeland, B., & Vaughn, B. (1981). Failure of "bond formation" as a cause of abuse, neglect, and maltreatment. *American Journal of Orthopsychiatry, 51*, 78–84.

Egeland, J. A., Gerhard, D. S., Pauls, D. L., Sussex, J. N., Kidd, K. K., et al. (1987). Bipolar affective disorders linked to DNA markers on chromosome 11. *Nature, 325*, 783–787.

Eiger, M. S., & Olds, S. W. (1987). *The complete book of breastfeeding*. New York: Workman.

Eilers, R. E., & Minifie, F. D. (1975). Fricative discrimination in early infancy. *Journal of Speech and Hearing Research, 18*, 158–167.

Eilers, R. E., & Oller, D. K. (1988). Precursors to speech. In R. Vasta (Ed.), *Annals of child development* (Vol. 5). Greenwich, Conn.: JAI Press.

Eisenberg, N. (1987). Self-attributions, social interaction, and moral development. In W. M. Kurtines & J. L. Gewirtz (Eds.), *Moral development through social interaction*. New York: John Wiley.

Eisenberg, N. (1990). Prosocial development in early and mid-adolescence. In R. Montemayor, G. R. Adams, & T. P. Gullotta (Eds.), *Advances in adolescent development: Vol. 2. From childhood to adolescence: A transitional period?* Newbury Park, Calif.: Sage Publications.

Eisenberg, R. B. (1976). *Auditory competence in early life*. Baltimore: University Park Press.

Eisenberg-Berg, N., & Hand, M. (1979). The relationship of preschoolers' reasoning about prosocial moral conflicts to prosocial behavior. *Child Development, 50*, 356–360.

Elder, G. H., Jr. (1974). *Children of the great depression*. Chicago: University of Chicago Press.

Elder, G. H., Jr. (1979). Historical change in life patterns and personality. In P. B. Baltes & O. G. Brim, Jr. (Eds.), *Life span development and behavior* (Vol. 2). New York: Academic Press.

Elder, G. H., Jr., Nguyen, T. Van, & Caspi, A. (1985). Linking family hardship to children's lives. *Child Development, 56*, 361–375.

Elicker, J., & Sroufe, L. A. (1989). Predicting peer competence and peer relationships in childhood from early parent-child relationships. In R. D. Parke & G. W. Ladd (Eds.), *Family-peer relationships: Modes of linkage*. Hillsdale, N.J.: Lawrence Erlbaum.

Elkind, D. (1967). Egocentrism in adolescence. *Child Development, 38*, 1025–1034.

Elkind, D. (1981a). *The hurried child: Growing up too fast too soon*. Reading, Mass.: Addison-Wesley.

Elkind, D. (1981b). Understanding the young adolescent. In L. D. Steinberg (Ed.), *The life cycle: Readings in human development*. New York: Columbia University Press.

Elkind, D. (1987). *Miseducation: Preschoolers at risk*. New York: Alfred A. Knopf.

Elkind, D., & Bowen, R. (1979). Imaginary audience behavior in children and adolescents. *Developmental Psychology, 15*, 38–44.

Elkington, J. (1986). *The poisoned womb*. Harmondsworth, Middlesex, England: Penguin Books.

Elliott, G. C. (1982). Self-esteem and self-presentation among the young as a function of age and gender. *Journal of Youth and Adolescence, 11*, 135–142.

Emery, A. E. H. (1983). *Elements of medical genetics* (6th ed.). Edinburgh and London: Churchill Livingstone.

Emery, A. E. H. (1984). Introduction — The principles of genetic counseling. In A. E. H. Emery & I. Pullen (Eds.), *Psychological aspects of genetic counseling*. New York: Academic Press.

Emery, A. E. H., & Pullen, I. (Eds.). (1984). *Psychological aspects of genetic counseling.* New York: Academic Press.

Emery, R. E. (1989). Family violence. *American Psychologist, 44,* 321–328.

Endsley, R. C., & Bradbard, M. R. (1981). *Quality day care: A handbook of choices for parents and caregivers.* Englewood Cliffs, N.J.: Prentice-Hall.

Enright, R., Shukla, D., & Lapsley, D. (1980). Adolescent egocentrism – sociocentrism in early and late adolescence. *Adolescence, 14,* 687–695.

Epling, W. F., Pierce, W. D., & Stefan, L. (1983). A theory of activity-based anorexia. *International Journal of Eating Disorders, 3,* 27–45.

Erickson, J. D., & Bjerkedal, T. (1981). Down's syndrome associated with father's age in Norway. *Journal of Medical Genetics, 18,* 22–28.

Erickson, M. T. (1987). *Behavior disorders of children and adolescents.* Englewood Cliffs, N.J.: Prentice-Hall.

Erikson, E. H. (1956). The problems of ego identity. *Journal of the American Psychoanalytic Association, 4,* 56–121.

Erikson, E. H. (1959). Identity and the life cycle: Selected papers. From *Psychological Issue Monograph Series,* 1. New York: International Universities Press.

Erikson, E. H. (1961). The roots of virtue. In J. Huxley (Ed.), *The humanist frame.* New York: Harper & Row.

Erikson, E. H. (1968). *Identity, youth and crisis.* New York: W. W. Norton.

Ernst, C., & Angst, J. (1983). *Birth order: Its influence on personality.* New York: Springer-Verlag.

Essman, E. J. (1984). Marijuana intoxication in rats: Interruption of recent memory and effect on brain concentration of Delta 9-tetrahydrocannabinol. *Psychological Reports, 55,* 563–567.

Ethical standards for research with children. (1973). *SRCD Newsletter,* Winter, 3–4.

Evans, R. I. (1989). *Albert Bandura: The man and his ideas – a dialogue.* New York: Praeger.

Eveleth, P. B., & Tanner, J. M. (1976). *Worldwide variation in human growth.* Cambridge, England: Cambridge University Press.

Eysenck, H. J., & Kamin, L. (1981). *Intelligence: The battle for the mind.* London: Macmillan.

Fagan, J., Piper, E., & Moore, M. (1986). Violent delinquents and urban youths. *Criminology, 24,* 439–468.

Fagan, J. F., III. (1974). Infant color perception. *Science, 183,* 973–975.

Falek, A. (1975). Ethical issues in human behavior genetics: Civil rights, informed consent, and ethics of intervention. In K. W. Schaie, V. F. Anderson, G. E. McClearn, & J. Money (Eds.), *Developmental human behavior genetics.* Lexington, Mass.: D. C. Heath.

Fantz, R. L. (1963). Pattern vision in newborn infants. *Science, 140,* 296–297.

Fantz, R. L. (1965). Visual perception from birth as shown by pattern selectivity. *Annals of the New York Academy of Science, 118,* 793–814.

Farleger, D. (1977, July). The battle over children's rights. *Psychology Today,* 89–91.

Fasick, F. A. (1988). Patterns of formal education in high school as *rites de passage. Adolescence, 23,* 457–471.

Fedoruk, G. M. (1989). Kindergarten screening for 1st-grade learning problems: The conceptual inadequacy of a child deficit model. *Childhood Education, 66,* 40–42.

Feingold, B. F. (1975a). Hyperkinesis and learning disabilities linked to artificial food flavors and colors. *American Journal of Nursing, 75,* 797–803.

Feingold, B. F. (1975b). *Why your child is hyperactive.* New York: Random House.

Fenson, L. (1987). The developmental progression of play. In A. W. Gottfried & C. C. Brown (Eds.), *Play interactions: The contribution of play materials and parental involvement to children's development.* Lexington, Mass.: D. C. Heath.

Ferri, E., & Robinson, H. (1976). *Coping alone.* Windsor, Berks., Great Britain: NFER Publishing.

Feuerstein, R. (1979). *The dynamic assessment of retarded performers: The learning potential assessment device, theory, instruments, and techniques.* Baltimore: University Park Press.

Field, T. M. (1987). Coping with separation stress by infants and young children. In T. M. Field, P. M. McCabe, & N. Schneiderman (Eds.), *Stress and coping.* Hillsdale, N.J.: Lawrence Erlbaum.

Finkelhor, D., and associates (Eds.). (1986). *A sourcebook on child sexual abuse.* Beverly Hills, Calif.: Sage.

Fischer, K. W. (1980). A theory of cognitive development: The control and construction of hierarchies of skills. *Psychological Review, 87,* 477–531.

Fischer, K. W., & Pipp, S. L. (1984). Development of the structures of unconscious thought. In K. Bowers &

D. Meichenbaum (Eds.), *The unconscious reconsidered*. New York: John Wiley.

Fischer, K. W., & Silvern, L. (1985). Stages and individual differences in cognitive development. *Annual Review of Psychology, 36,* 613–648.

Fisher, R. (1990). *Teaching children to think.* Oxford: Basil Blackwell.

Fisher, W. A., & Byrne, D. (1978). Sex differences in response to erotica? Love versus lust. *Journal of Personality and Social Psychology, 36,* 117–126.

Fishkin, J., Keniston, K., & MacKinnon, C. (1973). Moral reasoning and political ideology. *Journal of Personality and Social Psychology, 27,* 109–119.

Flavell, J. H. (1982). On cognitive development. *Child Development, 53,* 1–10.

Flavell, J. H. (1985). *Cognitive development* (2nd ed.). Englewood Cliffs, N.J.: Prentice-Hall.

Fogel, A. (1984). *Infancy: Infant, family, and society.* St. Paul, Minn.: West.

Fogel, A., Toda, S., & Kawai, M. (1988). Mother-infant face-to-face interaction in Japan and the United States: A laboratory comparison using 3-month-old infants. *Developmental Psychology, 3,* 398–406.

Formanek, R. (1982). On the origins of gender identity. In D. Mendell (Ed.), *Early female development: Current psychoanalytic views.* Jamaica, N.Y.: Spectrum, 1–24.

Fouts, R. S. (1987). Chimpanzee signing and emergent levels. In G. Greenberg & E. Tobach (Eds.), *Cognition, language and consciousness: Integrative levels.* Hillsdale, N.J.: Lawrence Erlbaum.

Fraiberg, S. (1974). Blind infants and their mothers: An examination of the sign system. In M. Lewis & L. A. Rosenblum (Eds.), *The effect of the infant on its caregiver.* New York: John Wiley.

Fraiberg, S. (1975). The development of human attachments in infants blind from birth. *Merrill-Palmer Quarterly, 21,* 315–334.

Fraiberg, S. (Ed.). (1980). *Clinical studies in infant mental health.* New York: Basic Books.

Francis, P. L., Self, P. A., & Horowitz, F. D. (1987). The behavioral assessment of the neonate: An overview. In J. D. Osofsky (Ed.), *Handbook of infant development.* New York: John Wiley.

Frankenburg, W. K., Dodds, J. B., Fandal, A. W., Kazuk, E., & Cohrs, M. (1975). *Denver Developmental Screening Test Reference Manual: Revised 1975 Edition.* Denver: University of Colorado Medical Center.

Frankenburg, W. K., Fandal, A. W., Sciarillo, W., & Burgess, D. (1981). The newly abbreviated and revised Denver Developmental Screening Test. *Journal of Pediatrics, 99,* 995–999.

Franklin, J. T. (1985). Alternative education as substance abuse prevention. *Journal of Alcohol and Drug Education, 30,* 12–23.

Frazier, A., & Lisonbee, L. K. (1950). Adolescent concerns with physique. *School Review, 58,* 397–405.

Freud, A. (1946). *The ego and the mechanisms of defense* (C. Baines, Trans.). New York: International Universities Press.

Freyberg, J. T. (1973). Increasing the imaginative play of urban disadvantaged kindergarten children through systematic training. In J. L. Singer (Ed.), *The child's world of make-believe.* New York: Academic Press.

Fried, P. A. (1986). Marijuana and human pregnancy. In I. J. Chasnoff (Ed.), *Drug use in pregnancy: Mother and child.* Boston, Mass.: MTP Press.

Friedan, B. (1983). *The second stage.* New York: Simon & Schuster.

Friedman, A. S. (1969). The family and the female delinquent: An overview. In O. Pollak & A. S. Friedman (Eds.), *Family dynamics and female sexual delinquency.* Palo Alto, Calif.: Science and Behavior Books.

Friedman, L. (1989). Mathematics and the gender gap: A meta-analysis of recent studies on sex differences in mathematical tasks. *Review of Educational Research, 59,* 185–213.

Frisch, R. E., & Revelle, R. (1970). Height and weight at menarche and a hypothesis of critical body weights and adolescent events. *Science, 169,* 397–398.

Furrow, D., Nelson, K., & Benedict, H. (1979). Mother's speech to children and syntactic development: Some simple relationships. *Journal of Child Language, 6,* 423–442.

Furstenberg, F. F., Jr., Brooks-Gunn, J., & Chase-Lansdale, L. (1989). Teenaged pregnancy and childbearing. *American Psychologist, 44,* 313–320.

Furth, H. (1980). Piagetian perspectives. In J. Sants (Eds.), *Developmental psychology and society.* London: Macmillan, 142–168.

Furth, H. G. (1973). *Deafness and learning: A psychosocial approach.* Belmont, Calif.: Wadsworth.

Gaddis, A., & Brooks-Gunn, J. (1985). The male experience of pubertal change. *Journal of Youth and Adolescence, 14,* 61–72.

Gagné, R. M., & Briggs, L. J. (1983). *Principles of instruction design* (3rd ed.). New York: Holt, Rinehart & Winston.

Galjaard, H. (1982). Basic research, early diagnosis and prenatal analysis of congenital disorders: A survey. In H. Galjaard (Ed.), *The future of prenatal diagnosis.* London: Churchill Livingstone, 1–10.

Galler, J. R. (Ed.). (1984). *Human nutrition: A comprehensive treatise: Vol. 5. Nutrition and behavior.* New York: Plenum.

Galton, F. (1896). *Hereditary genius: An enquiry into its laws and consequences.* London: Macmillan.

Gamble, T. J., & Zigler, E. (1986). Effects of infant day care: Another look at the evidence. *American Journal of Orthopsychiatry, 56,* 26–42.

Garbarino, J., & Crouter, A. (1977). The human ecology of child maltreatment: A conceptual model for research. *Journal of Marriage and the Family, 39,* 721–735.

Gardner, H. (1982, March). The making of a storyteller. *Psychology Today,* 48–53, 61–63.

Gardner, H. (1983). *Frames of mind: The theory of multiple intelligences.* New York: Basic Books.

Gardner, M. K. (1985). Cognitive psychological approaches to instructional task analysis. In W. W. Gordon (Ed.), *Review of Research in Education* (Vol. 12), Washington, D.C.: American Educational Research Association, 157–196.

Garmezy, N. (1976). Vulnerable and invulnerable children: Theory, research, and intervention. Master lecture on developmental psychology, American Psychological Association.

Garvey, C. (1977). *Play.* Cambridge, Mass.: Harvard University Press.

Gelles, R. J. (1979). Violence toward children in the United States. In R. Bourne & E. H. Newberger (Eds.), *Critical perspectives on child abuse.* Lexington, Mass.: D.C. Heath.

Gelman, R. (1978). Cognitive development. *Annual Review of Psychology, 29,* 297–332.

Gelman, R. (1982). Basic numerical abilities. In R. J. Sternberg (Ed.), *Advances in the psychology of human intelligence* (Vol. 1). Hillsdale, N.J.: Lawrence Erlbaum.

Gelman, R., & Gallistel, C. R. (1978). *The young child's understanding of number.* Cambridge, Mass.: Harvard University Press.

The gene hunt. (1989). *Time,* March 20, pp. 54–61.

Genesee, F. (1985). Second language learning through immersion: A review of U.S. programs. *Review of Educational Research, 55,* 541–546.

Gerber, M. (1958). The psycho-motor development of African children in the first year and the influence of maternal behavior. *Journal of Social Psychology, 47,* 185–195.

Gerbner, G. (1972). Violence in television drama: Trends and symbolic functions. In G. A. Comstock & E. A. Rubenstein (Eds.), *Television and social behavior* (Vol. 1). Washington, D.C.: U.S. Government Printing Office.

Gesell, A. (1925). *The mental growth of the pre-school child.* New York: Macmillan.

Getzels, J. W., & Jackson, P. W. (1962). *Creativity and intelligence.* New York: John Wiley.

Gewirtz, J. L. (1965). The course of infant smiling in four child-rearing environments in Israel. In B. M. Foss (Ed.), *Determinants of infant behavior 3.* London: Methuen.

Gewirtz, J. L., & Boyd, E. F. (1976). Mother-infant interaction and its study. In H. W. Reese (Ed.), *Advances in child development and behavior,* 142–160.

Gianino, A., & Tronick, E. Z. (1988). The mutual regulation model: The infant's self and interactive regulation coping and defense. In T. Field, P. McCabe, & N. Schneiderman (Eds.), *Stress and coping.* Hillsdale, N.J.: Lawrence Erlbaum.

Gibbs, J. C. (1987). Social processes in delinquency: The need to facilitate empathy as well as sociomoral reasoning. In W. M. Kurtines & J. L. Gewirtz (Eds.), *Moral development through social interaction.* New York: John Wiley.

Gibson, E. J., & Walk, R. D. (1960). The "visual cliff." *Scientific American, 202,* 64–71.

Gil, D. G. (1970). *Violence against children: Physical child abuse in the United States.* Cambridge, Mass.: Harvard University Press.

Gilligan, C. (1982). *In a different voice: Psychological theory and women's development.* Cambridge, Mass.: Harvard University Press.

Gilligan, C., Kohlberg, L., Lerner, J., & Belenky, M. (1971). *Moral reasoning about sexual dilemmas: The development of an interview and scoring system.* Technical Report of the Commission on Obscenity and Pornography (Vol. 1, 141–174). Washington, D.C.: U.S. Government Printing Office.

Ginott, H. (1965). *Between parent and child.* New York: Macmillan.

Ginott, H. (1969). *Between parent and teenager.* New York: Macmillan.

Gitomer, D. H., & Pellegrino, J. W. (1985). Developmental and individual differences in long-term memory retrieval. In R. F. Dillon (Ed.), *Individual differences in cognition* (Vol. 2). New York: Academic Press.

Glick, P. C. (1989). Remarried families, stepfamilies, and stepchildren: A brief demographic profile. *Family Relations, 38,* 24–27.

Goelman, H., Shapiro, E., & Pence, A. R. (1990). Family environment and family day care. *Family Relations, 39,* 14–19.

Golbus, M. S. (1982). Future uses of fetoscopy. In H. Galjaard (Ed.), *The future of prenatal diagnosis.* London: Churchill Livingstone, 128–132.

Gold, R. (1986). Failure on Piagetian tasks: Misinterpretation of the question? In C. Pratt, A. F. Garton, W. E. Tunmer, & A. R. Nesdale (Eds.), *Research issues in child development.* Boston: Allen & Unwin.

Goldberg, S. (1983). Parent-infant bonding: Another look. *Child Development, 54,* 1355–1382.

Goldgaber, D., Lerman, M. I., McBride, O. W., Saffiotti, U., & Gajdusek, D. C. (1987). Characterization and chromosomal localization of a DNA encoding brain amyloid of Alzheimer's disease. *Science, 235,* 877–880.

Goldsmith, H. H. (1983). Genetic influences on personality from infancy to adulthood. *Child Development, 54,* 331–355.

Goldsmith, J. P. (1990). Neonatal morbidity. In R. D. Eden, F. H. Boehm, & M. Haire (Eds.), *Assessment and care of the fetus: Physiological, clinical, and medicolegal principles.* Norwalk, Conn.: Appleton & Lange.

Goode, E. T. (1985). Medical aspects of the bulimic syndrome and bulimarexia. *Transactional Analysis Journal, 15,* 4–11.

Goodwin, R. (1980). Two decades of research into early language. In J. Sants (Ed.), *Developmental psychology and society.* London: Macmillan, 169–218.

Gordon, T. (1975). *P.E.T.: Parent effectiveness training.* New York: New American Library.

Gordon, T. (1976). *P.E.T. in action.* New York: Bantam Books.

Gottesman, I. I. (1974). Developmental genetics and ontogenetic psychology: Overdue detente and propositions from a matchmaker. In A. Pick (Ed.), *Minnesota symposia on child psychology, 12,* 55–80.

Gottesman, I. I., & Shields, J. (1982). *The schizophrenic puzzle.* New York: Cambridge University Press.

Gottman, J. M. (1977). Toward a definition of social isolation in children. *Child Development, 48,* 513–517.

Gottman, J. M., & Mettetal, G. (1987). Speculations about social and affective development: Friendship and acquaintanceship through adolescence. In J. M. Gottman & J. Parker (Eds.), *Conversations of friends.* New York: Cambridge University Press.

Gould, S. J. (1981). *The mismeasure of man.* New York: W. W. Norton.

Graham, J. M., Jr. (1985). The effects of alcohol consumption during pregnancy. In M. Marois (Ed.), *Prevention of physical and mental congenital defects.* New York: Alan R. Liss.

Grant, J. P. (Executive Director of the United Nation's Children's Fund, UNICEF). (1986). *The state of the world's children: 1986.* New York: Oxford University Press.

Green, K. D., Forehand, R., Beck, S. J., & Vosk, B. (1980). An assessment of the relationship among measures of children's social competence and children's academic achievement. *Child Development, 51,* 1149–1156.

Greenacre, P. (1959). Play in relation to creative imagination. *Psychoanalytic Studies of the Child, 14,* 61–80.

Greenberg, G., & Tobach, E. (1987). *Cognition, language and consciousness: Integrative levels.* Hillsdale, N.J.: Lawrence Erlbaum.

Greenberg, M. T. (1980). Social interaction between deaf preschoolers and their mothers: The effects of communication method and communication competence. *Developmental Psychology, 16,* 465–474.

Greene, J. (1975). *Thinking and language.* London: Methuen.

Greenspan, S. I., & Leberman, A. F. (1989). A quantitative approach to the clinical assessment of representational elaboration and differentiation in children two to four. In S. I. Greenspan & G. H. Pollock (Eds.), *The course of life: Vol II. Early Childhood.* Madison, Conn.: International Universities Press.

Griffin, S. (1985). Eating issues and fat issues. *Transactional Analysis Journal, 15,* 30–36.

Griffore, R. J. (1980). Toward the use of child development research in informed parenting. *Journal of Clinical Child Psychology,* Spring, 48–61.

Grindstaff, C. F. (1988). Adolescent marriage and childbearing: The long-term economic outcome, Canada in the 1980s. *Adolescence, 23,* 45–58.

Gronlund, N. E., & Holmlund, W. S. (1958). The value of elementary school sociometric status scores for predicting a pupil's adjustment in high school. *Educational Administration and Supervision, 44*, 255–260.

Grossman, J. J. (Ed.). (1983). *Manual on terminology and classification in mental retardation, 1983 revision.* Washington, D.C.: American Association on Mental Deficiency.

Grotevant, M. D., Scarr, S., & Weinberg, R. A. (1977). *Intellectual development in family constellations with adopted and natural children: A test of the Zajonc and Markus model.* Paper presented at a meeting of the Society for Research in Child Development, New Orleans.

Grow, L. J. (1979). *Early childrearing by young mothers: A research study.* New York: Child Welfare League of America.

Guidubaldi, J., & Cleminshaw, H. (1985). Divorce, family health, and child adjustment. *Family Relations, 34*, 35–41.

Guilford, J. P. (1950). Creativity. *American Psychologist, 5*, 444–454.

Guilford, J. P. (1959). Three faces of intellect. *American Psychologist, 14*, 469–479.

Guilleminault, C., Ariagno, R. L., Forno, L. S., Nagle, L., Baldwin, R., & Owen, M. (1979). Obstructive sleep apnea and near miss for SIDS: Report of an infant with sudden death. *Pediatrics, 63*, 837–843.

Gustafson, G. E., & Harris, K. L. (1990). Women's responses to young infants' cries. *Developmental Psychology, 26*, 144–152.

Haaf, R. A., Smith, P. H., & Smitley, S. (1983). Infant response to facelike patterns under fixed-trial and infant-control procedures. *Child Development, 54*, 172–177.

Haith, M. M. (1980). *Rules that babies look by: The organization of newborn visual activity.* Hillsdale, N.J.: Lawrence Erlbaum.

Haith, M. M. (1986). Sensory and perceptual processes in early infancy. *Journal of Pediatrics, 109*, 158–171.

Haith, M. M., & Campos, J. J. (1977). Human infancy. *Annual Review of Psychology, 28*, 251–293.

Hakuta, K., & Garcia, E. E. (1989). Bilingualism and education. *American Psychologist, 44*, 374–379.

Hall, G. S. (1891). The contents of children's minds on entering school. *Paediatric Seminars, 1*, 139–173.

Hall, G. S. (1916). *Adolescence* (2 vols.). New York: Appleton-Century-Crofts.

Hall, W. G., & Oppenheim, R. W. (1987). Developmental psychobiology: Prenatal, perinatal, and early postnatal aspects of behavioral development. *Annual Review of Psychology, 38*, 91–128.

Hallahan, D. P., & Heins, E. D. (1976). Issues in learning disabilities. In J. M. Kauffman & D. P. Hallahan (Eds.), *Teaching children with learning disabilities: Personal perspectives.* Columbus, Ohio: Charles E. Merrill.

Hallahan, D. P., & Kauffman, J. M. (1986). *Exceptional children: Introduction to special education* (3rd ed.). Englewood Cliffs, N.J.: Prentice-Hall.

Halonen, J. S., & Passman, R. H. (1978). Pacifiers' effects upon play and separations from the mother for the one-year-old in a novel environment. *Infant Behavior and Development, 1*, 70–78.

Hamner, T. J., & Turner, P. H. (1985). *Parenting in contemporary society.* Englewood Cliffs, N.J.: Prentice-Hall.

Hare, J. W. (Ed.). (1989). *Diabetes complicating pregnancy: The Joslin Clinic Method.* New York: Alan R. Liss.

Hargrove, L. J., & Poteet, J. A. (1984). *Assessment in special education: The education evaluation.* Englewood Cliffs, N.J.: Prentice-Hall.

Harlow, H. F. (1959). Love in infant monkeys. *Scientific American, 200*, 68–70.

Harlow, H. F., Harlow, M. K., & Suomi, S. J. (1971). From thought to therapy: Lessons from a primate laboratory. *American Scientist, 59*, 538–549.

Harlow, H. F., & Zimmerman, R. R. (1959). Affectional responses in the infant monkey. *Science, 130*, 421–432.

Harris, P. L. (1983). Infant cognition. In M. M. Haith & J. J. Campos (Eds.), *Handbook of child psychology: Vol. 2. Infancy and developmental psychobiology.* New York: John Wiley.

Harris, P. L., & Gross, D. (1988). Children's understanding of real and apparent emotion. In J. W. Astington, P. L. Harris, & D. R. Olson (Eds.), *Developing theories of mind.* New York: Cambridge University Press.

Harris, T. (1973). *I'm ok — You're ok.* New York: Avon Books.

Harrison, L. (1985). Effects of early supplemental stimulation programs for premature infants: Review of the literature. *Maternal-Child Nursing Journal, 14*, 69–90.

Harter, S. (1983). Developmental perspectives on the self-system. In P. H. Mussen (Ed.), *Handbook of child psychology* (4th ed.) (Vol. 4): *Socialization, personality, and social development* (E. M. Hetherington, Ed.). New York: John Wiley.

Harter, S. (1985a). Processes underlying the construct, maintenance and enhancement of the self-concept in children. In J. Suls & A. Greenwald (Eds.), *Psychological perspectives on the self* (Vol. 3). Hillsdale, N.J.: Lawrence Erlbaum.

Harter, S. (1985b). *The Self-Perception Profile for Children: Revision of the Perceived Competence Scale for Children*, Manual. Denver: University of Denver.

Harter, S. (1987). The determinants and mediational role of global self-worth in children. In N. Eisenberg (Ed.), *Contemporary topics in developmental psychology.* New York: Wiley.

Harter, S. (1988). Developmental processes in the construction of self. In T. D. Yawkey & J. E. Johnson (Eds.), *Integrative processes and socialization: Early to middle childhood.* Hillsdale, N.J.: Lawrence Erlbaum.

Harter, S. (1990). Processes underlying adolescent self-concept formation. In R. Montemayor, G. R. Adams, & T. P. Gullotta (Eds.), *Advances in adolescent development: Vol. 2. From childhood to adolescence: A transitional period?* Newbury Park, Calif.: Sage.

Hartup, W. W. (1975). The origins of friendship. In M. Lewis & L. A. Rosenblum (Eds.), *Friendship and peer relations.* New York: John Wiley.

Hartup, W. W. (1978). Children and their friends. In H. McGurk (Ed.), *Issues in childhood social development.* London: Methuen.

Hartup, W. W. (1983). Peer relations. In P. H. Mussen (Ed.), *Handbook of child psychology* (4th ed.) (Vol. 4): *Socialization, personality, and social development* (E. M. Hetherington, Ed.). New York: John Wiley, 103–196.

Hartup, W. W. (1989). Social relationships and their developmental significance. *American Psychologist, 44,* 120–126.

Hartup, W. W., Glazer, J. A., & Charlesworth, R. (1967). Peer reinforcement and sociometric status. *Child Development, 38,* 1017–1024.

Hartup, W. W., & Lempers, J. (1973). A problem in life span development: The interactional analysis of family attachments. In P. B. Baltes & K. W. Schaie (Eds.), *Life span developmental psychology: Personality and socialization.* New York: Academic Press.

Haskins, R. (1989). Beyond metaphor: The efficacy of early childhood education. *American Psychologist, 44,* 274–282.

Hass, A. (1979). *Teenage sexuality: A survey of teenage sexual behavior.* New York: Macmillan.

Hauser, R. M., & Sewell, W. H. (1985). Birth order and educational attainment in full sibships. *American Journal of Educational Research Journal, 22,* 1–23.

Hayes, K. J., & Hayes, C. (1951). Intellectual development of a home-raised chimpanzee. *Proceedings of the American Philosophical Society, 95,* 105–109.

Haywood, H. C., Meyers, C. E., & Switzky, H. N. (1982). Mental retardation. *Annual Review of Psychology, 33,* 309–342.

Hebb, D. O. (1966). *A textbook of psychology* (2nd ed.). Philadelphia: W. B. Saunders.

Heinonen, O. P., Slone, D., & Shapiro, S. (1983). *Birth defects and drugs in pregnancy.* Boston: John Wright.

Heisel, B. E., & Retter, K. (1981). Young children's storage behavior in a memory for location task. *Journal of Experimental Child Psychology, 31,* 250–364.

Held, D. F. (1984). *The intuitive approach to reading and learning disabilities: A practical alternative.* Springfield, Ill.: Charles C. Thomas.

Henderson, G., & Henderson, B. B. (1984). *Mending broken children: A parent's manual.* Springfield, Ill.: Charles C. Thomas.

Hendry, L. S. (1960). *Cognitive processes in a moral conflict situation.* Unpublished doctoral dissertation, Yale University.

Henggeler, S. W., & Cooper, P. F. (1983). Deaf child–hearing mother interaction: Extensiveness and reciprocity. *Journal of Pediatric Psychology, 8,* 83–95.

Henker, B., & Whalen, C. K. (1989). Hyperactivity and attention deficits. *American Psychologist, 44,* 216–223.

Herbst, D. S., & Miller, J. R. (1980). Nonspecific X-linked mental retardation. II. The frequency in British Columbia. *American Journal of Medical Genetics, 17,* 461.

Herzog, E., & Sudia, C. (1970). *Boys in fatherless homes.* Washington, D.C.: U.S. Department of Health, Education, & Welfare.

Hess, G. C. (1990). Sexual abstinence, a revived option for teenagers. *Modern Psychology, 1,* 19–21.

Hetherington, E. M., Cox, M., & Cox, R. (1979). Play and social interaction in children following divorce. *Journal of Social Issues, 35,* 26–49.

Hetherington, E. M., Stanley-Hagen, M., & Anderson, E. R. (1989). Marital transitions: A child's perspective. *American Psychologist, 44,* 303–312.

Higbee, K. L. (1977). *Your memory: How it works and how to improve it.* Englewood Cliffs, N.J.: Prentice-Hall.

Hinde, R. A. (1983). Ethology and child development. In P. H. Mussen (Ed.), *Handbook of child psychology* (4th ed.) (Vol. 2): *Infancy and developmental psychobiology* (M. M. Haith & J. J. Campos, Eds.). New York: John Wiley, 27–94.

Hinde, R. A. (1989). Ethological and relationship approaches. In R. Vasta (Ed.), *Annals of child development* (Vol. 6). Greenwich, Conn.: JAI Press.

Hindelang, M. J. (1981). Variations in sex-race-age-specific incidence of offending. *American Sociological Review, 46,* 461–474.

Ho, D. (1983). Asian concepts in behavioral science. *Bulletin of the Hong Kong Psychological Society, 10,* 41–49.

Ho, D. Y. F. (1987). Fatherhood in Chinese culture. In M. E. Lamb (Ed.). *The father's role: Cross-cultural perspectives.* Hillsdale, N.J.: Lawrence Erlbaum.

Hodapp, R. M., & Mueller, E. (1982). Early social development. In B. B. Wolman and others (Eds.), *Handbook of developmental psychology.* Englewood Cliffs, N.J.: Prentice-Hall.

Hofer, M. A. (1981). *The roots of human behavior: An introduction to the psychobiology of early development.* San Francisco: W. H. Freeman.

Hoffman, L. W. (1989). Effects of maternal employment in the two-parent family. *American Psychologist, 44,* 283–292.

Hoffman, M. L. (1975). Developmental synthesis of affect and cognition and its implications for altruistic motivation. *Developmental Psychology, 11,* 607–622.

Hoffman, M. L. (1976). Empathy, role-taking, guilt, and development of altruistic motives. In T. Likona (Ed.), *Moral development: Current theory and research.* New York: Holt, Rinehart & Winston.

Hoffman, M. L. (1978). Empathy: Its developmental and prosocial implications. In C. B. Keasey (Ed.), *Nebraska symposium on motivation* (Vol. 25). Lincoln: University of Nebraska Press.

Hoffman, M. L. (1979). Development of moral thought, feeling, and behavior. *American Psychologist, 34,* 958–966.

Hoge, R. D. (1988). Issues in the definition and measurement of the giftedness construct. *Educational Researcher, 17,* 12–66.

Holbrook, R. H., Jr.; Laros, R. K., Jr.; & Creasy, R. K. (1988), Evaluation of a risk-scoring system for predic-tion of preterm labor. *American Journal of Perinatology, 6,* 62.

Holland, A. J., Hall, A., Murray, R., Russell, G. F. M., & Crisp, A. H. (1984). Anorexia nervosa: A study of 34 twin pairs and one set of triplets. *British Journal of Psychiatry, 145,* 414–419.

Holmes, R. H., & Rahe, R. H. (1967). The social readjustment rating scale. *Journal of Psychosomatic Research, 11,* 213–218.

Holstein, C. B. (1976). Irreversible, stepwise sequence in the development of moral judgment: A longitudinal study of males and females. *Child Development, 47,* 51–61.

Honzik, M. P. (1984). Life-span development. *Annual Review of Psychology, 35,* 309–331.

Horn, J. (1983). The Texas Adoption Project. *Child Development, 54,* 268–275.

Horn, J. L. (1976). Human abilities: A review of research and theory in the early 1970's. In M. R. Rosenzweig & L. W. Porter (Eds.), *Annual review of psychology* (Vol. 27). Palo Alto, Calif.: Annual Reviews.

Horn, J. L., & Donaldson, G. (1980). Cognitive development in adulthood. In O. G. Brim, Jr., & J. Kagan (Eds.), *Constancy and change in human development.* Cambridge, Mass.: Harvard University Press.

Horton, D. L., & Mills, C. B. (1984). Human learning and memory. *Annual Review of Psychology, 35,* 361–394.

Hough, R. A., & Stevens, J. H., Jr. (1981). Social networks as supports for parenting. *Young Children, 36,* 50–59.

Hrncir, E. J. (1989). Children's play: The dynamic and spontaneous expression of the interface of emotion and cognition. *Child & Youth Care Quarterly, 18,* 171–175.

Hsu, L. Y. F. (1986). Prenatal diagnosis of chromosome abnormalities. In A. Milunsky (Ed.), *Genetic disorders and the fetus* (2nd ed.). New York: Plenum Press.

Hubel, D. H., & Wiesel, T. N. (1970). The period of susceptibility to the physiological effects of unilateral eye closure in kittens. *Journal of Physiology, 206,* 419–436.

Huesmann, L. R., & Eron, L. D. (Eds.) (1986a). *Television and the aggressive child: A cross-national comparison.* Hillsdale, N.J.: Lawrence Erlbaum.

Huesmann, L. R., & Eron, L. D. (1986b). The development of aggression in children of different cultures: Psychological processes and exposure to violence. In L. R. Huesmann & L. D. Eron (Eds.), *Television and the aggressive child: A cross-national comparison.* Hillsdale, N.J.: Lawrence Erlbaum.

Huesmann, L. R., Eron, L. D., Lefkowitz, M. M., & Walder, L. O. (1984). The stability of aggression over time and generations. *Developmental Psychology, 20,* 1120–1134.

Hughes, R., Tingle, B. A., & Sawin, D. B. (1981). Development of empathic understanding in children. *Child Development, 52,* 122–128.

Humphrey, J. N., & Humphrey, J. H. (1989). *Child development during the elementary school years.* Springfield, Ill.: Charles C. Thomas.

Hurlock, E. B. (1964). *Child development* (4th ed.). New York: McGraw-Hill.

Huston, A. C., Watkins, B. Q., & Kunkel, D. (1989). Public policy and children's television. *American Psychologist, 44,* 424–433.

Huston, A. C., & Wright, J. C. (1983). Children's processing of television: The informative functions of formal features. In J. Bryant & D. R. Anderson (Eds.), *Children's understanding of television: Research on attention and comprehension.* New York: Academic Press, 35–68.

Huston, A. C., Wright, J. C., Rice, M. L., Kerkman, D., & St. Peters, M. (1990). Development of television viewing patterns in early childhood: A longitudinal investigation. *Developmental Psychology, 26,* 409–420.

Hutt, S. J., Lenard, H. G., & Prechtl, H. F. R. (1969). Psychophysiology of the newborn. In L. P. Lipsitt & H. W. Reese (Eds.), *Advances in child development and behavior.* New York: Academic Press.

Hyde, J. S. (1986). *Understanding human sexuality* (3rd ed.). New York: McGraw-Hill.

Hyde, J. S., Fennema, E., & Lamon, S. J. (1990). Gender differences in mathematics performance: A meta-analysis. *Psychological Bulletin, 107,* 139–155.

Hyde, S., & Linn, M. C. (1986). *The psychology of gender: Advances through meta-analysis.* Baltimore: Johns Hopkins University Press.

Iennarella, R. S., Chisum, G. M., & Bianchi, J. (1986). A comprehensive treatment model for pregnant chemical users, infants and families. In I. J. Chasnoff (Ed.), *Drug use in pregnancy: Mother and child.* Boston: MTP Press.

Increase expected in AIDS in North America — UN agency. (1988). *The Edmonton Journal,* Dec. 1, p. A2.

Inhelder, B., & Piaget, J. (1958). *The growth of logical thinking from childhood to adolescence.* New York: Basic Books.

Inoff-Germain, G.; Arnold, G. S.,; Nottelmann, E. D.; Susman, E. J.; Cutler, G. B., Jr.; & Chrousos, G. P.

(1988). Relations between hormone levels and observational measures of aggressive behavior of young adolescents in family interactions. *Developmental Psychology, 24,* 129–139.

Intons-Peterson, M. J. (1988). *Gender concepts of Swedish and American youth.* Hillsdale, N.J.: Lawrence Erlbaum.

Isabell, B. J., & McKee, L. (1980). Society's cradle: An anthropological perspective on the socialisation of cognition. In J. Sants (Ed.), *Developmental psychology and society.* London: Macmillan, 327–365.

Izard, C. E. (1977). *Human emotions.* New York: Plenum.

Izard, C. E., & Malatesta, C. Z. (1987). Perspectives on emotional development I: Differential emotions theory of early emotional development. In J. D. Osofsky (Ed.), *Handbook of infant development* (2nd ed.). New York: Wiley.

Jacklin, C. N. (1989). Female and male: Issues of gender. *American Psychologist, 44,* 127–133.

Jacobson, J. L., & Wille, D. E. (1984). Influence of attachment and separation experience on separation distress at 18 months. *Developmental Psychology, 20,* 477–484.

Jacobson, S. W., Fein, G. G., Jacobson, J. L., Schwartz, P. M., & Dowler, J. K. (1985). Neonatal correlates of exposure to smoking, caffeine, and alcohol. *Infant and Behavior Development, 7,* 253–265.

Jacobson, S. W., & Kagan, J. (1979). Interpreting "imitative" responses in early infancy. *Science, 205,* 215–217.

Jaffe, B. F., & Luterman, D. M. (1980). The child with a hearing loss. In A. P. Scheiner & I. F. Abroms (Eds.), *The practical management of the developmentally disabled child.* St. Louis: C. V. Mosby, 250–268.

James, W. (1890). *The principles of psychology.* New York: Holt, Rinehart & Winston.

James, W. (1892). *Psychology: The briefer course.* New York: Henry Holt.

Jarvik, L. F., Klodin, V., & Matsuyama, S. S. (1973). Human aggression and the extra Y chromosome: Fact or fantasy? *American Psychologist, 28,* 674–682.

Jean-Gilles, M., & Crittenden, P. M. (1990). Maltreating families: A look at siblings. *Family Relations, 39,* 323–329.

Jensen, A. R. (1968). Social class, race, and genetics: Implications for education. *American Educational Research Journal, 5,* 1–42.

Jensen, W. A., et al. (1979). *Biology.* Belmont, Calif.: Wadsworth.

Jersild, A. T. (1963). *The psychology of adolescence* (2nd ed.). New York: Macmillan.

Johnson, B., & Morse, H. (1968). Injured children and their parents. *Children, 15,* 147–152.

Johnson, H. R., Myhre, S. A., Ruvalcaba, R. H. A., Thuline, H. C., & Kelley, V. C. (1970). Effects of testosterone on body image and behavior in Klinefelter's syndrome: A pilot study. *Developmental Medicine and Child Neurology, 12,* 454–460.

Johnson, J. E., & McGillicuddy-Delisi, A. (1983). Family environment factors and children's knowledge of rules and conventions. *Child Development, 54,* 218–226.

Johnson, J. E., & Yawkey, T. D. (1988). Play and integration. In T. D. Yawkey & J. E. Johnson (Eds.), *Integrative processes and socialization: Early to middle childhood.* Hillsdale, N.J.: Lawrence Erlbaum.

Johnson, J. H. (1986). *Life events as stressors in childhood and adolescence.* Beverly Hills, Calif: Sage.

Johnson, M. K., Bransford, J. D., & Solomon, S. (1973). Memory for tacit implications of sentences. *Journal of Experimental Psychology, 98,* 203–205.

Johnson, R. D. (1962). Measurements of achievement in fundamental skills of elementary school children. *Research Quarterly, 33,* 94–103.

Johnston, L. D., Bachman, J. G., & O'Malley, P. M. (1983). *Highlights from student drug use in America, 1975–1983.* Rockville, Md.: National Institute on Drug Abuse.

Johnston, L. D., O'Malley, P. M., and Bachman, J. G. (1986). *Drug use among American high school students, college students, and other young adults: National trends through 1985.* Rockville, Md.: National Institute on Drug Abuse.

Jones, E. F., and associates, (1986). *Teenage pregnancy in industrialized countries.* New Haven, Conn.: Yale University Press.

Jones, M. C. (1957). The later careers of boys who are early- or late-maturing. *Child Development, 28,* 113–128.

Jones, M. C. (1965). Psychological correlates of somatic development. *Child Development, 36,* 899–911.

Jones, M. C. (1974). Albert, Peter, and John B. Watson. *American Psychologist, 29,* 581–583.

Joy, L. A., Kimball, M., & Zabrack, M. L. (1977). *Television exposure and children's aggressive behavior.* Paper presented at the annual meeting of the Canadian Psychological Association, Vancouver, B.C.

Justice, E. (1985). Categorization as a preferred memory strategy: Developmental changes during elementary school. *Developmental Psychology, 21,* 1105–1110.

Kagan, J. (1976). Emergent themes in human development. *American Scientist, 64,* 186–196.

Kagan, J. (1978, August). The parental love trap. *Psychology Today,* 54–61, 91.

Kagan, J. (1982). The construct of difficult temperament: A reply to Thomas, Chess, and Korn. *Merrill-Palmer Quarterly, 28,* 21–24.

Kagan, J., Kearsley, R. B., & Zelazo, P. R. (1977). The effects of infant day care on psychological development. *Educational Quarterly, 1,* 109–142.

Kagan, J., Kearsley, R. B., & Zelazo, P. R. (1978). *Infancy: Its place in human development.* Cambridge, Mass.: Harvard University Press.

Kahn, A., & Blum, D. (1982). Phenothiazines and sudden infant death syndrome. *Pediatrics, 70,* 75–78.

Kaitz, M., Meschulach-Sarfaty, O., Auerbach, J., & Eidelman, A. (1988). A reexamination of newborn's ability to imitate facial expressions. *Developmental Psychology, 24,* 3–7.

Kalat, J. W. (1981). *Biological Psychology.* Belmont, Calif.: Wadsworth.

Kandel, D. B., & Logan, J. A. (1984). Patterns of drug use from adolescence to young adulthood: I. Period of risk for initiation, continued use, and discontinuation. *American Journal of Public Health, 74,* 660–666.

Kaplan, L. J. (1984). *Adolescence: The farewell to childhood.* New York: Simon & Schuster.

Kato, T. (1970). Chromosome studies in pregnant rhesus monkeys macaque given LSD-25. *Diseases of the Nervous System, 31,* 245–250.

Kavale, K., & Forness, S. (1985). *The science of learning disabilities.* San Diego, Calif.: College-Hill Press.

Kaye, K. (1977). Toward the origin of dialogue. In H. R. Schaffer (Ed.), *Studies in mother-infant interaction.* London: Academic Press.

Kazdin, A. E. (1989). Developmental psychopathology: Current research, issues, and directions. *American Psychologist, 44,* 180–187.

Kegan, R. (1982). *The evolving self: Problem and process in human development.* Cambridge, Mass.: Harvard University Press.

Kempe, R. S., & Kempe, C. H. (1984). *The common secret: Sexual abuse of children and adolescents.* New York: W. H. Freeman.

Kessen, W. (1965). *The child.* New York: John Wiley.

Kessen, W., Haith, M. H., & Salapatek, P. (1970). Human infancy: A bibliography and guide. In P. H. Mussen (Ed.), *Carmichael's manual of child psychology* (3rd ed.). New York: John Wiley.

Keyes, S., & Block, J. (1984). Prevalence and patterns of substance use among early adolescents. *Journal of Youth and Adolescence, 13,* 1–13.

Kinsey, A. C., Pomeroy, W. B., & Martin, C. E. (1948). *Sexual behavior in the human male.* Philadelphia: W. B. Saunders.

Kinsey, A. C., Pomeroy, W. B., Martin, C. E., & Gebhard, P. H. (1953). *Sexual behavior in the human female.* Philadelphia: W. B. Saunders.

Kirby, J. R., & Das, J. P. (1990). A cognitive approach to intelligence: Attention, coding, and planning. *Canadian Psychology, 31,* 320–331.

Kirk, S. (1979). *Educating exceptional children* (3rd ed.). Boston: Houghton Mifflin.

Klaus, M. H., & Kennell, H. H. (1983). *The beginnings of parent-infant attachment.* St. Louis: C. V. Mosby. (Originally published as *Maternal-infant bonding,* 1980.)

Klaus, M. H., Kreger, N., McAlpine, W., Steffa, M., & Kennell, J. (1972). Maternal attachment: Importance of the first post-partum days. *New England Journal of Medicine, 286,* 460–463.

Klein, M., & Stern, L. (1971). Low birth weight and the battered child syndrome. *American Journal of Diseases 1, 22,* 15–18.

Kleinginna, P. R., Jr., & Kleinginna, A. M. (1988). Current trends toward convergence of the behavioristic, functional, and cognitive perspectives in experimental psychology. *The Psychological Record, 38,* 369–392.

Kline, S. M. (1985). Achieving weight gain with anorexia and bulimic clients in a group setting. *Transactional Analysis Journal, 15,* 62–67.

Knuppel, R. A., & Angel, J. L. (1990). Diagnosis of fetal-maternal hemorrhage. In R. D. Eden, F. H. Boehm, & M. Haire (Eds.), *Assessment and care of the fetus: Physiological, clinical, and medicolegal principles.* Norwalk, Conn.: Appleton & Lange.

Knutson, J. F. (1978). Child abuse as an area of aggression research. *Journal of Pediatric Psychology, 3,* 20–27.

Kogan, N. (1983). Stylistic variation in childhood and adolescence: Creativity, metaphor, and cognitive style. In P. H. Mussen (Ed.), *Handbook of child psychology* (4th ed.) (Vol. 3): *Cognitive development* (J. H. Flavell & E. M. Markman, Eds.). New York: John Wiley, 630–706.

Kogan, N., & Pankove, E. (1972). Creative ability over a five-year span. *Child Development, 43,* 427–442.

Kohlberg, L. A. (1964). Development of moral character and moral ideology. In M. L. Hoffman & L. W. Hoffman (Eds.), *Review of Child Development Research* (Vol. 1). New York: Russell Sage Foundation.

Kohlberg, L. A. (1966). Cognitive-development analysis of children's sex-role concepts and attitudes. In E. Maccoby (Ed.), *The development of sex differences.* Stanford, Calif.: Stanford University Press.

Kohlberg, L. A. (1969). Stage and sequence: The cognitive-developmental approach to socialization. In D. Gosslin (Ed.), *Handbook of socialization theory and research.* Chicago: Rand McNally.

Kohlberg, L. A. (1978). Revisions in the theory and practice of moral development. *New Directions for Child Development, 2,* 83–87.

Kohlberg, L. A. (1980). *The meaning and measurement of moral development.* Worcester, Mass.: Clark University Press.

Kohlberg, L. A., & Candee, D. (1984). The relationship of moral judgment to moral action. In W. M. Kurtines & J. L. Gewirtz (Eds.), *Morality, moral behavior, and moral development.* New York: John Wiley.

Kolata, G. B. (1978). Behavioral teratology: Birth defects of the mind. *Science, 202,* 732–734.

Konner, M. (1982). Biological aspects of the mother-infant bond. In C. Parks & J. Stevenson-Hinde (Eds.), *The place of attachment in human behavior.* New York: Basic Books.

Kopp, C. B., & Kaler, S. R. (1989). Risk in infancy: Origins and implications. *American Psychologist, 44,* 224–230.

Kopp, C. B., & Parmelee, A. H. (1979). Prenatal and perinatal influences on infant behavior. In J. D. Osofsky (Ed.), *Handbook of infant development.* New York: John Wiley.

Kotelchuck, M. (1976). The infant's relationship to the father: Experimental evidence. In M. Lamb (Ed.), *The role of the father in child development.* New York: John Wiley.

Kovacs, M. (1989). Affective disorders in children and adolescents. *American Psychologist, 44,* 209–215.

Krikstone, B. J., & Levitt, R. A. (1975). Distorting drugs. In R. A. Levitt (Ed.), *Psychopharmacology: A biological approach.* Washington, D.C.: Hemisphere Publishing.

Kroupa, S. E. (1988). Perceived parental acceptance and female juvenile delinquency. *Adolescence, 23,* 143–155.

Kuhn, D. (1972). Mechanisms of change in the development of cognitive structures. *Child Development, 43,* 833–844.

Kuhn, D. (1984). Cognitive development. In M. H. Bornstein & M. E. Lamb (Eds.), *Developmental psychology: An advanced textbook.* Hillsdale, N.J.: Lawrence Erlbaum, 133–180.

Kurdek, L. A. (Ed.). (1983). *Children and divorce: New directions for child development.* San Francisco: Jossey-Bass.

Kurtines, W., & Grief, E. B. (1974). The development of moral thought: Review and evaluation of Kohlberg's approach. *Psychological Bulletin, 81,* 453–470.

Lachenmeyer, J. R., & Muni-Brander, P. (1988). Eating disorders in a nonclinical adolescent population: Implications for treatment. *Adolescence, 23* (90), 303–312.

Ladame, F., & Jeanneret, O. (1982). Suicide in adolescence: Some comments on epidemiology and prevention. *Journal of Adolescence, 5,* 355–366.

Lagercrantz, H., & Slotkin, T. A. (1986). The "stress" of being born. *Scientific American, 254,* 100–107.

Lamanna, M. A., & Riedmann, A. (1988). *Marriages and families: Making choices and facing change* (3rd ed.). Belmont, Calif.: Wadsworth.

Lamaze, F. (1972). *Painless childbirth: The Lamaze method.* New York: Pocket Books.

Lamb, M. E. (1980). The development of parent-infant attachments in the first two years of life. In F. A. Pedersen (Ed.), *The father-infant relationship: Observational studies in the family setting.* New York: Praeger, 21–42.

Lamb, M. E., Easterbrooks, M. A., & Holden, G. W. (1980). Reinforcement and punishment among preschoolers: Characteristics, effects, and correlates. *Child Development, 51,* 1230–1236.

Lamb, M. E., & Elster, A. B. (1985). Adolescent mother-infant-father relationships. *Developmental Psychology, 21,* 768–773.

Lamb, M. E., Frodi, M., Hwang, C., & Frodi, A. M. (1983). Effects of paternal involvement on infant preferences for mothers and fathers. *Child Development, 54,* 450–458.

Lambert, W. E. (1975). Culture and language as factors in learning and education. In A. Wolfgang (Ed.), *Educa-*

tion of immigrant students. Toronto: Ontario Institute for Studies in Education.

Landesman, S., & Ramey, C. (1989). Developmental psychology and mental retardation: Integrating scientific principles with treatment practices. *American Psychologist, 44,* 409–415.

Landry, R. (1987). Additive bilingualism, schooling, and special education: A minority group perspective. *Canadian Journal for Exceptional Children, 3,* 109–114.

Langlois, J. H., Roggman, L. A., & Rieser-Danner, L. A. (1990). Infants' differential social responses to attractive and unattractive faces. *Developmental Psychology, 26,* 153–159.

Langlois, J. H., & Stephan, C. W. (1981). Beauty and the beast: The role of physical attractiveness in the development of peer relations and social behavior. In S. S. Brehm, S. M. Kassin, & F. X. Gibbons (Eds.), *Developmental social psychology.* New York: Oxford University Press.

Lapsley, D. K. (1990). Continuity and discontinuity in adolescent social cognitive development. In R. Montemayor, G. R. Adams, & T. P. Gullotta (Eds.), *Advances in adolescent development: Vol. 2. From childhood to adolescence: A transitional period?* Newbury Park, Calif.: Sage.

Laszlo, J. I. (1986). Development of perceptual motor abilities in children from 5 years to adults. In C. Pratt, A. F. Garton, W. E. Tunmer, & A. R. Nesdale (Eds.), *Research issues in child development.* Boston: Allen & Unwin.

Lazar, I., Darlington, R., Murray, H., Royce, J., & Snipper, A. (1982). Lasting effects of early education: A report from the Consortium for Longitudinal Studies. *Monographs of the Society for Research in Child Development, 47,* no. 195.

Le monde au chevet de l'enfance menacée. (1990, September 29). *Le Monde,* p. 15.

Leboyer, F. (1975). *Birth without violence.* New York: Random House.

Lee, V. E., Brooks-Gunn, J., & Schnur, E. (1988). Does Head Start work? A 1-year follow-up comparison of disadvantaged children attending Head Start, no preschool, and other preschool programs. *Developmental Psychology, 24,* 210–222.

Lees, S. (1986). *Losing out: Sexuality and adolescent girls.* London: Hutchinson.

Lefkowitz, M., Eron, L., Walder, L., & Huesmann, L. R. (1972). Television violence and child aggression: A follow-up study. In G. A. Comstock & E. A. Rubinstein

(Eds.), *Television and social behavior* (Vol. 3). Washington, D.C.: U.S. Government Printing Office.

Lefrançois, G. R. (1967). Jean Piaget's developmental model: Equilibration-through-adaptation. *Alberta Journal of Educational Research, 13,* 161–171.

Lefrançois, G. R. (1973). *Of children: An introduction to child development.* Belmont, Calif.: Wadsworth.

Lefrançois, G. R. (1982). *Psychological theories and human learning* (2nd ed.). Monterey, Calif.: Brooks/Cole.

Lefrançois, G. R. (1983). *Psychology* (2nd ed.). Belmont, Calif.: Wadsworth.

Lenneberg, E. H. (1967). *Biological foundations of language.* New York: John Wiley.

Lenneberg, E. H. (1969). On explaining language. *Science, 164,* 635–643.

Lenneberg, E. H., Nichols, I. A., & Rosenberger, E. F. (1964). Primitive stages of language development in mongolism. In *Disorders of communication, Vol. 42: Research publications, A.R.N.M.D.* Baltimore: Williams & Wilkins.

Lerner, R. M. (1985). Individual and context in developmental psychology: Conceptual and theoretical issues. In J. R. Nesselroade & A. Von Eye (Eds.), *Individual development and social change: Explanatory analysis* (pp. 155–188). New York: Academic Press.

Lerner, R. M. (1987). The concept of plasticity in development. In J. J. Gallagher & C. T. Ramey (Eds.), *The malleability of children.* Baltimore: Brookes.

Lerner, R. M., & Busch-Rossnagel, N. A. (Eds.). (1981). *Individuals as producers of their development.* New York: Academic Press.

Lerner, R. M., & Korn, S. J. (1972). The development of body-build stereotypes in males. *Child Development, 43,* 908–920.

Lerner, R. M., Lerner, J. V., Winelle, M., Hooker, K., Lenez, K., and others. (1986). Children and adolescents in their contexts: Tests of the goodness of fit model. In R. Plomin & J. Dunn (Eds.), *The study of temperament: Changes, continuities and challenges.* Hillsdale, N.J.: Lawrence Erlbaum.

Lerner, R. M., & Shea, J. A. (1982). Social behavior in adolescence. In B. B. Wolman and others (Eds.), *Handbook of developmental psychology.* Englewood Cliffs, N.J.: Prentice-Hall.

Leslie, A. M. (1988). Some implications of pretense for mechanisms underlying the child's theory of mind. In J. W. Astington, P. L. Harris, & D. R. Olson (Eds.),

Developing theories of mind. New York: Cambridge University Press.

Lesser, H. (1977). *Television and the preschool child: A psychological theory of instruction and curriculum development.* New York: Academic Press.

Levine, R. A. (1987). Women's schooling, patterns of fertility, and child survival. *Educational Researcher, 16,* 21–27.

Lewin, R. (1975, September). Starved brains. *Psychology Today,* 29–33.

Lewis, M., & Lee-Painter, S. (1974). An interactional approach to the mother-infant dyad. In M. Lewis & L. A. Rosenblum (Eds.), *The effect of an infant on its caregiver.* New York: John Wiley.

Lewis, M., Sullivan, M. W., & Vasen, A. (1987). Making faces: Age and emotion differences in the posing of emotional expressions. *Developmental Psychology, 23,* 690–697.

Lewis, P. (1983). *Clinical pharmacology in obstetrics.* Boston: John Wright.

Liben, L. (1975). *Perspective-taking skills in young children: Seeing the world through rose-colored glasses.* Paper presented at the meeting of the Society for Research in Child Development, Denver, April.

Liberty, C., & Ornstein, P. A. (1973). Age differences in organization and recall: The effects of training in categorization. *Journal of Experimental Child Psychology, 15,* 169–186.

Lieberman, A. B. (1987). *Giving birth.* New York: St. Martin's Press.

Liggins, G. C. (1988). The onset of labor: An historical review. In C. T. Jones (Ed.), *Research in perinatal medicine (VII): Fetal and neonatal development.* Ithaca, N.Y.: Perinatology Press.

Linn, M. C., & Hyde, J. S. (1989). Gender, mathematics, and science. *Educational Researcher, 18,* 17–27.

Lipsitt, L. P. (1982). Infant learning. In T. M. Field, A. Huston, H. C. Quay, L. Troll, & G. E. Finley (Eds.), *Review of human development.* New York: John Wiley.

Lipsitt, L. P., Engen, T., & Kaye, H. (1963). Developmental changes in the olfactory threshold of the neonate. *Child Development, 34,* 371–376.

Lipsitt, L. P., & Levy, N. (1959). Electrotactual threshold in the neonate. *Child development, 30,* 547–554.

Locke, J. (1699). *Some thoughts concerning education* (4th ed.). London: A. & J. Churchills.

Lockhart, A. S. (1980). Motor learning and motor development during infancy and childhood. In C. B. Corbin (Ed.), *A textbook of motor development.* Dubuque, Iowa: Wm. C. Brown.

Loehlin, J. C. (1985). Fitting heredity-environment models jointly to twin and adoption data from the California Psychological Inventory. *Behavior Genetics, 15,* 199–221.

Loehlin, J. C., Willerman, L., & Horn, J. M. (1988). Human behavior genetics. *Annual Review of Psychology, 39,* 101–133.

Long, L., & Long, T. (1983). *The handbook for latchkey children and their parents.* New York: Arbor House.

Long, R. E. (1987). *AIDS.* (The Reference Shelf, Vol. 59, No. 3). New York: H. W. Wilson.

Lorenz, K. (1952). *King Solomon's ring.* London: Methuen.

Loro, A. D., & Orleans, C. S. (1981). Binge eating in obesity: Preliminary findings and guidelines for behavioral analysis and treatment. *Addictive Behaviors, 6,* 155–166.

Love, H., & Walthall, J. E. (1977). *A handbook of medical, educational, and psychological information for teachers of physically handicapped children.* Springfield, Ill.: Charles C. Thomas.

Lowery, C. R., & Settle, S. A. (1985). Effects of divorce on children: Differential impact of custody and visitation patterns. *Family Relations, 34,* 455–463.

Lozoff, B. (1989). Nutrition and behavior. *American Psychologist, 44,* 231–236.

Lynn, D. B. (1974). *The father: His role in child development.* Monterey, Calif.: Brooks/Cole.

Lynn, D. B. (1979). *Daughters and parents: Past, present and future.* Monterey, Calif.: Brooks/Cole.

Maccoby, E. E., & Jacklin, C. N. (1974). *The psychology of sex differences.* Stanford, Calif.: Stanford University Press.

Maccoby, E. E., & Jacklin, C. N. (1980). Sex differences in aggression: A rejoinder and reprise. *Child Development, 51,* 964–980.

Macfarlane, A. (1975). Olfaction in the development of social preferences in the human neonate. In Proceedings of CIBA Foundation Symposium, *Parent-infant interaction.* Amsterdam: Elsevier.

MacMillan, D. L. (1982). *Mental retardation in school and society* (2nd ed.). Boston: Little, Brown.

MacMillan, D. L., & Meyers, C. E. (1979). Educational labeling of handicapped learners. In D. C. Berliner (Ed.), *Review of research in education* (Vol. 7). Washington, D.C.: American Educational Research Association.

Madsen, M. C. (1971). Developmental and cross-cultural differences in the cooperation and competitive behavior of young children. *Journal of Cross-Cultural Psychology, 2,* 365–371.

Madsen, M. C., & Lancy, D. F. (1981). Cooperative and competitive behavior: Experiments related to ethnic identity and urbanization in Papua, New Guinea. *Journal of Cross-Cultural Psychology, 12,* 389–409.

Magnusson, D., & Backteman, G. (1978). Longitudinal stability of person characteristics: Intelligence and creativity. *Applied Psychological Measurement, 2,* 481–490.

Malina, R. M. (1990). Physical growth and performance during the transitional years (9 to 16). In R. Montemayor, G. R. Adams, & T. P. Gullotta (Eds.), *Advances in adolescent development: Vol. 2. From childhood to adolescence: A transitional period?* Newbury Park, Calif.: Sage.

Malina, R. M., & Bouchard, C. (1988). Subcutaneous fat distribution during growth. In C. Bouchard & F. E. Johnston (Eds.), *Fat distribution during growth and later health outcomes.* New York: Liss.

Malmquist, C. P. (1978). *Handbook of adolescence.* New York: Jason Aronson.

Mandler, J. M. (1984). Representation and recall in infancy. In M. Moscovitch (Ed.), *Infant memory.* New York: Plenum Press.

Marcia, J. E. (1966). Development and validation of ego-identity status. *Journal of Personality and Social Psychology, 3,* 551–558.

Marcia, J. E. (1980). Identity in adolescence. In J. Adelson (Ed.), *Handbook of adolescent psychology.* New York: Wiley.

Marcia, J. E., & Friedman, M. L. (1970). Ego identity status in college women. *Journal of Personality, 39,* 249–269.

Marland, S. P. (1972). *Education of the gifted and talented.* Washington, D.C.: U.S. Government Printing Office.

Marlatt, G. A., Baer, J. S., Donovan, D. M., & Kivlahan, D. R. (1988). Addictive behaviors: Etiology and treatment. *Annual Review of Psychology, 39,* 223–252.

Marsh, H. W. (1989). Sex differences in the development of verbal and mathematics constructs: The high school and beyond study. *American Educational Research Journal, 26,* 191–225.

Marsh, H. W., & Holmes, I. W. MacDonald (1990). Multidimensional self-concepts: Construct validation of responses by children. *American Educational Research Journal, 27,* 89–117.

Marsiglio, W. (1986). Teenage fatherhood: High school accreditation and educational attainment. In A. B. Elster & M. E. Lamb (Eds.), *Adolescent fatherhood*. Hillsdale, N.J.: Lawrence Erlbaum.

Marston, A. R., Jacobs, D. F., Singer, R. D., Widaman, K. F., & Little, T. D. (1988). Characteristics of adolescents at risk for compulsive overeating on a brief screening test. *Adolescence, 23*, 288–302.

Martin, H. (1976). *The abused child*. Cambridge, Mass.: Ballinger.

Martin, N., & Jardine, R. (1986). Eysenck's contributions to behaviour genetics. In S. Modgil & C. Modgil (Eds.), *Hans Eysenck: Consensus and controversy*. Philadelphia: Falmer.

Martin, R. P. (1989). Temperament and education: Implications for underachievement and learning disabilities. In W. B. Carey & S. C. McDevitt (Eds.), *Clinical and educational applications of temperament research*. Berwyn, Penn.: Swets North America.

Maslow, A. H. (1970). *Motivation and personality* (2nd ed.). New York: Harper & Row.

Mason, W. A., & Kenney, M. D. (1974). Redirection of filial attachments in rhesus monkeys: Dogs as mother surrogates. *Science, 183*, 1209–1211.

Masters, J. C. (1979). Interpreting "imitative" responses in early infancy. *Science, 205*, 215.

Masters, W. H., Johnson, V. E., & Kolodny, R. C. (1988). *Crisis: Heterosexual behavior in the age of AIDS*. New York: Grove Press.

Matsungaga, E., Tonomura, A., Oishi, H., & Kikuchi, Y. (1978). Re-examination of parental age effect in Down's syndrome. *Human Genetics, 40*, 259–268.

Maxim, G. W. (1989). *The very young* (3rd ed.). Columbus, Ohio: Charles E. Merrill.

Mayer, N. K., & Tronick, E. Z. (1985). Mother's turn-giving signals and infant turn-taking in mother-infant interaction. In T. M. Field & N. A. Fox (Eds.), *Social perception in infants*. Norwood, N.J.: Ablex.

Mazur, A. (1977). On Wilson's sociobiology. *American Journal of Sociology, 83*, 697–700.

McCall, R. B., Applebaum, M. I., & Hogarty, F. S. (1973). Developmental changes in mental test performance. *Monographs of the Society for Research in Child Development, 38*, No. 150.

McCartney, K., Bernieri, F., & Harris, M. J. (1990). Growing up and growing apart: A developmental meta-analysis of twin studies. *Psychological Bulletin, 107*, 226–237.

McCartney, K., & Jordan, E. (1990). Parallels between research on child care and research on school effects. *Educational Researcher, 19*, 21–27.

McClelland, D., Constantian, C. S., Regalado, D., & Stone, C. (1978, June). Making it to maturity. *Psychology Today*, 42–53, 114.

McCormick, M., Shapiro, S., & Starfield, B. (1984). High-risk young mothers: Infant mortality and morbidity in four areas in the United States, 1973–1978. *American Journal of Public Health, 74*, 18–23.

McGraw, M. B. (1943). *The neuromuscular maturation of the human infant*. New York: Columbia University Press.

McKay, J., Sinisterra, L., McKay, A., Gomez, H., & Lloreda, P. (1978). Improving cognitive ability in chronically deprived children. *Science, 200*, 270–278.

McKusick, V. A. (1986). *Mendelian inheritance in man* (7th ed.). Baltimore: Johns Hopkins University Press.

McNeill, D. (1970). *The acquisition of language: The study of developmental psycholinguistics*. New York: Harper & Row.

Mead, G. H. (1967). *Mind, self, and society*. (C. W. Norris, Ed.). Chicago: University of Chicago Press.

Meadow, K. P. (1975). Development of deaf children. In E. M. Hetherington (Ed.), *Review of child development research* (Vol. 5). Chicago: University of Chicago Press.

Mednick, S. A. (1962). The associative basis of the creative process. *Psychological Review, 69*, 220–232.

Meissner, S. J. (1965). Parental interaction of the adolescent boy. *Journal of Genetic Psychology, 107*, 225–233.

Melican, G. J., & Feldt, L. S. (1980). An empirical study of the Zajonc-Marcus hypothesis for achievement test scores declines. *American Educational Research Journal, 17*, 5–19.

Meline, C. W. (1976). Does the medium matter? *Journal of Communication, 26*, 81–89.

Meltzoff, A. N. (1988). Infant imitation after a 1-week delay: Long-term memory for novel acts and multiple stimuli. *Developmental Psychology, 24*, 470–476.

Meltzoff, A. N., & Moore, M. K. (1977). Imitation of facial and manual gestures by human neonates. *Science, 198*, 75–78.

Meltzoff, A. N., & Moore, M. K. (1979). Interpreting "imitative" responses in early infancy. *Science, 205*, 217–219.

Meltzoff, A. N., & Moore, M. K. (1983). Newborn infants imitate adult facial gestures. *Child Development, 54,* 702–709.

Meltzoff, A. N., & Moore, M. K. (1989). Imitation in newborn infants: Exploring the range of gestures imitated and the underlying mechanisms. *Developmental Psychology, 25,* 954–962.

Mercer, C. D., & Snell, M. E. (1977). *Learning theory research in mental retardation: Implications for teaching.* Columbus, Ohio: Charles E. Merrill.

Mercer, J. R. (1973). *Labeling the mentally retarded.* Berkeley: University of California Press.

Meyer, W. J. (1985). Summary, integration, and prospective. In J. B. Dusek (Ed.), *Teacher expectancies.* Hillsdale, N.J.: Laurence Erlbaum.

Mielke, K. W. (1983). Formative research on appeal and comprehension in 3-2-1 CONTACT. In J. Bryant & D. R. Anderson (Eds.), *Children's understanding of television: Research on attention and comprehension* (pp. 241–264). New York: Academic Press.

Miller, G. A. (1956). The magical number seven, plus or minus two: Some limits on our capacity for processing information. *Psychological Review, 63,* 81–97.

Miller, L. B., & Bizzell, R. P. (1983). Long-term effects of four preschool programs: Sixth, seventh, and eighth grades. *Child Development, 54,* 727–741.

Miller, S. A. (1981). *Certainty and necessity in the understanding of Piagetian concepts.* Paper presented at the Society for Research in Child Development meetings, Boston, April.

Minister of Supply and Services Canada (1989). *Canada Yearbook (1990).* Ottawa: Statistic Canada.

Mischel, W. (1979). On the interface of cognition and personality: Beyond the person-situation debate. *American Psychologist, 34,* 740–754.

Mitchell, A. (1985). *Children in the middle.* New York: Tavistock.

Mitchell, G. D., Arling, G. L., & Moller, G. W. (1967). Long term effects of maternal punishment on the behavior of monkeys. *Psychonomic Science,* 209–210.

Miyawaki, K., Strange, W., Verbrugge, R., Liberman, A. M., Jenkins, J. J., & Fujimura, O. (1975). An effect of linguistic experience: The discrimination of [r] and [l] by native speakers of Japanese and English. *Perception & Psychophysics, 18,* 331–340.

Moffitt, A. R. (1971). Consonant cue perception by 20–24 week old infants. *Child Development, 42,* 717–731.

Monachesi, E. D., & Hathaway, S. R. (1969). The personality of delinquents. In J. N. Butcher (Ed.), *MMPI: Research developments and clinical applications.* New York: McGraw-Hill, 207–219.

Moncrieff, C., Larner, M., Riley, D., Gunnarsson, L., & Henderson, C. R., Jr. (Eds.). (1990). *Extending families: The social networks of parents and their children.* New York: Cambridge University Press.

Money, J. (1975). Counselling in genetics and applied behavior genetics. In K. W. Schaie, V. F. Anderson, G. F. McClearn, & J. Money (Eds.), *Developmental human behavior genetics.* Lexington, Mass.: D. C. Heath.

Money, J., & Ehrhardt, A. A. (1968). Prenatal hormonal exposure: Possible effects on behavior in man. In R. P. Michael (Ed.), *Endocrinology and human behavior.* London: Oxford University Press.

Montemayor, R., & Eisen, M. (1977). The development of self-conceptions from childhood to adolescence. *Developmental Psychology, 13,* 314–319.

Montemayor, R., & Flannery, D. J. (1990). Making the transition from childhood to early adolescence. In R. Montemayor, G. R. Adams, & T. P. Gullotta (Eds.), *Advances in adolescent development: Vol. 2. From childhood to adolescence: A transitional period?* Newbury Park, Calif.: Sage.

Montemayor, R., & Van Komen, R. (1980). Age segregation of adolescents in and out of school. *Journal of Youth and Adolescence, 9,* 371–381.

Montessori, M. (1912). *The Montessori method.* New York: Frederick A. Stokes.

Montessori, M. (1967). *The absorbent mind.* New York: Holt, Rinehart & Winston.

Moore, R. C. (1986). *Childhood's domain: Play and place in child development.* London: Croom Helm.

Moran, J. D., III, & O'Brien, G. (1984). Relationship between parental child-rearing attitudes and preschoolers' moral judgements. *Psychological Reports, 55,* 893–894.

Moray, N. (1959). Attention and dichotic listening: Affective cues and the influence of instruction. *Quarterly Journal of Experimental Psychology, 11,* 56–60.

Moriarty, A. (1990). Deterring the molester and abuser: Pre-employment testing for child and youth care workers. *Child and Youth Care Quarterly, 18,* 59–65.

Morin, S. F. (1988). AIDS: The challenge to psychology. *American Psychologist, 43,* 838–842.

Morrison, E., Starks, K., Hyndman, C., & Ronzio, N. (1980). *Growing up sexual.* New York: Van Nostrand Reinhold.

Morrison, J. R., & Stewart, M. A. (1973). The psychiatric status of the legal families of adopted hyperactive children. *Archives of Genetic Psychiatry, 28,* 888–891.

Morsink, C. V. (1985). Learning disabilities. In W. H. Berdine & A. E. Blackhurst (Eds.), *An introduction to special education* (2nd ed.). Boston: Little, Brown.

Moskowitz, B. A. (1978). The acquisition of language. *Scientific American, 239,* 92–108.

Moynahan, E. D. (1973). The development of knowledge concerning the effect of categorization upon free recall. *Child Development, 44,* 238–245.

Mulhern, R. K., & Passman, R. H. (1979). The child's behavioral pattern as a determinant of maternal punitiveness. *Child Development, 15,* 417–423.

Mulhern, R. K., Jr., & Passman, R. H. (1981). Parental discipline as affected by the sex of the parent, the sex of the child, and the child's apparent responsiveness to discipline. *Developmental Psychology, 17,* 604–613.

Murray, J. P. (1973, June). Television and violence: Implications of the Surgeon General's research program. *American Psychologist,* 472–478.

Muuss, R. E. (1975). *Theories of adolescence* (3rd ed.). New York: Random House.

Muuss, R. E. (1988). Carol Gilligan's theory of sex differences in the development of moral reasoning during adolescence. *Adolescence, 23,* 229–243.

Naeye, R. L. (1980). Sudden infant death. *Scientific American, 242,* 56–62.

National Center for Health Statistics. (1981). *Vital statistics of the United States.* Hyattsville, Md.: Public Health Service.

Neal, J. H. (1983). Children's understanding of their parents' divorces. In L. A. Kurdek (Ed.), *Children and divorce: New directions for child development.* San Francisco: Jossey-Bass, 3–14.

Nealis, J. T. (1983). Epilepsy. In J. Umbriet (Ed.), *Physical disabilities and health impairment: An introduction* (pp. 74–85). Columbus, Ohio: Charles E. Merrill.

Nelson, K. E. (1989). Strategies for first language teaching. In M. L. Rice & R. L. Schiefelbusch (Eds.), *Teachability of language.* Baltimore: Brookes.

Newcomb, M. D., & Bentler, P. M. (1988). *Consequences of adolescent drug use: Impact on the lives of young adults.* Newbury Park, Calif.: Sage.

Newcomb, M. D., & Bentler, P. M. (1989). Substance use and abuse among children and teenagers. *American Psychologist, 44,* 242–248.

Newman, H. H., Freeman, F. N., & Holzinger, K. J. (1937). *Twins: A study of heredity and environment.* Chicago: University of Chicago Press.

Newsweek, January 6, 1969, p. 37.

Nicolaides, K. H., Thorpe-Beeston, J. G., & Nobel, P. (1990). Cordocentesis. In R. D. Eden, F. H. Boehm, & M. Haire (Eds.), *Assessment and care of the fetus: Physiological, clinical, and medicolegal principles.* Norwalk, Conn.: Appleton & Lange.

Nielsen Television Index: Report on television usage. (1984). Hackensack, N.J.: A. C. Nielsen Co.

Norcia, A. M., & Tyler, C. W. (1985). Spatial frequency sweep VEP: Visual acuity during the first year of life. *Vision Research, 25,* 1399–1408.

Nucci, L. P., & Turiel, E. (1978). Social interactions and the development of social concepts in preschool children. *Child Development, 49,* 400–407.

Oden, M. (1968). The fulfillment of promise: 40-year follow-up of the Terman gifted group. In R. S. Albert (Ed.), *Genius and eminence: The social psychology of creativity and exceptional achievement.* New York: Oxford University Press (1983).

Oden, S. (1988). Alternative perspectives on children's peer relationships. In T. D. Yawkey & J. E. Johnson (Eds.), *Integrative processes and socialization: Early to middle childhood.* Hillsdale, N.J.: Lawrence Erlbaum.

Offer, D., & Offer, J. (1975). *From teenage to young manhood: A psychological study.* New York: Basic Books.

Offer, D. O., Ostrov, E., Howard, K. (1981). *The adolescent: A psychological self-portrait.* New York: Basic Books.

Offer, D. O., Ostrov, E., Howard, K. (1984). *Patterns of adolescent self-image.* San Francisco: Jossey-Bass.

Offer, D. O., Ostrov, E., Howard, K., & Atkinson, R. (1988). *The teenage world: Adolescents' self-image in ten countries.* New York: Plenum Press.

O'Leary, K. D. (1984). *Mommy, I can't sit still!: Coping with hyperactive and aggressive children.* New York: New Horizon Press Publishers.

Olson, D. R. (1986). The cognitive consequences of literacy. *Canadian Psychology, 27,* 109–121.

Olson, G. M. (1981). The recognition of specific persons. In M. E. Lamb & L. R. Sherrod (Eds.), *Infant social cognition: Empirical and theoretical considerations.* Hillsdale, N.J.: Lawrence Erlbaum.

O'Neill, G. P. (1984). Some reflections on the integration of moderately mentally handicapped students (TMR) in Ontario schools. *Canadian Journal for Exceptional Children, 1,* 19–22.

Opper, S. (1977). Concept development in Thai urban and rural children. In P. R. Dasen (Ed.), *Piagetian psychology: Cross-cultural contributions.* New York: Gardner Press.

Ornstein, P. A., Baker-Ward, L., & Naus, M. J. (1988). The development of mnemonic skill. In F. E. Weinert & M. Perlmutter (Eds.), *Memory development: Universal changes and individual differences.* Hillsdale, N.J.: Lawrence Erlbaum.

Oster, H., Daily, L., & Goldenthal, P. (1989). Processing facial affect. In A. W. Young & H. D. Ellis (Eds.), *Handbook of research on face processing.* Amsterdam: North Holland.

Overton, W. F. (1973). On the assumptive base of the nature-nurture controversy: Additive versus interactive conceptions. *Human Development, 16,* 74–89.

Packard, V. (1968). *The sexual wilderness.* New York: Pocket Books.

Packard, V. (1983). *Our endangered children: Growing up in a changing world.* Boston: Little, Brown.

Page, E. B., & Grandon, G. M. (1979). Family configuration and mental ability: Two theories contrasted with U.S. data. *American Educational Research Journal, 16,* 257–272.

Paley, V. G. (1984). *Boys and girls: Superheroes in the doll corner.* Chicago: University of Chicago Press.

Paley, V. G. (1986). *Mollie is three: Growing up in School.* Chicago: University of Chicago Press.

Pallas, A. M., Natriello, G., & McDill, E. L. (1989). The changing nature of the disadvantaged population: Current dimensions and future trends. *Educational Researcher, 18,* 16–22.

Panzica, N. (1983). *Your teen and drugs: A parent's handbook on drug abuse.* New York: McGraw-Hill.

Paris, S. G., & Lindauer, B. K. (1976). The role of inference in children's comprehension and memory for sentences. *Cognitive Psychology, 8,* 217–227.

Paris, S. G., & Lindauer, B. K. (1982). Cognitive development in infancy. In B. B. Wolman and others (Eds.), *Handbook of developmental psychology.* Englewood Cliffs, N.J.: Prentice-Hall.

Parke, R. D. (1970). The role of punishment in the socialization process. In R. A. Hoppe, G. A. Milton, & E. C. Simmel (Eds.), *Early experiences and the process of socialization.* New York: Academic Press.

Parke, R. D. (1979). Perspectives on father-infant interaction. In J. D. Osofsky (Ed.), *Handbook of infant development.* New York: John Wiley.

Parke, R. D., & Collmer, C. W. (1975). Child abuse: An interdisciplinary analysis. In E. M. Hetherington (Ed.), *Review of child development research* (Vol. 5). Chicago: University of Chicago Press.

Parke, R. D., MacDonald, K. B., Burks, V. M., Carson, J., Bhavnagri, N., et al. (1989). Family and peer systems: In search of linkages. In K. Kreppner & R. M. Lerner (Eds.), *Family systems of life span development.* Hillsdale, N.J.: Lawrence Erlbaum.

Parmelee, A. H., Jr., & Sigman, M. D. (1983). Perinatal brain development and behavior. In P. H. Mussen (Ed.), *Handbook of child psychology* (4th ed.) (Vol. 2): *Infancy and developmental psychobiology* (M. M. Haith & J. J. Campos, Eds.). New York: John Wiley, 95–156.

Parnes. S. J., & Harding, H. E. (Eds.). (1962). *A sourcebook for creative thinking.* New York: Charles Scribner's.

Parten, M. B. (1932). Social participation among preschool children. *Journal of Abnormal Social Psychology, 27,* 243–270.

Passman, R. H. (1974). *The effects of mothers and security blankets upon learning in children (Should Linus bring his blanket to school?).* Paper presented at the American Psychological Association Convention, New Orleans, September.

Passman, R. H. (1976). Arousal reducing properties of attachment objects: Testing the functional limits of the security blanket relative to the mother. *Developmental Psychology, 12,* 468–469.

Passman, R. H. (1977). Providing attachment objects to facilitate learning and reduce distress: Effects of mothers and security blankets. *Developmental Psychology, 12,* 25–28.

Passman, R. H. (1987). Attachments to inanimate objects: Are children who have security blankets insecure? *Journal of Consulting and Clinical Psychology, 55,* 825–830.

Passman, R. H., & Adams, R. E. (1982). Preferences for mothers and security blankets and their effectiveness as reinforcers for young children's behaviors. *Journal of Child Psychology and Psychiatry, 23,* 223–236.

Passman, R. H., & Blackwelder, D. E. (1981). Rewarding and punishing by mothers: The influence of progressive changes in the quality of their son's apparent behavior. *Developmental Psychology, 17,* 614–619.

Passman, R. H., & Erck, T. W. (1978). Permitting maternal contact through vision alone: Films of mothers for promoting play and locomotion. *Developmental Psychology, 14,* 512–516.

Passman, R. H., & Halonen, J. S. (1979). A developmental survey of young children's attachments to inanimate objects. *The Journal of Genetic Psychology, 134,* 165–178.

Passman, R. H., & Longeway, K. P. (1982). The role of vision in maternal attachment: Giving 2-year-olds a photograph of their mother during separation. *Developmental Psychology, 18,* 530–533.

Passman, R. H., & Mulhern, R. K. (1977). Maternal punitiveness as affected by situational stress: An experimental analogue of child abuse. *Journal of Abnormal Psychology, 86,* 565–569.

Passman, R. H., & Weisberg, P. (1975). Mothers and blankets as agents for promoting play and exploration by young children in a novel environment: The effects of social and nonsocial attachment objects. *Development Psychology, 11,* 170–177.

Patton, J. M., Prillaman, D., & Tassel-Baska, J. V. (1990). The nature and extent of programs for the disadvantaged gifted in the United States and Territories. *Gifted Child Quarterly, 34,* 94–96.

Pavlov, I. P. (1927). *Conditioned reflexes.* London: Oxford University Press.

Pazulinec, R., Meyerrose, M., & Sajwaj, T. (1983). Punishment via response cost. In S. Axelrod & J. Apsche (Eds.), *The effects of punishment on human behavior.* New York: Academic Press.

Pearce, J. C. (1977). *Magical child: Rediscovering nature's plan for our children.* New York: Bantam Books.

Pearl, R., Bryan, T., & Herzog, A. (1990). Resisting or acquiescing to peer pressure to engage in misconduct: Adolescents' expectations of probable consequences. *Journal of Youth and Adolescence, 19,* 43–55.

Pearse, W. H. (1982). Trends in out-of-hospital births. *Obstetrics and Gynecology, 60,* 267–270.

Pearson, J. L., & Ferguson, L. R. (1989). Gender differences in patterns of spatial ability, environmental cognition, and math and English achievement in late adolescence. *Adolescence, 24,* 421–431.

Pedersen, F. A. (Ed.). (1980). *The father-infant relationship: Observational studies in the family setting.* New York: Praeger.

Penner, L. A., Thompson, J. K., & Coovert, D. L. (1991). Size overestimation among anorexics: Much ado about very little? *Journal of Abnormal Psychology, 100,* 90–93.

Perlmutter, M. (1980). Development of memory in the preschool years. In R. Greene & T. D. Yawkey (Eds.), *Childhood development.* Westport, Conn.: Technomic Publishing.

Peskin, H. (1973). Influence of the developmental schedule of puberty on learning and ego functioning. *Journal of Youth and Adolescence, 2,* 273–290.

Petersen, A. C. (1988). Adolescent development. *Annual Review of Psychology, 39,* 583–607.

Peterson, C., & Peterson, R. (1986). Parent-child interaction and daycare: Does quality of daycare matter? *Journal of Applied Developmental Psychology, 7,* 1–15.

Peterson, G. W., Leigh, G. K., & Day, R. D. (1984). Family stress theory and the impact of divorce on children. *Journal of Divorce, 7,* 1–20.

Pfeffer, C. R. (1981). Developmental issues among children of separation and divorce. In I. R. Stuart & L. E. Abt (Eds.), *Children of separation and divorce: Management and treatment.* New York: Van Nostrand, 20–33.

Phillips, D., McCartney, K., & Scarr, S. (1987). Child-care quality and children's social development. *Developmental Psychology, 23,* 537–543.

Piaget, J. (1923). *Le langage et la pensée chez l'enfant.* London: Kegan Paul.

Piaget, J. (1932). *The moral judgment of the child.* London: Kegan Paul.

Piaget, J. (1951). *Play, dreams and imitation in childhood.* New York: W. W. Norton.

Piaget, J. (1954). *The construction of reality in the child.* New York: Basic Books.

Piaget, J. (1961). The genetic approach to the psychology of thought. *Journal of Educational Psychology, 52,* 275–281.

Piaget, J. (1972). Intellectual development from adolescence to adulthood. *Human Development, 15,* 1–12.

Pill, C. J. (1990). Stepfamilies: Redefining the family. *Family Relations, 39,* 186–193.

Pinchbeck, I., & Hewitt, M. (1973). *Children in English society* (Vol. II): *From the eighteenth century to the Children Act of 1948.* London: Routledge & Kegan Paul.

Pines, M. (1966). *Revolution in learning: The years from birth to six.* New York: Harper & Row.

Pines, M. (1975). In praise of the "invulnerables." *APA Monitor*, December, 7.

Pines, M. (1978, September). Invisible playmates. *Psychology Today*, 38–42, 106.

Pines, M. (1979, January). Superkids. *Psychology Today*, 53–63.

Pines, M. (1982, February). Baby, you're incredible. *Psychology Today*, 48–53.

Pipes, P. L., Bumbals, J., & Pritkin, R. (1985). Collecting and assessing food intake information. In P. L. Pipes (Ed.), *Nutrition in infancy and childhood*. St. Louis: Times-Mirror/Mosby.

Pitcher, E. G., & Schultz, L. H. (1983). *Boys and girls at play: The development of sex roles*. New York: Praeger.

Placek, P. J. (1986). Commentary: Cesarean rates still rising. *Statistical Bulletin, 67*, 9.

Plomin, R. (1987). Developmental behavioral genetics and infancy. In J. D. Osofsky (Ed.), *Handbook of infant development* (2nd ed.). New York: John Wiley.

Plomin, R. (1989). Environment and genes: Determinants of behavior. *American Psychologist, 44*, 105–111.

Pogrebin, L. C. (1980). *Growing up free: Raising your child in the 80's*. New York: McGraw-Hill.

Pogue-Geile, M. F., & Rose, R. J. (1985). Developmental genetic studies of adult personality. *Developmental Psychology, 21*, 547–557.

Polivy, J., & Herman, C. P. (1985). Dieting and binging. A causal analysis. *American Psychologist, 40*, 193–201.

Polson, B., & Newton, M. (1984). *Not my kid: A family's guide to kids and drugs*. New York: Arbor House.

Pope, H. G., Hudson, J. I., Jurgelun-Todd, D., & Hudson, M. S. (1984). Prevalence of anorexia nervosa and bulimia in three student populations. *International Journal of Eating Disorders, 2*, 75–85.

Post, G., & Crowther, J. H. (1985). Variables that discriminate bulimic from nonbulimic adolescent females. *Journal of Youth and Adolescence, 14*, 85–99.

Prado, W. (1958). *Appraisal of performance as a function of the relative-ego-involvement of children and adolescents*. Unpublished doctoral dissertation, University of Oklahoma.

Preemies' diet seen key to progress. (1988). *Edmonton Journal*, Feb. 1, p. C1.

Premack, A. J., & Premack, D. (1972). Teaching language to an ape. *Scientific American, 227*, 92–99.

Premack, D. (1965). Reinforcement theory. In D. Levine (Ed.), *Nebraska Symposium on Motivation* (Vol. 13). Lincoln: University of Nebraska Press.

Pressley, M., Forrest-Pressley, D., & Elliott-Faust, D. J. (1988). What is strategy instructional enrichment and how to study it: Illustrations from research on children's prose memory and comprehension. In F. E. Weinert & M. Perlmutter (Eds.), *Memory development: Universal changes and individual differences*. Hillsdale, N.J.: Lawrence Erlbaum.

Preyer, W. (1888–1889). *The mind of the child* (2 vols.). New York: Appleton Century. (First published in German, 1882.)

Provine, R. R., & Westerman, J. A. (1979). Crossing the midline: Limits of early eye-hand behavior. *Child Development, 50*, 804–814.

Punch, J. (1983). The prevalence of hearing impairment. *ASHA, 25*, 27.

Putallaz, M., & Gottman, J. M. (1981). An interactional model of children's entry into peer groups. *Child Development, 52*, 986–994.

Pyles Honzik, M. K. (1932). Verbalization as a factor in learning. *Child Development, 3*, 108–113.

Quay, H. C. (1987). Intelligence. In H. C. Quay (Ed.), *Handbook of juvenile delinquency*. New York: John Wiley, 106–117.

Raeburn, J. A. (1984). Mental handicap. In E. H. Emery & I. Pullen (Eds.), *Psychological aspects of genetic counselling*. New York: Academic Press.

Ramsay, D., & Campos, J. (1975). Memory by the infant in an object notion task. *Developmental Psychology, 11*, 411–412.

Rank, O. (1929). *The trauma of birth*. New York: Harcourt Brace & World.

Ratner, H. H. (1980). The role of social context in memory development. In M. Perlmutter (Ed.), *Children's memory*. San Francisco: Jossey-Bass.

Rawlings, G., Reynolds, E. O. R., Steward, A., & Strang, L. B. (1971). Changing prognosis for infants of very low birth weight. *Lancet, 1*, 516–519.

Ray, W. Z., & Ravizza, R. (1985). *Methods toward a science of behavior and experience* (2nd ed.). Belmont, Calif.: Wadsworth.

Rayburn, W., Wilson, G., Schreck, J., Louwsma, G., & Hamman, J. (1982). Prenatal counseling: A state-wide telephone service. *Obstetrics and Gynecology, 60*, 243–246.

Rayna, S., Sinclair, H., & Stambak, M. (1989). Infants and physics. In H. Sinclair, M. Stambak, I. Lézine,

S. Rayna, & M. Verba (Eds.), *Infants and objects: The creativity of cognitive development.* New York: Academic Press.

Rebok, G. W., & Balcerak, L. J. (1989). Memory self-efficacy and performance differences in young and old adults: The effect of mnemonic training. *Developmental Psychology, 25,* 714–721.

Recommended Dietary Allowances (9th ed.). 1980. Washington, D.C.: National Academy of Sciences.

Redmond, M. (1985). Attitudes of adolescent males toward adolescent pregnancy and fatherhood. *Family Relations, 34,* 337–342.

Reese, H. W., & Overton, W. F. (1970). Models and theories of development. In L. R. Goulet & P. B. Baltes (Eds.), *Lifespan developmental psychology: Research and theory.* New York: Academic Press.

Reiss, I. L. (1966). *The social context of premarital sexual permissiveness.* New York: Holt, Rinehart & Winston.

Reissland, N. (1988). Neonatal imitation in the first hour of life: Observations in rural Nepal. *Developmental Psychology, 24,* 464–469.

Rheingold, H. L. (1985). Development as the acquisition of familiarity. *Annual Review of Psychology, 36,* 1–17.

Rheingold, H. L., & Cook, K. V. (1975). The contents of boys' and girls' rooms as an index of parents' behavior. *Child Development, 46,* 459–463.

Rice, B. (1982, February). The Hawthorne defect: Persistence of a flawed theory. *Psychology Today,* 71–74.

Rice, M. L. (1989). Children's language acquisition. *American Psychologist, 44,* 149–156.

Ringler, N. M., Kennell, J. H., Jarvella, R., Navojosky, B. J., & Klaus, M. H. (1975). Mother to child speech at two years: Effects of early post-natal contact. *Journal of Pediatrics, 86,* 141–144.

Ringwalt, C. L., & Palmer, J. H. (1989). Cocaine and crack users compared. *Adolescence, 24,* 851–859.

Roazen, P. (1975). *Freud and his followers.* New York: Alfred A. Knopf.

Roberts, D. F., & Bachan, C. M. (1981). Mass communication effects. *Annual Review of Psychology, 32,* 307–356.

Robinson, N. M., & Robinson, H. B. (1976). *The mentally retarded child: A psychological approach* (2nd ed.). New York: McGraw-Hill.

Robinson, S. (1989). Caring for childbearing women: The interrelationship between midwifery and medi-cal reponsibilities. In S. Robinson & A. M. Thomson (Eds.), *Midwives, research and childbirth* (Vol. 1). New York: Chapman and Hall.

Rochat, P. (1989). Object manipulation and exploration in 2- to 5-month-old infants. *Developmental Psychology, 25,* 871–884.

Roche, A. F., Lipman, R. S., Overall, J. E., & Hung, W. (1979). The effects of stimulant medication on the growth of hyperkinetic children. *Pediatrics, 63,* 847–850.

Rodeck, C. H. (1982). Fetal blood sampling. In H. Galjaard (Ed.), *The future of prenatal diagnosis.* London: Churchill Livingstone, 85–92.

Roethlisberger, S. J., & Dickson, W. J. (1939). *Management and the worker.* Cambridge, Mass.: Harvard University Press.

Roffwarg, H. P., Muzio, J. N., & Dement, W. C. (1966). Ontogenetic development of the human sleep-dream cycle. *Science, 152.* 604–619.

Rogers, C. R. (1951). *Client-centered therapy: Its current practice, implications, and theory.* Boston: Houghton Mifflin.

Rolison, M. A., & Medway, F. J. (1985). Teachers' expectations and attributions for student achievement: Effects of label, performance pattern, and special education intervention. *American Educational Research Journal, 22,* 561–573.

Romig, C. A., & Bakken, L. (1990). Teens at risk for pregnancy: The role of ego development and family processes. *Journal of Adolescents, 13,* 195–199.

Roscoe, B., & Kruger, T. L. (1990). AIDS: Late adolescents' knowledge and its influence on sexual behavior. *Adolescence, 25,* 39–48.

Rosengren, K. E., & Windahl, S. (1989). *Media matter: TV use in childhood and adolescence.* Norwood, N.J.: Ablex.

Rosenkoetter, L. I., Huston, A. C., & Wright, J. C. (1990). Television and the moral judgment of the young child. *Journal of Applied Developmental Psychology, 11,* 123–137.

Rosenthal, R. (1969). Experimenter expectancy and the reassuring nature of the null hypothesis decision procedure. *Psychological Bulletin Monographs Supplement, 70,* 30–47.

Rosenthal, R., & Jacobson, L. (1968a). *Pygmalion in the classroom: Teacher expectations and pupils' intellectual development.* New York: Holt, Rinehart & Winston.

Rosenthal, R., & Jacobson, L. (1968b). Teacher expectations for the disadvantaged. *Scientific American, 218,* 19–23.

Rosenthal, T. L., & Zimmerman, B. J. (1972). Modeling by exemplification and instruction in training conservation. *Developmental Psychology, 6,* 392–401.

Rosett, H. L., & Sander, L. W. (1979). Effects of maternal drinking on neonatal morphology and state regulation. In J. D. Osofsky (Ed.), *Handbook of infant development.* New York: John Wiley, 809–836.

Ross, A. O. (1980). *Psychological disorders of children: A behavioral approach to theory, research, and therapy* (2nd ed.). New York: McGraw-Hill.

Ross, H. S. (1982). Establishment of social games among toddlers. *Developmental Psychology, 18,* 509–518.

Rothbart, M. K. (1982). The concept of difficult temperament: A critical analysis of Thomas, Chess, and Korn, *Merrill-Palmer Quarterly, 28,* 35–40.

Rothstein, E. (1980). The scar of Sigmund Freud. *New York Review of Books,* October 9, 14–20.

Rousseau, J. J. (1911). *Emile, or on education* (Barbara Foxley, Trans.). London: Dent. (Originally published, 1762.)

Rovee-Collier, C. K. (1987). Learning and memory in infancy. In J. D. Osofsky (Ed.), *Handbook of infant development.* New York: John Wiley.

Rovee-Collier, C. K., Sullivan, M. W., Enright, M. L., Lucas, D., & Fagen, J. W. (1980). Reactivation of infant memory. *Science, 208,* 1159–1161.

Rubin, J. Z., Provenzano, J. J., & Luria, Z. (1974). The eye of the beholder: Parent's views on sex of newborns. *American Journal of Orthopsychiatry, 44,* 512–519.

Rubin, K. H., Maioni, T. L., & Hornung, M. (1976). Free play behaviors in middle- and lower-class preschoolers: Parten and Piaget revisited. *Child Development, 47,* 414–419.

Rubin, Z. (1980). *Children's friendships.* Cambridge, Mass.: Harvard University Press.

Runco, M. A. (1986a). Maximal performance on divergent thinking tests by gifted, talented, and nongifted children. *Psychology in the Schools, 23,* 308–315.

Runco, M. A. (1986b). Flexibility and originality in children's divergent thinking. *The Journal of Psychology, 120,* 345–352.

Runco, M. A., & Albert, R. S. (1986). Exceptional giftedness in early adolescence and intrafamilial divergent thinking. *Journal of Youth and Adolescence, 15,* 335–344.

Russell, J. A., & Ward, L. M. (1982). Environmental psychology. *Annual Review of Psychology, 33,* 651–688.

Sagan, C. (1977). *The dragons of Eden.* New York: Ballantine Books.

Sagov, S. E., Feinbloom, R. L., Spindel, P., & Brodsky, A. (1984). *Home births: A practitioner's guide to birth outside the hospital.* Rockville, Md.: Aspen Systems Corporation.

Sameroff, A. J. (1968). The components of sucking in the human newborn. *Journal of Experimental Child Psychology, 6,* 607–623.

Savin-Williams, R. C., & Small, S. A. (1986). The timing of puberty and its relationship to adolescent and parent perceptions of family interactions. *Developmental Psychology, 22,* 342–347.

Scarr, S. (1985). Constructing psychology: Making facts and fables for our times. *American Psychologist, 40,* 499–512.

Scarr, S., & Kidd, K. K. (1983). Developmental behavior genetics. In P. H. Mussen (Ed.), *Handbook of child psychology* (4th ed.) (Vol. 2): *Infancy and developmental psychobiology* (M. M. Haith & J. J. Campos, Eds.). New York: John Wiley, 345–434.

Scarr, S., & Salapatek, P. (1970). Patterns of fear development during infancy. *Merrill-Palmer Quarterly, 16,* 56–90.

Scarr, S., & Weinberg, R. A. (1983). The Minnesota Adoption Studies: Genetic differences and malleability. *Child Development, 54,* 260–267.

Scarr-Salapatek, S., & Williams, M. L. (1973). The effects of early stimulation on low-birth weight infants. *Child Development, 44,* 94–101.

The "scene" and the skinheads. (1990). *Edmonton Journal,* Nov. 18, E1.

Schaefer, C. E. (1969). Imaginary companions and creative adolescents. *Developmental Psychology, 1,* 747–749.

Schaffer, H. R. (1966). The onset of fear of strangers and the incongruity hypothesis. *Journal of Child Psychology and Psychiatry, 7,* 95–106.

Schaffer, H. R. (1984). *The child's entry into a social world.* New York: Academic Press.

Schaffer, H. R., Collis, G. M., & Parsons, G. (1977). Vocal interchange and visual regard in verbal and pre-verbal children. In H. R. Schaffer (Ed.), *Studies in mother-infant interaction.* London: Academic Press.

Schaie, K. W. (1965). A general model for the study of developmental problems. *Psychological Bulletin, 64,* 92–107.

Schardein, J. L. (1985). *Chemical induced birth defects.* New York: Marcel Dekker.

Scheiner, A. P., & McNabb, N. A. (1980). The child with mental retardation. In A. P. Scheiner & I. F. Abroms (Eds.), *The practical management of the developmentally disabled child* (pp. 184–220). St. Louis: C. V. Mosby.

Scher, J., & Dix, C. (1983). *Will my baby be normal? Everything you need to know about pregnancy.* New York: Dial Press.

Schiefelbusch, R. L., & McCormick, L. (1981). Language and speech disorders. In J. M. Kauffman & D. P. Hallahan (Eds.), *Handbook of Special Education.* Englewood Cliffs, N.J.: Prentice-Hall.

Schneider, B., Trehub, S. E., & Bull, D. (1980). High frequency sensitivity in infants. *Science, 207,* 1003–1004.

Schneider, W., Borkowsky, J. G., Kurtz, B. E., & Kerwin, K. (1986). Metamemory and motivation: A comparison of strategy use in German and American children. *Journal of Cross-Cultural Psychology, 17,* 315–336.

Schneider-Rosen, K., Braunwald, K. G., Carlson, V., & Cicchetti, D. (1985). Current perspectives in attachment theory: Illustration from the study of maltreated infants. In I. Bretherton & E. Waters (Eds.), Growing points of attachment theory and research. *Monographs of the Society for Research in Child Development, 50,* No. 209.

Schumer, F. (1983). *Abnormal psychology.* Lexington, Mass.: D.C. Heath.

Schunk, D. H. (1984). Self-efficacy perspective on achievement behavior. *Educational Psychologist, 19,* 48–58.

Schwartzman, H. B. (1987). A cross-cultural perspective on child-structured play activities and materials. In A. W. Gottfried & C. C. Brown (Eds.), *Play interactions: The contribution of play materials and parental involvement to children's development.* Lexington, Mass.: D. C. Heath.

Sears, R. R. (1984). Patterns of child rearing. In S. A. Mednick, M. Harway, & K. M. Finello (Eds.), *Handbook of longitudinal research* (Vol. 1): *Birth and childhood cohorts.* New York: Holt, Rinehart & Winston.

Sears, R. R., Maccoby, E. P., & Lewin, H. (1957). *Patterns of child rearing.* Evanston, Ill.: Row, Peterson.

Sebald, H. (1984). *Adolescence: A social psychological analysis* (3rd ed.). Englewood Cliffs, N.J.: Prentice-Hall.

Seligman, M. E. P. (1975). *Helplessness: On depression, development, and death.* San Francisco: W. H. Freeman.

Selman, R. L. (1976). Social-cognitive understanding: A guide to educational and clinical practice. In T. Lickona (Ed.), *Moral development and behavior: Theory, research and social issues.* New York: Holt, Rinehart & Winston.

Selman, R. L. (1980). *The growth of interpersonal understanding.* New York: Academic Press.

Selman, R. L. (1981). The child as friendship philosopher. In S. R. Asher & J. M. Gottman (Eds.), *The development of children's friendships.* New York: Cambridge University Press.

Selye, H. (1974). *Stress without distress.* Philadelphia: J. B. Lippincott.

Seymour, D. (1971). *Black children, black speech. Commonweal,* November, 19.

Shanklin, D. R., & Hodin, J. (1979). *Maternal nutrition and child health.* Springfield, Ill.: Charles C. Thomas.

Shantz, C. U. (1975). The development of social cognition. In E. M. Hetherington (Ed.), *Review of child development research* (Vol. 5). Chicago: University of Chicago Press.

Shantz, C. U. (1983). Social cognition. In P. H. Mussen (Ed.), *Handbook of child psychology* (Vol. 3): *Cognitive Development* (J. H. Flavell & E. M. Markman, Eds.). New York: John Wiley.

Shedler, J., & Block, J. (1990). Adolescent drug use and psychological health: A longitudinal inquiry. *American Psychologist, 45,* 612–630.

Shepard, L. A., Smith, M. L., & Vojir, C. P. (1983). Characteristics of pupils identified as learning disabled. *American Educational Research Journal, 20,* 309–331.

Shepherd-Look, D. L. (1982). Sex differentiation and the development of sex roles. In B. B. Wolman and others (Eds.), *Handbook of developmental psychology.* Englewood Cliffs, N. J.: Prentice-Hall.

Sherman, M., & Key, C. B. (1932). The intelligence of isolated mountain children. *Child Development, 3,* 279–290.

Sherman, M., & Sherman, I. C. (1929). *The process of human behavior.* New York: W. W. Norton.

Showers, C., & Cantor, N. (1985). Social cognition: A look at motivated strategies. *Annual Review of Psychology, 36,* 275–305.

Siegel, A. W., & White, S. H. (1982). The child study movement: Early growth and development of the symbolized child. In H. W. Reese (Ed.), *Advances in child development and behavior* (Vol. 17). New York: Academic Press.

Siegel, O. (1982). Personality development in adolescence. In B. B. Wolman and others (Eds.), *Handbook of developmental psychology.* Englewood Cliffs, N.J.: Prentice-Hall.

Siegler, R. S. (1989). Mechanisms of cognitive development. *Annual Review of Psychology, 40,* 353–379.

Siegler, R. S., & Liebert, R. M. (1972). Effects of presenting relevant rules and complete feedback on the conservation of liquid quantity task. *Developmental Psychology, 7,* 133–138.

Silverstein, F. S., & Johnston, M. V. (1990). Neurological assessment of children: The damaged child. In R. D. Eden, F. H. Boehm, & M. Haire (Eds.), *Assessment and care of the fetus: Physiological, clinical, and medicolegal principles.* Norwalk, Conn.: Appleton & Lange.

Sinclair, H., Stambak, M., Lézine, I., Rayna, S., & Verba, M. (Eds.). (1989). *Infants and objects: The creativity of cognitive development.* New York: Academic Press.

Singer, J. L. (Ed.). (1973). *The child's world of make-believe: Experimental studies of imaginative play.* New York: Academic Press.

Singer, J. L., & Singer, D. G. (1983). Implications of childhood television viewing for cognition, imagination, and emotion. In J. Bryant & D. R. Anderson (Eds.), *Children's understanding of television: Research on attention and comprehension* (pp. 265–297). New York: Academic Press.

Singer, R. S. (1982). Childhood, aggression and television. *Television and Children, 5,* 57–63.

Singh, J. A., & Zingg, R. N. (1942). *Wolf-children and feral man.* New York: Harper.

Skinner, B. F. (1953). *Science and human behavior.* New York: Macmillan.

Skinner, B. F. (1957). *Verbal behavior.* New York: Appleton-Century-Crofts.

Skinner, B. F. (1961). *Cumulative record* (Rev. ed.). New York: Appleton-Century-Crofts.

Skolnick, A. (1978). The myth of the vulnerable child. *Psychology Today,* February, 56–60, 65.

Sloan, D., Shapiro, S., & Mitchell, A. A. (1980). Strategies for studying the effects of the antenatal chemical environment on the fetus. In R. H. Schwarz & S. J. Yaffe (Eds.), *Drug and chemical risks to the fetus and newborn.* New York: Alan R. Liss.

Slobin, D. L. (1972, July). They learn the same way all around the world. *Psychology Today,* 71–74, 82.

Smith, C. A. (1947). The effect of wartime starvation in Holland upon pregnancy and its product. *American Journal of Obstetrics and Gynecology, 53,* 599–608.

Smith, C. L. (1979). Children's understanding of natural language hierarchies. *Journal of Experimental Child Psychology, 27,* 437–458.

Smith, D. A., & Graesser, A. C. (1981). Memory for actions in scripted activities as a function of typicality, retention interval, and retrieval task. *Memory and Cognition, 9,* 550–559.

Smith, P. B., Weinman, M., & Malinak, L. R. (1984). Adolescent mothers and fetal loss: What is learned from experience? *Psychological Reports, 55,* 775–778.

Smoll, F. L., & Schutz, R. W. (1990). Quantifying gender differences in physical performance: A developmental perspective. *Developmental Psychology, 26,* 360–369.

Snyder, L. A., Freifelder, D., & Hartl, D. L. (1985). *General genetics.* Boston: Jones & Bartlett.

Snyderman, M., & Rothman, S. (1987). Survey of expert opinion on intelligence and aptitude testing. *American Psychologist, 42,* 137–144.

Sorensen, R. C. (1973). *Adolescent sexuality in contemporary America.* New York: World.

Spearman, C. (1927). *The abilities of man.* New York: Macmillan.

Spellacy, W. N., Miller, S. J., & Winegar, A. (1986). Pregnancy after 40 years of age. *Obstetrics and Gynecology, 68,* 452–454.

Spezzano, C. (1981, May). Prenatal psychology: Pregnant with questions. *Psychology Today,* 49–57.

Spitz, R. A. (1945). Hospitalism: An inquiry into the genesis of psychiatric conditions in early childhood. Part 1. *Psychoanalytic Studies of the Child, 1,* 53–74.

Spitz, R. A. (1954). Unhappy and fatal outcomes of emotional deprivation and stress in infancy. In I. Galdston (Ed.), *Beyond the germ theory.* Washington, D.C.: Health Education Council.

Spock, B. (1976). *Baby and child care.* New York: Pocket Books.

Springer, C., & Wallerstein, J. S. (1983). Young adolescents' responses to their parents' divorces. In L. A. Kurdek (Ed.), *Children and divorce: New directions for child development* (pp. 15–28). San Francisco: Jossey-Bass.

Springer, N. S. (1982). *Nutritional casebook on developmental disabilities.* New York: Syracuse University Press.

Sroufe, L., & Waters, E. (1976). The ontogenesis of smiling and laughter: A perspective on the organization of development in infancy. *Psychological Review, 83,* 173–189.

Sroufe, L., & Wunsch, J. (1972). The development of laughter in the first year of life. *Child Development, 43,* 1326–1344.

Stall, R. D., Coates, T. J., & Hoff, C. (1988). Behavioral risk reduction for HIV infection among gay and bisexual men. *American Psychologist, 43,* 878–885.

Stambak, M., Sinclair, H., Verba, M., Moreno, L., & Rayna, S. (1989). Infants and logic. In H. Sinclair, M. Stambak, I. Lézine, S. Rayna, & M. Verba (Eds.), *Infants and objects: The creativity of cognitive development.* New York: Academic Press.

Starr, R. H. (1979). Child abuse. *American Psychologist, 34,* 872–878.

Starr, R. H. (1982). A research-based approach to the prediction of child abuse. In R. H. Starr, Jr. (Ed.), *Child abuse prediction: Policy implications.* Cambridge, Mass.: Ballinger.

Starr, R. H., Jr., Dietrich, K. N., & Fischoff, J. (1981). The contribution of children to their own abuse. Paper presented at a meeting of the Society for Research in Child Development, Boston, April.

Stein, P. J. (1983). Singlehood. In E. D. Macklin & R. H. Rubin (Eds.), *Contemporary families and alternative lifestyles: Handbook on research and theory* (pp. 27–48). Beverly Hills, Calif.: Sage.

Stein, Z., Susser, M., Saenger, G., & Marolla, F. (1975). *Famine and human development: The Dutch hunger winter of 1944–1945.* New York: Oxford University Press.

Steiner, J. E. (1979). Human facial expressions in response to taste and smell stimulation. In H. Reese & L. Lipsitt (Eds.), *Advances in child development and behavior* (Vol. 13). New York: Academic Press.

Stern, C. (1956). Hereditary factors affecting adoption. In *A Study of Adoption Practices* (Vol. 2). New York: Child Welfare League of America.

Stern, D. N., Spieker, S., Barnett, R. K., & MacKain, K. (1983). The prosody of maternal speech: Infant age and context related changes. *Journal of Child Language, 10,* 1–15.

Sternberg, R. J. (1984). A contextualist view of the nature of intelligence. *International Journal of Psychology, 19,* 307–334.

Sternberg, R. J. (1985). *Beyond IQ: A triarchic theory of intelligence.* New York: Cambridge University Press.

Stifter, C. A., & Fox, N. A. (1990). Infant reactivity: Physiological correlates of newborn and 5-month temperament. *Developmental Psychology, 26,* 582–588.

Stockman, J. A., III (1990). Fetal hematology. In R. D. Eden, F. H. Boehm, & M. Haire (Eds.), *Assessment and care of the fetus: Physiological, clinical, and medicolegal principles.* Norwalk, Conn.: Appleton & Lange.

Strangler, R. S., & Printz, A. M. (1980). DSM-III: Psychiatric diagnosis in a university population. *American Journal of Psychiatry, 137,* 937–940.

Straus, M. A., and Gelles, R. (1986). Societal change and change in family violence from 1975 to 1985 as revealed by two national surveys. *Journal of Marriage and the Family, 48,* 465–479.

Streissguth, A. P., Barr, H. M., & Martin, D. C. (1983). Maternal alcohol use and neonatal habituation assessed with the Brazelton scale. *Child Development, 54,* 1109–1118.

Streissguth, A. P., Landesman-Dwyer, S., Martin, J. C., & Smith, D. W. (1980). Teratogen effects of alcohol in humans and laboratory animals. *Science, 209,* 353–361.

Strelau, J. (1989). Temperament risk factors in children and adolescents as studied in Eastern Europe. In W. B. Carey & S. C. McDevitt (Eds.), *Clinical and educational applications of temperament research.* Berwyn, Penn.: Swets North America.

Stuart, R. B. (1969). Critical reappraisal and reformulation of selected "mental health" programs. In L. A. Hamerlynck, P. O. Davidson, & L. E. Acker (Eds.), *Behavior modification and mental health services.* Calgary, Alb.: University of Calgary Press.

Tan, A. S. (1976). TV beauty ads and role expectations of adolescent female viewers. *Journal Questionnaire, 53,* 271–279.

Tanner, J. M. (1955). *Growth at adolescence.* Springfield, Ill.: Charles C. Thomas.

Tanner, J. M. (1970). Physical growth. In P. H. Mussen (Ed.), *Carmichael's manual of child psychology* (3rd ed.). New York: John Wiley.

Tanner, J. M. (1975). Sequence, tempo, and individual variation in the growth and development of boys and girls aged twelve to sixteen. In R. E. Grinder (Ed.), *Studies in adolescence*. New York: Macmillan.

Task Force on Pediatric AIDS. (1989). Pediatric AIDS and human immunodeficiency virus infection. *American Psychologist, 44,* 258–264.

Tavris, C., & Baumgartner, A. I. (1983). How would your life be different if you'd been born a boy? *Redbook,* February, 99.

Teenage pregnancy: The problem that hasn't gone away. (1981). New York: The Alan Guttmacher Institute.

Television & your children. (1985). Ontario: TV Ontario: The Ontario Educational Communications Authority.

Telfer, M. A., Baker, D., Clark, G. R., & Richardson, C. E. (1968). Incidence of gross chromosomal errors among tall, criminal American males. *Science, 159,* 1249–1250.

Terman, L. M., assisted by B. T. Baldwin and others. (1925). *Genetic studies of genius* (Vol. 1). Stanford, Calif.: Stanford University Press.

Termine, N. T., & Izard, C. E. (1988). Infants' responses to their mother's expressions of joy and sadness. *Developmental Psychology, 24,* 223–229.

Terrace, H. S. (1985). In the beginning was the "Name." *American Psychologist, 40,* 1011–1028.

Thomas, A., & Chess, S. (1977). *Temperament and development*. New York: Brunner/Mazel.

Thomas, A., & Chess, S. (1981). The role of temperament in the contribution of individuals to their development. In R. M. Lerner & N. A. Busch-Rossnagel (Eds.), *Individual as producers of their development*. New York: Academic Press.

Thomas, A., Chess, S., & Birch, H. G. (1968). *Temperament and behavior disorders in children*. New York: New York University Press.

Thomas, A., Chess, S., & Birch, H. G. (1970). The origin of personality. *Scientific American, 223,* 102–109.

Thomas, J. W. (1980). Agency and achievement: Self-management and self-regard. *Review of Educational Research, 50,* 213–240.

Thomas, R. M. (1985). *Comparing theories of child development* (2nd ed.). Belmont, Calif.: Wadsworth.

Thompson, R. F. (1975). *Introduction to physiological psychology*. New York: Harper & Row.

Thorndike, R. L., & Hagen, E. (1977). *Measurement and evaluation in psychology and education* (4th ed.). New York: John Wiley.

Thorndike, R. L., Hagen, E., & Sattler, J. M. (1985). *Revised Stanford-Binet intelligence scale* (4th ed.). Boston: Houghton Mifflin.

Thorpe, W. H. (1963). *Learning and instinct in animals* (2nd ed.). London: Methuen.

Thurstone, L. L. (1938). Primary mental abilities. *Psychometric Monographs*, No. 1. Chicago: University of Chicago Press.

Timiras, P. S. (1972). *Developmental physiology and aging*. New York: Macmillan.

Torrance, E. P. (1966). Torrance's tests of creative thinking. *Norms technical manual*. Princeton, N.J.: Personnel Press.

Torrance, E. P. (1974). *Torrance tests of creative thinking*. Lexington, Mass.: Ginn.

Trawick-Smith, J. (1989). Play is not learning: A critical review of the literature. *Child & Youth Care Quarterly, 18,* 161–170.

Trent, J. W., & Crais, J. L. (1967). Commitment and conformity in the American college. *Journal of Social Issues, 22,* 34–51.

Trickett, P. K., & Susman, E. J. (1988). Parental perceptions of child-rearing practices in physically abusive and nonabusive families. *Developmental Psychology, 24,* 270–276.

Trofatter, K. F., Jr. (1990). Fetal immunology. In R. D. Eden, F. H. Boehm, & M. Haire (Eds.), *Assessment and care of the fetus: Physiological, clinical, and medicolegal principles*. Norwalk, Conn.: Appleton & Lange.

Tronick, E. Z. (1989). Emotions and emotional communication in infants. *American Psychologist, 44,* 112–119.

Tryon, R. C. (1940). Genetic differences in maze learning in rats. *Yearbook of the National Society for the Study of Education, 39,* 111–119.

Tsang, M. C. (1988). Cost analysis for educational policymaking: A review of cost studies in education in developing countries. *Review of Educational Research, 58,* 181–230.

Tuma, J. M. (1989). Mental health services for children. *American Psychologist, 44,* 188–195.

Tzuriel, D. (1989). Development of motivational and cognitive-informational orientations from third to ninth grades. *Journal of Applied Developmental Psychology, 10,* 107–121.

U.S. Bureau of the Census. (1981). *Statistical abstracts of the United States: 1981* (102nd ed.). Washington, D.C.: U.S. Government Printing Office.

U.S. Bureau of the Census. (1988). *Statistical abstracts of the United States 1987* (108th ed.). Washington, D.C.: U.S. Government Printing Office.

U. S. Bureau of the Census. (1990). *Statistical abstracts of the United States 1990* (110th ed.). Washington, D.C.: U.S. Government Printing Office.

U.S. Department of Health & Human Services. (1974). *Alcohol and health: New knowledge.* Second special report to the U.S. Congress. Washington, D.C.: U.S. Government Printing Office, June.

U.S. Department of Health & Human Services. (1981). *The health consequences of smoking: The changing cigarette: A report of the Surgeon General.* Washington, D.C.: U.S. Government Printing Office.

U.S. Department of Health & Human Services. (1989). *Monthly Vital Statistics Report,* Vol. 37, No. 11, Feb. 1989. Public Health Service, Centers for Disease Control. Washington, D.C.: U.S. Government Printing Office.

U.S. Department of Health, Education & Welfare. (1978). *Third special report to the U.S. Congress on alcohol and health.* Washington, D.C.: U.S. Government Printing Office.

U.S. Office of Education. (1975). *Estimated number of handicapped children in the United States, 1974–1975.* Washington, D.C.: Bureau of Education for the Handicapped.

Un bébé meurt apres un accouchement dans une piscine gonflable. (1990). *Le Monde,* Sept. 29, p. 13.

Valsiner, J. (1987). *Culture and the development of children's action: A cultural-historical theory of developmental psychology.* New York: John Wiley.

Valsiner, J. (Ed.). (1989). *Child development in cultural context.* Lewiston, N.Y.: Hogrefe and Huber.

Van Houten, R., & Doleys, D. M. (1983). Are social reprimands effective? In S. Axelrod & J. Apsche (Eds.), *The effects of punishment on human behavior.* New York: Academic Press.

Van Houten, R., Nau, P. A., MacKenzie-Keating, S., Sameoto, D., & Colavecchia, B. (1982). An analysis of some variables influencing the effectiveness of reprimands. *Journal of Applied Behavior Analysis, 15,* 65–83.

Vandell, D. L., Wilson, K. S., & Buchanan, N. R. (1980). Peer interaction in the first year of life: An examination of its structure, content, and sensitivity to toys. *Child Development, 51,* 481–488.

Vandenberg, B. R. (1987). Beyond the ethology of play. In A. W. Gottfried & C. C. Brown (Eds.), *Play interactions: The contribution of play materials and parental involvement to children's development.* Lexington, Mass.: D. C. Heath.

Vaughn, B., Gove, F., & Egeland, B. (1980). The relationship between out-of-home care and the quality of infant-mother attachment in an economically deprived population. *Child Development, 50,* 971–975.

Vaz, E., & Lodhi, A. (1979). *Crime and delinquency in Canada.* Scarborough, Ontario: Prentice-Hall.

Velandia, W., Grandon, G. M., & Page, E. B. (1978). Family size, birth order, and intelligence in a large South American sample. *American Educational Research Journal, 15,* 399–416.

Verhaaren, P., & Connor, F. P. (1981). Physical disabilities. In J. M. Kauffman & D. P. Hallahan (Eds.), *Handbook of special education* (pp. 248–289). Englewood Cliffs, N.J.: Prentice-Hall.

Visher, E. B., & Visher, J. S. (1982). *How to win as a stepfamily.* New York: Dembner.

Visher, E. B., & Visher, J. S. (1988). *Old loyalties, new ties.* New York: Brunner/Mazel.

Von Hofsten, C., & Lindhagen, K. (1979). Observations on the development of reaching for moving objects. *Journal of Experimental Child Psychology, 28,* 158–173.

Vorhees, C. V., & Mollnow, E. (1987). Behavioral teratogenesis: Long-term influences on behavior from early exposure to environmental agents. In J. D. Osofsky (Ed.), *Handbook of infant development.* New York: John Wiley.

Vygotsky, L. S. (1962). *Thought and language* (E. Hansmann & G. Vaker, Eds. and Trans.). New York: John Wiley.

Vygotsky, L. S. (1986). *Thought and language* (Translated and revised by A. Kozulin). Cambridge, Mass.: MIT Press.

Waddington, C. H. (1975). *The evolution of an evolutionist.* Edinburgh: Edinburgh University Press.

Wadsworth, B. J. (1989). *Piaget's theory of cognitive and affective development* (4th ed.). New York: Longman.

Walker, J. J. (1978). The gifted and talented. In E. L. Meyen (Ed.), *Exceptional children and youth: An introduction.* Denver: Love.

Walker, L. J. (1988). The development of moral reasoning. In R. Vasta (Ed.), *Annals of child development* (Vol 5). Greenwich, Conn.: JAI Press.

Wallach, M. A., & Kogan, N. (1965). *Modes of thinking in young children: A study of the creativity-*

intelligence distinction. New York: Holt, Rinehart & Winston.

Wallerstein, J. S. (1989). Children after divorce: Wounds that don't heal. *The New York Times Magazine,* January 23, 19–21, 41–44.

Wallerstein, J. S., Corbin, S. B., & Lewis, J. M. (1988). Children of divorce: A ten-year study. In E. M. Hetherington & J. Arasteh (Eds.), *Impact of divorce, single-parenting and stepparenting on children.* Hillsdale, N.J.: Lawrence Erlbaum.

Wallerstein, J. S., & Kelly, J. B. (1974). The effects of parental divorce: The adolescent experience. In E. J. Anthony & C. Koupernik (Eds.), *The child in his family: Children at psychiatric risk* (Vol. 3). New York: John Wiley.

Wallerstein, J. S., & Kelly, J. B. (1975). The effects of parental divorce: Experiences of the preschool child. *Journal of the American Academy of Child Psychiatry, 14,* 600–616.

Wallerstein, J. S., & Kelly, J. B. (1976). The effects of parental divorce: Experiences of the child in later latency. *American Journal of Orthopsychiatry, 46,* 256–269.

Wallerstein, J. S., & Kelly, J. (1980). *Surviving the break-up: How children actually cope with divorce.* New York: Basic Books.

Walsh, B. T. (1982). Endocrine disturbance in anorexia nervosa and depression. *Psychosomatic Medicine, 44,* 85–91.

Walters, G. C., & Grusec, J. E. (1977). *Punishment.* San Francisco: W. H. Freeman.

Wasserman, G. (1980). The nature and function of early mother-infant interaction. In B. L. Blum (Ed.), *Psychological aspects of pregnancy, birthing, and bonding.* New York: Human Sciences Press, 324–348.

Waterman, A. S. (1984). Identity formation: Discovery or creation? *Journal of Early Adolescence, 4,* 329–341.

Waterman, A. S. (1988). Identity status theory and Erikson's theory: Commonalities and differences. *Developmental Review, 8,* 185–208.

Waters, E. (1980). Traits, relationships and behavioral systems: The attachment construct and the organization of behavior and development. In K. Immelman, E. Barlow, M. Main, & L. Petrinovich (Eds.), *Development of behavior.* New York: Cambridge University Press.

Waters, E., Hay, D., & Richters, J. (1986). Infant-parent attachment and the origins of prosocial and antiso-cial behavior. In D. Olweus, J. Block, & M. Radke-Yarrow (Eds.), *Development of antisocial and prosocial behavior: Research, theories, and issues.* New York: Academic Press.

Watson, J. B. (1914). *Behavior: An introduction to comparative psychology.* New York: Holt, Rinehart & Winston.

Watson, J. B., & Rayner, R. (1920). Conditioned emotional reactions. *Journal of Experimental Psychology, 3,* 1–14.

Watts, W. D., & Wright, L. S. (1990). The relationship of alcohol, tobacco, marijuana, and other illegal drug use to delinquency among Mexican-American, black, and white adolescent males. *Adolescence, 25,* 171–181.

Weinberg, R. (1989). Intelligence and IQ. *American Psychologist, 44,* 98–104.

Weiner, B. (1979). A theory of motivation for some classroom experiences. *Journal of Educational Psychology, 71,* 3–25.

Weiner, B. (1980a). *Human motivation.* New York: Holt, Rinehart & Winston.

Weiner, B. (1980b). The role of affect in rational (attributional) approaches to human motivation. *Educational Researcher, 9,* 4–11.

Weisfeld, G. E. (1982). The nature-nurture issue and the integrating concept of function. In B. B. Wolman and others (Eds.), *Handbook of developmental psychology.* Englewood Cliffs, N.J.: Prentice-Hall.

Weiss, R. S. (1984). The impact of marital dissolution on income and consumption in single parent households. *Journal of Marriage and the Family, 46,* 115–127.

Weisskopf, M. (1987). Lead astray: The poisoning of America. *Discover, 8,* 76–77.

Wellman, H. M. (1988). The early development of memory strategies. In F. E. Weinert & M. Perlmutter (Eds.), *Memory development: Universal changes and individual differences.* Hillsdale, N.J.: Lawrence Erlbaum.

Werner, E. E., & Smith, R. S. (1982). *Vulnerable but invincible: A longitudinal study of resilient children and youth.* New York: McGraw-Hill.

Werry, J. S. (1972). The childhood psychoses. In H. C. Quay & J. S. Werry (Eds.), *Psychopathological disorders of childhood.* New York: John Wiley.

Wertham, F. (1954). *Seduction of the innocent.* New York: Rinehart.

Wertsch, J. V. (1985). *Vygotsky and the social formation of mind.* Cambridge, Mass.: Harvard University Press.

Wesley, F., & Wesley, C. (1977). *Sex-role psychology.* New York: Human Sciences Press.

White, B. L. (1985). *The first three years of life* (Rev. ed.). Englewood Cliffs, N.J.: Prentice-Hall.

Whitney, E. N., & Hamilton, E. M. N. (1984). *Understanding nutrition* (3rd ed.). St. Paul, Minn.: West.

Whorf, B. L. (1941). The relation of habitual thought and behavior to language. In L. Spier (Ed.), *Language, culture and personality.* Salt Lake City: University of Utah Press.

Whorf, B. L. (1956). *Language, thought and reality.* New York: John Wiley.

Willerman, L. (1973). Activity level and hyperactivity in twins. *Child Development, 44,* 288–293.

Willerman, L. (1979). Effects of families on intellectual development. *American Psychologist, 34,* 923–929.

Willig, A. (1985). A meta-analysis of selected studies on the effectiveness of bilingual education. *Review of Educational Research, 55,* 269–317.

Wilson, E. O. (1975). *Sociobiology: The new synthesis.* Cambridge, Mass.: Belknap.

Winn, M. (1985). *The plug-in drug* (Rev. ed.). New York: Viking Press.

Winnicott, O. (1971). *Playing and reality.* New York: Basic Books.

Winsten, S. (1949). *Days with Bernard Shaw.* New York: Vanguard.

Witkin, H. A., Mednick, S. A., Schulsinger, F., Bakkestrom, E., Christiansen, K. O., Goodenough, D. R., Hirschhorn, K., Lundesteen, C., Owen, D. R., Philip, J., Rubin, D. B., & Stocking, M. (1976). Criminality in XYY and XXY men. *Science, 193,* 547–555.

Wittrock, M. C. (1986). Students' thought processes. In M. C. Wittrock (Ed.), *Handbook of research on teaching* (3rd ed.). New York: Macmillan.

Wolff, P. H. (1959). Observations on newborn infants. *Psychosomatic Medicine, 21,* 110–118.

Wolff, P. H. (1963). Observations of the early development of smiling. In B. M. Foss (Ed.), *Determinants of infant behavior 2.* London: Methuen.

Wolff, P. H. (1966). The causes, controls, and organization of behavior in the neonate. *Psychological Issues, 5.*

Wolff, P. H. (1969). The natural history of crying and other vocalizations in early infancy. In B. Foss (Ed.), *Determinants of infant behavior 4.* London: Methuen.

Wolock, I., & Horowitz, B. (1984). Child maltreatment as a social problem: The neglect of neglect. *American Journal of Orthopsychiatry, 54,* 530–543.

Wood, B. S. (1981). *Children and communication: Verbal and nonverbal language development* (2nd ed.). Englewood Cliffs, N.J.: Prentice-Hall.

World Health Organization. (1989). *World Health Statistics Annual.* Geneva: World Health Organization.

Wright, H. F. (1960). Observational child study. In P. H. Mussen (Ed.), *Handbook of research methods in child development.* New York: John Wiley.

Yager, J. (1982). Family issues in the pathogenesis of anorexia nervosa. *Psychosomatic Medicine, 44,* 43–60.

Yamamoto, K. (1964). *Experimental scoring manual for Minnesota Tests of Creative Thinking and Writing.* Kent, Ohio: Bureau of Educational Research, Kent State University.

Yarrow, L. J., & Goodwin, M. S. (1973). The immediate impact of separation: Reactions of infants to a change in mother figures. In L. J. Stone, H. T. Smith, & L. B. Murphy (Eds.), *The competent infant: Research and commentary.* New York: Basic Books.

Young, K. T., & Zigler, E. (1986). Infant and toddler day care: Regulations and policy implications. *American Journal of Orthopsychiatry, 56,* 42–53.

Zabin, L. S., Hirsch, M. B., Streett, R., Emerson, M. R., Smith, M., Hardy, J. B., & King, T. M. (1988). The Baltimore pregnancy prevention program for urban teenagers: I. How did it work? *Family Planning Perspectives, 20,* 182–187.

Zajonc, R. B. (1976). Family configuration and intelligence. *Science, 192,* 227–236.

Zajonc, R. B., & Markus, G. B. (1975). Birth order and intellectual development. *Psychological Review, 82,* 74–88.

Zelnik, M., Kantner, J. F., & Ford, K. (1981). *Sex and pregnancy in adolescence.* Beverly Hills, Calif.: Sage.

Zelnik, M., & Shah, F. K. (1983). First intercourse among young Americans. *Family Planning Perspectives, 15,* 64–70.

Zigler, E., & Freedman, J. (1987). Early experience, malleability, and Head Start. In J. J. Gallagher & C. T. Ramey (Eds.), *The malleability of children.* Baltimore: Brookes.

Zuckerman, D. M., Singer, D. G., & Singer, J. L. (1980). Television viewing and children's reading and related classroom behavior. *Journal of Communication, 30,* 166–174.

AUTHOR INDEX

SUBJECT INDEX

Acknowledgments

Page 1: Michael Hayman/Stock Boston; *p. 16:* © Chester Higgins, Jr./Photo Researchers; *p. 21* (left): *The Happy Mother (Allegory of the Senses)*, Willem van Mieris/© The Art Institute of Chicago, all rights reserved; (right): Detroit Institute of Arts; *p. 22:* Cornell Capa/Magnum Photos; *p. 57:* Fred D. Bodin/ Stock Boston; *p. 58:* Michael Weisbrot & Family/Stock, Boston; *p. 65:* Elizabeth Crews; *p. 75:* Ken Heyman; *p. 81:* Jane Kramer/EKM-Nepenthe; *p. 87:* Nina Leen, *Life* Magazine © Time Inc.; *p. 89:* Elliott Erwitt/Magnum; *p. 105:* Carnegie Institute of Washington, Dept. Of Embryology, UC Davis; *p. 106* (top left, center, right): Carnegie Institute of Washington, Dept. Of Embryology, UC Davis; (bottom left): © 1982 Joel Gordon; (bottom right): © Mike Greenlar/The Image Works; *p. 107* (top): Carnegie Institute of Washington, Dept. Of Embryology, UC Davis; (bottom left): © Donald Dietz, 1981/Stock, Boston; (bottom right): © James Holland/Stock, Boston; *p. 108* (top left): Suzanne Arms/Jeroboam, Inc.; (top right): Giraudon, Paris; (bottom): Hella Hammid/Photo Researchers, Inc.; *p. 111:* Prints Old and Rare, San Francisco; *p. 127:* The Bettmann Archive; *p. 131:* National Foundation for the March of Dimes; *p. 132:* Evan Johnson/Jeroboam, Inc.; *p. 138* (left): Laimute E. Druskis/Jeroboam, Inc.; (right): Bob Daemmrich/ Stock, Boston; *p. 139:* Hiroji Jubota/Magnum; *p. 161:* Carnegie Institute of Washington, Dept. of Embryology, UC Davis; *p. 165:* Carnegie Institute of Washington, Dept. of Embryology, UC Davis; *p. 171:* © 1990 Ted Wood/Picture Group; *p. 176:* © 1990 Joel Gordon; *p. 186:* Brian Lanker/Topeka Capital-Journal; *p. 196:* Bill Aron/Jeroboam, Inc.; *p. 197:* David Hurn/Magnum; *p. 206* (top left, top right): Hickman Archives; (bottom right): Elizabeth Crews/Stock, Boston; (bottom left): Courtesy Roberta Broyer; (middle left): © Jerry Howard/Stock, Boston; *p. 207* (top left): Suzanne Arms/Jeroboam Inc.; (top right): © James R. Holland/Stock, Boston; (bottom right): Charles Harbutt/Actuality Inc.; (bottom left): Lionel Delevingne/Stock, Boston; *p. 208* (top): *Baby at Play*, Thomas Eakins, National Gallery of Art; (bottom): Rohn Engh/The Image Works; *p. 214:* Suzanne Arms/Jeroboam, Inc.; *p. 220:* © 1978 Joel Gordon; *p. 225:* Laima E. Druskis/Jeroboam, Inc.; *p. 227:* Hickman Archives; *p. 228:* William Vandivert/*Scientific American*; *p. 236:* The Lucy T. Howat Archives; *p. 239:* Elizabeth Crews; *p. 250:* David Powers; *p. 254:* Frank Siteman/Stock, Boston; *p. 273* (top left): Hickman Archives; (top right): Anna Kaufman Moon/ Stock, Boston; (bottom right): Tom Carter/Jeroboam, Inc.; (bottom left): Suzanne Arms/Jeroboam, Inc.; *p. 275:* Joanne Leonard/ Woodfin Camp & Associates; *p. 277:* Elliott Erwitt, Magnum; *p. 284:* Nik Wheeler/Black Star; *p. 291:* Harry Harlow/Wisconsin Primate Laboratory; *p. 295:* Suzanne Szasz/Photo Researchers; *p. 300:* Wayne Miller/Magnum; *p. 302:* David A. Krathwohl/Stock Boston; *p. 310:* Kent Reno/Jeroboam, Inc.; *p. 317:* © Allan Grant Productions; *p. 323:* Constance Stuart/Black Star; *p. 324* (top left): Edward Hicks; *Peaceable Kingdom,* reproduced through courtesy New York State Historical Association; (top right): Dorothea Lange Art Fund; (bottom): © 1991 Tom Levy/BAWRC; *p. 325* (top left): Chris Stewart/*San Francisco Chronicle*; (top right): Elizabeth Crews/Stock, Boston; (bottom right): Bob Daemmrich/Stock, Boston; (bottom left): © Elizabeth Crews; *p. 326* (right): © 1991 Tom Levy; (bottom left): J. R. Holland/Stock, Boston; *p. 331:* © 1991 Tom Levy; *p. 340:* EKM-Nepenthe; *p. 345:* © Elizabeth Crews/Stock, Boston; *p. 350:* Jean-Claude Lejeune/Stock, Boston; *p. 356:* Peter Menzel; *p. 358:* Billy Barnes; *p. 369:* Barbara Rios/Photo Researchers; *p. 389:* Jane Scherr/Jeroboam, Inc.; *p. 390:* Elizabeth Crews/The Image Works; *p. 395:* Elizabeth Crews; *p. 404:* Elizabeth Hamlin/Stock, Boston; *p. 417:* Jane Scherr/Jeroboam, Inc.; *p. 420:* Elizabeth Crews; *p. 435:* Elizabeth Crews; *p. 436* (top left): © 1991 by Tom Levy; (top right): *Snap the Whip*, Winslow Homer/The Metropolitan Museum of Art; (center right): Rick Smolan/Stock, Boston; (bottom right): © 1991 by Tom Levy; (bottom left): Jeroboam, Inc.; *p. 437* (top right): International Collection of Child Art/The University Museums, Illinois State University; (bottom right): Nita Winter Photography; (bottom left): Jill Freedman; *p. 438* (top): © 1991 Tom Levy/San Francisco Chronicle; (bottom): Elliott Erwitt/Magnum; *p. 443:* Kit Hedman/Jeroboam, Inc.; *p. 448:* Elizabeth Crews; *p. 450:* Elizabeth Crews/Stock, Boston; *p. 462:* Karen R. Preuss/Jeroboam, Inc.; *p. 477:* Danny Lyon/Magnum; *p. 482:* Joseph Schuyler/Stock, Boston; *p. 490:* Evan Johnson/Jeroboam, Inc.; *p. 502:* Photo Researchers; *p. 510:* Jean-Claude Lejeune/Stock, Boston; *p. 513:* Peter Southwick/Stock, Boston; *p. 523:* Elizabeth Crews; *p. 525:* Evan Johnson; *p. 527:* Photo Researchers, Inc.; *p. 530:* Steve Hansen/Stock, Boston; *p. 539:* Sybil Shelton/Peter Arnold; *p. 544:* UPI/Bettmann Newsphotos; *p. 563:* Hickman Archives; *p. 564* (left): © 1991 by Tom Levy; (top right): Nita Winter Photography; (bottom right): Peter Southwick/Stock, Boston; *p. 565* (top left): Steve & Mary Skjold/The Image Works; (top right): *The Butt — Shooting a Cherry,* 1848, William Mulready/Art Resource; (bottom): Nita Winter Photography; *p. 566* (top left): Elizabeth Crews; (top right): © Ursula Markus/Photo Researchers; (bottom): © Tom Levy/BAWRC; *p. 571:* Dan Chidester/The Image Works; *p. 577:* Evan Johnson/Jeroboam, Inc.; *p. 581:* Susan Rosenberg/Photo Researchers; *p. 591:* Ellis Herwig/Stock, Boston; *p. 592:* Peter Menzel/Stock, Boston; *p. 594:* Tony Freeman/Photo Edit; *p. 599:* Alan Carey/The Image Works; *p. 609:* Alan Carey/The Image Works; *p. 629:* Michael Weisbrot & Family/Stock, Boston; *p. 631:* Will McIntyre/Photo Researchers; *p. 633:* Sylvia Johnson/Woodfin Camp & Associates; *p. 644:* Planned Parenthood Federation of America; *p. 649:* H. Armstrong Roberts; *p. 654:* Dorothy Littel/Stock, Boston; *p. 669:* Jim Mahoney/The Image Works; *p. 675:* Elizabeth Crews; *p. 683:* The Lucy T. Howat Archives.